To our families and students, who give meaning and enjoyment to our lives.
*—CCN and DJW*

# Preface

The measurement of joint motion is an important component of a thorough physical examination of the extremities and spine, one which helps health professionals identify impairments and assess rehabilitative status. The need for a comprehensive text with sufficient written detail and photographs to allow for the standardization of goniometric measurement methods—both for the purposes of teaching and clinical practice led to the development of the first edition of the *Measurement of Joint Motion: A Guide to Goniometry* in 1985. Our approach included a discussion and illustration of testing position, stabilization, end-feel, and goniometer alignment for each measurable joint in the body. The resulting text was extremely well received by a variety of health professional educational programs and was used as a reference in many clinical settings.

In the years following initial publication, a considerable amount of research on the measurement of joint motion appeared in the literature. Consequently, a second edition, published in 1995, included a chapter on the reliability and validity of joint measurement as well as joint-specific research sections in each existing chapter. We also expanded the text by adding structure, osteokinematics, arthrokinematics, capsular and noncapsular patterns of limitation, and functional ranges of motion for each joint.

The third edition included extensive new research findings related to joint motion. New to the third edition was the inclusion of muscle length testing at joints where muscle length is often a factor affecting range of motion. This addition integrated the measurement procedures used in this book with the American Physical Therapy Association's *Guide to Physical Therapy Practice*. Inclinometer techniques for measuring range of motion of the spine were added to coincide with current practice in some clinical settings. Illustrations were included to accompany anatomical descriptions so that the reader had a visual reminder of the joint structures involved in range of motion. New illustrations of bony anatomical landmarks and photographs of surface anatomy were added to help the reader align the goniometer accurately.

In the fourth edition we reorganized the content in Chapters 4 to 13 to create a more logical progression from anatomical descriptions of joint structures and landmarks used in goniometer alignment directly to the measurement procedures. Information summarizing research findings now follows, rather than precedes, the measurement procedures. This restructuring makes it easier for readers that are focused on learning measurement technique, as well as readers that are focused on reviewing the research literature for evidence-based practice, to find what they are seeking. Similar to earlier editions we have incorporated new information on normative range of motion values for various age and gender groups, as well as the range of motion needed to perform common functional tasks. We added current information on the effects of subject characteristics, such as body mass, occupational and recreational activities, and the effects of the testing process, such as the testing position and type of measuring instrument, on range of motion. In the fourth edition we added and restructured more measurement techniques to the spine chapters and added several commonly used methods to assess finger and thumb range of motion. The TMJ chapter was enhanced with clear photographs and illustrations of measurement techniques. In addition, over 90 new photographs and illustrations replaced many of the older, dated art work.

This book continues to present goniometry logically and clearly. Chapter 1 discusses basic concepts regarding the use of goniometry to assess range of motion and muscle length in patient evaluation. Arthrokinematic and osteokinematic movements, elements of active and passive range of motion, hypomobility, hypermobility, and factors affecting joint motion are included. The inclusion of end-feels and capsular and noncapsular patterns of joint limitation introduces readers to current concepts in orthopedic manual therapy and encourages them to consider joint structure while measuring joint motion.

Chapter 2 takes the reader through a step-by-step process to master the techniques of goniometric evaluation, including: positioning, stabilization, instruments used for measurement, goniometer alignment, and the recording of results. Exercises that help develop necessary psychomotor skills and demonstrate direct application of theoretical concepts facilitate learning.

Chapter 3 discusses the validity and reliability of measurement. The results of validity and reliability studies on the measurement of joint motion are summarized to help the reader focus on ways of improving and interpreting goniometric measurements. Mathematical methods of evaluating reliability are shown along with examples and exercises so that the readers can assess their reliability in taking measurements.

Chapters 4 to 13 present detailed information on goniometric testing procedures for the upper and lower extremities, spine, and temporomandibular joint. When appropriate, muscle length testing procedures are also included. The text presents the anatomical landmarks, testing position, stabilization, testing motion, normal end-feel, and goniometer alignment for each joint and motion, in a format that reinforces a consistent approach to evaluation. The extensive use of photographs and captions eliminates the need for repeated demonstrations by an instructor and provides the reader with a permanent reference for visualizing the procedures. Also included is information on joint structure, osteokinematic and arthrokinematic motion, and capsular patterns of restrictions. A review of current literature regarding normal range of motion values; the effects of age, gender, and other factors on range of motion; functional range of motion; and reliability and validity of measurement procedures are also presented for each body region to assist the reader to comply with evidence-based practice.

We hope this book makes the teaching and learning of goniometry easier and improves the standardization and thus the reliability and validity of this examination tool. We believe that the fourth edition provides a comprehensive coverage of the clinical measurement of joint motion and muscle length. We hope that the additions will motivate health professionals to conduct research and to use research results in evaluation. We encourage our readers to provide us with feedback on our current efforts to bring you a high-quality, user-friendly text.

CCN
DJW

# Acknowledgments

We are very grateful for the contributions of the many people who were involved in the development and production of this text. Photographer Jocelyn Molleur applied her skill and patience during many sessions at the physical therapy laboratory at the University of Massachusetts Lowell to produce the high-quality photographs that appear in both the third and fourth editions. Her efforts combined with those of Lucia Grochowska Littlefield, who took the photographs for the first edition, are responsible for an important feature of the book. Timothy Malone, an artist from Ohio, used his talents, knowledge of anatomy, and good humor to create the excellent illustrations that appear in this edition. We also offer our thanks to Colleen DeCotret, Alexander White, Claudia Van Bibber, and University of Massachusetts Lowell physical therapy students: Rachel Blakeslee, Rebecca D'Amour, and Chris Fournier who graciously agreed to be subjects for the new photographs and provided painstaking research support for the fourth edition.

We wish to express our appreciation to these dedicated professionals at F. A. Davis: Margaret Biblis, Publisher, and Melissa Duffield, Acquisitions Editor, for their encouragement and commitment to excellence. Our thanks are also extended to George Lang, Manager of Content Development; David Orzechowski, Managing Editor; Robert Butler, Production Manager; Karen Carter, Developmental Editor; Carolyn O'Brien, Manager of Art and Design; Katharine L. Margeson, Illustration Coordinator; Elizabeth Stepchin, Developmental Associate; Stephanie Casey, Administrative Assistant; and Jean-Francois Vilain, Former Publisher for the first and second editions. We are very grateful to the numerous students, faculty, and clinicians who over the years have used the book or formally reviewed portions of the manuscript and offered insightful comments and helpful suggestions that have improved this text.

Finally, we wish to thank our families: Cynthia's daughter, Alexandra, and her daughters, Taylor and Kimberly; and Joyce's husband, Jonathan, sons, Alexander and Ethan, and parents, Dorothy and Emerson, for their continuing encouragement and support. We will always be appreciative.

# Reviewers

**Joni Goldwasser Barry, PT, DPT, NCS**
Assistant Professor
School of Health Professions
Maryville University
St. Louis, Missouri

**Rebekah R. Bower, MS, ATC, LAT**
Education Coordinator
Athletic Training Education Program
Health, Phys. Ed. & Recreation Department
Wright State University
Dayton, Ohio

**Marc Campo, PT, MS, OSC, Cert. MDT**
Assistant Professor
Physical Therapy Department
Mercy College
Dobbs Ferry, New York

**Gary Steven Chleboun, PhD, PT**
Professor
School of Physical Therapy
Ohio University
Athens, Ohio

**Liz L. Harrison, DPT, BPT, MSc, PhD**
Professor and Associate Dean
School of Physical Therapy
University of Saskatchewan
Saskatoon, Saskatchewan, Canada

**Suchita Kulkarni-Lambore, PT, PhD**
Associate Professor
Physical Therapy Department
Chatham College
Pittsburgh, Pennsylvania

**Teresa Seefeld, PT, ATC**
Assistant Professor
Athletic Training Department
University of Mary
Bismarck, North Dakota

# Contents

# INTRODUCTION TO GONIOMETRY

## OBJECTIVES

On completion of Part I, the reader will be able to:

1. **Define:**
   - Goniometry
   - Planes and axes
   - Range of motion
   - End-feel
   - Muscle length testing
   - Reliability
   - Validity

2. **Identify the appropriate planes and axes for each of the following motions:**

   Flexion–extension, abduction–adduction, and rotation

3. **Compare:**
   - Active and passive ranges of motion
   - Arthrokinematic and osteokinematic motions
   - Soft, firm, and hard end-feels
   - Hypomobility and hypermobility
   - Capsular and noncapsular patterns of restricted motion
   - One-joint, two-joint, and multijoint muscles
   - Reliability and validity
   - Intratester and intertester reliability

4. **Explain the importance of:**
   - Testing positions
   - Stabilization

   - Clinical estimates of range of motion
   - Palpating bony landmarks
   - Recording starting and ending positions

5. **Describe the parts of universal, fluid, and pendulum goniometers**

6. **List:**
   - Six-step explanation sequence
   - 12-step testing sequence
   - 10 items included in recording

7. **Perform a goniometric evaluation of the elbow joint including:**
   - Clear explanation of the procedure
   - Positioning of a subject in the testing position
   - Adequate stabilization of the proximal joint component
   - Correct determination of the end of the range of motion
   - Correct identification of the end-feel
   - Palpation of the correct bony landmarks
   - Accurate alignment of the goniometer
   - Correct reading of the goniometer and recording of the measurement

8. **Perform and interpret intratester and intertester reliability tests including standard deviation, coefficient of variation, correlation coefficients, and standard error of measurement.**

# Chapter 1

# Basic Concepts

This book is designed to serve as a guide to learning the technique of human joint measurement called goniometry. Background information on principles and procedures necessary for an understanding of goniometry is found in Part 1. Practice exercises are included at appropriate intervals to help the examiner apply this information and develop the psychomotor skills necessary for competency in goniometry. The validity and reliability of goniometric measurements are explored to encourage thoughtful and appropriate use of these techniques in clinical practice. Procedures for the goniometric examination of joint range of motion and muscle length testing of the upper extremity, lower extremity, and spine and temporomandibular joint are presented in Parts II, III, and IV, respectively.

## Goniometry

The term goniometry is derived from two Greek words, *gonia*, meaning angle, and *metron*, meaning measure. Therefore, goniometry refers to the measurement of angles, in particular the measurement of angles created at human joints by the bones of the body. The examiner obtains these measurements by placing the parts of the measuring instrument, called a goniometer, along the bones immediately proximal and distal to the joint being evaluated. Goniometry may be used to determine both a particular joint position and the total amount of motion available at a joint.

**Example:** The elbow joint is evaluated by placing the parts of the measuring instrument on the humerus (proximal segment) and the forearm (distal segment) and measuring either a specific joint position or the total arc of motion (Fig. 1.1).

Goniometry is an important part of a comprehensive examination of joints and surrounding soft tissue. A comprehensive examination typically begins by interviewing the subject and reviewing records to obtain an accurate description of current symptoms; functional abilities; occupational, social, and recreational activities; and medical history. Observation of the body to assess bone and soft tissue contour, as well as skin and nail condition, usually follows the interview. Gentle

FIGURE 1.1 The left upper extremity of a subject in the supine position is shown. The parts of the measuring instrument have been placed along the proximal (humerus) and distal (radius) segments and centered over the axis of the elbow joint. When the distal segment has been moved toward the proximal segment (elbow flexion), a measurement of the arc of motion can be obtained.

145°

Distal segment

Proximal segment

Tim Malone

palpation is used to determine skin temperature and the quality of soft tissue deformities and to locate pain symptoms in relation to anatomical structures. Anthropometric measurements such as leg length, circumference, and body volume may be indicated.

The performance of active joint motions by the subject during the examination allows the examiner to screen for abnormal movements and gain information about the subject's willingness to move. If abnormal active motions are found, the examiner performs passive joint motions in an attempt to determine reasons for joint limitation. Performing passive joint motions enables the examiner to assess the tissue that is limiting the motion, detect pain, and make an estimate of the amount of motion. Goniometry is used to measure and document the amount of active and passive joint motion as well as abnormal fixed joint positions. Resisted isometric muscle contractions, joint integrity and mobility tests, and special tests for specific body regions are used in conjunction with goniometry to help identify the injured anatomical structures. Tests to assess muscle performance and neurological function are often included. Diagnostic imaging procedures and laboratory tests may be required.

Goniometric data used in conjunction with other information can provide a basis for the following:

- Determining the presence or absence of impairment
- Establishing a diagnosis
- Developing a prognosis, treatment goals, and plan of care
- Evaluating progress or lack of progress toward rehabilitative goals
- Modifying treatment
- Motivating the subject
- Researching the effectiveness of therapeutic techniques or regimens (for example, measuring outcomes following exercises, medications, and surgical procedures)
- Fabricating orthoses and adaptive equipment

## ◯ Joint Motion

### Arthrokinematics

Motion at a joint occurs as the result of movement of one joint surface in relation to another. **Arthrokinematics** is the term used to refer to the movement of joint surfaces. The movements of joint surfaces are described as slides (or glides), spins, and rolls.[1,2] A **slide (glide)**, which is a translatory motion, is the sliding of one joint surface over another, as when a braked wheel skids (Fig. 1.2). A **spin** is a rotary motion, similar to the spinning of a toy top. All points on the moving joint surface rotate around a fixed axis of motion (Fig. 1.3). A **roll** is a rotary motion similar to the rolling of the bottom of a rocking chair on the floor or the rolling of a tire on the road (Fig. 1.4).

In the human body, slides, spins, and rolls usually occur in combination with each other and result in angular movement of the shafts of the bones. The combination of the sliding and rolling is referred to as roll-sliding or roll-gliding[3] and

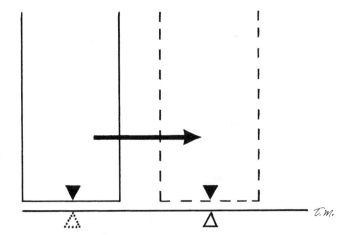

**FIGURE 1.2** A slide is a translatory motion in which the same point on the moving joint surface comes in contact with new points on the opposing surface, and all the points on the moving surface travel the same amount of distance.

**FIGURE 1.3** A spin is a rotary motion in which all the points on the moving surface rotate around a fixed central axis. The points on the moving joint surface that are closer to the axis of motion will travel a smaller distance than the points further from the axis.

allows for increased motion at a joint by postponing the joint compression and separation that would occur at either side of the joint during a pure roll. The direction of the rolling and sliding components of a roll-slide will vary depending on the shape of the moving joint surface.[2,3] If a convex joint surface is moving, the convex surface will roll in the same direction as the angular motion of the shaft of the bone but will slide in the opposite direction (Fig. 1.5A). If a concave joint surface is moving, the concave surface will roll and slide in the same direction as the angular motion of the shaft of the bone (Fig. 1.5B).

Arthrokinematic motions are examined for amount of motion, tissue resistance at the end of the motion (end-feel),

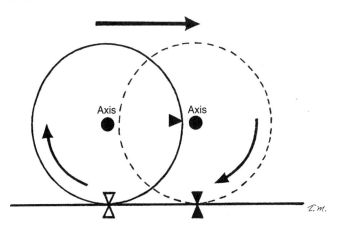

**FIGURE 1.4** A roll is a rotary motion in which new points on the moving joint surface come in contact with new points on the opposing surface. The axis of rotation has also moved, in this case to the right.

and effect on the patient's symptoms.[4] The ranges of arthrokinematic motions are very small and cannot be measured with a goniometer or standard ruler. Instead, arthrokinematic motions are subjectively compared to the same motion on the contralateral side of the body, or compared to an examiner's past experience testing people of similar age and gender as the patient. These motions are also called accessory or joint play motions.

## Osteokinematics

**Osteokinematics** refers to the gross movement of the shafts of bones rather than the movement of joint surfaces. The movements of the shafts of bones are usually described in

terms of the rotary or angular motion produced, as if the movement occurs around a fixed axis of motion. Goniometry measures the angles created by the rotary motion of the shafts of the bones. Some translatory shifting of the axis of motion usually occurs during movement; however, most clinicians find the description of osteokinematic movement in terms of just rotary motion to be sufficiently accurate and use goniometry to measure osteokinematic movements.

## Planes and Axes

Osteokinematic motions are classically described as taking place in one of the three **cardinal planes** of the body (sagittal, frontal, transverse) around three corresponding **axes** (medial–lateral, anterior–posterior, vertical). The three planes lie at right angles to one another, whereas the three axes lie at right angles both to one another and to their corresponding planes.

The **sagittal plane** proceeds from the anterior to the posterior aspect of the body. The median sagittal plane divides the body into right and left halves. The motions of flexion and extension occur in the sagittal plane (Fig. 1.6). The axis around which the motions of flexion and extension occur may be envisioned as a line that is perpendicular to the sagittal plane and proceeds from one side of the body to the other. This axis is called a **medial–lateral axis**. All motions in the sagittal plane take place around a medial–lateral axis.

The **frontal plane** proceeds from one side of the body to the other and divides the body into front and back halves. The motions that occur in the frontal plane are abduction and adduction (Fig. 1.7). The axis around which the motions of abduction and adduction take place is an **anterior–posterior axis**. This axis lies at right angles to the frontal plane and proceeds from

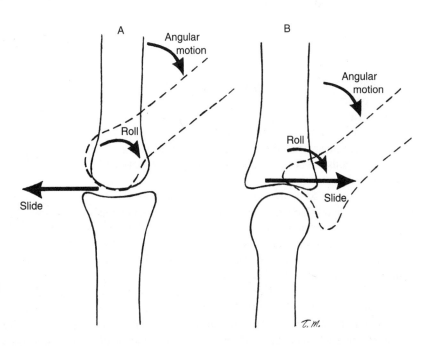

**FIGURE 1.5** (A) If the joint surface of the moving bone is convex, sliding is in the opposite direction to the rolling and angular movement of the bone. (B) If the joint surface of the moving bone is concave, sliding is in the same direction as the rolling and angular movement of the bone.

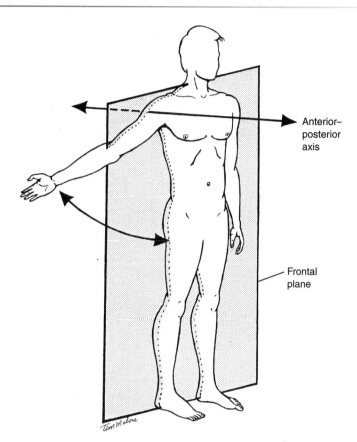

**FIGURE 1.7** The frontal plane, indicated by the shaded area, proceeds from one side of the body to the other. Motions in this plane, such as abduction and adduction of the upper and lower extremities, take place around an anterior–posterior axis.

**FIGURE 1.6** The shaded areas indicate the sagittal plane. This plane proceeds from the anterior aspect of the body to the posterior aspect. Motions in this plane, such as flexion and extension of the upper and lower extremities, take place around a medial–lateral axis.

the anterior to the posterior aspect of the body. Therefore, the anterior–posterior axis lies in the sagittal plane.

The **transverse plane** is horizontal and divides the body into upper and lower portions. The motion of rotation occurs in the transverse plane around a vertical axis (Fig. 1.8A and B). The **vertical axis** lies at right angles to the transverse plane and proceeds in a cranial to caudal direction.

The motions described previously are considered to occur in a single plane around a single axis. Combination motions such as circumduction (flexion–abduction–extension–adduction) are possible at many joints, but because of the limitations imposed by the uniaxial design of the measuring instrument, only motion occurring in a single plane can be measured in goniometry.

The type of motion that is available at a joint varies according to the structure of the joint. Some joints, such as the interphalangeal joints of the digits, permit a large amount of motion in only one plane around a single axis: flexion and extension in the sagittal plane around a medial–lateral axis. A

joint that allows motion in only one plane is described as having 1 **degree of freedom of motion.** The interphalangeal joints of the digits have 1 degree of freedom of motion. Other joints, such as the glenohumeral joint, permit motion in three planes around three axes: flexion and extension in the sagittal plane around a medial–lateral axis, abduction and adduction in the frontal plane around an anterior–posterior axis, and medial and lateral rotation in the transverse plane around a vertical axis. The glenohumeral joint has three degrees of freedom of motion.

The planes and axes for each joint and joint motion to be measured are presented in Chapters 4 through 13.

## Range of Motion

**Range of motion (ROM)** is the arc of motion that occurs at a joint or a series of joints.[5] The starting position for measuring all ROM, except rotations in the transverse plane, is anatomical position. Three notation systems have been used to define ROM: the 0 to 180 degree system, the 180 to 0 degree system, and the 360 degree system.

In the **0 to 180 degree notation system**, the upper-extremity and lower-extremity joints are at 0 degrees for flexion–extension and abduction–adduction when the body is in the anatomical position (Fig. 1.9A). A body position in which the extremity joints are halfway between medial (internal) and lateral (external) rotation is 0 degrees for the ROM in rotation (Fig. 1.9B). Normally, a ROM begins at 0 degrees and proceeds in an arc toward 180 degrees. This 0 to 180 degree system of notation, also called the **neutral zero method,** is widely used throughout the world. First described by Silver[6] in 1923, its use has been supported by many authorities, including Cave and Roberts,[7] Moore,[8] the American Academy

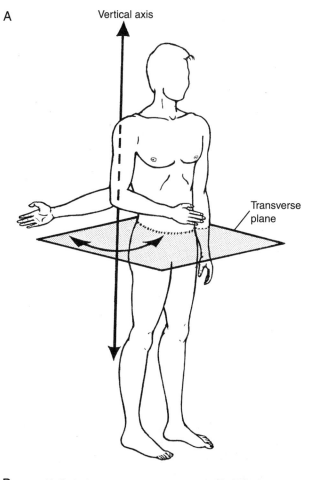

A

Vertical axis

Transverse plane

**FIGURE 1.8** The transverse plane is indicated by the shaded area. Movements in this plane take place around a vertical axis. These motions include rotation of the shoulder (A), head (B), and hip, as well as pronation and supination of the forearm.

B

Vertical axis                    Vertical axis

Anatomical position

A

Neutral position

B

**FIGURE 1.9** (A) In the anatomical position, the forearm is supinated so that the palms of the hands face anteriorly. (B) When the forearm is in a neutral position (with respect to rotation), the palm of the hand faces the side of the body.

of Orthopaedic Surgeons,[9,10] and the American Medical Association.[11]

**Example:** The ROM for shoulder flexion, which begins with the shoulder in the anatomical position (0 degrees) and ends with the arm overhead in full flexion (180 degrees), is expressed as 0 to 180 degrees.

In the preceding example, the portion of the extension ROM from full shoulder flexion back to the zero starting position does not need to be measured because this ROM represents the same arc of motion that was measured in flexion. However, the portion of the extension ROM that is available beyond the zero starting position must be measured (Fig. 1.10). Documentation of extension ROM usually incorporates only the extension that occurs beyond the zero starting position. The term **extension,** as it is used in this manual, refers to both the motion that is a return from full flexion to the zero starting position and the motion that normally occurs beyond the zero starting position. The term **hyperextension** is used to describe a greater than normal extension ROM.

Two other systems of notation have been described. The **180 to 0 degree notation system** defines anatomical position as 180 degrees.[12] ROM begins at 180 degrees and proceeds in an arc toward 0 degrees. The **360 degree notation system** also defines anatomical position as 180 degrees.[13,14] The motions of flexion and abduction begin at 180 degrees and proceed in an arc

**FIGURE 1.10** Flexion and extension of the shoulder begin with the shoulder in the anatomical position. The ROM in flexion proceeds anteriorly from the zero position through an arc toward 180 degrees. The long, bold arrow shows the ROM in flexion, which is measured in goniometry. The ROM in extension proceeds posteriorly from the zero position through an arc toward 180 degrees. The short, bold arrow shows the ROM in extension, which is measured in goniometry.

toward 0 degrees. The motions of extension and adduction begin at 180 degrees and proceed in an arc toward 360 degrees. These two notation systems are more difficult to interpret than the 0 to 180 degree notation system and are infrequently used. Therefore, we have not included them in this text.

## Active Range of Motion

**Active range of motion (AROM)** is the arc of motion attained by a subject during unassisted voluntary joint motion. Having a subject perform active ROM provides the examiner with information about the subject's willingness to move, coordination, muscle strength, and joint ROM. If pain occurs during active ROM, it may be due to contracting or stretching of "contractile" tissues, such as muscles, tendons, and their attachments to bone. Pain may also be due to stretching or pinching of noncontractile (inert) tissues, such as ligaments, joint capsules, bursa, fascia, and skin. Testing active ROM is a good screening technique to help focus a physical examination. If a subject can complete active ROM easily and painlessly, further testing of that motion is probably not needed.

If, however, active ROM is limited, painful, or awkward, the physical examination should include additional testing to clarify the problem.

## Passive Range of Motion

**Passive range of motion (PROM)** is the arc of motion attained by an examiner without assistance from the subject. The subject remains relaxed and plays no active role in producing the motion. Normally passive ROM is slightly greater than active ROM[15–17] because each joint has a small amount of available motion that is not under voluntary control. The additional passive ROM that is available at the end of the normal active ROM is due to the stretch of tissues surrounding the joint and the reduced bulk of relaxed compared to contracting muscles. This additional passive ROM helps to protect joint structures because it allows the joint to absorb extrinsic forces.

Testing passive ROM provides the examiner with information about the integrity of the joint surfaces and the extensibility of the joint capsule and associated ligaments, muscles, fascia, and skin. To focus on these issues, passive ROM rather than active ROM should be tested in goniometry. Unlike active ROM, passive ROM does not depend on the subject's muscle strength and coordination. Comparisons between passive ROMs and active ROMs provide information about the amount of motion permitted by the associated joint structures (passive ROM) relative to the subject's ability to produce motion at a joint (active ROM). In cases of impairment such as muscle weakness, passive ROMs and active ROMs may vary considerably.

**Example:** An examiner may find that a subject with a muscle paralysis has a full passive ROM but no active ROM at the same joint. In this instance, the joint surfaces and the extensibility of the joint capsule, ligaments, muscles, tendons, fascia, and skin are sufficient to allow full passive ROM. The lack of muscle strength prevents active motion at the joint.

The examiner should test passive ROM prior to performing a manual muscle test of muscle strength because the grading of manual muscle tests is based on completion of the joint ROM. An examiner must know the extent of the passive ROM before initiating a manual muscle test.

If pain occurs during passive ROM, it is often due to moving, stretching, or pinching of noncontractile (inert) structures. Pain occurring at the end of passive ROM may be due to stretching of contractile structures as well as noncontractile structures. Pain during passive ROM is not due to active shortening (contracting) of contractile tissues. By comparing which motions (active versus passive) cause pain and noting the location of the pain, the examiner can begin to determine which injured tissues are involved. Having the subject perform resisted isometric muscle contractions midway through the ROM, so that no tissues are being stretched, can help to isolate contractile structures. Having the examiner perform joint play mobility and joint integrity tests on the subject can help determine which noncontractile structures are involved. Careful consideration of the end-feel and location of tissue tension and pain during passive ROM also adds information about structures that are limiting ROM.

## End-Feel

The amount of passive ROM is determined by the unique structure of the joint being tested. Some joints are structured so that the joint capsules limit the end of the ROM in a particular direction, whereas other joints are so structured that ligaments limit the end of a particular ROM. Other normal limitations to motion include passive tension in soft tissue such as muscles, fascia, and skin; soft tissue approximation; and contact of joint surfaces.

The type of structure that limits a ROM has a characteristic feel that may be detected by the examiner who is performing the passive ROM. This feeling, which is experienced by an examiner as a barrier to further motion at the end of a passive ROM, is called the **end-feel.** Developing the ability to determine the character of the end-feel requires practice and sensitivity. Determination of the end-feel must be carried out slowly and carefully to detect the end of the ROM and to distinguish among the various normal and abnormal end-feels. The ability to detect the end of the ROM is critical to the safe and accurate performance of goniometry. The ability to distinguish among the various end-feels helps the examiner identify the type of limiting structure. Cyriax,[18] Kaltenborn,[3] and Paris[19] have described a variety of normal (physiological) and abnormal (pathological) end-feels. Table 1.1, which describes normal end-feels, and Table 1.2, which describes abnormal end-feels, have been adapted from the works of these authors.

In Chapters 4 through 13 we describe what we believe are the normal end-feels and the structures that limit the ROM for each joint and motion. Because of the paucity of specific literature in this area, these descriptions are based on our experience in evaluating joint motion and on information obtained from established anatomy[20,21] and biomechanics texts.[22–28] Considerable controversy exists among experts concerning the structures that limit the ROM in some parts of the body. Also, normal individual variations in body structure may cause instances in which the end-feel differs from our description.

Examiners should practice trying to distinguish among the end-feels. In Chapter 2, Exercise 1 is included for this purpose. However, some additional topics regarding positioning and stabilization must be addressed before this exercise can be completed.

## Hypomobility

The term **hypomobility** refers to a decrease in passive ROM that is substantially less than normal values for that joint, given the subject's age and gender. The end-feel occurs early in the ROM and may be different in quality from what is expected. The limitation in passive ROM may be due to a variety of causes including abnormalities of the joint surfaces; passive shortening of joint capsules, ligaments, muscles, fascia, and skin; and inflammation of these structures. Hypomobility has been associated with many orthopedic conditions such as osteoarthritis,[29,30] rheumatoid arthritis,[31] adhesive capsulitis,[32,33] and spinal disorders.[34, 35] Decreased ROM is a common consequence of immobilization after fractures[36,37] and scar development after burns.[38,39] Neurological conditions such as stroke, head trauma, cerebral palsy, and complex regional pain syndrome[40] can also result in hypomobility owing to loss of voluntary movement, increased muscle tone, immobilization, and pain. In addition, metabolic conditions such as diabetes have been associated with limited joint motion.[41–43]

### Capsular Patterns of Restricted Motion

Cyriax[18] has proposed that pathological conditions involving the entire joint capsule cause a particular pattern of restriction involving all or most of the passive motions of the joint. This pattern of restriction is called a **capsular pattern.** The restrictions do not involve a fixed number of degrees for each motion, but rather a fixed proportion of one motion relative to another motion.

**Example:** The capsular pattern for the elbow joint is a greater limitation of flexion than of extension. The elbow joint normally has a passive flexion ROM of

## TABLE 1.1 Normal End-Feels

| End-Feel | Description | Example |
|---|---|---|
| Soft | Soft tissue approximation | Knee flexion (contact between soft tissue of posterior leg and posterior thigh) |
| Firm | Muscular stretch | Hip flexion with the knee straight (passive elastic tension of hamstring muscles) |
| | Capsular stretch | Extension of metacarpophalangeal joints of fingers (tension in the anterior capsule) |
| | Ligamentous stretch | Forearm supination (tension in the palmar radioulnar ligament of the inferior radioulnar joint, interosseous membrane, oblique cord) |
| Hard | Bone contacting bone | Elbow extension (contact between the olecranon process of the ulna and the olecranon fossa of the humerus) |

**TABLE 1.2    Abnormal End-Feels**

| End-Feel | Description | Example |
|---|---|---|
| Soft | Occurs sooner or later in the ROM than is usual or in a joint that normally has a firm or hard end-feel. Feels boggy. | Soft tissue edema<br>Synovitis |
| Firm | Occurs sooner or later in the ROM than is usual or in a joint that normally has a soft or hard end-feel. | Increased muscular tonus<br>Capsular, muscular, ligamentous, and fascial shortening |
| Hard | Occurs sooner or later in the ROM than is usual or in a joint that normally has a soft or firm end-feel. A bony grating or bony block is felt. | Chondromalacia<br>Osteoarthritis<br>Loose bodies in joint<br>Myositis ossificans<br>Fracture |
| Empty | No real end-feel because pain prevents reaching end of ROM. No resistance is felt except for patient's protective muscle splinting or muscle spasm. | Acute joint inflammation<br>Bursitis<br>Abscess<br>Fracture<br>Psychogenic disorder |

0 to 150 degrees. If the capsular involvement is mild, the subject might lose the last 15 degrees of flexion and the last 5 degrees of extension so that the passive flexion ROM is 5 to 135 degrees. If the capsular involvement is more severe, the subject might lose the last 30 degrees of flexion and the first 10 degrees of extension so that the passive flexion ROM is 10 to 120 degrees.

Capsular patterns vary from joint to joint (Table 1.3). The capsular patterns for each joint, as presented by Cyriax[18] and Kaltenborn,[3] are listed in the beginning of Chapters 4 through 13. Studies are needed to test the hypotheses regarding the cause of capsular patterns and to determine the capsular pattern for each joint. Several studies[44–46] have examined the construct validity of Cyriax's capsular pattern in patients with arthritis or arthrosis of the knee. Although differing opinions exist, the findings seem to support the concept of a capsular pattern of restriction for the knee but with more liberal interpretation of the proportions of limitation than suggested by Cyriax.[18] Two studies[46,47] examining capsular patterns for the hip found decreases in all hip motions in osteoarthritic hips as compared to nonosteoarthritic hips, but raised questions concerning specific patterns of limitation proposed by Kaltenborn[3] and Cyriax.[18]

Hertling and Kessler[48] have thoughtfully extended Cyriax's concepts on causes of capsular patterns. They suggest that conditions resulting in a capsular pattern of restriction can be classified into two general categories: (1) conditions in which there is considerable joint effusion or synovial inflammation, and (2) conditions in which there is relative capsular fibrosis.

Joint effusion and synovial inflammation accompany conditions such as traumatic arthritis, infectious arthritis, acute rheumatoid arthritis, and gout. In these conditions the joint capsule is distended by excessive intra-articular synovial fluid, causing the joint to maintain a position that allows the greatest intra-articular joint volume. Pain triggered by stretching the capsule and muscle spasms that protect the capsule from further insult inhibit movement and cause a capsular pattern of restriction.

Relative capsular fibrosis often occurs during chronic low-grade capsular inflammation, immobilization of a joint, and the resolution of acute capsular inflammation. These conditions increase the relative proportion of collagen compared with that of mucopolysaccharide in the joint capsule, or they change the structure of the collagen. The resulting decrease in extensibility of the entire capsule causes a capsular pattern of restriction.

## Noncapsular Patterns of Restricted Motion

A limitation of passive motion that is not proportioned similarly to a capsular pattern is called a **noncapsular pattern** of restricted motion.[18,48] A noncapsular pattern is usually caused by a condition involving structures other than the entire joint capsule. Internal joint derangement, adhesion of a part of a joint capsule, ligament shortening, muscle strains, and muscle contractures are examples of conditions that typically result in noncapsular patterns of restriction. Noncapsular patterns usually

## TABLE 1.3 Capsular Pattern of Extremity Joints

| Joint | Restricted Motions |
|---|---|
| Glenohumeral joint | Greatest loss of lateral rotation, moderate loss of abduction, minimal loss of medial rotation. |
| Elbow complex (humeroulnar, humeroradial, proximal radioulnar joints) | Loss of flexion greater than loss of extension. Rotations full and painless except in advanced cases. |
| Forearm (proximal and distal radioulnar joints) | Equal loss of supination and pronation, only occurring if elbow has marked restrictions of flexion and extension. |
| Wrist (radiocarpal and midcarpal joints) | Equal loss of flexion and extension, slight loss of ulnar and radial deviation (Cyriax). |
| | Equal loss of all motions (Kaltenborn). |
| Hand | |
| Carpometacarpal joint—digit 1 | Loss of abduction (Cyriax). Loss of abduction greater than extension (Kaltenborn). |
| Carpometacarpal joint—digits 2–5 | Equal loss of all motions. |
| Metacarpophalangeal and interphalangeal joints | Equal loss of flexion and extension (Cyriax). |
| | Restricted in all motions, but loss of flexion greater than loss of other motions (Kaltenborn). |
| Hip | Greatest loss of medial rotation and flexion, some loss of abduction, slight loss of extension. Little or no loss of adduction and lateral rotation (Cyriax). |
| | Greatest loss of medial rotation, followed by less restriction of extension, abduction, flexion, and lateral rotation (Kaltenborn). |
| Knee (tibiofemoral joint) | Loss of flexion greater than extension. |
| Ankle (talocrural joint) | Loss of plantarflexion greater than dorsiflexion. |
| Subtalar joint | Loss of inversion (varus). |
| Midtarsal joint | Loss of inversion (adduction and medial rotation); other motions full. |
| Foot | |
| Metatarsophalangeal joint—digit 1 | Loss of extension greater than flexion. |
| Metatarsophalangeal joint—digits 2–5 | Loss of flexion greater than extension. |
| Interphalangeal joints | Loss of extension greater than flexion. |

Reproduced with permission from Dyrek, DA: Assessment and treatment planning strategies for musculoskeletal deficits. In O'Sullivan, SB, and Schmitz, TJ (eds): Physical Rehabilitation: Assessment and Treatment, ed 3. FA Davis, Philadelphia, 1994.
Capsular patterns are from Cyriax[18] and Kaltenborn.[3]

involve only one or two motions of a joint, in contrast to capsular patterns, which involve all or most motions of a joint.[3,18]

**Example:** A strain of the biceps muscle may result in pain and restriction at the end of the range of passive elbow extension. The passive motion of elbow flexion would not be affected.

## Hypermobility

The term **hypermobility** refers to an increase in passive ROM that exceeds normal values for that joint, given the subject's age and gender. For example, in adults the normal ROM for extension at the elbow joint is about 0 degrees.[10] A ROM measurement of 30 degrees or more of extension at the elbow is well beyond normal ROM and is indicative of a hypermobile joint in an adult. Children have some normally occurring specific instances of increased ROM as compared with adults. For example, neonates 6 to 72 hours old have been found to have a mean ankle dorsiflexion passive ROM of 59 degrees,[50] which contrasts with mean adult ROM values of between 12 and 20 degrees.[9,51] The increased motion that is present in these children is normal for their age. If the increased motion persists beyond the expected age range, it would be considered abnormal and hypermobility would be present.

Hypermobility is due to the laxity of soft tissue structures such as ligaments, capsules, and muscles that normally prevent excessive motion at a joint. In some instances the hypermobility may be due to abnormalities of the joint surfaces. A frequent cause of hypermobility is trauma to a joint. Hypermobility also occurs in serious hereditary disorders of connective tissue such as Ehlers-Danlos syndrome, Marfan syndrome, rheumatic diseases, and osteogenesis imperfecta. One of the typical physical abnormalities of Down syndrome is hypermobility. In this instance generalized hypotonia is thought to be an important contributing factor to the hypermobility.

Hypermobility syndrome (HMS) or benign joint hypermobility syndrome (BJHS) is used to describe otherwise-healthy individuals who have generalized hypermobility accompanied by musculoskeletal symptoms.[52,53] An inherited abnormality in collagen and regular physical exercise are thought to be responsible for the joint laxity in these individuals.[54,55] Traditionally, the diagnosis of HMS involves the exclusion of other conditions, a score of at least "4" on the Beighton scale (Table 1-4), and arthralgia for longer than 3 months in four or more joints.[56–58] Some researchers have noted that these criteria are inadequate for children because scores greater than "4" on the Beighton scale have been found in 65 percent of a sample of 1120 children ages 4 to 7 years in Brazil.[55] Other criteria have also been proposed, including additional joint motions and extra-articular signs.[53,54,58]

## TABLE 1.4 Beighton Hypermobility Score

| The Ability to | Points |
|---|---|
| Passively appose thumb to forearm | |
|   Right | 1 |
|   Left | 1 |
| Passively extend fifth MCP joint more than 90 degrees | |
|   Right | 1 |
|   Left | 1 |
| Hyperextend elbow more than 10 degrees | |
|   Right | 1 |
|   Left | 1 |
| Hyperextend knee more than 10 degrees | |
|   Right | 1 |
|   Left | 1 |
| Place palms on floor by flexing trunk with knees straight | 1 |
| Total Beighton Score = sum of points. | 0–9 |

Adapted from Beighton, P, Solomon, L, and Soskolne, CL: Articular mobility in an African population. Ann Rheum Dis 32:23, 1973.

According to Grahame,[53] the following joint motions should also be considered: shoulder lateral rotation greater than 90 degrees, cervical spine lateral flexion greater than 60 degrees, distal interphalangeal joint hyperextension greater than 60 degrees, and first metatarsophalangeal joint extension greater than 90 degrees.

## Factors Affecting Range of Motion

ROM varies among individuals and is influenced by factors such as age, gender, and whether the motion is performed actively or passively. A fairly extensive amount of research on the effects of age and gender on ROM has been conducted for the upper and lower extremities as well as the spine. Other factors relating to subject characteristics such as body mass index (BMI), occupational activities, and recreational activities may affect ROM, but have not been as extensively researched as age and gender. In addition, factors relating to the testing process, such as the testing position, type of instrument employed, experience of the examiner, and even time of day have been identified as affecting ROM measurements. A brief summary of research findings that examine age and gender effects on ROM is presented later in this chapter. To assist the examiner, more detailed information about the effects of age and gender on the featured joints is presented at the end of Chapters 4 through 13. Information on the effects of subject characteristics and the testing process is included if available.

Ideally, to determine whether a ROM is impaired, the value of the ROM of the joint under consideration should be compared with ROM values from people of the same age and gender and from studies that used the same method of measurement. Often such comparisons are not possible because age-related and gender-related norms have not been established for all groups. In such situations the ROM of the joint should be compared with the same joint of the individual's contralateral extremity, providing that the contralateral extremity is not impaired or used selectively in athletic or occupational activities. Most studies have found little difference between the ROM of the right and left extremities.[29,51,59–65] A few studies[16,66–68] have found slightly less ROM in some joints of the upper extremity on the dominant or right side as compared with the contralateral side, which Allender and coworkers[66] attribute to increased exposure to stress. If the contralateral extremity is inappropriate for comparison, the individual's ROM may be compared with average ROM values in handbooks of the American Academy of Orthopaedic Surgeons[9,10] and other standard texts.[11,69–73] However, in many of these texts, the populations from which the values were derived, as well as the testing positions and type of measuring instruments used, are not identified.

Mean ROM values published in several standard texts and studies are summarized at the beginning of the Range of Motion Testing Procedures for each motion and in tables at the end of Chapters 4 through 13. The ROM values presented should serve as only a general guide to identifying normal versus impaired ROM. Considerable differences in mean

ROM values are sometimes noted between the various references.

## Age

Numerous studies have been conducted to determine the effects of age on ROM of the extremities and spine. General agreement exists among investigators regarding the age-related effects on the ROM of the extremity joints of new-borns, infants, and young children up to about 2 years of age.[50,74–78] These age effects are joint and motion specific but do not seem to be affected by gender; both males and females are affected similarly. The youngest age groups have more hip flexion, hip abduction, hip lateral rotation, ankle dorsiflexion, and elbow motion as compared to adults. Limitations in hip extension, knee extension, and plantar flexion are considered to be normal for these youngest age groups. Mean values for these age groups differ by more than 2 standard deviations from mean values for adults published by the American Academy of Orthopaedic Surgeons,[9] the American Medical Association,[11] and Boone and Azen.[51] Therefore, age-appropriate norms should be used whenever possible for newborns, infants, and young children up to 2 years of age.

Most investigators who have studied a wide range of age groups have found that older adult groups have somewhat less ROM of the extremities than younger adult groups. These age-related changes in the ROM of older adults also are joint and motion specific and may affect males and females differently. Allander and associates[66] found that wrist flexion–extension, hip rotation, and shoulder rotation ROM decreased with increasing age, whereas flexion ROM in the metacarpophalangeal (MCP) joint of the thumb showed no consistent loss of motion. Roach and Miles[79] generally found a small decrease (3 to 5 degrees) in mean active hip and knee motions between the youngest age group (25 to 39 years) and the oldest age group (60 to 74 years). Except for hip extension ROM, these decreases represented less than 15 percent of the arc of motion. Stubbs, Fernandez, and Glenn[67] found a decrease of between 4 percent and 30 percent in 11 of 23 joints studied in men between the ages of 25 and 54 years. James and Parker[15] found systematic decreases in 10 active and passive lower-extremity motions in subjects who were between 70 and 92 years of age.

As with the extremities, age-related effects on spinal ROM appear to be motion specific. Investigators have reached varying conclusions regarding how large a decrease in ROM occurs with increasing age. Moll and Wright[80] found an initial increase in thoracolumbar spinal mobility (flexion, extension, lateral flexion) in subjects from 15 to 34 years of age, followed by a progressive decrease with increasing age. These authors concluded that age alone may decrease spinal mobility from 25 percent to 52 percent by the seventh decade, depending on the motion. Loebl[81] found that thoracolumbar spinal mobility (flexion–extension) decreases with age an average of 8 degrees per decade. Fitzgerald and colleagues[82] found a systematic decrease in lateral flexion and extension of the lumbar spine at 20-year intervals but no differences in rotation and forward flexion. Youdas and associates[83] found that with each decade both females and males lose approximately 5 degrees

of active motion in neck extension and 3 degrees in lateral flexion and rotation. Chen and colleagues,[84] in a review of the literature regarding the effects of aging on cervical spine ROM, concluded that active cervical ROM decreased by 4 degrees per decade, which is similar to the findings of Youdas and associates.

## Gender

The effects of gender on the ROM of the extremities and spine also appear to be joint and motion specific. If gender differences in the amount of ROM are found, females are more often reported to have slightly greater ROM than males. In general, gender differences appear to be more prevalent in adults than in young children.

Bell and Hoshizaki[85] found that females across an age range of 18 to 88 years had more flexibility than males in 14 of 17 joint motions tested. Beighton, Solomon, and Soskolne,[56] in a study of an African population, found that females between 0 and 80 years of age were more mobile than their male counterparts. Walker and coworkers,[86] in a study of 28 joint motions in 60 to 84 year olds, reported that 8 motions were greater in females and 4 motions were greater in males, whereas the other motions showed little gender difference. Kalscheur and associates[87] measured 24 upper-extremity and cervical motions in men and women between the ages of 63 and 86 years. Gender differences were noted for 14 of the motions, and in all cases the older women had greater active ROM than the older men. Looking at the thoracolumbar spine, Moll and Wright[80] found that female left lateral flexion exceeded male left lateral flexion by 11 percent. However, male mobility exceeded female mobility in thoracolumbar flexion and extension.

## ⟳ Muscle Length Testing

Maximal **muscle length** is the greatest extensibility of a muscle-tendon unit.[5] It is the maximal distance between the proximal and the distal attachments of a muscle to bone. Clinically, muscle length is not measured directly; instead, it is measured indirectly by determining the maximal passive ROM of the joint(s) crossed by the muscle.[88–90] Muscle length, in addition to the integrity of the joint surfaces and the extensibility of the capsule, ligaments, fascia, and skin, affects the amount of passive ROM of a joint. The purpose of testing muscle length is to ascertain whether hypomobility or hypermobility is caused by the length of the inactive antagonist muscle or other structures. By ascertaining which structures are involved, the health professional can choose more specific and more effective treatment procedures.

Muscles can be categorized by the number of joints they cross from their proximal to their distal attachments. **One-joint muscles** cross and therefore influence the motion of only one joint. **Two-joint muscles** cross and influence the motion of two joints, whereas multi-joint muscles cross and influence multiple joints.

No difference exists between the indirect measurement of the length of a one-joint muscle and the measurement of passive joint ROM in the direction opposite to the muscle's active motion. Usually, one-joint muscles have sufficient length to allow full passive ROM at the joint they cross. If a one-joint muscle is shorter than normal, passive ROM in the direction opposite to the muscle's action is decreased and the end-feel is firm owing to a muscular stretch. At the end of the ROM the examiner may be able to palpate tension within the muscle-tendon unit if the structures are superficial. In addition, the subject may complain of pain in the region of the tight muscle and tendon. These signs and symptoms help to confirm muscle shortness as the cause of the joint limitation.

If a one-joint muscle is abnormally lax, passive tension in the capsule and ligaments may initially maintain a normal ROM. However, with time, these joint structures often lengthen as well and passive ROM at the joint increases. Because the indirect measurement of the length of one-joint muscles is the same as the measurement of passive joint ROM, we have not presented specific muscle length tests for one-joint muscles.

**Example:** The length of one-joint hip adductors such as the adductor longus, adductor magnus, and adductor brevis is assessed by measuring passive hip abduction ROM. The indirect measurement of the length of these hip adductor muscles is identical to the measurement of passive hip abduction ROM (Fig. 1.11).

In contrast to one-joint muscles, the length of two-joint and multi-joint muscles is usually not sufficient to allow full passive ROM to occur simultaneously at all joints crossed by these muscles.[91] This inability of a muscle to lengthen and allow full ROM at all of the joints the muscle crosses is termed **passive insufficiency.** If a two-joint or multi-joint muscle crosses a joint the examiner is assessing for ROM, the subject must be positioned so that passive tension in the muscle does not limit the joint's ROM. To allow full ROM at the joint under consideration and to ensure sufficient length in the muscle, the muscle must be put on slack at all of the joints the muscle crosses that are not being assessed. A muscle is put on slack by passively approximating the origin and insertion of the muscle.

**Example:** The triceps is a two-joint muscle that extends the elbow and shoulder. The triceps is passively insufficient during full shoulder flexion and full elbow flexion. When an examiner assesses elbow flexion ROM, the shoulder must be in a neutral position so there is sufficient length in the triceps to allow full flexion at the elbow (Fig. 1.12).

To assess the length of a two-joint muscle, the subject is positioned so that the muscle is lengthened over the proximal or distal joint that the muscle crosses. One joint is held in position while the examiner attempts to further lengthen the muscle by moving the second joint through full ROM. The end-feel in this situation is firm owing to the development of passive tension in the stretched muscle. The length of the two-joint muscle is indirectly assessed by measuring the passive ROM in the direction opposite to the muscle's action at the second joint.

**Example:** To assess the length of a two-joint muscle such as the triceps, the shoulder is positioned and held in full flexion. The elbow is flexed until tension is felt in the triceps, creating a firm end-feel. The length of the triceps is determined by measuring passive ROM of elbow flexion with the shoulder in flexion (Fig. 1.13).

**FIGURE 1.11** The indirect measurement of the muscle length of one-joint hip adductors is the same as measurement of passive hip abduction ROM.

**FIGURE 1.12** During the measurement of elbow flexion ROM, the shoulder must be in neutral to avoid passive insufficiency of the triceps, which would limit the ROM.

The length of multi-joint muscles is assessed in a manner similar to that used in assessing the length of two-joint muscles. However, the subject is positioned and held so that the muscle is lengthened over all of the joints that the muscle crosses except for one last joint. The examiner attempts to further lengthen the muscle by moving the last joint through full ROM. Again, the end-feel is firm owing to tension in the stretched muscle. The length of the multi-joint muscle is indirectly determined by measuring passive ROM in the direction opposite to the muscle's action at the last joint to be moved. Commonly used muscle length tests that indirectly assess two-joint and multi-joint muscles have been included in Chapters 4 through 12 as appropriate.

**FIGURE 1.13** To assess the length of the two-joint triceps muscle, elbow flexion is measured while the shoulder is positioned in flexion.

# REFERENCES

1. MacConaill, MA, and Basmajian, JV: Muscles and Movement: A Basis for Human Kinesiology, ed 2. Robert E. Krieger, New York, 1977.
2. Kisner, C, and Colby, LA: Therapeutic Exercise, ed 5. FA Davis, Philadelphia, 2007.
3. Kaltenborn, FM: Manual Mobilization of the Extremity Joints, ed 5. Olaf Norlis Bokhandel, Oslo, 1999.
4. White, DJ: Musculoskeletal Examination. In O'Sullivan, SB, and Schmitz, TJ (eds): Physical Rehabilitation, ed 5. FA Davis, Philadelphia, 2007.
5. American Physical Therapy Association: Guide to Physical Therapist Practice, ed 2. Phys Ther 81:9, 2001.
6. Silver, D: Measurement of the range of motion in joints. J Bone Joint Surg 21:569, 1923.
7. Cave, EF, and Roberts, SM: A method for measuring and recording joint function. J Bone Joint Surg 18:455, 1936.
8. Moore, ML: The measurement of joint motion. Part II: The technic of goniometry. Phys Ther Rev 29:256, 1949.
9. American Academy of Orthopaedic Surgeons: Joint Motion: Methods of Measuring and Recording. AAOS, Chicago, 1965.
10. Greene, WB, and Heckman, JD (eds): The Clinical Measurement of Joint Motion. American Academy of Orthopaedic Surgeons, Rosemont, IL, 1994.
11. American Medical Association: Guides to the Evaluation of Permanent Impairment, ed 5. Cocchiarella, L, and Andersson, GBJ (editors). AMA, Chicago, 2001.
12. Clark, WA: A system of joint measurement. J Orthop Surg 2:687, 1920.
13. West, CC: Measurement of joint motion. Arch Phys Med Rehabil 26:414, 1945.
14. Cole, TM, and Tobis, JS: Measurement of Musculoskeletal Function. In Kottke, FJ, and Lehmann, JF (eds): Krusenn's Handbook of Physical Medicine and Rehabilitation, ed 4. WB Saunders, Philadelphia, 1990.
15. James, B, and Parker, AW: Active and passive mobility of lower limb joints in elderly men and women. Am J Phys Med Rehabil 68:162, 1989.
16. Gunal, I, et al: Normal range of motion of the joints of the upper extremity in male subjects, with special reference to side. J Bone Joint Surg (Am) 78(A):1401, 1996.
17. Smahel, Z, and Klimova, A: The influence of age and exercise on the mobility of hand joints: 1: Metacarpophalangeal joints of the three-phalangeal fingers. Acta Chirurgiae Plasticae 46:81, 2004.
18. Cyriax, J: Textbook of Orthopaedic Medicine: Diagnosis of Soft Tissue Lesions, ed 8. Bailliere Tindall, London, 1982.
19. Paris, SV: Extremity Dysfunction and Mobilization. Institute Press, Atlanta, 1980.
20. Standring, S (ed): Grey's Anatomy, ed 39. Elsevier, New York, 2005.
21. Moore, KL, and Dalley, AF: Clinically Oriented Anatomy, ed 5. Lippincott, Williams & Wilkins, Baltimore, 2005.
22. Kapandji, IA: Physiology of the Joints, Vol 1, ed 2. Churchill Livingstone, London, 1970.
23. Kapandji, IA: Physiology of the Joints, Vol 2, ed 2. Williams & Wilkins, Baltimore, 1970.
24. Kapandji, IA: Physiology of the Joints, Vol 3, ed 2. Churchill Livingstone, London, 1970.
25. Steindler, A: Kinesiology of the Human Body. Charles C. Thomas, Springfield, IL, 1955.
26. Gowitzke, BA, and Milner, M: Understanding the Scientific Basis for Human Movement, ed 3. Williams & Wilkins, Baltimore, 1988.
27. Levangie, PL, and Norkin, CC: Joint Structure and Function: A Comprehensive Analysis, ed 4. FA Davis, Philadelphia, 2005.
28. Newmann, DA: Kinesiology of the Musculoskeletal System. Mosby, St. Louis, Mo, 2002.
29. Steultjens, MPM, et al: Range of joint motion and disability in patients with osteoarthritis of the knee or hip. Rheumatology 39:955, 2000.
30. Messier, SP, et al: Osteoarthritis of the knee: Effects on gait, strength, and flexibility. Arch Phys Med Rehabil 73:29, 1992.
31. Goodson, A, et al: Direct, quantitative clinical assessment of hand function: Usefulness and reproducibility. Manual Ther 12:144, 2007.
32. Stam, HW: Frozen shoulder: A review of current concepts. Physiotherapy 80:588, 1994.
33. Roubal, PJ, Dobritt, D, and Placzek, JD: Glenohumeral gliding manipulation following interscalene brachial plexus block in patients with adhesive capsulitis. J Orthop Sports Phys Ther 24:66, 1996.
34. Hagen, KB, et al: Relationship between subjective neck disorders and cervical spine mobility and motion-related pain in male machine operators. Spine 22:1501, 1997.
35. Hermann, KM, and Reese, CS: Relationship among selected measures of impairment, functional limitation, and disability in patients with cervical spine disorders. Phys Ther 81:903, 2001.
36. MacKenzie, EJ, et al: Physical impairment and functional outcomes six months after severe lower extremity fractures. J Trauma 34:528, 1993.
37. Chesworth, BM, and Vandervoort, AA: Comparison of passive stiffness variables and range of motion in uninvolved and involved ankle joints of patients following ankle fractures. Phys Ther 75:254, 1995.
38. Richard, RL, and Ward, RS: Burns. In O'Sullivan, SB and Schmitz, TJ (eds): Physical Rehabilitation: Assessment and Treatment, ed 5. FA Davis, Philadelphia, 2005.
39. Johnson, J, and Silverberg, R: Serial casting of the lower extremity to correct contractures during the acute phase of burn care. Phys Ther 75:262, 1995.
40. Field, J: Measurement of finger stiffness in algodystrophy. Hand Clin 19:511, 2003.
41. Schulte, L, et al: A quantitative assessment of limited joint mobility in patients with diabetes. Arthritis Rheum 10:1429, 1993.
42. Rao, SR, et al: Increased passive ankle stiffness and reduced dorsiflexion range of motion in individuals with diabetes mellitus. Foot & Ankle International 27:617, 2006.
43. Sauseng, S, Kastenbauer, T, and Irsigler, K: Limited joint mobility in selected hand and foot joints in patients with type 1 diabetes mellitus: A methodology comparison. Diab Nutr Metab 15:1, 2002.
44. Fritz, JM, et al: An examination of the selective tissue tension scheme, with evidence for the concept of a capsular pattern of the knee. Phys Ther 78:1046, 1998.
45. Hayes, KW, Petersen, C, and Falconer, J: An examination of Cyriax's passive motion tests with patients having osteoarthritis of the knee. Phys Ther 74:697, 1994.
46. Biji, D, et al: Validity of Cyriax's concept capsular pattern for the diagnosis of osteoarthritis of hip and/or knee. Scand J Rheumatol 27:347, 1998.
47. Klassbo, M, and Harms-Ringdahl, K: Examination of passive ROM and capsular pattern in the hip. Physiotherapy Research International 8:1, 2003.
48. Dyrek, DA: Assessment and treatment planning strategies for musculoskeletal deficits. In O'Sullivan, SB, and Schmitz, TJ (eds): Physical Rehabilitation: Assessment and Treatment, ed 3. FA Davis, Philadelphia, 1994.
49. Hertling, DH, and Kessler, RM: Management of Common Musculoskeletal Disorders, ed 4. Lippincott, Williams & Wilkins, Philadelphia, 2005.
50. Waugh, KG, et al: Measurement of selected hip, knee and ankle joint motions in newborns. Phys Ther 63:1616, 1983.
51. Boone, DC, and Azen, SP: Normal range of motion of joints in male subjects. J Bone Joint Surg Am 61:756, 1979.
52. Everman, DB, and Robin, NH: Hypermobility syndrome. Pediatr Rev 19:111, 1998.
53. Grahame, R: Hypermobility not a circus act. Int J Clin Pract 54:314, 2000.
54. Russek, LN: Hypermobility syndrome. Phys Ther 79:59, 1999.
55. Lamari, NM, Chueire, AG, and Cordeiro, JA: Analysis of joint mobility patterns among preschool children. Sao Paulo Med:123:119, 2005.
56. Beighton, P, Solomon, L, and Soskolne, CL: Articular mobility in an African population. Ann Rheum Dis 32:23, 1973.
57. Remvig, L, Jensen, DV, and Ward, RC: Are diagnostic criteria for general joint hypermobility and benign joint hypermobility syndrome based on reproducible and valid tests? A review of the literature. J Rheumatol 34:798, 2007.
58. Bird, HA: Joint hypermobility: Report from Special Interest Groups of the annual meeting of the British Society of Rheumatology. Br J Rheumatol 31:205, 1992.
59. Roaas, A, and Andersson, GB: Normal range of motion of the hip, knee and ankle joints in male subjects, 30–40 years of age. Acta Othop Scand 53:205, 1982.
60. Chang, DE, Buschbacher, LP, and Edlich, RF: Limited joint mobility in power lifters. Am J Sports Med 16:280, 1988.
61. Ahlberg, A, Moussa, M, and Al-Nahdi, M: On geographical variations in the normal range of joint motion. Clin Orthop Rel Res 234:229, 1988.
62. Schwarze, DJ, and Denton, JR: Normal values of neonatal limbs: An evaluation of 1000 neonates. J Res Pediatr Orthop 13:758, 1993.
63. Stefanyshyn, DJ, and Ensberg, JR: Right to left differences in the ankle joint complex range of motion. Med Sci Sports Exerc 26:551, 1993.
64. Mosley, AM, Crosbie, J, and Adams, R: Normative data for passive ankle plantar flexion-dorsiflexion flexibility. Clin Biomech 16:514, 2001.

65. Escalanate, A, et al: Determinants of hip and knee flexion range: Results from the San Antonio Longitudinal Study of Aging. Arthritis Care Res 12:8, 1999.

66. Allender, E, et al: Normal range of joint movements in shoulder, hip, wrist and thumb with special reference to side: A comparison between two populations. Int J Epidemiol 3:253, 1974.

67. Stubbs, NB, Fernandez, JE, and Glenn, WM: Normative data on joint ranges of motion for 25- to 54-year old males. Int J Ind Ergonomics 12:265, 1993.

68. Escalante, A, Lichtenstein, MJ, and Hazuda, HP: Determinants of shoulder and elbow flexion range: Results from the San Antonio longitudinal study of aging. Arthritis Care Res 12:277, 1999.

69. Hoppenfeld, S: Physical Examination of the Spine and Extremities. Appleton-Century-Crofts, New York, 1976.

70. Kendall, FP, et al: Muscles: Testing and Function with Posture and Pain, ed 5. Lippincott, Williams & Wilkins, Philadelphia, 2005.

71. Esch, D, and Lepley, M: Evaluation of Joint Motion: Methods of Measurement and Recording. University of Minnesota Press, Minneapolis, 1974.

72. Palmer, ML, and Epler, M: Fundamentals of Musculoskeletal Assessment Techniques. Lippincott, Williams & Wilkins, Philadelphia, 1998.

73. Reese, NB, and Bandy, WD: Joint Range of Motion and Muscle Length Testing. WB Saunders, Philadelphia, 2002.

74. Drews, JE, Vraciu, JK, and Pellino, G: Range of motion of the joints of the lower extremities of newborns. Phys Occup Ther Pediatr 4:49, 1984.

75. Phelps, E, Smith, LJ, and Hallum, A: Normal range of hip motion of infants between nine and 24 months of age. Dev Med Child Neurol 27:785, 1985.

76. Wanatabe, H, et al: The range of joint motions of the extremities in healthy Japanese people: The differences according to age. Nippon Seikeigeka Gakkai Zasshi 53:275, 1979. Cited in Walker, JM: Musculoskeletal development: A review. Phys Ther 71:878, 1991.

77. Schwarze, DJ, and Denton, JR: Normal values of neonatal limbs: An evaluation of 1000 neonates. J Pediatr Orthop 13:758, 1993.

78. Broughton, NS, Wright, J, and Menelaus, MB: Range of knee motion in normal neonates. J Pediatr Orthop 13:263, 1993.

79. Roach, KE, and Miles, TP: Normal hip and knee active range of motion: The relationship to age. Phys Ther 71:656, 1991.

80. Moll, JMH, and Wright, V: Normal range of spinal mobility. Ann Rheum Dis 30:381, 1971.

81. Loebl, WY: Measurement of spinal posture and range of spinal movement. Ann Phys Med 9:103, 1967.

82. Fitzgerald, GK, et al: Objective assessment with establishment of normal values for lumbar spinal range of motion. Phys Ther 63:1776, 1983.

83. Youdas, JW, et al: Normal range of motion of the cervical spine: An initial goniometric study. Phys Ther 72:770, 1992.

84. Chen, J, et al: Meta-analysis of normative cervical motion. Spine 24:1571, 1999.

85. Bell, RD, and Hoshizaki, TB: Relationship of age and sex with range of motion: Seventeen joint actions in humans. Can J Appl Sci 6:202, 1981.

86. Walker, JM, et al: Active mobility of the extremities in older subjects. Phys Ther 64:919, 1984.

87. Kalscheur, JA, Costello, PS, and Emery, LJ: Gender differences in range of motion in older adults. Physical & Occupational Therapy in Geriatrics 22:77, 2003.

88. Gajdosik, RL, et al: Comparison of four clinical tests for assessing hamstring muscle length. J Orthop Sports Phys Ther 18:614, 1993.

89. Tardieu, G, Lespargot, A, and Tardieu, C: To what extent is the tibia-calcaneum angle a reliable measurement of the triceps surae length: Radiological correction of the torque-angle curve. Eur J Appl Physiol 37:163, 1977.

90. Gajdosik, RL: Passive extensibility of skeletal muscle: Review of the literature with clinical implications. Clin Biomech 16:87, 2001.

91. Gajdosik, RL, Hallett, JP, and Slaughter, LL: Passive insufficiency of two-joint shoulder muscles. Clin Biomech 9:377, 1994.

# Chapter 2

# Procedures

Competency in goniometry requires that the examiner acquire the following knowledge and develop the following skills.

The examiner must have knowledge of the following for each joint and motion:

1. Joint structure and function
2. Normal end-feels
3. Testing positions
4. Stabilization required
5. Anatomical bony landmarks
6. Instrument alignment

The examiner must have the skill to perform the following for each joint and motion:

1. Position and stabilize correctly
2. Move a body part through the appropriate range of motion (ROM)
3. Determine the end of the ROM and end-feel
4. Palpate the appropriate bony landmarks
5. Align the measuring instrument with landmarks
6. Read the measuring instrument
7. Record measurements correctly

## ◯ Positioning

Positioning is an important part of goniometry because it is used to place the joints in a zero starting position and helps to stabilize the proximal joint segment. Positioning affects the amount of tension in soft tissue structures (capsule, ligaments, muscles) surrounding a joint. A testing position in which one or more of these soft tissue structures become taut results in a more limited ROM than a position in which the same structures become lax. As can be seen in the following example, the use of different testing positions alters the ROM obtained for hip flexion.

**Example:** A testing position in which the knee is flexed yields a greater hip flexion ROM than a testing position in which the knee is extended. When the knee is extended, hip flexion is prematurely limited by tension in the hamstring muscles.

It is important that examiners use the same testing position during successive measurements of a joint ROM so that the relative amounts of tension in the soft tissue structures are the same as in previous measurements. In this manner, a comparison of ROM measurements taken in the same position should yield similar results. When different testing positions are used for successive measurements of a joint ROM, more variability is added to the measurement[1–10] and no basis for comparison exists. If testing positions vary, it is difficult to determine if differences in successive measurements are the result of changes in the testing position or a true change in joint ROM.

**Testing positions** refer to the positions of the body that we recommend for obtaining goniometric measurements. The series of testing positions that are presented in this text are designed to do the following:

1. Place the joint in a starting position of 0 degrees
2. Permit a complete ROM
3. Provide stabilization for the proximal joint segment

If a testing position cannot be attained because of restrictions imposed by the environment or limitations of the subject, the examiner must use creativity to decide how to obtain a particular joint measurement. The alternative testing position that is created must serve the same three functions as the recommended testing position. The examiner must describe the position precisely in the subject's records so that the same position can be used for all subsequent measurements.

Testing positions involve a variety of body positions such as supine, prone, sitting, and standing. When an examiner intends to test several joints and motions during one testing session, the goniometric examination should be planned to avoid moving the subject unnecessarily. For example, if the subject is prone, all possible measurements in this position should be taken before the subject is moved into another position. Table 2.1, which lists joint measurements by body

| TABLE 2.1 | Joint Measurements by Body Position | | | |
|---|---|---|---|---|
| | **Prone** | **Supine** | **Sitting** | **Standing** |
| Shoulder | Extension | Flexion | | |
| | | Abduction | | |
| | | Medial rotation | | |
| | | Lateral rotation | | |
| Elbow | | Flexion | | |
| Forearm | | | Pronation | |
| | | | Supination | |
| Wrist | | | All motions | |
| Hand | | | All motions | |
| Hip | Extension | Flexion | Medial rotation | |
| | | Abduction | Lateral rotation | |
| | | Adduction | | |
| Knee | | Flexion | | |
| Ankle and foot | Subtalar inversion | Dorsiflexion | Dorsiflexion | |
| | Subtalar eversion | Plantar flexion | Plantar flexion | |
| | | Inversion | Inversion | |
| | | Eversion | Eversion | |
| | | Midtarsal inversion | Midtarsal inversion | |
| | | Midtarsal eversion | Midtarsal eversion | |
| Toes | | All motions | All motions | |
| Cervical spine | | | Flexion | |
| | | | Extension | |
| | | | Lateral flexion | |
| | | Rotation (I) | Rotation | |
| Thoracolumbar spine | | | Rotation | Flexion |
| | | | | Extension |
| | | | | Lateral flexion |
| | | | | Rotation (I) |
| Temporomandibular joint | | | Depression | |
| | | | Protrusion | |
| | | | Lateral excursion | |

I = measured with inclinometer(s)

position, has been designed to help the examiner plan a goniometric examination.

## ⌀ Stabilization

The testing position helps to stabilize the subject's body and proximal joint segment so that a motion can be isolated to the joint being examined. Isolating the motion to one joint helps to ensure that a true measurement of the motion is obtained, rather than a measurement of combined motions that occur at

a series of joints. Positional stabilization may be supplemented by manual stabilization provided by the examiner.

**Example:** Measurement of medial rotation of the hip joint is performed with the subject in a sitting position (Fig. 2.1A). The pelvis (proximal segment) is partially stabilized by the body weight, but the subject is moving her trunk and pelvis during hip rotation. Additional stabilization should be provided by the examiner and the subject (Fig. 2.1B). The examiner provides manual stabilization for the pelvis by exerting a downward pressure on the iliac crest of the side

**FIGURE 2.1** (A) The consequences of inadequate stabilization. The examiner has failed to stabilize the subject's pelvis and trunk; therefore, a lateral tilt of the pelvis and lateral flexion of the trunk accompany the motion of hip medial rotation. The range of medial rotation appears greater than it actually is because of the added motion from the pelvis and trunk. (B) The use of proper stabilization. The examiner uses her right hand to stabilize the pelvis (keeping the pelvis from raising off the table) during the passive range of motion (ROM). The subject assists in stabilizing the pelvis by placing her body weight on the left side. The subject keeps her trunk straight by placing both hands on the table.

being tested. The subject is instructed to shift her body weight over the hip being tested to help keep the pelvis stabilized.

For most measurements, the amount of manual stabilization applied by an examiner must be sufficient to keep the proximal joint segment fixed during movement of the distal joint segment. If both the distal and the proximal joint segments are allowed to move during joint testing, the end of the ROM is difficult to determine. Learning how to stabilize requires practice because the examiner must stabilize with one hand while simultaneously moving the distal joint segment with the other hand. Sometimes in the case of the hip a second person may be necessary to help either with stabilizing the proximal joint segment or with holding the distal joint segment after the end of the ROM has been determined, so that the goniometer can be accurately aligned. The techniques of stabilizing the proximal joint segment and of determining the end of a ROM (end-feel) are basic to goniometry and must be mastered prior to learning how to use the goniometer. **Exercise 1 on page 22** is designed to help the examiner learn how to stabilize and determine the end of the ROM and end-feel.

## ⊘ Measurement Instruments

A variety of instruments are used to measure joint motion. These instruments range from simple paper tracings and tape measures to electrogoniometers and motion analysis systems. An examiner may choose to use a particular instrument based upon the purpose of the measurement (clinical versus research); the motion being measured; and the instrument's accuracy, availability, cost, ease of use, and size.

### Universal Goniometer

The **universal goniometer** is the instrument most commonly used to measure joint position and motion in the clinical setting. Moore[11,12] designated this type of goniometer as "universal" because of its versatility. It can be used to measure joint position and ROM at almost all joints of the body. The majority of measurement techniques presented in this book demonstrate the use of the universal goniometer.

Universal goniometers may be constructed of plastic (Fig. 2.2) or metal (Fig. 2.3) and are produced in many sizes

# Exercise 1

## Determining the End of the Range of Motion and End-Feel

This exercise is designed to help the examiner determine the end of the ROM and to differentiate among the three normal end-feels: soft, firm, and hard.

**ELBOW FLEXION: Soft End-Feel**

**ACTIVITIES:** See Figure 5.13 in Chapter 5.

1. Select a subject.
2. Position the subject supine with the arm placed close to the side of the body. A towel roll is placed under the distal end of the humerus to allow space for full elbow extension. The forearm is placed in full supination with the palm of the hand facing the ceiling.
3. With one hand, stabilize the distal end of the humerus (proximal joint segment) to prevent flexion of the shoulder.
4. With the other hand, slowly move the forearm through the full passive range of elbow flexion until you feel resistance limiting the motion.
5. Gently push against the resistance until no further flexion can be achieved. Carefully note the quality of the resistance. This soft end-feel is caused by compression of the muscle bulk of the anterior forearm with that of the anterior upper arm.
6. Compare this soft end-feel with the soft end-feel found in knee flexion (see ROM Testing Procedures for Knee Flexion and Figure 9.6 in Chapter 9).

**ANKLE DORSIFLEXION: Firm End-Feel**

**ACTIVITIES:** See Figure 10.11 in Chapter 10.

1. Select a subject.
2. Place the subject sitting so that the lower leg is over the edge of the supporting surface and the knee is flexed at least 30 degrees.
3. With one hand, stabilize the distal end of the tibia and fibula to prevent knee extension and hip motions.
4. With the other hand on the plantar surface of the metatarsals, slowly move the foot through the full passive range of ankle dorsiflexion until you feel resistance limiting the motion.
5. Push against the resistance until no further dorsiflexion can be achieved. Carefully note the quality of the resistance. This firm end-feel is caused by tension in the Achilles tendon, the posterior portion of the deltoid ligament, the posterior talofibular ligament, the calcaneo-fibular ligament, the posterior joint capsule, and the wedging of the talus into the mortise formed by the tibia and fibula.
6. Compare this firm end-feel with the firm end-feel found in metacarpophalangeal (MCP) extension of the fingers (see ROM Testing Procedures for Fingers MCP Extension and Figure 7.12 in Chapter 7).

**ELBOW EXTENSION: Hard End-Feel**

**ACTIVITIES:**

1. Select a subject.
2. Position the subject supine with the arm placed close to the side of the body. A small towel roll is placed under the distal end of the humerus to allow full elbow extension. The forearm is placed in full supination with the palm of the hand facing the ceiling.
3. With one hand resting on the towel roll and holding the posterior, distal end of the humerus, stabilize the humerus (proximal joint segment) to prevent extension of the shoulder.
4. With the other hand, slowly move the forearm through the full passive range of elbow extension until you feel resistance limiting the motion.
5. Gently push against the resistance until no further extension can be attained. Carefully note the quality of the resistance. When the end-feel is hard, it has no give to it. This hard end-feel is caused by contact between the olecranon process of the ulna and the olecranon fossa of the humerus.
6. Compare this hard end-feel with the hard end-feel usually found in radial deviation of the wrist (see ROM Testing Procedures for Radial Deviation and Figure 6.12 in Chapter 6).

**FIGURE 2.2** Plastic universal goniometers are available in different shapes and sizes. Some goniometers have full-circle bodies (A,B,C,E), whereas others have half-circle bodies (D). The 14-inch goniometer (A) is used to measure large joints such as the hip, knee, and shoulder. Six- to 8-inch goniometers (B,C,D) are used to assess midsized joints such as the wrist and ankle. The small goniometer (E) has been cut in length from a 6-inch goniometer (C) to make it easier to measure the fingers and toes.

**FIGURE 2.3** These metal goniometers are of different sizes but all have half-circle bodies. Metal goniometers with full-circle bodies are also available. The smallest goniometer (D) is specifically designed to lie on the dorsal or ventral surface of the fingers and toes while measuring joint motion. Goniometers A and B have a cut-out portion on the moving arm, whereas goniometers C and D have pointers on the moving arm to enable the reading of the scale on the bodies.

and shapes but adhere to the same basic design. Typically the design includes a body and two thin extensions called arms—a stationary arm and a moving arm (Fig. 2.4).

The **body** of a universal goniometer resembles a protractor and may form a half circle or a full circle (Fig. 2.5). The scales on a half-circle goniometer read from 0 to 180 degrees and from 180 to 0 degrees. The scales on a full-circle instrument may read either from 0 to 180 degrees and from 180 to 0 degrees, or from 0 to 360 degrees and from 360 to 0 degrees. Sometimes full-circle instruments have both 180-degree and 360-degree scales.

**FIGURE 2.4** The body of this universal goniometer forms a half circle. The stationary arm is an integral part of the body of the goniometer. The moving arm is attached to the body by a rivet so that it can be moved independently from the body. In this example, a cut-out portion, sometimes referred to as a "window," is found in the center and at the end of the moving arm. The windows permit the examiner to read the scale on the body of the goniometer.

Increments on the scales may vary from 1 to 10 degrees, but 1- and 5-degree increments are the most common.

Traditionally, the **arms** of a universal goniometer are designated as moving or stationary according to how they are attached to the body of the goniometer (Fig. 2.4). The **stationary arm** is a structural part of the body of the goniometer and cannot be moved independently from the body. The **moving arm** is attached to the center of the body of most plastic goniometers by a rivet that permits the arm to move freely on the body. The moving arm may have one or more of the following features: a pointed end, a black or white line extending the length of the arm, or a cut-out portion (window). Goniometers that are used to measure ROM on radiographs have an opaque white line extending the length of the arms and opaque markings on the body. These features help the examiner to read the scales.

The length of the arms varies among instruments from approximately 1 to 14 inches. These variations in length represent an attempt on the part of the manufacturers to adapt the size of the instrument to the size of the joints.

**Example:** A universal goniometer with 14-inch arms is appropriate for measuring motion at the knee joint because the arms are long enough to permit alignment with the greater trochanter of the femur and the lateral malleolus of the tibia (Fig. 2.6A). A universal goniometer with short arms would be difficult to use because the arms do not extend a sufficient distance along the femur and tibia to permit alignment with the bony landmarks (Fig. 2.6B). A goniometer with long arms would be awkward for measuring the MCP joints of the hand.

**FIGURE 2.5** The body of the goniometer may be either a half circle (top) or a full circle (bottom).

**FIGURE 2.6** Selecting the right-sized goniometer makes it easier to measure joint motion. (A) The examiner is using a full-circle instrument with long arms to measure knee flexion ROM. The arms of the goniometer extend along the distal and proximal segments of the joint to within a few inches of the bony landmarks (black dots) that are used to align the arms. The proximity of the ends of the arms to the landmarks makes alignment easy and helps ensure that the arms are aligned accurately. (B) The small half-circle metal goniometer is a poor choice for measuring knee flexion ROM because the landmarks are so far from the ends of the goniometer's arms that accurate alignment is difficult.

## Gravity-Dependent Goniometers (Inclinometers)

Although not as common as the universal goniometer, several other types of manual goniometers may be found in the clinical setting. **Gravity-dependent goniometers** or **inclinometers** use gravity's effect on pointers and fluid levels to measure joint position and motion (Fig. 2.7). The **pendulum**

**goniometer** consists of a 360-degree protractor with a weighted pointer hanging from the center of the protractor. This device was first described by Fox and Van Breeme[13] in 1934. The **fluid (bubble) goniometer**, which was developed by Schenkar[14] in 1956, has a fluid-filled circular chamber containing an air bubble. It is similar to a carpenter's level but, being circular, has a 360-degree scale. Other inclinometers such as the Myrin OB Goniometer and the cervical range of

**FIGURE 2.7** Each of these gravity-dependent goniometers uses a weighted pointer (A,B,D) or bubble (C) to indicate the position of the goniometer relative to the vertical pull of gravity. All of these inclinometers have a rotating dial so that the scale can be zeroed with the pointer or bubble in the starting position.

motion device (CROM) use a pendulum needle that reacts to gravity to measure motions in the frontal and sagittal planes and use a compass needle that reacts to the earth's magnetic field to measure motions in the horizontal plane. A fairly large selection of manual inclinometers and a few digital inclinometers are commercially available. Generally these instruments are more expensive than universal goniometers.

Inclinometers are either attached to or held on the distal segment of the joint being measured. The angle between the long axis of the distal segment and the line of gravity is noted. Inclinometers may be easier to use in certain situations than universal goniometers because they do not have to be aligned with bony landmarks or centered over the axis of motion. However, it is critical that the proximal segment of the joint being measured be positioned vertically or horizontally to obtain accurate measurements; otherwise, adjustments must be made in determining the measurement.[12,15] Inclinometers are also difficult to use on small joints[16] and where there is soft tissue deformity or edema.[12,15]

Although universal and gravity-dependent goniometers may be available within a clinical setting, they should not be used interchangeably.[17–20] For example, an examiner should not use a universal goniometer on Tuesday and an inclinometer on Wednesday to measure a subject's knee ROM. The two instruments may provide slightly different results, making comparisons for judging changes in ROM inappropriate.

## Electrogoniometers

**Electrogoniometers**, introduced by Karpovich and Karpovich[21] in 1959, are used primarily in research to obtain dynamic joint measurements. Most devices have two arms, similar to those of the universal goniometer, which are attached to the proximal and distal segments of the joint being measured.[22–25]

A potentiometer is connected to the two arms. Changes in joint position cause the resistance in the potentiometer to vary. The resulting change in voltage can be used to indicate the amount of joint motion. Potentiometers measuring angular displacement have also been integrated with strain gauges[26,27] and isokinetic dynamometers[28] for measuring resistive torque. Flexible electrogoniometers with two plastic end-blocks connected by a flexible strain gauge have been designed to measure angular displacement between the end-blocks in one or two planes of motion.[19,29]

Some electrogoniometers resemble pendulum goniometers.[30,31] Changes in joint position cause a change in contact between the pendulum and the small resistors. Contact with the resistors produces a change in electric current, which is used to indicate the amount of joint motion.

Electrogoniometers are expensive and take time to calibrate accurately and attach to the subject. Given these drawbacks, electrogoniometers are used more often in research than in clinical settings. Radiographs, photographs, film, videotapes, and computer-assisted video motion analysis systems are other joint measurement methods used more commonly in research settings.

## Visual Estimation

Although some examiners make visual estimates of joint position and motion rather than use a measuring instrument, we do not recommend this practice. Several authors suggest the use of visual estimates in situations in which the subject has excessive soft tissue covering physical landmarks.[32,33] Most authorities report more accurate and reliable measurements with a goniometer than with visual estimates.[34–40] Even when produced by a skilled examiner, visual estimates yield only subjective information in contrast to goniometric measurements, which yield objective information. However, estimates are useful in the learning process. Visual estimates made prior to goniometric measurements help to reduce errors attributable to incorrect reading of the goniometer. If the goniometric measurement is not in the same quadrant as the estimate, the examiner is alerted to the possibility that the wrong scale is being read.

After the examiner has read and studied this section on measurement instruments, **Exercise 2** should be completed. Given the adaptability and widespread use of the universal goniometer in the clinical setting, this book focuses on teaching the measurement of joint motion using a universal goniometer.

## Alignment

**Goniometer alignment** refers to the alignment of the arms of the goniometer with the proximal and distal segments of the joint being evaluated. Instead of depending on soft tissue contour, the examiner should use bony **anatomical landmarks** to more accurately visualize the joint segments. These landmarks, which have been identified for all joint measurements, should be exposed so that they may be identified easily and also palpated (Fig. 2.8). The landmarks should be learned and adhered to when taking all measurements. The careful visualization, palpation, and alignment of the arms of the goniometer with the landmarks improve the accuracy and consistency of the measurements.

The stationary arm is often aligned parallel to the longitudinal axis of the proximal segment of the joint, and the moving arm is aligned parallel to the longitudinal axis of the distal segment of the joint (Fig. 2.9). In some situations, because of limitations imposed by either the goniometer or the subject (Fig. 2.10A), it may be necessary to reverse the alignment of the two arms so that the moving arm is aligned with the proximal part and the stationary arm is aligned with the distal part (Fig. 2.10B). Therefore, we have decided to use the term **proximal arm** to refer to the arm of the goniometer that is aligned with the proximal segment of the joint. The term **distal arm** refers to the arm aligned with the distal

# Exercise 2

## The Universal Goniometer

The following activities are designed to help the examiner become familiar with the universal goniometer.

**EQUIPMENT:** Full-circle and half-circle universal goniometers made of plastic and metal.

**ACTIVITIES:**

1. Select a goniometer.
2. Identify the type of goniometer selected (full-circle or half-circle) by noting the shape of the body.
3. Differentiate between the moving and the stationary arms of the goniometer. (Remember that the stationary arm is an integral part of the body of the goniometer.)
4. Observe the moving arm to see if it has a cut-out portion.
5. Find the line in the middle of the moving arm and follow it to a number on the scale.
6. Study the body of the goniometer and answer the following questions:
   a. Is the scale located on one or both sides?
   b. Is it possible to read the scale through the body of the goniometer?
   c. What intervals are used?
   d. Does the body contain one, two, or more scales?
7. Hold the goniometer in both hands. Position the arms so that they form a continuous straight line. When the arms are in this position, find the scale that reads 0 degrees.
8. Keep the stationary arm fixed in place and shift the moving arm while watching the numbers on the scale, either at the tip of the moving arm or in the cut-out portion. Shift the moving arm from 0 to 45, 90, 150, and 180 degrees.
9. Keep the stationary arm fixed and shift the moving arm from 0 degrees through an estimated 45-degree arc of motion. Compare the visual estimate with the actual arc of motion by reading the scale on the goniometer. Try to estimate other arcs of motion and compare the estimates with the actual arc of motion.
10. Keep the moving arm fixed in place and move the stationary arm through different arcs of motion.
11. Repeat steps 2 to 10 using different goniometers.

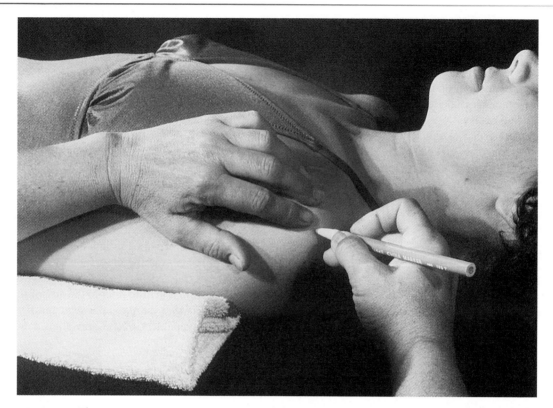

**FIGURE 2.8** The examiner is using a grease pencil to mark the location of the subject's left acromion process. Note that the patient's clothing has been removed so that the bony landmark can be easily visualized. The examiner is using the index and middle fingers of her left hand to palpate the bony landmark.

**FIGURE 2.9** When using a full-circle goniometer to measure ROM of elbow flexion, the stationary arm is usually aligned parallel to the longitudinal axis of the proximal part (subject's humerus) and the moving arm is aligned parallel to the longitudinal axis of the distal part (subject's forearm). However, if the arms of the goniometer are reversed, the same angle will be measured.

segment of the joint (Fig. 2.11). The anatomical landmarks provide reference points that help to ensure that the alignment of the arms is correct.

The **fulcrum** of the goniometer may be placed over the approximate location of the axis of motion of the joint being measured. However, because the axis of motion changes during movement, the location of the fulcrum must be adjusted accordingly. Moore[12] suggests that careful alignment of the proximal and distal arms ensures that the fulcrum of the goniometer is located at the approximate axis of motion. Therefore, alignment of the arms of the goniometer with the proximal and distal joint segments should be emphasized more than placement of the fulcrum over the approximate axis of motion.

Errors in measuring joint position and motion with a goniometer can occur if the examiner is not careful. When aligning the arms and reading the scale of the goniometer, the examiner must be at eye level with the goniometer to avoid parallax. If the examiner is higher or lower than the goniometer, the alignment and scales may be distorted. Often a goniometer will have several scales, one going from 0 to 180 degrees and another going from 180 to 0 degrees. Examiners must carefully determine which scale is correct for the measurement. If a visual estimate is made before the measurement is taken, gross errors caused by reading the wrong scale

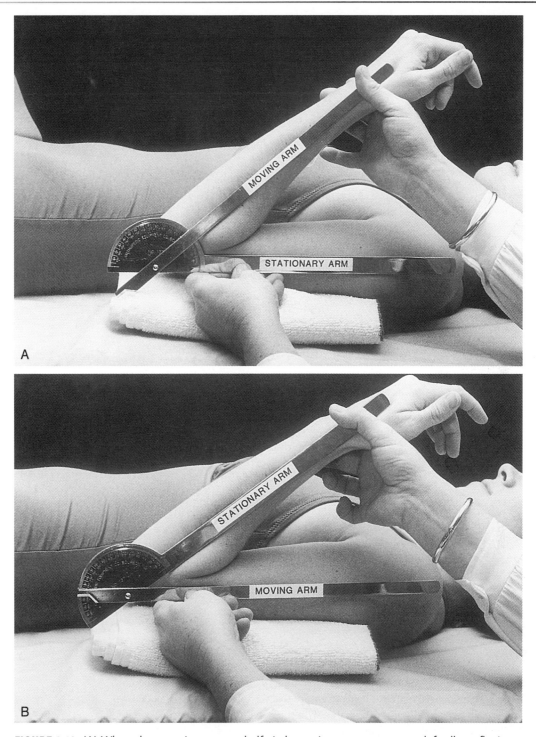

**FIGURE 2.10** (A) When the examiner uses a half-circle goniometer to measure left elbow flexion, aligning the moving arm with the subject's forearm causes the pointer to move beyond the goniometer body, which makes it impossible to read the scale. (B) Reversing the arms of the instrument so that the stationary arm is aligned parallel to the distal part and the moving arm is aligned parallel to the proximal part causes the pointer to remain on the body of the goniometer, enabling the examiner to read the scale along the pointer.

will be obvious. Another source of error is misinterpretation of the intervals on the scale. For example, the smallest interval of a particular goniometer may be 5 degrees, but an examiner may believe the interval represents 1 degree. In this case the examiner would incorrectly read 91 degrees instead of 95 degrees.

After the examiner has read this section on alignment, Exercise 3 should be completed.

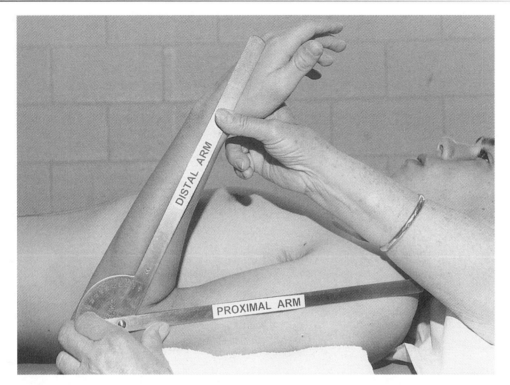

**FIGURE 2.11** Throughout the book we use the term "proximal arm" to indicate the arm of the goniometer that is aligned with the proximal segment of the joint being examined. The term "distal arm" is used to indicate the arm of the goniometer that is aligned with the distal segment of the joint. During the measurement of elbow flexion, the proximal arm is aligned with the humerus, and the distal arm is aligned with the forearm.

# Exercise 3

## Goniometer Alignment for Elbow Flexion

The following activities are designed to help the examiner learn how to align and read the goniometer.

**EQUIPMENT:** Full-circle and half-circle universal goniometers of plastic and metal in various sizes and a skin-marking pencil.

**ACTIVITIES:** See Figures 5.9 to 5.15 in Chapter 5.

1. Select a goniometer and a subject.
2. Position the subject so that he or she is supine. The subject's right arm should be positioned so that it is close to the side of the body with the forearm in supination (palm of hand faces the ceiling). A towel roll placed under the distal humerus helps to ensure that the elbow is fully extended.
3. Locate and mark each of the following landmarks with the pencil: acromion process, lateral epicondyle of the humerus, radial head, and radial styloid process.
4. Align the proximal arm of the goniometer along the longitudinal axis of the humerus, using the acromion process and the lateral epicondyle as reference landmarks. Make sure that you are positioned so that the goniometer is at eye level during the alignment process.
5. Align the distal arm of the goniometer along the longitudinal axis of the radius, using the radial head and the radial styloid process as reference landmarks.
6. The fulcrum should be close to the lateral epicondyle. Check to make sure that the body of the goniometer is not being deflected by the supporting surface.
7. Recheck the alignment of the arms and readjust the alignment as necessary.
8. Read the scale on the goniometer.
9. Remove the goniometer from the subject's arm and place it nearby so it is handy for measuring the next joint position.

10. Move the subject's forearm into various positions in the flexion ROM, including the end of the flexion ROM. At each joint position, align and read the goniometer. Remember that you must support the subject's forearm while aligning the goniometer.
11. Repeat steps 3 to 10 on the subject's left upper extremity.
12. Repeat steps 4 to 10 using goniometers of different sizes and shapes.
13. Answer the following questions:
    a. Did the length of the goniometer arms affect the accuracy of the alignment? Explain.
    b. What length goniometer arms would you recommend as being the most appropriate for this measurement? Why?
    c. Did the type of goniometer used (full-circle or half-circle) affect either joint alignment or the reading of the scale? Explain.
    d. Did the side of the body that you were testing make a difference in your ability to align the goniometer? Why?

## ○ Recording

Goniometric measurements are recorded in numerical tables, in pictorial charts, or within the written text of an evaluation. Regardless of which method is used, recordings should provide enough information to permit an accurate interpretation of the measurement. The following items are recommended to be included in the recording:

1. Subject's name, age, and gender
2. Examiner's name
3. Date and time of measurement
4. Make and type of goniometer used
5. Side of the body, joint, and motion being measured (for example, left knee flexion)
6. ROM, including the number of degrees at the beginning and end of the motion
7. Type of motion being measured (that is, passive or active motion)
8. Any subjective information, such as discomfort or pain, that is reported by the subject during the testing
9. Any objective information obtained by the examiner during testing, such as a protective muscle spasm, crepitus, or capsular or noncapsular pattern of restriction
10. A complete description of any deviation from the recommended testing positions

If a subject has normal pain-free ROM during active or passive motion, the ROM may be recorded as normal (N) or within normal limits (WNL). To determine whether the ROM is normal, the examiner should compare the ROM of the joint being tested with ROM values from people of the same age and gender, and from studies that used the same method of measurement. A selection of normal ROM values for adults is presented at the beginning of testing procedures for each motion. Text and ROM tables that report normal values by age with information on gender and methods of measurement are presented in Research Findings in Chapters 4 through 13. The ROM of the joint being tested may also be compared with the same joint of the subject's contralateral extremity, provided that the contralateral extremity is neither impaired nor used selectively in athletic or occupational activities.

If passive ROM appears to be decreased or increased when compared with normal values, the ROM should be measured and recorded. Recordings should include both the starting and the ending joint positions to define the ROM. A recording that includes only the total ROM, such as 50 degrees of flexion, gives no information as to where a motion begins and ends. Likewise, a recording that lists –20 degrees (minus 20 degrees) of flexion is open to misinterpretation because the lack of flexion could occur at either the end or the beginning of the ROM.

A motion such as flexion that begins at 0 degrees and ends at 50 degrees of flexion is recorded as 0–50 degrees of flexion (Fig. 2.12A). A motion that begins with the joint flexed at 20 degrees and ends at 70 degrees of flexion is recorded as 20–70 degrees of flexion (Fig. 2.12B). The total ROM is the same (50 degrees) in both instances, but the arcs of motion are different.

Because both the starting and the ending joint positions have been recorded, the measurement can be interpreted correctly. If we assume that the normal ROM for this movement is 0 to 140 degrees, the subject who has a flexion ROM of 0–50 degrees lacks motion at the end of the flexion ROM. The subject with a flexion ROM of 20–70 degrees lacks motion both at the beginning and at the end of the flexion ROM. The term **hypomobile** may be applied to both of these joints because both joints have a less-than-normal ROM.

Sometimes the opposite situation exists, in which a joint has a greater-than-normal range of motion and is **hypermobile.** If an elbow joint is hypermobile, the starting position for measuring elbow flexion may be in hyperextension rather than at 0 degrees. If the elbow was hyperextended 20 degrees in the starting position, the beginning of the flexion ROM would be recorded as 20 degrees of hyperextension (Fig. 2.13). To clarify that the 20 degrees represents hyperextension rather than limited flexion, a "0" representing the zero starting position, which is now within the ROM, is included. A ROM that begins at 20 degrees of hyperextension and ends at 140 degrees of flexion is recorded as 20–0–140 degrees of flexion.

Some authorities have suggested the use of plus (+) and minus (−) signs to indicate hypomobility and hypermobility. However, the use of these signs varies depending

A

0°–50°

B

20°–70°

**FIGURE 2.12** A recording of ROM should include the beginning of the range as well as the end. (A) In this illustration, the motion begins at 0 degrees and ends at 50 degrees so that the total ROM is 50 degrees. (B) In this illustration, the motion begins at 20 degrees of flexion and ends at 70 degrees, so that the total ROM is 50 degrees. For both subjects, the total ROM is the same, 50 degrees, even though the arcs of motion are different.

on the authority consulted. To avoid confusion, we have omitted the use of plus and minus signs. A ROM that does not start with 0 degrees or ends prematurely indicates hypomobility. The addition of zero, representing the usual starting position within the ROM, indicates hypermobility.

## Numerical Tables

Numerical tables typically list joint motions in a column down the center of the form (Fig. 2.14). Space to the left of the central column is reserved for measurements taken on the left side of the subject's body; space to the right is reserved for measurements taken on the right side of the body. The examiner's initials and the date of testing are

noted at the top of the measurement columns. Subsequent measurements are recorded on the same form and identified by the examiner's initials and the date at the top of the appropriate measurement column. This format makes it easy to compare a series of measurements to identify problem motions and then to track rehabilitative response over time.

## Pictorial Charts

Pictorial charts may be used in isolation or combined with numerical tables to record ROM measurements. Pictorial charts usually include a diagram of the normal starting and ending positions of the motion (Fig. 2.15).

20°–0°–140°

*Tim Malone*

**FIGURE 2.13** This subject has 20 degrees of hyperextension at his elbow. In this case, motion begins at 20 degrees of hyperextension and proceeds through the 0-degree position to 140 degrees of flexion.

| | | JW | JW | Examiner | JW | | | |
|---|---|---|---|---|---|---|---|---|
| | | 4/1/08 | 3/18/08 | Date | 3/18/08 | | | |
| | | | | Hip | | | | |
| | | 0-98 | 0-73 | Flexion | 0-118 | | | |
| | | 0-5 | 0-5 | Extension | 0-12 | | | |
| | | 0-28 | 0-18 | Abduction | 0-32 | | | |
| | | 0-12 | 0-6 | Adduction | 0-15 | | | |
| | | 0-35 | 0-24 | Medial Rotation | 0-42 | | | |
| | | 0-40 | 0-35 | Lateral Rotation | 0-44 | | | |
| | | | | Comments: | | | | |

Name Paul Jones  Age 57  Gender M  
Left  Right

**FIGURE 2.14** This numerical table records the results of ROM measurements of a subject's left and right hips. The examiner has recorded her initials and the date of testing at the top of each column of ROM measurements. Note that the right hip was tested once, on March 18, 2008, and the left hip was tested twice, once on March 18, 2008, and again on April 1, 2008.

## Sagittal–Frontal–Transverse–Rotation Method

Another method of recording, which may be included in a written text or formatted into a table, is the **sagittal–frontal–transverse–rotation (SFTR) recording method**, developed by Gerhardt and Russe.[41,42] Although it is not commonly used in the United States, it is used in a few countries in Europe and has been described by the American Medical Association.[43] In the SFTR method, three numbers are used to describe all motions in a given plane. The first and last numbers indicate the ends of the ROM in that plane. The middle

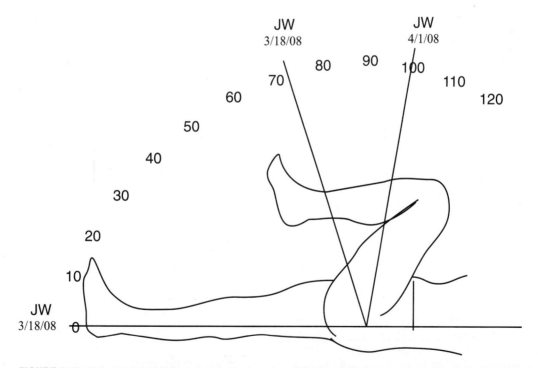

**FIGURE 2.15** This pictorial chart records the results of flexion ROM measurements of a subject's left hip. For measurements taken on March 18, 2008, note the 0 to 73 degrees of left hip flexion; for measurements taken on April 1, 2008, note the 0 to 98 degrees of left hip flexion. (Adapted with permission from Range of Motion Test, New York University Medical Center, Rusk Institute of Rehabilitation Medicine.)

number indicates the starting position, which would be 0 in normal motion.

In the **sagittal plane,** represented by S, the first number indicates the end of the extension ROM, the middle number indicates the starting position, and the last number indicates the end of the flexion ROM.

**Example:** If a subject has 50 degrees of shoulder extension and 170 degrees of shoulder flexion, these motions would be recorded: Shoulder S: 50–0–170 degrees.

In the **frontal plane,** represented by F, the first number indicates the end of the abduction ROM, the middle number indicates the starting position, and the last number indicates the end of the adduction ROM. The ends of spinal ROM in the frontal plane (lateral flexion) are listed to the left first and to the right last.

**Example:** If a subject has 45 degrees of hip abduction and 15 degrees of hip adduction, these motions would be recorded: Hip F: 45–0–15 degrees.

In the **transverse plane,** represented by T, the first number indicates the end of the horizontal abduction ROM, the middle number indicates the starting position, and the last number indicates the end of the horizontal adduction ROM.

**Example:** If a subject has 30 degrees of shoulder horizontal abduction and 135 degrees of shoulder horizontal adduction, these motions would be recorded: Shoulder T: 30–0–135 degrees.

**Rotation** is represented by R. Lateral rotation ROM, including supination and eversion, is listed first; medial rotation ROM, including pronation and inversion, is listed last. Rotation ROM of the spine to the left is listed first; rotation ROM to the right is listed last. Limb position during measurement is noted if it varies from anatomical position. "F90" would indicate that a measurement was taken with the limb positioned in 90 degrees of flexion.

**Example:** If a subject has 35 degrees of lateral rotation ROM of the hip and 45 degrees of medial rotation ROM of the hip, and these motions were measured with the hip in 90 degrees of flexion, these motions would be recorded: Hip R: (F90) 35–0–45 degrees.

Hypomobility is noted by the lack of 0 as the middle number or by less-than-normal values for the first and last numbers, which indicate the ends of the ROM.

**Example:** If elbow flexion ROM was limited and a subject could move only between 20 and 90 degrees of flexion, it would be recorded: Elbow S: 0–20–90 degrees. The starting position is 20 degrees of flexion, and the end of the ROM is 90 degrees of flexion.

A fixed-joint limitation, ankylosis is indicated by the use of only two numbers. The zero starting position is included to clarify in which motion the fixed position occurs.

**Example:** An elbow fixed in 40 degrees of flexion would be recorded: Elbow S: 0–40 degrees.

## American Medical Association Guides to Evaluation Method

Another system of recording restricted motion has been described by the American Medical Association in the Guides to the Evaluation of Permanent Impairment.[43] This book provides ratings of permanent impairment for all major body systems, including the respiratory, cardiovascular, digestive, and visual systems. The longest chapter focuses on impairment evaluation of the extremities, spine, and pelvis. Restricted active motion, ankylosis, amputation, sensory loss, vascular changes, loss of strength, pain, joint crepitation, joint swelling, joint instability, and deformity are measured and converted to percentage of impairment for the body part. The total percentage of impairment for the body part is converted to the percentage of impairment for the extremity and, finally, to a percentage of impairment for the entire body. Often these permanent impairment ratings are used, along with other information, to determine the patient's level of disability and the amount of monetary compensation to be expected from the employer or the insurer. Physicians and therapists working with patients with permanent impairments who are seeking compensation for their disabilities should refer to this book for more detail.

The system of recording restricted motion found in the Guides to the Evaluation of Permanent Impairment also uses the 0 to 180 degree notation method. The neutral starting position is recorded as 0 degrees with motions progressing toward 180 degrees. However, the recording system proposed in the Guides to the Evaluation of Permanent Impairment does differ from other recording systems described in our text. In this system, when extension exceeds the neutral starting position, it is referred to as hyperextension and is expressed with the plus (+) symbol. For example, motion at the metacarpophalangeal (MCP) joint of a finger from 15 degrees of hyperextension to 45 degrees of flexion would be recorded as +15 to 45 degrees. The plus (+) symbol is used to emphasize the fact that the joint has hyperextension.

In this system, the minus (–) symbol is used to emphasize the fact that a joint has an extension limitation. When the neutral (zero) starting position cannot be attained, an extension limitation exists and is expressed with the minus symbol. For example, motion at the MCP joint of a finger from 15 degrees of flexion to 45 degrees of flexion would be recorded as –15 to 45 degrees. It should be noted that the American Academy of Orthopaedic Surgeons[40] does not use the minus (–) symbol to indicate an extension limitation or hypomobility.

## ○ Procedures

Prior to beginning a goniometric evaluation, the examiner must do the following:

- Determine which joints and motions need to be tested
- Organize the testing sequence by body position
- Gather the necessary equipment, such as goniometers, towel rolls, and recording forms
- Prepare an explanation of the procedure for the subject

## Explanation Procedure

The listed steps and the example that follow provide the examiner with a suggested format for explaining the goniometric testing procedure to a subject.

### Steps

1. Introduce self and explain purpose
2. Explain and demonstrate goniometer
3. Explain and demonstrate anatomical landmarks
4. Explain and demonstrate testing position
5. Explain and demonstrate examiner's and subject's roles
6. Confirm subject's understanding

Lay rather than technical terms are used in the example so that the subject can understand the procedure. During the explanation, the examiner should try to establish a good rapport with the subject and enlist the subject's participation in the evaluation process. After reading the example, the examiner should practice **Exercise 4 on page 36.**

**Example:** Explanation of Goniometric Testing Procedure for Measuring Elbow Flexion

**1. Introduce Self and Explain Purpose**
*Introduction:* My name is _____. I am a (occupational title).
*Explanation:* I understand that you have been having some difficulty moving your elbow. I am going to measure the amount of motion that you have at your elbow joint to see if it is equal to, less than, or greater than normal. I will use this information to plan a treatment program and assess its effectiveness.
*Demonstration:* The examiner flexes and extends his or her own elbow so that the subject is able to observe a joint motion.

**2. Explain and Demonstrate Goniometer**
*Explanation:* The instrument that I will be using to obtain the measurements is called a goniometer. It is similar to a protractor, but it has two extensions called arms. It is placed on the outside of your body, next to your elbow.
*Demonstration:* The examiner shows the goniometer to the subject and encourages the subject to ask questions. The examiner shows the subject how the goniometer is used by holding it next to his or her own elbow.

**3. Explain and Demonstrate Anatomical Landmarks**
*Explanation:* To obtain accurate measurements, I will need to identify some anatomical landmarks. These landmarks help me to align the arms of the goniometer. Because these landmarks are important, I may

have to ask you to remove certain articles of clothing, such as your shirt. Also, to locate some of the landmarks, I may have to press my fingers against your skin.
*Demonstration:* The examiner shows the subject an easily identified anatomical landmark such as the radial styloid process.

**4. Explain and Demonstrate Recommended Testing Positions**
*Explanation:* Certain testing positions have been established to help make joint measurements easier and more accurate. Whenever possible, I would like you to assume these positions. If you need some help in getting into a particular position, I will be happy to assist you. Please let me know if you need assistance.
*Demonstration:* The sitting or supine positions.

**5. Explain and Demonstrate Examiner's and Subject's Roles During Active Motion**
*Explanation:* I will ask you to move your arm in exactly the same way that I move your arm.
*Demonstration:* The examiner takes the subject's arm through a passive ROM and then asks the subject to perform the same motion.

**6. Explain and Demonstrate Examiner's and Subject's Roles During Passive Motion**
*Explanation:* I will move your arm and take a measurement. You should relax and let me do all of the work. These measurements should not cause discomfort. Please let me know if you have any discomfort and I will stop moving your arm.
*Demonstration:* The examiner moves the subject's arm gently and slowly through the range of elbow flexion.

**7. Confirm Subject's Understanding**
*Explanation:* Do you have any questions? Are you ready to begin?

## Testing Procedure

The testing procedure is initiated after the explanation has been given and the examiner is assured that the subject understands the nature of the testing process. The testing procedure consists of the following 12-step sequence of activities.

### Steps

1. Place the subject in the testing position.
2. Stabilize the proximal joint segment.
3. Move the distal joint segment to the zero starting position. If the joint cannot be moved to the zero starting position, it should be moved as close as possible to the zero starting position. Slowly move the distal joint segment to the end of the passive ROM and determine the end-feel. Ask the subject if there was any discomfort during the motion.
4. Make a visual estimate of the ROM.
5. Return the distal joint segment to the starting position.
6. Palpate the bony anatomical landmarks.
7. Align the goniometer.
8. Read and record the starting position. Remove the goniometer.

9. Stabilize the proximal joint segment.
10. Move the distal segment through the full ROM.
11. Replace and realign the goniometer. Palpate the anatomical landmarks again if necessary.
12. Read and record the ROM.

**Exercise 5,** which is based on the 12-step sequence, affords the examiner an opportunity to use the testing procedure for an evaluation of the elbow joint. This exercise should be practiced until the examiner is able to perform the activities sequentially without reference to the exercise.

# Exercise 4

## Explanation of Goniometric Testing Procedure

**EQUIPMENT:** A universal goniometer.

**ACTIVITIES:** Practice the following six steps with a subject.

1. Introduce yourself and explain the purpose of goniometric testing. Demonstrate a joint ROM on yourself.
2. Show the goniometer to your subject and demonstrate how it is used to measure a joint ROM.
3. Explain why bony landmarks must be located and palpated. Demonstrate how you would locate a bony landmark on yourself, and explain why clothing may have to be removed.
4. Explain and demonstrate why changes in position may be required.
5. Explain the subject's role in the procedure. Explain and demonstrate your role in the procedure.
6. Obtain confirmation of the subject's understanding of your explanation.

# Exercise 5

## Testing Procedure for Goniometric Measurement of Elbow Flexion ROM

**EQUIPMENT:** A universal goniometer, skin-marking pencil, recording form, and pencil.

**ACTIVITIES:** See Figures 5.9 to 5.15 in Chapter 5.

1. Place the subject in a supine position, with the arm to be tested positioned close to the side of the body. Place a towel roll under the distal end of the humerus to allow full elbow extension. Position the forearm in full supination, with the palm of the hand facing the ceiling.
2. Stabilize the distal end of the humerus to prevent flexion of the shoulder.
3. Move the forearm to the zero starting position and determine whether there is any motion (extension) beyond zero. Move to the end of the passive range of flexion. Evaluate the end-feel. Usually the end-feel is soft because of compression of the muscle bulk on the anterior forearm in conjunction with that on the anterior humerus. Ask the subject if there was any discomfort during the motion. Refer to Figure 5.13.
4. Make a visual estimate of the beginning and end of the ROM.
5. Return the forearm to the starting position.
6. Palpate the bony anatomical landmarks (acromion process, lateral epicondyle of the humerus, radial head, and radial styloid process) and mark with a skin pencil. Refer to Figures 5.9 to 5.12.
7. Align the arms and the fulcrum of the goniometer. Align the proximal arm with the lateral midline of the humerus, using the acromion process and lateral epicondyle for reference. Align the distal arm along the lateral midline of the radius, using the radial head and the radial styloid process for reference. The fulcrum should be close to the lateral epicondyle of the humerus.
8. Read the goniometer and record the starting position. Refer to Figure 5.14. Remove the goniometer.
9. Stabilize the proximal joint segment (humerus).
10. Perform the passive ROM, making sure that you complete the available range.
11. When the end of the ROM has been attained, replace and realign the goniometer. Palpate the anatomical landmarks again if necessary. Refer to Figure 5.15.
12. Read the goniometer and record your reading. Compare your reading with your visual estimate to make sure that you are reading the correct scale on the goniometer.

# REFERENCES

1. Rothstein, JM, Miller, PJ, and Roettger, F: Goniometric reliability in a clinical setting. Phys Ther 63:1611, 1983.
2. Ekstrand, J, et al: Lower extremity goniometric measurements: A study to determine their reliability. Arch Phys Med Rehabil 63:171, 1982.
3. Sabar, JS, et al: Goniometric assessment of shoulder range of motion: Comparison of testing in supine and sitting positions. Arch Phys Med Rehabil 79:64,1998.
4. Marshall, MM, Morzall, JR, and Shealy, JE: The effects of complex wrist and forearm posture on wrist range of motion. Human Factors 41:205, 1999.
5. Werner, SL, and Plancher, KD: Biomechanics of wrist injuries in sports. Clin Sports Med 17:407, 1998.
6. Simoneau, GG, et al: Influence of hip position and gender on active hip internal and external rotation. J Orthop Sports Phys Ther 28:158, 1998.
7. Bierma-Zeinstra, SMA, et al: Comparison between two devices for measuring hip joint motions. Clin Rehabil 12:497, 1998.
8. Van Dillen, LR, et al: Effect of knee and hip position on hip extension range of motion in individuals with and without low back pain. J Orthop Sports Phys Ther 30:307, 2000.
9. Mecagni, C, et al: Balance and ankle range of motion in community-dwelling women aged 64–87 years: A correlation study. Phys Ther 80:1004, 2000.
10. Bennell, K, et al: Hip and ankle range of motion and hip muscle strength in young female ballet dancers and controls. Br J Sports Med 33:340, 1999.
11. Moore, ML: The measurement of joint motion. Part II: The technic of goniometry. Phys Ther Rev 29:256, 1949.
12. Moore, ML: Clinical assessment of joint motion. In Basmajian, JV (ed): Therapeutic Exercise, ed 3. Williams & Wilkins, Baltimore, 1978.
13. Fox, RF, and Van Breemen, J: Chronic Rheumatism, Causation and Treatment. Churchill, London, 1934, p 327.
14. Schenkar, WW: Improved method of joint motion measurement. N Y J Med 56:539, 1956.
15. Miller, PJ: Assessment of joint motion. In Rothstein, JM (ed): Measurement in Physical Therapy. Churchill Livingstone, New York, 1985.
16. Clarkson, HM: Musculoskeletal Assessment: Joint Range of Motion and Manual Muscle Strength, ed 2. Lippincott Williams & Wilkins, Philadelphia, 2000.
17. Petherick, M, et al: Concurrent validity and intertester reliability of universal and fluid-based goniometers for active elbow range of motion. Phys Ther 68:966, 1988.
18. Rheault, W, et al: Intertester reliability and concurrent validity of fluid-based and universal goniometers for active knee flexion. Phys Ther 68:1676, 1988.
19. Goodwin, J, et al: Clinical methods of goniometry: A comparative study. Disabil Rehabil 14:10, 1992.
20. Rome, K, and Cowieson, F: A reliability study of the universal goniometer, fluid goniometer, and electrogoniometer for the measurement of ankle dorsiflexion. Foot Ankle 17:28, 1996.
21. Karpovich, PV, and Karpovich, GP: Electrogoniometer: A new device for study of joints in action. Fed Proc 18:79, 1959.
22. Kettelkamp, DB, et al: An electrogoniometric study of knee motion in normal gait. J Bone Joint Surg Am 52:775, 1970.
23. Knutzen, KM, Bates, BT, and Hamill, J: Electrogoniometry of postsurgical knee bracing in running. Am J Phys Med Rehabil 62:172, 1983.
24. Carey, JR, Patterson, JR, and Hollenstein, PJ: Sensitivity and reliability of force tracking and joint-movement tracking scores in healthy subjects. Phys Ther 68:1087, 1988.
25. Torburn, L, Perry, J, and Gronley, JK: Assessment of rearfoot motion: Passive positioning, one-legged standing, gait. Foot Ankle 19:688:1998.
26. Vandervoort, AA, et al: Age and sex effects on mobility of the human ankle. J Gerontol 47:M17, 1992.
27. Chesworth, BM, and Vandervoort, AA: Comparison of passive stiffness variables and range of motion in uninvolved and involved ankle joints of patients following ankle fractures. Phys Ther 75:253, 1995.
28. Gajdosik, RL, Vander Linden, DW, and Williams, AK: Influence of age on length and passive elastic stiffness characteristics of the calf muscles-tendon unit of women. Phys Ther 79:827, 1999.
29. Ball, P, and Johnson, GR: Reliability of hindfoot goniometry when using a flexible electrogoniometer. Clin Biomech 8:13, 1993.
30. Clapper, MP, and Wolf, SL: Comparison of the reliability of the Ortho-ranger and the standard goniometer for assessing active lower extremity range of motion. Phys Ther 68:214, 1988.
31. Greene, BL, and Wolf, SL: Upper extremity joint movement: Comparison of two measurement devices. Arch Phys Med Rehabil 70:288, 1989.
32. American Academy of Orthopaedic Surgeons: Joint Motion: A Method of Measuring and Recording. AAOS, Chicago, 1965.
33. Rowe, CR: Joint measurement in disability evaluation. Clin Orthop 32:43, 1964.
34. Watkins, MA, et al: Reliability of goniometric measurements and visual estimates of knee range of motion obtained in a clinical setting. Phys Ther 71:90, 1991.
35. Youdas, JW, Carey, JR, and Garrett, TR: Reliability of measurements of cervical spine range of motion: Comparison of three methods. Phys Ther 71:98, 1991.
36. Low, JL: The reliability of joint measurement. Physiotherapy 62:227, 1976.
37. Moore, ML: The measurement of joint motion. Part I: Introductory review of the literature. Phys Ther Rev 29:195, 1949.
38. Salter, N: Methods of measurement of muscle and joint function. J Bone Joint Surg Br 34:474, 1955.
39. Minor, MA, and Minor, SD: Patient Evaluation Methods for the Health Professional. Reston Publishing, Reston, VA, 1985.
40. Greene, WB, and Heckman JD (eds): The Clinical Measurement of Joint Motion. American Academy of Orthopaedic Surgeons, Rosemont, IL, 1994.
41. Gerhardt, JJ, and Russe, OA: International SFTR Method of Measuring and Recording Joint Motion. Hans Huber, Bern, 1975.
42. Gerhardt, JJ: Clinical measurement of joint motion and position in the neutral-zero method and SFTR: Basic principles. Int Rehabil Med 5:161, 1983.
43. Cocchisrella, L and Andersson, GBJ (eds): Guides to the Evaluation of Permanent Impairment, ed 5. American Medical Association, Milwaukee, 2001.

# VALIDITY AND RELIABILITY

## ◯ Validity

For goniometry to provide meaningful information, measurements must be valid and reliable. Currier[1] states that **validity** is "the degree to which an instrument measures what it is purported to measure; the extent to which it fulfills its purpose." Stated in another way, the validity of a measurement refers to how well the measurement represents the true value of the variable of interest. The purpose of goniometry is to measure the angle created at a joint by the adjacent bones of the body. Therefore, a valid goniometric measurement is one that truly represents the actual joint angle. The joint angle is used to describe a specific joint position or, if a beginning and ending joint position are compared, a range of motion (ROM).

### Face Validity

There are four main types of validity: face validity, content validity, criterion-related validity, and construct validity.[2–5] Most support for the validity of goniometry is in the form of face, content, and criterion-related validity. **Face validity** indicates that the instrument generally appears to measure what it proposes to measure—that it is plausible.[2–5] Much of the literature on goniometric measurement does not specifically address the issue of validity; rather, it assumes that the angle created by aligning the arms of a universal goniometer with bony landmarks truly represents the angle created by the proximal and distal bones composing the joint. One infers that changes in goniometer alignment reflect changes in joint angle and represent a range of joint motion. Portney and Watkins[3] report that face validity is easily established for some tests, such as the measurement of ROM, because the instrument measures the variable of interest through direct observation.

### Content Validity

**Content validity** is determined by judging whether or not an instrument adequately measures and represents the domain of content—the substance—of the variable of interest.[2–5] Both content and face validity are based on subjective opinion. However, face validity is the most basic and elementary form of validity, whereas content validity involves more rigorous and careful consideration. Gajdosik and Bohannon[6] state, "Physical therapists judge the validity of most ROM measurements based on their anatomical knowledge and their applied skills of visual inspection, palpation of bony landmarks, and accurate alignment of the goniometer. Generally, the accurate application of knowledge and skills, combined with interpreting the results as measurement of ROM only, provide sufficient evidence to ensure content validity."

## Criterion-Related Validity

**Criterion-related validity** justifies the validity of the measuring instrument by comparing measurements made with the instrument to a well-established gold standard of measurement—the criterion.[2–5] If the measurements made with the instrument and criterion are taken at approximately the same time, **concurrent validity** is tested. Concurrent validity is a type of criterion-related validity.[3,7] Criterion-related validity can be assessed objectively with statistical methods. In terms of goniometry, an examiner may question the construction of a particular goniometer on a very basic level and consider whether the degree units of the goniometer accurately represent the degree units of a circle. The angles of the goniometer can be compared with known angles of a protractor—the criterion. Usually the construction of goniometers is adequate, and the issue of validity focuses on whether the goniometer accurately measures the angle of joint position and ROM in a subject.

### Criterion-Related Validity Studies of Extremity Joints

The best gold standard used to establish criterion-related validity of goniometric measurements of joint position and ROM is radiography. Several studies that examined extremity joints for the concurrent validity of goniometric and radiographic measurements are discussed below. When available, summaries of additional studies comparing goniometry to radiographs and/or photographs are included in the Research Findings sections of Chapters 4 to 13. Gogia and associates[8] measured the knee position of 30 subjects with radiography and with a universal goniometer. Knee positions ranged from

0 to 120 degrees. High correlation (correlation coefficient [r] = 0.97) and agreement (intraclass correlation coefficient [ICC] = 0.98) were found between the two types of measurements. Therefore goniometric measurement of knee joint position was considered to be valid. Enwemeka[9] studied the validity of measuring knee ROM with a universal goniometer by comparing the goniometric measurements taken on 10 subjects with radiographs. No significant differences were found between the two types of measurements when ROM was within 30 to 90 degrees of flexion (mean difference between the two measurements ranged from 0.5 to 3.8 degrees). However, a significant difference was found when ROM was within 0 to 15 degrees of flexion (mean difference 4.6 degrees). Ahlback and Lindahl[10] found that a joint-specific goniometer used to measure hip flexion and extension in 14 subjects closely agreed with radiographic measurements. Kato and coworkers[11] compared the accuracy of three types of goniometers aligned on the lateral and dorsal surfaces of the proximal interphalangeal joints of the 16 fixated fingers to radiographs. Mean differences between the goniometers and radiographs ranged from 0.5 to 3.3 degrees.

### Criterion-Related Validity Studies of the Spine

Various instruments used to measure ROM of the spine have also been compared with a radiographic criterion, although some researchers question the use of radiographs as the gold standard given the variability of ROM measurement taken from spinal radiographs.[12] Three studies that contrasted cervical range of motion measurements taken with gravity-dependent goniometers with those recorded on radiographs found concurrent validity to be high. Herrmann,[13] in a study of 11 subjects, noted a high correlation (r = 0.97) and agreement (ICC = 0.98) between radiographic measures and pendulum goniometer measures of head and neck flexion–extension. Ordway and colleagues[14] simultaneously measured cervical flexion and extension in 20 healthy subjects with a cervical range of motion device (CROM), a computerized tracking system, and radiographs. There were no significant differences between measurements taken with the CROM and radiographic angles determined by an occipital line and a vertical line, although there were differences between the CROM and the radiographic angles between the occiput and C-7. Tousignant and coworkers[15] measured cervical flexion and extension in 31 subjects with a CROM goniometer and radiographs that included cervical and upper thoracic motion. They found a high correlation between the two measurements (r = 0.97).

Studies that compared clinical ROM measurement methods for the lumbar spine with radiographic results report high to low validity. Macrae and Wright[16] measured lumbar flexion in 342 subjects by using a tape measure, according to the Schober and modified Schober method, and compared these results with those shown in radiographs. Their findings support the validity of these measures: correlation coefficient values between the Schober method and the radiographic evidence were 0.90 (standard error = 6.2 degrees) and between the modified Schober and the radiographs were 0.97 (standard error = 3.3 degrees). Portek and associates,[17] in a study of 11 males, found no significant difference between lumbar flexion and extension ROM measurement taken with a skin distraction method and single inclinometer compared with radiographic evidence, but correlation coefficients were low (0.42 to 0.57). Comparisons may have been inappropriate because measurements were made sequentially rather than concurrently, with subjects in varying testing positions. Radiographs and skin distraction methods were performed on standing subjects, whereas inclinometer measurements were performed in subjects sitting for flexion and prone for extension.

Burdett, Brown, and Fall,[18] in a study of 27 subjects, found a fair correlation between measurements taken with a single inclinometer and radiographs for lumbar flexion (r = 0.73) and a very poor correlation for lumbar extension (r = 0.15). Mayer and coworkers[19] measured lumbar flexion and extension in 12 patients with a single inclinometer, double inclinometer, and radiographs. No significant difference was noted between measurements. Saur and colleagues,[20] in a study of 54 patients, found lumbar flexion ROM measurement taken with two inclinometers correlated highly with radiographs (r = 0.98). Extension ROM measurement correlated with radiographs to a fair degree (r = 0.75). Samo and associates[21] used double inclinometers and radiographs to measure 30 subjects held in a position of flexion and extension. Radiographs resulted in flexion values that were 11 to 15 degrees greater than those found with inclinometers and extension values that were 4 to 5 degrees less than those found with inclinometers.

## Construct Validity

**Construct validity** is the ability of an instrument to measure an abstract concept (construct)[3] or to be used to make an inferred interpretation.[7] There is a movement within rehabilitative medicine to develop and validate measurement tools to identify functional limitations and predict disability.[22] Joint ROM may be one such measurement tool. In Chapters 4 through 13 on measurement procedures, we have included the results of research studies that report joint ROM observed during functional tasks. These findings begin to quantify the joint motion needed to avoid functional limitations. Several researchers have artificially restricted joint motion with splints or braces and examined the effect on function.[23–25] It appears that many functional tasks can be completed with severely restricted elbow or wrist ROM, providing other adjacent joints are able to compensate.

Some studies have measured the correlation between ROM values and the ability to perform functional tasks in patient populations. A study by Hermann and Reese[26] examined the relationship among impairments, functional limitations, and disability in 80 patients with cervical spine disorders. The highest correlation (r = 0.82) occurred between impairment measures and functional limitation measures, with ROM contributing more to the relationship than the other two impairment measures of cervical muscle force and pain. Triffitt[27] found significant correlations between the amount of shoulder ROM and the ability to perform nine functional activities in 125 patients with shoulder symptoms. Wagner and colleagues[28] measured passive ROM of wrist flexion, extension, radial and ulnar deviation, and the strength of the wrist extensor and flexor muscles in 18 boys with Duchenne muscular dystrophy. A highly significant negative correlation was found between difficulty performing functional hand tasks and radial deviation ROM (r = −0.76 to −0.86) and between difficulty performing functional hand tasks and wrist extensor strength (r = −0.61 to −0.83).

## ⟳ Reliability

The **reliability** of a measurement refers to the amount of consistency between successive measurements of the same variable on the same subject under the same conditions. A goniometric measurement is highly reliable if successive measurements of a joint angle or ROM, on the same subject and under the same conditions, yield the same results. A highly reliable measurement contains little measurement error. Assuming that a measurement is valid and highly reliable, an examiner can confidently use its results to determine a true absence, presence, or change in dysfunction. For example, a highly reliable goniometric measurement could be used to determine the presence of joint ROM limitation, to evaluate patient progress toward rehabilitative goals, and to assess the effectiveness of therapeutic interventions.

A measurement with poor reliability contains a large amount of measurement error. An unreliable measurement is inconsistent and does not produce the same results when the same variable is measured on the same subject under the same conditions. A measurement that has poor reliability is not dependable and should not be used in the clinical decision-making process.

### Summary of Goniometric Reliability Studies

The reliability of goniometric measurement has been the focus of many research studies. Given the variety of study designs and measurement techniques, it is difficult to compare the results of many of these studies. However, some findings noted in several studies can be summarized. An overview of such findings is presented here. More information on reliability studies that pertain to the featured joint is reviewed in Chapters 4 through 13. Readers may also wish to refer to several review articles and book chapters on this topic.[6,29–31]

The measurement of joint position and ROM of the extremities with a universal goniometer has generally been found to have good-to-excellent reliability. Numerous reliability studies have been conducted on joints of the upper and lower extremities. Some studies have examined the reliability of measuring joints held in a fixed position, whereas others have examined the reliability of measuring passive or active

ROM. Studies that measured a fixed joint position usually have reported higher reliability values than studies that measured ROM.[8,13,32,33] This finding is expected because more sources of variation and error are present in measuring ROM than in measuring a fixed joint position. Additional sources of error in measuring ROM include movement of the joint axis, variations in manual force applied by the examiner during passive ROM, and variations in a subject's effort during active ROM.

The reliability of goniometric ROM measurements varies somewhat depending on the joint and motion. ROM measurements of upper-extremity joints have been found by several researchers to be more reliable than ROM measurements of lower-extremity joints,[34,35] although opposing results have also been reported.[36] Even within the upper or lower extremities there are differences in reliability between joints and motions. For example, Hellebrandt, Duvall, and Moore,[37] in a study of upper-extremity joints, noted that measurements of wrist flexion, medial rotation of the shoulder, and abduction of the shoulder were less reliable than measurements of other motions of the upper extremity. Low[38] found ROM measurements of wrist extension to be less reliable than measurements of elbow flexion. Greene and Wolf[39] reported ROM measurements of shoulder rotation and wrist motions to be more variable than elbow motion and other shoulder motions. Reliability studies on ROM measurement of the cervical and thoracic spine in which a universal goniometer was used have generally reported lower reliability values than studies of the extremity joints.[18,40–43] Many devices and techniques have been developed to try to improve the reliability of measuring spinal motions. Gajdosik and Bohannon[6] suggested that the reliability of measuring certain joints and motions might be adversely affected by the complexity of the joint. Measurement of motions that are influenced by movement of adjacent joints or multijoint muscles may be less reliable than measurement of motions of simple hinge joints. Difficulty palpating bony landmarks and passively moving heavy body parts may also play a role in reducing the reliability of measuring ROM of the lower extremity and spine.[6,34]

Many studies of joint measurement methods have found intratester reliability to be higher than intertester reliability.[18,32–38,40,41,43–63] Reliability was higher when successive measurements were taken by the same examiner than when successive measurements were taken by different examiners. This is true for studies that measured joint position and ROM of the extremities and spine with universal goniometers and other devices such as joint-specific goniometers, pendulum goniometers, tape measures, and flexible rulers. Only a few studies found intertester reliability to be higher than intratester reliability.[64–67] In most of these studies, the time interval between repeated measurements by the same examiner was considerably greater than the time interval between measurements by different examiners.

The reliability of goniometric measurements is affected by the measurement procedure. Several studies found that intertester reliability improved when all the examiners used consistent, well-defined testing positions and measurement methods.[45,47,48,68] Intertester reliability was lower if examiners used a variety of positions and measurement methods.

Several investigators have examined the reliability of using the mean (average) of several goniometric measurements compared with using one measurement. Low[38] recommends using the mean of several measurements made with the goniometer to increase reliability over one measurement. Early studies by Cobe[69] and Hewitt[70] also used the mean of several measurements. However, Boone and associates[34] found no significant difference between repeated measurements made by the same examiner during one session and suggested that one measurement taken by an examiner is as reliable as the mean of repeated measurements. Rothstein, Miller, and Roettger,[48] in a study on knee and elbow ROM, found that intertester reliability determined from the means of two measurements improved only slightly from the intertester reliability determined from single measurements.

The authors of some texts on goniometric methods suggest the use of universal goniometers with longer arms to measure joints with large body segments such as the hip and shoulder.[29,71,72] Goniometers with shorter arms are recommended to measure joints with small body segments such as the wrist and fingers. Robson,[73] using a mathematical model, determined that goniometers with longer arms are more accurate in measuring an angle than goniometers with shorter arms. Goniometers with longer arms reduce the effects of errors in the placement of the goniometer axis. However, Rothstein, Miller, and Roettger[48] found no difference in reliability among large plastic, large metal, and small plastic universal goniometers used to measure knee and elbow ROM. Riddle, Rothstein, and Lamb[46] also reported no difference in reliability between large and small plastic universal goniometers used to measure shoulder ROM.

Numerous studies have compared the measurement values and reliability of different types of devices used to measure joint ROM. Universal, pendulum, and fluid goniometers; joint-specific devices; tape measures; and wire tracing are some of the devices that have been compared. Studies comparing clinical measurement devices have been conducted on the shoulder,[37,39] elbow,[32,37,39,57,74,75] wrist,[32,39] hand,[33,60,76,77] hip,[78,79] knee,[48,78,80,81] ankle,[78,82] cervical spine,[40,41,65,83] and thoracolumbar spine.[17,21,42,63,84–91] Many studies have found differences in values and reliability between measurement devices, whereas some studies have reported no differences.

In conclusion, on the basis of reliability studies and our clinical experience, we recommend the following procedures to improve the reliability of goniometric measurements (Table 3.1). Examiners should use consistent, well-defined testing positions and carefully palpated anatomical landmarks to align the arms of the goniometer. During successive measurements of passive ROM, examiners should strive to apply the same amount of manual force to move the subject's body. During successive measurements of active ROM, the subject should be urged to exert the same effort to perform a motion. To reduce measurement variability, it is prudent to take repeated measurements on a subject with the same type of measurement device. For example, an examiner should take all repeated measurements of a ROM with a universal goniometer, rather than taking the first measurement with a universal goniometer and the second measurement with an inclinometer. We believe most examiners find it easier and more accurate to use a large universal goniometer when measuring joints with large body segments and a small goniometer when measuring joints with small body segments. Inexperienced examiners may wish to take several measurements and record the mean (average) of those measurements to improve reliability, but one measurement is usually sufficient for more experienced examiners using good technique. Finally, it is important to remember that successive measurements are more reliable if taken by the same examiner rather than by different examiners.

The mean standard deviation of repeated ROM measurement of extremity joints taken by one examiner using a universal goniometer has been found to range from 4 to 5 degrees.[34,36] Therefore, to show improvement or worsening of a joint motion measured by the same examiner, a difference of about 5 degrees (1 standard deviation) to 10 degrees (2 standard deviations) is necessary. The mean standard deviation increased to 5 to 6 degrees for repeated measurements taken by different examiners,[34,36] so that a difference of about 6 (1 standard deviation) to 12 degrees (2 standard deviations) is necessary to show true change in this situation. These values serve as a general guideline only and will vary depending on the joint and motion being tested, the examiners and procedures used, and the individual being tested. Refer to the Research Findings section of Chapters 4 to 13 for more joint-specific information on reliability.

| TABLE 3.1 | Recommendations for Improving the Reliability of Goniometric Measurements |
| --- | --- |

- Use consistent, well-defined positions.
- Use consistent, well-defined, and carefully palpated anatomical landmarks to align the goniometer.
- Use the same amount of manual force to move subject's body part during successive measurements of passive ROM.
- Urge subject to exert the same effort to move the body part during successive measurements of active ROM.
- Use the same device to take successive measurements.
- Use a goniometer that is suitable in size to the joint being measured.
- If examiner is less experienced, record the mean of several measurements rather than a single measurement.
- Have the *same* examiner, rather than a *different* examiner, take successive measurements.

## Statistical Methods of Evaluating Measurement Reliability

Clinical measurements are prone to three main sources of variation: (1) true biological variation, (2) temporal variation, and (3) measurement error.[92] **True biological variation** refers to variation in measurements from one individual to another, caused by factors such as age, sex, race, genetics, medical history, and condition. **Temporal variation** refers to variation in measurements made on the same individual at different times, caused by changes in factors such as a subject's medical (physical) condition, activity level, emotional state, and circadian rhythms. **Measurement error** refers to variation in measurements made on the same individual under the same conditions at different times, caused by factors such as the examiners (testers), measuring instruments, and procedural methods. For example, the skill level and experience of the examiners, the accuracy of the measurement instruments, and the standardization of the measurement methods affect the amount of measurement error. Reliability reflects the degree to which a measurement is free of measurement error; therefore, highly reliable measurements have little measurement error.

Statistics can be used to assess variation in numerical data and hence to assess measurement reliability.[92,93] A digression into statistical methods of testing and expressing reliability is included to assist the examiner in correctly interpreting goniometric measurements and in understanding the literature on joint measurement. Several statistics—the standard deviation, coefficient of variation, Pearson product moment correlation coefficient, intraclass correlation coefficient, and standard error of measurement—are discussed. Examples that show the calculation of these statistical tests are presented. For additional information, including the assumptions underlying the use of these statistical tests, the reader is referred to the cited references.

At the end of this chapter, two exercises are included for examiners to assess their reliability in obtaining goniometric measurements. Many authors recommend that clinicians conduct their own studies to determine reliability among their staff and patient population. Miller[30] has presented a step-by-step procedure for conducting such studies.

### Standard Deviation

In the medical literature, the statistic most frequently used to indicate variation is the standard deviation.[92,93] The **standard deviation** is the square root of the mean of the squares of the deviations from the data mean. The standard deviation is symbolized as **SD**, **s**, or **sd**. If we denote each data observation as $x$ and the number of observations as $n$, and the summation notation $\Sigma$ is used, then the mean that is denoted by $\bar{x}$, is as follows:

$$\text{mean} = \bar{x} = \frac{\Sigma x}{n}$$

Two formulas for the standard deviation are given below. The first is the definitional formula; the second is the computational formula. Both formulas give the same result. The definitional formula is easier to understand, but the computational formula is easier to calculate.

$$\text{Standard deviation} = \text{SD} = \sqrt{\frac{\Sigma (x - \bar{x})^2}{n-1}}$$

$$\text{SD} = \sqrt{\frac{\Sigma (x)^2 - \frac{(\Sigma x)^2}{n}}{n-1}}$$

The standard deviation has the same units as the original data observations. If the data observations have a normal (bell-shaped) frequency distribution, 1 standard deviation above and below the mean includes about 68 percent of all the observations, and 2 standard deviations above and below the mean include about 95 percent of the observations.

It is important to note that several standard deviations may be determined from a single study and represent different sources of variation.[92] Two of these standard deviations are discussed here. One standard deviation that can be determined represents mainly **inter**subject variation around the mean of measurements taken of a group of subjects, indicating biological variation. This standard deviation may be of interest in deciding whether a subject has an abnormal ROM in comparison with other people of the same age and gender. Another standard deviation that can be determined represents **intra**subject variation around the mean of measurements taken of an individual, indicating measurement error. This is the standard deviation of interest to indicate measurement reliability.

An example of how to determine these two standard deviations is provided. Table 3.2 presents ROM measurements taken on five subjects. Three repeated measurements (observations) were taken on each subject by the same examiner.

The **standard deviation indicating biological variation** (intersubject variation) is determined by first calculating the mean ROM measurement for each subject. The mean ROM measurement for each of the five subjects is found in the last column of Table 3.2. The grand mean of the mean ROM measurement for each of the five subjects equals 56 degrees. The grand mean is symbolized by $\bar{X}$. The standard deviation is determined by finding the differences between each of the five subjects' means and the grand mean. The differences are squared and added together. The sum is used in the definitional formula for the standard deviation. Calculation of the standard deviation indicating biological variation is found in Table 3.3.

In the example, the standard deviation indicating biological variation equals 13.6 degrees. This standard deviation denotes primarily intersubject variation. Knowledge of intersubject variation may be helpful in deciding whether a subject has an abnormal ROM in comparison with other people of the same age and gender. If a normal distribution of the measurements is assumed, one way of interpreting this standard deviation is to predict that about 68 percent of all the subjects' mean ROM measurements

| TABLE 3.2 | Three Repeated ROM Measurements (in Degrees) Taken on Five Subjects | | | | |
| --- | --- | --- | --- | --- | --- |
| Subject | First Measurement | Second Measurement | Third Measurement | Total | Mean of Three Measurements ($\bar{x}$) |
| 1 | 57 | 55 | 65 | 177 | 59 |
| 2 | 66 | 65 | 70 | 201 | 67 |
| 3 | 66 | 70 | 74 | 210 | 70 |
| 4 | 35 | 40 | 42 | 117 | 39 |
| 5 | 45 | 48 | 42 | 135 | 45 |

Grand mean ($\bar{X}$) $= \dfrac{(59 + 67 + 70 + 39 + 45)}{5} = 56$ degrees.

| TABLE 3.3 | Calculation of the Standard Deviation Indicating Biological Variation in Degrees | | | |
| --- | --- | --- | --- | --- |
| Subject | Mean of Three Measurements ($\bar{x}$) | Grand Mean ($\bar{X}$) | ($\bar{x} - \bar{X}$) | ($\bar{x} - \bar{X}$)$^2$ |
| 1 | 59 | 56 | 3 | 9 |
| 2 | 67 | 56 | 11 | 121 |
| 3 | 70 | 56 | 14 | 196 |
| 4 | 39 | 56 | −17 | 289 |
| 5 | 45 | 56 | −11 | 121 |

$\Sigma(\bar{x} - \bar{X})^2 = 9 + 121 + 196 + 289 + 121 = 736$ degrees; $SD = \sqrt{\dfrac{\Sigma(\bar{x} - \bar{X})^2}{(n-1)}} = \sqrt{\dfrac{736}{(5-1)}} = 13.6$ degrees.

would fall between 42.4 degrees and 69.6 degrees (plus or minus 1 standard deviation around the grand mean of 56 degrees). We would expect that about 95 percent of all the subjects' mean ROM measurements would fall between 28.8 degrees and 83.2 degrees (plus or minus 2 standard deviations around the grand mean of 56 degrees).

**The standard deviation indicating measurement error** (intrasubject variation) also is determined by first calculating the mean ROM measurement for each subject. However, this standard deviation is determined by finding the differences between each of the three repeated measurements taken on a subject and the mean of that subject's measurements. The differences are squared and added together. The sum is used in the definitional formula for the standard deviation. Using the information on subject 1 in the example, the calculation of the standard deviation indicating measurement error is shown in Table 3.4.

Referring to Table 3.2 for information on the each of the other subjects and using the same procedure as shown in Table 3.4, the standard deviation for subject 1 = 5.3 degrees, the standard deviation for subject 2 = 2.6 degrees, the

standard deviation for subject 3 = 4.0 degrees, the standard deviation for subject 4 = 3.6 degrees, and the standard deviation for subject 5 = 3.0 degrees. The mean standard deviation for all of the subjects combined is determined by

| TABLE 3.4 | Calculation of the Standard Deviation Indicating Measurement Error in Degrees for Subject 1 | | |
| --- | --- | --- | --- |
| Measurements (x) | Mean ($\bar{x}$) | (x − $\bar{x}$) | (x − $\bar{x}$)$^2$ |
| 57 | 59 | −2 | 4 |
| 55 | 59 | −4 | 16 |
| 65 | 59 | 6 | 36 |

$SD = \sqrt{\dfrac{\Sigma(x - \bar{x})^2}{(n - 1)}} = \sqrt{\dfrac{56}{2}} = 5.3$ degrees summing the five subjects' standard deviations and dividing by the number of subjects, which is 5:

$$SD = \frac{5.3 + 2.6 + 4.0 + 3.6 + 3.0}{5} = \frac{18.5}{5} = 3.7 \text{ degrees}$$

In the example, the standard deviation indicating intrasubject variation equals 3.7 degrees. This standard deviation is appropriate for indicating measurement error, especially if the repeated measurements on each subject were taken within a short period of time. Note that in this example the standard deviation indicating measurement error (3.7 degrees) is much smaller than the standard deviation indicating biological variation (13.6 degrees). One way of interpreting the standard deviation for measurement error is to predict that about 68 percent of the repeated measurements on a subject would fall within 3.7 degrees (1 standard deviation) above and below the mean of the repeated measurements of a subject because of measurement error. We would expect that about 95 percent of the repeated measurements on a subject would fall within 7.4 degrees (2 standard deviations) above and below the mean of the repeated measurements of a subject, again because of measurement error. The smaller the standard deviation, the less the measurement error and the better the reliability.

## Coefficient of Variation

Sometimes it is helpful to consider the percentage of variation rather than the standard deviation, which is expressed in the units of the data observation (measurement). The **coefficient of variation** is a measure of variation that is relative to the mean and standardized so that the variations of different variables can be compared. The coefficient of variation is the standard deviation divided by the mean and multiplied by 100 percent. It is a percentage and is not expressed in the units of the original observation. The coefficient of variation is symbolized by **CV** and the formula is as follows:

$$\text{coefficient of variation} = CV = \frac{SD}{\bar{x}} (100)\%$$

For the example presented in Table 3.2, the coefficient of variation indicating biological variation uses the standard deviation for biological variation (standard deviation = 13.6 degrees).

$$CV = \frac{SD}{\bar{x}} (100)\% = \frac{13.6}{56} (100)\% = 24.3\%$$

The coefficient of variation indicating measurement error uses the standard deviation for measurement error (standard deviation = 3.7 degrees).

$$CV = \frac{SD}{\bar{x}} (100)\% = \frac{3.7}{56} (100)\% = 6.6\%$$

In this example the coefficient of variation for measurement error (6.6 percent) is less than the coefficient of variation for biological variation (24.3 percent).

Another name for the coefficient of variation indicating measurement error is the **coefficient of variation of replication.**[94] The lower the coefficient of variation of replication, the lower the measurement error and the better the reliability.

This statistic is especially useful in comparing the reliability of two or more variables that have different units of measurement (for example, comparing ROM measurement methods recorded in inches versus degrees).

## Correlation Coefficients

Correlation coefficients are traditionally used to measure the relationship between two variables. They result in a number from −1 to +1, which indicates how well an equation can predict one variable from another variable.[2–4,92] A +1 describes a perfect positive linear (straight-line) relationship, whereas a −1 describes a perfect negative linear relationship. A correlation coefficient of 0 indicates that there is no linear relationship between the two variables. Correlation coefficients are used to indicate measurement reliability because it is assumed that two repeated measurements should be highly correlated and approach +1. One interpretation of correlation coefficients used to indicate reliability is that 0.90 to 0.99 equals high reliability, 0.80 to 0.89 equals good reliability, 0.70 to 0.79 equals fair reliability, and 0.69 and below equals poor reliability.[95] Another interpretation offered by Portney and Watkins[3] states that correlation coefficients higher than 0.75 indicate good reliability, whereas those less than 0.75 indicate poor to moderate reliability.

### Pearson Product Moment Correlation Coefficient

Because goniometric measurements produce ratio level data, the **Pearson product moment correlation coefficient** has been the correlation coefficient usually calculated to indicate the reliability of pairs of goniometric measurements. The Pearson product moment correlation coefficient is symbolized by *r*, and its formula is presented following this paragraph. If this statistic is used to indicate reliability, *x* symbolizes the first measurement and *y* symbolizes the second measurement.

$$r = \frac{\Sigma(x - \bar{x})(y - \bar{y})}{\sqrt{\Sigma(x - \bar{x})^2} \sqrt{\Sigma(y - \bar{y})^2}}$$

Referring to the example in Table 3.2, the Pearson correlation coefficient can be used to determine the relationship between the first and the second ROM measurements on the five subjects. Calculation of the Pearson product moment correlation coefficient for this example is found in Table 3.5. The resulting value of *r* = 0.98 indicates a highly positive linear relationship between the first and the second measurements. In other words, the two measurements are highly correlated.

$$r = \frac{\Sigma(x - \bar{x})(y - \bar{y})}{\sqrt{\Sigma(x - \bar{x})^2} \sqrt{\Sigma(y - \bar{y})^2}}$$

$$= \frac{650.6}{\sqrt{738.8} \sqrt{597.2}} = \frac{650.6}{(27.2)(24.4)} = 0.98$$

The Pearson product moment correlation coefficient indicates association between the pairs of measurements rather than agreement. Therefore, to decide whether the two

| TABLE 3.5 | Calculation of the Pearson Product Moment Correlation Coefficient for the First (x) and Second (y) ROM Measurements in Degrees | | | | | | |
|---|---|---|---|---|---|---|---|
| Subject | x | y | $(x - \bar{x})$ | $(y - \bar{y})$ | $(x - \bar{x})(y - \bar{y})$ | $(x - \bar{x})^2$ | $(y - \bar{y})^2$ |
| 1 | 57 | 55 | 3.2 | −0.6 | −1.92 | 10.24 | 0.36 |
| 2 | 66 | 65 | 12.2 | 9.4 | 114.68 | 148.84 | 88.36 |
| 3 | 66 | 70 | 12.2 | 14.4 | 175.68 | 148.84 | 207.36 |
| 4 | 35 | 40 | −18.8 | −15.6 | 293.28 | 353.44 | 243.36 |
| 5 | 45 | 48 | −8.8 | −7.6 | 68.88 | 77.44 | 57.76 |
| | | | | | $\Sigma = 650.60$ | $\Sigma = 738.80$ | $\Sigma = 597.20$ |

$$\bar{x} = \frac{57 + 66 + 66 + 35 + 45}{5} = 53.8 \text{ degrees; } \bar{y} = \frac{55 + 65 + 70 + 40 + 48}{5} = 55.6 \text{ degrees.}$$

measurements are identical, the equation of the straight line best representing the relationship should be determined. If the equation of the straight line representing the relationship includes a slope $b$ equal to 1 and an intercept $a$ equal to 0, then an $r$ value that approaches +1 also indicates that the two measurements are identical. The equation of a straight line is $y = a + bx$, with $x$ symbolizing the first measurement, $y$ the second measurement, $a$ the intercept, and $b$ the slope. The equation for a slope is

$$\text{slope} = b = \frac{\Sigma (x - \bar{x})(y - \bar{y})}{\Sigma (x - \bar{x})^2}$$

The equation for an intercept is $intercept = a = \bar{y} - b\bar{x}$

For our example, the slope and intercept are calculated as follows:

$$b = \frac{\Sigma (x - \bar{x})(y - \bar{y})}{\Sigma (x - \bar{x})^2} = \frac{650.6}{738.8} = 0.88$$
$$intercept = a = \bar{y} - b\bar{x} = 55.6 - 0.88(53.8) = 8.26$$

The equation of the straight line best representing the relationship between the first and the second measurements in the example is $y = 8.26 + 0.88x$. Although the $r$ value indicates high correlation, the two measurements are not identical given the linear equation.

One concern in interpreting correlation coefficients is that the value of the correlation coefficient is markedly influenced by the range of the measurements.[3,93,96] The greater the biological variation between individuals for the measurement, the more extreme the $r$ value, so that $r$ is closer to −1 or +1. Another limitation is the fact that the Pearson product moment correlation coefficient can evaluate the relationship between only two variables or measurements at a time.

### Intraclass Correlation Coefficient

To avoid the need for calculating and interpreting both the correlation coefficient and a linear equation, some investigators use the **intraclass correlation coefficient (ICC)** to evaluate reliability. The ICC also allows the comparison of two or more measurements at a time; one can think of it as an average correlation among all possible pairs of measurements.[96]

This statistic is determined from an analysis of variance model, which compares different sources of variation. The ICC is conceptually expressed as the ratio of the variance associated with the subjects, divided by the sum of the variance associated with the subjects plus error variance.[97] The theoretical limits of the ICC are between 0 and +1; +1 indicates perfect agreement (no error variance), whereas 0 indicates no agreement (large amount of error variance).

There are six different formulas for determining ICC values based on the design of the study, the purpose of the study, and the type of measurement.[3,97,98] Three models have been described, each with two different forms. In Model 1, each subject is tested by a different set of testers, and the testers are considered representative of a larger population of testers—to allow the results to be generalized to other testers. In Model 2, each subject is tested by the same set of testers, and again the testers are considered representative of a larger population of testers. In Model 3, each subject is tested by the same set of testers, but the testers are the only testers of interest—the results are not intended to be generalized to other testers. The first form of all three models is used when single measurements (1) are compared, whereas the second form is used when the means of multiple measurements (k) are compared. The different formulas for the ICC are identified by two numbers enclosed by parentheses. The first number indicates the model, and the second number indicates the form. For further discussion, examples, and formulas, the reader is urged to refer to the referenced texts[3] and articles.[97–99]

In our example, a repeated measures analysis of variance was conducted and the ICC (3,1) was calculated as 0.94. This ICC model was used because each measurement was taken by the same tester, there was only an interest in applying the results to this tester, and single measurements were compared rather than the means of several measurements. This ICC value indicates a high reliability between the three repeated measurements. However, this value is slightly lower than the Pearson product moment correlation coefficient, perhaps due to the variability added by the third measurement on each subject.

Like the Pearson product moment correlation coefficient, the ICC is also influenced by the range of measurements between the subjects. As the group of subjects becomes more homogeneous, the ability of the ICC to detect agreement is reduced and the ICC can erroneously indicate poor reliability.[3,97,100] Because correlation coefficients are sensitive to the range of the measurements and do not provide an index of reliability in the units of the measurement, some experts prefer the use of the standard deviation of the repeated measurements (intrasubject standard deviation) or the standard error of measurement to assess reliability.[4,100,101]

### Standard Error of Measurement

The standard error of measurement is the final statistic that we review here to evaluate reliability. It has received support because of its practical interpretation in estimating measurement error in the same units as the measurement. According to DuBois,[102] "The **standard error of measurement** is the likely standard deviation of the error made in predicting true scores when we have knowledge only of the obtained scores." The true scores (measurements) are forever unknown, but several formulas have been developed to estimate this statistic. The standard error of measurement is symbolized as **SEM**, **SE$_{meas}$**, or **S$_{meas}$**. If the standard deviation indicating biological variation is denoted SD$_x$, a correlation coefficient such as the intraclass correlation coefficient is denoted ICC, and the Pearson product moment correlation coefficient is denoted r, the formulas for the SEM are as follows:

$$SEM = SD_x \sqrt{1 - ICC}$$

or

$$SEM = SD_x \sqrt{1 - r}$$

The SEM can also be determined from a repeated measures analysis of variance model. The SEM is equivalent to the square root of the mean square of the error.[103,104] Because the SEM is a special case of the standard deviation, 1 standard error of measurement above and below the observed measurement includes the true measurement 68 percent of the time. Two standard errors of measurement above and below the observed measurement include the true measurement 95 percent of the time.

It is important to note that another statistic, the standard error of the mean, is often confused with the standard error of measurement. The standard error of the mean is symbolized as SEM, SE$_M$, SE$_{\bar{x}}$, or S$_{\bar{x}}$.[2,4,92,93] The use of the same or similar symbols to represent different statistics has added much confusion to the reliability literature. These two statistics are not equivalent, nor do they have the same interpretation. The standard error of the mean is the standard deviation of a distribution of means taken from samples of a population.[1,2,93] It describes how much variation can be expected in the means from future samples of the same size. Because we are interested in the variation of individual measurements when evaluating reliability rather than the variation of means, the standard deviation of the repeated measurements or the standard error of measurement are the appropriate statistical tests to use.[105]

Let us return to the example and calculate the standard error of the measurement. The value for the ICC is 0.94. The value for SD$_x$, the standard deviation indicating biological variation among the 5 subjects, is 13.6.

$$SEM = SD_x \sqrt{1 - ICC}$$

$$13.6 \sqrt{1 - 0.94} = 13.6 \sqrt{0.06} = 3.3 \text{ degrees}$$

Likewise, if we use the results of the repeated measures analysis of variance to calculate the SEM, the SEM equals the square root of the mean square of the error = $\sqrt{10.9}$ = 3.3 degrees. In this example, about two-thirds of the time the true measurement would be within 3.3 degrees of the observed measurement.

## Exercises to Evaluate Reliability

Exercises 6 and 7 have been included to help examiners assess their reliability in obtaining goniometric measurements. Calculations of the standard deviation and coefficient of variation are included in the belief that understanding is reinforced by practical application. **Exercise 6** examines **intratester reliability**. Intratester reliability refers to the amount of agreement between repeated measurements of the same joint position or ROM by the same examiner (tester). An intratester reliability study answers the question: How accurately can an examiner reproduce his or her own measurements? **Exercise 7** examines **intertester reliability**. Intertester reliability refers to the amount of agreement between repeated measurements of the same joint position or ROM by different examiners (testers). An intertester reliability study answers the question: How accurately can one examiner reproduce measurements taken by other examiners?

# Exercise 6

## Intratester Reliability

1. Select a subject and a universal goniometer.
2. Measure elbow flexion ROM on your subject three times, following the steps outlined in Chapter 2, Exercise 5.
3. Record each measurement on the recording form (see opposite page) in the column labeled $x$. A measurement is denoted by $x$.
4. Compare the measurements. If a discrepancy of more than 5 degrees exists between measurements, recheck each step in the procedure to make sure that you are performing the steps correctly, and then repeat this exercise.
5. Continue practicing until you have obtained three successive measurements that are within 5 degrees of each other.
6. To gain an understanding of several of the statistics used to evaluate intratester reliability, calculate the standard deviation and coefficient of variation by completing the following steps.
   a. Add the three measurements together to determine the sum of the measurements. $\Sigma$ is the symbol for summation. Record the sum at the bottom of the column labeled $x$.
   b. To determine the **mean**, divide this sum by 3, which is the number of measurements. The number of measurements is denoted by $n$. The mean is denoted by $\bar{x}$. Space to calculate the mean is provided on the recording form.
   c. To continue the process of calculating the **standard deviation**, subtract the mean from each of the three measurements and record the results in the column labeled $x - \bar{x}$. Space to calculate the standard deviation is provided on the recording form.
   d. Square each of the numbers in the column labeled $x - \bar{x}$, and record the results in the column labeled $(x - \bar{x})^2$.
   e. Add the three numbers in column $(x - \bar{x})^2$ to determine the sum of the squares. Record the results at the bottom of the column labeled $(x - \bar{x})^2$.
   f. Divide this sum by 2, which is the number of measurements minus 1 ($n - 1$). Then find the square root of this number.
   g. To determine the **coefficient of variation,** divide the standard deviation by the mean. Multiply this number by 100 percent. Space to calculate the coefficient of variation is provided on the recording form.
7. Repeat this procedure with other joints and motions after you have learned the testing procedures.

# RECORDING FORM FOR EXERCISE 6. INTRATESTER RELIABILITY

Follow the steps outlined in Exercise 6. Use this form to record your measurements and the result of your calculations.

Subject's Name _____ Date _____

Examiner's Name _____

Joint and Motion _____ Right or Left Side _____

Passive or Active Motion _____ Type of Goniometer _____

| Measurement | $x$ | $x - \bar{x}$ | $(x - \bar{x})^2$ | $x^2$ |
|---|---|---|---|---|
| 1 | | | | |
| 2 | | | | |
| 3 | | | | |
| $n = 3$ | $\Sigma x =$ | | $\Sigma(x - \bar{x})^2 =$ | $\Sigma x^2 =$ |

$$\text{Mean of the three measurements} = \bar{x} = \frac{\Sigma x}{n} =$$

$$\text{Standard deviation} = \sqrt{\frac{\Sigma (x - \bar{x})^2}{n - 1}} =$$

$$\text{or use SD} = \sqrt{\frac{\Sigma x^2 - \frac{(\Sigma x)^2}{n}}{n - 1}}$$

$$\text{Coefficient of variation} = \frac{\text{SD}}{\bar{x}} (100)\% =$$

# Exercise 7

## Intertester Reliability

1. Select a subject and a universal goniometer.
2. Measure elbow flexion ROM on your subject once, following the steps outlined in Chapter 2, Exercise 5.
3. Ask two other examiners to measure the same elbow flexion ROM on your subject, using your goniometer and following the steps outlined in Chapter 2, Exercise 5.
4. Record each measurement on the recording form (see opposite page) in the column labeled $x$. A measurement is denoted by $x$.
5. Compare the measurements. If a discrepancy of more than 5 degrees exists between measurements, repeat this exercise. The examiners should observe one another's measurements to discover differences in technique that might account for variability, such as faulty alignment, lack of stabilization, or reading the wrong scale.
6. To gain an understanding of several of the statistics used to evaluate intertester reliability, calculate the mean deviation, standard deviation, and coefficient of variation by completing the following steps.
    a. Add the three measurements together to determine the sum of the measurements. $\Sigma$ is the symbol for summation. Record the sum at the bottom of the column labeled $x$.
    b. To determine the **mean,** divide this sum by 3, which is the number of measurements. The number of measurements is denoted by $n$. The mean is denoted by $\bar{x}$. Space to calculate the mean is provided on the recording form.
    c. To continue the process of calculating the **standard deviation**, subtract the mean from each of the three measurements, and record the results in the column labeled $x - \bar{x}$. Space to calculate the standard deviation is provided on the recording form.
    d. Square each of the numbers in the column labeled $x - \bar{x}$, and record the results in the column labeled $(x - \bar{x})^2$.
    e. Add the three numbers in column $(x - x)^2$ to determine the sum of the squares. Record the results at the bottom of column $(x - \bar{x})^2$.
    f. Divide this sum by 2, which is the number of measurements minus 1 $(n - 1)$. Then find the square root of this number.
    g. To determine the **coefficient of variation,** divide the standard deviation by the mean. Multiply this number by 100 percent. Space to calculate the coefficient of variation is provided on the recording form.
7. Repeat this exercise with other joints and motions after you have learned the testing procedures.

# RECORDING FORM FOR EXERCISE 7. INTERTESTER RELIABILITY

Follow the steps outlined in Exercise 7. Use this form to record your measurements and the results of your calculations.

Subject's Name _____ Date _____

Examiner 1. Name _____

Examiner 2. Name _____ Joint and Motion _____

Examiner 3. Name _____ Right or Left Side _____

Passive or Active Motion _____ Type of Goniometer _____

| Measurement | $x$ | $x - \bar{x}$ | $(x - \bar{x})^2$ | $x^2$ |
|---|---|---|---|---|
| 1 | | | | |
| 2 | | | | |
| 3 | | | | |
| $n = 3$ | $\Sigma x =$ | | $\Sigma(x - \bar{x})^2 =$ | $\Sigma x^2 =$ |

$$\text{Mean of the three measurements} = \bar{x} = \frac{\Sigma x}{n} =$$

$$\text{Standard deviation} = \sqrt{\frac{\Sigma (x - \bar{x})^2}{n - 1}}$$

$$\text{or use SD} = \sqrt{\frac{\Sigma x^2 - \frac{(\Sigma x)^2}{n}}{n - 1}}$$

$$\text{Coefficient of variation} = \frac{\text{SD}}{\bar{x}} (100)\% =$$

# REFERENCES

1. Currier, DP: Elements of Research in Physical Therapy, ed 3. Williams & Wilkins, Baltimore, 1990, p 171.
2. Kerlinger, FN: Foundations of Behavioral Research, ed 2. Holt, Rinehart, & Winston, New York, 1973.
3. Portney, LG, and Watkins, MP: Foundations of Clinical Research: Applications to Practice, ed 2. Prentice-Hall, Upper Saddle River, NJ, 2000.
4. Rothstein, JM: Measurement and Clinical Practice: Theory and Application. In Rothstein, JM (ed): Measurement in Physical Therapy. Churchill Livingstone, New York, 1985.
5. Sims, J, and Arnell, P: Measurement validity in physical therapy research. Phys Ther 73:102, 1993.
6. Gajdosik, RL, and Bohannon, RW: Clinical measurement of range of motion: Review of goniometry emphasizing reliability and validity. Phys Ther 67:1867, 1987.
7. American Physical Therapy Association: Standards for tests and measurements in physical therapy practice. Phys Ther 71:589, 1991.
8. Gogia, PP, et al: Reliability and validity of goniometric measurements at the knee. Phys Ther 67:192, 1987.
9. Enwemeka, CS: Radiographic verification of knee goniometry. Scand J Rehabil Med 18:47, 1986.
10. Ahlback, SO, and Lindahl, O: Sagittal mobility of the hip-joint. Acta Orthop Scand 34:310, 1964.
11. Kato, M, et al: The accuracy of goniometric measurements of proximal interphalangeal joints in fresh cadavers: Comparison between methods of measurement, types of goniometers, and fingers. J Hand Ther 20:12, 2007.
12. Chen, J, et al: Meta-analysis of normative cervical motion. Spine 24:1571, 1999.
13. Herrmann, DB: Validity study of head and neck flexion-extension motion comparing measurements of a pendulum goniometer and roentgenograms. J Orthop Sports Phys Ther 11:414, 1990.
14. Ordway, NR, et al: Cervical sagittal range-of-motion analysis using three methods: Cervical range-of-motion device, space, and radiography. Spine 22:501, 1997.
15. Tousignant, M, et al: Criterion validity of the cervical range of motion (CROM) goniometer for cervical flexion and extension. Spine 25:324, 2000.
16. Macrae, JF, and Wright, V: Measurement of back movement. Ann Rheum Dis 28:584, 1969.
17. Portek, I, et al: Correlation between radiographic and clinical measurement of lumbar spine movement. Br J Rheumatol 22:197, 1983.
18. Burdett, RG, Brown, KE, and Fall, MP: Reliability and validity of four instruments for measuring lumbar spine and pelvic positions. Phys Ther 66:677, 1986.
19. Mayer, TG, et al: Use of noninvasive techniques for quantification of spinal range-of-motion in normal subjects and chronic low-back dysfunction patients. Spine 9:588, 1984.
20. Saur, PM, et al: Lumbar range of motion: Reliability and validity of the inclinometer technique in the clinical measurement of trunk flexibility. Spine 21:1332, 1996.
21. Samo, DG, et al: Validity of three lumbar sagittal motion measurement methods: Surface inclinometers compared with radiographs. J Occup Environ Med 39:209, 1997.
22. Campbell, SK: Commentary: Measurement validity in physical therapy research. Phys Ther 73:110, 1993.
23. Vasen, AP, et al: Functional range of motion of the elbow. J Hand Surg 20A:288, 1995.
24. Cooper, JE, et al: Elbow joint restriction: Effect on functional upper limb motion during performance of three feeding activities. Arch Phys Med Rehabil 74:805, 1993.
25. Nelson, DL: Functional wrist motion. Hand Clin 13:83, 1997.
26. Hermann, KM, and Reese, CS: Relationships among selected measures of impairment, functional limitation, and disability in patients with cervical spine disorder. Phys Ther 81:903, 2001.
27. Triffitt, PD: The relationship between motion of the shoulder and the stated ability to perform activities of daily living. J Bone Joint Surg 80:41, 1998.
28. Wagner, MB, et al: Assessment of hand function in Duchenne muscular dystrophy. Arch Phys Med Rehabil 74:801, 1993.
29. Moore, ML: Clinical assessment of joint motion. In Basmajian, JV (ed): Therapeutic Exercise, ed 3. Williams & Wilkins, Baltimore, 1978.
30. Miller, PJ: Assessment of joint motion. In Rothstein, JM (ed): Measurement in Physical Therapy. Churchill Livingstone, New York, 1985.
31. Lea, RD, and Gerhardt, JJ: Current concepts review: Range-of-motion measurements. J Bone Joint Surg Am 77:784, 1995.
32. Grohmann, JEL: Comparison of two methods of goniometry. Phys Ther 63:922, 1983.
33. Hamilton, GF, and Lachenbruch, PA: Reliability of goniometers in assessing finger joint angle. Phys Ther 49:465, 1969.
34. Boone, DC, et al: Reliability of goniometric measurements. Phys Ther 58:1355, 1978.
35. Pandya, S, et al: Reliability of goniometric measurements in patients with Duchenne muscular dystrophy. Phys Ther 65:1339, 1985.
36. Bovens, AMP, et al: Variability and reliability of joint measurements. Am J Sport Med 18:58, 1990.
37. Hellebrandt, FA, Duvall, EN, and Moore, ML: The measurement of joint motion. Part III: Reliability of goniometry. Phys Ther Rev 29:302, 1949.
38. Low, JL: The reliability of joint measurement. Physiotherapy 62:227, 1976.
39. Greene, BL, and Wolf, SL: Upper extremity joint movement: Comparison of two measurement devices. Arch Phys Med Rehabil 70:299, 1989.
40. Tucci, SM, et al: Cervical motion assessment: A new, simple and accurate method. Arch Phys Med Rehabil 67:225, 1986.
41. Youdas, JW, Carey, JR, and Garrett, TR: Reliability of measurements of cervical spine range of motion: Comparison of three methods. Phys Ther 71:2, 1991.
42. Fitzgerald, GK, et al: Objective assessment with establishment of normal values for lumbar spine range of motion. Phys Ther 63:1776, 1983.
43. Nitschke, JE, et al: Reliability of the American Medical Association Guides' model for measuring spinal range of motion. Spine 24:262, 1999.
44. Mayerson, NH, and Milano, RA: Goniometric measurement reliability in physical medicine. Arch Phys Med Rehabil 65:92, 1984.
45. Watkins, MA, et al: Reliability of goniometric measurements and visual estimates of knee range of motion obtained in a clinical setting. Phys Ther 71:90, 1991.
46. Riddle, DL, Rothstein, JM, and Lamb, RL: Goniometric reliability in a clinical setting: Shoulder measurements. Phys Ther 67:668, 1987.
47. Ekstrand, J, et al: Lower extremity goniometric measurements: A study to determine their reliability. Arch Phys Med Rehabil 63:171, 1982.
48. Rothstein, JM, Miller, PJ, and Roettger, RF: Goniometric reliability in a clinical setting: Elbow and knee measurements. Phys Ther 63:1611, 1983.
49. Solgaard, S, et al: Reproducibility of goniometry of the wrist. Scand J Rehabil Med 18:5, 1986.
50. Patel, RS: Intratester and intertester reliability of the inclinometer in measuring lumbar flexion [abstract]. Phys Ther 72:S44, 1992.
51. Lovell, FW, Rothstein, JM, and Personius, WJ: Reliability of clinical measurements of lumbar lordosis taken with a flexible rule. Phys Ther 69:96, 1989.
52. Bartlett, JD, et al: Hip flexion contractures: A comparison of measurement methods. Arch Phys Med Rehabil 66:620, 1985.
53. Jonson, SR, and Gross, MT: Intraexaminer reliability, interexaminer reliability, and mean values for nine lower extremity skeletal measures in healthy naval midshipmen. J Orthop Sports Phys Ther 25:253, 1997
54. Elveru, RA, Rothstein, JM, and Lamb, RL: Goniometric reliability in a clinical setting. Phys Ther 68:672, 1988.
55. Diamond, JE, et al: Reliability of a diabetic foot evaluation. Phys Ther 69:797, 1989.
56. MacDermid, JC, et al: Intratester and intertester reliability of goniometric measurement of passive lateral shoulder rotation. J Hand Ther 12:187, 1999.
57. Armstrong, AD, et al: Reliability of range-of-motion measurement in the elbow and forearm. J Shoulder Elbow Surg 7:573, 1998.
58. Boon, AJ, and Smith, J: Manual scapular stabilization: Its effect on shoulder rotational range of motion Arch Phys Med Rehabil 81:978, 2000.
59. Horger, MM: The reliability of goniometric measurements of active and passive wrist motions. Am J Occup Ther 44:342, 1990.
60. Ellis, B, Bruton, A, and Goddard, JR: Joint angle measurement: A comparative study of the reliability of goniometry and wire tracing for the hand. Clin Rehabil 11:314, 1997.
61. Pellecchia, GL, and Bohannon, RW: Active lateral neck flexion range of motion measurements obtained with a modified goniometer. Reliability and estimates of normal. J Manipulative Physiol Ther 21:443, 1998.
62. Nilsson, N: Measuring passive cervical motion: A study of reliability. J Manipulative Physiol Ther 18:293, 1995.
63. Williams, R, et al: Reliability of the modified-modified Schober and double inclinometer methods for measuring lumbar flexion and extension. Phys Ther 73:26, 1993.

64. Defibaugh, JJ: Measurement of head motion. Part II: An experimental study of head motion in adult males. Phys Ther 44:163, 1964.
65. Balogun, JA, et al: Inter- and intratester reliability of measuring neck motions with tape measure and Myrin Gravity-Reference Goniometer. J Orthop Sports Phys Ther 10:248, 1989.
66. Capuano-Pucci, D, et al: Intratester and intertester reliability of the cervical range of motion. Arch Phys Med Rehabil 72:338, 1991.
67. LaStayo, PC, and Wheeler, DL: Reliability of passive wrist flexion and extension goniometric measurements: A multicenter study. Phys Ther 74:162, 1994.
68. Mayer, TG, et al: Spinal range of motion. Spine 22:1976, 1997.
69. Cobe, HM: The range of active motion at the wrist of white adults. J Bone Joint Surg Br 10:763, 1928.
70. Hewitt, D: The range of active motion at the wrist of women. J Bone Joint Surg Br 10:775, 1928.
71. Palmer, ML, and Epler, M: Clinical Assessment Procedures in Physical Therapy, ed 2. JB Lippincott, Philadelphia, 1998.
72. Clarkson, HM: Musculoskeletal Assessment: Joint Range of Motion and Manual Muscle Strength, ed 2. Williams & Wilkins, Baltimore, 2000.
73. Robson, P: A method to reduce the variable error in joint range measurement. Ann Phys Med 8:262, 1966.
74. Goodwin, J, et al: Clinical methods of goniometry: A comparative study. Disabil Rehabil 14:10, 1992.
75. Petherick, M, et al: Concurrent validity and intertester reliability of universal and fluid-based goniometers for active elbow range of motion. Phys Ther 68:966, 1988.
76. Brown, A, et al: Validity and reliability of the Dexter hand evaluation and therapy system in hand-injured patients. J Hand Ther 13:37, 2000.
77. Weiss, PL, et al: Using the Exos Handmaster to measure digital range of motion: Reliability and validity. Med Eng Phys 16:323, 1994.
78. Clapper, MP, and Wolf, SL: Comparison of the reliability of the Orthoranger and the standard goniometer for assessing active lower extremity range of motion. Phys Ther 68:214, 1988.
79. Ellison, JB, Rose, SJ, and Sahrman, SA: Patterns of hip rotation: A comparison between healthy subjects and patients with low back pain. Phys Ther 70:537, 1990.
80. Rheault, W, et al: Intertester reliability and concurrent validity of fluid-based and universal goniometers for active knee flexion. Phys Ther 68:1676, 1988.
81. Bartholomy, JK, Chandler, RF, and Kaplan, SE: Validity analysis of fluid goniometer measurements of knee flexion [abstract]. Phys Ther 80:S46, 2000.
82. Rome, K, and Cowieson, F: A reliability study of the universal goniometer, fluid goniometer, and electrogoniometer for the measurement of ankle dorsiflexion. Foot Ankle Int 17:28, 1996.
83. White, DJ, et al: Reliability of three methods of measuring cervical motion [abstract]. Phys Ther 66:771, 1986.
84. Reynolds, PMG: Measurement of spinal mobility: A comparison of three methods. Rheumatol Rehabil 14:180, 1975.
85. Miller, MH, et al: Measurement of spinal mobility in the sagittal plane: New skin distraction technique compared with established methods. J Rheumatol 11:4, 1984.
86. Gill, K, et al: Repeatability of four clinical methods for assessment of lumbar spinal motion. Spine 13:50, 1988.
87. Lindahl, O: Determination of the sagittal mobility of the lumbar spine. Acta Orthop Scand 37:241, 1966.
88. White, DJ, et al: Reliability of three clinical methods of measuring lateral flexion in the thoracolumbar pine [abstract]. Phys Ther 67:759, 1987.
89. Mayer, RS, et al: Variance in the measurement of sagittal lumbar range of motion among examiners, subjects, and instruments. Spine 20:1489, 1995.
90. Chen, SP, et al: Reliability of the lumbar sagittal motion measurement methods: Surface inclinometers. J Occup Environ Med 39:217, 1997.
91. Breum, J, Wilberg, J, and Bolton, JE: Reliability and concurrent validity of the BROM II for measuring lumbar mobility. J Manipulative Physiol Ther 18:497, 1995.
92. Colton, T: Statistics in Medicine. Little, Brown, Boston, 1974.
93. Dawson-Saunders, B, and Trapp, RG: Basic and Clinical Biostatistics. Appleton & Lange, Norwalk, CT, 1990.
94. Francis, K: Computer communication: Reliability. Phys Ther 66:1140, 1986.
95. Blesh, TE: Measurement in Physical Education, ed 2. Ronald Press, New York, 1974. Cited by Currier, DP: Elements of Research in Physical Therapy, ed 3. Williams & Wilkins, Baltimore, 1990.
96. Bland, JM, and Altman, DG: Measurement error and correlation coefficients [statistics notes]. BMJ 313:41, 1996.
97. Lahey, MA, Downey, RG, and Saal, FE: Intraclass correlations: There's more there than meets the eye. Psychol Bull 93:586, 1983.
98. Shout, PE, and Fleiss, JL: Intraclass correlations: Uses in assessing rater reliability. Psychol Bull 86:420, 1979.
99. Krebs, DE: Computer communication: Intraclass correlation coefficients. Phys Ther 64:1581, 1984.
100. Stratford, P: Reliability: Consistency or differentiating among subjects? [letters to the editor]. Phys Ther 69:299, 1989.
101. Bland, JM, and Altman, DG: Measurement error [statistics notes]. BMJ 312:1654, 1996.
102. DuBois, PH: An Introduction to Psychological Statistics. Harper & Row, New York, 1965, p 401.
103. Stratford, P: Use of the standard error as a reliability index of interest: An applied example using elbow flexor strength data. Phys Ther 77:745, 1997.
104. Eliasziw, M, et al: Statistical methodology for the concurrent assessment of interrater and intrarater reliability: Using goniometric measurement as an example. Phys Ther 74:777, 1994.
105. Bartko, JJ: Rationale for reporting standard deviations rather than standard errors of the mean. Am J Psychiatry 142:1060, 1985.

# UPPER-EXTREMITY TESTING

## OBJECTIVES

ON COMPLETION OF PART II, THE READER WILL BE ABLE TO:

1. **Identify:**
   - Appropriate planes and axes for each upper-extremity joint motion
   - Structures that limit the end of the range of motion
   - Expected normal end-feels

2. **Describe:**
   - Testing positions used for each upper-extremity joint motion and muscle length test
   - Goniometer alignment
   - Capsular pattern of restricted motion
   - Range of motion necessary for selected functional activities

3. **Explain:**
   - How age, gender, and other factors can affect the range of motion
   - How sources of error in measurement can affect testing results

4. **Perform a goniometric measurement of any upper-extremity joint including:**
   - A clear explanation of the testing procedure
   - Proper positioning of the subject

- Adequate stabilization of the proximal joint component
- Correct determination of the end of the range of motion
- Correct identification of the end-feel
- Palpation of the appropriate bony landmarks
- Accurate alignment of the goniometer and correct reading and recording

5. **Plan goniometric measurements of the shoulder, elbow, wrist, and hand that are organized by body position.**

6. **Assess intratester and intertester reliability of goniometric measurements of the upper-extremity joints using methods described in Chapter 3.**

7. **Perform tests of muscle length at the shoulder, elbow, wrist, and hand including:**
   - A clear explanation of the testing procedure
   - Proper positioning of the subject in the starting position
   - Adequate stabilization
   - Use of appropriate testing motion
   - Correct identification of the end-feel
   - Accurate alignment of the goniometer and correct reading and recording

The testing positions, stabilization techniques, end-feels, and goniometer alignment for the joints of the upper extremities are presented in Chapters 4 through 7. The goniometric evaluation should follow the 12-step sequence presented in Exercise 5 in Chapter 2.

# The Shoulder

## ◯ Structure and Function

### Glenohumeral Joint

#### Anatomy

The glenohumeral joint is a synovial ball-and-socket joint. The ball is the convex head of the humerus, which faces medially, superiorly, and posteriorly with respect to the shaft of the humerus (Fig. 4.1).[1,2] The socket is formed by the concave glenoid fossa of the scapula and faces laterally, superiorly, and anteriorly. The socket is shallow and smaller than the humeral head but is deepened and enlarged by the fibrocartilaginous glenoid labrum. The joint capsule is thin and lax, blends with the glenoid labrum, and is reinforced by the tendons of the rotator cuff muscles and by the glenohumeral (superior, middle, inferior) and coracohumeral ligaments (Fig. 4.2).

#### Osteokinematics

The glenohumeral joint has 3 degrees of freedom. The motions permitted at the joint are flexion–extension, abduction–adduction, and medial–lateral rotation.[1,2] In addition, horizontal abduction and horizontal adduction are functional motions performed at the level of the shoulder and are created by combining abduction and extension, and adduction and flexion, respectively. Full range of motion (ROM) of the shoulder requires humeral, scapular, and clavicular motion at the glenohumeral, sternoclavicular, acromioclavicular, and scapulothoracic joints.

#### Arthrokinematics

Motion at the glenohumeral joint occurs as a rolling and sliding of the head of the humerus on the glenoid fossa. The convex joint surface of the head of the humerus slides in the opposite direction and rolls in the same direction as the osteokinematic movements of the shaft of the humerus.[2,3] The sliding motions help to maintain contact between the head of the humerus and the glenoid fossa of the scapular during the rolling motions and reduce translational movement of the axis of rotation in the humerus. During abduction the surface of the humeral head slides inferiorly while rolling superiorly.[2–5] The opposite motions occur during adduction. In medial rotation and flexion, the surface of the humeral head slides posteriorly and rolls anteriorly.[4,5] In lateral rotation and extension, the surface of the humeral head slides anteriorly and rolls posteriorly on the glenoid fossa.[4,5] Arthrokinematic motions during flexion and extension have also been described as a spin.[3]

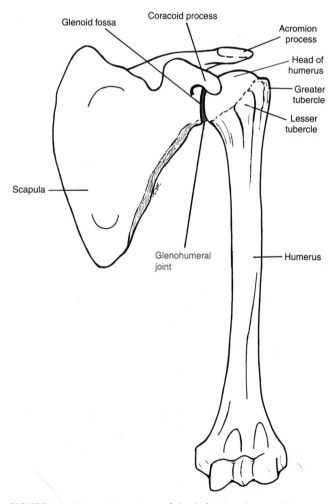

Glenoid fossa

Coracoid process

Acromion process

Head of humerus

Greater tubercle

Lesser tubercle

Scapula

Glenohumeral joint

Humerus

**FIGURE 4.1** An anterior view of the left glenohumeral joint.

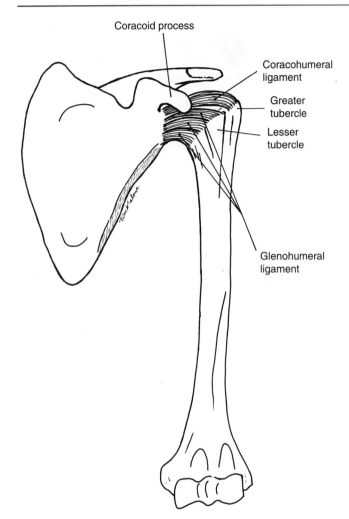

**FIGURE 4.2** An anterior view of the left glenohumeral joint showing the coracohumeral and glenohumeral ligaments.

## Capsular Pattern

The greatest restriction of passive motion is in lateral rotation, followed by some restriction in abduction and less restriction in medial rotation.[5,6]

## Sternoclavicular Joint

### Anatomy

The sternoclavicular (SC) joint is a synovial joint linking the medial end of the clavicle with the sternum and the cartilage of the first rib (Fig. 4.3A). The joint surfaces are saddle-shaped.[1,2] The clavicular joint surface is convex cephalocaudally and concave anteroposteriorly. The opposing joint surface, located at the notch formed by the manubrium of the sternum and the first costal cartilage, is concave cephalocaudally and convex anteroposteriorly. An articular disc divides the joint into two separate compartments.

The associated joint capsule is strong and reinforced by anterior and posterior sternoclavicular ligaments (Fig. 4.3B). These ligaments limit anterior–posterior movement of the medial end of the clavicle. The costoclavicular ligament, which extends from the inferior surface of the medial end of the clavicle to the first rib, limits clavicular elevation and

protraction. The interclavicular ligament extends from one clavicle to another and limits excessive inferior movement of the clavicle.[7]

### Osteokinematics

The SC joint has 3 degrees of freedom, and motion consists of movement of the clavicle on the sternum. These motions are described by the movement at the lateral end of the clavicle. Clavicular motions include elevation–depression, protraction–retraction, and anterior–posterior rotation.[2,7]

### Arthrokinematics

During clavicular elevation and depression, the convex portion of the joint surface of the clavicle slides on the concave manubrium in the opposite direction and rolls in the same direction as movement of the lateral end of the clavicle.[2–5] In protraction and retraction, the concave portion of the clavicular joint surface slides and rolls on the convex surface of the manubrium in the same direction as the lateral end of the clavicle.[2–5] In rotation, the clavicular joint surface spins on the opposing joint surface. In summary, the clavicle slides inferiorly in elevation, superiorly in depression, anteriorly in protraction, and posteriorly in retraction.

## Acromioclavicular Joint

### Anatomy

The acromioclavicular (AC) joint is a synovial joint linking the scapula and the clavicle. The scapular joint surface is a

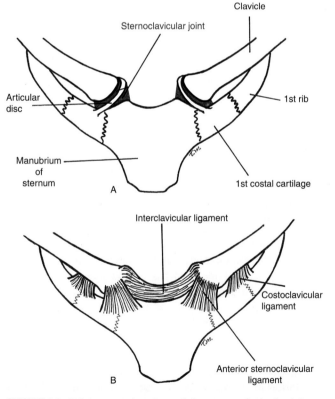

**FIGURE 4.3 (A)** An anterior view of the sternoclavicular joint showing the bone structures and articular disc. **(B)** An anterior view of the SC joint showing the interclavicular, sternoclavicular, and costoclavicular ligaments.

shallow concave facet located on the medial aspect of the acromion of the scapula (Fig. 4.4).[4,5] The clavicular joint surface is a slightly convex facet located on the lateral end of the clavicle. However, in some individuals the joint surfaces may be flat or the reverse pattern of convex–concave shapes.[1] The joint contains a fibrocartilaginous disc and is surrounded by a weak joint capsule. The superior and inferior acromioclavicular ligaments reinforce the capsule (Fig. 4.5). The coracoclavicular ligament, which extends between the clavicle and the scapular coracoid process, provides additional stability.

## Osteokinematics

The AC joint has 3 degrees of freedom and permits movement of the scapula on the clavicle in three planes.[2] Numerous terms have been used to describe these motions. **Tilting** (tipping) is movement of the scapula in the sagittal plane around a coronal axis. During anterior tilting the superior border of the scapula and glenoid fossa move anteriorly, whereas the inferior angle moves posteriorly. During posterior tilting (tipping) the superior border of the scapula and glenoid fossa move posteriorly, whereas the inferior angle moves anteriorly.

**Upward** and **downward rotations** of the scapula occur in the frontal plane around an anterior–posterior axis. During upward rotation the glenoid fossa moves cranially, whereas during downward rotation the glenoid fossa moves caudally.

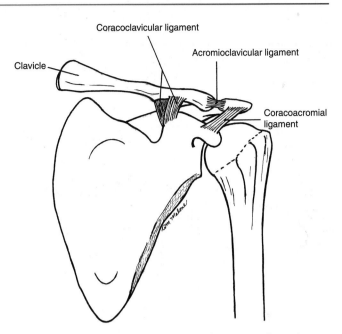

**FIGURE 4.5** An anterior view of the left acromioclavicular joint showing the coracoclavicular, acromioclavicular, and coracoacromial ligaments.

**Protraction** and **retraction** of the scapula occur in the transverse plane around a vertical axis. During protraction (also termed medial rotation, or winging) the glenoid fossa moves medially and anteriorly, whereas the vertebral border of the scapula moves away from the spine. During retraction (also termed lateral rotation) the glenoid fossa moves laterally and posteriorly, whereas the vertebral border of the scapula moves toward the spine. The terms abduction–adduction have been used by various authors to indicate the motions of upward rotation–downward rotation as well as protraction–retraction.[5,7]

## Arthrokinematics

If the acromial facet is concave in shape, the acromial facet will slide and roll on the lateral end of the clavicle in the same direction as osteokinematic movement of the scapula.[5]

# Scapulothoracic Joint

## Anatomy

The scapulothoracic joint is considered to be a functional rather than an anatomical joint. The joint surfaces are the anterior surface of the scapula and the posterior surface of the thorax.

## Osteokinematics

The motions that occur at the scapulothoracic joint are caused by the independent or combined motions of the sternoclavicular and acromioclavicular joints. These motions include scapular elevation–depression, upward–downward rotation, anterior–posterior tilting, protraction–retraction, and medial–lateral rotation.[1,2]

## Arthrokinematics

Motion consists of a sliding of the scapula on the thorax.

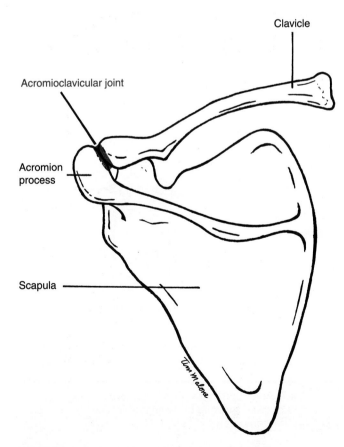

**FIGURE 4.4** A posterior–superior view of the left acromioclavicular joint.

# RANGE OF MOTION TESTING PROCEDURES: Shoulder

Full ROM of the shoulder requires movement at the glenohumeral, SC, AC, and scapulothoracic joints. To make measurements more informative, we suggest using two methods of measuring the ROM of the shoulder. One method measures passive motion primarily at the glenohumeral joint. The other method measures passive ROM at all the joints included in the shoulder complex.

We have found the method that measures primarily glenohumeral motion is helpful in identifying glenohumeral joint problems within the shoulder complex. The ability to differentiate and quantify ROM at the glenohumeral joint from other joints in the shoulder complex is important in diagnosing and treating many shoulder conditions. This method of measuring glenohumeral motion requires the use of passive motion and careful stabilization of the scapula. Active motion is avoided because it results in synchronous motion throughout the shoulder complex, making isolation of glenohumeral motion difficult. Certain studies have begun establishing some normative values (Table 4.2 in Research Findings) and assessing the reliability of this glenohumeral measurement method.

The second method measures full motion of the shoulder complex and is useful in evaluating the functional ROM of the shoulder. This more traditional method of assessing shoulder motion incorporates the stabilization of the thoracic spine and rib cage. Tissue resistance to further motion is typically due to the stretch of structures connecting the clavicle to the sternum, and the scapula to the ribs and spine. ROM values for shoulder complex motion are presented in Tables 4.1, 4.3, and 4.4 in Research Findings. Both methods of measuring the ROM of the shoulder are presented in the following discussions of stabilization techniques and end-feels. However, the alignment of the goniometer is the same for measuring glenohumeral and shoulder complex motions.

## Landmarks for Testing Procedure

**FIGURE 4.6** An anterior view of the humerus, clavicle, sternum, and scapula showing surface anatomy landmarks for aligning the goniometer.

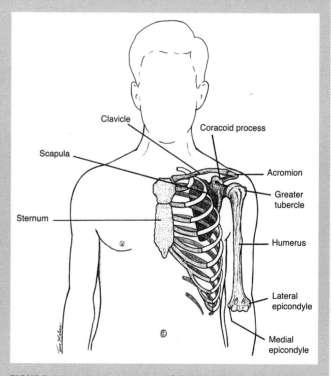

**FIGURE 4.7** An anterior view of the humerus, clavicle, sternum, and scapula showing bony anatomical landmarks for aligning the goniometer.

## Landmarks for Testing Procedure (continued)

**FIGURE 4.8** A lateral view of the upper arm showing surface anatomy landmarks for aligning the goniometer.

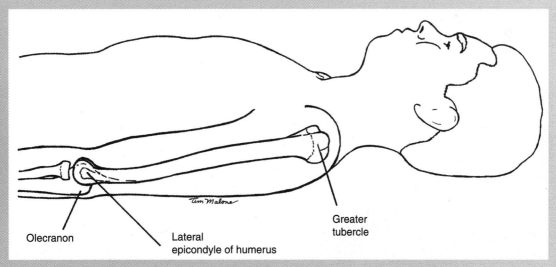

Olecranon

Lateral
epicondyle of humerus

Greater
tubercle

**FIGURE 4.9** A lateral view of the upper arm showing bony anatomical landmarks for aligning the goniometer.

# FLEXION

Motion occurs in the sagittal plane around a medial–lateral axis. Normal shoulder complex flexion ROM for adults is 180 degrees according to the American Academy of Orthopaedic Surgeons (AAOS),[8,9] 180 degrees according to the American Medical Association (AMA),[10] and 165 degrees according to Boone and Azen.[11] Normal glenohumeral flexion ROM for adults is 106 degrees according to Lannan, Lehman, and Toland[12] and 97 degrees according to Rundquist and coworkers[13] for a small sample of older subjects. See Tables 4.1 to 4.4 in Research Findings for additional normal ROM values by age and gender.

## Testing Position

Place the subject supine, with the knees flexed to flatten the lumbar spine. Position the shoulder in 0 degrees of abduction, adduction, and rotation. Place the elbow in extension so that tension in the long head of the triceps muscle does not limit the motion. Position the forearm in 0 degrees of supination and pronation so that the palm of the hand faces the body.

## Stabilization

### Glenohumeral Flexion

Stabilize the scapula to prevent posterior tilting, upward rotation, and elevation of the scapula.

### Shoulder Complex Flexion

Stabilize the thorax to prevent extension of the spine and movement of the ribs. The weight of the trunk may assist stabilization.

## Testing Motion

Flex the shoulder by lifting the humerus off the examining table, bringing the hand up over the subject's head. Maintain the extremity in neutral abduction and adduction during the motion. Slight rotation is allowed to occur as needed to attain maximal flexion.

### Glenohumeral Flexion

The end of glenohumeral flexion ROM occurs when resistance to further motion is felt and attempts to overcome the resistance cause upward rotation, posterior tilting, or elevation of the scapula (Fig. 4.10).

### Shoulder Complex Flexion

The end of shoulder complex flexion ROM occurs when resistance to further motion is felt and attempts to overcome the resistance cause extension of the spine or motion of the ribs (Fig. 4.11).

**FIGURE 4.10** The end of glenohumeral flexion ROM. The examiner stabilizes the lateral border of the scapula with her hand. The examiner is able to determine that the end of the ROM has been reached because any attempt to move the extremity into additional flexion causes the lateral border of the scapula to move anteriorly and laterally.

**FIGURE 4.11** The end of shoulder complex flexion ROM. The examiner stabilizes the subject's trunk and ribs with her hand. The examiner is able to determine that the end of the ROM has been reached because any attempt to move the extremity into additional flexion causes extension of the spine and movement of the ribs.

## Normal End-Feel
### Glenohumeral Flexion
The end-feel is firm because of tension in the posterior band of the coracohumeral ligament; the posterior joint capsule; and the posterior deltoid, teres minor, teres major, and infraspinatus muscles.

### Shoulder Complex Flexion
The end-feel is firm because of tension in the costo-clavicular ligament and SC capsule and ligaments, and the latissimus dorsi, sternocostal fibers of the pectoralis major and pectoralis minor, and rhomboid major and minor muscles.

## Goniometer Alignment
This goniometer alignment is used for measuring glenohumeral and shoulder complex flexion (Figs. 4.12 through 4.14).

1. Center **fulcrum** of the goniometer over the lateral aspect of the greater tubercle.
2. Align **proximal arm** parallel to the midaxillary line of the thorax.
3. Align **distal arm** with the lateral midline of the humerus. Depending on how much flexion and rotation occur, the lateral epicondyle of the humerus or the olecranon process of the ulnar may be helpful references.

**FIGURE 4.12** The alignment of the goniometer at the beginning of glenohumeral and shoulder complex flexion ROM.

**FIGURE 4.13** The alignment of the goniometer at the end of glenohumeral flexion ROM. The examiner's hand supports the subject's extremity and maintains the goniometer's distal arm in correct alignment over the lateral epicondyle. The examiner's other hand releases its stabilization and aligns the goniometer's proximal arm with the lateral midline of the thorax.

**FIGURE 4.14** The alignment of the goniometer at the end of shoulder complex flexion ROM. More motion is noted during shoulder complex flexion than in glenohumeral flexion.

# 🖋 EXTENSION

Motion occurs in the sagittal plane around a medial–lateral axis. Normal shoulder complex extension ROM for adults is 50 degrees according to the AMA,[10] 57 degrees according to Boone and Azen,[11] and 60 degrees according to the AAOS.[8] Normal glenohumeral extension ROM for adults is 20 degrees as cited by Lannan, Lehman, and Toland.[12] See Tables 4.1 to 4.4 in Research Findings for additional normal ROM values by age and gender.

## Testing Position

Position the subject prone, with the face turned away from the shoulder being tested. A pillow is not used under the head. Place the shoulder in 0 degrees of abduction, adduction, and rotation. Position the elbow in slight flexion so that tension in the long head of the biceps brachii muscle will not restrict the motion. Place the forearm in 0 degrees of supination and pronation so that the palm of the hand faces the body.

## Stabilization

### Glenohumeral Extension

Stabilize the scapula at the inferior angle or at the acromion and coracoid processes to prevent elevation and anterior tilting (inferior angle moves posteriorly) of the scapula.

### Shoulder Complex Extension

The examining table and the weight of the trunk stabilize the thorax to prevent forward flexion of the spine. The examiner can also stabilize the trunk to prevent rotation of the spine.

## Testing Motion

Extend the shoulder by lifting the humerus off the examining table. Maintain the extremity in neutral abduction and adduction during the motion.

### Glenohumeral Extension

The end of ROM occurs when resistance to further motion is felt and attempts to overcome the resistance cause anterior tilting or elevation of the scapula (Fig. 4.15).

### Shoulder Complex Extension

The end of ROM occurs when resistance to further motion is felt and attempts to overcome the resistance cause forward flexion or rotation of the spine (Fig. 4.16).

**FIGURE 4.15** The end of glenohumeral extension ROM. The examiner is stabilizing the inferior angle of the scapula with her hand. The examiner is able to determine that the end of the ROM in extension has been reached because any attempt to move the humerus into additional extension causes the scapula to tilt anteriorly and to elevate, causing the inferior angle of the scapula to move posteriorly. Alternatively, the examiner may stabilize the acromion and coracoid processes of the scapula.

**FIGURE 4.16** The end shoulder complex extension ROM. The examiner stabilizes the subject's trunk and ribs with her hand. The examiner is able to determine that the end of the ROM has been reached because any attempt to move the extremity into additional extension causes flexion and rotation of the spine.

## Normal End-Feel
### Glenohumeral Extension
The end-feel is firm because of tension in the anterior band of the coracohumeral ligament; anterior joint capsule; and clavicular fibers of the pectoralis major, coracobrachialis, and anterior deltoid muscles.

### Shoulder Complex Extension
The end-feel is firm because of tension in the SC capsule and ligaments and in the serratus anterior muscle.

## Goniometer Alignment
This goniometer alignment is used for measuring glenohumeral and shoulder complex extension (Figs. 4.17 to 4.19).

1. Center **fulcrum** of the goniometer over the lateral aspect of the greater tubercle.
2. Align **proximal arm** parallel to the midaxillary line of the thorax.
3. Align **distal arm** with the lateral midline of the humerus, using the lateral epicondyle of the humerus for reference.

**FIGURE 4.17** The alignment of the goniometer at the beginning of glenohumeral and shoulder complex extension ROM.

**FIGURE 4.18** The alignment of the goniometer at the end of glenohumeral extension ROM. The examiner's left hand supports the subject's extremity and holds the distal arm of the goniometer in correct alignment over the lateral epicondyle of the humerus.

**FIGURE 4.19** The alignment of the goniometer at the end of shoulder complex extension ROM. The examiner's hand that formerly stabilized the subject's trunk now positions the goniometer.

# ● ABDUCTION

Motion occurs in the frontal plane around an anterior–posterior axis. Normal shoulder complex abduction ROM for adults is 180 degrees according to the AAOS[8] and AMA[10] and 183 degrees according to Boone and Azen.[11] Normal glenohumeral abduction ROM for adults is 129 degrees as noted by Lannan, Lehman, and Toland,[12] 100 degrees according to Rundquist and coworkers[13] for a small sample of older subjects, and ranging from 90 to 120 degrees in Levangie and Norkin.[2] See Tables 4.1 to 4.4 in Research Findings for additional normal ROM values by age and gender.

## Testing Position

Position the subject supine, with the shoulder in lateral rotation and 0 degrees of flexion and extension so that the palm of the hand faces anteriorly. If the humerus is not laterally rotated, contact between the greater tubercle of the humerus and the upper portion of the glenoid fossa or the acromion process will restrict the motion. The elbow should be extended so that tension in the long head of the triceps does not restrict the motion.

## Stabilization

### Glenohumeral Abduction

Stabilize the scapula to prevent upward rotation and elevation of the scapula.

### Shoulder Complex Abduction

Stabilize the thorax to prevent lateral flexion of the spine. The weight of the trunk may assist stabilization.

## Testing Motion

Abduct the shoulder by moving the humerus laterally away from the subject's trunk. Maintain the upper extremity in lateral rotation and neutral flexion and extension during the motion.

### Glenohumeral Abduction

The end of ROM occurs when resistance to further motion is felt and attempts to overcome the resistance cause upward rotation or elevation of the scapula (Fig. 4.20).

### Shoulder Complex Abduction

The end of ROM occurs when resistance to further motion is felt and attempts to overcome the resistance cause lateral flexion of the spine (Fig. 4.21).

**FIGURE 4.20** The end of the ROM of glenohumeral abduction. The examiner stabilizes the lateral border of the scapula with her hand to detect upward rotation of the scapula. Alternatively, the examiner may stabilize the acromion and coracoid processes of the scapula to detect elevation of the scapula.

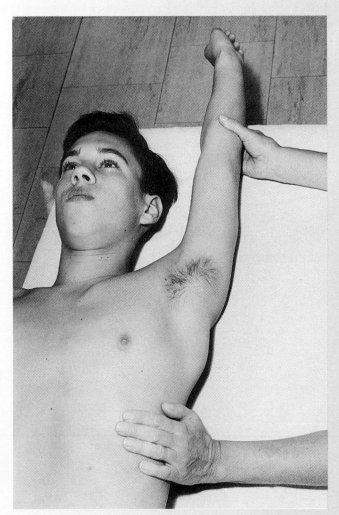

**FIGURE 4.21** The end of the ROM of shoulder complex abduction. The examiner stabilizes the subject's trunk and ribs with her hand to detect lateral flexion of the spine and movement of the ribs.

## Normal End-Feel
### Glenohumeral Abduction
The end-feel is usually firm because of tension in the middle and inferior bands of the gleno-humeral ligament, inferior joint capsule, and the teres major and clavicular fibers of the pectoralis major muscles.

### Shoulder Complex Abduction
The end-feel is firm because of tension in the costocla-vicular ligament; sternoclavicular capsule and ligaments; and latissimus dorsi, sternocostal fibers of the pectoralis major, and major and minor rhomboid muscles.

## Goniometer Alignment
This goniometer alignment is used for measuring glenohumeral and shoulder complex abduction (Figs. 4.22 to 4.24).

1. Center **fulcrum** of the goniometer close to the anterior aspect of the acromial process.
2. Align **proximal arm** so that it is parallel to the mid-line of the anterior aspect of the sternum.
3. Align **distal arm** with the anterior midline of the humerus. Depending on the amount of abduction and lateral rotation that has occurred, the medial epicondyle may be a helpful reference.

**FIGURE 4.22** The align-ment of the goniometer at the beginning of gleno-humeral and shoulder complex abduction ROM.

**FIGURE 4.23** The alignment of the goniometer at the end of glenohumeral abduction ROM. The examining table or the examiner's hand can support the subject's extremity and align the goniometer's distal arm with the anterior midline of the humerus. The examiner's other hand has released its stabilization of the scapula and is holding the proximal arm of the goniometer parallel to the sternum.

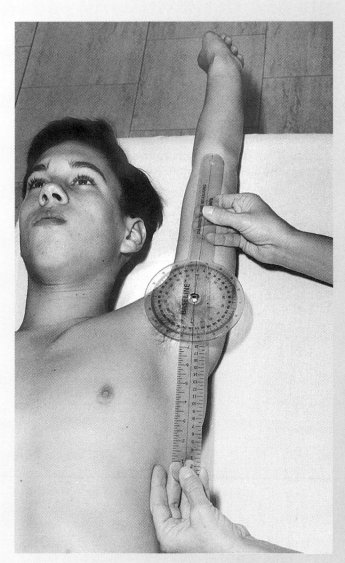

**FIGURE 4.24** The alignment of the goniometer at the end of shoulder complex abduction ROM. The humerus has laterally rotated, and the medial epicondyle is now a helpful anatomical landmark for aligning the distal arm of the goniometer. Note that the placement of the stationary and moving arms of the goniometer with the proximal and distal joint segments have switched from that in Fig. 4.23, but both placements will give an accurate measurement of the angle at the end of motion.

# ● ADDUCTION

Motion occurs in the frontal plane around an anterior-posterior axis. Adduction is not usually measured and recorded because it is the return to the zero starting position from full abduction.

# ● MEDIAL (INTERNAL) ROTATION

When the subject is in anatomical position, the motion occurs in the transverse plane around a vertical axis. When the subject is in the testing position, the motion occurs in the sagittal plane around a medial-lateral (coronal) axis. Normal shoulder complex medial rotation for adults is 67 degrees according to Boone and Azen,[11] 70 degrees according to the AAOS,[8] and 90 degrees according to the AMA.[10] Normal glenohumeral medial rotation for adults is 49 degrees according to Lannan, Lehman, and Toland,[12] and for older childern it is 54 degrees according to Ellenbecker[14] and 63 degrees according to Boon and Smith.[15] See Tables 4.1 to 4.4 in Research Findings for additional normal ROM values by age and gender.

## Testing Position

Position the subject supine, with the arm being tested in 90 degrees of shoulder abduction. Place the forearm perpendicular to the supporting surface and in 0 degrees of supination and pronation so that the palm of the hand faces the feet. Rest the full length of the humerus on the examining table. The elbow is not supported by the examining table. Place a pad under the humerus so that the humerus is level with the acromion process.

## Stabilization

### Glenohumeral Medial Rotation

In the beginning of the ROM, stabilization is often needed at the distal end of the humerus to keep the shoulder in 90 degrees of abduction. Toward the end of the ROM, the clavicle and corocoid and acromion processes of the scapula are stabilized to prevent anterior tilting and protraction of the scapula.

### Shoulder Complex Medial Rotation

Stabilization is often needed at the distal end of the humerus to keep the shoulder in 90 degrees of abduction. The thorax may be stabilized by the weight of the subject's trunk or with the examiner's hand to prevent flexion or rotation of the spine.

## Testing Motion

Medially rotate the shoulder by moving the forearm anteriorly, bringing the palm of the hand toward the floor. Maintain the shoulder in 90 degrees of abduction and the elbow in 90 degrees of flexion during the motion.

### Glenohumeral Medial Rotation

The end of ROM occurs when resistance to further motion is felt and attempts to overcome the resistance cause an anterior tilt or protraction of the scapula (Fig. 4.25).

### Shoulder Complex Medial Rotation

The end of ROM occurs when resistance to further motion is felt and attempts to overcome the resistance cause flexion or rotation of the spine (Fig. 4.26).

**FIGURE 4.25** The end of glenohumeral medial (internal) rotation ROM. The examiner stabilizes the acromion and coracoid processes of the scapula. The examiner is able to determine that the end of the ROM has been reached because any attempt to move the extremity into additional medial rotation causes the scapula to tilt anteriorly or protract. The examiner should also maintain the shoulder in 90 degrees of abduction and the elbow in 90 degrees of flexion during the motion.

**FIGURE 4.26** The end of shoulder complex medial (internal) rotation ROM. The examiner stabilizes the distal end of the humerus to maintain the shoulder in 90 degrees of abduction and the elbow in 90 degrees of flexion during the motion. Resistance is noted at the end of medial rotation of the shoulder complex because attempts to move the extremity into further motion cause the spine to flex or rotate. The clavicle and scapula are allowed to move as they participate in shoulder complex motions.

## Normal End-Feel

### Glenohumeral Medial Rotation

The end-feel is firm because of tension in the posterior joint capsule and the infraspinatus and teres minor muscles.

### Shoulder Complex Medial Rotation

The end-feel is firm because of tension in the sternoclavicular capsule and ligaments, the costoclavicular ligament, and the major and minor rhomboid and trapezius muscles.

## Goniometer Alignment

This goniometer alignment is used for measuring glenohumeral and shoulder complex medial rotation (Figs. 4.27 to 4.29).

1. Center **fulcrum** of the goniometer over the olecranon process.
2. Align **proximal arm** so that it is either perpendicular to or parallel with the floor.
3. Align **distal arm** with the ulna, using the olecranon process and ulnar styloid for reference.

**FIGURE 4.27** The alignment of the goniometer at the beginning of medial rotation ROM of the glenohumeral and shoulder complex.

**FIGURE 4.28** The alignment of the goniometer at the end of medial rotation ROM of the glenohumeral joint. The examiner uses one hand to support the subject's forearm and the distal arm of the goniometer. The examiner's other hand holds the body and the proximal arm of the goniometer.

**FIGURE 4.29** The alignment of the goniometer at the end medial rotation ROM of the shoulder complex.

# ● LATERAL (EXTERNAL) ROTATION

When the subject is in anatomical position, the motion occurs in the transverse plane around a vertical axis. When the subject is in the testing position, the motion occurs in the sagittal plane around a medial-lateral (coronal) axis. Normal shoulder complex lateral rotation for adults is 90 degrees according to the AAOS[8] and AMA[10] and 100 degrees according to Boone and Azen.[11] Normal glenohumeral medial rotation for adults is 94 degrees according to Lannan, Lehman, and Toland,[12] and for older children it is 104 degrees according to Ellenbecker[14] and 108 degrees according to Boon and Smith.[15] See Tables 4.1 to 4.4 in Research Findings for additional normal ROM values by age and gender.

## Testing Position

Position the subject supine, with the arm being tested in 90 degrees of shoulder abduction. Place the forearm perpendicular to the supporting surface and in 0 degrees of supination and pronation so that the palm of the hand faces the feet. Rest the full length of the humerus on the examining table. The elbow is not supported by the examining table. Place a pad under the humerus so that the humerus is level with the acromion process.

## Stabilization

### Glenohumeral Lateral Rotation

At the beginning of the ROM, stabilization is often needed at the distal end of the humerus to keep the shoulder in 90 degrees of abduction. Toward the end of the ROM, the spine of the scapula is stabilized to prevent posterior tilting and retraction.

### Shoulder Complex Lateral Rotation

Stabilization is often needed at the distal end of the humerus to keep the shoulder in 90 degrees of abduction. To prevent extension or rotation of the spine, the thorax may be stabilized by the weight of the subject's trunk or by the examiner's hand.

## Testing Motion

Rotate the shoulder laterally by moving the forearm posteriorly, bringing the dorsal surface of the palm of the hand toward the floor. Maintain the shoulder in 90 degrees of abduction and the elbow in 90 degrees of flexion during the motion.

### Glenohumeral Lateral Rotation

The end of ROM occurs when resistance to further motion is felt and attempts to overcome the resistance cause a posterior tilt or retraction of the scapula (Fig. 4.30).

### Shoulder Complex Lateral Rotation

The end of ROM occurs when resistance to further motion is felt and attempts to overcome the resistance cause extension or rotation of the spine (Fig. 4.31).

**FIGURE 4.30** The end of lateral rotation ROM of the glenohumeral joint. The examiner's hand stabilizes the spine of the scapula. The end of the ROM is reached when additional motion causes the scapula to posteriorly tilt or retract and push against the examiner's hand.

**FIGURE 4.31** The end of lateral rotation ROM of the shoulder complex. The examiner stabilizes the distal humerus to prevent shoulder abduction beyond 90 degrees. The elbow is maintained in 90 degrees of flexion during the motion.

## Normal End-Feel
### Glenohumeral Lateral Rotation
The end-feel is firm because of tension in the anterior joint capsule; the three bands of the glenohumeral ligament; the coracohumeral ligament; and the subscapularis, the teres major, and the clavicular fibers of the pectoralis major muscles.

### Shoulder Complex Lateral Rotation
The end-feel is firm because of tension in the SC capsule and ligaments and in the latissimus dorsi, sternocostal fibers of the pectoralis major, pectoralis minor, and serratus anterior muscles.

## Goniometer Alignment
This goniometer alignment is used for measuring glenohumeral and shoulder complex lateral rotation (Figs. 4.32 to 4.34).

1. Center **fulcrum** of the goniometer over the olecranon process.
2. Align **proximal arm** so that it is either parallel to or perpendicular to the floor.
3. Align **distal arm** with the ulna, using the olecranon process and ulnar styloid for reference.

**FIGURE 4.32** The alignment of the goniometer at the beginning of lateral rotation ROM of the glenohumeral joint and shoulder complex.

**FIGURE 4.33** The alignment of the goniometer at the end of lateral rotation ROM of the glenohumeral joint. The examiner's hand supports the subject's forearm and the distal arm of the goniometer. The examiner's other hand holds the body and proximal arm of the goniometer. The placement of the examiner's hands would be reversed if the subject's right shoulder were being tested.

**FIGURE 4.34** The alignment of the goniometer at the end of lateral rotation ROM of the shoulder complex.

# ⊘ Research Findings

## Effects of Age, Gender, and Other Factors

Table 4.1 shows normal values of shoulder complex ROM for adults from four sources.[8,10,11,16] In general, these values range from 155 to 180 degrees for shoulder complex flexion, 50 to 60 degrees for extension, 165 to 180 degrees for abduction, 50 to 90 degrees for medial rotation, and 85 to 100 degrees for lateral rotation. The data on age, gender, and number of subjects that were measured to obtain the values reported for the AAOS[8] and AMA[10] were not reported. Information on the subjects in the studies by Boone and Azen[11] and Greene and Wolf[16] are noted in Table 4.1; both studies measured active ROM using a universal goniometer. Unless otherwise noted in this section, Research Findings, the reader should assume that shoulder ROM refers to shoulder complex ROM.

Few studies have specifically measured glenohumeral ROM using clinical tools such as a universal goniometer. In general, the overall ratio of glenohumeral to scapulothoracic motion during flexion and abduction is given as 2:1.[2,17–19] Therefore, about two-thirds of shoulder complex motion is attributed to the glenohumeral joint and one-third to the combined SC and AC joints. Table 4.2 shows normal values of glenohumeral ROM obtained from three sources.[12,14,15] These three studies used manual stabilization of the scapula and universal goniometers to obtain glenohumeral measurements. In another study of 56 healthy male and female athletes ages 13 to 18 years, Awan, Smith, and Boon[20] found mean medial rotation for the glenohumeral joint to be between 63.2 and 70.2 degrees with the scapula manually stabilized and between 60.6 and 70.7 degrees using visualized movement of the scapula to determine end range. Rundquist and coworkers[13] also provide some glenohumeral ROM data measured with electromagnetic tracking sensors on the humerus and scapula in 10 asymptomatic subjects (mean age = 51 years).

More studies are needed to establish normative values for glenohumeral ROM, especially in older adults.

### Age

A review of shoulder complex ROM values presented in Table 4.3 shows very slight differences among children from birth through adolescence. Values from the study by Wanatabe and coworkers[21] were derived from measurements of passive ROM of Japanese males and females. The mean values listed from Boone[22] were derived from measurements of active ROM taken with a universal goniometer on Caucasian males. Although the values obtained from Wanatabe and coworkers[21] for infants are greater than those obtained from Boone[22] for children between the ages of 1 and 19 years, it is difficult to compare values across studies. Within one study, Boone[22] and Boone and Azen[11] found that shoulder ROM varied little in boys between 1 and 19 years of age.

There is some indication that children have greater values than adults for certain shoulder complex motions. Wanatabe and coworkers[21] found that the ROM in shoulder extension and lateral rotation was greater in Japanese infants than the average values typically reported for adults. Boone and Azen[11] found significantly greater active ROM in all shoulder motions except for abduction in male children between 1 and 19 years of age compared with male adults between 20 and 54 years of age.

Table 4.4 summarizes the effects of age on shoulder complex ROM in adults. There appears to be a trend for older adults (between 60 and 93 years of age) to have lower values than younger adults (between 20 and 39 years of age) for the motions of extension, lateral rotation, and abduction. It is interesting to note that the standard deviations for the older groups are much larger than the values reported for the younger groups. The larger standard deviations appear to indicate that ROM is more variable in the older groups than in the younger groups. However, the fact that the measurements of the two oldest groups were obtained by different investigators should be considered when drawing conclusions from this information.

| TABLE 4.1 | Shoulder Complex Motion: Normal Values for Adults in Degrees From Selected Sources |

| | AAOS[8] | AMA[10] | Boone and Azen[11] 20–54 yrs n = 56 Males | | Greene and Wolf[16] 18–55 yrs n = 20 Males and Females | |
|---|---|---|---|---|---|---|
| *Motion* | | | *Mean* | *(SD)* | *Mean* | *(SD)* |
| Flexion | 180 | 180 | 165.0 | (5.0) | 155.8 | (1.4) |
| Extension | 60 | 50 | 57.3 | (8.1) | — | — |
| Abduction | 180 | 180 | 182.7 | (9.0) | 167.6 | (1.8) |
| Medial rotation | 70 | 90 | 67.1 | (4.1) | 48.7 | (2.8) |
| Lateral rotation | 90 | 90 | 99.6 | (7.6) | 83.6 | (3.0) |

**TABLE 4.2**  Glenohumeral Motion: Normal Values in Degrees From Selected Sources

| | Lannan et al[12] | | Boon & Smith[15] | | Ellenbecker et al[14] | | Ellenbecker et al[14] | |
| | 21–40 yrs n = 60 Males and Females | | 12-18 yrs n = 50 Males and Females | | 11–17 yrs n = 113 Males | | 11–17 yrs n = 90 Females | |
| Motion | Mean | (SD) | Mean | (SD) | Mean | (SD) | Mean | (SD) |
|---|---|---|---|---|---|---|---|---|
| Flexion | 106.2 | (10.2) | — | — | — | — | — | — |
| Extension | 20.1 | (5.8) | — | — | — | — | — | — |
| Abduction | 128.9 | (9.1) | — | — | — | — | — | — |
| Medial rotation | 49.2 | (9.0) | 62.8 | (12.7) | 50.9 | (12.6) | 56.3 | (10.3) |
| Lateral rotation | 94.2 | (12.2) | 108.1 | (14.1) | 102.8 | (10.9) | 104.6 | (10.3) |

**TABLE 4.3**  Effects of Age on Shoulder Complex Motions for Newborns Through Adolescents: Normal Values in Degrees

| | Wanatabe et al[21] | Boone[22] | | | | | |
| | 0–2 yrs n = 45 Males and Females | 1–5 yrs n = 19 Males | | 6–12 yrs n = 17 Males | | 13–19 yrs n = 17 Males | |
| Motion | Range of Means | Mean | (SD) | Mean | (SD) | Mean | (SD) |
|---|---|---|---|---|---|---|---|
| Flexion | 172–180 | 168.8 | (3.7) | 169.0 | (3.5) | 167.4 | (3.9) |
| Extension | 79–89 | 68.9 | (6.6) | 69.6 | (7.0) | 64.0 | (9.3) |
| Medial rotation | 72–90 | 71.2 | (3.6) | 70.0 | (4.7) | 70.3 | (5.3) |
| Lateral rotation | 118–134 | 110.0 | (10.0) | 107.4 | (3.6) | 106.3 | (6.1) |
| Abduction | 177–187 | 186.3 | (2.6) | 184.7 | (3.8) | 185.1 | (4.3) |

**TABLE 4.4**  Effects of Age on Shoulder Complex Motion in Adults 20 to 93 Years of Age: Normal Values in Degrees

| | Boone[22] | | | | | | | | Walker et al[23] | | Downey et al[24] | |
| | 20–29 yrs n = 19 Males | | 30–39 yrs n = 18 Males | | 40–54 yrs n = 19 Males | | 60–85 yrs n = 30 Males | | | | 61–93 yrs n = 140 Female and 60 Male Shoulders | |
| Motion | Mean | (SD) | Mean | (SD) | Mean | (SD) | Mean | (SD) | Mean | (SD) | Mean | (SD) |
|---|---|---|---|---|---|---|---|---|---|---|---|---|
| Flexion | 164.5 | (5.9) | 165.4 | (3.8) | 165.1 | (5.2) | 160.0 | (11.0) | | | 165.0 | (10.7) |
| Extension | 58.3 | (8.3) | 57.5 | (8.5) | 56.1 | (7.9) | 38.0 | (11.0) | | | — | — |
| Medial rotation | 65.9 | (4.0) | 67.1 | (4.2) | 68.3 | (3.8) | 59.0 | (16.0) | | | 65.0 | (11.7) |
| Lateral rotation | 100.0 | (7.2) | 101.5 | (6.9) | 97.5 | (8.5) | 76.0 | (13.0) | | | 80.6 | (11.0) |
| Abduction | 182.6 | (9.8) | 182.8 | (7.7) | 182.6 | (9.8) | 155.0 | (22.0) | | | 157.9 | (17.4) |

In addition to the evidence for age-related changes presented in Tables 4.3 and 4.4, West[25] Clarke and coworkers,[26] and Allander and associates[27] have also identified age-related trends. West[25] found that older subjects had between 15 and 20 degrees less shoulder complex flexion ROM and 10 degrees less extension ROM than younger subjects. Subjects ranged in age from the first decade to the eighth decade. Clarke and coworkers[26] found significant decreases with age in passive glenohumeral lateral rotation, total rotation, and abduction in a study that included 60 normal males and females ranging in age from 21 to 80 years. Mean reduction in these three glenohumeral ROMs in those aged 71 to 80 years, compared with those aged 21 to 30 years, ranged from 7 to 29 degrees. Allander and associates,[27] in a study of 517 females and 203 males aged 33 to 70 years, also found that passive shoulder complex rotation ROM significantly decreased with increasing age.

## Gender

Several studies have noted that females have greater shoulder complex ROM than males. Walker and coworkers,[23] in a study of 30 men and 30 women between 60 and 84 years of age, found that women had statistically significant greater ROM than their male counterparts in all shoulder motions studied except for medial rotation. The mean differences for women were 20 degrees greater than those of males for shoulder abduction, 11 degrees greater for shoulder extension, and 9 degrees greater for shoulder flexion and lateral rotation. Allander and associates,[27] in a study of passive shoulder rotation in 208 Swedish women and 203 men aged 45 to 70 years, likewise found that women had a greater ROM in total shoulder rotation than men. Escalante, Lichenstein, and Hazuda[28] studied shoulder flexion in 687 community-dwelling adults aged 65 to 74 years and found that women had 3 degrees more flexion than men.

Gender differences have also been noted in glenohumeral ROM. Clarke and associates,[26] in a study that included 60 males and 60 females, found that females had greater glenohumeral ROM for shoulder abduction as well as lateral and total rotation. Six age groups with subjects between 20 and 40 years of age were included in the study. These gender differences were present in all age groups. Males had, on average, 92 percent of the ROM of their female counterparts, the difference being most marked in abduction. Lannan, Lehman, and Toland,[12] in a study of 40 women and 20 men aged 21 to 40 years, found that women had statistically significant greater amounts of glenohumeral flexion, extension, abduction, and medial and lateral rotation than men. The mean differences typically varied between 3 and 8 degrees. Boon and Smith,[15] in a study of 32 females and 18 males aged 12 to 18 years, reported that females had significantly more lateral and total rotation than males. The mean difference in lateral and total rotation was 4.5 and 9.1 degrees, respectively. Ellenbecker and colleagues[14] studied 113 male and 90 female elite tennis players aged 11 to 17 years (see Table 4.2). Their data seem to indicate that the females had greater ROM than males for glenohumeral medial and lateral rotation, although no statistical tests focused on the effect of gender on ROM.

## Testing Position

A subject's posture and testing position have been shown to affect certain shoulder complex motions. Kebaetse, McClure, and Pratt,[29] in a study of 34 healthy adults, measured active shoulder abduction and scapula ROM while subjects were sitting in both erect and slouched trunk postures. There was significantly less active shoulder abduction ROM in the slouched than in the erect postures (mean difference = 23.6 degrees). The slouched posture also resulted in more scapula elevation during 0 to 90 degrees of abduction and less scapula posterior tilting in the interval between 90-degree and maximal abduction.

Sabari and associates[30] studied 30 adult subjects and noted greater amounts of active and passive shoulder abduction measured in the supine than in the sitting position. The mean differences in abduction ranged from 3.0 to 7.1 degrees. On visual inspection of the data there were also greater amounts of shoulder flexion in the supine versus the sitting position; however, these differences did not attain significance.

## Body Mass Index

Escalante, Lichenstein, and Hazuda[28] studied shoulder complex flexion ROM in 695 community-dwelling subjects, aged 65 to 74 years, who participated in the San Antonio Longitudinal Study of Aging. They found no relationship between shoulder flexion and body mass index.

## Sports

Several studies of professional and collegiate baseball players have found a significant increase in lateral rotation ROM and a decrease in medial rotation ROM of the shoulder complex in the dominant shoulder compared with the nondominant shoulder. These differences have been found in position players as well as in pitchers. Bigliani and coworkers[31] studied 148 professional baseball players (72 pitchers and 76 position players) with no history of shoulder problems. Mean lateral rotation ROM measured with the shoulder in 90 degrees of abduction was 113.5 degrees in the dominant arm and 99.9 degrees in the nondominant arm. Mean medial rotation ROM, recorded as the highest vertebral level reached behind the back and converted to a numerical value, was significantly less in the dominant arm. There were no significant differences between the dominant and the nondominant arms in shoulder flexion and shoulder lateral rotation measured with the arm at the side of the body. A study by Baltaci, Johnson, and Kohl[32] of 15 collegiate pitchers and 23 position players had similar findings. Pitchers had an average of 14 degrees more lateral rotation and 11 degrees less medial rotation in the dominant versus nondominant shoulders. Position players had an average of 8 degrees more lateral rotation and 10 degrees less medial rotation in the dominant shoulder. All measurements of rotation were taken with the shoulder in 90 degrees of abduction.

Decreases in shoulder medial rotation ROM have also been noted in the dominant (playing) compared with the nondominant (nonplaying) arms of tennis players. Chinn, Priest, and Kent,[33] in a study of 83 national and international men and women tennis players aged 14 to 50 years, found a significant decrease in active medial rotation ROM of the shoulder complex in the playing versus the nonplaying arm (mean difference = 6.8 degrees in males, 11.9 degrees in females). Men also had a significant increase in lateral rotation ROM in the playing compared with the nonplaying arm. A study by Kibler and colleagues[34] of 39 members of the U. S. Tennis Association National Tennis Team and touring professional program, found a decrease in passive glenohumeral medial rotation ROM, an increase in glenohumeral lateral rotation ROM, and a decrease in total rotation ROM in the playing versus the nonplaying arm. The differences in medial rotation ROM increased with age and years of tournament play. A study by Ellenbecker and associates[14] of 203 junior elite tennis players aged 11 to 17 years reported a significant decrease in active medial rotation ROM and total rotation ROM of the glenohumeral joint in the playing versus the nonplaying arm. The average differences in medial rotation ROM were 11 degrees in the 113 males and 8 degrees in the 90 females. There were no significant differences in glenohumeral lateral rotation ROM between playing and nonplaying arms.

Power lifters were found to have decreased ROM in shoulder complex flexion, extension, and medial and lateral rotation compared with nonlifters in a study by Chang, Buschbacher, and Edlich.[35] Ten male power lifters and 10

aged-matched male nonlifters were included in the study. The authors suggest that athletic training programs that emphasize muscle-strengthening exercise without stretching exercise may cause progressive loss of ROM.

## Functional Range of Motion

Numerous activities of daily living (ADL) require adequate shoulder ROM. Tiffitt,[36] in a study of 25 patients, found a significant correlation between the amount of specific shoulder complex motions and the ability to perform activities such as combing the hair, putting on a coat, washing the back, washing the contralateral axilla, using the toilet, reaching a high shelf, lifting above the shoulder level, pulling, and sleeping on the affected side. Flexion and adduction ROM correlated best with the ability to comb the hair, whereas medial and lateral rotation ROM correlated best with the ability to wash the back.

Several studies[37–39] have examined the ROM that occurs during certain functional tasks (Table 4.5). A large amount of abduction (112 degrees) and lateral rotation is required to reach behind the head for activities such as grooming the hair (Fig 4.35), positioning a necktie, and fastening a dress zipper. Maximal flexion (148 degrees) is needed to reach a high shelf (Fig. 4.36), whereas less flexion (36 to 52 degrees) is needed for self-feeding tasks (Fig 4.37). To reach behind the back for

| TABLE 4.5 | Maximal Shoulder Complex Motion Necessary for Functional Activities: Mean Values in Degrees | | | |
|---|---|---|---|---|
| **Activity** | **Motion** | **Mean** | **(SD)** | **Source** |
| Eating | Flexion | 52 | (8) | Matsen*[37] |
| | Flexion | 36 | (14) | Safaee-Rad et al†[38] |
| | Abduction | 22 | (7) | Safaee-Rad et al |
| | Medial rotation | 18 | (10) | Safaee-Rad et al |
| | Horizontal adduction‡ | 87 | (29) | Matsen |
| Drinking with a cup | Flexion | 43 | (16) | Safaee-Rad et al |
| | Abduction | 31 | (9) | Safaee-Rad et al |
| | Medial rotation | 23 | (12) | Safaee-Rad et al |
| Washing axilla | Flexion | 52 | (14) | Matsen |
| Combing hair | Horizontal adduction | 104 | (12) | Matsen |
| | Abduction | 112 | (10) | Matsen |
| | Horizontal adduction | 54 | (27) | Matsen |
| Maximal elevation | Flexion/abduction | 148 | (11) | Matsen |
| Maximal reaching up back | Horizontal adduction | 55 | (17) | Matsen |
| | Extension | 56 | (13) | Matsen |
| | Horizontal abduction‡ | 69 | (11) | Matsen |
| Reaching perineum | Extension | 38 | (10) | Matsen |
| | Horizontal abduction | 86 | (13) | Matsen |

* Eight normal subjects were assessed with electromagnetic sensors on the humerus.
† Ten normal male subjects were assessed with a three-dimensional video recording system.
‡ The 0-degree starting position for measuring horizontal adduction and horizontal abduction was in 90 degrees of abduction.

**FIGURE 4.35** Reaching behind the head requires a large amount of abduction (112 degrees)[37] and lateral rotation of the shoulder.

tasks such as fastening a bra (Fig 4.38), tucking in a shirt, and reaching the perineum to perform hygiene activities, 38 to 56 degrees of extension and considerable medial rotation and horizontal abduction are necessary. Horizontal adduction is needed for activities performed in front of the body such as washing the contralateral axilla (104 degrees) and eating (87 degrees). If patients have difficulty performing certain functional activities, evaluation and treatment procedures need to focus on the shoulder motions necessary for the activity. Likewise, if patients have known limitations in shoulder ROM, therapists and physicians should anticipate patient difficulty in performing these tasks, and adaptations should be suggested.

## Reliability and Validity

The intratester and intertester reliability of measurements of shoulder motions with a universal goniometer have been studied by many researchers. Most of these studies have presented evidence that intratester reliability is better than intertester reliability. Reliability varied according to the motion being measured. In other words, the reliability of measuring certain shoulder motions was better than the reliability of measuring other motions.

Hellebrandt, Duvall, and Moore,[40] in a study of 77 patients, found the intratester reliability of measurements of active ROM

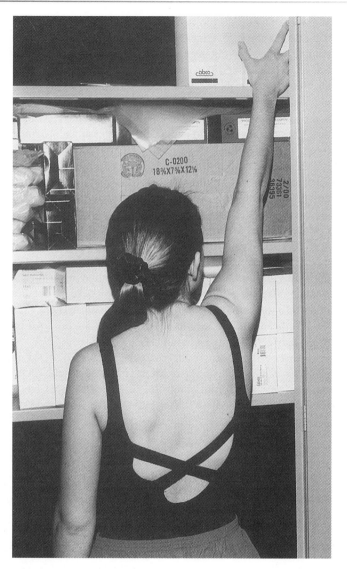

**FIGURE 4.36** Reaching objects on a high shelf requires 148 degrees of shoulder flexion.[37]

of shoulder complex abduction and medial rotation to be less than the intratester reliability of shoulder flexion, extension, and lateral rotation. The mean difference between the repeated measurements ranged from 0.2 to 1.5 degrees. Measurements were taken with a universal goniometer and devices designed by the U.S. Army for specific joints. For most ROM measurements taken throughout the body, the universal goniometer was a more dependable tool than the special devices.

Boone and coworkers[41] examined the reliability of measuring passive ROM for lateral rotation of the shoulder complex, elbow extension–flexion, wrist ulnar deviation, hip abduction, knee extension–flexion, and foot inversion. Four physical therapists used universal goniometers to measure these motions in 12 normal males once a week for 4 weeks. Measurement of lateral rotation ROM of the shoulder was found to be more reliable than that of the other motions tested. For all motions except lateral rotation of the shoulder, intratester reliability was noted to be greater than intertester reliability. Intratester and

**FIGURE 4.37** Feeding tasks require 36 to 52 degrees of shoulder flexion.[37,38]

**FIGURE 4.38** Reaching behind the back to fasten a bra or bathing suit requires 56 degrees of extension, 69 degrees of horizontal abduction,[37] and a large amount of medial rotation of the shoulder.

intertester reliability were similar (r = 0.96 and 0.97, respectively) for lateral rotation ROM.

Pandya and associates,[42] in a study in which five testers measured the range of shoulder complex abduction of 150 children and young adults with Duchenne muscular dystrophy, found that the intratester intraclass correlation coefficient (ICC) for measurements of shoulder abduction was 0.84. The intertester reliability for measuring shoulder abduction was lower (ICC = 0.67). In comparison with measurements of elbow and wrist extension, the measurement of shoulder abduction was less reliable.

Riddle, Rothstein, and Lamb[43] conducted a study to determine intratester and intertester reliability for passive ROM measurements of the shoulder complex. Sixteen physical therapists, assessing in pairs, used two different-sized universal goniometers (large and small) for their measurements on 50 patients. Patient position and goniometer placement during measurements were not controlled. ICC values for intratester reliability for all motions ranged from 0.87 to 0.99. ICC values for intertester reliability for flexion, abduction, and lateral rotation ranged from 0.84 to 0.90. Intertester reliability

was considerably lower for measurements of horizontal abduction, horizontal adduction, extension, and medial rotation, with ICC values ranging from 0.26 to 0.55. The authors concluded that passive ROM measurements for all shoulder motions can be reliable when taken by the same physical therapist, regardless of whether large or small goniometers are used. Measurements of flexion, abduction, and lateral rotation can be reliable when assessed by different therapists. However, because repeated measurements of horizontal abduction, horizontal adduction, extension, and medial rotation were unreliable when taken by more than one tester, these measurements should be taken by the same therapist.

Greene and Wolf[16] compared the reliability of the Ortho Ranger, an electronic pendulum goniometer, with that of a standard universal goniometer for active upper-extremity motions in 20 healthy adults. Shoulder complex motions were measured three times with each instrument during three sessions that occurred over a 2-week period. Both instruments demonstrated high intrasession correlations (ICCs ranged from 0.98 to 0.87), but correlations were higher and 95 percent confidence levels were much lower for the universal goniometer. Measurements of medial rotation and lateral rotation were less reliable than measurements of flexion, extension, abduction, and adduction. There were significant differences between measurements taken with the Ortho Ranger and the universal goniometer. Interestingly, there were significant differences in measurements between sessions for both instruments. The authors noted that the daily variations that were found might have been caused by normal fluctuation in ROM, as suggested by Boone and colleagues,[41] or by daily differences in subjects' efforts while performing active ROM.

Bovens and associates,[44] in a study of the variability and reliability of nine joint motions throughout the body, used a universal goniometer to examine active lateral rotation ROM of the shoulder complex with the arm at the side. Three physician testers and eight healthy subjects participated in the study. Intratester reliability coefficients for lateral rotation of the shoulder ranged from 0.76 to 0.83, whereas the intertester reliability coefficient was 0.63. Mean intratester standard deviations for the measurements taken on each subject ranged from 5.0 to 6.6 degrees, whereas the mean intertester standard deviation was 7.4 degrees. The measurement of lateral rotation ROM of the shoulder was more reliable than ROM measurements of the forearm and wrist. Mean standard deviations between repeated measurement of shoulder lateral rotation ROM were similar to those of the forearm and larger than those of the wrist.

Sabari and associates[30] examined intrarater reliability in the measurement of active and passive shoulder complex flexion and abduction ROM when 30 adults were positioned in supine and sitting positions. The ICCs between two trials by the same tester for each procedure ranged in value from 0.94 to 0.99, indicating high intratester reliability, regardless of whether the measurements were active or passive or whether they were taken with the subject in the supine or the sitting position. ICCs between measurements taken in supine compared with those taken in sitting positions ranged from 0.64 to 0.81. There were no significant differences between comparable flexion measurements taken in supine and sitting positions. However, significantly greater abduction ROM was found in the supine than in the sitting position.

In a study by MacDermid and colleagues,[45] two experienced physical therapists measured passive shoulder complex rotation ROM in 34 patients with a variety of shoulder pathologies. A universal goniometer was used to measure lateral rotation with the shoulder in 20 to 30 degrees of abduction. Intratester ICCs (0.88 and 0.93) and intertester ICCs (0.85 and 0.80) were high. Intratester standard errors of measurement (SEMs; 4.9 and 7.0 degrees) and intertester SEMs (7.5 and 8.0 degrees) also indicated good reliability. The SEMs indicate that differences of 5 to 7 degrees could be attributed to measurement error when the same tester repeats a measurement and about 8 degrees could be attributed to measurement error when different testers take a measurement.

Boon and Smith[15] studied 50 high school athletes to determine the reliability of measuring passive shoulder rotation ROM with and without manual stabilization of the scapula. Four experienced physical therapists working in pairs took goniometric measurements with the shoulder in 90 degrees of abduction and repeated those measurements 5 days later. Scapular stabilization, which resulted in more isolated glenohumeral motion, produced significantly smaller ROM values than when the scapula was not stabilized. According to the authors, intratester reliability for medial rotation was poor for nonstabilized motion (ICC = 0.23, SEM = 20.2 degrees) and good for stabilized motion (ICC = 0.60, SEM = 8.0). The authors state that intratester reliability for lateral rotation was good for both nonstabilized (ICC = 0.79, SEM = 5.6) and stabilized motion (ICC = 0.53, SEM = 9.1). Intertester reliability for medial rotation improved from nonstabilized motion (ICC = 0.13, SEM = 21.5) to stabilized motion (ICC = 0.38, SEM = 10.0) and was comparable for both nonstabilized and stabilized lateral rotation (ICC = 0.84, SEM = 4.9 and ICC = 0.78, SEM = 6.6), respectively.

Hayes and coworkers[46] measured the intratester reliability of active shoulder flexion, abduction, and lateral rotation ROM in nine patients using one tester, and the intertester reliability of active shoulder motion in eight patients using four testers. A universal goniometer was aligned with the humerus and various planes of motion with the subjects in sitting for flexion and abduction and in supine for lateral rotation. Intratester reliability ICC values for the universal goniometer ranged from 0.53 to 0.65, and SEM values ranged from 14 to 23 degrees. Intertester reliability ICC values for the universal goniometer ranged from 0.64 to 0.69, and SEM values ranged from 14 to 25 degrees. The reliability of using visual estimation and still photography to measure shoulder ROM was also studied and produced similar results. However, the use of a tape measure to note distance between T1 and the thumb during reaching behind the back produced even worse ICC values of 0.39 and SEM values of 6 centimeters.

The reliability of measurement devices other than a universal goniometer for assessing shoulder ROM has also been studied and is briefly mentioned here. Intratester and intertester reliability for the different motions and methods varied widely. Green and associates[47] investigated the reliability of measuring active shoulder complex ROM with a Plurimeter-V inclinometer in six patients with shoulder pain and stiffness. Tiffitt, Wildin, and Hajioff[48] studied the reliability of using an inclinometer to measure active shoulder complex motions in 36 patients with shoulder disorders. Valentine and Lewis[49] included 45 subjects with and without shoulder symptoms in a study of the intratester reliability of shoulder flexion and abduction using a gravity dependent inclinometer, lateral rotation using a tape measure, and medial rotation using visual estimation. Bower[50] and Clarke and coworkers[26] examined the reliability of measuring passive glenohumeral motions with a hydrogoniometer. Croft and colleagues[51] investigated the reliability of observing shoulder complex flexion and lateral rotation, and sketching the ROMs onto diagrams that were then measured with a protractor.

# REFERENCES

1. Standring, S (ed): Gray's Anatomy, ed 39. Elsevier, New York, 2005.
2. Ludewig, PM, and Borstead, JD: The shoulder complex. In Levangie, P, and Norkin, C (eds): Joint Structure and Function: A Comprehensive Analysis, ed 4. FA Davis, Philadelphia, 2005.
3. Neumann, DA: Kinesiology of the Musculoskeletal System. Mosby, St. Louis, MO, 2002.
4. Kisner, C, and Colby, LA: Therapeutic Exercise, ed 5. FA Davis, Philadelphia, 2007.
5. Kaltenborn, FM: Manual Mobilization of the Extremity Joints, ed 5. Olaf Norlis Bokhandel, Oslo,1999.
6. Cyriax, JH, and Cyriax, PJ: Illustrated Manual of Orthopaedic Medicine. Butterworths, London, 1983.
7. Culham, E, and Peat, M: Functional anatomy of the shoulder complex. J Orthop Sports Phys Ther 18:342, 1993.
8. American Academy of Orthopaedic Surgeons: Joint Motion: Method of Measuring and Recording. AAOS, Chicago, 1965.
9. Greene, WB, and Heckman, JD: The Clinical Measurement of Joint Motion. American Academy of Orthopaedic Surgeons, Rosemont, IL, 1994.
10. Cocchiarella, L, and Andersson, GBJ: American Medical Association: Guides to the Evaluation of Permanent Impairment, ed 5. AMA, Chicago, 2001.
11. Boone, DC, and Azen, SP: Normal range of motion in male subjects. J Bone Joint Surg Am 61:756, 1979.
12. Lannan, D, Lehman, T, and Toland, M: Establishment of normative data for the range of motion of the glenohumeral joint. Master of Science Thesis, University of Massachusetts, Lowell, MA, 1996
13. Rundquist, PJ, et al: Shoulder kinematics in subjects with frozen shoulder. Arch Phys Med Rehabil 84:1473, 2003.
14. Ellenbecker, TS, et al: Glenohumeral joint internal and external rotation range of motion in elite junior tennis players. J Orthop Sports Phys Ther 24:336, 1996.
15. Boon, AJ, and Smith, J: Manual scapular stabilization: Its effect on shoulder rotational range of motion. Arch Phys Med Rehabil 81:978, 2000.
16. Greene, BL, and Wolf, SL: Upper extremity joint movement: Comparison of two measurement devices. Arch Phys Med Rehabil 70:288, 1989.
17. Soderberg, GL: Kinesiology: Application to Pathological Motion. Williams & Wilkins, Baltimore, 1986.
18. Doody, SG, Freedman, L, and Waterland, JC: Shoulder movements during abduction in the scapular plane. Arch Phys Med Rehabil 51:595, 1970.
19. Poppen, NK, and Walker, PS: Forces at the glenohumeral joint in abduction. Clin Orthop 135:165, 1978.
20. Awan, R, Smith, J, and Boon, AJ: Measuring shoulder internal rotation range of motion: A comparison of 3 techniques. Arch Phys Med Rehabil 83:1229, 2002.
21. Wanatabe, H, et al: The range of joint motions of the extremities in healthy Japanese people: The difference according to age. Nippon Seikeigeka Gakkai Zasshi 53:275, 1979. Cited by Walker, JM: Musculoskeletal development: A review. Phys Ther 71:878, 1991.
22. Boone, DC: Techniques of measurement of joint motion. (Unpublished supplement to Boone, DC, and Azen, SP: Normal range of motion in male subjects. J Bone Joint Surg Am 61:756, 1979.)
23. Walker, JM, et al: Active mobility of the extremities in older subjects. Phys Ther 64:919, 1984.
24. Downey, PA, Fiebert, I, and Stackpole-Brown, JB: Shoulder range of motion in persons aged sixty and older [abstract]. Phys Ther 71:S75, 1991.
25. West, CC: Measurement of joint motion. Arch Phys Med Rehabil 26:414, 1945.
26. Clarke, GR, et al: Preliminary studies in measuring range of motion in normal and painful stiff shoulders. Rheumatol Rehabil 14:39, 1975.
27. Allander, E, et al: Normal range of joint movement in shoulder, hip, wrist and thumb with special reference to side: A comparison between two populations. Int J Epidemiol 3:253, 1974.
28. Escalante, A, Lichenstein, MJ, and Hazuda, HP: Determinants of shoulder and elbow flexion range: Results from the San Antonio longitudinal study of aging. Arthritis Care Res 12:277, 1999.
29. Kebaetse, M, McClure, P, and Pratt, NA: Thoracic position effect on shoulder range of motion, strength, and three-dimensional scapular kinematics. Arch Phys Med Rehabil 80:945, 1999.
30. Sabari, JS, et al: Goniometric assessment of shoulder range of motion: Comparison of testing in supine and sitting positions. Arch Phys Med Rehabil 79:64, 1998.
31. Bigliani, LU, et al: Shoulder motion and laxity in the professional baseball player. Am J Sports Med 25:609, 1997.
32. Baltaci, G, Johnson, R, and Kohl H: Shoulder range of motion characteristics in collegiate baseball players. J Sports Med Phys Fitness 41:236, 2001.
33. Chinn, CJ, Priest, JD, and Kent, BA: Upper extremity range of motion, grip strength and girth in highly skilled tennis players. Phys Ther 54:474, 1974.
34. Kibler, WB, et al: Shoulder range of motion in elite tennis players: Effect of age and years of tournament play. Am J Sports Med 24:279, 1996.
35. Chang, DE, Buschbacker, LP, and Edlich, RF: Limited joint mobility in power lifters. Am J Sports Med 16:280, 1988.
36. Tiffitt, PD: The relationship between motion of the shoulder and the stated ability to perform activities of daily living. J Bone Joint Surg 80:41, 1998.
37. Matsen, FA, et al: Practical Evaluation and Management of the Shoulder. WB Saunders, Philadelphia, 1994.
38. Safaee-Rad, R, et al: Normal functional range of motion of upper limb joints during performance of three feeding activities. Arch Phys Med Rehabil 71:505, 1990.
39. Van Andel, CJ, et al: Complete 3D kinematics of upper extremity functional tasks. Gait Posture (2007), doi:10.1016/j.gaitpost 2007.03.002.
40. Hellebrandt, FA, Duvall, EN, and Moore, ML: The measurement of joint motion. Part III: Reliability of goniometry. Phys Ther Rev 29:302, 1949.
41. Boone, DC, et al: Reliability of goniometric measurements. Phys Ther 58:1355, 1978.
42. Pandya, S, et al: Reliability of goniometric measurements in patients with Duchenne muscular dystrophy. Phys Ther 65:1339, 1985.
43. Riddle, DL, Rothstein, JM, and Lamb, RL: Goniometric reliability in a clinical setting: Shoulder measurements. Phys Ther 67:668, 1987.
44. Bovens, AMP, et al: Variability and reliability of joint measurements. Am J Sports Med 18:58, 1990.
45. MacDermid, JC, et al: Intratester and intertester reliability of goniometric measurement of passive lateral shoulder rotation. J Hand Ther 12:187, 1999.
46. Hayes, K, et al: Reliability of five methods for assessing shoulder range of motion. Australian J Physiother 47:289, 2001.
47. Green, A, et al: A standardized protocol for measurement of range of movement of the shoulder using the Plurimeter-V inclinometer and assessment of its intrarater and interrater reliability. Arthritis Care Res 11:43, 1998.
48. Tiffitt, PD, Wildin, C, and Hajioff, D: The reproducibility of measurement of shoulder movement. Acta Orthop Scand 70:322, 1999.
49. Valentine, RE, and Lewis, JS: Intraobserver reliability of 4 physiologic movements of the shoulder in subjects with and without symptoms. Arch Phys Med Rehabil 87:1242, 2006.
50. Bower, KD: The hydrogoniometer and assessment of glenohumeral joint motion. Aust J Physiother 28:12, 1982.
51. Croft, P, et al: Observer variability in measuring elevation and external rotation of the shoulder. Br J Rheumatol 33:942, 1994.

# The Elbow and Forearm

## ⭕ Structure and Function

### Humeroulnar and Humeroradial Joints

#### Anatomy

The humeroulnar and humeroradial joints between the upper arm and the forearm are considered to be a hinged compound synovial joint (Figs. 5.1 and 5.2). The proximal joint surface of the humeroulnar joint consists of the convex trochlea located on the anterior medial surface of the distal humerus. The distal joint surface is the concave trochlear notch on the proximal ulna.

The proximal joint surface of the humeroradial joint is the convex capitulum located on the anterior lateral surface of the distal humerus. The concave radial head on the proximal end of the radius is the opposing joint surface.

The joints are enclosed in a large, loose, weak joint capsule that also encloses the superior radioulnar joint. Medial and lateral collateral ligaments reinforce the sides of the capsule and help to provide medial–lateral stability (Figs. 5.3 and 5.4).[1]

When the arm is in the anatomical position of full elbow extension and supination, the long axes of the humerus and the forearm form an acute angle at the elbow. This angle is called the "carrying angle" (Fig. 5.5) and is approximately 10 to 12 degrees in men and 13 to 17 degrees in women.[2,3] The carrying angle of the dominant arm is reported to be slightly greater (1.5 degrees) than the nondominant arm and slightly greater (2 degrees) in adults than in children.[4] An angle that is greater (more acute) than average is called "cubitus valgus."[5] An angle that is less than average is called "cubitus varus."

#### Osteokinematics

The humeroulnar and humeroradial joints have 1 degree of freedom; flexion–extension occurs in the sagittal plane

**FIGURE 5.1** An anterior view of the right elbow showing the humeroulnar and humeroradial joints.

**FIGURE 5.2** A posterior view of the right elbow showing the humeroulnar and humeroradial joints.

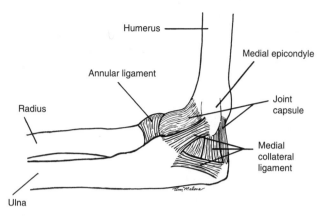

**FIGURE 5.3**  A medial view of the right elbow showing the medial (ulnar) collateral ligament, annular ligament, and joint capsule.

around a medial–lateral (coronal) axis. In elbow flexion and extension, the axis of rotation lies approximately through the center of the trochlea.[3]

### Arthrokinematics

At the humeroulnar joint, posterior sliding of the concave trochlear notch of the ulna on the convex trochlea of the humerus continues during extension until the ulnar olecranon process enters the humeral olecranon fossa. In flexion, the ulna slides anteriorly along the humerus until the coronoid process of the ulna reaches the floor of the coronoid fossa of the humerus or until soft tissue in the anterior aspect of the elbow blocks further flexion.

At the humeroradial joint, the concave radial head slides posteriorly on the convex surface of the capitulum during extension. In flexion, the radial head slides anteriorly until the rim of the radial head enters the radial fossa of the humerus.

### Capsular Pattern

Most authorities agree that the range of motion (ROM) in flexion is more limited than in extension.[7–9] Only in severe

**FIGURE 5.5**  An anterior view of the right upper extremity showing the carrying angle between the longitudinal midline of the humerus and forearm.

cases would supination and pronation be slightly limited.[7] The literature varies as to the proportions of limitation in the capsular pattern for the elbow. For example, according to Cyriax, 30 degrees of limitation in flexion would typically correspond to about 10 degrees of limitation in extension.[7] Kaltenborn notes "that with flexion limited to 90 degrees (60-degree limitation) there is only 10 degrees of limited extension."[8]

## Superior and Inferior Radioulnar Joints

### Anatomy

The ulnar portion of the superior radioulnar joint includes both the radial notch located on the lateral aspect of the proximal ulna and the annular ligament (Fig. 5.6). The radial notch and the annular ligament form a concave joint surface. The radial aspect of the joint is the convex head of the radius.

The ulnar component of the inferior radioulnar joint is the convex ulnar head (see Fig. 5.6). The opposing articular surface is the ulnar notch of the radius.

The interosseous membrane, a broad sheet of collagenous tissue linking the radius and ulna, provides stability for both joints (Fig. 5.7). The following three structures provide stability for the superior radioulnar joint: the annular and quadrate ligaments and the oblique cord. Stability of

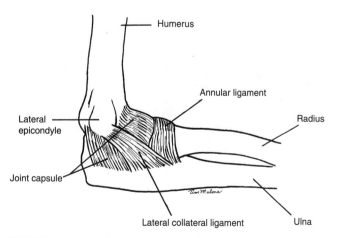

**FIGURE 5.4**  A lateral view of the right elbow showing the lateral (radial) collateral ligament, annular ligament, and joint capsule.

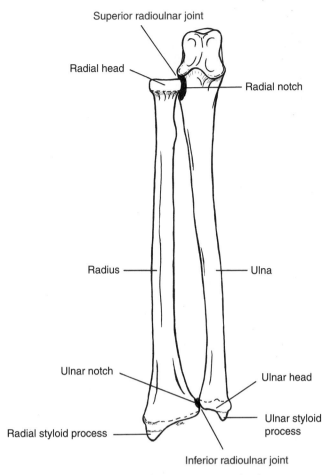

**FIGURE 5.6** Anterior view of the superior and inferior radioulnar joints of the right forearm.

**FIGURE 5.7** Anterior view of the superior and inferior radioulnar joints showing the annular ligament, quadrate ligament, oblique cord, interosseous membrane, anterior radioulnar ligament, and articular disc.

the inferior radioulnar joint is provided by the articular disc and the anterior and posterior radioulnar ligaments (Fig. 5.8).[1]

## Osteokinematics

The superior and inferior radioulnar joints are mechanically linked. Therefore, motion at one joint is always accompanied by motion at the other joint. The axis for motion is a longitudinal axis extending from the radial head to the ulnar head. The mechanically linked joint is a synovial pivot joint with 1 degree of freedom. The motions permitted are pronation and supination. In pronation the radius crosses over the ulna, whereas in supination the radius and ulna lie parallel to one another.

## Arthrokinematics

At the superior radioulnar joint the convex rim of the radial head spins within the annular ligament and the concave radial notch of the ulna during pronation and supination. The articular surface on the radial head spins posteriorly during pronation and anteriorly during supination.

At the inferior radioulnar joint the concave surface of the ulnar notch on the radius slides over the ulnar head. The concave articular surface of the radius slides anteriorly (in the same direction as the hand) during pronation and slides

posteriorly (in the same direction as the hand) during supination.

## Capsular Pattern

The capsular pattern is an equal limitation of supination and pronation according to Cyriax and Cyriax[7] and Kaltenborn.[8]

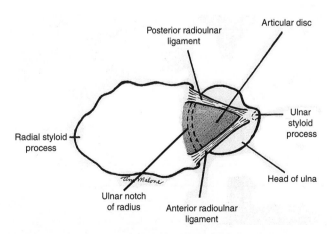

**FIGURE 5.8** Distal aspect of the inferior radioulnar joint showing the articular disc and radioulnar ligaments.

# RANGE OF MOTION TESTING PROCEDURES: Elbow and Forearm

## Landmarks for Testing Procedures

**FIGURE 5.9** Anterior view of the right upper extremity showing surface anatomy landmarks for goniometer alignment during the measurement of elbow and forearm ROM.

**FIGURE 5.10** Anterior view of the right upper extremity showing bony anatomical landmarks for goniometer alignment during the measurement of elbow and forearm ROM.

## Landmarks for Testing Procedures (continued)

FIGURE 5.11 Posterior view of the right upper extremity showing surface anatomy landmarks for goniometer alignment during the measurement of elbow and forearm ROM.

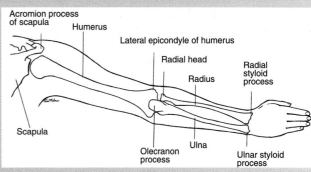

FIGURE 5.12 Posterior view of the right upper extremity showing anatomical landmarks for goniometer alignment during the measurement of elbow and forearm ROM.

# ELBOW FLEXION

Motion occurs in the sagittal plane around a medial–lateral axis. Normal ROM values for adults range from 140 degrees according to the American Medical Association (AMA)[12] to 150 degrees according to the American Academy of Orthopaedic Surgeons (AAOS).[10,11] See Research Findings and Tables 5.1 to 5.3 for additional normal ROM values by age and gender.

## Testing Position

Position the subject supine, with the shoulder in 0 degrees of flexion, extension, and abduction so that the arm is close to the side of the body. Place a pad under the distal end of the humerus to allow full elbow extension. Position the forearm in full supination with the palm of the hand facing the ceiling.

## Stabilization

Stabilize the humerus to prevent flexion of the shoulder. The pad under the distal humerus and the examining table prevent extension of the shoulder.

## Testing Motion

Flex the elbow by moving the hand toward the shoulder. Maintain the forearm in supination during the motion (Fig. 5.13). The end of flexion ROM occurs when resistance to further motion is felt and attempts to overcome the resistance cause flexion of the shoulder.

## Normal End-Feel

Usually the end-feel is soft because of compression of the muscle bulk of the anterior forearm with that of the anterior upper arm. If the muscle bulk is small, the end-feel may be hard because of contact between the coronoid process of the ulna and the coronoid fossa of the humerus and because of contact between the head of the radius and the radial fossa of the humerus. The end-feel may be firm because of tension in the posterior joint capsule, the lateral and medial heads of the triceps muscle, and the anconeus muscle.

## Goniometer Alignment

See Figures 5.14 and 5.15.

1. Center **fulcrum** of the goniometer over the lateral epicondyle of the humerus.
2. Align **proximal arm** with the lateral midline of the humerus, using the center of the acromion process for reference.
3. Align **distal arm** with the lateral midline of the radius, using the radial head and radial styloid process for reference.

**FIGURE 5.13** End of elbow flexion ROM. The examiner's hand stabilizes the humerus, but it must be positioned so it does not limit the motion.

**FIGURE 5.14** Alignment of the goniometer at the beginning of elbow flexion ROM. A towel is placed under the distal humerus to ensure that the supporting surface does not prevent full elbow extension. As can be seen in this photograph, the subject's elbow is in about 5 degrees of hyperextension.

**FIGURE 5.15** Alignment of the goniometer at the end of elbow flexion ROM. The proximal and distal arms of the goniometer have been switched from the starting position so that the ROM can be read from the pointer on the body of this 180-degree goniometer.

# ● ELBOW EXTENSION

Motion occurs in the sagittal plane around a medial–lateral axis. Elbow extension ROM is not usually measured and recorded separately because it is the return to the starting position from the end of elbow flexion ROM. If recorded, the normal extension ROM value for adults is 0 degrees.[10–12] See Research Findings and Tables 5.1 to 5.3 for additional normal ROM values by age and gender.

## Testing Position, Stabilization, and Goniometer Alignment

The testing position, stabilization, and alignment are the same as those used for elbow flexion.

## Testing Motion

Extend the elbow by moving the hand dorsally toward the examining table. Maintain the forearm in supination during the motion. The end of extension ROM occurs when resistance to further motion is felt and attempts to overcome the resistance cause extension of the shoulder.

## Normal End-Feel

Usually the end-feel is hard because of contact between the olecranon process of the ulna and the olecranon fossa of the humerus. Sometimes the end-feel is firm because of tension in the anterior joint capsule, the collateral ligaments, and the brachialis muscle.

# ● FOREARM PRONATION

Motion occurs in the transverse plane around a vertical axis when the subject is in the anatomical position. When the subject is in the testing position, the motion occurs in the frontal plane around an anterior–posterior axis. Normal ROM values for adults are 76 degrees according to Boone and Azen[13] and 84 degrees according to Greene and Wolf.[14] Both the AMA[12] and the AAOS[10,11] state that normal pronation ROM is 80 degrees. See Research Findings and Tables 5.1 to 5.3 for additional normal ROM values by age and gender.

## Testing Position

Position the subject sitting, with the shoulder in 0 degrees of flexion, extension, abduction, adduction, and rotation so that the upper arm is close to the side of the body. Flex the elbow to 90 degrees, and support the forearm. Initially position the forearm midway between supination and pronation so that the thumb points toward the ceiling.

## Stabilization

Stabilize the distal end of the humerus to prevent medial rotation and abduction of the shoulder.

## Testing Motion

Pronate the forearm by moving the distal radius in a volar direction so that the palm of the hand faces the floor. See Figure 5.16. The end of pronation ROM occurs when resistance to further motion is felt and attempts to overcome the resistance cause medial rotation and abduction of the shoulder.

## Normal End-Feel

The end-feel may be hard because of contact between the ulna and the radius, or it may be firm

**FIGURE 5.16** End of pronation ROM. The subject is sitting on the edge of a table, and the examiner is standing facing the subject. The examiner uses one hand to hold the elbow close to the subject's body and in 90 degrees of elbow flexion, helping to prevent both medial rotation and abduction of the shoulder. The examiner's other hand pushes on the radius rather than on the subject's hand. If the examiner pushes on the subject's hand, movement of the wrist may be mistaken for movement at the radioulnar joints.

because of tension in the dorsal radioulnar ligament of the inferior radioulnar joint, the interosseous membrane, and the supinator muscle.

## Goniometer Alignment
See Figures 5.17 and 5.18.

1. Center **fulcrum** of the goniometer laterally and proximally to the ulnar styloid process.

2. Align **proximal** arm parallel to the anterior midline of the humerus.
3. Place **distal arm** across the dorsal aspect of the forearm, just proximal to the styloid processes of the radius and ulna, where the forearm is most level and free of muscle bulk. The distal arm of the goniometer should be parallel to the styloid processes of the radius and ulna.

**FIGURE 5.17** Alignment of the goniometer in the beginning of pronation ROM. The goniometer is placed laterally to the distal radioulnar joint. The arms of the goniometer are aligned parallel to the anterior midline of the humerus.

**FIGURE 5.18** Alignment of the goniometer at the end of pronation ROM. The examiner uses one hand to hold the proximal arm of the goniometer parallel to the anterior midline of the humerus. The examiner's other hand supports the forearm and assists in placing the distal arm of the goniometer across the dorsum of the forearm just proximal to the radial and ulnar styloid process. The fulcrum of the goniometer is proximal and lateral to the ulnar styloid process.

# ● FOREARM SUPINATION

Motion occurs in the transverse plane around a longitudinal axis when the subject is in the anatomical position. When the subject is in the testing position, the motion occurs in the frontal plane around an anterior–posterior axis. Normal ROM values for adults are 92 degrees according to Gunal and coworkers,[15] 82 degrees according to Boone and Azen,[13] and 77 degrees according to Greene and Wolf.[14] Both the AMA[12] and the AAOS[10,11] state that normal supination ROM is 80 degrees. See Research Findings and Tables 5.1 to 5.3 for additional normal ROM values by age and gender.

## Testing Position

Position the subject sitting, with the shoulder in 0 degrees of flexion, extension, abduction, adduction, and rotation so that the upper arm is close to the side of the body. Flex the elbow to 90 degrees, and support the forearm. Initially position the forearm midway between supination and pronation so that the thumb points toward the ceiling.

## Stabilization

Stabilize the distal end of the humerus to prevent lateral rotation and adduction of the shoulder.

**FIGURE 5.19** End of supination ROM. The examiner uses one hand to hold the elbow close to the subject's body and in 90 degrees of elbow flexion, preventing lateral rotation and adduction of the shoulder. The examiner's other hand pushes on the distal radius while supporting the forearm.

## Testing Motion

Supinate the forearm by moving the distal radius in a dorsal direction so that the palm of the hand faces the ceiling. See Figure 5.19. The end of supination ROM occurs when resistance to further motion is felt and attempts to overcome the resistance cause lateral rotation and adduction of the shoulder.

## Normal End-Feel

The end-feel is firm because of tension in the palmar radioulnar ligament of the inferior radioulnar joint, oblique cord, interosseous membrane, and pronator teres and pronator quadratus muscles.

## Goniometer Alignment

See Figures 5.20 and 5.21.

1. Place **fulcrum** of the goniometer medially and just proximally to the ulnar styloid process.
2. Align **proximal arm** parallel to the anterior midline of the humerus.
3. Place **distal arm** across the ventral aspect of the forearm, just proximal to the styloid processes, where the forearm is most level and free of muscle bulk. The distal arm of the goniometer should be parallel to the styloid processes of the radius and ulna.

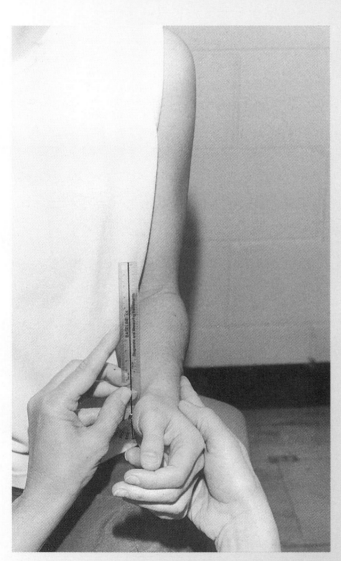

**FIGURE 5.20** Alignment of the goniometer at the beginning of supination ROM. The body of the goniometer is medial to the distal radioulnar joint, and the arms of the goniometer are parallel to the anterior midline of the humerus.

**FIGURE 5.21** Alignment of the goniometer at the end of supination ROM. The examiner uses one hand to hold the proximal arm of the goniometer parallel to the anterior midline of the humerus. The examiner's other hand supports the forearm while holding the distal arm of the goniometer across the volar surface of the forearm just proximal to the radial and ulnar styloid process. The fulcrum of the goniometer is proximal and medial to the ulnar styloid process.

# MUSCLE LENGTH TESTING PROCEDURES:
## Elbow and Forearm

### ● BICEPS BRACHII

The biceps brachii muscle crosses the glenohumeral, humeroulnar, humeroradial, and superior radioulnar joints. The short head of the biceps brachii originates proximally from the coracoid process of the scapula (Fig. 5.22). The long head originates from the supraglenoid tubercle of the scapula. The biceps brachii attaches distally to the radial tuberosity.

When the biceps brachii contracts, it flexes the elbow and shoulder and supinates the forearm. The muscle is passively lengthened by placing the shoulder and elbow in full extension and the forearm in pronation. If the biceps brachii is short, it limits elbow extension when the shoulder is positioned in full extension.

If elbow extension is limited regardless of shoulder position, the limitation is caused by abnormalities of the joint surfaces, by shortening of the anterior joint capsule and collateral ligaments, or by muscles that cross only the elbow such as the brachialis and brachioradialis.

### Starting Position

Position the subject supine at the edge of the examining table. See Figure 5.23. Flex the elbow and position the shoulder in full extension and 0 degrees of abduction, adduction, and rotation.

**FIGURE 5.22** A lateral view of the left upper extremity showing the origins and insertion of the biceps brachii while being stretched over the glenohumeral, elbow, and superior radioulnar joints.

Labels in figure:
Supraglenoid tubercle
Coracoid process
Glenoid fossa
Acromion process
Long head of the biceps
Short head of the biceps
Radial tuberosity
Ulna
Radius

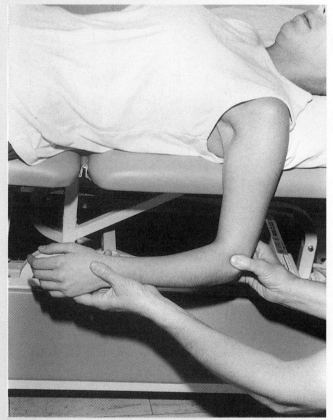

**FIGURE 5.23** Starting position for testing the length of the biceps brachii.

## Stabilization

The examiner stabilizes the subject's humerus. The examining table and passive tension in the serratus anterior muscle help to stabilize the scapula.

## Testing Motion

Extend the elbow while holding the forearm in pronation. See Figures 5.24 and 5.22. The end of the testing motion occurs when resistance is felt and additional elbow extension causes shoulder flexion.

## Normal End-Feel

The end-feel is firm because of tension in the biceps brachii muscle.

## Goniometer Alignment

See Figure 5.25.

1. Center **fulcrum** of the goniometer over the lateral epicondyle of the humerus.
2. Align **proximal arm** with the lateral midline of the humerus, using the center of the acromion process for reference.
3. Align **distal arm** with the lateral midline of the ulna, using the ulna styloid process for reference.

**FIGURE 5.24** End of the testing motion for the length of the biceps brachii. The examiner uses one hand to stabilize the humerus in full shoulder extension while the other hand holds the forearm in pronation and moves the elbow into extension.

**FIGURE 5.25** Alignment of the goniometer at the end of testing the length of the biceps brachii. The examiner releases the stabilization of the humerus and now uses her hand to position the goniometer.

## ● TRICEPS BRACHII

The triceps brachii muscle crosses the glenohumeral and humeroulnar joints. The long head of the triceps brachii muscle originates proximally from the infraglenoid tubercle of the scapula (Fig. 5.26). The lateral head of the triceps brachii originates from the posterior and lateral surfaces of the humerus, whereas the medial head originates from the posterior and medial surfaces of the humerus. All parts of the triceps brachii insert distally on the olecranon process of the ulna. When this muscle contracts, it extends the shoulder and elbow. The long head of the triceps brachii is passively lengthened by placing the shoulder and elbow in full flexion. If the long head of the triceps brachii is short, it limits elbow flexion when the shoulder is positioned in full flexion.

If elbow flexion is limited regardless of shoulder position, the limitation is due to abnormalities of the joint surfaces or shortening of the posterior capsule or muscles that cross only the elbow, such as the anconeus and the lateral and medial heads of the triceps brachii.

### Starting Position

Position the subject supine, close to the edge of the examining table. Extend the elbow and position the shoulder in full flexion and 0 degrees of abduction, adduction, and rotation. Supinate the forearm (Fig. 5.27).

### Stabilization

The examiner stabilizes the subject's humerus. The weight of the subject's trunk on the examining table and the passive tension in the latissumus dorsi, pectoralis minor, and rhomboid major and minor muscles help to stabilize the scapula.

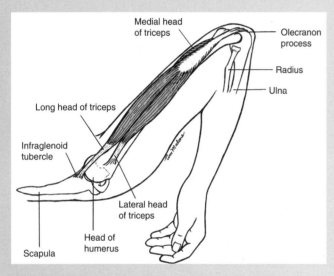

**FIGURE 5.26** A lateral view of the left upper extremity showing the origins and insertions of the triceps brachii while being stretched over the glenohumeral and elbow joints.

**FIGURE 5.27** Starting position for testing the length of the triceps brachii.

## Testing Motion

Flex the elbow by moving the hand closer to the shoulder. See Figures 5.28 and 5.26. The end of the testing motion occurs when resistance is felt and additional elbow flexion causes shoulder extension.

## Normal End-Feel

The end-feel is firm because of tension in the long head of the triceps brachii muscle.

## Goniometer Alignment

See Figure 5.29.

1. Center **fulcrum** of the goniometer over the lateral epicondyle of the humerus.
2. Align **proximal arm** with the lateral midline of the humerus, using the center of the acromion process for reference.
3. Align **distal arm** with the lateral midline of the radius, using the radial styloid process for reference.

**FIGURE 5.28** End of the testing motion for the length of the triceps brachii. The examiner uses one hand to stabilize the humerus in full shoulder flexion and the other hand to move the elbow into flexion.

**FIGURE 5.29** Alignment of the goniometer at the end of testing the length of the triceps brachii. The examiner uses one hand to continue to stabilize the humerus and align the proximal arm of the goniometer. The examiner's other hand holds the elbow in flexion and aligns the distal arm of the goniometer with the radius.

## ◯ Research Findings

### Effects of Age, Gender, and Other Factors

Table 5.1 provides normal elbow and forearm ROM values for adults.[10–15] In addition to the sources listed in Table 5.1, Goodwin and coworkers[16] found mean active elbow flexion to be 148.9 degrees in 23 females between 18 and 31 years of age. Petherick and associates[17] found mean active elbow flexion to be 145.8 degrees in 10 males and 20 females with a mean age of 24.0 years. Sanya and Chinyelu[18] studied 50 healthy adults (27 females and 23 males) between 20 and 71 years of age and found mean active elbow flexion to be 137.8 degrees. All of these sources used universal goniometers to obtain measurements. Fiebert, Fuhri, and New[19] measured elbow flexion and forearm motions with the Ortho Ranger (electronic inclinometer) and elbow extension with a universal goniometer in 124 men and women, 60 to 99 years of age. They found mean passive elbow flexion ROM to be 147 degrees, elbow extension –1 degree, pronation 84 degrees, and supination 85 degrees.

### Age

A comparison of cross-sectional studies of normal ROM values for various age groups suggests that elbow and forearm ROM decreases slightly with increasing age. The elbow and forearm ROM values in infants reported by Wanatabe and colleagues[20] and in young male children aged 1 to 7 years reported by Hacker and coworkers[21] as noted in Table 5.2 are generally greater than the normal values for adult males found in Tables 5.1 and 5.3. However, it can be difficult to compare values obtained from various studies because subject selection and measurement methods can differ.

Within one study of 109 males ranging in age from 18 months to 54 years, Boone and Azen[13] noted a significant difference in elbow flexion and supination between subjects age 19 years or younger and those older than 19 years. Further analyses found that the group between 6 and 12 years of age had more elbow flexion and extension than other age groups. The youngest group (between 18 months and 5 years) had a significantly greater amount of pronation and supination than other age groups. However, the greatest differences between the age groups were small: 6.8 degrees of flexion, 4.4 degrees of supination, 3.9 degrees of pronation, and 2.5 degrees of extension.[22]

Older persons appear to have difficulty fully extending their elbows to 0 degrees. Walker and associates[23] found that the older men and women (between 60 and 84 years of age) in their study were unable to extend their elbows to 0 degrees to attain a neutral starting position for flexion. The mean value for the starting position was 6 degrees in men and 1 degree in women. Boone and Azen[13] also found that the oldest subjects in their study (between 40 and 54 years of age) had lost elbow extension and began flexion from a slightly flexed position. Bergstrom and colleagues,[24] in a study of 52 women and 37 men aged 79 years, found that 11 percent had flexion contractures of the right elbow greater than 5 degrees, and 7 percent had bilateral flexion contractures.

Kalscheur and associates[25] examined the effects of age in a study of 61 older women aged 63 to 83 years and the effects of age and gender in the same sample of 61 older women and 25 older men aged 66 to 86 years.[26] Depending on the linear regression models used, they found that elbow flexion declined about 0.1 to 0.2 degrees per year from age 65 to 85 years; pronation declined about 0.1 to 0.4 degrees per year, and supination declined about 0.0 to 1.0 degrees per year. It was projected that over a 20-year period elbow flexion could be expected to decline approximately 3 degrees, pronation 4 degrees, and right supination 6 degrees.[26] Only declines in right supination and pronation ROM were statistically significant.

### Gender

Studies seem to concur that females have more elbow flexion and extension ROM than males, but results are unclear

| TABLE 5.1 | Normal Elbow and Forearm ROM Values for Adults in Degrees From Selected Sources |

| | AAOS[10,11] | AMA[12] | Boone & Azen[13] 20–54 yrs* n = 56 Males | Greene & Wolf[14] 18–55 yrs* n = 20 Males and Females | Gunal et al[15] 18–22 yrs† n = 1000 Males |
|---|---|---|---|---|---|
| *Motion* | | | *Mean (SD)* | *Mean (SD)* | *Mean (SD)* |
| Flexion | 150 | 140 | 140.5 (4.9) | 145.3 (1.2) | 144.2 (5.8) |
| Extension | 0 | 0 | 0.3 (2.7) | | 4.9 (11.1) |
| Pronation | 80 | 80 | 75.0 (5.3) | 84.4 (2.2) | |
| Supination | 80 | 80 | 81.1 (4.0) | 76.9 (2.1) | 91.7 (9.6) |

SD = standard deviation.
* Values are for active ROM measured with a universal goniometer.
† Values are for passive ROM measured with a universal goniometer. Values are extrapolated from tables.

| TABLE 5.2 | Effects of Age on Elbow and Forearm Motion: Normal Values in Degrees for Newborns, Children, and Adolescents | | | | |
|---|---|---|---|---|---|
| | Wanatabe et al[20] | Hacker er al[21] | Boone[22] | | |
| | 2 wks–2 yrs*<br>n = 45<br>Males and Females | 1–7 yrs<br>n = 72<br>Males | 18 mos–5 yrs†<br>n = 19<br>Males | 6–12 yrs†<br>n = 17<br>Males | 13–19 yrs†<br>n = 17<br>Males |
| Motion | Range of Means | Mean (SD) | Mean (SD) | Mean (SD) | Mean (SD) |
| Flexion | 148–158 | 151.4 (1.8) | 144.9 (5.7) | 146.5 (4.0) | 144.9 (6.0) |
| Extension | | 1.1 (3.9) | 0.4 (3.4) | 2.1 (3.2) | 0.1 (3.8) |
| Pronation | 90–96 | | 78.9 (4.4) | 76.9 (3.6) | 74.1 (5.3) |
| Supination | 81–93 | | 84.5 (3.8) | 82.9 (2.7) | 81.8 (3.2) |

SD = standard deviation.
* Values are for passive ROM.
† Values are for active ROM measured with a universal goniometer.

concerning gender effects on forearm supination and pronation ROM.

Bell and Hoshizaki,[27] using a Leighton Flexometer, studied the ROM of 124 females and 66 males between the ages of 18 and 88 years. Females had significantly more elbow flexion than males. Extrapolating from a graph, the mean differences between males and females ranged from 14 degrees in subjects aged 32 to 44 years to 2 degrees in subjects older than 75 years. Although females had greater supination–pronation ROM than males, this increase was not statistically significant.

Salter and Darcus,[28] measuring forearm supination–pronation with a specialized arthrometer in 20 males and 5 females between the ages of 16 and 29 years, found that the females had an average of 8 degrees more forearm rotation than males, although the difference was not statistically significant.

Escalante, Lichenstein, and Hazuda,[29] in a study of 695 community-dwelling older subjects between 65 and 74 years of age, found that females had an average of 4 degrees more elbow flexion than males.

Thirty older females and 30 older males, aged 60 to 84 years, were included in a study by Walker and coworkers.[23] Females had significantly more flexion ROM (1–148 degrees) than males (5–139 degrees), but males had significantly more supination (83 degrees) than females (65 degrees). Females had more pronation ROM than males, but the difference was not significant.

Kalscheru and coworkers[26] found that older women had more elbow and forearm ROM than older men in a study of a 61 women and 25 men ranging in age from 63 to 86 years. These gender differences were statistically significant for elbow flexion and pronation with mean differences of 6.2 and 4.9 degrees, respectively. There was no significant difference in supination ROM between the men and women.

### Body Mass Index

Body mass index (BMI) was found by Escalante, Lichenstein, and Hazuda[29] to be inversely associated with elbow flexion in 695 older subjects. Each unit increase in BMI ($kg/m^2$) was

| TABLE 5.3 | Effects of Age on Active Elbow and Forearm Motion: Normal Values in Degrees for Adult Males 20 to 85 Years of Age | | | |
|---|---|---|---|---|
| | Boone[22] | | Walker et al[23] | |
| | 20–29 yrs<br>n = 19 | 30–39 yrs<br>n = 18 | 40–54 yrs<br>n = 19 | 60–85 yrs<br>n = 30 |
| Motion | Mean (SD) | Mean (SD) | Mean (SD) | Mean (SD) |
| Flexion | 140.1 (5.2) | 141.7 (3.2) | 139.0 (14.0) | 139.7 (5.8) |
| Extension | 0.7 (3.2) | 0.7 (1.7) | –6.0* (5.0) | –0.4* (3.0) |
| Pronation | 76.2 (3.9) | 73.6 (4.3) | 68.0 (9.0) | 75.0 (7.0) |
| Supination | 80.1 (3.7) | 81.7 (4.2) | 83.0 (11.0) | 81.4 (4.0) |

SD = standard deviation.
* The minus sign indicates flexion.

significantly associated with a 0.22 decrease in degrees of elbow flexion. Hacker and coworkers[21] also found an association between increased BMI and decreased elbow ROM in 72 healthy boys ages 1 to 7 years.

### Right Versus Left Side

Studies comparing ROM between the right and left sides or between the dominant and nondominant limbs have generally found no clinically relevant differences in elbow and forearm ROM. Studies that had large numbers of subjects had the statistical power to find differences of 2 to 3 degrees to be significant. If differences were found, the left or nondominant side had more motion.

Boone and Azen[13] studied 109 males between the ages of 18 months and 54 years who were subdivided into six age groups. They found no significant differences between right and left elbow flexion, extension, supination, and pronation, except for the age group of subjects between 20 and 29 years of age, whose elbow flexion ROM was greater on the left than on the right. This one significant finding was attributed to chance. Hacker and colleagues[21] found no significant difference between sides for elbow ROM in 72 healthy boys aged 1 to 7 years. Gunal and coworkers,[15] in a study of 1000 males between 18 to 22 years of age, found significantly greater elbow flexion, extension, and supination ROM on the left as compared to the right; mean differences were 2.6 degrees, 2.0 degrees, and 2.2 degrees, respectively. Chang, Buschbacher, and Edlich[30] studied 10 power lifters and 10 age-matched non-lifters, all of whom were right handed, and found no differences between sides in elbow and forearm ROM.

Studies on older subjects have noted similar results. Escalante, Lichenstein, and Hazudal,[29] in a study of 695 older subjects, found significantly greater elbow flexion on the left than on the right, but the difference averaged only 2 degrees. Kalscheur and coworkers[25] reported no significant differences between sides for elbow flexion and pronation ROM in a study of 61 older women. A statistically significant difference between sides was noted for pronation ROM, with the left side being an average of 3.0 degrees greater than the right.

### Sports

It appears that the frequent use of the upper extremities in sport activities may reduce elbow and forearm ROM. Possible causes for this association include muscle hypertrophy, muscle tightness, and joint trauma from overuse.

Chinn, Priest, and Kent,[31] in a study of 53 male and 30 female national and international tennis players, found significantly less active ROM in pronation (mean difference = 5.8 degrees) and supination (4.6 degrees) in the playing arms of all subjects. Male players also demonstrated a significant decrease (4.1 degrees) in elbow extension in the playing arm versus the nonplaying arm. Chang, Buschbacher, and Edlich[30] studied 10 power lifters and 10 age-matched nonlifters and found less active elbow flexion in the power lifters than in the nonlifters. No significant differences were found between the two groups for supination and pronation ROM. Wright and colleagues[32] noted an average decrease of 7.9 degrees for

elbow extension ROM and 5.5 degrees for elbow flexion ROM in the dominant versus the nondominant arm of 33 professional pitchers. No significant differences were noted between the dominant and nondominant sides for supination and pronation ROM.

## Functional Range of Motion

The amount of elbow and forearm motion that occurs during activities of daily living has been studied by several investigators. Table 5.4 has been adapted from the works of Morrey and associates,[33] Packer and colleagues,[34] and Safaee-Rad and coworkers.[35] Morrey and associates[33] used a triaxial electrogoniometer to measure elbow and forearm motion in 33 normal subjects during performance of 15 activities. They concluded that most of the activities of daily living that were studied required a total arc of about 100 degrees of elbow flexion (between 30 and 130 degrees) and 100 degrees of rotation (50 degrees of supination and 50 degrees of pronation). Using a telephone necessitated the greatest total ROM. The greatest amount of flexion was required to reach the back of the head (144 degrees), whereas feeding tasks such as drinking from a cup (Fig. 5.30) and eating with a fork required about 130 degrees of flexion. Reaching the shoes and rising from a chair (Fig. 5.31) required the greatest amount of extension. Among the tasks studied, the greatest amount of supination was needed for eating with a fork. Reading a newspaper (Fig. 5.32), pouring from a pitcher, and cutting with a knife required the most pronation.

Five healthy subjects participated in a study by Packer and colleagues,[34] which examined elbow ROM during three functional tasks. A uniaxial electrogoniometer was used to determine ROM required for using a telephone, for rising from a chair to a standing position, and for eating with a spoon. A range of 15 to 140 degrees of flexion was needed for these three activities. This ROM is slightly greater than the arc reported by Morrey and associates, but the activities that required the minimal and maximal flexion angles did not differ. The authors suggest that the height of the chair, the type of chair arms, and the positioning of the telephone could account for the different ranges found in the studies.

Safaee-Rad and coworkers[35] used a three-dimensional video system to measure ROM during three feeding activities: eating with a spoon, eating with a fork, and drinking from a handled cup. Ten healthy males participated in the study. The feeding activities required approximately 70 to 130 degrees of elbow flexion, 40 degrees of pronation, and 60 degrees of supination. Drinking with a cup required the greatest arc of elbow flexion (58 degrees) of the three activities, whereas eating with a spoon required the least (22 degrees). Eating with a fork required the greatest arc of pronation–supination (97 degrees), whereas drinking from a cup required the least (28 degrees). Maximum ROM values during feeding tasks were comparable with those reported by Morrey and associates. However, minimum values varied, possibly owing to the different chair and table heights used in the two studies.

| TABLE 5.4 | Elbow and Forearm Motion During Functional Activities: Mean Values in Degrees | | | | | | |

| Activity | Flexion | | | Pronation | Supination | | Source |
|---|---|---|---|---|---|---|---|
| | *Min* | *Max* | *Arc* | *Max* | *Max* | *Arc* | |
| Use telephone | 42.8 | 135.6 | 92.8 | 40.9 | 22.6 | 63.5 | Morrey[33] |
| | 75 | 140 | 65 | | | | Packer[34] |
| Rise from chair | 20.3 | 94.5 | 74.2 | 33.8 | –9.5* | 24.3 | Morrey |
| | 15 | 100 | 85 | | | | Packer |
| Open door | 24.0 | 57.4 | 33.4 | 35.4 | 23.4 | 58.8 | Morrey |
| Read newspaper | 77.9 | 104.3 | 26.4 | 48.8 | –7.3* | 41.5 | Morrey |
| Pour pitcher | 35.6 | 58.3 | 22.7 | 42.9 | 21.9 | 64.8 | Morrey |
| Put glass to mouth | 44.8 | 130.0 | 85.2 | 10.1 | 13.4 | 23.5 | Morrey |
| Drink from cup | 71.5 | 129.2 | 57.7 | –3.4† | 31.2 | 27.8 | Safaee-Rad[35] |
| Cut with knife | 89.2 | 106.7 | 17.5 | 41.9 | –26.9* | 15.0 | Morrey |
| Eat with fork | 85.1 | 128.3 | 43.2 | 10.4 | 51.8 | 62.2 | Morrey |
| | 93.8 | 122.3 | 28.5 | 38.2 | 58.8 | 97.0 | Safaee-Rad |
| Eat with spoon | 101.2 | 123.2 | 22.0 | 22.9 | 58.7 | 81.6 | Safaee-Rad |
| | 70 | 115 | 45 | | | | Packer |

* The minus sign indicates pronation.
† The minus sign indicates supination.

**FIGURE 5.30** Drinking from a cup requires about 130 degrees of elbow flexion.

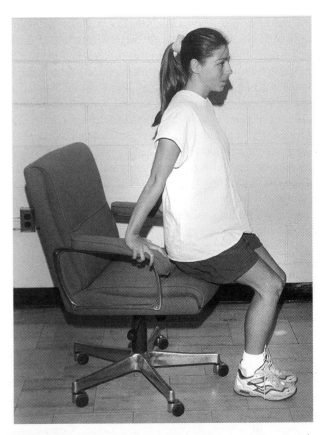

**FIGURE 5.31** Studies report that rising from a chair using the upper extremities requires a large amount of elbow and wrist extension.

**FIGURE 5.32** Approximately 50 degrees of pronation occur during the action of reading a newspaper.

Marco and coworkers[36] studied the performance of 20 activities of daily living in 10 subjects using a goniometer and torsiometer system. They concluded that eating activities required the least motion (53 to 129 degrees of elbow flexion ROM), instrument use such as writing and telephoning demanded a moderate amount of motion (44 to 130 degrees of elbow flexion ROM), and dressing activities required the greatest motion (10 to 140 degrees of elbow flexion ROM). Most instrument and dressing activities required pronation. The use of a spoon required the greatest supination (55 degrees).

Several investigators have taken a different approach in determining the amount of elbow and forearm motion needed for activities of daily living. Vasen and associates[37] studied the ability of 50 healthy adults to comfortably complete 12 activities of daily living while their elbows were restricted in an adjustable Bledsoe brace. Forty-nine subjects were able to complete all of the tasks with the elbow motion limited to between 75 and 120 degrees of flexion. Subjects used compensatory motions at adjacent normal joints to complete the activities. Cooper and colleagues[38] studied upper-extremity motion in subjects during three feeding tasks, with the elbow unrestricted and then fixed in 110 degrees of flexion with a splint. The 19 subjects were assessed with a video-based, three-dimensional motion analysis system while they were drinking with a handled cup, eating with a fork, and eating with a spoon. Compensatory motions to accommodate the fixed elbow occurred to a large extent at the shoulder and to a lesser extent at the wrist.

## Reliability

A number of studies have examined the reliability of the measuring elbow and forearm ROM. Most investigators have found the intratester and intertester reliability of measuring ROM with a universal goniometer at these joints to be good to excellent. However, studies indicate that larger differences in repeated measurements are needed to detect meaningful change when examining forearm supination and pronation as compared to elbow flexion and extension. Comparisons between ROM measurements taken with different devices have also been conducted, giving some indication of the concurrent validity of these devices with the universal goniometer. It is recommended that clinicians use the same device and alignment method to improve reliability because they are not interchangeable.

In a study published in 1949 by Hellebrandt, Duvall, and Moore,[39] one therapist repeatedly measured 13 active upper-extremity motions, including elbow flexion and extension and forearm pronation and supination, in 77 patients. The differences between the means of two trials ranged from 0.1 degrees for elbow extension to 1.5 degrees for supination. A significant difference between the measurements was noted for elbow flexion, although the difference between the means was only 1.0 degrees. Significant differences were also noted between measurements taken with a universal goniometer and those obtained by means of specialized devices, leading the author to conclude that different measuring devices could not be used interchangeably. The universal goniometer was generally found to be the more reliable device.

Boone and colleagues[40] examined the reliability of measuring six passive motions, including elbow extension–flexion. Four physical therapists used universal goniometers to measure these motions in 12 normal males weekly for 4 weeks. They found that intratester reliability (r = 0.94) was slightly higher than intertester reliability (r = 0.88).

Rothstein, Miller, and Roettger[41] found high intratester and intertester reliability for passive ROM of elbow flexion and extension. Their study involved 12 testers who used three different commonly used universal goniometers (large plastic, small plastic, and large metal) to measure 24 patients. Pearson product-moment correlation values ranged from 0.89 to 0.97 for elbow flexion and extension ROM, whereas intraclass correlation coefficient (ICC) values ranged from 0.85 to 0.95.

Grohmann,[42] in a study involving 40 testers and one subject, found that no significant differences existed between elbow measurements obtained by an over-the-joint method for goniometer alignment and the traditional lateral method. Differences between the means of the measurements were less than 2 degrees. The elbow was held in two fixed positions (an acute and an obtuse angle) by a plywood stabilizing device.

Petherick and associates,[17] in a study in which two testers measured 30 healthy subjects, found that intertester reliability for measuring active elbow ROM with a fluid-based goniometer was higher than with a universal goniometer. The Pearson product-moment correlation between the two devices was 0.83, whereas a significant difference was found between the two devices. The authors concluded that no concurrent validity existed between the fluid-based and the universal goniometers and that these instruments could not be used interchangeably.

Greene and Wolf[14] compared the reliability of the Ortho Ranger, an electronic pendulum goniometer, with the reliability of a universal goniometer for active upper-extremity motions in 20 healthy adults. Elbow flexion and extension were measured three times for each instrument during each session. The three sessions were conducted by one physical therapist during a 2-week period. Within-session reliability was higher for the universal goniometer, as indicated by ICC values and 95 percent confidence intervals. Measurements taken with the Ortho Ranger correlated poorly with those taken with the universal goniometer (r = 0.11 to 0.21), and there was a significant difference in measurements between the two devices.

Goodwin and coworkers[16] evaluated the reliability of a universal goniometer, a fluid goniometer, and an electrogoniometer for measuring active elbow ROM in 23 healthy women. Three testers took three consecutive readings using each type of goniometer, on two occasions that were 4 weeks apart. Significant differences were found between types of goniometers, testers, and replications. Measurements taken with the universal and fluid goniometers correlated the best (r = 0.90), whereas the electrogoniometer correlated poorly with the universal goniometer (r = 0.51) and fluid goniometer (r = 0.33). Intratester and intertester reliability was high during each occasion, with correlation coefficients greater than 0.98 and 0.90, respectively. Intratester reliability between occasions was highest for the universal goniometer. ICC values ranged from 0.61 to 0.92 for the universal goniometer, 0.53 to 0.85 for the fluid goniometer, and 0.00 to 0.61 for the electrogoniometer. Similar to other researchers, the authors do not advise the interchangeable use of different types of goniometers in the clinical setting.

Armstrong and associates[43] examined the intratester, intertester, and interdevice reliability of active ROM measurements of the elbow and forearm in 38 surgical patients. Five testers measured each motion twice with each of the three devices: a universal goniometer, an electrogoniometer, and a mechanical rotation measuring device. Intratester reliability was high (r values generally greater than 0.90) for all three devices and all motions. Intertester reliability was high for pronation and supination with all three devices. Intertester reliability for elbow flexion and extension was high for the electrogoniometer and moderate for the universal goniometer. Measurements taken with different devices varied widely. The authors concluded that meaningful changes in intratester ROM taken with a universal goniometer occur with 95 percent confidence if they are greater than 6 degrees for flexion, 7 degrees for extension, and 8 degrees for pronation and supination. Meaningful changes in intertester ROM taken with a universal goniometer occur if they are greater than 10 degrees for flexion, extension, and pronation and greater than 11 degrees for supination.

Two examiners measured the active ROM of several upper-extremity joints in 29 patients with reflex sympathetic dystrophy with either an inclinometer or universal goniometer in a study by Geertzen and coworkers.[44] Each examiner measured the motions of each patient once per session, and the session was repeated 30 minutes later. The smallest detectable difference, defined as the smallest amount of change in a variable that can be measured with statistical significance, for elbow flexion and extension with a universal goniometer was 9.6 and 12.1 degrees on the affected side and 7.1 and 12.1 degrees on the nonaffected side, respectively. The smallest detectable difference for supination measured with an inclinometer was 19.3 degrees on the affected side and 16.5 degrees on the nonaffected side. Correlation coefficients between repeated measurements

ranged from 0.57 to 0.84 for flexion, 0.66 to 0.92 for elbow extension, and 0.85 to 0.94 for supination. The authors concluded that random error, followed by observer and patient–observer interaction were the most important sources of variation in these patients with reflex sympathetic dystrophy.

A study by Gajdosik[45] of 31 healthy subjects compared three methods of measuring active ROM for supination and pronation. All three methods aligned the stationary arm of a universal goniometer parallel to the humerus. However, Method I aligned the movable arm of the goniometer with a pencil held in the hand. Method II placed the movable arm of the goniometer over the anterior or posterior surface of the distal forearm, and Method III aligned the movable arm of the goniometer parallel to a visualized line connecting the distal radius and ulna. There was a significant difference in values between the three methods, with Method I having the greatest amount of supination and the least amount of pronation. All methods were highly reliable with ICC values ranging from 0.81 to 0.97 for three trials by one tester in one session and from 0.86 to 0.96 for two sessions conducted 30 minutes apart. The author noted that Method I was the most reliable but was confounded during supination by movement of the fourth and fifth metacarpals. Methods II and III were recommended as reliable and more valid for clinical use but should not be used interchangeably.

Flower and associates[46] measured passive supination and pronation ROM in 30 orthopedic patients (31 wrists) with a traditional 6-inch universal goniometer aligned with the humerus and placed on the distal forearm and a new offset goniometer with a tubular handle and plumbline design. Three therapists measured each motion with each device once per session and repeated the session 20 minutes later. Intraclass correlation coefficients for supination were 0.95 for both the universal and new goniometer and 0.79 and 0.87 for pronation with the universal and new goniometer, respectively. Average standard error of the measurement for supination was 3.7 degrees for both the universal and new goniometer and 7.0 and 6.2 degrees for pronation with the universal and new goniometer, respectively. The authors stated that the difference in reliability between the two methods is probably not clinically significant.

Karagiannopoulos, Sitler, and Michlovitz[47] assessed the reliability of two methods of measuring a functional combination of active forearm and wrist rotation in 20 injured and 20 noninjured subjects. One method placed the stationary arm of a universal goniometer vertically and aligned the movable arm with a pencil held in the hand. The second method utilized an investigator-constructed tubular handle attached to a single-arm plumbline goniometer. Measurements were taken three times with each method by the two examiners during one session. Reliability was high and error was low for both methods and subject groups. Intratester and intertester ICC values ranged from 0.86 to 0.98 and from 0.91 to 0.96, respectively. Intratester SEM values ranged from 1.4 to 2.1 degrees, whereas intertester SEM values ranged from 2.2 to 3.9 degrees. To assess functional supination and pronation, the authors recommended the clinical use of the handheld pencil method over the slightly more reliable plumbline method because of the simplicity and greater availability of the equipment for the handheld pencil method.

## Validity

We are unaware of any published studies that report criterion-related validity of elbow and forearm ROM measurements taken with a universal goniometer to radiographs. However, if photographic measurements are accepted as valid, then some indication of criterion-related validity may be provided by comparing goniometric and photographic measurements. In a study by Fish and Wingate,[48] 46 physical therapy students used plastic and metal universal goniometers to measure the angle of an elbow fixed in approximately 50 and 135 degrees of flexion by a splint. In some cases the landmarks were prelabeled, whereas in others the testers had to palpate and identify the landmarks for goniometer alignment. Measurements were also determined from photographs of the prelabeled, fixed elbow. In addition, passive elbow flexion ROM was measured in the unsplinted elbow. There were small but significant differences (ranging from 0.6 to 5.1 degrees) between the means of the goniometric measurements as compared to the photographic measurements, except in one case. The standard deviation of the measurements increased from a low of 0.7 to 1.1 degrees with photographic measurements to a high of 3.4 to 4.2 degrees with passive ROM. The authors proposed that small systematic errors in alignment of the goniometer, identification of bony landmarks, and variations in the amount of torque applied by the tester may account for these differences.

# REFERENCES

1. Levangie, PK, and Norkin, CC: Joint Structure and Function: A Comprehensive Analysis, ed 4. FA Davis, Philadelphia, 2005.
2. Amis, AA, and Miller, JH: The elbow. Clin Rheum Dis 8:571, 1982.
3. Van Roy, P, et al: Arthro-kinematics of the elbow: Study of the carrying angle. Ergonomics 48:11, 2005.
4. Yilmaz, E, et al: Variation of carrying angle with age, sex, and special reference to side. Orthopedics 28:1360, 2005.
5. Hoppenfeld, S: Physical Examination of the Spine and Extremities. Appleton-Century-Crofts, New York, 1977.
6. Morrey, BF, and Chao, EYS: Passive motion of the elbow joint. J Bone Joint Surg Am 58:50, 1976.
7. Cyriax, JH, and Cyriax, PJ: Illustrated Manual of Orthopaedic Medicine. Butterworths, London, 1983.
8. Kaltenborn, FM: Manual Mobilization of the Extremity Joints, ed 5. Olaf Norlis Bokhandel, Oslo, 1999.
9. Magee, DJ: Orthopedic Physical Assessment, ed. 4. WB Saunders, Philadelphia, 2006.
10. American Academy of Orthopaedic Surgeons: Joint Motion: Methods of Measuring and Recording. AAOS, Chicago, 1965.
11. Green, WB, and Heckman, JD (eds): The Clinical Measurement of Joint Motion. American Academy of Orthopaedic Surgeons, Rosemont, IL, 1994.
12. American Medical Association: Guides to the Evaluation of Permanent Impairment, ed 5. Cocchiarella, L and Andersson, GBJ (eds). AMA, Chicago, 2001.
13. Boone, DC, and Azen, SP: Normal range of motion in male subjects. J Bone Joint Surg Am 61:756, 1979.
14. Greene, BL, and Wolf, SL: Upper extremity joint movement: Comparison of two measurement devices. Arch Phys Med Rehabil 70:288, 1989.
15. Gunal, I, et al: Normal range of motion of the joints of the upper extremity in male subjects, with special reference to side. J Bone Joint Surg (Am) 78(A):1401, 1996.
16. Goodwin, J, et al: Clinical methods of goniometry: A comparative study. Disabil Rehabil 14:10, 1992.
17. Petherick, M, et al: Concurrent validity and intertester reliability of universal and fluid-based goniometers for active elbow range of motion. Phys Ther 68:966, 1988.
18. Sanya, AO, and Chinyelu SO: Range of motion in selected joints of diabetic and non-diabetic subjects. African J Health Sci 6:17, 1999.
19. Fiebert, I, Fuhri, JR, and New, MD: Elbow, forearm and wrist passive range of motion in persons aged sixty and older. Phys Occup Ther Geriatr 10:17, 1992.
20. Wanatabe, H, et al: The range of joint motions of the extremities in healthy Japanese people: The difference according to age. Nippon Seikeigeka Gakkai Zasshi 53:275, 1979. (Cited in Walker, JM: Musculoskeletal development: A review. Phys Ther 71:878, 1991.)
21. Hacker, MR, Funk, SM, and Manco-Johnson, MJ: The Colorado Hemophilia Paediatric Joint Physical Examination Scale: Normal values and interrater reliability. Haemophilia 13:71, 2007.
22. Boone, DC: Techniques of measurement of joint motion. (Unpublished supplement to Boone, DC, and Azen, SP: Normal range of motion in male subjects. J Bone Joint Surg Am 61:756, 1979.)
23. Walker, JM, et al: Active mobility of the extremities in older subjects. Phys Ther 64:919, 1984.
24. Bergstrom, G, et al: Prevalence of symptoms and signs of joint impairment. Scand J Rehabil Med 17:173, 1985.
25. Kalscheur, JA, Emery, LJ, and Costello, PS: Range of motion in older women. Phys Occup Ther Geriatr 16:77, 1999.
26. Kalscheur, JA, Costello, PS, and Emery, LJ: Gender differences in range of motion in older adults. Phys Occup Ther Geriatr 22:77, 2003.
27. Bell, RD, and Hoshizaki, TB: Relationships of age and sex with range of motion of seventeen joint actions in humans. Can J Appl Spt Sci 6:202, 1981.
28. Salter, N, and Darcus, HD: The amplitude of forearm and of humeral rotation. J Anat 87:407, 1953.
29. Escalante, A, Lichenstein, MJ, and Hazuda, HP: Determinants of shoulder and elbow flexion range: Results from the San Antonio Longitudinal Study of Aging. Arthritis Care Res 12:277, 1999.
30. Chang, DE, Buschbacher, LP, and Edlich, RF: Limited joint mobility in power lifters. Am J Sports Med 16:280, 1988.
31. Chinn, CJ, Priest, JD, and Kent, BA: Upper extremity range of motion, grip strength and girth in highly skilled tennis players, Phys Ther 54:474, 1974.
32. Wright, RW, et al: Elbow range of motion in professional baseball pitchers. Am J Sports Med 34:190, 2006.
33. Morrey, BF, Askew, KN, and Chao, EYS: A biomechanical study of normal functional elbow motion. J Bone Joint Surg Am 63:872, 1981.
34. Packer, TL, et al: Examining the elbow during functional activities. Occup Ther J Res. 10:323, 1990.
35. Safaee-Rad, R, et al: Normal functional range of motion of upper limb joints during performance of three feeding activities. Arch Phys Med Rehabil 71:505, 1990.
36. Marco, SC, et al: Kinematic analysis of the elbow in the activities of daily living. Rehabilitacion 33:293, 1999.
37. Vasen, AP, et al: Functional range of motion of the elbow. J Hand Surg 20A:288, 1995.
38. Cooper, JE, et al: Elbow joint restriction: Effect on functional upper limb motion during performance of three feeding activities. Arch Phys Med Rehabil 74:805, 1993.
39. Hellebrandt, FA, Duvall, EN, and Moore, ML: The measurement of joint motion. Part III: Reliability of goniometry. Phys Ther Rev 29:302, 1949.
40. Boone, DC, et al: Reliability of goniometric measurements. Phys Ther 58:1355, 1978.
41. Rothstein, JM, Miller, PJ, and Roettger, RF: Goniometric reliability in a clinical setting: Elbow and knee measurements. Phys Ther 63:1611, 1983.
42. Grohmann, JEL: Comparison of two methods of goniometry. Phys Ther 63:922, 1983.
43. Armstrong, AD, et al: Reliability of range-of-motion measurement in the elbow and forearm. J Shoulder Elbow Surg 7:573, 1998.
44. Geertzen, JHB, et al: Variation in measurements of range of motion: A study in reflex sympathetic dystrophy patients. Clin Rehabil 12:254, 1998.
45. Gajdosik, RL: Comparison and reliability of three goniometric methods for measuring forearm supination and pronation. Percept Mot Skills 93:353, 2001.
46. Flower, KR, et al: Intrarater reliability of a new method and instrumentation for measuring passive supination and pronation: A preliminary study. J Hand Ther 14:30, 2001.
47. Karagiannopoulos, C, Sitler, M, and Michlovitz, S: Reliability of 2 functional goniometric methods for measuring forearm pronation and supination active range of motion. J Orthop Sports Phys Ther 33:523, 2003.
48. Fish, DR, and Wingate, L: Sources of goniometric error at the elbow. Phys Ther 65:1666, 1985.

# Chapter 6

# The Wrist

## ⟲ Structure and Function

### Radiocarpal and Midcarpal Joints

#### Anatomy

The wrist is comprised of two joints, the radiocarpal and midcarpal joints, both of which are important to function. The radiocarpal joint lies closer to the forearm, whereas the midcarpal joint is closer to the hand. The proximal joint surface of the radiocarpal joint consists of the distal radius and radioulnar articular disc (Fig. 6.1; see also Fig. 5.7).[1] The disc connects the medial aspect of the distal radius to the distal ulna. The distal radius and the disc form a continuous concave surface.[2,3] The distal joint surface includes three bones from the proximal carpal row—the scaphoid, lunate, and triquetrum—which are connected by interosseous ligaments to form a

convex surface (Fig. 6.1). The radius articulates with the scaphoid and lunate, whereas the radioulnar disc articulates with the triquetrum and, to a lesser extent, the lunate. The pisiform, although found in the proximal row of carpal bones, does not participate in the radiocarpal joint. The joint is enclosed by a strong capsule and is reinforced by the palmar radiocarpal, ulnocarpal, dorsal radiocarpal, ulnar collateral, and radial collateral ligaments and numerous intercarpal ligaments (Figs. 6.2 and 6.3).

The midcarpal joint is distal to the radiocarpal joint. The predominant central and ulnar portions of the midcarpal joint consist of the concave surfaces of the scaphoid, lunate, and triquetrum proximally and the convex surfaces of the capitate and hamate distally (Fig. 6.1). On the radial side of the midcarpal joint, a smaller convex surface of the scaphoid contacts the concave surfaces of the trapezium and trapezoid. The midcarpal

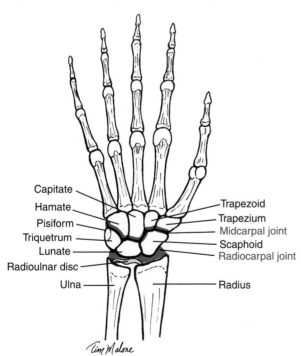

**FIGURE 6.1** An anterior (palmar) view of the right wrist showing the radiocarpal and midcarpal joints.

Capitate
Hamate
Pisiform
Triquetrum
Lunate
Radioulnar disc
Ulna

Trapezoid
Trapezium
Midcarpal joint
Scaphoid
Radiocarpal joint
Radius

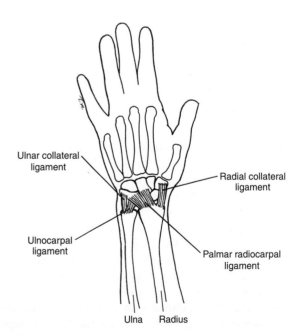

**FIGURE 6.2** An anterior (palmar) view of the right wrist showing the palmar radiocarpal, ulnocarpal, and collateral ligaments.

Ulnar collateral ligament
Radial collateral ligament
Ulnocarpal ligament
Palmar radiocarpal ligament
Ulna   Radius

**115**

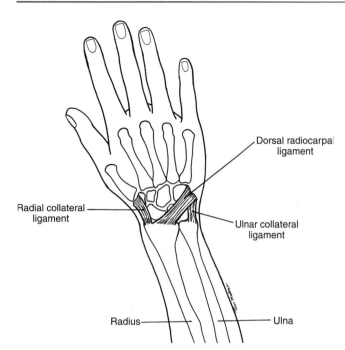

Radial collateral ligament

Dorsal radiocarpal ligament

Ulnar collateral ligament

Radius

Ulna

**FIGURE 6.3** A posterior view of the right wrist showing the dorsal radiocarpal and collateral ligaments.

joint has a joint capsule that is continuous with each intercarpal joint and some carpometacarpal and intermetacarpal joints. Many of the ligaments that reinforce the radiocarpal joint also support the midcarpal joint (Figs. 6.2 and 6.3).

## Osteokinematics

The radiocarpal and midcarpal joints are of the condyloid type, with 2 degrees of freedom.[2] The wrist complex (radiocarpal and midcarpal joints) permits flexion–extension in the sagittal plane around a medial–lateral axis and radial–ulnar deviation in the frontal plane around an anterior–posterior axis. Both joints contribute to these motions.[4–6] Some sources also report that a small amount of supination–pronation occurs at the wrist complex,[7] but this rotation is not usually measured in the clinical setting.

## Arthrokinematics

Motion at the radiocarpal joint occurs because the convex surfaces of the proximal row of carpals roll and slide on the concave surfaces of the radius and radioulnar disc. The proximal row of carpals rolls in the same direction but slides in the opposite direction to movement of the hand.[3,8,9] The carpals slide dorsally on the radius and disc during wrist flexion and ventrally toward the palm during wrist extension. During ulnar deviation, the carpals roll in an ulnar direction and slide in a radial direction. During radial deviation, they roll in a radial direction and slide in an ulnar direction.

Motion at the midcarpal joint occurs because the distal row of carpals rolls and slides on the proximal row of carpals. The distal joint surface is predominantly convex and rolls in the same direction and slides in the opposite direction to the

osteokinematic movements of the wrist, but there is more complexity at the midcarpal joint than at the radiocarpal joint. During flexion, the large and markedly convex surfaces of the capitate and hamate roll ventrally and slide dorsally on the concave surfaces of the scaphoid, lunate, and triquetrum.[3,8,9] The smaller, shallow surfaces of the trapezium and trapezoid are slightly concave and roll and slide ventrally on the convex surface of the scaphoid with flexion. The movements during extension are opposite to that of flexion.

During radial deviation at the midcarpal joint, the convex surfaces of the capitate and hamate roll in a radial direction and slide in an ulnar direction on the concave surfaces of the scaphoid, lunate, and triquetrum. However, the concave surfaces of the trapezium and trapezoid roll and slide slightly dorsally on the scaphoid during radial deviation.[2,9,10] With ulnar deviation, the surfaces on the capitate and hamate roll in an ulnar direction and slide in a radial direction. The joint surfaces of the trapezium and trapezoid roll and slide slightly ventrally.

## Capsular Pattern

Cyriax and Cyriax[11] report that the capsular pattern at the wrist is an equal limitation of flexion and extension and a slight limitation of radial and ulnar deviation. Kaltenborn[3] notes that the capsular pattern is an equal restriction in all motions.

# RANGE OF MOTION TESTING PROCEDURES: Wrist

## Landmarks for Testing Procedures

**FIGURE 6.4** Posterior view of the upper extremity showing surface anatomy landmarks for goniometer alignment during the measurement of wrist ROM.

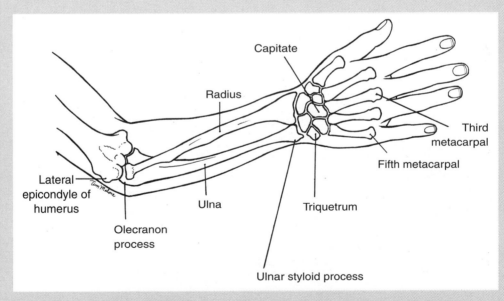

**FIGURE 6.5** Posterior view of the upper extremity showing bony anatomical landmarks for goniometer alignment during the measurement of wrist ROM.

## ● Wrist Flexion

This motion occurs in the sagittal plane around a medial–lateral axis. Wrist flexion is sometimes referred to as volar or palmar flexion. Normal range of motion (ROM) values for adults are 60 degrees according to the American Medical Association (AMA),[12] 80 degrees according to the American Academy of Orthopaedic Surgeons (AAOS),[13,14] and 75 degrees according to Boone and Azen.[15] Refer to Research Findings and Tables 6.1 to 6.3 for additional normal ROM values by age and gender.

### Testing Position

Position the subject sitting next to a supporting surface with the shoulder abducted to 90 degrees, the elbow flexed to 90 degrees, and the palm of the hand facing the ground. In this position the forearm will be midway between supination and pronation. Rest the forearm on the supporting surface, but leave the hand free to move. Avoid radial or ulnar deviation of the wrist and flexion of the fingers. If the fingers are flexed, tension in the extensor digitorum communis, extensor indicis, and extensor digiti minimi muscles will restrict the motion.

### Stabilization

Stabilize the radius and ulna to prevent supination or pronation of the forearm and motion of the elbow.

### Testing Motion

Flex the wrist by pushing on the dorsal surface of the third metacarpal, moving the hand toward the floor (Fig. 6.6). Maintain the wrist in 0 degrees of radial and ulnar deviation. The end of flexion ROM occurs when resistance to further motion is felt and attempts to overcome the resistance cause the forearm to lift off the supporting surface.

### Normal End-Feel

The end-feel is firm because of tension in the dorsal radiocarpal ligament and the dorsal joint capsule. Tension in the extensor carpi radialis brevis and longus and extensor carpi ulnaris muscles may also contribute to the firm end-feel.

### Goniometer Alignment

See Figures 6.7 and 6.8.

1. Center **fulcrum** on the lateral aspect of the wrist over the triquetrum.
2. Align **proximal arm** with the lateral midline of the ulna, using the olecranon and ulnar styloid processes for reference.
3. Align **distal arm** with the lateral midline of the fifth metacarpal. Do not use the soft tissue of the hypothenar eminence for reference.

**FIGURE 6.6**   The end of wrist flexion ROM. Only about three-quarters of the subject's forearm is supported by the examining table so that there is sufficient space for the hand to complete the motion.

**FIGURE 6.7** The alignment of the goniometer at the beginning of wrist flexion ROM.

**FIGURE 6.8** At the end of wrist flexion ROM the examiner uses one hand to align the distal arm of the gonimeter with the fifth metacarpal while maintaining the wrist in flexion. The examiner exerts pressure on the middle of the dorsum of the subject's hand and avoids exerting pressure directly on the fifth metacarpal because such pressure will distort the goniometer alignment.

## Alternative Goniometer Alignment: Dorsal Aspect

This alternative goniometer alignment is recommended by LaStoya and Wheeler,[16] although edema may make accurate alignment over the dorsal surfaces of the forearm and hand difficult. Intratester reliability is similar to lateral alignment technique (intraclass correlation coefficient [ICC] = 0.87 to 0.92).

1. Center **fulcrum** over the capitate on the dorsal aspect of the wrist joint.
2. Align **proximal arm** with the dorsal midline of the forearm.
3. Align **distal arm** with the dorsal aspect of the third metacarpal.

## ● Wrist Extension

Motion occurs in the sagittal plane around a medial–lateral axis. Wrist extension is sometimes referred to as dorsal flexion. Normal ROM values for adults are 60 degrees according to the AMA,[12] 70 degrees according to the AAOS,[13,14] and 74 degrees according to Boone and Azen.[15] See Research Findings and Tables 6.1 to 6.3 for additional normal ROM values by age and gender.

### Testing Position

Position the subject sitting next to a supporting surface with the shoulder abducted to 90 degrees, the elbow flexed to 90 degrees, and the palm of the hand facing the ground. In this position the forearm will be midway between supination and pronation. Rest the forearm on the supporting surface, but leave the hand free to move. Avoid radial or ulnar deviation of the wrist and extension of the fingers. If the fingers are held in extension, tension in the flexor digitorum superficialis and profundus muscles will restrict the motion.

### Stabilization

Stabilize the radius and ulna to prevent supination or pronation of the forearm and motion of the elbow.

### Testing Motion

Extend the wrist by pushing evenly across the palmar surface of the metacarpals, moving the hand in a dorsal direction toward the ceiling (Fig. 6.9). Maintain the wrist in 0 degrees of radial and ulnar deviation. The end of extension ROM occurs when resistance to further motion is felt and attempts to overcome the resistance cause the forearm to lift off of the supporting surface.

### Normal End-Feel

Usually the end-feel is firm because of tension in the palmar radiocarpal ligament, ulnocarpal ligament, and palmar joint capsule. Tension in the palmaris longus, flexor carpi radialis, and flexor carpi ulnaris muscles may also contribute to the firm end-feel. Sometimes the end-feel is hard because of contact between the radius and the carpal bones.

### Goniometer Alignment

See Figures 6.10 and 6.11.

1. Center **fulcrum** on the lateral aspect of the wrist over the triquetrum.
2. Align **proximal arm** with the lateral midline of the ulna, using the olecranon and ulnar styloid process for reference.
3. Align **distal arm** with the lateral midline of the fifth metacarpal. Do not use the soft tissue of the hypothenar eminence for reference.

**FIGURE 6.9** At the end of the wrist extension ROM, the examiner stabilizes the subject's forearm with one hand and uses her other hand to hold the subject's wrist in extension. The examiner is careful to distribute pressure equally across the subject's metacarpals.

**FIGURE 6.10** The alignment of the goniometer at the beginning of wrist extension ROM.

**FIGURE 6.11** At the end of the ROM of wrist extension, the examiner aligns the distal goniometer arm with the fifth metacarpal while holding the wrist in extension. The examiner avoids exerting excessive pressure on the fifth metacarpal.

## Alternative Goniometer Alignment: Palmar Aspect

This alternative goniometer alignment is recommended by LaStayo and Wheeler,[16] although edema may make accurate alignment over the palmar surfaces of the forearm and hand difficult. Intratester reliability is similar to lateral alignment technique (ICC = 0.80 to 0.84).

1. Center **fulcrum** on the palmar surface of the wrist joint at the level of the capitate.
2. Align **proximal arm** with the palmar midline of the forearm.
3. Align **distal arm** with the palmar midline of the third metacarpal.

## • Wrist Radial Deviation

Motion occurs in the frontal plane around an anterior–posterior axis. Radial deviation is sometimes referred to as radial flexion or abduction. Normal ROM values for adults are 20 degrees according to the AMA[12] and AAOS[13,14] and 25 degrees according to Greene and Wolf.[17] See Research Findings and Tables 6.1 to 6.3 for additional normal ROM values by age and gender.

### Testing Position

Position the subject sitting next to a supporting surface with the shoulder abducted to 90 degrees, the elbow flexed to 90 degrees, and the palm of the hand facing the ground. In this position the forearm will be midway between supination and pronation. Rest the forearm and hand on the supporting surface.

### Stabilization

Stabilize the radius and ulna to prevent pronation or supination of the forearm and elbow flexion beyond 90 degrees.

### Testing Motion

Radially deviate the wrist by moving the hand toward the thumb (Fig. 6.12). Maintain the wrist in 0 degrees of flexion and extension, and avoid rotating the hand. The end of radial deviation ROM occurs when resistance to further motion is felt and attempts to overcome the resistance cause the elbow to flex.

### Normal End-Feel

Usually the end-feel is hard because of contact between the radial styloid process and the scaphoid, but it may be firm because of tension in the ulnar collateral ligament, the ulnocarpal ligament, and the ulnar portion of the joint capsule. Tension in the extensor carpi ulnaris and flexor carpi ulnaris muscles may also contribute to the firm end-feel.

### Goniometer Alignment

See Figures 6.13 and 6.14.

1. Center **fulcrum** on the dorsal aspect of the wrist over the capitate.
2. Align **proximal arm** with the dorsal midline of the forearm. If the shoulder is in 90 degrees of abduction and the elbow is in 90 degrees of flexion, the lateral epicondyle of the humerus can be used for reference.
3. Align **distal arm** with the dorsal midline of the third metacarpal. Do not use the third phalanx for reference.

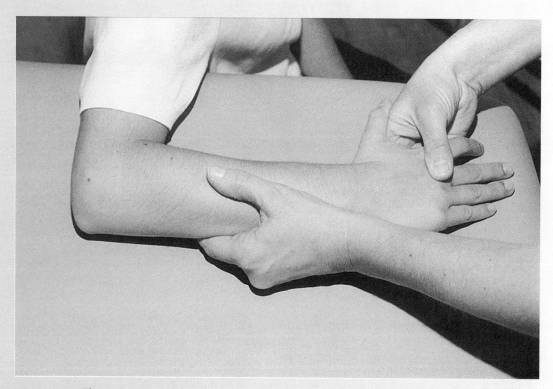

**FIGURE 6.12** The examiner stabilizes the subject's forearm to prevent flexion of the elbow beyond 90 degrees when the wrist is moved into radial deviation. The examiner avoids moving the wrist into either flexion or extension.

**FIGURE 6.13** The alignment of the goniometer at the beginning of radial deviation ROM. The examining table can be used to support the hand.

**FIGURE 6.14** The alignment of the goniometer at the end of radial deviation ROM. The examiner must center the fulcrum over the dorsal surface of the capitate. If the fulcrum shifts to the ulnar side of the wrist, there will be an incorrect measurement of excessive radial deviation.

## ● WRIST ULNAR DEVIATION

Motion occurs in the frontal plane around an anterior–posterior axis. Ulnar deviation is sometimes referred to as ulnar flexion or adduction. Normal ROM values for adults are 30 degrees according to the AMA[12] and AAOS[13,14] and 39 degrees according to Greene and Wolf.[17] See Research Findings and Tables 6.1 to 6.3 for additional normal ROM values by age and gender.

### Testing Position

Position the subject sitting next to a supporting surface with the shoulder abducted to 90 degrees, the elbow flexed to 90 degrees, and the palm of the hand facing the ground. In this position the forearm will be midway between supination and pronation. Rest the forearm and hand on the supporting surface.

### Stabilization

Stabilize the radius and ulna to prevent pronation or supination of the forearm and less than 90 degrees of elbow flexion.

### Testing Motion

Deviate the wrist in the ulnar direction by moving the hand toward the little finger (Fig. 6.15). Maintain the wrist in 0 degrees of flexion and extension, and avoid rotating the hand. The end of ulnar deviation ROM occurs when resistance to further motion is felt and attempts to overcome the resistance cause the elbow to extend.

### Normal End-Feel

The end-feel is firm because of tension in the radial collateral ligament and the radial portion of the joint capsule. Tension in the extensor pollicis brevis and abductor pollicis longus muscles may contribute to the firm end-feel.

### Goniometer Alignment

See Figures 6.16 and 6.17.

1. Center **fulcrum** on the dorsal aspect of the wrist over the capitate.
2. Align **proximal** arm with the dorsal midline of the forearm. If the shoulder is in 90 degrees of abduction and the elbow is in 90 degrees of flexion, the lateral epicondyle of the humerus can be used for reference.
3. Align **distal** arm with the dorsal midline of the third metacarpal. Do not use the third phalanx for reference.

**FIGURE 6.15** The examiner uses one hand to stabilize the subject's forearm and maintain the elbow in 90 degrees of flexion. The examiner's other hand moves the wrist into ulnar deviation, being careful not to flex or extend the wrist.

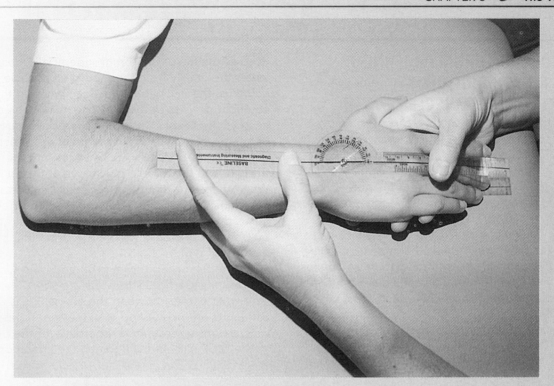

**FIGURE 6.16** The alignment of the goniometer at the beginning of ulnar deviation ROM. Sometimes if a half-circle goniometer is used, the proximal and distal arms of the goniometer will have to be reversed so that the pointer remains on the body of the goniometer at the end of the ROM.

**FIGURE 6.17** The alignment of the goniometer at the end of the ulnar deviation ROM. The examiner must center the fulcrum over the dorsal surface of the capitate. If the fulcrum shifts to the radial side of the wrist, there will be an incorrect measurement of excessive ulnar deviation.

## MUSCLE LENGTH TESTING PROCEDURES: Wrist

### ⬤ FLEXOR DIGITORUM PROFUNDUS AND FLEXOR DIGITORUM SUPERFICIALIS MUSCLE LENGTH

The flexor digitorum profundus crosses the elbow, wrist, metacarpophalangeal (MCP), proximal interphalangeal (PIP), and distal interphalangeal (DIP) joints. The flexor digitorum profundus originates proximally from the upper three-fourths of the ulna, the coronoid process of the ulna, and the interosseus membrane (Fig. 6.18). This muscle inserts distally onto the palmar surface of the bases of the distal phalanges of the fingers. When it contracts, it flexes the MCP, PIP, and DIP joints of the fingers and flexes the wrist. The flexor digitorum profundus is passively lengthened by placing the elbow, wrist, MCP, PIP, and DIP joints in extension.

The **flexor digitorum superficialis** crosses the elbow, wrist, MCP, and PIP joints. The humeroulnar head of the flexor digitorum superficialis muscle originates proximally from the medial epicondyle of the humerus, the ulnar collateral ligament, and the coronoid process of the ulna (Fig. 6.19). The radial head of the flexor digitorum superficialis muscle originates proximally from the anterior surface of the radius. It inserts distally via two slips into the sides of the bases of the middle phalanges of the fingers. When the flexor digitorum superficialis contracts, it flexes the MCP and PIP joints of the fingers and flexes the wrist. The muscle is passively lengthened by placing the elbow, wrist, MCP, and PIP joints in extension.

If the flexor digitorum profundus and flexor digitorum superficialis muscles are short, they will limit wrist extension when the elbow, MCP, PIP, and DIP joints are positioned in extension. If passive wrist extension is limited regardless of the position of the MCP, PIP, and DIP joints, the limitation is

Flexor digitorum profundus

**FIGURE 6.18** An anterior view of the right forearm showing the attachments of the flexor digitorum profundus muscle.

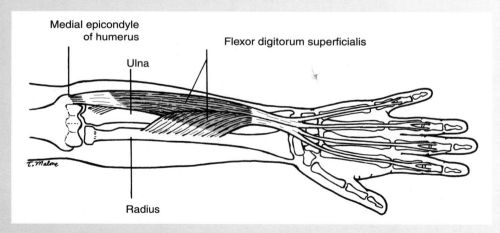

Medial epicondyle of humerus

Flexor digitorum superficialis

Ulna

Radius

**FIGURE 6.19** An anterior view of the right forearm and hand showing the attachments of the flexor digitorum superficialis muscle.

due to abnormalities of wrist joint surfaces or shortening of the palmar joint capsule, palmar radiocarpal ligament, ulnocarpal ligament, palmaris longus, flexor carpi radialis, or flexor carpi ulnaris muscles.

## Starting Position

Position the subject sitting next to a supporting surface with the upper extremity resting on the surface. Place the elbow, MCP, PIP, and DIP joints in extension (Fig. 6.20). Pronate the forearm and place the wrist in neutral.

**FIGURE 6.20** The starting position for testing the length of the flexor digitorum profundus and flexor digitorum superficialis muscles.

## Stabilization
Stabilize the forearm to prevent elbow flexion.

## Testing Motion
Hold the MCP, PIP, and DIP joints in extension while extending the wrist (Figs. 6.21 and 6.22). The end of the testing motion occurs when resistance is felt and additional wrist extension causes the fingers or elbow to flex.

## End-Feel
The end-feel is firm because of tension in the flexor digitorum profundus and flexor digitorum superficialis muscles.

**FIGURE 6.21** The end of the testing motion for the length of the flexor digitorum profundus and flexor digitorum superficialis muscles. The examiner uses one hand to stabilize the forearm, while the other hand holds the fingers in extension and moves the wrist into extension. The examiner has moved her right thumb from the dorsal surface of the fingers to allow a clearer photograph, but keeping the thumb placed on the dorsal surface would help to prevent the fingers from flexing at the PIP joints.

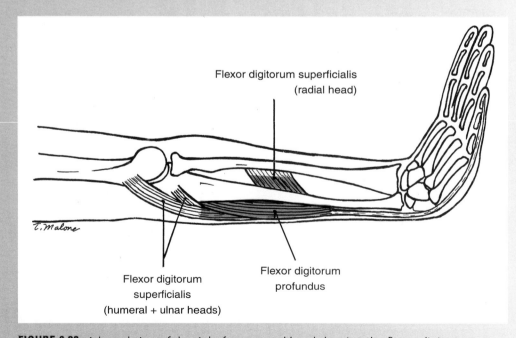

Flexor digitorum superficialis
(radial head)

Flexor digitorum
superficialis
(humeral + ulnar heads)

Flexor digitorum
profundus

**FIGURE 6.22** A lateral view of the right forearm and hand showing the flexor digitorum profundus and flexor digitorum superficialis being stretched over the elbow, wrist, MCP, PIP, and DIP joints.

## Goniometer Alignment
See Figure 6.23.

1. Center **fulcrum** on the lateral aspect of the wrist over the triquetrum.
2. Align **proximal arm** with the lateral midline of the ulna, using the olecranon and ulnar styloid process for reference.
3. Align **distal arm** with the lateral midline of the fifth metacarpal. Do not use the soft tissue of the hypothenar eminence for reference.

**FIGURE 6.23** The alignment of the goniometer at the end of testing the length of the flexor digitorum profundus and flexor digitorum superficialis muscles.

# ● EXTENSOR DIGITORUM, EXTENSOR INDICIS, AND EXTENSOR DIGITI MINIMI MUSCLE LENGTH

The extensor digitorum, extensor indicis, and extensor digiti minimi muscles cross the elbow; wrist; and MCP, PIP, and DIP joints. When these muscles contract, they extend the MCP, PIP, and DIP joints of the fingers and extend the wrist. These muscles are passively lengthened by placing the elbow in extension and the wrist, MCP, PIP, and DIP joints in full flexion.

The **extensor digitorum** originates proximally from the lateral epicondyle of the humerus and inserts distally onto the middle and distal phalanges of the fingers via the extensor hood (Fig. 6.24). The **extensor indicis** originates proximally from the posterior surface of the ulna and the interosseous membrane. This muscle inserts distally onto the extensor hood of the index finger. The **extensor digiti minimi** also originates proximally from the lateral epicondyle of the humerus but inserts distally onto the extensor hood of the little finger.

If the extensor digitorum, extensor indicis, and extensor digiti minimi muscles are short, they will limit wrist flexion when the elbow is positioned in extension and the MCP, PIP, and DIP joints are positioned in full flexion. If wrist flexion is limited regardless of the position of the MCP, PIP, and DIP joints, the limitation is due to abnormalities of joint surfaces of the wrist or shortening of the dorsal joint capsule, dorsal radiocarpal ligament, extensor carpi radialis longus, extensor carpi radialis brevis, or extensor carpi ulnaris muscles.

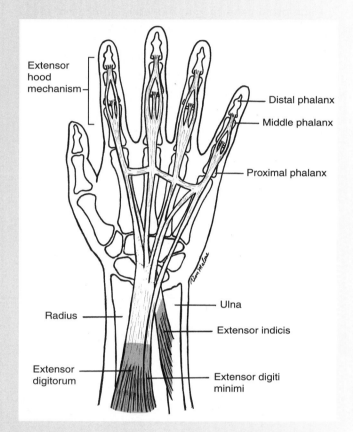

**FIGURE 6.24** A posterior view of the right forearm and hand showing the distal attachments of the extensor digitorum, extensor indicis, and extensor digiti minimi muscles.

## Starting Position

Position the subject sitting next to a supporting surface. The upper arm and the forearm should rest on the supporting surface, but the hand should be free to move into flexion. Place the elbow in full extension and the MCP, PIP, and DIP joints in full flexion (Fig. 6.25). Place the forearm in pronation and the wrist in neutral.

## Stabilization

Stabilize the forearm to prevent elbow flexion.

## Testing Motion

Hold the MCP, PIP, and DIP joints in full flexion while flexing the wrist (Figs. 6.26 and 6.27). The end of the testing motion occurs when resistance is felt and additional wrist flexion causes the fingers to extend or the elbow to flex.

## Normal End-Feel

The end-feel is firm because of tension in the extensor digitorum, extensor indicis, and extensor digiti minimi muscles.

**FIGURE 6.25** The starting position for testing the length of the extensor digitorum, extensor indicis, and extensor digiti minimi muscles. The hand is positioned off the end of the examining table to allow room for finger and wrist flexion.

**FIGURE 6.26** The end of the testing motion for the length of the extensor digitorum, extensor indicis, and extensor digiti minimi muscles. One of the examiner's hands stabilizes the forearm, while the other hand holds the fingers in full flexion and moves the wrist into flexion.

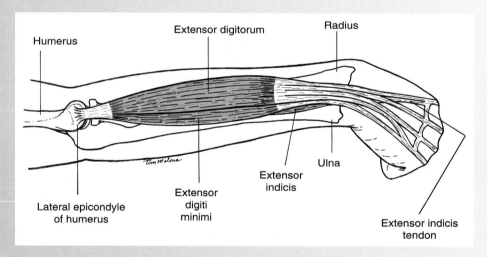

**FIGURE 6.27** A posterior view of the right forearm and hand showing the extensor digitorum, extensor indicis, and extensor digiti minimi muscles stretched over the elbow, wrist, MCP, PIP, and DIP joints.

## Goniometer Alignment
See Figure 6.28.

1. Center **fulcrum** on the lateral aspect of the wrist over the triquetrum.
2. Align **proximal arm** with the lateral midline of the ulna, using the olecranon and ulnar styloid process for reference.
3. Align **distal arm** with the lateral midline of the fifth metacarpal. Do not use the soft tissue of the hypothenar eminence for reference.

**FIGURE 6.28** The alignment of the goniometer at the end of testing the length of the extensor digitorum, extensor indicis, and extensor digiti minimi muscles.

## ⟨⟩ Research Findings

### Effects of Age, Gender, and Other Factors

Table 6.1 provides normal wrist ROM values for adults as reported by the AAOS,[12–15,17,18] AMA,[12] Boone and Azen,[15] Greene and Wolf,[17] and Ryu and associates.[18] In general, these values range from 60 to 80 degrees for flexion, 60 to 75 degrees for extension, 20 to 25 degrees for radial deviation, and 30 to 40 degrees for ulnar deviation. Other studies that provide wrist ROM data for adults between the ages of 20 to 60 years include Solgaard and colleagues,[19] Solveborn and Olerud,[20] and Stubbs and coworkers.[21]

### Age

Most studies support a small, gradual decrease in the amount of wrist motion with increasing age. Age-related ROM changes appear to be most marked in young children and seniors, whereas changes in young and middle-aged adults seem minimal.

Table 6.2 provides normative wrist ROM values for newborns and children. Although caution must be used in drawing conclusions from comparisons between values obtained by different researchers, the mean flexion and extension values for infants from Wanatabe and coworkers[22] are larger than values for males aged 18 months to 19 years reported by Boone and Azen.[15,23] Within the study by Boone and Azen, wrist flexion and ulnar and radial deviation motions for the youngest age group (18 months to 5 years) were significantly larger than the values for other age groups (see Tables 6.2 and 6.3). Wrist extension values were significantly larger for males 6 to 12 years of age than for those in the other age groups.

Table 6.3 provides wrist ROM values in male adults from 20 to 54 years of age. Boone and Azen[15,23] found a significant difference in wrist flexion and extension ROM between males younger than or equal to 19 years of age and those who were older. However, the effects of age on wrist motion in adults from 20 to 54 years of age appear to be very slight. A study by Stubbs and associates[21] placed 55 male subjects between the ages of 25 and 54 years into three age groups. There was

## TABLE 6.1 Normal Wrist ROM Values for Adults in Degrees from Selected Sources

| | AAOS[13,14] | AMA[12] | Boone and Azen[15] | Greene and Wolf[17] | Ryu et al[18] |
|---|---|---|---|---|---|
| | | | 20–54 yrs<br>n = 56<br>Males | 18–55 yrs<br>n = 20<br>Males and Females | n = 40<br>Males and Females |
| Motion | | | Mean (SD) | Mean (SD) | Mean |
| Flexion | 80 | 60 | 74.8 (6.6) | 73.3 (2.1) | 79.1 |
| Extension | 70 | 60 | 74.0 (6.6) | 64.9 (2.2) | 59.3 |
| Radial deviation | 20 | 20 | 21.1 (4.0) | 25.4 (2.0) | 21.1 |
| Ulnar deviation | 30 | 30 | 35.3 (3.8) | 39.2 (2.1) | 37.7 |

## TABLE 6.2 Effects of Age on Wrist ROM in Newborns, Children, and Adolescents: Normal Values in Degrees

| | Wanatabe et al[22] | Boone and Azen[15,23] | | |
|---|---|---|---|---|
| | 2 wks–2 yrs<br>n = 45<br>Males and Females | 18 mos–5 yrs<br>n = 19<br>Males | 6–12 yrs<br>n = 17<br>Males | 13–19 yrs<br>n = 17<br>Males |
| Motion | Range of Means | Mean (SD) | Mean (SD) | Mean (SD) |
| Flexion | 88–96 | 82.2 (3.8) | 76.3 (5.6) | 75.4 (4.5) |
| Extension | 82–89 | 76.1 (4.9) | 78.4 (5.9) | 72.9 (6.4) |
| Radial deviation | | 24.2 (3.7) | 21.3 (4.1) | 19.7 (3.0) |
| Ulnar deviation | | 38.7 (3.6) | 35.4 (2.4) | 35.7 (4.2) |

| TABLE 6.3 | Effects of Age on Wrist ROM in Men 20 to 54 Years Old: Normal Values in Degrees | | | | | |
|---|---|---|---|---|---|---|
| | Boone and Azen[15,23] | | | Stubbs et al[21] | | |
| | 20–29 yrs n = 19 | 30–39 yrs n = 18 | 40–54 yrs n = 19 | 25–34 yrs n = 15 | 35–44 yrs n = 20 | 45–54 yrs n = 20 |
| Motion | Mean (SD) | Mean (SD) | Mean (SD) | Mean (SD) | Mean (SD) | Mean (SD) |
| Flexion | 76.8 (5.5) | 74.9 (4.0) | 72.8 (8.9) | 70.6 (9.3) | 73.5 (10.4) | 68.9 (8.4) |
| Extension | 77.5 (5.1) | 72.8 (6.9) | 71.6 (6.3) | 78.3 (11.8) | 76.4 (10.4) | 76.7 (11.7) |
| Radial deviation | 21.4 (3.6) | 20.3 (3.1) | 21.6 (5.1) | 23.8 (9.5) | 22.5 (7.9) | 18.9 (7.9) |
| Ulnar deviation | 35.1 (3.8) | 36.1 (2.9) | 34.7 (4.5) | 51.1 (9.0) | 49.9 (7.0) | 44.1 (4.3) |

no significant difference among the age groups for wrist flexion, extension, and radial deviation ROM. A significant difference in ulnar deviation (7 degrees) was found between the oldest and the youngest age groups, with the oldest group having less motion.

Wrist ROM values in males 60 years of age and older are presented in Table 6.4. Flexion and extension ROM in these older adults, as presented by Walker and associates,[24] Chaparro and colleagues,[25] and Kalscheur and coworkers[26] are less than the values for the age groups presented in Table 6.3. Chaparro and colleagues[25] further subdivided the 62 male subjects in their study into four age groups: 60 to 69 years of age, 70 to 79 years of age, 80 to 89 years of age, and 90 years of age and older. They found a trend of decreasing ROM with increasing age, with the oldest group having significantly lower wrist flexion and ulnar deviation values than the two youngest groups.

Four other studies offer additional information on the effects of age on wrist motion. Hewitt,[27] in a study of 112 females between 11 and 45 years of age, found slight differences in the average amount of active motion in various age groups, but no statistical analyses were performed. Allander and coworkers,[28] in a study of 309 Icelandic females, 208 Swedish females, and 203 Swedish males ranging in age from 33 to 70 years, found that with increasing age there was a decrease in flexion and extension ROM at both wrists. Males lost an average of 2.2 degrees of motion every 5 years. Bell and Hoshizaki[29] studied 124 females and 66 males ranging in age from 18 to 88 years. A significant negative correlation was noted between ROM and age for wrist flexion–extension and radial–ulnar deviation in females and for wrist flexion–extension in males. As age increased, wrist motions generally decreased. There was a significant difference among the five age groups of females for all wrist motions, although the difference was not significant for males. Kalscheur and associates,[30] in a study of 61 women between the ages of 63 and 85 years, found a significant linear relationship between age and right wrist flexion and extension with ROM decreasing an average of 0.4 to 0.5 degrees per year in these older women. The relationships between age and left wrist motions were not statistically significant.

## Gender

The following four studies offer evidence of gender effects on the wrist joint, with most supporting the belief that women have slightly more wrist ROM than men. Cobe,[31] in a study of 100 college men and 15 women ranging in age from 20 to 30 years, found that women had a greater active ROM in all motions at the wrist than men. Allander and coworkers[28] compared wrist flexion and extension ROM in 203 Swedish men and 208 Swedish women between the ages of 45 and more than 70 years of age and noted that women had significantly greater motion than men. Both studies measured active motion with joint-specific mechanical devices. Walker and associates,[24] in a study of 30 men and 30 women aged 60 to 84 years, found that the women had more active wrist extension and flexion than the men, whereas the men had more ulnar and radial deviation than the women. These differences were statistically significant for wrist extension (4 degrees) and ulnar deviation (5 degrees). Chaparro and colleagues[25]

| TABLE 6.4 | Effects of Age on Wrist ROM in Men Older Than 60 Years: Normal Values in Degrees | | |
|---|---|---|---|
| | Walker et al[24] | Chaparro et al[25] | Kalscheur et al[26] |
| | 60–85 yrs n = 30 | 60–90+ yrs n = 62 | 66–86 yrs n = 25 |
| Motion | Mean (SD) | Mean (SD) | Mean (SD) |
| Flexion | 62.0 (12.0) | 50.8 (13.8) | 64.9 (8.7) |
| Extension | 61.0 (6.0) | 44.0 (9.9) | 58.2 (10.9) |
| Radial deviation | 20.0 (6.0) | | |
| Ulnar deviation | 28.0 (7.0) | 35.0 (9.5) | |

examined wrist flexion, extension, and ulnar deviation ROM in 62 men and 85 women from 60 to more than 90 years of age. Women had significantly greater wrist extension (6.4 degrees) and ulnar deviation (3.0 degrees) than men. Kalscheur and coworkers[26] found that women had more wrist flexion and extension ROM than men in a study of 61 women and 25 men between the ages of 63 and 86 years. These differences ranged from 1.7 to 5.3 degrees and were statistically significant for right wrist flexion (5.0 degrees) and left wrist extension (5.3 degrees).

## Right Versus Left Sides

Study results vary as to whether there is a difference between left and right wrist ROM. Boone and Azen,[15] in a study of 109 normal males between 18 months and 54 years of age, found no significant difference in wrist flexion, extension, and radial and ulnar deviation between sides. Likewise, Chang, Buschbacher, and Edlich[32] found no significant difference between right and left wrist flexion and extension in the 10 power lifters and 10 nonlifters who were their subjects. Solgaard and coworkers[19] studied 8 males and 23 females aged 24 to 65 years. Right and left wrist extension and radial deviation differed significantly, but the differences were small and not significant when the total range (i.e., flexion and extension) was assessed. The authors stated that the opposite wrist could be satisfactorily used as a reference.

In contrast, several studies have found the left wrist to have greater ROM than the right wrist. Cobe[31] measured wrist motions in the positions of pronation and supination in 100 men and 15 women. He found that men had greater ROM in their left wrist than in their right for all motions except ulnar deviation measured in pronation. However, he reported that the women had greater wrist motion on the right except for extension in pronation and radial deviation in supination. No statistical tests were conducted in the 1928 study, but Allander and associates[28] reported that a recalculation of the original data collected by Cobe found a significantly greater ROM on the left in men. Cobe[31] suggests that the heavy work that men performed using their right extremities may account for the decrease in right-side motion in comparison with left-side motion. A study by Kalscheur and associates[30] found a significantly greater range of left wrist extension and right wrist flexion as compared to the contralateral side in 61 older women. The mean differences between sides were small, ranging from 3 to 5 degrees.

Allander and associates,[28] in a study subgroup of 309 Icelandic women aged 34 to 61 years, found no significant difference between the right and the left wrists. However, a subgroup of 208 women and 203 Swedish men in the study showed significantly smaller ranges of wrist flexion and extension on the right than on the left, independent of gender. The authors state that these differences may be due to a higher level of exposure to trauma of the right hand in a predominantly right-handed society. Solveborn and Olerud[20] measured wrist ROM in 16 healthy subjects in addition to 123 patients with unilateral tennis elbow. Among the healthy subjects a significantly greater ROM was found for wrist flexion and extension

on the left compared with the right. However, mean differences between sides were only 2 degrees. The authors concurred with Boone and Azen[15] that a patient's healthy limb can be used to establish a norm for comparing with the affected side.

## Testing Position

Several studies have reported differences in wrist ROM depending on the testing position of the forearm during measurement. These findings support the use of consistent forearm positions during wrist measurements. Cobe,[31] in a study of 100 men and 15 women, found that ulnar deviation ROM was greater in supination, whereas radial deviation was greater in pronation. It is interesting that the total amount of ulnar and radial deviation combined was similar between the two positions. Hewitt[27] measured wrist ROM in 112 females in supination and pronation and found that ulnar deviation was greater in supination, whereas radial deviation, flexion, and extension were greater in pronation. Werner and Plancher,[6] in a review article, also stated that ulnar deviation has a greater ROM when the forearm is supinated than when the forearm is pronated. They noted that radial and ulnar deviation ROMs become minimal when the wrist is fully flexed or extended. No specific references for these observations were cited.

Spilman and Pinkston[28] examined the effect of three frequently used goniometric testing positions on active wrist radial and ulnar deviation ROM in 100 subjects (63 males, 37 females). In Position One the subject's arm was at the side, with the elbow flexed to 90 degrees and the forearm fully pronated. In Position Two the shoulder was in 90 degrees of flexion, with the elbow extended and the hand prone. In Position Three the subject's shoulder was in 90 degrees of abduction, with the elbow in 90 degrees of flexion and the hand prone (in this position the forearm is in neutral pronation). Ulnar deviation and the total range of radial and ulnar deviation were significantly greater when measured in Position Three. Radial deviation was significantly greater when the subject was in Position Three or Position Two than in Position One. The differences between the means for the three positions were small—approximately 3 degrees.

Wrist ROM values have also been found to vary if different wrist positions are used during testing. It appears that the greatest ROM values are obtained with the wrist in a neutral position. Marshall, Morzall, and Shealy[34] evaluated 35 men and 19 women for wrist ROM in one plane of motion while the subjects were fixed in secondary wrist and forearm positions. For example, during the measurement of radial and ulnar deviation, the wrist was alternatively positioned in 0 degrees, 40 degrees of flexion, and 40 degrees of extension. During the measurement of flexion and extension the wrist was positioned in 0 degrees, 15 degrees radial deviation, and 25 degrees ulnar deviation. The effects of the secondary wrist and forearm postures, although statistically significant, were generally small (less than 5 degrees), with most motions having the greatest range with the wrist in neutral. However, radial deviation ROM was greatest when performed in wrist extension. The authors believed that the changes that occur in wrist ROM with positional alterations might have been due to changes in contact between articular surfaces and tautness of ligaments that span the wrist region. In a study of 10 subjects performing active circumduction, Li and associates[35] found that maximum ROM in flexion and extension occurred with the wrist near 0 degrees of radial and ulnar deviation. Likewise, maximum ROM in radial and ulnar deviation occurred with the wrist near 0 degrees of flexion and extension. Wrist deviation from the neutral position in one plane of motion reduced wrist ROM in other planes of motions.

## Functional Range of Motion

Several investigators have examined the range of motion that occurs at the wrist during activities of daily living (ADLs) and during the placement of the hand on the body areas necessary for personal care. Tables 6.5 and 6.6 are adapted from the works of Brumfield and Champoux,[36] Ryu and associates,[18] Safaee-Rad and colleagues,[37] and Cooper and coworkers.[38] Differences in ROM values reported for certain functional tasks were most likely the result of variations in task definitions, measurement methods, and subject selection. However, in spite of the range of values reported, certain trends are evident.

A review of Table 6.5 shows that the majority of ADLs required wrist extension and ulnar deviation. Drinking activities generally required the least amount of extension (6 to 24 degrees) and the smallest arc of motion (13 to 20 degrees). Using the telephone (Fig. 6.29), turning a steering wheel or a doorknob and rising from a chair (see Fig. 5.31) required the greatest amounts of extension (40 to 63 degrees) and arc of motion (43 to 85 degrees). Turning a doorknob (Fig. 6.30) involved the greatest amount of flexion (40 degrees). The greatest amounts of ulnar deviation (27 to 32 degrees) were noted while rising from a chair, turning a doorknob and steering wheel, and pouring from a pitcher.

Table 6.6 provides information on wrist position during the placement of the hand on the body areas commonly touched during personal care. The majority of positions required wrist flexion and less overall wrist motion than the ADLs presented in Table 6.5. Among the positions studied, placing the palm to the front of the chest consistently required the greatest amount of wrist flexion, whereas placing the palm to the sacrum required the greatest amount of ulnar deviation.

Brumfield and Champoux[36] used a uniaxial electrogoniometer to determine the range of wrist flexion and extension during 15 ADLs performed by 12 men and 7 women. They determined that ADLs such as eating, drinking, and using a telephone were accomplished with 5 degrees of flexion to 35 degrees of extension. Personal care activities that involved

---

**TABLE 6.5** Wrist ROM During Functional Activities: Mean Values in Degrees

| Activity | Extension* | | | Ulnar Deviation† | | | Source |
|---|---|---|---|---|---|---|---|
| | Min | Max | Arc | Min | Max | Arc | |
| Put glass to mouth | 11.2 | 24.0 | 12.8 | — | — | — | Brumfield[36] |
| Drink from glass | 2 | 22 | 20 | 5 | 20 | 15 | Ryu‡[18] |
| Drink from handled cup | −7.5* | 5.9 | 13.4 | 8.3 | 16.1 | 7.8 | Safaee-Rad[37] |
| Eat with fork | 9.3 | 36.5 | 27.7 | — | — | — | Brumfield |
| | 3.3 | 17.7 | 14.4 | 3.2 | −4.9† | 8.1 | Safaee-Rad |
| Feeding tasks: fork, spoon, cup | −6.8* | 20.9 | 27.2 | 18.7 | −2.4† | 21.1 | Cooper (males)[38] |
| Cut with knife | −3.5* | 20.2 | 23.7 | — | — | — | Brumfield |
| | −30* | −5 | 25 | 12 | 27 | 15 | Ryu |
| Pour from pitcher | 8.7 | 29.7 | 21.0 | — | — | — | Brumfield |
| | −20* | 22 | 42 | 12 | 32 | 20 | Ryu |
| Turn doorknob | −40* | 45 | 85 | −2† | 32 | 34 | Ryu |
| Use telephone | −0.1* | 42.6 | 42.7 | — | — | — | Brumfield |
| | −15 | 40 | 55 | −10† | 12 | 22 | Ryu |
| Turn steering wheel | −15* | 45 | 60 | −17† | 27 | 44 | Ryu |
| Rise from chair | 0.6 | 63.4 | 62.8 | — | — | — | Brumfield |
| | −10* | 60 | 70 | 5 | 30 | 25 | Ryu |

*The minus sign denotes flexion.
†The minus sign denotes radial deviation.
‡Values from Ryu et al were extrapolated from graphs.

| TABLE 6.6 | Wrist Motions During Hand Placement Needed for Personal Care Activities: Mean Values in Degrees | | | | |
|---|---|---|---|---|---|
| | Extension | Flexion | Ulnar Deviation | Radial Deviation | |
| **Activity** | **Mean (SD)** | **Mean (SD)** | **Mean (SD)** | **Mean (SD)** | **Source** |
| Hand to top of head | — — | 2.3 (12.5) | — — | — — | Brumfield[36] |
| | — — | 20.9 (13.9) | 16.1 (12.7) | — — | Ryu[18] |
| Hand to occiput | 12.7 (9.9) | — — | — — | — — | Brumfield |
| | — — | 0.9 (17.6) | 9.7 (11.9) | — — | Ryu |
| Hand to front of chest | — — | 18.9 (8.9) | — — | — — | Brumfield |
| | — — | 24.5 (16.7) | — — | 5.1 (10.3) | Ryu |
| Hand to sacrum | — — | 0.6 (9.8) | — — | — — | Brumfield |
| | — — | 19.5 (19.3) | 47.8 (16.8) | — — | Ryu |
| Hand to foot | 14.2 (10.6) | — — | — — | — — | Brumfield |
| | 0.8 (14.6) | — — | 8.7 (12.2) | — — | Ryu |

**FIGURE 6.29** Using a telephone requires approximately 40 degrees of wrist extension.

**FIGURE 6.30** Turning a doorknob requires 40 degrees of wrist flexion and 45 degrees of wrist extension.

placing the hand on the body required 20 degrees of flexion to 15 degrees of extension. The authors concluded that an arc of wrist motion of 45 degrees (10 degrees of flexion to 35 degrees of extension) is sufficient to perform most of the activities studied.

Palmer and coworkers[39] used a triaxial electrogoniometer to study 10 normal subjects while they performed 52 tasks. A range of 33 degrees of flexion, 59 degrees of extension, 23 degrees of radial deviation, and 22 degrees of ulnar deviation was used in performing ADLs and personal hygiene. During these tasks the average amount of motion was about 5 degrees of flexion, 30 degrees of extension, 10 degrees of radial deviation, and 15 degrees of ulnar deviation. ROM values for individual tasks were not presented in the study.

Ryu and associates[18] found that 31 examined tasks could be performed with 54 degrees of flexion, 60 degrees of extension, 17 degrees of radial deviation, and 40 degrees of ulnar deviation. The 20 men and 20 women were evaluated with a biaxial electrogoniometer during performance of palm placement activities, personal care and hygiene, diet and food preparation, and miscellaneous ADLs.

Studies by Safaee-Rad and coworkers[37] and Cooper and coworkers[38] examined wrist ROM with a video-based three-dimensional motion analysis system during three feeding tasks: drinking from a cup, eating with a fork, and eating with a spoon. The 10 males studied by Safaee-Rad and coworkers used from 10 degrees of wrist flexion to 25 degrees of extension and from 20 degrees of ulnar deviation to 5 degrees of radial deviation during the tasks. Cooper and coworkers examined 10 males and 9 females during feeding tasks, with the elbow unrestricted and then fixed in 110 degrees of flexion. With the elbow unrestricted, males used from 7 degrees of wrist flexion to 21 degrees of extension and from 19 degrees of ulnar deviation to 2 degrees of radial deviation. Females had similar values for flexion and extension but used from

3 degrees of ulnar deviation to 18 degrees of radial deviation. Both studies found that drinking from a cup required less of an arc of wrist motion than eating with a fork or spoon.

Nelson[40] took a different approach to determining the amount of wrist motion necessary for carrying out functional tasks. He evaluated the ability of 9 males and 3 females to perform 123 ADLs with a splint on the dominant wrist that limited motion to 5 degrees of flexion, 6 degrees of extension, 7 degrees of radial deviation, and 6 degrees of ulnar deviation. All 123 activities could be completed with the splint in place, with 9 activities having a mean difficulty rating of greater than or equal to 2 (could be done with minimal difficulty or frustration and with satisfactory outcome). The most difficult activities included putting on/taking off a brassiere (Fig. 6.31), washing legs/back, writing, dusting low surfaces, cutting vegetables, handling a sharp knife, cutting meat, using a can opener, and using a manual eggbeater. It should be noted that these subjects were pain free and had normal shoulders and elbows to compensate for the restricted wrist motions. The ability to generalize these results to a patient population with pain and multiply involved joints may be limited.

Repetitive trauma disorders such as carpal tunnel syndrome and wrist/hand tendinitis have been noted to occur more frequently in performing certain types of work, sports, and artistic endeavors. To elucidate the cause of these higher incidences of injury, studies have been conducted on the wrist positions used and the amount and frequency of wrist motions required during grocery bagging,[41] grocery scanning,[42] piano playing,[43] industrial work,[44] and handrim wheelchair propulsion[45,46] and in playing sports such as basketball, baseball pitching, and golf.[6,47] The reader is advised to refer directly to these studies to gain information about the amount of wrist ROM that occurs during these activities. In general, an association has been noted between activities that require extreme wrist postures and the prevalence of hand/wrist tendinitis.[48] Tasks that involve repeated wrist flexion and extreme wrist extension, repetitive work with the hands, and repeated force applied to the base of the palm and wrist have been associated with carpal tunnel syndrome.[49]

## Reliability

In early studies of wrist motion conducted by Hewitt[27] and Cobe[31] in the 1920s, both authors observed considerable differences in repeated measurements of active wrist motions. These differences were attributed to a lack of motor control on the part of the subjects in expending maximal effort. Cobe suggested that only average values have much validity and that changes in ROM should exceed 5 degrees to be considered clinically significant.

Later studies of intratester and intertester reliability were conducted by numerous researchers. The majority of these investigators found that intratester reliability was greater than intertester reliability, that reliability varied according to the motion being tested, and that different instruments should not be used interchangeably during joint measurement.

Hellebrandt, Duvall, and Moore[50] found that wrist motions measured with a universal goniometer were more reliable than those measured with a joint-specific device. Measurements of wrist flexion and extension were less reliable than measurements of radial and ulnar deviation, although mean differences between successive measurements taken with a universal goniometer by a skilled tester were 1.1 degrees for flexion and 0.9 degrees for extension. The mean differences between successive measurements increased to 5.4 degrees for flexion and 5.7 degrees for extension when successive measurements were taken with different instruments.

In a study by Low,[51] 50 testers using a universal goniometer visually estimated and then measured the author's active wrist extension and elbow flexion. Five testers also took 10 repeated measurements over the course of 5 to 10 days. Mean error improved from 12.8 degrees for visual estimates to 7.8 degrees for goniometric measurement. Intraobserver error was less than interobserver error. The measurement of wrist extension was less reliable than the measurement of elbow flexion, with mean errors of 7.8 and 5.0 degrees, respectively.

Boone et al[52] conducted a study in which four testers using a universal goniometer measured ulnar deviation on 12 male volunteers. Measurements were repeated over a period of 4 weeks. Intratester reliability was found to be

**FIGURE 6.31** A large amount of wrist flexion is needed to fasten a bra or bathing suit. This is one of the most difficult activities to perform if wrist motion is limited.

better than intertester reliability. The authors concluded that to determine true change when more than one tester measures the same motion, differences in motion should exceed 5 degrees.

In a study by Bird and Stowe,[53] two observers repeatedly measured active and passive wrist ROM in three subjects. They concluded that interobserver error was greatest for extension (±8 degrees) and least for radial and ulnar deviation (±2 to 3 degrees). Error during passive ROM measurements was slightly greater than during active ROM measurements.

Greene and Wolf[17] compared the reliability of the Ortho-Ranger, an electronic pendulum goniometer, with a universal goniometer for active upper-extremity motions in 20 healthy adults. Wrist ROM was measured by one therapist three times with each instrument during each of three sessions over a 2-week period. There was a significant difference between instruments for wrist extension and ulnar deviation. Within-session reliability was slightly higher for the universal goniometer (ICC = 0.91 to 0.96) than for the OrthoRanger (ICC = 0.88 to 0.92). The 95 percent confidence level, which represents the variability around the mean, ranged from 7.6 to 9.3 degrees for the goniometer and from 18.2 to 25.6 degrees for the Ortho-Ranger. The authors concluded that the OrthoRanger provided no advantages over the universal goniometer.

Solgaard and coworkers[19] found intratester standard deviations of 5 to 8 degrees and intertester standard deviations of 6 to 10 degrees in a study of wrist and forearm motions involving 31 healthy subjects. Measurements were taken with a universal goniometer by four testers on three different occasions. The coefficients of variation (percent variation) between testers were greater for ulnar and radial deviation than for flexion, extension, pronation, and supination.

Horger[54] conducted a study in which 13 randomly paired therapists performed repeated measurements of active and passive wrist motions on 48 patients. Therapists were free to select their own method of measurement with a universal goniometer. The six specialized hand therapists used an ulnar alignment for flexion and extension, whereas the nonspecialized therapists used a radial goniometer alignment. Intratester reliability of both active and passive wrist motions were highly reliable (all ICCs higher than 0.90) for all motions. Intratester reliability was consistently higher than intertester reliability (ICC 0.66 to 0.91). Standard errors of measurements (SEM) ranged from 2.6 to 4.4 for intratester values and from 3.0 to 8.2 for intertester values. Agreement between measures was better for flexion and extension than for radial and ulnar deviation. Intertester reliability coefficients for measurements of active motion (ICC = 0.78 to 0.91) were slightly higher than were coefficients for passive motion (ICC = 0.66 to 0.86) except for radial deviation. Generally, reliability was higher for the specialized therapists than for the nonspecialized therapists. The author determined that the presence of pain reduced the reliability of both active and passive measurements, but active measurements were affected more than passive measurements.

LaStayo and Wheeler[16] studied the intratester and intertester reliability of passive ROM measurements of wrist flexion and extension in 120 patients as measured by 32 randomly paired therapists, who used three goniometric alignments (ulnar, radial, and dorsal–volar). The reliability of measuring wrist flexion ROM was consistently higher than that of measuring extension ROM. Mean intratester ICCs for wrist flexion were 0.86 for radial, 0.87 for ulnar, and 0.92 for dorsal alignment. Mean intratester ICCs for wrist extension were 0.80 for radial, 0.80 for ulnar, and 0.84 for volar alignment. The authors recommended that these three alignments, although generally having good reliability, should not be used interchangeably because there were some significant differences between the measurements taken with the three alignments. The authors suggested that the dorsal–volar alignment should be the technique of choice for measuring passive wrist flexion and extension, given its higher reliability. In an invited commentary on this study, Flower[55] suggested using the fifth metacarpal, which is easier to visualize and align with the distal arm of the goniometer in the ulnar technique, rather than the third metacarpal, which was used in the study. Flower noted that the presence and fluctuation of edema on the dorsal surface of the hand may reduce the reliability of the dorsal alignment and necessitate the use of the ulnar (fifth metacarpal) alignment in the clinical setting.

## Validity

We are unaware of any published studies that report criterion-related validity of wrist ROM measurements taken with a goniometer to radiographs. However, several studies have examined construct validity between impairment measures, such as wrist ROM, and ratings of functional limitation or disability. A review of 32 published wrist outcome instruments noted that ROM was the most frequently included variable, present in 82 percent of the outcome instruments.[56]

Wagner and colleagues[57] measured passive ROM of wrist flexion, extension, radial and ulnar deviation, and the strength of the wrist extensor and flexor muscles in 18 boys with Duchenne muscular dystrophy. A highly significant negative correlation was found between difficulty performing functional hand tasks and radial deviation ROM ($r = -0.76$ to $-0.86$) and between difficulty performing functional hand tasks and wrist extensor strength ($r = -0.61$ to $-0.83$).

The relationship between wrist ROM and activity limitation, pain, and disability following wrist fractures has been examined. Tremayne and associates,[58] in a study of 20 patients with distal radius fractures, found strong, significant correlations ($r = -0.51$ to $-0.76$) between grip strength and tasks in the Jebsen Test of Hand Function (JTHF) and weaker correlations ($r = -0.17$ to $-0.55$) between wrist extenson ROM and tasks in the JTHF. In a subset of 11 patients with Colles' type fractures, there were significant correlations ($r = -0.74$ to $-0.84$) between wrist extension ROM and three of seven tasks (turning cards, stimulated feeding, and lifting large light objects) included in the JTHF.

In a study of 120 patients with distal radius fractures, MacDermid and coworkers[59] found that higher patient-rated pain and disability scores 6 months post-injury (6-month Patient-Rated Wrist Evaluation [PRWE] scores) were moderately associated (r = −0.41) with lower composite ROM scores. Composite ROM scores were based on wrist flexion, extension, ulnar and radial deviation, supination, pronation, and finger flexion.

Karnezis and Fragkiadakis,[60] in a study of 25 patients recovering from distal radial fractures, reported correlations between the "Function Score" of the PRWE score and grip strength (r = 0.80), wrist extension ROM (r = 0.78), pronation (r = 0.70), supination (r = 0.63), and wrist flexion (r = 0.62).

They concluded that grip strength, followed by wrist extension and forearm pronation, were the most sensitive clinical indicators of return of wrist function. In another report of 31 patients recovering from distal radial fracture, the same authors noted that flexion–extension and pronation–supination arcs of motion (expressed as percentages of the unaffected side) were not significantly associated with total PRWE scores in a multiple regression model that included grip strength, age, gender, presence of high-energy injury, and intra-articular fracture.[61] The possibility that some of the variables included in the regression model may be inadvertent markers for diminished ROM values may have affected the findings.

# REFERENCES

1. Linscheid, RL: Kinematic considerations of the wrist. Clin Orthop 202:27, 1986.
2. Austin, NM: The Wrist and Hand Complex. In Levangie, PK, and Norkin, CC (eds): Joint Structure and Function: A Comprehensive Analysis, ed 4. FA Davis, Philadelphia, 2005.
3. Kaltenborn, FM: Manual Mobilization of the Joints, Vol l: The Extremities, ed 5. Olaf Norlis Bokhandel, Oslo, Norway, 1999.
4. Sarrafian, SH, Melamed, JL, and Goshgarian, GM: Study of wrist motion in flexion and extension. Clin Orthop 126:153, 1977.
5. Youm, Y, et al: Kinematics of the wrist: I. An experimental study of radial–ulnar deviation and flexion–extension. J Bone Joint Surg (Am) 60:423, 1978.
6. Werner, SL, and Plancher, KD: Biomechanics of wrist injuries in sports. Clin Sports Med 17:407, 1998.
7. Ritt, M, et al: Rotational stability of the carpus relative to the forearm. J Hand Surg 20A:305, 1995.
8. Neumann, DA: Kinesiology of the Musculoskeletal System. Mosby, St. Louis, 2002.
9. Kisner, C, and Colby, LA: Therapeutic Exercise: Foundations and Techniques, ed 5. FA Davis, Philadelphia, 2007.
10. Kapandji, IA, and Kandel, MJ: The Physiology of the Joints, Vol 1, ed 5. Churchill-Livingstone, Edinburgh, 1997.
11. Cyriax, JH, and Cyriax, PJ: Illustrated Manual of Orthopaedic Medicine. Butterworths, London, 1983.
12. American Medical Association: Guides to the Evaluation of Permanent Impairment, ed 5. AMA, Chicago, 2001.
13. American Academy of Orthopaedic Surgeons: Joint Motion: Methods of Measuring and Recording. AAOS, Chicago, 1965.
14. Greene, WB, and Heckman, JD (eds):The Clinical Measurement of Joint Motion. American Academy of Orthopaedic Surgeons, Rosemont, IL, 1994.
15. Boone, DC, and Azen, SP: Normal range of motion in male subjects. J Bone Joint Surg (Am) 61:756, 1979.
16. LaStayo, PC, and Wheeler, DL: Reliability of passive wrist flexion and extension measurements: A multicenter study. Phys Ther 74:162, 1994
17. Greene, BL, and Wolf, SL: Upper extremity joint movement: Comparison of two measurement devices. Arch Phys Med Rehabil 70:288, 1989.
18. Ryu, J, et al: Functional ranges of motion of the wrist joint. J Hand Surg 16A:409, 1991.
19. Solgaard, S, et al: Reproducibility of goniometry of the wrist. Scand J Rehabil Med 18:5, 1986.
20. Solveborn, SA, and Olerud, C: Radial epicondylalgia (tennis elbow): Measurement of range of motion of the wrist and the elbow. J Orthop Sports Phys Ther 23:251, 1996.
21. Stubbs, NB, Fernandez, JE, and Glenn, WM: Normative data on joint ranges of motion of 25- to 54-year-old males. International Journal of Industrial Ergonomics 12; 265, 1993.
22. Wanatabe, H, et al: The range of joint motions of the extremities in healthy Japanese people: The difference according to age. Nippon Seikeigeka Gokkai Zasshi 53:275, 1979. (Cited in Walker, JM: Musculoskeletal development: A review. Phys Ther 71:878, 1991.)
23. Boone, DC: Techniques of measurement of joint motion. (Unpublished supplement to Boone, DC, and Azen, SP: Normal range of motion in male subjects. J Bone Joint Surg [Am] 61:756, 1979.)
24. Walker, JM, et al: Active mobility of the extremities in older subjects. Phys Ther 64:919, 1984.
25. Chaparro, A, et al: Range of motion of the wrist: Implications for designing computer input devices for the elderly. Disabil Rehabil 22:633:2000.
26. Kalscheur, JA, et al: Gender differences in range of motion in older adults. Phys Occup Ther Geriatr 22:77, 2003.
27. Hewitt, D: The range of active motion at the wrist of women. J Bone Joint Surg (Br) 26:775, 1928.
28. Allander, E, et al: Normal range of joint movements in shoulder, hip, wrist and thumb with special reference to side: A comparison between two populations. Int J Epidemiol 3:253, 1974.
29. Bell, RD, and Hoshizaki, TB: Relationships of age and sex with range of motion of seventeen joint actions in humans. Can J Appl Spt Sci 6:202, 1981.
30. Kalscheur, JA, et al: Range of motion in older women. Phys Occup Ther Geriatr 16:77, 1999.
31. Cobe, HM: The range of active motion of the wrist of white adults. J Bone Joint Surg (Br) 26:763, 1928.
32. Chang, DE, Buschbacher, LP, and Edlich, RF: Limited joint mobility in power lifters. Am J Sports Med 16:280, 1988.
33. Spilman, HW, and Pinkston, D: Relation of test positions to radial and ulnar deviation. Phys Ther 49:837, 1969.
34. Marshall, MM, Morzall, JR, and Shealy, JE: The effects of complex wrist and forearm posture on wrist range of motion. Human Factors 41:205, 1999.
35. Li, ZM, et al: Coupling between wrist flexion–extension and radial–ulnar deviation. Clin Biomech 20:177, 2005.
36. Brumfield, RH, and Champoux, JA: A biomechanical study of normal functional wrist motion. Clin Orthop 187:23, 1984.
37. Safaee-Rad, R, et al: Normal functional range of motion of upper limb joints during performance of three feeding tasks. Arch Phys Med Rehabil 71:505, 1990.
38. Cooper, JE, et al: Elbow joint restriction: Effect on functional upper limb motion during performance of three feeding tasks. Arch Phys Med Rehabil 74:805, 1993.
39. Palmer, AK, et al: Functional wrist motion: A biomechanical study. J Hand Surg 10A:39, 1985.
40. Nelson, DL: Functional wrist motion. Hand Clin 13:83, 1997.
41. Estill, CF, and Kroemer, KH: Evaluation of supermarket bagging using a wrist motion monitor. Hum Factors 40:624, 1998.
42. Marras, WS, et al: Quantification of wrist motion during scanning. Hum Factors 37:412, 1995.
43. Wagner, CH: The pianist's hand: Anthropometry and biomechanics. Ergonomics 31:97, 1988.
44. Marras, WS, and Schoenmarklin, RW: Wrist motions in industry. Ergonomics 36:341, 1995.
45. Veeger, DHEJ, et al: Wrist motion in handrim wheelchair propulsion. J Rehabil Res Dev 35:305, 1998.
46. Wei, S, et al: Wrist kinematic characterization of wheelchair propulsion in various seating positions: Implication to wrist pain. Clin Biomech 18:S46, 2003.
47. Ohinishi, N, et al: Analysis of wrist motion during basketball shooting. In Nakamura, RL, Linscheid, RL, and Miura, T (eds): Wrist Disorder: Current Concepts and Challenges. New York, Springer-Verlag, 1992.
48. Bernard, BP (ed): Musculoskeletal disorders and workplace factors. Cincinnati, Ohio: National Institute of Occupational Safety and Health. 1997.
49. Armstrong, TJ, et al: Ergonomic considerations in hand and wrist tendinitis. J Hand Surg 12A: 830, 1982.
50. Hellebrandt, FA, Duvall, EN, and Moore, ML: The measurement of joint motion. Part III: Reliability of goniometry. Phys Ther Rev 29:302, 1949.
51. Low, JL: The reliability of joint measurement. Physiotherapy 62:227, 1976.
52. Boone, DC, et al: Reliability of goniometric measurements. Phys Ther 58:1355, 1978.
53. Bird, HA, and Stowe, J: The wrist. Clin Rheum Dis 8:559, 1982.
54. Horger, MM: The reliability of goniometric measurements of active and passive wrist motions. Am J Occup Ther 44:342, 1990.
55. Flower, KR: Invited commentary. Phys Ther 74:174, 1994.
56. Bialocerkowski, AE, et al: A systematic review of the content and quality of wrist outcome instruments. Int J Qual Health Care 12:149, 2000.
57. Wagner, MB, et al: Assessment of hand function in Duchenne muscular dystrophy. Arch Phys Med Rehabil 74:801, 1993.
58. Tremayne, A, et al: Correlation of impairment and activity limitation after wrist fracture. Physiother Res Int 7:90, 2002.
59. MacDermid, JC, et al: Patient versus injury factors as predictors of pain and disability six months after a distal radius fracture. J Clin Epidemiol 55:849, 2002.
60. Karnezis, IA, and Fragkiadakis, EG: Objective clinical parameters and patient-rated wrist function. J Bone Joint Surg (Br) 85-B supplement I:7, 2003.
61. Karnezis, IA, and Fragkiadakis, EG: Association between objective clinical variables and patient-rated disability of the wrist. J Bone Joint Surg (Br) 84-B:967, 2002.

# The Hand

## ⚲ Structure and Function

### Fingers: Metacarpophalangeal Joints

#### Anatomy

The metacarpophalangeal (MCP) joints of the fingers are composed of the convex distal end of each metacarpal and the concave base of each proximal phalanx (Fig. 7.1). The joints are enclosed in fibrous capsules (Figs. 7.2 and 7.3). The anterior portion of each capsule has a fibrocartilaginous thickening called the palmar plate (palmar ligament), which is loosely attached to the metacarpals and firmly attached to the proximal phalanx.[1,2] Ligamentous support is provided by palmar, collateral, and deep transverse metacarpal ligaments.

#### Osteokinematics

The MCP joints are biaxial condyloid joints that have 2 degrees of freedom, allowing flexion–extension in the sagittal plane and abduction–adduction in the frontal plane. Abduction–adduction is possible with the MCP joints positioned in extension, but it is limited with the MCP joints in flexion because of tightening of the collateral ligaments.[2] A small amount of passive axial rotation has been reported at the MCP joints,[2-4] but this motion is not usually measured in the clinical setting.

#### Arthrokinematics

The concave base of the phalanx slides and rolls on the convex head of the metacarpal in the same direction as movement of the shaft of the phalanx.[5] During flexion the base of the phalanx slides and rolls anteriorly toward the palm, whereas during extension the base of the phalanx slides and rolls dorsally. In

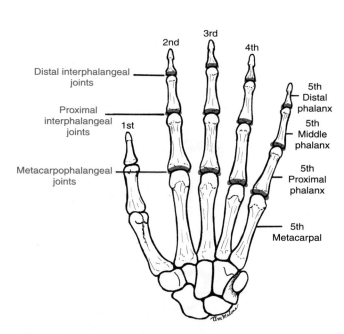

**FIGURE 7.1** An anterior (palmar) view of the hand showing metacarpophalangeal, proximal interphalangeal, and distal interphalangeal joints.

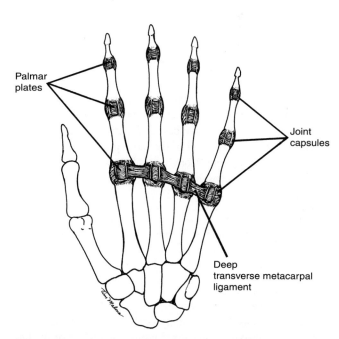

**FIGURE 7.2** An anterior (palmar) view of the hand showing joint capsules and palmar plates of the metacarpophalangeal, proximal interphalangeal, and distal interphalangeal joints and the deep transverse metacarpal ligament.

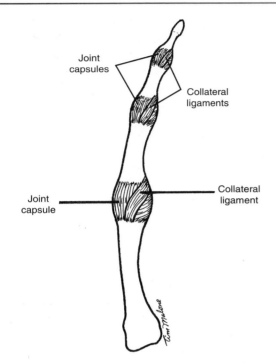

**FIGURE 7.3** A lateral view of a finger showing joint capsules and collateral ligaments of the metacarpophalangeal, proximal interphalangeal, and distal interphalangeal joints.

abduction, the base of the phalanx slides and rolls in the same direction as the movement of the finger.

## Capsular Pattern

Cyriax and Cyriax[6] report that the capsular pattern is an equal restriction of flexion and extension. Kaltenborn[7] notes that all motions are restricted with more limitation in flexion.

## Fingers: Proximal Interphalangeal and Distal Interphalangeal Joints

### Anatomy

The structure of both the proximal interphalangeal (PIP) and the distal interphalangeal (DIP) joints is very similar (see Fig. 7.1). Each phalanx has a concave base and a convex head. The joint surfaces comprise the head of the more proximal phalanx and the base of the adjacent, more distal phalanx. Each joint is supported by a joint capsule, a palmar plate, and two collateral ligaments (see Figs. 7.2 and 7.3).[1,2]

### Osteokinematics

The PIP and DIP joints of the fingers are classified as synovial hinge joints with 1 degree of freedom: flexion–extension in the sagittal plane.

### Arthrokinematics

Motion of the joint surfaces includes a sliding and rolling of the concave base of the more distal phalanx on the convex head of the proximal phalanx. Sliding and rolling of the base of the moving phalanx occurs in the same direction as the movement of the shaft.[5] For example, in PIP flexion the base of the middle phalanx slides and rolls toward the palm. In PIP

extension, the base of the middle phalanx slides and rolls toward the dorsum of the hand.

## Capsular Pattern

The capsular pattern is an equal restriction of both flexion and extension, according to Cyriax and Cyriax.[6] Kaltenborn[7] notes that all motions are restricted with more limitation in flexion.

## Thumb: Carpometacarpal Joint

### Anatomy

The carpometacarpal (CMC) joint of the thumb is the articulation between the trapezium and the base of the first metacarpal (Fig. 7.4). The saddle-shaped trapezium is concave in the sagittal plane and convex in the frontal plane (Fig. 7.5).[1,5] The base of the first metacarpal has a reciprocal shape that conforms to that of the trapezium, so that the base of the metacarpal is convex in the sagittal plane and concave in the frontal plane. The joint capsule is thick but lax and is reinforced by radial, ulnar, palmar, and dorsal ligaments (Fig. 7.6).[1,2]

### Osteokinematics

The first CMC joint is a saddle joint with 2 degrees of freedom: flexion–extension in the frontal plane parallel to the palm and abduction–adduction in the sagittal plane perpendicular to the palm.[1,5] These planes of movement for the CMC joint of the thumb are at right angles to the planes of movement of the fingers because the trapezium is anterior to the other carpals, effectively rotating the palmar surface of the thumb medially.[1,8] The laxity of the joint capsule also permits

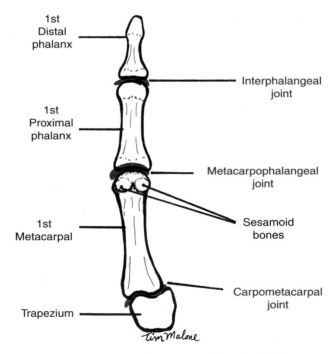

**FIGURE 7.4** An anterior (palmar) view of the thumb showing carpometacarpal, metacarpophalangeal, and interphalangeal joints.

**FIGURE 7.5** The saddle-shaped joint surface of the trapezium at the first carpometacarpal (CMC) joint is convex in the frontal plane (flexion–extension) and concave in the sagittal plane (abduction–adduction). The base of the metacarpal of the thumb has a shape that is reciprocal to that of the trapezium. Reproduced with permission from Levangie, PL, and Norkin, CC: Joint Structure and Function: A Comprehensive Analysis, ed 4. FA Davis, Philadelphia, 2005.

some axial rotation. This rotation allows the thumb to move into position for contact with the fingers during opposition. The sequence of motions that combines with rotation and results in opposition is as follows: abduction, flexion, medial axial rotation, and adduction.[1,5] Reposition returns the thumb to the starting position.

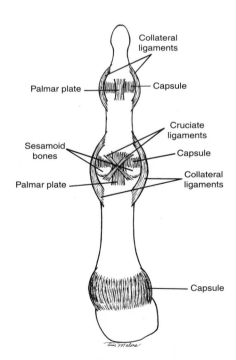

**FIGURE 7.6** An anterior (palmar) view of the thumb showing joint capsules, collateral ligaments, palmar plates, and cruciate (intersesamoid) ligaments.

### Arthrokinematics

The concave joint surface of the first metacarpal slides and rolls on the convex surface of the trapezium in the same direction as the metacarpal shaft to produce flexion–extension.[5,7] During flexion, the base of the metacarpal slides and rolls in an ulnar direction. During extension, it slides and rolls in a radial direction.

To produce abduction–adduction the convex joint surface of the first metacarpal slides on the concave portion of the trapezium in the opposite direction to the shaft of the metacarpal but rolls in the same direction as the shaft of the metacarpal.[5,7] Therefore, the base of the metacarpal slides toward the dorsal surface of the hand and rolls toward the palmar surface of the hand during abduction. The base of the first metacarpal slides toward the palmar surface of the hand and rolls toward the dorsal surface of the hand during adduction.

### Capsular Pattern

The capsular pattern is a limitation of abduction according to Cyriax and Cyriax.[6] Kaltenborn[7] reports limitations in abduction and extension.

## Thumb: Metacarpophalangeal Joint

### Anatomy

The metacarpophalangeal (MCP) joint of the thumb is the articulation between the convex head of the first metacarpal and the concave base of the first proximal phalanx (see Fig. 7.4). The joint is reinforced by a joint capsule, palmar plate, two sesamoid bones on the palmar surface, two intersesamoid ligaments (cruciate ligaments), and two collateral ligaments (see Fig. 7.6).[1]

### Osteokinematics

The MCP joint is a condyloid joint with 2 degrees of freedom.[1,8] The motions permitted are flexion–extension and a minimal amount of abduction–adduction. Motions at this joint are more restricted than at the MCP joints of the fingers.

### Arthrokinematics

At the MCP joint the concave base of the proximal phalanx slides and rolls on the convex head of the first metacarpal in the same direction as the shaft of the phalanx.[5,7] The base of the proximal phalanx moves toward the palmar surface of the thumb in flexion and toward the dorsal surface of the thumb in extension.

### Capsular Pattern

The capsular pattern for the MCP joint is a restriction of motion in all directions, but flexion is more limited than extension.[6,7]

## Thumb: Interphalangeal Joint

### Anatomy

The interphalangeal (IP) joint of the thumb is identical in structure to the IP joints of the fingers. The head of the proximal phalanx is convex, and the base of the distal phalanx is concave (see Fig. 7.4). The joint is supported by a joint capsule, a palmar plate, and two lateral collateral ligaments (see Fig. 7.6).

## Osteokinematics

The IP joint is a synovial hinge joint with 1 degree of freedom: flexion–extension.

## Arthrokinematics

At the IP joint the concave base of the distal phalanx slides and rolls on the convex head of the proximal phalanx, in the same direction as the shaft of the phalanx.[5,7] The base of the distal phalanx moves toward the palmar surface of the thumb in flexion and toward the dorsal surface of the thumb in extension.

## Capsular Pattern

The capsular pattern is an equal restriction in both flexion and extension according to Cyriax.[6] Kaltenborn[7] notes that all motions are restricted with more limitation in flexion.

# RANGE OF MOTION TESTING PROCEDURES:
## Fingers

Included in this section are common clinical techniques for measuring joint motions of the fingers and thumb. These techniques, which often place the goniometer on the dorsal surface of the digits, are appropriate for evaluating motions in the majority of people. Groth and Ehretsman found that dorsal placement of the goniometer was preferred by 73 percent of 231 surveyed therapists.[9] However, swelling and bony deformities sometimes require that the examiner either measure the MCP and IP joints from the lateral aspect or create alternative evaluation techniques. Photocopies, photographs, and tracings of the hand at the beginning and end of the range of motion (ROM) may be helpful.

 **Landmarks for Testing Procedures**

**FIGURE 7.7** Posterior view of the right hand showing surface anatomy landmarks for goniometer alignment during measurement of finger range of motion.

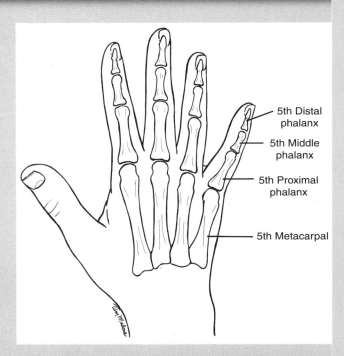

5th Distal phalanx

5th Middle phalanx

5th Proximal phalanx

5th Metacarpal

**FIGURE 7.8** Posterior view of the right hand showing bony anatomical landmarks for goniometer alignment during the measurement of finger range of motion. The index, middle, ring, and little fingers each have a metacarpal and a proximal, middle, and distal phalanx.

# ● FINGERS: METACARPOPHALANGEAL FLEXION

Motion occurs in the sagittal plane around a medial–lateral axis. Normal ROM values for adults are 90 degrees according to the American Association of Orthopaedic Surgeons (AAOS)[10] and the American Medical Association (AMA)[11] and 100 degrees according to Hume and coworkers.[12] MCP flexion appears to increase slightly in an ulnar direction from the index finger to the little finger. See Research Findings and Tables 7.1 and 7.2 for additional normal ROM values.

## Testing Position

Place the subject sitting, with the forearm and hand resting on a supporting surface. Place the forearm midway between pronation and supination, the wrist in 0 degrees of flexion, extension, and radial and ulnar deviation and the MCP joint in a neutral position relative to abduction and adduction. Avoid extreme flexion of the PIP and DIP joints of the finger being examined.

## Stabilization

Stabilize the metacarpal to prevent wrist motion. Do not hold the MCP joints of the other fingers in extension because tension in the transverse metacarpal ligament will restrict the motion.

## Testing Motion

Flex the MCP joint by pushing on the dorsal surface of the proximal phalanx, moving the finger toward the palm (Fig. 7.9). Maintain the MCP joint in a neutral position relative to abduction and adduction. The end of flexion ROM occurs when resistance to further motion is felt and attempts to overcome the resistance cause the wrist to flex.

## Normal End-Feel

The end-feel may be hard because of contact between the palmar aspect of the proximal phalanx and the metacarpal, or it may be firm because of tension in the dorsal joint capsule and the collateral ligaments.

## Goniometer Alignment

See Figures 7.10 and 7.11.

1. Center **fulcrum** of the goniometer over the dorsal aspect of the MCP joint.
2. Align **proximal arm** over the dorsal midline of the metacarpal.
3. Align **distal arm** over the dorsal midline of the proximal phalanx.

**FIGURE 7.9** During flexion of the metacarpophalangeal (MCP) joint, the examiner uses one hand to stabilize the subject's metacarpal and to maintain the wrist in a neutral position. The index finger and the thumb of the examiner's other hand grasp the subject's proximal phalanx to move it into flexion.

**FIGURE 7.10** The alignment of the goniometer at the beginning of metacarpophalangeal (MCP) flexion range of motion. In this photograph, the examiner is using a 6-inch plastic goniometer in which the arms have been trimmed to approximately 2 inches to make it easier to align over the small joints of the hand. Most examiners use goniometers with arms that are 6 inches or shorter when measuring ROM in the hand.

**FIGURE 7.11** At the end of metacarpophalangeal (MCP) flexion range of motion, the examiner uses one hand to hold the proximal goniometer arm in alignment and to stabilize the subject's metacarpal. The examiner's other hand maintains the proximal phalanx in MCP flexion and aligns the distal goniometer arm. Note that the goniometer arms make direct contact with the dorsal surfaces of the metacarpal and proximal phalanx, causing the fulcrum of the goniometer to lie somewhat distal and dorsal to the MCP joint.

# ● FINGERS: METACARPOPHALANGEAL EXTENSION

Motion occurs in the sagittal plane around a medial-lateral axis. Normal ROM values for adults are 20 degrees according to the AMA[11] and 45 degrees according to the AAOS.[10] Passive MCP extension ROM is greater than active extension. Mallon, Brown, and Nunley[13] report that extension ROM at the MCP joints is equal across all fingers, whereas Skvarilova and Plevkova[14] and Smahel and Klimova[15] note that the little finger has the greatest amount of MCP extension. See Research Findings and Tables 7.1 and 7.2 for additional normal ROM values.

## Testing Position

Position the subject sitting, with the forearm and hand resting on a supporting surface. Place the forearm midway between pronation and supination; the wrist in 0 degrees of flexion, extension, and radial and ulnar deviation; and the MCP joint in a neutral position relative to abduction and adduction. Avoid extension or extreme flexion of the PIP and DIP joints of the finger being tested. (If the PIP and DIP joints are positioned in extension, tension in the flexor digitorum superficialis and profundus muscles may restrict the motion. If the PIP and DIP joints are positioned in full flexion, tension in the lumbricalis and interossei muscles will restrict the motion.)

## Stabilization

Stabilize the metacarpal to prevent wrist motion. Do not hold the MCP joints of the other fingers in full flexion because tension in the transverse metacarpal ligament will restrict the motion.

## Testing Motion

Extend the MCP joint by pushing on the palmar surface of the proximal phalanx, moving the finger away from the palm (Fig. 7.12). Maintain the MCP joint in a neutral position relative to abduction and adduction. The end of extension ROM occurs when resistance to further motion is felt and attempts to overcome resistance cause the wrist to extend.

## Normal End-Feel

The end-feel is firm because of tension in the palmar joint capsule and in the palmar plate.

## Goniometer Alignment

See Figures 7.13 and 7.14 for alignment of the goniometer over the dorsal aspect of the fingers.

1. Center **fulcrum** of the goniometer over the dorsal aspect of the MCP joint.
2. Align **proximal arm** over the dorsal midline of the metacarpal.
3. Align **distal arm** over the dorsal midline of the proximal phalanx.

**FIGURE 7.12** During metacarpophalangeal (MCP) extension, the examiner uses her index finger and thumb to grasp the subject's proximal phalanx and to move the phalanx dorsally. The examiner's other hand maintains the subject's wrist in the neutral position, stabilizing the metacarpal.

**FIGURE 7.13** A full-circle, 6-inch plastic goniometer is being used to measure the beginning range of motion for metacarpophalangeal (MCP) extension. The proximal arm of the goniometer is slightly longer than necessary for optimal alignment. If a goniometer of the right size is not available, the examiner can cut the arms of a plastic model to a suitable length.

**FIGURE 7.14** The alignment of the goniometer at the end of metacarpophalangeal (MCP) extension. The body of the goniometer is aligned over the dorsal aspect of the MCP joint, whereas the goniometer arms are aligned over the dorsal aspect of the metacarpal and proximal phalanx.

## Alternative Goniometer Alignment: Palmar Aspect

See Figure 7.15 for alignment of the goniometer over the palmar aspect of the finger. This alignment should not be used if swelling or hypertrophy is present in the palm of the hand.

1. Center **fulcrum** of the goniometer over the palmar aspect of the MCP joint.
2. Align **proximal arm** over the palmar midline of the metacarpal.
3. Align **distal arm** over the palmar midline of the proximal phalanx.

**FIGURE 7.15** An alternative alignment of a finger goniometer over the palmar aspect of the proximal phalanx, the metacarpophalangeal joint, and the metacarpal. The shorter goniometer arm must be used over the palmar aspect of the proximal phalanx so that the proximal interphalangeal and distal interphalangeal joints are allowed to relax in flexion.

# ● FINGERS: METACARPOPHALANGEAL ABDUCTION

Motion occurs in the frontal plane around an anterior–posterior axis. No sources were found for normal abduction ROM values measured with a universal goniometer at the MCP joint. Some values have been reported for the maximal angles between adjacent fingers using tracings[15], and between fingers and the midline of the hand using a gravity-based goniometer.[16]

## Testing Position

Position the subject sitting, with the forearm and hand resting on a supporting surface. Place the wrist in 0 degrees of flexion, extension, and radial and ulnar deviation; the forearm in full pronation so that the palm of the hand faces the ground; and the MCP joint in 0 degrees of flexion and extension.

## Stabilization

Stabilize the metacarpal to prevent wrist motions.

## Testing Motion

Abduct the MCP joint by pushing on the medial surface of the proximal phalanx, moving the finger away from the midline of the hand (Fig. 7.16). Maintain the MCP joint in a neutral position relative to flexion and extension. The end of abduction ROM occurs when resistance to further motion is felt and attempts to overcome the resistance cause the wrist to move into radial or ulnar deviation.

## Normal End-Feel

The end-feel is firm because of tension in the collateral ligaments of the MCP joints, the fascia of the web space between the fingers, and the palmar interossei muscles.

## Goniometer Alignment

See Figures 7.17 and 7.18.

1. Center **fulcrum** of the goniometer over the dorsal aspect of the MCP joint.
2. Align **proximal arm** over the dorsal midline of the metacarpal.
3. Align **distal arm** over the dorsal midline of the proximal phalanx.

**FIGURE 7.16** During metacarpophalangeal (MCP) abduction, the examiner uses the index finger of one hand to press against the subject's metacarpal and prevent radial deviation at the wrist. With the other index finger and thumb holding the distal end of the proximal phalanx, the examiner moves the subject's second MCP joint into abduction.

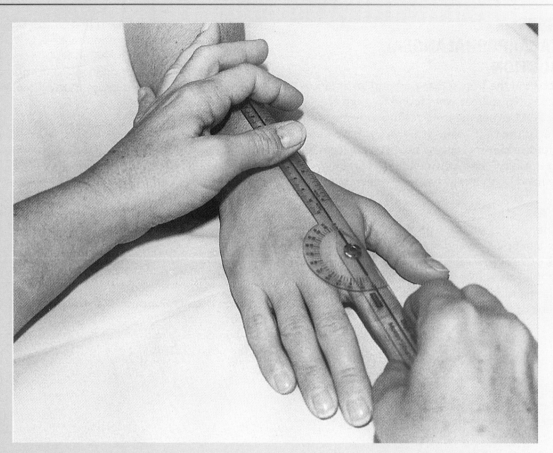

**FIGURE 7.17** The alignment of the goniometer at the beginning of metacarpophalangeal abduction range of motion.

**FIGURE 7.18** At the end of metacarpophalangeal (MCP) abduction, the examiner aligns the arms of the goniometer with the dorsal midline of the metacarpal and proximal phalanx rather than with the contour of the hand and finger.

# ● FINGERS: METACARPOPHALANGEAL ADDUCTION

Motion occurs in the frontal plane around an anterior–posterior axis. MCP adduction is not usually measured and recorded because it is the return from full abduction to the 0 starting position. There is very little adduction ROM beyond the 0 starting position. No sources were found for normal MCP adduction ROM values.

# ● FINGERS: PROXIMAL INTERPHALANGEAL FLEXION

Motion occurs in the sagittal plane around a medial–lateral axis. Normal ROM values for adults are 100 degrees according to the AAOS[10] and the AMA[11] and 105 degrees according to Hume and coworkers[12] and Mallon, Brown, and Nunley.[13] PIP flexion ROM is equal for all the fingers.[13] See Research Findings and Tables 7.1 and 7.2 for additional normal ROM values.

## Testing Position

Place the subject sitting, with the forearm and hand resting on a supporting surface. Position the forearm in 0 degrees of supination and pronation; the wrist in 0 degrees of flexion, extension, and radial and ulnar deviation; and the MCP joint in 0 degrees of flexion, extension, abduction, and adduction. (If the wrist and MCP joints are positioned in full flexion, tension in the extensor digitorum communis, extensor indicis, or extensor digiti minimi muscles will restrict the motion. If the MCP joint is positioned in full extension, tension in the lumbricalis and interossei muscles will restrict the motion.)

## Stabilization

Stabilize the proximal phalanx to prevent motion of the MCP joint.

## Testing Motion

Flex the PIP joint by pushing on the dorsal surface of the middle phalanx, moving the finger toward the palm (Fig. 7.19). The end of flexion ROM occurs when resistance to further motion is felt and attempts to overcome the resistance cause the MCP joint to flex.

## Normal End-Feel

Usually, the end-feel is hard because of contact between the palmar aspect of the middle phalanx and the proximal phalanx. In some individuals, the end-feel may be soft because of compression of soft tissue between the palmar aspect of the middle and proximal phalanges. In other individuals, the end-feel may be firm because of tension in the dorsal joint capsule and the collateral ligaments.

## Goniometer Alignment

See Figures 7.20 and 7.21.

1. Center **fulcrum** of the goniometer over the dorsal aspect of the PIP joint.
2. Align **proximal arm** over the dorsal midline of the proximal phalanx.
3. Align **distal arm** over the dorsal midline of the middle phalanx.

**FIGURE 7.19** During proximal interphalangeal (PIP) flexion, the examiner stabilizes the subject's proximal phalanx with her thumb and index finger. The examiner uses her other thumb and index finger to move the subject's PIP joint into full flexion.

**FIGURE 7.20** The alignment of the goniometer at the beginning of proximal interphalangeal (PIP) flexion range of motion.

**FIGURE 7.21** At the end of proximal interphalangeal (PIP) flexion, the examiner continues to stabilize and align the proximal goniometer arm over the dorsal midline of the proximal phalange with one hand. The examiner's other hand maintains the PIP joint in flexion and aligns the distal goniometer arm with the dorsal midline of the middle phalanx.

# ● FINGERS: PROXIMAL INTERPHALANGEAL EXTENSION

Motion occurs in the sagittal plane around a medial–lateral axis. PIP extension is usually recorded as the starting position for PIP flexion ROM. Normal ROM values for adults are 0 degrees according to the AAOS[10] and the AMA.[11] Mallon, Brown, and Nunley[13] report a mean of 7 degrees of active PIP extension and 16 degrees of passive PIP extension. PIP extension is generally equal for all fingers.[13] See Research Findings and Tables 7.1 and 7.2 for additional normal ROM values.

## Testing Position

Place the subject sitting, with the forearm and hand resting on a supporting surface. Position the forearm in 0 degrees of supination and pronation; the wrist in 0 degrees of flexion, extension, and radial and ulnar deviation; and the MCP joint in 0 degrees of flexion, extension, abduction, and adduction. (If the MCP joint and wrist are extended, tension in the flexor digitorum superficialis and profundus muscles will restrict the motion.)

## Stabilization

Stabilize the proximal phalanx to prevent motion of the MCP joint.

## Testing Motion

Extend the PIP joint by pushing on the palmar surface of the middle phalanx, moving the finger away from the palm. The end of extension ROM occurs when resistance to further motion is felt and attempts to overcome the resistance cause the MCP joint to extend.

## Normal End-Feel

The end-feel is firm because of tension in the palmar joint capsule and palmar plate (palmar ligament).

## Goniometer Alignment

1. Center **fulcrum** of the goniometer over the dorsal aspect of the PIP joint.
2. Align **proximal arm** over the dorsal midline of the proximal phalanx.
3. Align **distal arm** over the dorsal midline of the middle phalanx.

# FINGERS: DISTAL INTERPHALANGEAL FLEXION

Motion occurs in the sagittal plane around a medial–lateral axis. Normal ROM values for adults range from 70 degrees according to the AMA[11] to 90 degrees according to the AAOS.[10] Hume and coworkers[12] and Skvarilova and Plevkova[14] report a mean of 85 degrees of active DIP flexion. DIP flexion ROM is generally equal for all fingers.[13] See Research Findings and Tables 7.1 and 7.2 for additional normal ROM values.

## Testing Position

Position the subject sitting, with the forearm and hand resting on a supporting surface. Place the forearm in 0 degrees of supination and pronation; the wrist in 0 degrees of flexion, extension, and radial and ulnar deviation; and the MCP joint in 0 degrees of flexion, extension, abduction, and adduction. Place the PIP joint in approximately 70 to 90 degrees of flexion. (If the wrist and the MCP and PIP joints are fully flexed, tension in the extensor digitorum communis, extensor indicis, or extensor digiti minimi muscles may restrict DIP flexion. If the PIP joint is extended, tension in the oblique retinacular ligament may restrict DIP flexion.)

## Stabilization

Stabilize the middle and proximal phalanx to prevent further flexion of the PIP joint.

## Testing Motion

Flex the DIP joint by pushing on the dorsal surface of the distal phalanx, moving the finger toward the palm (Fig. 7.22). The end of flexion ROM occurs when resistance to further motion is felt and attempts to overcome the resistance cause the PIP joint to flex.

## Normal End-Feel

The end-feel is firm because of tension in the dorsal joint capsule, collateral ligaments, and oblique retinacular ligament.

## Goniometer Alignment

See Figures 7.23 to 7.25.

1. Center **fulcrum** of the goniometer over the dorsal aspect of the DIP joint.
2. Align **proximal arm** over the dorsal midline of the middle phalanx.
3. Align **distal arm** over the dorsal midline of the distal phalanx.

**FIGURE 7.22** During distal interphalangeal (DIP) flexion, the examiner uses one hand to stabilize the middle phalanx and keep the proximal interphalangeal joint in 70 to 90 degrees of flexion. The examiner's other hand pushes on the distal phalanx to flex the DIP joint.

**FIGURE 7.23** Measurement of the beginning of distal interphalangeal (DIP) flexion range of motion is being conducted by means of a half-circle plastic goniometer with 6-inch arms that have been trimmed to accommodate the small size of the DIP joint.

**FIGURE 7.24** The alignment of the goniometer at the end of distal interphalangeal (DIP) flexion range of motion. Note that the fulcrum of the goniometer lies distal and dorsal to the proximal interphalangeal joint axis so that the arms of the goniometer stay in direct contact with the dorsal surfaces of the middle and distal phalanges.

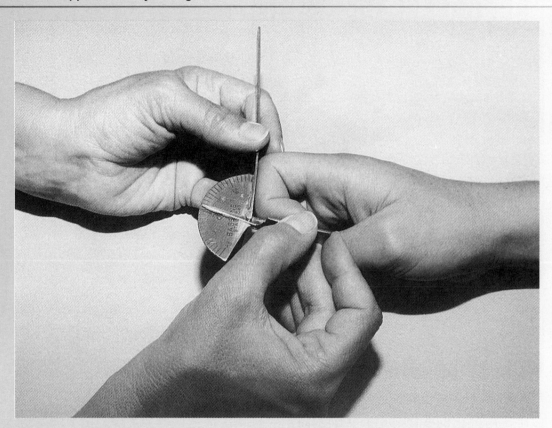

**FIGURE 7.25** Distal interphalangeal flexion range of motion also can be measured by using a finger goniometer that is placed on the dorsal surface of the middle and distal phalanges. This type of goniometer is appropriate for measuring the small joints of the fingers, thumb, and toes.

## ● FINGERS: DISTAL INTERPHALANGEAL EXTENSION

Motion occurs in the sagittal plane around a medial–lateral axis. DIP extension is usually recorded as the starting position for DIP flexion ROM. Most references, such as the AAOS[10] and the AMA,[11] report normal ROM values to be 0 degrees. However, Mallon, Brown, and Nunley[13] report a mean of 8 degrees of active DIP extension and 20 degrees of passive DIP extension. DIP extension ROM is generally equal for all fingers.[13] See Research Findings and Tables 7.1 and 7.2 for additional normal ROM values.

### Testing Position
Position the subject sitting, with the forearm and hand resting on a supporting surface. Place the forearm in 0 degrees of supination and pronation; the wrist in 0 degrees of flexion, extension, and radial and ulnar deviation; and the MCP joint in 0 degrees of flexion, extension, abduction, and adduction. Position the PIP joint in approximately 70 to 90 degrees of flexion. (If the PIP joint, MCP joint, and wrist are fully extended, tension in the flexor digitorum profundus muscle may restrict DIP extension.)

### Stabilization
Stabilize the middle and proximal phalanx to prevent extension of the PIP joint.

### Testing Motion
Extend the DIP joint by pushing on the palmar surface of the distal phalanx, moving the finger away from the palm. The end of extension ROM occurs when resistance to further motion is felt and attempts to overcome the resistance cause the PIP joint to extend.

### Normal End-Feel
The end-feel is firm because of tension in the palmar joint capsule and the palmar plate (palmar ligament).

### Goniometer Alignment
1. Center **fulcrum** of the goniometer over the dorsal aspect of the DIP joint.
2. Align **proximal arm** over the dorsal midline of the middle phalanx.
3. Align **distal arm** over the dorsal midline of the distal phalanx.

# ● FINGERS: COMPOSITE FLEXION OF THE MCP, PIP, AND DIP JOINTS

Composite finger flexion (CFF) is a simple method of quickly assessing multiple joints in a finger to indicate the functional ability to make a fist. However, a disadvantage of CFF is the inability to localize an impairment or response to treatment in a specific joint. Normally when the MCP, PIP, and DIP joints are maximally flexed, the distance between the fingertip and the distal palmar crease of the hand is zero. Ellis and Bruton[17] report that repeated CFF measurements fell within 5 to 6 mm 95 percent of the time when taken by the same tester and fell within 7 to 9 mm 95 percent of the time when taken by different testers.

## Testing Position

Place the subject sitting, with the forearm and hand resting on a supporting surface. Position the forearm in neutral supination and pronation and the wrist in 0 degrees of flexion, extension, and radial and ulnar deviation. Alternatively, the forearm could be positioned in full supination.

## Stabilization

Stabilize the metacarpals to prevent motion of the wrist.

## Testing Motion

Flex the MCP, PIP, and DIP joints by pushing on the dorsal surface of the finger, moving the finger toward the palm. The end of flexion ROM occurs when resistance to further motion is felt and attempts to overcome the resistance cause the wrist to flex.

## Normal End-Feel

Usually, the end-feel is soft because of contact between the palmar aspect of the proximal, middle, and distal phalanx and palm of the hand. In other individuals, the end-feel may be firm because of tension in the dorsal joint capsules and the collateral ligaments.

## Measurement Method

See Figures 7.26 and 7.27. Measure the perpendicular distance between the distal palmar crease and the tip of the finger.[18,19] Alternatively, the distance between the distal palmar crease and the distal corner of the nail bed on the radial border of the finger can be measured.[17]

**FIGURE 7.26** Composite finger flexion (CFF) is determined by measuring the distance between the distal palmar crease and the tip of the finger at the end of flexion of the MCP, PIP, and DIP joints. Normally, the tip of the finger is able to touch the palm at the distal palmar crease. This subject has limited range of motion.

# RANGE OF MOTION TESTING PROCEDURES: Thumb

## Landmarks for Testing Procedures

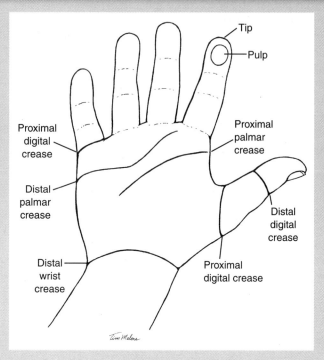

**FIGURE 7.27** A, B Anterior (palmar) view of the right hand showing the digital and palmar creases used for measuring composite finger flexion and CMC opposition of the thumb.

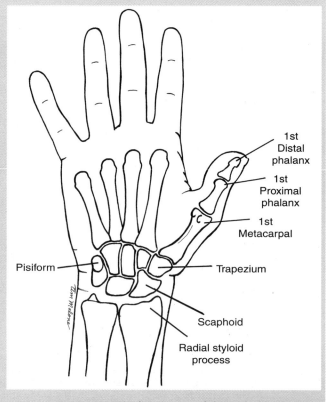

**FIGURE 7.28** Anterior (palmar) view of the right hand showing surface anatomy landmarks for goniometer alignment during the measurement of thumb range of motion.

**FIGURE 7.29** Anterior (palmar) view of the right hand showing bony anatomical landmarks for goniometer alignment during the measurement of thumb range of motion.

## Landmarks for Testing Procedures (continued)

**FIGURE 7.30** Posterior view of the right hand showing surface anatomy landmarks for goniometer alignment during the measurement of thumb range of motion.

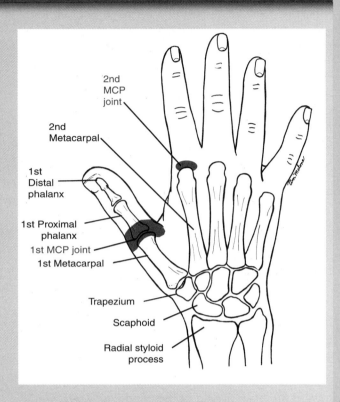

**FIGURE 7.31** Posterior view of the right hand showing bony anatomical landmarks for goniometer alignment during the measurement of thumb range of motion.

# THUMB: CARPOMETACARPAL FLEXION

Motion occurs in the plane of the hand. When the subject is in the anatomical position, the motion occurs in the frontal plane around an anterior–posterior axis. Normal ROM is 15 degrees according to the AAOS.[10]

## Testing Position

Position the subject sitting, with the forearm and hand resting on a supporting surface. Place the forearm in full supination; the wrist in 0 degrees of flexion, extension, and radial and ulnar deviation; and the CMC joint of the thumb in 0 degrees of abduction. The MCP and IP joints of the thumb are relaxed in a position of slight flexion. (If the MCP and IP joints of the thumb are positioned in full flexion, tension in the extensor pollicis longus and brevis muscles may restrict the motion.)

## Stabilization

Stabilize the carpals, radius, and ulna to prevent wrist motions. Movement of the wrist will affect the accuracy of the ROM measurement.

## Testing Motion

Flex the CMC joint of the thumb by pushing on the dorsal surface of the metacarpal, moving the thumb toward the ulnar aspect of the hand (Fig. 7.32). Maintain the CMC joint in 0 degrees of abduction.

The end of flexion ROM occurs when resistance to further motion is felt and attempts to overcome the resistance cause the wrist to deviate ulnarly.

## Normal End-Feel

The end-feel may be soft because of contact between muscle bulk of the thenar eminence and the palm of the hand, or it may be firm because of tension in the dorsal joint capsule and the extensor pollicis brevis and abductor pollicis brevis muscles.

## Goniometer Alignment

See Figures 7.33 and 7.34.

1. Center **fulcrum** of the goniometer over the palmar aspect of the first CMC joint.
2. Align **proximal arm** with the ventral midline of the radius using the ventral surface of the radial head and radial styloid process for reference.
3. Align **distal arm** with the ventral midline of the first metacarpal.

   In the beginning position for flexion and extension, the goniometer will indicate an angle of approximately 30 to 50 degrees rather than 0 degrees, depending on the shape of the hand and wrist position. The difference between the beginning-position degrees and the end-position degrees is the ROM. For example, a measurement that begins at 35 degrees and ends at 15 degrees should be recorded as 0 to 20 degrees.

**FIGURE 7.32** During carpometacarpal (CMC) flexion, the examiner uses the index finger and thumb of one hand to stabilize the carpals, radius, and ulna to prevent ulnar deviation of the wrist. The examiner's other index finger and thumb flex the CMC joint by moving the first metacarpal medially.

**FIGURE 7.33** The alignment of the goniometer at the beginning of carpometacarpal (CMC) flexion range of motion of the thumb. Note that the goniometer does not read 0 degrees.

**FIGURE 7.34** At the end of carpometacarpal (CMC) flexion range of motion, the examiner uses the hand that was stabilizing the wrist to align the proximal arm of the goniometer with the radius. The examiner's other hand maintains CMC flexion and aligns the distal arm of the goniometer with the first metacarpal. During the measurement, the examiner must be careful not to move the subject's wrist further into ulnar deviation or the goniometer reading will be incorrect (too high).

## Alternative Goniometer Alignment
See Figures 7.35 and 7.36.

1. Center **fulcrum** of the goniometer over the palmar aspect of the first CMC joint.
2. Align **proximal arm** with an imaginary line between the palmar surfaces of the trapezium and pisiform. This line is often parallel to the distal wrist crease (refer to Figure 7.27).
3. Align **distal arm** with the ventral midline of the first metacarpal.

This alternative alignment method avoids errors in ROM measurement due to inadvertent movement of the wrist. The goniometer in the beginning position will indicate an angle of approximately 40 to 70 degrees rather than 0 degrees, depending on the shape and size of the hand. The difference between the beginning-position degrees and the end-position degrees is the ROM.

**FIGURE 7.35** An alternative method of measuring the beginning of carpometacarpal (CMC) flexion aligns the proximal arm of the goniometer with the palmar surface of the trapezium and pisiform. Note that the goniometer does not read 0 degrees.

**FIGURE 7.36** An alternative method of aligning the goniometer to measure the end of carpometacarpal (CMC) flexion range of motion. The difference between the degrees on the goniometer at the beginning and the end positions is the range of motion.

# ● THUMB: CARPOMETACARPAL EXTENSION

Motion occurs in the plane of the hand. When the subject is in the anatomical position, the motion occurs in the frontal plane around an anterior–posterior axis. This motion is sometimes called radial abduction. Reported values for CMC thumb extension ROM are 35 degrees according to the AMA[11] (this is the difference between an angle of 15 degrees of separation between the first and second metacarpal at the beginning of the motion and an angle of 50 degrees at the end of the motion), and vary from 20 degrees to 80 degrees according to the AAOS.[10,18] However, the measurement methods used by the AAOS and the AMA appear to differ from the method suggested here.

## Testing Position

Position the subject sitting, with the forearm and hand resting on a supporting surface. Place the forearm in full supination; the wrist in 0 degrees of flexion, extension, and radial and ulnar deviation; and the CMC joint of the thumb in 0 degrees of abduction.

The MCP and IP joints of the thumb are relaxed in a position of slight flexion. (If the MCP and IP joints of the thumb are positioned in full extension, tension in the flexor pollicis longus muscle may restrict the motion.)

## Stabilization

Stabilize the carpals, radius, and ulna to prevent wrist motions.

## Testing Motion

Extend the CMC joint of the thumb by pushing on the palmar surface of the metacarpal, moving the thumb toward the radial aspect of the hand (Fig. 7.37). Maintain the CMC joint in 0 degrees of abduction. The end of extension ROM occurs when resistance to further motion is felt and attempts to overcome the resistance cause the wrist to deviate radially.

## Normal End-Feel

The end-feel is firm because of tension in the anterior joint capsule and the flexor pollicis brevis, adductor pollicis, opponens pollicis, and first dorsal interossei muscles.

**FIGURE 7.37** During carpometacarpal (CMC) extension of the thumb, the examiner uses one hand to stabilize the carpals, radius, and ulna thereby preventing radial deviation of the subject's wrist. The examiner's other hand is used to pull the first metacarpal laterally into extension.

## Goniometer Alignment
See Figures 7.38 and 7.39.

1. Center **fulcrum** of the goniometer over the palmar aspect of the first CMC joint.
2. Align **proximal arm** with the ventral midline of the radius, using the ventral surface of the radial head and the radial styloid process for reference.
3. Align **distal arm** with the ventral midline of the first metacarpal.

In the beginning positions for flexion and extension, the goniometer will indicate an angle of approximately 30 to 50 degrees rather than 0 degrees, depending on the shape of the hand and wrist position. The difference between the beginning-position degrees and the end-position degrees is the ROM. For example, a measurement that begins at 35 degrees and ends at 55 degrees should be recorded as 0 to 20 degrees.

**FIGURE 7.38** The goniometer alignment for measuring the beginning of carpometacarpal (CMC) extension range of motion is the same as for measuring the beginning of CMC flexion.

**FIGURE 7.39** The alignment of the goniometer at the end of carpometacarpal (CMC) extension range of motion of the thumb. The examiner must be careful to move only the CMC joint into extension and not to change the position of the wrist during the measurement.

## Alternative Goniometer Alignment
See Figures 7.40 and 7.41.

1. Center **fulcrum** of the goniometer over the palmar aspect of the first CMC joint.
2. Align **proximal arm** with an imaginary line between the palmar surface of the trapezium and pisiform. This line is often parallel to the distal wrist crease (refer to Figure 7.27).
3. Align **distal arm** with the ventral midline of the first metacarpal.

This alternative alignment method avoids errors in ROM measurement due to inadvertent movement of the wrist. The goniometer in the beginning position will indicate an angle of 40 to 70 degrees rather than 0 degrees, depending on the shape and size of the hand. The difference between the beginning and the end-position degrees is the ROM. For example, a measurement that begins at 50 degrees and ends at 30 degrees should be recorded as 0 to 20 degrees.

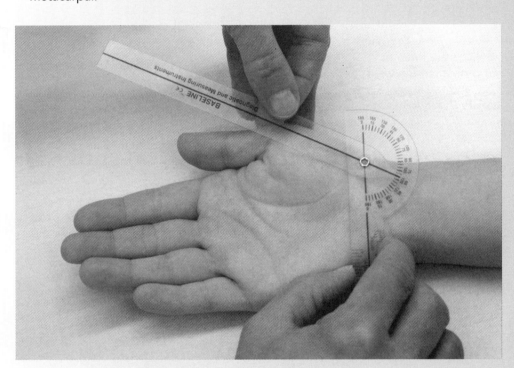

**FIGURE 7.40** The alternative method of measuring the beginning of CMC extension is the same as the alternative method for measuring the beginning of CMC flexion.

**FIGURE 7.41** The alternative method of aligning the goniometer to measure the end of CMC extension ROM.

## ● THUMB: CARPOMETACARPAL ABDUCTION

Motion occurs at a right angle to the palm of the hand. When the subject is in the anatomical position, the motion occurs in the sagittal plane around a medial–lateral axis. This motion is sometimes called palmar abduction. Abduction ROM is 70 degrees according to the AAOS[10,18]. However, the measurement method used by the AAOS appears to differ from the method suggested here.

### Testing Position
Position the subject sitting, with the forearm and hand resting on a supporting surface. Place the forearm midway between supination and pronation; the wrist in 0 degrees of flexion, extension, and radial and ulnar deviation; and the CMC, MCP, and IP joints of the thumb in 0 degrees of flexion and extension.

### Stabilization
Stabilize the carpals and the second metacarpal to prevent wrist motions.

### Testing Motion
Abduct the CMC joint by moving the metacarpal away from the palm of the hand (Fig. 7.42). The end of abduction ROM occurs when resistance to further motion is felt and attempts to overcome the resistance cause the wrist to flex.

### Normal End-Feel
The end-feel is firm because of tension in the fascia and the skin of the web space between the thumb and the index finger. Tension in the adductor pollicis and first dorsal interossei muscles also contributes to the firm end-feel.

### Goniometer Alignment
See Figures 7.43 and 7.44.

1. Center **fulcrum** of the goniometer over the lateral aspect of the radial styloid process.
2. Align **proximal arm** with the lateral midline of the second metacarpal, using the center of the second MCP joint for reference.
3. Align **distal arm** with the lateral midline of the first metacarpal, using the center of the first MCP joint for reference.

Note that the proximal surface of the first metacarpal contacts the trapezium, while the proximal surface of the second metacarpal contacts the trapezoid. Contact of the metacarpals with two

**FIGURE 7.42** During carpometacarpal (CMC) abduction, the examiner uses one hand to stabilize the subject's second metacarpal. Her other hand grasps the subject's first metacarpal just proximal to the metacarpophalangeal joint to move it away from the palm and into abduction.

different carpals and the palmar position of the trapezium relative to the trapezoid create difficulties in identifying a fulcrum and alignment for the arms of the goniometer in this motion. We have chosen the radial styloid process and the first and second

MCP joints as easily identifiable landmarks to indicate CMC abduction of the thumb. As the motion progresses toward the end of CMC abduction, these landmarks will be better aligned with the first and second metacarpals.

**FIGURE 7.43** At the beginning of carpometacarpal (CMC) abduction range of motion, the distal end of the subject's first metacarpal of the thumb lies over the second metacarpal of the index finger.

**FIGURE 7.44** The alignment of the goniometer at the end of carpometacarpal (CMC) abduction range of motion.

## ● THUMB: CARPOMETACARPAL ADDUCTION

Motion occurs at a right angle to the palm of the hand. When the subject is in the anatomical position, the motion occurs in the sagittal plane around a medial–lateral axis. Adduction of the CMC joint of the thumb is not usually measured and recorded separately because it is the return to the 0 starting position from full abduction.

## ● THUMB: CARPOMETACARPAL OPPOSITION

This motion is a combination of abduction, flexion, medial axial rotation (pronation), and adduction at the CMC joints of the thumb. Contact between the tip of the thumb and the base of the little finger (proximal digital crease) is usually possible at the end of opposition ROM, providing that some flexion at the MCP and IP joints of the thumb is allowed. If no flexion of the MCP and IP joints of the thumb is allowed, there will be a distance of several centimeters between the thumb and base of the little finger at the end of opposition. Many methods of measuring CMC opposition have been suggested.[10,11,18–21] It is important to note the landmarks that are being used and the amount of motion allowed at the MCP and IP joints of

the thumb so that there is consistency between repeated measurements on an individual.

### Testing Position

Position the subject sitting with the forearm and hand resting on a supporting surface. Place the forearm in full supination and the wrist in 0 degrees of flexion, extension, and radial and ulnar deviation.

### Stabilization

Stabilize the fifth metacarpal to prevent motion at the fifth CMC joint and wrist.

### Testing Motion

Grasp the first metacarpal and move it away from the palm of the hand (abduction) and then in an ulnar direction toward the base of the little finger (flexion and adduction), allowing the first metacarpal to medially rotate (Fig. 7.45). The end of opposition ROM occurs when contact is made between the tip of the thumb and the base of the little finger, if some flexion of the MCP and IP joints of the thumb is allowed (Fig. 7.46). If no flexion is allowed at the MCP and IP joints, the end of opposition will occur when resistance to further motion is felt and attempts to overcome the resistance cause the wrist to deviate or the forearm to pronate.

**FIGURE 7.45** Midway through the range of motion of carpometacarpal (CMC) opposition, the metacarpal of the thumb is in abduction, flexion, and medial rotation. The fifth metacarpal is stabilized by the examiner.

**FIGURE 7.46** At the end of the range of opposition the tip of the subject's thumb is normally in contact with the base of the little finger. The thumb has moved through carpometacarpal (CMC) abduction, flexion, medial rotation, and adduction, while the metacarpophalangeal (MCP) joint is allowed to flex.

## Normal End-Feel

The end-feel may be soft because of contact between the muscle bulk of the thenar eminence and the palm or between the tip of the thumb with the base of the little finger. In some individuals it may be firm because of tension in the CMC joint capsule, fascia, and skin of the web space between the thumb and the index finger and tension in the adductor pollicis, first dorsal interossei, extensor pollicis brevis, and extensor pollicis longus muscles.

## Measurement Method

The goniometer is not commonly used to measure the angular range of opposition. Instead, a ruler is often used to measure the shortest distance between the **tip of the thumb** and the center of the **proximal digital crease of the little finger** at the end of opposition (Fig. 7.47).[10,18]

Alternately, the shortest distance between the center of the **proximal digital crease of the thumb** and the **distal palmar crease directly over the fifth MCP joint** can be measured (Fig. 7.48). In this manner, motion at the MCP and IP joints of the thumb will not affect the measurement of opposition.

The AMA *Guides to the Evaluation of Permanent Impairment*[11] recommends measuring the longest distance from the **flexion crease of the thumb IP joint** to the **distal palmar crease directly over the third MCP joint** (Fig. 7.49). However, this measurement method seems more consistent with the measurement of CMC abduction. A distance of less than 8 cm is considered impaired.[11]

**FIGURE 7.47** The range of motion (ROM) in opposition can be determined by measuring the shortest distance between the tip of the thumb and the proximal digital crease of the little finger. The examiner is using the arm of a goniometer to measure, but any ruler would suffice. This subject's hand does not have full ROM in opposition.

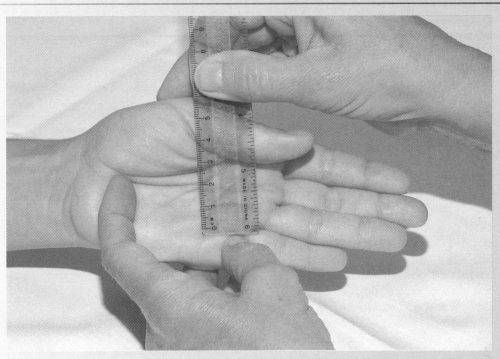

**FIGURE 7.48** Another method of measuring thumb opposition is to record the distance between the proximal digital crease of the thumb and the distal palmar crease over the fifth metacarpophalangeal (MCP) joint.

**FIGURE 7.49** In an alternative method of measuring thumb opposition proposed by the American Medical Association, the examiner uses a ruler to find the longest possible distance between the distal palmar crease directly over the metacarpophalangeal joint of the middle finger and the flexion crease of the thumb interphalangeal joint. (From Stanley, BG, and Tribuzi, SM: Concepts in Hand Rehabilitation. FA Davis, Philadelphia, 1992, p 546, with permission.)

# ● THUMB: METACARPOPHALANGEAL FLEXION

Motion occurs in the frontal plane around an anterior–posterior axis when the subject is in the anatomical position. Normal ROM values for adults are 50 degrees according to the AAOS,[10,18] 60 degrees according to the AMA,[11] and 55 degrees according to DeSmet and colleagues.[22] See Research Findings and Table 7.3 for additional normal ROM values.

## Testing Position
Position the subject sitting, with the forearm and hand resting on a supporting surface. Place the forearm in full supination; the wrist in 0 degrees of flexion, extension, and radial and ulnar deviation; the CMC joint of the thumb in 0 degrees of flexion, extension, abduction, adduction, and opposition; and the IP joint of the thumb in 0 degrees of flexion and extension. (If the wrist and IP joint of the thumb are positioned in full flexion, tension in the extensor pollicis longus muscle will restrict the motion.)

## Stabilization
Stabilize the first metacarpal to prevent wrist motion and flexion of the CMC joint of the thumb.

## Testing Motion
Flex the MCP joint by pushing on the dorsal aspect of the proximal phalanx, moving the thumb toward the ulnar aspect of the hand (Fig. 7.50). The end of flexion ROM occurs when resistance to further motion is felt and attempts to overcome the resistance cause the CMC joint to flex.

## Normal End-Feel
The end-feel may be hard because of contact between the palmar aspect of the proximal phalanx and the first metacarpal, or it may be firm because of tension in the dorsal joint capsule, the collateral ligaments, and the extensor pollicis brevis muscle.

## Goniometer Alignment
See Figures 7.51 and 7.52.

1. Center **fulcrum** of the goniometer over the dorsal aspect of the MCP joint.
2. Align **proximal arm** over the dorsal midline of the metacarpal.
3. Align **distal arm** with the dorsal midline of the proximal phalanx.

**FIGURE 7.50** During metacarpophalangeal (MCP) flexion of the thumb, the examiner uses the index finger and thumb of one hand to stabilize the subject's first metacarpal and maintain the wrist in a neutral position. The examiner's other index finger and thumb grasp the subject's proximal phalanx to move it into flexion.

**FIGURE 7.51** The alignment of the goniometer on the dorsal surfaces of the first metacarpal and proximal phalanx at the beginning of metacarpophalangeal (MCP) flexion range of motion of the thumb. If a bony deformity or swelling is present, the goniometer may be aligned with the lateral surface of these bones.

**FIGURE 7.52** At the end of metacarpophalangeal (MCP) flexion, the examiner uses one hand to stabilize the subject's first metacarpal and align the proximal arm of the goniometer. The examiner uses her other hand to maintain the proximal phalanx in flexion and align the distal arm of the goniometer.

# ● THUMB: METACARPOPHALANGEAL EXTENSION

Motion occurs in the frontal plane around an anterior–posterior axis when the subject is in the anatomical position. Normal extension ROM values are 0 degrees according to the AAOS,[10,18] 40 degrees according to the AMA,[11] and 14 degrees (actively) and 23 degrees (passively) according to Skvarilova and Plevkova.[14] See Research Findings and Table 7.3 for additional normal ROM values.

## Testing Position

Position the subject sitting, with the forearm and hand resting on a supporting surface. Place the forearm in full supination; the wrist in 0 degrees of flexion, extension, and radial and ulnar deviation; the CMC joint of the thumb in 0 degrees of flexion, extension, abduction, and opposition; and the IP joint of the thumb in 0 degrees of flexion and extension. (If the wrist and the IP joint of the thumb are positioned in full extension, tension in the flexor pollicis longus muscle may restrict the motion.)

## Stabilization

Stabilize the first metacarpal to prevent motion at the wrist and at the CMC joint of the thumb.

## Testing Motion

Extend the MCP joint by pushing on the palmar surface of the proximal phalanx, moving the thumb toward the radial aspect of the hand. The end of extension ROM occurs when resistance to further motion is felt and attempts to overcome the resistance cause the CMC joint to extend.

## Normal End-Feel

The end-feel is firm because of tension in the palmar joint capsule, palmar plate (palmar ligament), intersesamoid (cruciate) ligaments, and flexor pollicis brevis muscle.

## Goniometer Alignment

1. Center **fulcrum** of the goniometer over the dorsal aspect of the MCP joint.
2. Align **proximal arm** over the dorsal midline of the metacarpal.
3. Align **distal arm** with the dorsal midline of the proximal phalanx.

# • THUMB: INTERPHALANGEAL FLEXION

Motion occurs in the frontal plane around an anterior–posterior axis when the subject is in the anatomical position. Normal ROM values for adults are 67 degrees according to Jenkins and associates[23] and 80 degrees according to the AAOS,[10,18] AMA,[11] DeSmet and colleagues,[22] and Skvarilova and Plevkova.[14] See Research Findings and Table 7.3 for additional normal ROM values.

## Testing Position

Position the subject sitting, with the forearm and hand resting on a supporting surface. Place the forearm in full supination; the wrist in 0 degrees of flexion, extension, and radial and ulnar deviation; the CMC joint in 0 degrees of flexion, extension, abduction, and opposition; and the MCP joint of the thumb in 0 degrees of flexion and extension. (If the wrist and MCP joint of the thumb are flexed, tension in the extensor pollicis longus muscle may restrict the motion. If the MCP joint of the thumb is fully extended, tension in the abductor pollicis brevis and the oblique fibers of the adductor pollicis may restrict the motion through their insertion into the extensor mechanism.)

## Stabilization

Stabilize the proximal phalanx to prevent flexion or extension of the MCP joint.

## Testing Motion

Flex the IP joint by pushing on the dorsal surface of the distal phalanx, moving the tip of the thumb toward the ulnar aspect of the hand (Fig. 7.53). The end of flexion ROM occurs when resistance to further motion is felt and attempts to overcome the resistance cause the MCP joint to flex.

## Normal End-Feel

Usually, the end-feel is firm because of tension in the collateral ligaments and the dorsal joint capsule. In some individuals, the end-feel may be hard because of contact between the palmar aspect of the distal phalanx, the palmar plate, and the proximal phalanx.

**FIGURE 7.53** During interphalangeal (IP) flexion of the thumb, the examiner uses one hand to stabilize the proximal phalanx and keep the metacarpophalangeal joint in 0 degrees of flexion and the carpometacarpal joint in 0 degrees of flexion, abduction, and opposition. The examiner uses her other index finger and thumb to flex the distal phalanx.

## Goniometer Alignment
See Figures 7.54 and 7.55.

1. Center **fulcrum** of the goniometer over the dorsal surface of the IP joint.
2. Align **proximal arm** with the dorsal midline of the proximal phalanx.

3. Align **distal arm** with the dorsal midline of the distal phalanx.

**FIGURE 7.54** The alignment of the goniometer at the beginning of interphalangeal (IP) flexion range of motion. The arms of the goniometer are placed on the dorsal surfaces of the proximal and distal phalanges. However, the arms of the goniometer could instead be placed on the lateral surfaces of the proximal and distal phalanges if the nail protruded or if there was a bony prominence or swelling.

**FIGURE 7.55** The alignment of the goniometer at the end of interphalangeal (IP) flexion range of motion. The examiner holds the arms of the goniometer so that they maintain close contact with the dorsal surfaces of the proximal and distal phalanges.

# • THUMB: INTERPHALANGEAL EXTENSION

Motion occurs in the frontal plane around an anterior–posterior axis when the subject is in the anatomical position. Normal extension ROM at the IP joint of the thumb is 20 degrees according to the AAOS,[10] 30 degrees according to the AMA,[11] and 23 degrees (actively) and 35 degrees (passively) according to Skvarilova and Plevkova.[14] See Research Findings and Table 7.3 for additional normal ROM values.

## Testing Position

Position the subject sitting, with the forearm and hand resting on a supporting surface forearm. Place the forearm in full supination; the wrist in 0 degrees of flexion, extension, and radial and ulnar deviation; the CMC joint of the thumb in 0 degrees of flexion, extension, abduction, and opposition; and the MCP joint of the thumb in 0 degrees of flexion and extension. (If the wrist and MCP joint of the thumb are extended, tension in the flexor pollicis longus muscle may restrict the motion.)

## Stabilization

Stabilize the proximal phalanx to prevent extension or flexion of the MCP joint.

## Testing Motion

Extend the IP joint by pushing on the palmar surface of the distal phalanx, moving the thumb toward the radial aspect of the hand. The end of extension ROM occurs when resistance to further motion is felt and attempts to overcome the resistance cause the MCP joint to extend.

## Normal End-Feel

The end-feel is firm because of tension in the palmar joint capsule and the palmar plate (palmar ligament).

## Goniometer Alignment

1. Center **fulcrum** of the goniometer over the dorsal surface of the IP joint.
2. Align **proximal arm** with the dorsal midline of the proximal phalanx.
3. Align **distal arm** with the dorsal midline of the distal phalanx.

# MUSCLE LENGTH TESTING PROCEDURES: Fingers

## ● LUMBRICALS, PALMAR INTEROSSEI, AND DORSAL INTEROSSEI

The lumbrical, palmar interossei, and dorsal interossei muscles cross the MCP, PIP, and DIP joints. The first and second lumbricals originate proximally from the radial sides of the tendons of the flexor digitorum profundus of the index and middle fingers, respectively (Fig. 7.56). The third lumbrical originates on the ulnar side of the tendon of the flexor digitorum profundus of the middle finger and the radial side of the tendon of the ring finger. The fourth lumbrical originates on the ulnar side of the tendon of the flexor digitorum profundus of the ring finger and the radial side of the tendon of the little finger. Each lumbrical passes to the radial side of the corresponding finger and inserts distally into the extensor mechanism of the extensor digitorum profundus.

The first palmar **interossei muscle** originates proximally from the ulnar side of the metacarpal of the index finger and inserts distally into the ulnar side of the proximal phalanx and the extensor mechanism of the extensor digitorum profundus of the same finger (Fig. 7.57). The second and third palmar interossei muscles originate proximally from the radial sides of the metacarpal of the ring and little fingers, respectively, and insert distally into the ulnar side of the proximal phalanx and the extensor mechanism of the extensor digitorum profundus of the same fingers.

The four **dorsal interossei** are bipenniform muscles that originate proximally from two adjacent metacarpals (Fig. 7.58): the first dorsal interossei from the metacarpals of the thumb and index finger, the second from the metacarpals of the index and middle fingers, the third from the metacarpals of the middle and ring fingers, and the fourth from the metacarpals of the ring and little fingers. The dorsal interossei insert distally into the bases of the proximal phalanges and the extensor mechanism of the extensor digitorum profundus of the same fingers.

When these muscles contract, they flex the MCP joints and extend the PIP and DIP joints. These muscles are passively lengthened by placing the MCP joints in extension and the PIP and DIP joints in full flexion. If the lumbricals and the palmar and dorsal interossei are short, they will limit MCP extension when the PIP and DIP joints are positioned in full flexion.

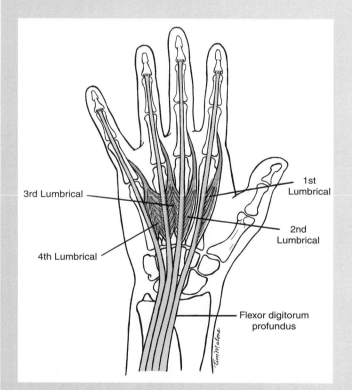

**FIGURE 7.56** An anterior (palmar) view of the right hand showing the proximal attachments of the lumbricals. The lumbricals insert distally into the extensor digitorum on the posterior surface of the hand.

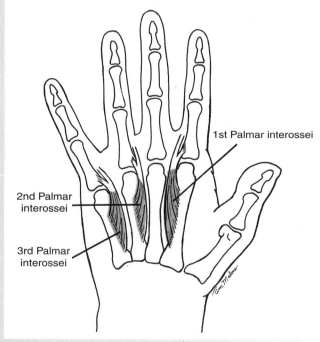

**FIGURE 7.57** An anterior (palmar) view of the right hand showing the proximal and distal attachments of the palmar interossei. The palmar interossei also attach distally to the extensor digitorum on the posterior surface of the hand.

If MCP flexion is limited regardless of the position of the PIP and DIP joints, the limitation is due to abnormalities of the joint surfaces of the MCP joint or shortening of the palmar joint capsule and the palmar plate.

## Starting Position
Position the subject sitting, with the forearm and hand resting on a supporting surface. Place the forearm midway between pronation and supination and the wrist in 0 degrees of flexion, extension, and radial and ulnar deviation. Flex the MCP, PIP, and DIP joints (Fig. 7.59). The MCP joints should be in a neutral position relative to abduction and adduction.

## Stabilization
Stabilize the metacarpals and the carpal bones to prevent wrist motion.

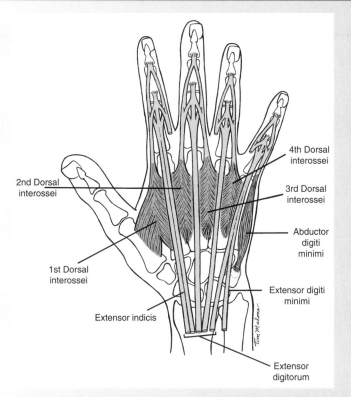

**FIGURE 7.58** A posterior view of the right hand showing the proximal attachments of the dorsal interossei on the metacarpals and the distal attachments into the extensor mechanism of the extensor digitorum, extensor indicis, and extensor digiti minimi muscles.

**FIGURE 7.59** The starting position for testing the length of the lumbricals and the palmar and dorsal interossei. The examiner uses one hand to stabilize the subject's wrist and the other hand to position the subject's metacarpophalangeal, proximal interphalangeal, and distal interphalangeal joints in full flexion.

## Testing Motion

Hold the PIP and DIP joints in full flexion while extending the MCP joint (Figs. 7.60 and 7.61). All of the fingers may be screened together, but if abnormalities are found, testing should be conducted on individual fingers. The end of flexion ROM occurs when resistance to further motion is felt and attempts to overcome the resistance cause the PIP, DIP, or wrist joints to extend.

## Normal End-Feel

The end-feel is firm because of tension in the lumbrical, palmar, and dorsal interossei muscles.

## Goniometer Alignment

See Figure 7.62.

1. Center **fulcrum** of the goniometer over the dorsal aspect of the MCP joint.
2. Align **proximal arm** over the dorsal midline of the metacarpal.
3. Align **distal arm** over the dorsal midline of the proximal phalanx.

**FIGURE 7.60** The end of the motion for testing the length of the lumbricals and the palmar and dorsal interossei. The examiner holds the subject's proximal interphalangeal and distal interphalangeal joints in full flexion while moving the metacarpophalangeal joint into extension.

1st Lumbrical

Extensor digitorum

1st Dorsal interossei

**FIGURE 7.61** A lateral view of the right hand showing the first lumbrical and the first dorsal interossei muscles being stretched over the metacarpophalangeal, proximal interphalangeal, and distal interphalangeal joints.

**FIGURE 7.62** The alignment of the goniometer at the end of testing the length of the lumbricals and the palmar and dorsal interossei muscles. The arms of the goniometer are placed on the dorsal midline of the metacarpal and proximal phalanx of the finger being tested.

# Research Findings

## Effects of Age, Gender, and Other Factors

Table 7.1 provides a summary of ROM values for the MCP, PIP, and DIP joints of the fingers. Certain trends are evident, although the values reported by the sources in Table 7.1 vary. The PIP joints, followed by the MCP and DIP joints, have the greatest amount of flexion. The MCP joints have the greatest amount of extension, whereas the PIP joints have the least amount of extension. Total active motion (TAM) is the sum of flexion and extension ROM of the MCP, PIP, and DIP joints of a digit. Normal TAM values range from 290 to 310 degrees for the fingers.

Mallon, Brown, and Nunley[13]; Skvarilova and Plevkova[14]; and Smahel and Klimova[15,24] also studied joint motion in individual fingers (Table 7.2). Some differences in ROM values are noted between the fingers. Flexion ROM at the MCP joints seems to increase linearly in an ulnar direction from the index finger to the little finger.[13–15] Mallon, Brown, and Nunley[13] report that extension at the MCP joints is approximately equal for all fingers. However, Skvarilova and Plevkova[14] and Smahel and Klimova[15] note that the little finger has the greatest amount of MCP extension. PIP flexion and extension and DIP flexion are generally equal for all fingers.[13] Some passive extension beyond neutral is possible at the DIP joints, with a minor increase in a radial direction from the little finger toward the index finger.[13]

Only the MCP joints of the fingers have a considerable amount of abduction–adduction. The amount of abduction–adduction varies with the position of the MCP joint. Abduction–adduction ROM is greatest in extension and least in full flexion. The collateral ligaments of the MCP joints are slack and allow full abduction in extension. However, the collateral ligaments tighten and restrict abduction in the fully flexed position.[1,3] Some authors note that the index and little fingers have a greater ROM in abduction–adduction than the middle and ring fingers,[1] whereas others report that the little finger has the greatest MCP abduction.[16]

Table 7.3 presents ROM values for the joints of the thumb. The greatest amount of flexion and extension ROM is reported at the IP joint.[10,11,14,18,22,23,25] Studies by Joseph[26] and Yoshida and coworkers[25] have identified two general anatomical shapes of the metacarpal head of the thumb. MCP joints with a round versus a flat metacarpal head had greater motion and may account for some of the variations seen in MCP values. Sauseng and coworkers[27] and Shaw and Morris[28] also present some normative data on MCP and IP flexion of the thumb. Very little data are available for normal values of motions at the CMC joint.

### Age

Goniometric studies focusing on the effects of age on ROM typically exclude the joints of the fingers and thumb. However, among the limited number of studies that examined aging effects in the hand there appears to be less finger and thumb ROM with increasing age. DeSmet and colleagues[22] found a significant correlation between decreasing MCP and IP flexion of

| TABLE 7.1 | | Active Finger Motion: Normal Values in Degrees from Selected Sources | | | | | |
|---|---|---|---|---|---|---|---|
| | | AAOS[10,18] | AMA[11] | Hume[12] | Mallon*[13] | Skvarilova†[14] | Smahel†[15,24] |
| | | | | 26–28 yrs n = 35 Males | 18–35 yrs n = 60 Males, 60 Females | 20–25 yrs n = 100 Males, 100 Females | 18–28 yrs n = 52 Males, 49 Females |
| Joint | Motion | | | Mean | Mean | Mean (SD) | Mean (SD) |
| MCP | Flexion | 90 | 90 | 100 | 95 | 91.0 (6.2) | 91.9 (8.0) |
| | Extension | 45 | 20 | 0 | 20 | 25.8 (6.7) | 24.8 (7.2) |
| PIP | Flexion | 100 | 100 | 105 | 105 | 107.9 (5.6) | 110.7 (5.3) |
| | Extension | 0 | 0 | 0 | 7 | — | — |
| DIP | Flexion | 90 | 70 | 85 | 68 | 84.5 (7.9) | 81.3 (7.0) |
| | Extension | 0 | 0 | 0 | 8 | — | — |
| Total active motion | | — | — | 290 | 303 | 309.2 (6.6) | 308.7 (6.8) |

AAOS = American Association of Orthopaedic Surgeons; AMA = American Medical Association; DIP = distal interphalangeal; MCP = metacarpophalangeal; PIP = proximal interphalangeal; SD = standard deviation.
* Values were averaged from both genders and all fingers.
† Values were averaged from both genders, both hands, and all fingers and were converted from a 360-degree to a 180-degree recording system.

| TABLE 7.2 | Individual Finger Motion: Mean Values in Degrees From Selected Sources |

| Finger | Joint | Motion | Mallon[13] Passive ROM 18–35 yrs | | Skvarilova*[14] Passive ROM 20–25 yrs | | Smahel*[15,24] Active ROM 18–28 yrs | |
| | | | Male n = 60 | Female n = 60 | Male n = 100 | Female n = 100 | Male n = 52 | Female n = 49 |
|---|---|---|---|---|---|---|---|---|
| Index | MCP | Flexion | 94 | 95 | 97 | 97 | 87 | 87 |
| | | Extension | 29 | 56 | 55 | 56 | 22 | 26 |
| | PIP | Flexion | 106 | 107 | 115 | 117 | 111 | 113 |
| | | Extension | 11 | 19 | — | — | — | — |
| | DIP | Flexion | 75 | 75 | 87 | 95 | 78 | 80 |
| | | Extension | 22 | 24 | — | — | — | — |
| Middle | MCP | Flexion | 98 | 100 | 102 | 104 | 95 | 94 |
| | | Extension | 34 | 54 | 48 | 48 | 20 | 24 |
| | PIP | Flexion | 110 | 112 | 115 | 118 | 111 | 114 |
| | | Extension | 10 | 20 | — | — | — | — |
| | DIP | Flexion | 80 | 79 | 87 | 98 | 84 | 83 |
| | | Extension | 19 | 23 | — | — | — | — |
| Ring | MCP | Flexion | 102 | 103 | 104 | 102 | 94 | 93 |
| | | Extension | 29 | 60 | 48 | 49 | 21 | 25 |
| | PIP | Flexion | 110 | 108 | 115 | 119 | 112 | 115 |
| | | Extension | 14 | 20 | — | — | — | — |
| | DIP | Flexion | 74 | 76 | 83 | 92 | 80 | 78 |
| | | Extension | 17 | 18 | — | — | — | — |
| Little | MCP | Flexion | 107 | 107 | 107 | 104 | 93 | 93 |
| | | Extension | 48 | 62 | 63 | 65 | 27 | 32 |
| | PIP | Flexion | 111 | 110 | 111 | 113 | 104 | 106 |
| | | Extension | 13 | 21 | — | — | — | — |
| | DIP | Flexion | 72 | 72 | 89 | 102 | 83 | 84 |
| | | Extension | 15 | 21 | — | — | — | — |

DIP = distal interphalangeal; MCP = metacarpophalangeal; PIP = proximal interphalangeal.
* Values were converted from a 360-degree to a 180-degree recording system.

the thumb and increasing age. The 58 females and 43 males who were included in the study ranged in age from 16 to 83 years. Smahel and Klimova,[15,24] in studies of 101 university students, 60 senior citizens, and 52 pianists, found that the senior citizens had significantly less MCP, PIP, and DIP ranges of motion in the fingers than the university students, except for total abduction (ability to spread fingers) of the MCP joints in females. The mean age differences were 6.3 degrees for active MCP flexion, 6.1 degrees for active MCP extension, 20.4 degrees for passive MCP extension, 9.1 degrees for active PIP flexion, and 9.5 degrees for active DIP flexion. The age differences in ROM were generally greater in males than in females.

Measures of hypermobility that include motions of the thumb and little finger have shown a decrease with age. Beighton, Solomon, and Soskolne[29] used passive apposition of the thumb (with wrist flexion) to the anterior aspect of the forearm and passive hyperextension of the MCP joint of the fifth finger beyond 90 degrees as indicators of hypermobility in a study of 456 men and 625 women in an African village. They found that joint laxity decreased with age. Lamari and coworkers,[30] in a study that included similar measures of hypermobility in the thumb/wrist and little finger of 1120 healthy Brazilian children between the ages of 4 to 7 years, found that lower hypermobility scores were associated with increasing age, even within this limited age range. Overall, 76 percent of the children were able to apposition the thumb to the forearm and 53 percent were able to hyperextend the MCP joint of the little finger beyond 90 degrees. Significant age differences were present in both genders for thumb apposition but only in boys for little finger hyperextension.

| TABLE 7.3 | Thumb Motion: Mean Values in Degrees from Selected Sources | | | | | | |
|---|---|---|---|---|---|---|---|

| | | AAOS[10,18] | AMA[11] | Jenkins[23] 16-72 yrs n = 50 Males, 69 Females | DeSmet[22] 16-83 yrs n = 43 Males, 58 Females | Yoshida[25] 18-63 yrs n = 51 Males, 49 Females | Skvarilova*[14] 20-25 yrs n=100 Males, 100 Females | |
|---|---|---|---|---|---|---|---|---|
| Joint | Motion | | | Active Mean (SD) | Mean (SD) | Active Mean (SD) | Active Mean (SD) | Passive Mean (SD) |
| CMC | Abduction | 70 | | | | | | |
| | Flexion | 15 | | | | | | |
| | Extension | 20, 80 | 35† | | | | | |
| MCP | Flexion | 50 | 60 | 59 (11) | 54.0 (13.7) | 77 | 57.0 (10.7) | 67.0 (9.0) |
| | Extension | 0 | 40 | | | 35 | 13.7 (10.5) | 22.6 (10.9) |
| IP | Flexion | 80 | 80 | 67 (11) | 79.8 (10.2) | 81 | 79.1 (8.7) | 85.8 (8.3) |
| | Extension | 20 | 30 | | | 33 | 23.2 (13.3) | 34.7 (13.3) |

CMC = carpometacarpal; IP = interphalangeal; MCP = metacarpophalangeal; SD = standard deviation.
* Values were recalculated to include both thumbs for both genders and were converted from a 360-degree to a 180-degree recording system.
† The AMA reports that in this plane of motion the minimal angle of separation between the first and second metacarpal is 15 degrees, whereas the maximal angle of separation between the first and second metacarpals is 50 degrees. The ROM value of 35 degrees is the difference between these two measurements.

One study by Allander and associates[31] found that active flexion and passive extension of the MCP joint of the thumb demonstrated no consistent pattern of age-related effects in a study of 517 women and 208 men (between 33 and 70 years of age). These authors stated that the typical reduction in mobility with age resulting from degenerative arthritis found in other joints may be exceeded by an accumulation of ligamentous ruptures that reduce the stability of the first MCP joint.

### Gender
Studies that examined the effect of gender on the ROM of the fingers reported varying results. Mallon, Brown, and Nunley[13] found no significant effect of gender on the amount of flexion in any joints of the fingers. However, in this study women generally had more extension at all joints of the fingers than men. Skvarilova and Plevkova[14] found that PIP flexion, DIP flexion, and MCP extension of the fingers were greater in women than in men, whereas MCP flexion of the fingers was greater in men. Smahel and Klimova[15] reported that MCP extension was significantly greater in women versus men in both groups of young and older adults, whereas no gender differences were noted in MCP flexion. In a study of PIP and DIP joint ROM of the fingers, Smahel and Klimova[24] found that women had greater PIP flexion than men, but they did not differ in DIP flexion (see Table 7.2).

Several studies have found no significant differences between males and females in the ROM of the thumb, whereas other studies have reported more mobility in females. Joseph[26] used radiographs to examine MCP and IP flexion ROM of the thumb in 90 males and 54 females; no significant differences were found between the two groups. He found two general shapes of MCP joints, round and flat, with the round MCP joints having greater range of flexion. Shaw and Morris[28] noted no differences in MCP and IP flexion ROM between 199 males and 149 females aged 16 to 86 years. Likewise, DeSmet and colleagues,[22] as well as Jenkins and associates,[23] found no differences in MCP and IP flexion of the thumb owing to gender.

Allander and associates[31] found that, in some age groups, females showed more mobility in the MCP joint of the thumb than their male counterparts. Skvarilova and Plevkova[14] noted that MCP flexion and extension of the thumb were greater in females, whereas gender differences were small and unimportant at the IP joint. Yoshida and associates,[25] in a study of 51 healthy men, 49 healthy women, and 70 cadavers, identified two general shapes of the metacarpal head: round and flat. The female gender was associated with greater MCP joint ROM and a higher prevalence of a round metacarpal head. No gender differences were noted in ROM at the IP joint. Beighton, Solomon, and Soskolne[29] in a study of 456 men and 625 women of an African village; Fairbank, Pynsett, and Phillips[32] in a study of 227 male and 219 female adolescents; and Lamari and coworkers[30] in a study of 1120 young Brazilian children measured passive apposition of the thumb toward the anterior surface of the forearm and hyperextension of the MCP joints of the fifth or middle fingers. All three studies reported an increase in laxity in females as compared with males.

### Right Versus Left Sides
The studies that have compared ROM in the right and left joints of the fingers have generally found no significant difference

between sides or only a small increase in motion on the left side. Mallon, Brown, and Nunley,[13] in a study in which half of the 120 subjects were right-handed and the other half left-handed, noted no difference between sides in finger motions at the MCP, PIP, and DIP joints. Skvarilova and Plevkova[14] reported only small right-left differences in the majority of the joints of the fingers and thumb in 200 subjects. Only MCP extension of the fingers and thumb and IP flexion of the thumb seemed to have greater ROM values on the left. Smahel and Klimova,[15,24] in studies of 101 university students, 60 senior citizens, and 52 pianists, found that in all three groups MCP joint ROM of the fingers was greater in the left hand. However, in most instances, ROM differences between the left and right hands were not significant for PIP and DIP joints of the fingers.

Similar to findings in studies of the fingers, most studies have reported no difference in ROM between the right and left thumbs. Joseph[26] and Shaw and Morris,[28] in a study of 144 and 248 subjects, respectively, found no significant difference between sides in MCP and IP flexion ROM of the thumb. DeSmet and colleagues[22] examined 101 healthy subjects and reported no difference between sides for the MCP and IP joints of the thumb. No difference between sides in IP flexion of the thumb was found by Jenkins and associates[23] in a study of 119 subjects. A statistically significant greater amount of MCP flexion was reported for the right thumb than for the left; however, this difference was only 2 degrees. Allander and associates[31] also found no differences attributed to side in MCP motions of the thumb in 720 subjects.

### Testing Position

Mallon, Brown, and Nunley,[13] in addition to establishing normative ROM values for the fingers, also studied passive joint ROM while positioning the next most proximal joint in maximal flexion and extension. The DIP joint had significantly more flexion (18 degrees) when the PIP joint was flexed than when the PIP joint was extended. This finding has been cited as an indication of abnormal tightness of the oblique retinacular ligament (Landsmeer's ligament).[33] However, the results of Mallon, Brown, and Nunley's study[13] suggest that this finding is normal. The MCP joint had about 6 degrees more flexion when the wrist was extended than when the wrist was flexed, although this difference was not statistically significant. The extensor digitorum, extensor indicis, and extensor digiti minimi were more slack to allow greater flexion of the MCP joint when the wrist was extended than when flexed. There was no effect on PIP motion with changes in MCP joint position.

Knutson and associates[34] examined eight subjects to study the effect of seven wrist positions on the torque required to passively move the MCP joint of the index finger. The findings indicated that in many wrist positions, extrinsic tissues (those that cross more than one joint) such as the extensor digitorum, extensor indicis, flexor digitorum superficialis, and flexor digitorum profundus muscles offered greater restraint to MCP flexion and extension than intrinsic tissues (those that cross only one joint). Intrinsic tissues offered greater resistance to passive moment at the MCP joint when the wrist was flexed or extended enough to slacken the extrinsic tissues.

## Functional Range of Motion

Joint motion, muscular strength and control, sensation, adequate finger length, and sufficient palm width and depth are necessary for a hand that is capable of performing functional, occupational, and recreational activities. Numerous classification systems and terms for describing functional hand patterns have been proposed.[23,35–38] Some common patterns include (1) finger-thumb prehension such as tip (Fig. 7.63), pulp, lateral, and three-point pinch (Fig. 7.64); (2) full-hand prehension, also called a power grip or cylindrical grip (Fig. 7.65); (3) nonprehension, which requires parts of the hand to be used as an extension of the upper extremity; and (4) bilateral prehension, which requires use of the palmar surfaces of both hands.[36] Texts by Stanley and Tribuzi,[39] Mackin and associates,[40] and the American Society of Hand Therapists[19] have reviewed many functional patterns and tests for the hand.

Table 7.4 summarizes the active ROM of the dominant fingers and thumb during 11 activities of daily living that

FIGURE 7.63 Picking up a coin is an example of finger–thumb prehension that requires use of the tips or pulps of the digits. In this photograph the pulp of the thumb and the tip of the index finger are being used.

FIGURE 7.64 Writing usually requires finger–thumb prehension in the form of a three-point pinch.

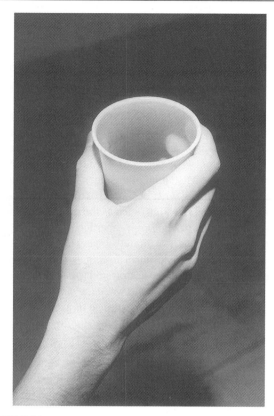

**FIGURE 7.65** Holding a cylinder such as a cup requires full-hand prehension (power grip). The amount of metacarpophalangeal and proximal interphalangeal flexion varies, depending on the diameter of the cylinder.

| TABLE 7.4 | Finger and Thumb Motions During 11 Functional Activities: Values in Degrees[12] | | |
|---|---|---|---|
| **Motion** | **Range** | **Mean** | **SD** |
| Finger MCP flexion | 33–73 | 61 | (12) |
| PIP flexion | 36–86 | 60 | (12) |
| IP flexion | 20–61 | 39 | (14) |
| Thumb MCP flexion | 10–32 | 21 | (5) |
| IP flexion | 2–43 | 18 | (5) |

IP = interphalangeal; MCP = metacarpophalangeal; PIP = proximalinterphalangeal; SD = standard deviation.
The 11 functional activities include holding a telephone, can, fork, scissors, toothbrush, and hammer; using a zipper and comb; turning a key; printing with a pen; and unscrewing a jar.

require various types of finger–thumb prehension or full-hand prehension. Hume and coworkers[12] used an electrogoniometer and a universal goniometer to study 35 right-handed men aged 26 to 28 years during performance of these 11 tasks. Of the tasks that were included, holding a soda can required the least amount of finger and thumb motion, whereas holding a toothbrush required the most motion.

Lee and Rim[41] examined the amount of motion required at the joints of the fingers to grip five different-size cylinders. Data were collected from four subjects by means of markers and multi-camera photogrammetry. As cylinder diameter decreased, the amount of flexion of the MCP and PIP joints increased. However, DIP joint flexion remained constant with all cylinder sizes.

Sperling and Jacobson-Sollerman[42] used movie film in their study of the grip pattern of 15 men and 15 women aged 19 to 56 years during serving, eating, and drinking activities. The use of different digits, types of grips, contact surfaces of the hand, and relative position of the digits was reported; however, ROM values were not included.

## Reliability

Several studies have been conducted to assess the reliability of goniometric measurements in the hand. Most studies found that ROM measurements of the fingers and thumb that were taken with universal goniometers and finger goniometers were highly reliable. Measurements taken over the dorsal surface of the digits appear to be similar to those taken laterally. Consistent with other regions of the body, measurements of finger and thumb ROM taken by one examiner are more reliable than measurements taken by several examiners. Research studies support the opinions of Bear-Lehman and Abreu[43] and Adams, Greene, and Topoozian,[19] which are that the margin of error is generally accepted to be 5 degrees for goniometric measurement of joints in the hand, provided that measurements are taken by the same examiner and that standardized techniques are employed.

Hamilton and Lachenbruch[44] had seven testers take measurements of MCP, PIP, and DIP flexion in one subject whose fingers were held in a fixed position. The daily measurements were taken for 4 days with three types of goniometers. These authors found intertester reliability was lower than intratester reliability. No significant differences existed between measurements taken with a dorsal (over-the-joint) finger goniometer, a universal goniometer, or a pendulum goniometer.

Groth and coworkers[45] had 39 therapists measure the PIP and DIP joints of the index and middle fingers of one patient, both dorsally and laterally, using either a 6-inch plastic universal goniometer or a DeVore metal finger goniometer. No significant difference in measurements was found between the two instruments. No differences were found between the dorsal and lateral measurement methods for seven of the eight joint motions, with mean differences ranging from 2 to 0 degrees. In a subset of six therapists, intertester reliability was high for both methods, with intraclass correlation coefficients (ICCs) ranging from 0.86 for lateral methods to 0.99 for dorsal methods.

Weiss and associates[46] compared measurements of index finger MCP, PIP, and DIP joint positions taken by a dorsal metal finger goniometer with those taken by the Exos Handmaster, a Hall-effect instrumented exoskeleton. Twelve subjects were measured with each device during one session by one examiner and again within 2 weeks of the initial session. Test-retest reliability was high for both devices, with ICCs ranging from 0.98 to 0.99. Mean differences between sessions for each instrument were statistically significant but less than 1 degree. Measurements taken by the finger goniometer and those taken by the Exos Handmaster were significantly different (mean difference = 7 degrees) but highly correlated (r = 0.89 to 0.94).

Ellis, Bruton, and Goddard[47] placed one subject in two splints while a total of 40 therapists measured the MCP, PIP, and DIP joints of the middle finger by means of a dorsal finger goniometer and a wire tracing. Each therapist measured each joint three times with each device. The goniometer consistently produced smaller ranges and smaller standard deviations than the wire tracing, indicating better reliability for the goniometer. The 95 percent confidence limit for the difference between measurements ranged from 3.8 to 9.9 degrees for the goniometer and 8.9 to 13.2 degrees for the wire tracing. Both methods had more variability when distal joints were measured, possibly because of the shorter levers used to align the goniometer or wire. Intratester reliability was always higher than intertester reliability.

Brown and colleagues[48] evaluated the ROM of the MCP, PIP, and DIP joints of two fingers in 30 patients to calculate total active motion (TAM) by means of the dorsal finger goniometer and the computerized Dexter Hand Evaluation and Treatment System. Three therapists measured each finger three times with each device during one session. Intratester and intertester reliability were high for both methods, with ICCs ranging from 0.97 to 0.99. The mean difference between methods ranged from 0.1 degrees to 2.4 degrees.

Goldsmith and Juzl[49] studied the intratester reliability of measuring active ROM of the MCP, PIP, and DIP joints of the fingers in 12 healthy subjects and intertester reliability in 12 patients with hand conditions. A universal goniometer adapted for measuring the hand (one short arm) was applied over the dorsal surface. The two therapists each took three measurements of flexion and extension at each joint in one session to assess intratester reliabilty and one measurement of flexion and extension at each involved joint in one session to assess intertester reliabilty. Both intratester and interester reliability were high with correlation coefficients greater than 0.99. When agreement was defined as within 3 degrees, the percent agreement was 93.9 to 94.6 percent for intratester reliability and 67.7 percent for interester reliability. When agreement was defined as within 5 degrees, the percent agreement was 99.7 percent to 100 percent for intratester reliability and 87.1 percent for intertester reliability.

Sauseng and coworkers[27] in a study of 50 patients with type 1 diabetes mellitus and 44 healthy controls, measured active ROM of the fifth MCP joint, first MCP joint, first IP joint, wrist, ankle, and first metatarsal phalangeal joint with a pocket goniometer. Each motion was measured three times by one tester. The coefficients of variation for the measurements were between 1.3 percent and 8.2 percent. The ROM of all tested joints was significantly lower in the diabetic versus the control group except for the first IP and MTP joints.

The distance between the fingertip pulp and distal palmar crease has been suggested as a simple and quick method of estimating total finger flexion ROM at the MCP, PIP, and DIP joints.[18,19] Ellis and Bruton[17] examined the intratester and intertester reliability of composite finger flexion (CFF) and compared it to dorsal goniometric measures of PIP flexion of the index, middle, and ring fingers. One hand was splinted in three positions and measured three times by 51 therapists at 18 hospital sites with a ruler and goniometer. Intratester goniometric measurements fell within 4 to 5 degrees of each other 95 percent of the time, whereas intertester goniometric measurements fell within 7 to 9 degrees of each other 95 percent of the time. CFF measures fell within 5 to 6 mm of each other 95 percent of the time for intratester measurements and within 7 to 9 mm of each other for intertester measurements. After scaling the two methods to allow comparison, the goniometer provided better reliability than CFF for measurements taken by the same tester, but both methods were equally reliable for measurements taken by different testers. The authors suggested that CFF may be a useful alternative when multiple joint measures are needed or when goniometry is impractical.

## Validity

Goniometric measurements of the fingers have been compared to radiographs, digital photographs, and disability measures in patient populations. In a study by Groth and coworkers,[45] active ROM of the PIP and DIP joints of the index and middle fingers of one patient who had sustained a crush injury with multiple fractures was measured by 39 therapists over a 3-day period. Measurements were made dorsally and laterally using either a DeVore metal finger goniometer or a 6-inch plastic universal goniometer. Prior to the goniometer measurements, radiographs were taken. In terms of concurrent validity, there were significant differences in measurements obtained from radiographs versus those from goniometers except for laterally measured index finger PIP extension and flexion. Differences between radiographic and mean goniometric measurements ranged from 1 to 2 degrees for laterally and dorsally measured index finger PIP motions to 14 degrees for laterally and dorsally measured middle finger PIP motions. The authors noted that concurrent validity was inconclusive because some of these differences may have been due to variations in the patient instructions for performing active motion, patient positioning, and patient fatigue with multiple active measurements.

Kato and coworkers[50] compared the accuracy of three therapists measuring PIP joint angles using three types of universal goniometers to lateral x-ray films in 16 fingers fixated with Kirschner wires from four cadavers. Each examiner used a 6-inch plastic goniometer with 6-inch arms, a plastic goniometer with a 3.5-inch and a 1-inch arm, and a metal goniometer with 1.5-inch arms to take measurements on the lateral and dorsal surfaces of the fingers. Intertester reliability was good with Pearson correlation coefficients ranging from 0.80 to 0.82. The mean angle discrepancies between the goniometers and x-rays ranged from 1.2 to 3.3 degrees (SD = 3.5 to 6.0 degrees) for the lateral method and from 0.5 to 2.9 degrees (SD = 3.5 to 6.4 degrees) for the dorsal method. There was no difference in angle discrepancies between types of goniometer using the lateral method. However, with two testers using the dorsal method the angle discrepancy was greater with the plastic goniometer with 6-inch arms, perhaps due to having longer arms than the other two goniometers.

In a study by Georgeu and associates,[51] one therapist measured full active flexion and extension of the MCP, PIP, and DIP joints of the little or ring finger in 20 patients. A digital camera, aligned with the MCP joint with the hand placed in a stabilizing device, was integrated with a computer to also determine ROM. There was a high correlation between the two methods ($r^2 = 0.975$). The photograph-computer method averaged 1 degree (95-percent confidence interval = 0 to 2 degrees, SD = 6 degrees) greater than the goniometer method but was not significantly different. The 95 percent level of agreement was –11 to 13 degrees.

Goodson and associates[52] measured ROM of the wrist, MCP and IP joints of the fingers with goniometers applied to the dorsal surface, pinch/grip strength, and pain and disability scoring (Cochin Scale) in 10 patients with rheumatoid arthritis, 10 patients with osteoarthritis, and 10 healthy control subjects. ROM and pinch/grip measurements were able to clearly discriminate between patient groups, which pain and disability scales were unable to do. Patients with rheumatoid arthritis had the greatest reduction in ROM of the MCP, followed by wrist and PIP joints. Patients with osteoarthritis had the greatest reduction in ROM at the DIP followed by the PIP joints. In the rheumatoid arthritis group, ROM of the MCP joints correlated with disability scores ($R^2 = 0.31$) and time since initial diagnosis ($R^2 = 0.32$). Wrist ROM was also related to time since diagnosis ($R^2 = 0.37$). The authors concluded that ROM and pinch/grip strength may more accurately reflect functional impairment associated with arthritis than pain and disability measures.

Field[53] studied 100 patients with Colles fractures of the wrist for the development of algodystrophy (complex regional pain syndrome). ROM of the PIP, DIP, and MCP joints of the fingers was measured at 1, 5, and 9 weeks on the dorsal surfaces with a finger goniometer and summed to generate a total ROM value for the hand. Pain response to pressure was assessed with a dolorimeter. Swelling was assessed using a water displacement method. Differences between the affected and unaffected hands were used in statistical tests. At 9 weeks postfracture, 24 patients were diagnosed with algodystrophy. Goniometry ROM measurements at 1 week showed a sensitivity of 96 percent and a specificity of 59 percent in predicting the development of algodystrophy. The cutoff for a positive test appeared to be about 70 degrees of ROM loss in the affected hand. The combination of dolorimetry and goniometry resulted in a sensitivity of 96 percent and improved specificity to 73 percent.

MacDermid and coworkers[54] studied the validity of using fingertip pulp-to-palm distance versus total finger flexion (also called composite finger flexion) to predict disability as measured by an upper-extremity disability score (Disabilities of the Arm, Shoulder, and Hand, or DASH). Active MCP, PIP, and DIP flexion of the most severely affected finger was measured in 50 patients by one examiner who used a dorsally placed electrogoniometer NK Hand Assessment System. A micrometer tool was used to measure pulp-to-palm distance in the same patients. The correlation between pulp-to-palm distance and total active flexion was –0.46 to –0.51, indicating that the measures were related but were not interchangeable. The relationship between DASH scores and total active flexion was stronger ($r = 0.45$) than the relationship between DASH scores and pulp-to-palm distances ($r = 0.21$ to $0.30$). The authors suggested that total active motion is a more functional measure than pulp-to-palm distance and that pulp-to-palm distance "should only be used to monitor individual patient progress and not to compare outcomes between patients or groups of patients."

# REFERENCES

1. Levangie, PL, and Norkin, CC: Joint Structure and Function: A Comprehensive Analysis, ed 4. FA Davis, Philadelphia, 2005.
2. Standring, S (ed): Gray's Anatomy, ed 39. Elsevier, New York, 2005.
3. Tubiana, R: Architecture and functions of the hand. In Tubiana, R, Thomine, JM, and Mackin, E (eds): Examination of the Hand and Upper Limb. WB Saunders, Philadelphia, 1984.
4. Krishnan, J, and Chipchase, L: Passive axial rotation of the metacarpophalangeal joint. J Hand Surg 22B:270, 2000.
5. Newmann, DA: Kinesiology of the Musculoskeletal System. Mosby, St. Louis, 2002.
6. Cyriax, JH, and Cyriax, PJ: Illustrated Manual of Orthopaedic Medicine. Butterworths, London, 1983.
7. Kaltenborn, FM: Manual Mobilization of the Joints: The Extremities, ed 5. Olaf Norlis Bokhandel, Oslo, Norway, 1999.
8. Ranney, D: The hand as a concept: Digital differences and their importance. Clin Anat 8:281, 1995.
9. Groth, GN, and Ehretsman, RL: Goniometry of the proximal and distal interphalangeal joints, part I: A survey of instrumentation and placement preferences. J Hand Ther 14:18, 2001.
10. American Academy of Orthopaedic Surgeons: Joint Motion: Methods of Measuring and Recording. AAOS, Chicago, 1965.
11. Cocchiarella, L, and Andersson, GBJ (eds): American Medical Association: Guides to the Evaluation of Permanent Impairment, ed 5. AMA Press, Chicago, 2001.
12. Hume, M, et al: Functional range of motion of the joints of the hand. J Hand Surg (Am) 15:240, 1990.
13. Mallon, WJ, Brown, HR, and Nunley, JA: Digital ranges of motion: Normal values in young adults. J Hand Surg (Am) 16:882, 1991.
14. Skvarilova, B, and Plevkova, A: Ranges of joint motion of the adult hand. Acta Chir Plast 38:67, 1996.
15. Smahel, Z, and Klimova, A: The influence of age and exercise on the mobility of hand joints: 1: Metacarpophalangeal joints of the three-phalangeal fingers. Acta Chirurgiae Plasticae 46:81, 2004.
16. Gurbuz, H, Mesut, R, and Turan, FN: Measurement of active abduction of metacarpophalangeal joints via electronic digital inclinometric technique. It J Anat Embryol 111:9, 2006.
17. Ellis, B, and Bruton, A: A study to compare the reliability of composite finger flexion with goniometry for measurement of range of motion in the hand. Clin Rehabil 16:562, 2002.
18. Greene, WB, and Heckman, JD (eds): The Clinical Measurement of Joint Motion. American Academy of Orthopaedic Surgeons, Rosemont, Ill., 1994.
19. Adams, LS, Greene, LW, and Topoozian, E: Range of motion. In American Society of Hand Therapists: Clinical Assessment Recommendations, ed 2. ASHT, Chicago, 1999.
20. Clarkson, HM: Joint Motion and Function Assessment. Lippincott Williams & Wilkins. Philadelphia, 2005.
21. Reese, NB, and Bandy, WD: Joint Range of Motion and Muscle Length Testing. WB Saunders, Philadelphia, 2002.
22. DeSmet, L, et al: Metacarpophalangeal and interphalangeal flexion of the thumb: Influence of sex and age, relation to ligamentous injury. Acta Orthop Belg 59:357, 1993.
23. Jenkins, M, et al: Thumb joint motion: What is normal? J Hand Surg (Br) 23:796, 1998.
24. Smahel, Z, and Klimova, A: The influence of age and exercise on the mobility of hand joints: 2: Interphalangeal joints of the three-phalangeal fingers. Acta Chirurgiae Plasticae 46:122, 2004.
25. Yoshida, R, et al: Motion and morphology of the thumb metacarpophalangeal joint. J Hand Surg 28A: 753, 2003.
26. Joseph, J: Further studies of the metacarpophalangeal and interphalangeal joints of the thumb. J Anat 85:221, 1951.
27. Sauseng, S, Kastenbauer, T, and Irsigler, K: Limited joint mobility in selected hand and foot joints in patients with type 1 diabetes mellitus: A methodology comparison. Diab Nutr Metab 15:1, 2002.
28. Shaw, SJ, and Morris, MA: The range of motion of the metacarpophalangeal joint of the thumb and its relationship to injury. J Hand Surg (Br) 17:164, 1992.
29. Beighton, P, Solomon, L, and Soskolne, CL: Articular mobility in an African population. Ann Rheum Dis 32:413, 1973.
30. Lamari, NM, Chueire, AG, and Cordeiro, JA: Analysis of joint mobility patterns among preschool children. Sao Paulo Med 123:119, 2005.
31. Allander, E, et al: Normal range of joint movements in shoulder, hip, wrist and thumb with special reference to side: A comparison between two populations. Int J Epidemiol 3:253, 1974.
32. Fairbank, JCT, Pynsett, PB, and Phillips, H: Quantitative measurements of joint mobility in adolescents. Ann Rheum Dis 43:288, 1984.
33. Nicholson, B: Clinical evaluation. In Stanley, BG, and Tribuzi, SM: Concepts in Hand Rehabilitation. FA Davis, Philadelphia, 1992.
34. Knutson, JS, et al: Intrinsic and extrinsic contributions to the passive moment at the metacarpophalangeal joint. J Biomech 33:1675, 2000.
35. Casanova, JS, and Grunert, BK: Adult prehension: Patterns and nomenclature for pinches. J Hand Ther 2:231, 1989.
36. Melvin, J: Rheumatic Disease: Occupation Therapy and Rehabilitation, ed 2. FA Davis, Philadelphia, 1982.
37. Swanson, AB: Evaluation of disabilities and record keeping. In Swanson, AB: Flexible Implant Resection Arthroplasty in the Hand and Extremities. CV Mosby, St Louis, 1973.
38. Napier, JR: Prehensile movements of the human hand. J Anat 89:564, 1955.
39. Totten, PA, and Flinn-Wagner, S: Functional evaluation of the hand. In Stanley, BG, and Tribuzi, SM (eds): Concepts in Hand Rehabilitation. FA Davis, Philadelphia, 1992.
40. Mackin, E, et al: Hunter, Mackin & Callahan's Rehabilitation of the Hand and Upper Extremity (ed 5). Elsevier, St Louis, 2002.
41. Lee, JW, and Rim, K: Measurement of finger joint angles and maximum finger forces during cylinder grip activity. J Biomed Eng 13:152, 1991.
42. Sperling, L, and Jacobson-Sollerman, C: The grip pattern of the healthy hand during eating. Scand J Rehabil Med 9:115, 1977.
43. Bear-Lehman, J, and Abreu, BC: Evaluating the hand: Issues in reliability and validity. Phys Ther 69:1025, 1989.
44. Hamilton, GF, and Lachenbruch, PA: Reliability of goniometers in assessing finger joint angle. Phys Ther 49:465, 1969.
45. Groth, G, et al: Goniometry of the proximal and distal interphalangeal joints. Part II: Placement preferences, interrater reliability, and concurrent validity. J Hand Ther 14:23, 2001.
46. Weiss, PL, et al: Using the Exos Handmaster to measure digital range of motion: Reliability and validity. Med Eng Phys 16:323, 1994.
47. Ellis, B, Bruton, A, and Goddard, JR: Joint angle measurement: A comparative study of the reliability of goniometry and wire tracing for the hand. Clin Rehabil 11:314, 1997.
48. Brown, A, et al: Validity and reliability of the Dexter Hand Evaluation and Therapy System in hand-injured patients. J Hand Ther 13:37, 2000.
49. Goldsmith, N, and Juzl, E: Inter-rater reliability of two trained raters using a goniometer for the measurement of finger joints. Br J Hand Ther 3:12, 1998.
50. Kato, M, et al: The accuracy of goniometric measurements of proximal interphalangeal joints in fresh cadavers: Comparison between methods of measurement, types of goniometers, and fingers. J Hand Ther 20:12, 2007.
51. Georgeu, GA, Mayfield, S, and Logan, AM: Lateral digital photography with computer-aided goniometry versus standard goniometry for recording finger joint angles. J Hand Surg 27B:184, 2002.
52. Goodson, A, et al: Direct, quantitative clinical assessment of hand function: Usefulness and reproducibility. Manual Ther 12:144, 2007.
53. Field, J: Measurement of finger stiffness in algodystrophy. Hand Clin 19:511, 2003.
54. MacDermid, JC, et al: Validity of pulp-to-palm distance as a measure of finger flexion. J Hand Surg 26B:432, 2001.

# LOWER-EXTREMITY TESTING

## OBJECTIVES

ON COMPLETION OF PART III, THE READER WILL BE ABLE TO:

### 1. Identify:

- Appropriate planes and axes for each lower-extremity joint motion
- Structures that limit the end of the range of motion
- Expected normal end-feels

### 2. Describe:

- Testing positions used for each lower-extremity joint motion and muscle length test
- Goniometer alignment
- Capsular pattern of limitation
- Range of motion necessary for selected functional activities at each major lower-extremity joint

### 3. Explain:

- How age, gender, and other variables may affect the range of motion
- How sources of error in measurement may affect testing results

### 4. Perform a goniometric measurement of any lower-extremity joint, including:

- A clear explanation of the testing procedure
- Proper positioning of the subject

- Adequate stabilization of the proximal joint component
- Use of appropriate testing motion
- Correct determination of the end of the range of motion
- Correct identification of the end-feel
- Palpation of the appropriate bony landmarks
- Accurate alignment of the goniometer and correct reading and recording of goniometric measurements

### 5. Plan goniometric measurements of the hip, knee, ankle, and foot that are organized by body position.

### 6. Assess the intratester and intertester reliability of goniometric measurements of the lower-extremity joints using methods described in Chapter 3.

### 7. Perform tests of muscle length at the hip, knee, and ankle, including:

- A clear explanation of the testing procedure
- Proper placement of the subject in the starting position
- Adequate stabilization
- Use of appropriate testing motion
- Correct identification of end-feel
- Accurate alignment of the goniometer and correct reading and recording

The testing positions, stabilization techniques, testing motions, end-feels, and goniometer alignment for the joints of the lower extremities are presented in Chapters 8 through 10. The goniometric evaluation should follow the 12-step sequence that was presented in Exercise 5 in Chapter 2.

# Chapter 8

# The Hip

## Structure and Function

### Iliofemoral Joint

#### Anatomy

The hip joint, or coxa, links the lower extremity with the trunk. The proximal joint surface is the acetabulum, which is formed superiorly by the ilium, posteroinferiorly by the ischium, and anteroinferiorly by the pubis (Fig. 8.1). The concave acetabulum faces laterally, inferiorly, and anteriorly and is deepened by a fibrocartilaginous acetabular labrum.[1] The distal joint surface is the convex head of the femur. The joint is enclosed by a strong, thick capsule, which is reinforced anteriorly by the iliofemoral and pubofemoral ligaments (Fig. 8.2) and posteriorly by the ischiofemoral ligament (Fig. 8.3).

#### Osteokinematics

The hip is a synovial ball-and-socket joint with 3 degrees of freedom. Motions permitted at the joint are flexion–extension in the sagittal plane around a medial–lateral axis, abduction–adduction in the frontal plane around an anterior–posterior axis, and medial and lateral rotation in the transverse plane around a vertical or longitudinal axis.[1] The axis of motion goes through the center of the femoral head.

#### Arthrokinematics

In an open kinematic (non–weight-bearing) chain, the convex femoral head rolls in the same direction and slides in the opposite direction, to movement of the shaft of the femur. In flexion, the femoral head rolls anteriorly and slides posteriorly and inferiorly on the acetabulum, whereas in extension, the femoral head rolls posteriorly and slides anteriorly and superiorly. In medial rotation, the femoral head rolls anteriorly

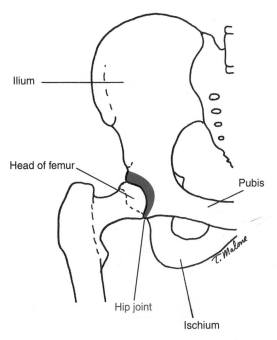

**FIGURE 8.1** An anterior view of the right hip joint.

**FIGURE 8.2** An anterior view of the right hip joint showing the iliofemoral and pubofemoral ligaments.

**FIGURE 8.3** A posterior view of the right hip joint showing the ischiofemoral ligament.

and slides posteriorly on the acetabulum. During lateral rotation, the femoral head rolls posteriorly and slides anteriorly. In abduction, the femoral head rolls superiorly and slides inferiorly, whereas in adduction, the femoral head rolls inferiorly and slides superiorly.

## Capsular Pattern

The capsular pattern is characterized by a marked restriction of medial rotation accompanied by limitations in flexion and abduction. A slight limitation may be present in extension, but no limitation is present in either lateral rotation or adduction.[2]

# RANGE OF MOTION TESTING PROCEDURES: Hip

## Landmarks for Testing Procedures

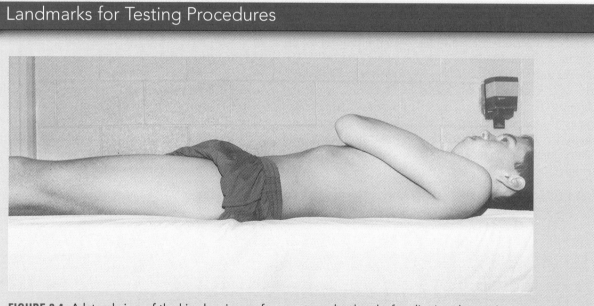

**FIGURE 8.4** A lateral view of the hip showing surface anatomy landmarks for aligning the goniometer for measuring hip flexion and extension.

**FIGURE 8.5** A lateral view of the hip showing bony anatomical landmarks for aligning the goniometer.

## Landmarks for Testing Procedures (continued)

**FIGURE 8.6** An anterior view of the hip showing surface anatomy landmarks for aligning the goniometer.

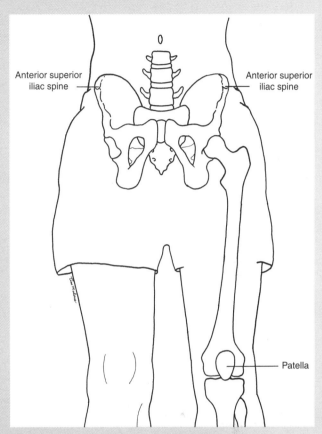

**FIGURE 8.7** An anterior view of the pelvis showing the anatomical landmarks for aligning the goniometer for measuring abduction and adduction.

# ● HIP FLEXION

Motion occurs in the sagittal plane around a medial–lateral axis. Hip flexion range of motion (ROM) for adults is 120 degrees according to the American Academy of Orthopaedic Surgeons (AAOS)[3] and 100 degrees according to the American Medical Association (AMA).[4] The mean ROM for males and females ranges from a mean of 122 degrees for ages 25 to 39 years to 118 degrees for ages 60 to 74 years according to Roach and Miles.[5] See Tables 8.1 to 8.4 in the Research Findings section for additional normal ROM values by age and gender.

## Testing Position

Place the subject in the supine position, with the knees extended and both hips in 0 degrees of abduction, adduction, and rotation.

## Stabilization

Stabilize the pelvis with one hand to prevent posterior tilting or rotation. Keep the contralateral lower extremity flat on the table in the neutral position to provide additional stabilization.

## Testing Motion

Flex the hip by lifting the thigh off the table. Allow the knee to flex passively during the motion to reduce tension in the hamstring muscles. Maintain the extremity in neutral rotation and abduction and adduction throughout the motion (Fig. 8.8). The end of the ROM occurs when resistance to further motion is felt and attempts at overcoming the resistance cause posterior tilting of the pelvis.

## Normal End-Feel

The end-feel is usually soft because of contact between the muscle bulk of the anterior thigh and the lower abdomen. However, the end-feel may be firm because of tension in the posterior joint capsule and the gluteus maximus muscle.

## Goniometer Alignment

See Figures 8.9 and 8.10.

1. Center **fulcrum** of the goniometer over the lateral aspect of the hip joint, using the greater trochanter of the femur for reference.
2. Align **proximal arm** with the lateral midline of the pelvis.
3. Align **distal arm** with the lateral midline of the femur, using the lateral epicondyle as a reference.

**FIGURE 8.8** The end of hip flexion passive ROM. The placement of the examiner's hand on the pelvis allows the examiner to stabilize the pelvis and to detect any pelvic motion.

**FIGURE 8.9** Goniometer alignment in the supine starting position for measuring hip flexion ROM.

**FIGURE 8.10** At the end of the left hip flexion ROM, the examiner uses one hand to align the distal goniometer arm and to maintain the hip in flexion. The examiner's other hand shifts from the pelvis to hold the proximal goniometer arm aligned with the lateral midline of the subject's pelvis.

# ● HIP EXTENSION

Motion occurs in a sagittal plane around a medial–lateral axis. Normal hip extension ROM is 30 degrees for adults according to the AMA[4] and 20 degrees according to the AAOS.[3] Normal hip extension ROM for adults ages 40 to 59 years is 18 degrees according to Roach and Miles.[5] See Tables 8.1 to 8.4 in the Research Findings section for additional normal ROM values by age and gender.

## Testing Position

Place the subject in the prone position, with both knees extended and the hip to be tested in 0 degrees of abduction, adduction, and rotation. A pillow may be placed under the abdomen for comfort, but no pillow should be placed under the head.

## Stabilization

Hold the pelvis with one hand to prevent an anterior tilt (an assistant could help stabilize the pelvis). Keep the contralateral extremity flat on the table to provide additional pelvic stabilization.

## Testing Motion

Extend the hip by raising the lower extremity from the table (Fig. 8.11). Maintain the knee in extension throughout the movement to ensure that tension in the two-joint rectus femoris muscle does not limit the hip extension ROM. The end of the ROM occurs when resistance to further motion of the femur is felt and attempts at overcoming the resistance cause anterior tilting of the pelvis and/or extension of the lumbar spine.

## Normal End-Feel

The end-feel is firm because of tension in the anterior joint capsule and the iliofemoral ligament and, to a lesser extent, the ischiofemoral and pubofemoral ligaments. Tension in various muscles that flex the hip, such as the iliopsoas, sartorius, tensor fasciae latae, gracilis, and adductor longus, may contribute to the firm end-feel.

## Goniometer Alignment

See Figures 8.12 and 8.13.

1. Center **fulcrum** of the goniometer over the lateral aspect of the hip joint, using the greater trochanter of the femur for reference.
2. Align **proximal arm** with the lateral midline of the pelvis.
3. Align **distal arm** with the lateral midline of the femur, using the lateral epicondyle as a reference.

**FIGURE 8.11** The subject's right lower extremity at the end of hip extension ROM. The examiner uses one hand to support the distal femur and maintain the hip in extension while her other hand grasps the pelvis at the level of the anterior superior iliac spine. Because the examiner's hand is on the subject's pelvis, the examiner is able to detect pelvic tilting.

**FIGURE 8.12** Goniometer alignmment in the prone starting position for measuring hip extension ROM.

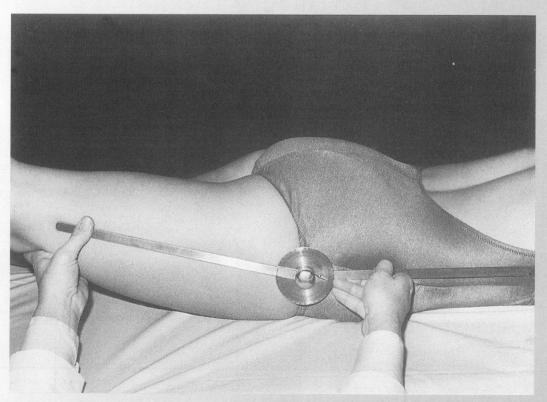

**FIGURE 8.13** At the end of hip extension ROM, the examiner uses one hand to hold the proximal goniometer arm in alignment. The examiner's other hand supports the subject's femur and keeps the distal goniometer arm in alignment.

# ● HIP ABDUCTION

Motion occurs in the frontal plane around an anterior–posterior axis. Normal ROM in abduction is 40 degrees according to the AMA[4] and 42 degrees for adult males and females ages 40 to 59 years according to Roach and Miles.[5] See Tables 8.1 to 8.5 in the Research Findings section for additional normal ROM values by age and gender.

## Testing Position

Place the subject in the supine position, with the knees extended and the hips in 0 degrees of flexion, extension, and rotation.

## Stabilization

Keep a hand on the pelvis to prevent lateral tilting and rotation. Watch the trunk for lateral trunk flexion.

## Testing Motion

Abduct the hip by sliding the lower extremity laterally (Fig. 8.14). Do not allow lateral rotation or flexion of the hip. The end of the ROM occurs when resistance to further motion of the femur is felt and attempts to overcome the resistance cause lateral pelvic tilting, pelvic rotation, or lateral flexion of the trunk.

## Normal End-Feel

The end-feel is firm because of tension in the inferior (medial) joint capsule, pubofemoral ligament, ischiofemoral ligament, and inferior band of the iliofemoral ligament. Passive tension in the adductor magnus, adductor longus, adductor brevis, pectineus, and gracilis muscles may contribute to the firm end-feel.

## Goniometer Alignment

See Figures 8.15 and 8.16.

1. Center **fulcrum** of the goniometer over the anterior superior iliac spine (ASIS) of the extremity being measured.
2. Align **proximal** arm with an imaginary horizontal line extending from one ASIS to the other.
3. Align **distal** arm with the anterior midline of the femur, using the midline of the patella for reference.

**FIGURE 8.14** The left lower extremity at the end of the hip abduction ROM. The examiner uses one hand to pull the subject's leg into abduction. (The examiner's grip on the ankle is designed to prevent lateral rotation of the hip.) The examiner's other hand not only stabilizes the pelvis but also is used to detect pelvic motion.

**FIGURE 8.15** In the starting position for measuring hip abduction ROM, the goniometer is at 90 degrees. This position is considered to be the 0-degree starting position. Therefore, the examiner must transpose her reading from 90 degrees to 0 degrees. For example, an actual reading of 90 to 120 degrees on the goniometer is recorded as 0 - 30 degrees.

**FIGURE 8.16** Goniometer alignment at the end of the abduction ROM. The examiner has determined the end-feel and has moved her right hand from stabilizing the pelvis to hold the goniometer in correct alignment.

## ● HIP ADDUCTION

Motion occurs in a frontal plane around an anterior–posterior axis. Normal adduction ROM for adults is 20 degrees according to the AMA.[4] See Tables 8.1 to 8.5 in the Research Findings section for additional normal ROM values by age and gender.

### Testing Position

Place the subject in the supine position, with both knees extended and the hip being tested in 0 degrees of flexion, extension, and rotation. Abduct the contralateral extremity to provide sufficient space to complete the full ROM in adduction.

### Stabilization

Stabilize the pelvis to prevent lateral tilting.

### Testing Motion

Adduct the hip by sliding the lower extremity medially toward the contralateral lower extremity (Fig. 8.17). Place one hand at the knee to move the extremity into adduction and to maintain the hip in neutral flexion and rotation. The end of the ROM occurs when resistance to further adduction is felt and attempts to overcome the resistance cause lateral pelvic tilting, pelvic rotation, and/or lateral trunk flexion.

**FIGURE 8.17** At the end of the hip adduction ROM, the examiner maintains the hip in adduction with one hand and stabilizes the pelvis with her other hand.

## Normal End-Feel

The end-feel is firm because of tension in the superior (lateral) joint capsule and the superior band of the iliofemoral ligament. Tension in the gluteus medius and minimus and the tensor fasciae latae muscles may also contribute to the firm end-feel.

## Goniometer Alignment

See Figures 8.18 and 8.19.

1. Center **fulcrum** of the goniometer over the ASIS of the extremity being measured.
2. Align **proximal arm** with an imaginary horizontal line extending from one ASIS to the other.
3. Align **distal arm** with the anterior midline of the femur, using the midline of the patella for reference.

**FIGURE 8.18** The alignment of the goniometer is at 90 degrees. Therefore, when the examiner records the measurement, she will have to transpose the reading so that 90 degrees is equivalent to 0 degrees. For example, an actual reading of 90 to 60 degrees is recorded as 0 - 30 degrees.

**FIGURE 8.19** At the end of the hip adduction ROM, the examiner uses one hand to hold the goniometer body over the subject's anterior superior iliac spine. The examiner prevents hip rotation by maintaining a firm grasp at the subject's knee with her other hand.

## ● HIP MEDIAL (INTERNAL) ROTATION

Motion occurs in a transverse plane around a vertical axis when the subject is in anatomical position. Normal medial rotation ROM for adults is 40 degrees according to the AMA[4] and 45 degrees according to the AAOS.[3] Normal medial rotation ROM for adults ages 40 to 59 years is 31 degrees according to Roach and Miles.[5] See Tables 8.1 to 8.5 in the Research Findings section for additional normal ROM values by age and gender.

### Testing Position

Seat the subject on a supporting surface, with the knees flexed to 90 degrees over the edge of the surface. Place the hip in 0 degrees of abduction and adduction and in 90 degrees of flexion. Place a towel roll under the distal end of the femur to maintain the femur in a horizontal plane.

### Stabilization

Stabilize the distal end of the femur to prevent abduction, adduction, or further flexion of the hip. Avoid rotations and lateral tilting of the pelvis.

### Testing Motion

Place one hand at the distal femur to provide stabilization, and use the other hand at the distal tibia to move the lower leg laterally. The hand performing the motion also holds the lower leg in a neutral position to prevent rotation at the knee joint (Fig. 8.20). The end of the ROM occurs when attempts at resistance are felt and attempts at further motion cause tilting of the pelvis or lateral flexion of the trunk.

**FIGURE 8.20** The left lower extremity at the end of the ROM of hip medial rotation. One of the examiner's hands is placed on the subject's distal femur to prevent hip flexion and abduction. Her other hand pulls the lower leg laterally.

**FIGURE 8.21** In the starting position for measuring hip medial rotation, the fulcrum of the goniometer is placed over the patella. Both arms of the instrument are together.

## Normal End-Feel

The end-feel is firm because of tension in the posterior joint capsule and the ischiofemoral ligament. Tension in the following muscles may also contribute to the firm end-feel: piriformis, obturatorii (internus and externus), gemelli (superior and inferior), quadratus femoris, gluteus medius (posterior fibers), and gluteus maximus.

## Goniometer Alignment

See Figures 8.21 and 8.22.

1. Center **fulcrum** of the goniometer over the anterior aspect of the patella.
2. Align **proximal arm** so that it is perpendicular to the floor or parallel to the supporting surface.
3. Align **distal arm** with the anterior midline of the lower leg, using the crest of the tibia and a point midway between the two malleoli for reference.

## Testing Position: Prone

Position subject prone with both legs extended. Flex the knee to 90 degrees in the leg to be tested. (The other leg should remain flat on the table with the knee extended.) Place a strap across the pelvis for stabilization. Goniometer alignment is the same as in the sitting position (Fig. 8.23). Note: This position should only be used if the rectus femoris is of normal length.

**FIGURE 8.22** At the end of hip medial rotation ROM, the proximal arm of the goniometer hangs freely so that it is perpendicular to the floor.

**FIGURE 8.23** Hip medial rotation in the prone testing position with the goniometer aligned at the end of the motion. Note that a strap is placed across the pelvis for stabilization.

# ● HIP LATERAL (EXTERNAL) ROTATION

Motion occurs in a transverse plane around a longitudinal axis when the subject is in anatomical position. Normal lateral rotation ROM for adults is 50 degrees according to the AMA[4] and 45 degrees according to the AAOS.[3] The normal ROM value for lateral rotation for adults ages 40 to 59 years is 32 degrees according to Roach and Miles.[5] See Tables 8.1 to 8.5 for additional normal ROM values by age and gender.

## Testing Position

Seat the subject on a supporting surface with knees flexed to 90 degrees over the edge of the surface. Place the hip in 0 degrees of abduction and adduction and in 90 degrees of flexion. Flex the contralateral knee beyond 90 degrees to allow the hip being measured to complete its full range of lateral rotation.

## Stabilization

Stabilize the distal end of the femur to prevent abduction or further flexion of the hip. Avoid rotation and lateral tilting of the pelvis.

## Testing Motion

Place one hand at the distal femur to provide stabilization, and place the other hand on the distal fibula to move the lower leg medially (Fig. 8.24). The hand on the fibula also prevents rotation at the knee joint. The end of the motion occurs when resistance is felt and attempts at overcoming the resistance cause tilting of the pelvis or trunk lateral flexion.

**FIGURE 8.24** The left lower extremity is at the end of the ROM of hip lateral rotation. The examiner places one hand on the subject's distal femur to prevent hip flexion and hip abduction. The subject assists with stabilization by placing her hands on the supporting surface and shifting her weight over her left hip. The subject flexes her right knee to allow the left lower extremity to complete the ROM.

**FIGURE 8.25** Goniometer alignment in the starting position for measuring hip lateral rotation.

## Normal End-Feel

The end-feel is firm because of tension in the anterior joint capsule, iliofemoral ligament, and pubofemoral ligament. Tension in the anterior portion of the gluteus medius, gluteus minimus, adductor magnus, adductor longus, pectineus, and piriformis muscles also may contribute to the firm end-feel.

## Goniometer Alignment

See Figures 8.25 and 8.26.

1. Center **fulcrum** of the goniometer over the anterior aspect of the patella.
2. Align **proximal arm** so that it is perpendicular to the floor or parallel to the supporting surface.
3. Align **distal arm** with the anterior midline of the lower leg, using the crest of the tibia and a point midway between the two malleoli for reference.

## Testing Position: Prone

Position the subject prone with both legs extended. Flex the knee to 90 degrees in the leg to be tested. (The other leg should remain flat on the table with the knee extended.) Place a strap across the pelvis for stabilization. Goniometer alignment is the same as in the sitting position (Fig. 8.27). Note: This position should be used only if the rectus femoris is of normal length.

**FIGURE 8.26** At the end of hip lateral rotation ROM the examiner uses one hand to support the subject's leg and to maintain alignment of the distal goniometer arm.

**FIGURE 8.27** Hip lateral rotation in the prone testing position with the goniometer aligned at the end of the motion. Note that a strap is placed across the pelvis for stabilization.

# MUSCLE LENGTH TESTING PROCEDURES: Hip

## ● HIP FLEXORS: THOMAS TEST

The iliacus and psoas major muscles flex the hip in the sagittal plane of motion. The rectus femoris flexes the hip in the sagittal plane but also extends the knee. Other muscles, because of their attachments, create hip flexion in combination with other motions. The sartorius flexes, abducts, and laterally rotates the hip while flexing the knee. The tensor fascia lata abducts, flexes, and medially rotates the hip and extends the knee. Several muscles that primarily adduct the hip, such as the pectineus, adductor longus, and adductor brevis, also lie anterior to the axis of the hip joint and can contribute to hip flexion. Short muscles that flex the hip limit hip extension ROM. Hip extension can also be limited by abnormalities of the joint surfaces, shortness of the anterior joint capsule, and short iliofemoral and ischiofemoral ligaments.

The anatomy of the major muscles that flex the hip is illustrated in Figure 8.28A and B. The **iliacus** originates proximally from the upper two thirds of the iliac fossa, the inner lip of the iliac crest, the lateral aspect (ala) of the sacrum, and the sacroiliac and iliolumbar ligaments. It inserts distally on the lesser trochanter of the femur. The **psoas major** originates proximally from the sides of the vertebral bodies and intervertebral discs of T12-L5 and the transverse processes of L1-L5. It inserts distally on the lesser trochanter of the femur. These two muscles are commonly referred to as the **iliopsoas**. If the iliopsoas is short, it limits hip extension without pulling the hip in another direction of motion; the thigh remains in the sagittal plane. Knee position does not affect the length of the iliopsoas muscle.

The **rectus femoris** arises proximally from two tendons: the anterior tendon from the anterior inferior iliac spine and the posterior tendon from a groove superior to the brim of the acetabulum (see Fig. 8.28B). It inserts distally into the base of the patella and into the tibial tuberosity via the patellar ligament. A short rectus femoris limits hip extension and knee flexion. If the rectus femoris is short and hip extension is attempted, the knee passively moves into extension to accommodate the shortened muscle. Sometimes, when the rectus femoris is shortened and hip extension is attempted, the knee remains flexed but hip extension is limited.

The **sartorius** (see Fig. 8.28A) arises proximally from the ASIS and the upper aspect of the iliac notch. It inserts distally into the proximal aspect of the medial tibia. If the sartorius is short, it limits hip extension, hip adduction, and knee extension. If the sartorius is short and hip extension is attempted, the hip passively moves into hip abduction and knee flexion to accommodate the short muscle.

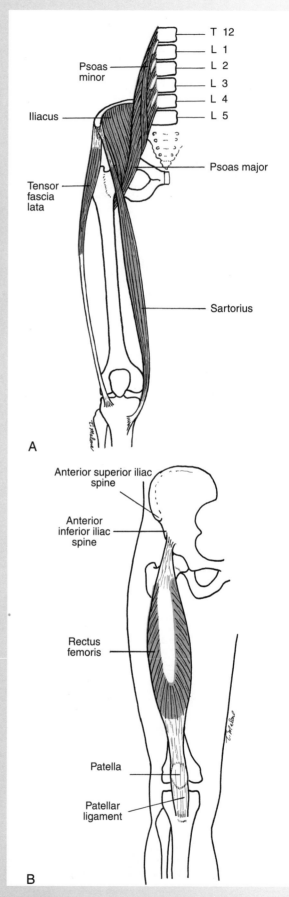

**FIGURE 8.28** An anterior view of the hip flexor muscles.

The **tensor fascia lata (TFL)** arises proximally from the anterior aspect of the outer lip of the iliac crest and the lateral surface of the ASIS and iliac notch (see Fig. 8.28A). It inserts distally into the iliotibial band of the fascia lata about one-third of the distance down the thigh. The iliotibial band inserts into the lateral anterior surface of the proximal tibia. When the tensor fascia lata is short, it can limit hip adduction, extension and lateral rotation, and knee flexion. If hip extension is attempted, the hip passively moves into abduction and medial rotation to accommodate the short muscle.

The **pectineus** originates from the pectineal line of the pubis and inserts in a line from the lesser trochanter to the linea aspera of the femur. The **adductor longus** arises proximally from the anterior aspect of the pubis and inserts distally into the linea aspera of the femur. The **adductor brevis** originates from the inferior ramus of the pubis. It inserts into a line that extends from the lesser trochanter to the linea aspera and the proximal part of the linea aspera just posterior to the pectineus and proximal part of the adductor longus. Shortness of these muscles limits hip abduction and extension. If these muscles are short and hip extension is attempted,

the hip passively moves into adduction to accommodate the shortened muscles.

## Starting Position

Place the subject in the sitting position at the end of the examining table, with the lower thighs, knees, and legs off the table. Assist the subject into the supine position by supporting the subject's back and flexing the hips and knees (Fig. 8.29). This sequence is used to avoid placing a strain on the subject's lower back while the starting test position is being assumed. Once the subject is supine, flex the hips by bringing the knees toward the chest just enough to flatten the low back and pelvis against the table (Fig. 8.30). In this position, the pelvis is in about 10 degrees of posterior pelvic tilt. Avoid pulling the knees too far toward the chest because this will cause the low back to go into excessive flexion and the pelvis to go into an exaggerated posterior tilt. This low back and pelvis position gives the appearance of tightness in the hip flexors when, in fact, no tightness is present.

**FIGURE 8.29** The examiner assists the subject into the starting position for testing the length of the hip flexors. Ordinarily the examiner stands on the same side as the hip being tested to visualize the hip region and take measurements, but the examiner is standing on the contralateral side for the photograph.

**FIGURE 8.30**  The starting position for testing the length of the hip flexors. Both knees and hips are flexed so that the low back and pelvis are flat on the examining table.

## Stabilization

Either the examiner or the subject holds the hip not being tested in flexion (knee toward the chest) to maintain the low back and pelvis flat against the examining table.

## Testing Motion

Information as to which muscles are short can be gained by varying the position of the knee and carefully observing passive motions of the hip and knee while hip extension is attempted. Extend the hip being tested by lowering the thigh toward the examining table. The knee is relaxed in approximately 80 degrees of flexion. The lower extremity should remain in the sagittal plane.

If the thigh lies flat on the examining table and the knee remains in 80 degrees of flexion, the iliopsoas and rectus femoris muscles are of normal length[6] (Figs. 8.31 and 8.32). At the end of the test, the hip is in 10 degrees of extension because the pelvis is being held in 10 degrees of posterior tilt. At this point, the test would be concluded.

**FIGURE 8.31** The end of the motion for testing the length of the hip flexors. The subject has normal length of the right hip flexors: the hip is able to extend to 10 degrees (thigh is flat on table), the knee remains in 80 degrees of flexion, and the lower extremity remains in the sagittal plane. Ordinarily the examiner would stand on the side of the hip being tested, but she has moved to the other side so that a photograph could be taken.

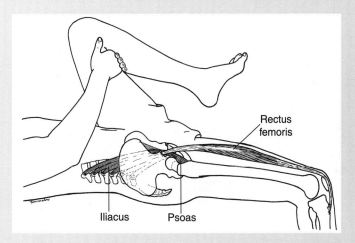

**FIGURE 8.32** A lateral view of the hip showing the hip flexors at the end of the Thomas test.

If the thigh does not lie flat on the table, hip extension is limited and further testing is needed to determine the cause (Fig. 8.33). Repeat the starting portion by flexing the hips and bringing the knee toward the chest. Extend the hip by lowering the thigh toward the examining table, but this time support the knee in extension (Fig. 8.34). When the knee is held in extension, the rectus femoris is slack over the knee joint. If the hip extends with the knee held in extension so that the thigh is able to lie on the examining table, the rectus femoris can be ascertained as being short. If the hip cannot extend with the knee held in extension and the thigh does not lie on the examining table, the iliopsoas, anterior joint capsule, iliofemoral ligament, and ischiofemoral ligament may be short.

When the hip is extending toward the examining table, observe carefully to see if the lower extremity stays in the sagittal plane. If the hip moves into lateral rotation and abduction, the sartorius muscle may be short. If the hip moves into medial rotation and abduction, the tensor fascia lata may be short. The Ober test can be used specifically to check the length of the tensor fasciae latae. If the hip moves into adduction, the pectineus, adductor longus, and adductor brevis may be short. Hip abduction ROM can be measured to test more specifically for the length of the hip adductors.

### Normal End-Feel

When the knee remains flexed at the end of hip extension ROM, the end-feel is firm owing to tension in the rectus femoris. When the knee is extended at the end of hip extension ROM, the end-feel is firm owing to tension in the anterior joint capsule, iliofemoral ligament, ischiofemoral ligament, and iliopsoas muscle. If one or more of the following muscles are shortened, they may also contribute to a firm end-feel: sartorius, tensor fascia lata, pectineus, adductor longus, and adductor brevis.

### Goniometer Alignment

See Figure 8.35.

1. Center **fulcrum** of the goniometer over the lateral aspect of the hip joint, using the greater trochanter of the femur for reference.
2. Align **proximal arm** with the lateral midline of the pelvis.
3. Align **distal arm** with the lateral midline of the femur, using the lateral epicondyle for reference.

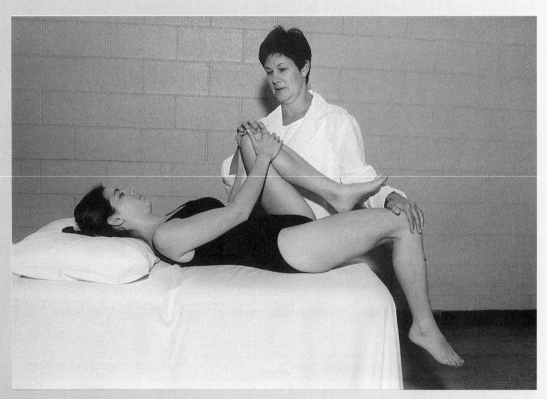

**FIGURE 8.33** This subject has restricted hip extension. Her thigh is unable to lie on the table with the knee flexed to 80 degrees. Further testing is needed to determine which structures are short.

**FIGURE 8.34** Because the subject had restricted hip extension at the end of the testing motion (see Fig. 8.33), the testing motion needs to be modified and repeated. This time, the knee is held in extension when the extremity is lowered toward the table. At the end of the test, the hip extends to 10 degrees, and the thigh lies flat on the table. Therefore, one may conclude that the rectus femoris is short and that the iliopsoas, anterior joint capsule, and iliofemoral and ischiofemoral ligaments are of normal length.

**FIGURE 8.35** Goniometer alignment for measuring the length of the hip flexors.

# ● THE HAMSTRINGS: SEMITENDINOSUS, SEMIMEMBRANOSUS, AND BICEPS FEMORIS: STRAIGHT LEG RAISING TEST

The hamstring muscles, composed of the semitendinosus, semimembranosus, and biceps femoris, cross two joints—the hip and the knee. When they contract, they extend the hip and flex the knee. The **semitendinosus** originates proximally from the ischial tuberosity and inserts distally on the proximal aspect of the medial surface of the tibia (Fig. 8.36A). The **semimembranosus** originates from the ischial tuberosity and inserts on the posterior medial aspect of the medial condyle of the tibia (Fig. 8.36B). The long head of the **biceps femoris** originates from the ischial tuberosity and the sacrotuberous ligament, whereas the short head of the biceps femoris originates proximally from the lateral lip of the linea aspera, the lateral supracondylar line, and the lateral intermuscular septum (Fig. 8.36A). The biceps femoris inserts onto the head of the fibula with a small portion extending to the lateral condyle of the tibia and the lateral collateral ligament.

The hamstring muscles cross the hip and knee joints, and if the hamstrings are short, they can limit both hip flexion and knee extension. Hip flexion is limited when the hamstrings are short and the knee is held in full extension. However, if hip flexion is limited when the knee is flexed, abnormalities of the joint surfaces, shortness of the posterior joint capsule, or a short gluteus maximus may be present.

Hamstring length can be measured using either the straight leg raising (SLR) method, wherein the angle between the pelvis and the thigh is measured, or by the distal hamstring length method, wherein the angle between the thigh and the lower leg is measured. The SLR test is presented in the following section, and the distal hamstring length test, also called the popliteal angle (or PA) test, is covered in the knee chapter.

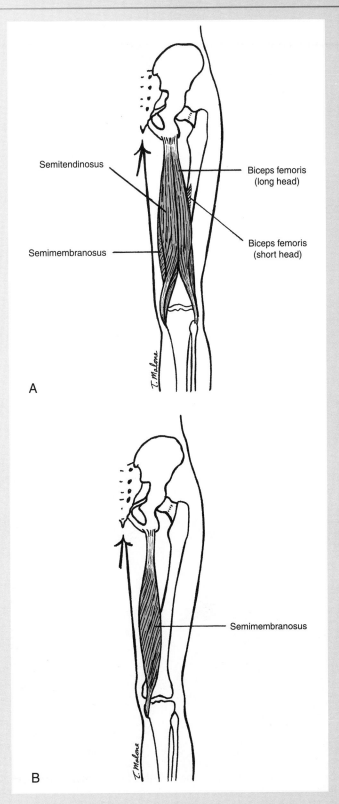

**FIGURE 8.36**  A posterior view of the hip showing the hamstring muscles (*A* and *B*).

## Starting Position

Place the subject in the supine position, with both knees extended and hips in 0 degrees of flexion, extension, abduction, adduction, and rotation (Fig. 8.37). If possible, remove clothing covering the ilium and low back so the pelvis and lumbar spine can be observed during the test.

## Stabilization

Hold the knee of the lower extremity being tested in full extension. Keep the other lower extremity flat on the examining table to stabilize the pelvis and prevent excessive amounts of posterior pelvic tilt and lumbar flexion. Usually, the weight of the lower extremity provides adequate stabilization, but a strap securing the thigh to the examining table can be added if necessary.

## Testing Motion

Flex the hip by lifting the lower extremity off the table (Figs. 8.38 and 8.39). Keep the knee in full extension by applying firm pressure to the anterior thigh. As the hip flexes, the pelvis and low back should flatten against the examining table. The end of the testing motion occurs when resistance is felt from tension in the posterior thigh and further flexion of the hip causes knee flexion, posterior pelvic tilt, or lumbar flexion. If the hip can flex to between 70 and 80 degrees with the knee extended, the test indicates normal length of the hamstring muscles.[6]

In a study of 214 adults (106 men and 106 women) aged 20 to 79 years, Youdas and associates[7] measured hip flexion ROM in the SLR test and found that females had a mean hip flexion range of 76.3 (standard deviation [SD] = 9.5) degrees and males had a mean range of 68.5 (SD = 6.8) degrees.

**FIGURE 8.37**   The starting position for testing the length of the hamstring muscles with the straight leg raising test (SLR).

**FIGURE 8.38** The end of the testing motion for the length of the hamstring muscles. The subject has normal length of the hamstrings: the hip can be passively flexed to 70 to 80 degrees with the knee held in full extension.

Biceps femoris

**FIGURE 8.39** A lateral view of the hip showing the biceps femoris at the end of the testing motion for the length of the hamstrings.

Shortness of muscles in the hip and lumbar region influences the results of the SLR test. If the subject has short hip flexors on the side that is not being tested, the pelvis is held in an anterior tilt when that lower extremity is lying on the examining table. An anterior pelvic tilt decreases the distance that the leg being tested can lift off the examining table, thus giving the appearance of less hamstring length than is actually present. To remedy this situation, have the subject flex the hip not being tested by resting the foot on the table or by supporting the thigh with a pillow (Fig. 8.40). This position slackens the short hip flexors and allows the low back and pelvis to flatten against the examining table. Be careful to avoid an excessive amount of posterior pelvic tilt and lumbar flexion.

If the subject has short lumbar extensors, the low back has an excessive lordotic curve and the pelvis is in an anterior tilt. The distance that the leg can lift off the examining table is decreased if the pelvis is in an anterior tilt, giving the appearance of less hamstring length than is actually present. In this case, the examiner needs to carefully align the proximal arm of the goniometer with the lateral midline of the pelvis when measuring hip flexion ROM and not be misled by the height of the lower extremity from the examining table.

**FIGURE 8.40**  If the subject has shortness of the contralateral hip flexors, flex the contralateral hip to prevent an anterior pelvic tilt.

## Normal End-Feel

The end-feel is firm owing to tension in the semimembranosus, semitendinosus, and biceps femoris muscles.

## Goniometer Alignment

See Figure 8.41.

1. Center **fulcrum** of the goniometer over the lateral aspect of the hip joint, using the greater trochanter of the femur for reference.
2. Align **proximal arm** with the lateral midline of the pelvis.
3. Align **distal arm** with the lateral midline of the femur, using the lateral epicondyle for reference.

**FIGURE 8.41** Goniometer alignment for measuring the length of the hamstring muscles. Another examiner will need to take the measurement while the first examiner supports the leg being tested.

# ● TENSOR FASCIA LATA AND ILIOTIBIAL BAND: OBER TEST

The **tensor fascia lata** crosses two joints—the hip and knee. When this muscle contracts, it abducts, flexes, and medially rotates the hip and extends the knee. The tensor fascia lata arises proximally from the anterior aspect of the outer lip of the iliac crest and the lateral surface of the ASIS and the iliac notch (Fig. 8.42). It attaches distally into the iliotibial band of the fascia lata about one-third of the way down the thigh. The **iliotibial band** inserts into the lateral tuberosity of the tibia, the head of the fibula, the lateral condyle of the femur, and the lateral patellar retinaculum. If the tensor fascia lata is short, it limits hip adduction and to a lesser extent hip extension, hip lateral rotation, and knee flexion. Shortening of this structure has been cited as a contributing cause of low-back pain,[8] iliotibial band friction syndrome,[9] and patellofemoral pain due to lateral tracking and tilting of the patella.[10]

Some authors have stated that the tensor fasciae latae is of normal length when the hip adducts to the examining table.[11,12] However, according to Kendall and colleagues,[6] stabilization of the pelvis to prevent a lateral tilt and avoidance of hip flexion and medial rotation will limit hip adduction to 10 degrees during the testing motion, which causes the thigh to drop only slightly below the horizontal position. More conservative hip adduction values have been reported as normal by Cade and associates,[13] who found that only 7 of 50 young female subjects had normal (or not short) Ober test values when the horizontal leg position or 0 degrees of adduction was used as the test parameter.

Gajdosik, Sandler, and Marr[14] used a universal goniometer centered at the ipsilateral ASIS to determine the effects of knee position and gender on Ober test values for 49 adults aged 20 to 43 years. The 26 women in the study had a range of 3 degrees of adduction to 16 degrees of abduction, whereas the 23 men had a range of 4 degrees of adduction to 15 degrees of abduction. According to Wang,[15] a normal value for 36 healthy subjects with a mean age of 24.3 years was found to be 17.8 degrees of adduction measured at the lateral femoral epicondyle at the knee with an inclinometer. Reese and Bandy[16] also used an inclinometer over the distal femur to measure the hip adduction position in 61 healthy subjects with a mean age of 24 years. The authors obtained a mean value of 18.9 degrees of adduction (SD = 7.6 degrees), which is similar to the value obtained by Wang.

## Starting Position

Place the subject in the sidelying position, with the hip being tested uppermost. Position the subject near the edge of the examining table, so that the examiner can stand directly behind the subject. Initially, extend the uppermost knee and place the hip in 0 degrees of flexion, extension, adduction, abduction, and rotation. The patient flexes the bottom hip and knee to stabilize the trunk, flatten the lumbar curve, and keep the pelvis in a slight posterior tilt.

## Stabilization

Place one hand on the iliac crest to stabilize the pelvis. Firm pressure is usually required to prevent the pelvis from laterally tilting during the testing motion. Having the patient flex the bottom hip and knee can also help to stabilize the trunk and pelvis.

## Testing Motion

Support the leg being tested by holding the medial aspect of the knee and the lower leg. Flex the hip and the knee to 90 degrees (Fig. 8.43). Keep the knee flexed and move the hip into abduction and extension to position the tensor fascia lata over the greater trochanter of the femur (Fig. 8.44). Test the length of the tensor fascia lata and iliotibial

**FIGURE 8.42** A lateral view of the left hip showing the tensor fascia lata muscle (in red) and the iliotibial band.

**FIGURE 8.43** The first step in the testing motion for the length of the tensor fascia lata and iliotibial band is to flex the hip and knee.

**FIGURE 8.44** The next step in the testing motion for the length of the tensor fascia lata and iliotibial band is to abduct and extend the hip.

band by lowering the leg into hip adduction and bringing it down toward the examining table (Figs. 8.45 and 8.46). Do not allow the pelvis to tilt laterally or the hip to flex because these motions slacken the muscle. Keep the knee flexed to control medial rotation of the hip and to maintain the stretch of the muscle. If the thigh drops to slightly below horizontal (10 degrees of hip adduction), the test is negative and the tensor fascia lata and iliotibial band are of normal length.[6] If the thigh remains above horizontal in hip abduction, the tensor fasciae latae and iliotibial band may be tight.

## Normal End-Feel
The end-feel is firm owing to tension in the tensor fascia lata.

## Goniometer Alignment
See Figure 8.47.

1. Center **fulcrum** of the goniometer over the ASIS of the extremity being measured.
2. Align **proximal arm** with an imaginary line extending from one ASIS to the other.
3. Align **distal arm** with the anterior midline of the femur, using the midline of the patella for reference.

Note that at least 0 degrees of hip extension is needed to perform length testing of the tensor fascia lata and iliotibial band. If the iliopsoas is tight, it prevents the proper positioning of the tensor fascia lata over the greater trochanter. If the rectus femoris is short, the knee may be extended during the test,[6] but extreme care must be taken to avoid medial rotation of the hip as the leg is lowered into adduction. This change in test position is called a Modified Ober test.

**FIGURE 8.45**  The end of the testing motion for the length of the tensor fascia lata and iliotibial band. The examiner is firmly holding the iliac crest to prevent a lateral tilt of the pelvis while the hip is lowered into adduction. No flexion or medial rotation of the hip is allowed. The subject has a normal length of the tensor fascia lata and iliotibial band; the thigh drops to slightly below horizontal.

**FIGURE 8.46** An anterior view of the hip showing the tensor fascia lata and iliotibial band at the end of the Ober test.

**FIGURE 8.47** Goniometer alignment for measuring the length of the tensor fascia lata and iliotibial band. The examiner stabilizes the pelvis and positions the leg being tested while another examiner takes the measurement. If another examiner is not available, a visual estimate will have to be made.

## TENSOR FASCIA LATA AND ILIOTIBIAL BAND: MODIFIED OBER TEST

The Modified Ober test was first proposed by the Kendalls in 1952 to reduce strain in the medial aspect of the knee joint, to reduce tension on the patella, and to reduce the influence of a tight two-joint rectus femoris muscle.[6] Gajdosik, Sandler, and Marr[14] suggest that the two tests yield different results and should not be used interchangeably. The results of the authors' study using a universal goniometer showed that there was a difference between men and women, with men having a range of 20 degrees of adduction to 3 degrees of abduction, whereas women had a range of 11 degrees of adduction to 5 degrees of abduction. Reese and Bandy[16] determined that the hip adduction position measured with an inclinometer over the lateral femoral epicondyle was 23.4 degrees (SD = 7.0 degrees) in the Modified Ober test.

### Starting Position

The starting position is the same as for the Ober test except that the knee is held in extension throughout the test.

### Stabilization

Stabilization is essentially the same as in the Ober test, but a second person may be needed to assist in either holding the extended leg or in stabilizing the pelvis.

### Testing Motion

The testing motion is the same as for the Ober test, but medial rotation may be more of a concern and must be prevented. The end of the test occurs when the pelvis begins to tilt laterally or the leg stops dropping.

### Goniometer Alignment

Goniometer alignment is the same as in the Ober test (Fig. 8.48).

**FIGURE 8.48** The extended position of the knee is shown at the end of the Modified Ober test.

## Research Findings

### Effects of Age, Gender, and Other Factors

Table 8.1 shows nomal hip range of motion (ROM) values from various sources. The age, gender, measurement instrument used, and number of subjects measured to obtain the AAOS[3] and AMA[4] values were not reported. In Table 8.1, the 9.8 degrees of hip extension motion reported by Boone and Azen[17] is much smaller than the degrees listed by the other authors.[3–5,18] This finding is most likely due to the fact that very young children who often have limitations in hip extension were included in Boone and Azen's study.

### Age

Researchers tend to agree that age affects hip ROM[19–25] and that the effects are motion specific in neonates, infants, children, and adults. In neonates some motions are larger than in other age groups and some motions are considerably smaller. Table 8.2 shows passive ROM values for neonates as reported in five studies.[19–23] All values presented in Table 8.2 were obtained by means of a universal goniometer. A comparison of the neonates' passive ROM values shown in Table 8.2 with the values of older children and adults shown in Table 8.1 reveals that the neonates studied have larger passive ROM in most hip motions except for extension, which is limited. The neonates' ROM in hip lateral and medial rotation and abduction is much larger than the ROM values of adults and older children for the same motions. Also, the relationship between hip lateral and medial rotation appears to differ from that found in a majority of older children and adults. Hip lateral rotation values for the neonates are considerably greater than the values for medial rotation, whereas in children and adults the lateral rotation values are either about the same or less than the values for medial rotation.[25]

Kozic and colleagues,[26] in a study of passive lateral and medial rotation in 1140 children aged 8 to 9 years, found that 90 percent of the children had less than 10 degrees difference between lateral and medial rotation. Ellison and coworkers,[27] in a study of 100 healthy adults and 50 patients with back problems, found that only 27 percent of healthy subjects compared with 48 percent of patients had greater lateral rotation than medial rotation. The large number of patients who had greater lateral than medial rotation suggests a rotational imbalance that may be related to back problems.

However, as seen in Table 8.2 and Table 8.3, the most dramatic effect of age is on hip extension ROM in newborns and infants because they are unable to extend the hip from full flexion to the neutral position (returning to 0 degrees from the end of the flexion ROM).[15–22] Waugh and associates[19] found that all 40 infants tested lacked complete hip extension, with limitations ranging from 21.7 degrees to 68.3 degrees. Forero, Okamura, and Larson[25] found that all 60 healthy, full-term neonates studied had hip extension limitations that ranged from 17 to 39 degrees, with a mean range of 30 degrees. Schwarze and Denton[20] found mean limitations of 19 degrees for boys and 21 degrees for girls, and Broughton, Wright, and Menelaus[21] found a mean hip extension limitation of 34.1 degrees in 57 boys and girls.

Limitations in hip extension found in the very young are considered to be normal and to decrease with age, as seen in Table 8.3. The term "physiological limitation of motion" has been used by Waugh and associates[19] and Walker[29] to describe the normal hip extension limitation of motion in infants. According to Walker,[29] movement into extension evolves without the need for intervention and should not be considered pathological in newborns and infants. The extension limitation has been attributed to the increased flexor tone that is present in neonates and infants and to the flexed position of the hip in the womb. Usually, a return from flexion to the neutral position is attained in children by 2 years of age, and

| TABLE 8.1 | Hip Motion: Normal Values in Degrees | | | | | | |
|---|---|---|---|---|---|---|---|
| | AAOS[3] | AMA[4] | Boone and Azen[17] | Svenningsen et al[18] | | Roach and Miles[5] |
| | | | 18 mos – 54 yrs Males n = 109 | 23 yrs Males n = 102 | 23 yrs Females n = 104 | 25 – 47yrs Males and Females n = 1683 |
| *Motion* | | | Mean (SD) | Mean | Mean | Mean (SD) |
| Flexion | 120 | 100 | 122.3 (6.1) | 137 | 141 | 121.0 (13.0) |
| Extension | 20 | 30 | 9.8 (6.8) | 23 | 26 | 19.0 (8.0) |
| Abduction | | 40 | 45.9 (9.3) | 40 | 42 | 42.0 (11.0) |
| Adduction | | 20 | 26.9 (4.1) | 29 | 30 | |
| Medial rotation | 45 | 40* | 47.3 (6.0) | 38 | 52 | 32.0 (8.0) |
| Lateral rotation | 45 | 50* | 47.2 (6.3) | 43 | 41 | 32.0 (9.0) |

SD = standard deviation.
* Measurements taken with subjects in the supine position.

| TABLE 8.2 | Age Effects on Hip Motion in Neonates 6 Hours to 4 Weeks of Age: Normal Values in Degrees | | | | |
|---|---|---|---|---|---|
| | Waugh et al[19] | Drews et al[22] | Schwarze and Denton[20] | Broughton et al[21] | Wanatabe et al[23] | Forero et al[25] |
| | 6 – 65 hrs n = 40 | 12 hrs – 6 days n = 54 | 1 – 3 days n = 1000 | 1 – 7 days n = 57 | 4 wks n = 62 | 1 – 3 days n = 60 |
| Motion | Mean (SD) | Mean (SD) | Mean | Mean (SD) | Mean | Mean (SD) |
| Flexion | — | — | — | — | 138.0 | 127.5 (4.8) |
| Extension* | 46.3 (8.2)† | 28.3 (6.0)‡ | 20.0 | 34.1 (6.3) | 12.0 | 29.9 (4.0) |
| Abduction | — | 55.5 (9.5)† | 78.0† | — | 51.0 | 38.9 (5.1) |
| Adduction | — | 6.4 (3.9)† | 15.0† | — | — | 17.3 (3.5) |
| Medial rotation | — | 79.8 (9.3)† | 58.0 | — | 24.0 | 76.0 (5.6) |
| Lateral rotation | — | 113.7 (10.4)† | 80.0 | — | 66.0 | 91.9 (3.0) |

SD = standard deviation.
* All values in this row represent the magnitude of the extension limitation.
† Tested with subjects in the supine position.
‡ Tested with subjects in the side-lying position.

extension ROM beginning at the neutral position usually approaches adult values by early adolescence.

Broughton, Wright, and Menelaus[21] found that by 6 months of age, mean hip extension limitations in infants had decreased to 7.5 degrees, and 27 of 57 subjects had no limitation. However, Phelps, Smith, and Hallum[24] found that 100 percent of the 9- and 12-month-old infants tested (n = 50) had some degree of hip extension limitation. At 18 months of age, 89 percent of infants had limitations, and at 24 months, 72 percent still had limitations.

In Table 8.4, very little difference is evident between the ROM values for hip flexion and hip abduction across the life span of 4 to 74 years in contrast to hip medial and lateral rotation, which have the greatest decrease in ROM. Roach and Miles[5] have suggested that differences in active ROM representing less than 10 percent of the arc of motion are of little clinical significance and that any substantial loss of mobility in individuals between 25 and 74 years of age should

be viewed as abnormal and not attributable to aging. In the data from Roach and Miles,[5] hip extension was the only motion in which the difference between the youngest and the oldest groups constituted a decrease of more than 20 percent of the available arc of motion.

Although Svenningsen and associates[18] studied hip ROM in fairly young subjects (761 males and females aged 4 to 28 years), these authors found that even in this limited age span, the ROM for most hip motions showed a decrease with increasing age. However, the reductions in ROM varied according to the motion. Decreases in flexion, abduction, medial rotation, and total rotation were greater than decreases in extension, adduction, and lateral rotation.

Nonaka and associates,[30] in a study of 77 healthy male volunteers aged 15 to 73 years, found that passive hip ROM decreased progressively with increasing age, but no change was observed in knee ROM in the same population. The authors suggested that most activities of daily living can be

| TABLE 8.3 | Hip Extension Limitations in Infants and Young Children 4 Weeks to 5 Years of Age: Values in Degrees | | | | |
|---|---|---|---|---|---|
| Wanatabe et al[23] | Broughton et al[21] | Phelps et al[24] | | Boone[28] | |
| 4–8 mos n = 54 | 3 mos n = 57 | 6 mos n = 57 | 9 mos n = 25 | 18 mos n = 18 | 1–5 yrs n = 19 |
| Mean (SD) | Mean (SD) | Mean (SD) | Mean (SD) | Mean (SD) | Mean (SD) |
| 4.0 | 18.9 (6.0) | 7.5 (5.7) | 10.0 (2.6) | 4.0 (3.2) | 0.8 (3.4) |

SD = standard deviation.

| TABLE 8.4 | Age Effects on Hip Motion in Individuals 4 to 74 Years of Age: Normal Values in Degrees | | | | | | |
|---|---|---|---|---|---|---|---|

| | Svenningsen[18] | | Boone[28] | | Roach and Miles[5] | | |
| | Female | Male | Males | | Males and Females | | |
| | 4 yrs<br>n = 52 | 4 yrs<br>n = 51 | 6–12 yrs<br>n = 17 | 13–19 yrs<br>n = 17 | 25–39 yrs<br>n = 433 | 40–59 yrs<br>n = 727 | 60–74 yrs<br>n = 523 |
| Motion | Mean | Mean | Mean (SD) | Mean (SD) | Mean (SD) | Mean (SD) | Mean (SD) |
| Flexion | 151 | 149 | 124.4 (5.9) | 122.6 (5.2) | 122.0 (12) | 120.0 (14) | 118.0 (13) |
| Extension | 29 | 28 | 10.4 (7.5) | 11.6 (5.0) | 22.0 (8) | 18.0 (7) | 17.0 (8) |
| Abduction | 55 | 53 | 48.1 (6.3) | 46.8 (6.0) | 44.0 (11) | 42.0 (11) | 39.0 (12) |
| Adduction | 30 | 30 | 27.6 (3.8) | 26.3 (2.9) | — | — | — |
| Medial rotation | 60 | 51 | 48.4 (4.8) | 47.1 (5.2) | 33.0 (7) | 31.0 (8) | 30.0 (7) |
| Lateral rotation | 44 | 48 | 47.5 (3.2) | 47.4 (5.2) | 34.0 (8) | 32.0 (8) | 29.0 (9) |

SD = standard deviation.

performed without maximal lengthening of hip joint muscles. Therefore, loss of hip ROM with increasing age may result from shortening of muscles or connective tissue due to reduced compliance of joint structures and degenerative changes in spinal alignment as a result of a decrease in physical activities that stretch the musculature surrounding the hip.

A number of other researchers have investigated age or gender effects on hip ROM.[31–34] Allander and colleagues[31] measured hip ROM in a population of 517 females and 203 males between 33 and 70 years of age. These authors found that older groups had significantly less hip rotation ROM than younger groups.

Walker and colleagues[32] measured all active hip motions in 30 women and 30 men ranging from 60 to 84 years of age. Although Walker and colleagues[32] found no differences in hip ROM between the group aged 60 to 69 years and the group aged 75 to 84 years, both age groups demonstrated a reduced ability to attain a neutral starting position for hip flexion. The mean starting position for both groups for measurements of flexion ROM was 11 degrees instead of 0 degrees. The mean ROM values obtained for both age groups for hip rotation, abduction, and adduction were 14 to 25 degrees less than the average values published by the AAOS.[3] This finding appears to provide support for the use of age-appropriate norms.

James and Parker[34] measured active and passive ROM at the hip, knee, and ankle in 80 healthy men and women ranging from 70 years to 92 years of age. Measurements of hip abduction ROM were taken with a universal goniometer. All other measurements were taken with a Leighton flexometer. Systematic decreases in both active and passive ROM were found in subjects between 70 and 92 years of age. Hip abduction decreased the most with age and was 33.4 percent less in the oldest group of men and women (those aged 85 to 92 years) compared with the youngest group (those aged 70 to 74 years). Medial and lateral rotation also decreased considerably, but the decrease was not as great as that seen in abduction. In contrast, hip flexion with the knee either extended or flexed was least affected by age, with a significant reduction occurring only in those older than 85 years of age. Passive ROM was greater than active ROM for all joint motions tested, with the largest difference (7 degrees) occurring in hip flexion with the knee flexed.

In a large study by Steinberg and colleagues,[35] passive hip ROM was compared in 1320 female dancers aged 8 to 16 years and 223 nondancers of similar age. Hip flexion and medial and lateral rotation decreased in both groups with increasing age, whereas hip abduction decreased significantly with increasing age only in the dancers. Hip extension ROM was found to increase with age in both groups, but the increase was only significant in the dancer group.

## Gender

The effects of gender on hip ROM are usually age and motion specific and account for only a relatively small amount of total variance in measurement. Gender effects have been found in both children and adults, but these effects have not been found in neonates and infants. Phelps, Smith, and Hallum[24] found no gender differences in hip rotation in 86 infants and young children (aged 9 to 24 months). Forero, Okamura, and Larson[25] found no significant gender differences in any of six hip motions in 60 neonates (26 females and 34 males).

Some studies have found that female children and adults have greater hip flexion ROM than males.[18,33,34] Boone and coworkers[33] found significant differences for most hip motions when gender comparisons were made for three age groupings of males and females. These findings were age and motion specific. Female children (1 to 9 years of age), young adult females (21 to 29 years of age), and older adult females (61 to 69 years of age) had significantly more hip flexion than their male counterparts. However, female children and young adult females had less hip adduction and lateral rotation than males in comparison groups.

Both young adult females and older adult females had less hip extension ROM than males.

Svenningson and associates[18] measured the passive ROM of 1552 hips in 761 healthy females and males between 4 and 28 years of age. Females of all age groups had greater passive ROM than males for total passive ROM, total rotation, medial rotation, and abduction. The following two findings agreed with Boone's findings: female children in the 11- and 15-year-old age groups and female adults had greater passive ROM in hip flexion than males in the same age groups, and females in the 4- and 6-year-old groups and female adults had less hip lateral rotation than males in the same age groups. However, females had more hip adduction than males, which is opposite to Boone's findings.

Allander and colleagues[31] determined that in five of eight age groups tested, females had a greater amount of hip rotation than males. Walker and colleagues[32] found that 30 females aged 60 to 84 years had 14 degrees more ROM in hip medial rotation than their male counterparts. Simoneau and coworkers[36] discovered that females (with a mean age of 21.8 years) had higher mean values in both medial and lateral rotation than age-matched male subjects. The authors used a universal metal goniometer to measure active ROM of hip rotation in 39 females and 21 males.

James and Parker[34] found that women were significantly more mobile than men in 7 of the 10 motions tested at the hip, knee, and ankle. At the hip, women had greater mobility than men in all hip motions except abduction. Men and women had similar mean values in hip flexion ROM, both with the knee flexed and with the knee extended, in the group aged 70 to 74 years, but in the group between 70 and 85-plus years of age, men had an approximate 25 percent decrease in ROM, whereas women had a decrease of only about 11 percent.

In a study by Youdas and colleagues,[7] two testers used a 360-degree goniometer to measure hamstring length by two methods (straight leg raising and popliteal angle) in 214 adults (108 women and 106 men) aged 20 to 79 years. A significant gender effect was found in both testing methods, with women having approximately 8 degrees more motion than men in the SLR test and 11 degrees more motion than men in the popliteal angle test.

In contrast to the previously mentioned studies, Hu and associates,[37] using a photographic method, found no significant gender differences in all six hip motions in 51 male and 54 female healthy Chinese subjects between the ages of 65 and 85 years living in Beijing, China.

Sanya and Obi[38] found no significant gender differences between 50 male and female patients with diabetes and a control group of 50 healthy subjects. Both groups ranged in age from 21 to 71 years.

### Body Mass Index

Increases in body mass index (BMI) seem to decrease the ROM at the hip. Kettunen and colleagues[39] found that former elite athletes with a high BMI had lower total amounts of hip passive ROM compared with former elite athletes with a low BMI. Subjects in the study included 117 former elite athletes

between the ages of 45 and 68 years. Measurements were taken by means of a Myrin inclinometer with the subjects in the prone position.

Escalante and coworkers[40] determined that there was a loss of at least 1 degree of passive range of motion in hip flexion for each unit increase in BMI in a group of 687 community-dwelling elders (those who were 65 to 78 years of age). Subjects who were severely obese had an average of 18 degrees less hip flexion than nonobese subjects as measured in the supine position with an inclinometer. BMI explained a higher proportion of the variance in hip flexion ROM than any other variable examined by the authors.

Lichtenstein and associates[41] studied interrelationships among the variables in the study by Escalante and coworkers[40] and concluded that BMI could be considered a primary direct determinant of hip flexion passive ROM. However, Bennell and associates[42] found no effect of BMI on active ROM in hip rotation in a study comparing 77 novice ballet dancers and 49 age-matched controls between the ages of 8 and 11 years. The control subjects, who had a higher BMI than the dancers, also had a significantly greater range of lateral and medial hip rotation.

### Testing Position

Simoneau and coworkers[36] found that measurement position (sitting versus prone) had little effect on active hip medial rotation ROM in 60 healthy male and female college students (aged 18 to 21 years), but position had a significant effect on lateral rotation ROM. Lateral rotation measured in the sitting position was statistically less (mean = 36 degrees) than it was when measured on subjects in the prone position (mean = 45 degrees). Bierma-Zeinstra and associates[43] found that both lateral and medial rotation ROMs were significantly less when measured in two males and seven females aged 21 to 43 years in the sitting and supine positions compared to measurements taken in the prone position (Table 8.5). However, Schwarze and Denton[20] found no difference in passive ROM measurements of hip medial and lateral rotation with neonates in the prone position compared to measurements of the 1000 neonates taken in the supine position.

Van Dillen and coworkers[44] compared the effects of knee and hip position on passive hip extension ROM in 10 patients (mean age = 33 years) with low-back pain and 35 healthy subjects (mean age = 31 years). Both groups had less hip extension when the hip was in neutral abduction than when the hip was fully abducted. Both groups also displayed less hip extension ROM when the knee was flexed to 80 degrees than when the knee was fully extended. This finding lends support for Kendall and colleagues,[6] who maintain that changing the knee joint angle during the Thomas test for hip flexor length can affect the passive ROM in hip extension.

Gajdosik, Sandler, and Marr[14] found that changing the position from knee flexion in the Ober test to knee extension in the Modified Ober test changed the angle of hip adduction in 49 subjects (26 women and 23 men). The knee flexed position limited hip adduction more than the knee extended position.

| TABLE 8.5 | Effects of Position on Hip ROM: Normal Values in Degrees | | | |
|---|---|---|---|---|
| Author | Motion | Position | | |
| | | Seated | Prone | Supine |
| | | Mean (SD) | Mean (SD) | Mean |
| Simoneau et al[36] | Lateral rotation* | 36 (7) | 45 (10) | — |
| | Medial rotation* | 33 (7) | 36 (9) | — |
| | Total rotation* | 69 (9) | 81 (12) | — |
| Bierma-Zeinstra et al[43] | Lateral rotation* | 33.9 | 47.0 | 33.1 |
| | Medial rotation* | 33.6 | 46.3 | 36.0 |
| | Lateral rotation† | 37.6 | 51.9 | 34.2 |
| | Medial rotation† | 38.8 | 53.2 | 39.9 |

SD = standard deviation.
* Active ROM measured with a universal goniometer.
† Passive ROM measured with a universal goniometer.

## Arts and Sports

A sampling of articles related to the effects of ballet and other forms of dance, ice hockey, and running on ROM are presented in the following paragraphs. As expected, the effects of the activity on ROM vary with the activity and involve motions that are specific to the particular activity.

Gilbert, Gross, and Klug[45] conducted a study of 20 female ballet dancers (aged 11 to 14 years) to determine the relationship between the dancer's ROM in hip lateral rotation and the turnout angle. An ideal turnout angle is a position in which the longitudinal axes of the feet are rotated 180 degrees from each other. The authors found that turnout angles were significantly greater (between 13 and 17 degrees) than measurements of hip lateral rotation ROM. This finding indicated that the dancers were using excessive movements at the knee and ankle to attain an acceptable degree of turnout. According to the authors, the use of compensatory motions at the knee and ankle predisposes the dancers to injury. The dancers had had 3 years of classical ballet training and still had not been able to attain the degree of hip lateral rotation that would give a 180-degree turnout angle. Consequently, the authors suggest that hip ROM may be genetically determined.

Bennell and associates[42] determined that age-matched control subjects had significantly greater active ROM in hip lateral and medial rotation than a group of 77 ballet dancers (aged 8 to 11 years), although there was no significant difference in the degree of turnout between the two groups. The amount of non-hip lateral rotation was 40 percent in the dancers compared to 20 percent in the control subjects. Non-hip lateral rotation increases torsional forces on the medial aspect of the knee, ankle, and foot in the young dancers and puts this group at high risk of injury. Similar to the findings of Gilbert, Gross, and Klug,[45] the authors found no relationship between number of years of training and lateral rotation ROM, which again suggests a genetic component of ROM.

The authors hypothesized that a shortening of the hip extensors (resulting from constant use) and the dancers' avoidance of full hip medial rotation might account for the fact that the dancers had less hip medial rotation than the control subjects.

Tyler and colleagues[46] found that a group of 25 professional male ice hockey players had about 10 degrees less hip extension ROM than a group of 25 matched control subjects. The authors postulated that the loss of hip extension in the hockey players was probably due to tight anterior hip capsule structures and tight iliopsoas muscles. The flexed hip and knee posture assumed by the players during skating probably contributed to the muscle shortness and loss of hip extension ROM.

Van Mechelen and colleagues[47] used goniometry to measure hip ROM in 16 male runners who had sustained running injuries during the year but who were fit at the time of the study. No right–left differences in hip ROM were found either in the previously injured group or in a control group of runners who had not sustained an injury. However, hip ROM in the injured group was on average 59.4 degrees, or about 10 degrees less than the average ROM of 68.1 degrees in runners without injuries.

## Disability

Steultjens and associates[48] used a universal goniometer to measure bilateral active assistive ROM at the hip and knee in 198 patients with osteoarthritis (OA) of the hip or knee. Generally a decrease in hip ROM was associated with an increase in disability, but that association was motion specific. Hip flexion contractures were present in 15 percent of the patients, whereas contractures at the knee were found in 31.5 percent of the patients. Twenty-five percent of the variation in disability levels was accounted for by differences in ROM.

Mollinger and Steffan,[49] in a study of 111 nursing home residents, found a mean hip extension of only 4 degrees.

Beissner, Collins, and Holmes,[50] in a study of 22 men and 58 women with an average age of 81 years, concluded that lower-extremity passive ROM and upper-extremity muscle force were important predictors of function for elderly individuals living in assisted living residences or skilled nursing facilities. Conversely, upper-extremity ROM and age were the strongest predictors of function in elderly individuals residing in independent living situations.

Sanya and Obi[38] measured the hip flexion and extension ROM in 50 diabetic and 50 non-diabetic age-matched control subjects aged 21 to 72 years. The men and women with diabetes had less right (mean = 92.1 degrees) and left hip flexion (mean = 91.7 degrees) than control subjects, whose mean right hip flexion was 110.4 degrees and left hip flexion was 111.0 degrees. Hip extension ROM was also less in the group with diabetes, but the differences were not as large as the differences in hip flexion ROM. The authors suggested that the decreased mobility in this group of patients may affect their ability to perform normal activities of daily living and that people involved in their care should be aware that patients with diabetes may have decreases in ROM that go unnoticed.

## Functional Range of Motion

Table 8.6 shows the hip flexion ROM necessary for selected functional activities as reported in several sources. An adequate ROM at the hip is important for meeting mobility demands such as walking, climbing stairs (Fig. 8.49), and performing many activities of daily living that require sitting and bending. According to Magee,[51] ideal functional ranges are 120 degrees of flexion, 0 degrees of abduction, and 20 degrees of lateral rotation. However, as can be seen in Table 8.6, considerably less ROM is necessary for gait on level surfaces.[52]

Livingston, Stevenson, and Olney[53] studied ascent and descent on stairs of different dimensions, using 15 female subjects between 19 and 26 years of age. McFayden and Winter[54] also studied stairclimbing; however, these authors used eight repeated trials of one subject.

Protopapadaki and colleagues[55] compared the ROM required for stair ascent and descent in 33 healthy young individuals using a Vicon Motion Analysis System. No significant difference in hip ROM was found between right and left

**FIGURE 8.49** Ascending stairs requires between 47 and 66 degrees of hip flexion, depending on stair dimensions.[53]

| TABLE 8.6 | Hip Flexion Range of Motion Required for Functional Activities: Normal Values in Degrees From Selected Sources | | | |
|---|---|---|---|---|
| | Livingston, et al[53] | Ranchos Los Amigos Medical Center[39] | McFayden and Winter[54] | Protopapadaki et al[55] |
| Activity | Range | Range | Mean (SD) | Mean (SD) |
| Walking on level surfaces | 0–30 | 0–30 | 44 (4.5) | — |
| Ascending stairs | 1–0–66 | — | 60 | 65.1 (7.1) |
| Descending stairs | 1–0–45 | — | 66 (0.1) | 49.0 (7.8) |

legs in the 16 males and 17 females (aged 18 to 39 years). The mean hip flexion ROM of 65.1 degrees required for stair ascent was greater than the hip flexion ROM of 40.0 degrees required for descent on stairs with 18-cm risers and a tread length of 28.5 cm.

In a study to determine the effects of age-related ROM on functional activity, Oberg, Krazinia, and Oberg[56] measured hip and knee active ROM with an electrogoniometer during gait in 240 healthy male and female individuals aged 10 to 79 years of age. Age-related changes were slightly more pronounced at slow gait speeds than at fast speeds, but the rate of changes was less than 1 degree per decade, and no distinct pattern was evident, except that hip flexion–extension appeared to be affected less than other motions.

Other functional and self-care activities require a larger ROM at the hip. For example, sitting requires at least 90 to 112 degrees of hip flexion with the knees flexed (Fig. 8.50). Additional hip flexion ROM (120 degrees) is necessary for putting on socks (Fig. 8.51), squatting (115 degrees), and stooping (125 degrees).[54]

The daily activities of various cultures may require a different set of functional ROM values. Hemmerich and coworkers[57] used a Fastrak electromagnetic tracking system to assess

**FIGURE 8.51** Putting on socks requires 120 degrees of flexion, 20 degrees of abduction, and 20 degrees of lateral rotation.[51]

hip, knee, and ankle ROM in 30 healthy Indian subjects (10 women and 20 men) with an average age of 48 years. The daily activities of this group of subjects included squatting with heels up or down, kneeling with ankles either dorsiflexed or plantarflexed, and sitting cross-legged on the floor. The mean maximum amount of hip flexion for squatting with the heels down was 95.4 degrees. Sitting cross-legged required a mean maximal angle of hip flexion of 83.5 degrees, a mean maximal angle of hip abduction of 34 degrees, and a mean maximal angle of hip lateral rotation of 37 degrees. The authors suggested that the prayer positions of Muslims and customs of other cultures may involve additional ROM at the hips, knees, and ankles.

## Reliability and Validity

Studies of the reliability of hip measurements have included both active and passive motion and different types of measuring instruments. Also, reliability has been assessed in different age and patient populations.[58–63] Therefore, comparisons among studies are difficult. Boone and associates[64] and Clapper and

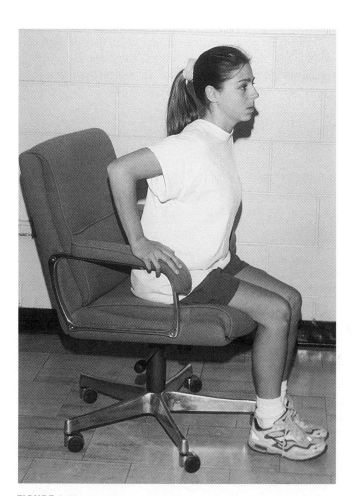

**FIGURE 8.50** Sitting in a chair with an average seat height requires 112 degrees of hip flexion.[51]

Wolf[65] investigated the reliability of measurements of active ROM, whereas other researchers[27,44,47,60,61,66–68] studied passive motion. Bierma-Zeinstra and associates[43] studied the reliability of both active and passive ROM. Table 8.7 and Table 8.8 provide a sampling of intratester and intertester reliability studies.

Boone and associates[64] conducted a study in which four physical therapists used a universal goniometer to measure active hip abduction ROM in 12 healthy male volunteers aged 26 to 54 years. Three measurements were taken by each tester at each of four sessions scheduled on a weekly basis for 4 weeks. Intratester reliability for hip abduction was r = 0.75, with a total standard deviation between measurements of 4 degrees taken by the same testers. Intertester reliability for hip abduction was r = 0.55, with a total standard deviation of 5.2 degrees between measurements taken by different testers.

Clapper and Wolf[65] compared the reliability of the Ortho-Ranger (Orthotronics, Daytona Beach, Fla.), an electronic computed pendulum goniometer, with that of the universal goniometer in a study of active hip motion involving 10 males and 10 healthy females between the ages of 23 and 40 years. The authors found that the universal goniometer showed significantly less variation within sessions than the Ortho-Ranger, except for measurements of hip adduction and lateral rotation. The authors concluded that the universal goniometer was a more reliable instrument than the OrthoRanger, and, due to the poor correlation between the two instruments, the authors cautioned that the instruments should not be used interchangeably

Ekstrand and associates[66] measured the passive ROM of hip flexion, extension, and abduction in 22 healthy men aged 20 to 30 years in two testing series. In the first series, the testing procedures were not controlled. In the second series, procedures were standardized and anatomical landmarks were indicated. The intratester coefficient of variation was lower than the intertester coefficient of variation for both series, but standardization of procedures improved reliability considerably.

Ellison and coworkers[27] compared passive ROM measurements of hip rotation taken with an inclinometer and a universal goniometer and found no significant differences between the means. Both instruments were found to be reliable, but the authors preferred the inclinometer because it was easier to use.

Bierma-Zeinstra and associates[43] compared the reliability of hip ROM measurements taken with an electronic inclinometer with those taken by a universal goniometer. The two instruments showed equal intratester reliability for both active and passive hip ROM in general and passive hip flexion and passive extension ROM. The intratester reliability of the inclinometer was higher than that of the goniometer for passive hip lateral rotation and sitting medial rotation. The goniometer had higher reliability for active and passive medial rotation in the prone position. The authors concluded that because the inclinometer and goniometer do not result in the same ROM values, the instruments should not be used interchangeably.

Gajdosik, Sandler, and Marr[14] assessed the intratester reliability of measurements of hip abduction or adduction during both the Ober and Modified Ober tests. One therapist administered all of the tests, and an assistant positioned and

| TABLE 8.7 | Intratester Reliability | | | | |
|---|---|---|---|---|---|
| Author | n | Sample | Position | Motion | ICC |
| Van Dillen et al[44] | 35 | Healthy subjects | Supine: Hip in neutral and knee in 80 degrees flexion | Extension | Right hip 0.70<br>Left hip 0.89 |
| | | | Hip in neutral and knee in full extension | Extension | Right hip 0.72<br>Left hip 0.76 |
| | | | Hip in full abduction and knee in 80 degrees flexion | Extension | Right hip 0.87<br>Left hip 0.76 |
| | | | Hip in full abduction flexion and knee in full extension | Extension | Right hip 0.96<br>Left hip 0.90 |
| Ellison et al[27] | 22 | Healthy subjects | Prone: hip in neutral position and knee flexed to 90 degrees | Medial rotation<br>Lateral rotation | Right hip 0.99<br>Right hip 0.96 |
| Cadenhead et al[68] | 6 | Adults with cerebral palsy | Supine<br>Prone<br>Supine | Abduction<br>Extension<br>Lateral rotation | Right hip 0.99<br>Right hip 0.98<br>Right hip 0.79 |

ICC = intraclass correlation coefficient.

| TABLE 8.8 | Intertester Reliability | | | | |
|---|---|---|---|---|---|
| Author | n | Sample | Position | Motion | ICC |
| Simoneau et al[36] | 60 | Healthy subjects (18–27 yrs) | Prone | Medial rotation | 0.82, 0.96, 0.97 |
| | | | Seated | Medial rotation | 0.89, 0.85, 0.93 |
| | | | Prone | Lateral rotation | 0.89, 0.79, 0.98 |
| | | | Seated | Lateral rotation | 0.90, 0.76, 0.95 |
| Ellison et al[27] | 22 | Healthy subjects (20–41 yrs) | Prone | Left medial rotation | 0.98 |
| | | | Prone | Left lateral rotation | 0.97 |
| | | | Prone | Right medial rotation | 0.99 |
| | | | Prone | Right lateral rotation | 0.96 |
| | 15 | Adults with back pain (23–61 yrs) | Prone | Left medial rotation | 0.97 |
| | | | Prone | Left lateral rotation | 0.95 |
| | | | Prone | Right medial rotation | 0.96 |
| | | | Prone | Right lateral rotation | 0.95 |

ICC = intraclass correlation coefficient.

read the universal goniometer. The intraclass correlation coefficients (ICCs) among three trials for women were 0.87 for the Ober test and 0.92 for the Modified Ober test. The ICCs for men were slightly lower, with an ICC of 0.83 for the Ober test and an ICC of 0.82 for the Modified Ober test.

Reese and Bandy,[16] in a study involving 61 healthy subjects with a mean age of 24 years, used an inclinometer to determine the intratester reliability of the repeated measurements of the Ober and Modified Ober tests. Intertester reliability was greater than an ICC of 0.90 for both tests using the inclinometer. T tests showed a significant difference in hip adduction ROM between the Ober test (18.9 degrees) and the Modified Ober test (23.4 degrees), but the actual difference between the two tests was 4.5 degrees.

Youdas and associates[7] had two experienced testers measure hamstring length with a 360-degree goniometer using the passive SLR test in 214 adults (108 women and 106 men between the ages of 20 and 79 years. ICCs were 0.97 for the right side and 0.98 for the left side.

Piva and colleagues[69] determined the intertester reliability of measurements of the length of the hamstrings, tensor fasciae latae, and the quadriceps. Two pairs of testers took the measurements with an inclinometer in 30 subjects with a mean age of 28.1 years. All ICCs were higher than 0.80. (Hamstring length ICC = 0.92 and tensor fascia latae ICC = 0.97).

Steinberg and associates[35] calculated intratester reliability coefficients on test-retest ROM measurements on 20 subjects. Intratester Pearson values ranged from r = 0.90 for hip medial rotation to r = 0.96 for both hip abduction and hip flexion. Predictably, intertester reliability r values were lower, ranging from 0.74 to 0.95.

In a study by Pandya and colleagues,[60] five physical therapists using universal goniometers measured passive joint motions including hip extension in 105 children and adolescents, aged 1 to 20 years, who had Duchenne muscular dystrophy. The intratester reliability for measurements of hip extension was good (ICC = 0.85), and the intertester reliability for measurements of hip extension was fair (ICC = 0.74). The results indicated the need for the same examiner to take measurements for long-term follow-up and to assess the results of therapeutic intervention.

McWhirk and Glanzman[58] employed two therapists (one with 10 years of experience and one with 1 year of experience) to measure abduction and extension ROM in both hips of 25 children aged 2 to 18 years with spastic cerebral palsy. To achieve the standarized positioning recommended by Norkin and White, the therapists assisted each other to help support and stabilize the limbs. Hip extension was measured using the Thomas test and was the least reliable intertester measurement with ICC = 0.58 (95 percent confidence interval (CI) for mean absolute difference = 3.96 ± 1.87 degrees), but intertester reliability for hip abduction ROM had an ICC of 0.91 (95 percent CI for mean absolute difference = 3.47 ± 1.47 degrees). The authors demonstrated that therapists with differing levels of pediatric experience can achieve moderate to high levels of intertester reliability. The effect of a strict protocol and the use of a second person to either stabilize or help hold the test limb in patients with cerebral palsy appeared to contribute to the high level of reliability.

Kilgour, McNair, and Stott[62] conducted a study in which three testers used a pediatric plastic goniometer with 10-cm moveable arms to measure straight leg raise, popliteal angle, prone hip extension, and hip extension in supine in the Thomas test and other joints in 25 children with spastic cerebral palsy aged 6 to 17 years and 25 age- and sex-matched healthy controls. The ICCs for intrasessional measures for straight leg raise (hip flexion) and for the popliteal angle were 0.95 and higher in both groups. The ICCs for the Thomas tests were poor for both groups, although there were low median absolute differences. Intersessional variation in both groups was high, indicating that the measurement variability was not influenced by the presence of spasticity. Measurement of a fixed joint by the three physical therapists was very reliable, with a maximum difference of 5 degrees and a between-sessions difference of 6.5 degrees. Therefore, the authors concluded that a major source of error in the study was difficulty in determining the correct end-range joint positioning.

Mutlu and associates [63] conducted a study in which passive range of motion was measured in 38 patients aged 18 to 108 months with spastic cerebral palsy. Three physical therapists used a 360-degree goniometer to measure each child's hip ROM once in each session on two different occasions 1 week apart. The highest intertester reliability (ICC = 0.95) was for hip extension using the Thomas test, and the lowest (ICC = 0.61) was for hip abduction. Intrareliability and interreliability was also high for hip flexion with the knee flexed and the opposite leg extended.

Croft and associates [61] had six clinicians use a fluid-filled inclinometer called a Plurimeter to take passive hip flexion and rotation ROM measurements of both hips in six patients with osteoarthritis involving only one hip joint. The results showed that the degree of agreement among testers was greatest for measurements of hip flexion.

Cibulka and colleagues, [67] in a study of passive ROM in medial and lateral hip rotation in 100 patients with low-back pain, determined that for this group of patients, measurements of rotation taken in the prone position were more reliable than those taken in the sitting position.

Holm and associates [59] compared the reliability of goniometric and visual measurements in 25 patients with hip osteoarthritis symptoms and a mean age of 64 years. Two teams consisting of two therapists each and one team consisting of a single experienced therapist took passive standardized goniometric measurements using a half-circle metal goniometer. The fourth team was an orthopedic surgeon who made visual estimates. Each team took measurements on two occasions with a week between sessions. There were highly significant differences in degrees between measurements made by the single persons when compared to measurements made by two people working together, except for internal rotation. The authors concluded that to obtain the most accurate results, measurements should be performed by two people working together. No significant differences were found between goniometric measurements and visual estimates or between measurements from the first and second sessions for the same team with the exception of hip abduction. Reproducibility of meaurements was best for hip flexion.

Cliborne and associates [70] determined the ROM and intratester reliability of hip flexion in 22 patients with osteoarthritis of the knee (mean age = 61.2 years) and 17 subjects without symptoms. Intratester reliability for hip flexion for two pairs of testers using an inclinometer was an ICC of 0.94 (95% CI = 0.89–0.97).

Owen and colleagues [71] followed the goniometric protocols used by the AAOS to measure 82 children aged 4 to 10 years with femoral shaft fractures at 15 and 24 months post-fracture. Hip abduction and adduction were measured in the supine position, and hip rotation was measured in the prone position. Active hip extension was measured using the Thomas test. The most reliable measure was for hip flexion ROM, but that was low with an ICC of 0.48 (95% CI = 0.29–0.63). The authors concluded that standarized protocols for hip ROM in this population had low reliability because only when differences in rotation exceeded at least 30 degrees and ROM in flexion–extension exceeded 50 degrees could clinicians conclude that true change has occurred.

In a reliability and validity study by Sprigle and associates, [72] radiographs were taken as 10 healthy male subjects sat in erect, anterior, and posterior postures. An electromagnetic tracking device (Flock of Birds) was used to digitize the anterior and posterior superior iliac spines as a 6 degree of freedom sensor was mounted on the thigh and sacrum. The variables were pelvic tilt and hip thigh flexion angle. Intratester reliability was calculated using nine radiographs and two testers. Intertester reliability was calculated from 30 radiographs and two testers. The ICCs for both intratester and intertester reliability were 0.98 or higher. Validity was determined by comparison of Flock of Birds measurements with radiographic measurements.

# REFERENCES

1. Levangie, PK, and Norkin, CC: Joint Structure and Function: A Comprehensive Analysis, ed 4. FA Davis, Philadelphia, 2005.
2. Cyriax, JH, and Cyriax, PJ: Illustrated Manual of Orthopaedic Medicine. Butterworths, London, 1983.
3. Greene, WB, and Heckman, JD (eds): American Academy of Orthopaedic Surgeons: The Clinical Measurement of Joint Motion. AAOS, Chicago, 1994.
4. American Medical Association: Guides to the Evaluation of Permanent Impairment, ed 5. Cocchiarella, L and Andersson, GBL (eds). AMA, Chicago, 2000.
5. Roach, KE, and Miles, TP: Normal hip and knee active range of motion: The relationship to age. Phys Ther 71:656, 1991.
6. Kendall, FP, et al: Muscles: Testing and Function with Posture and Pain, ed 5. Lippincott Williams and Wilkins, Baltimore, 2005.
7. Youdas, JW, et al:The influence of gender and age on hamstring length in healthy adults. J Orthop Sports Phys Ther 35:246, 2005.
8. Ober, FR: The role of the iliotibial band and fascia lata as a factor in the causation of low-back disabilities and sciatica. J Bone Joint Surg 18:105, 1936.
9. Noble, HB, Hajek, MR, and Porter, M: Diagnosis and treatment of iliotibial band tightness in runners. Phys Sports Med 10:67, 1982.
10. McConnell, J: The physical therapist's approach to patellofemoral disorders. Clin Sports Med 21:363, 2002.
11. Hoppenfeld, S: Physical Examination of the Spine and Extremities. Appleton-Century-Crofts, New York, 1976, p 167.
12. Gose, JC, and Schweizer, P: Iliotibial band tightness. J Orthop Sports Phys Ther 10:399, 1989.
13. Cade, DL, et al: Indirectly measuring length of the iliotibial band and related hip structures: A correlational analysis of four adduction tests. Abstract Platform Presentation at APTA Mid-Winter. Tex J Orthop Sports Phys Ther 31:A22, 2001.
14. Gajdosik, RL, Sandler, MM, and Marr, HL: Influence of knee position and gender on the Ober test for length of the iliotibial band. Clin Biomech 18:77, 2003.
15. Wang, T-G, et al: Assessment of stretching of the iliotibial tract with Ober and Modified Ober Tests: An Ultrasonographic study. Arch Phys Med Rehabil 87:1407-1410, 2006.
16. Reese, NB, and Bandy, WD: Use of an inclinometer to measure flexibility of the iliotibial band using the Ober Test and the Modified Ober Test: Differences in magnitude and reliability of measurement. J Orthop Sports Phys Ther 33:326, 2003.
17. Boone, DC, and Azen, SP: Normal range of motion of joints in male subjects. J Bone Joint Surg Am 61:756, 1979.
18. Svenningsen, S, et al: Hip motion related to age and sex. Acta Orthop Scand 60:97, 1989.
19. Waugh, KG, et al: Measurement of selected hip, knee and ankle joint motions in newborns. Phys Ther 63:1616, 1983.
20. Schwarze, DJ, and Denton, JR: Normal values of neonatal limbs: An evaluation of 1000 neonates. J Pediatr Orthop 13:758, 1993.
21. Broughton, NS, Wright, J, and Menelaus, MB: Range of knee motion in normal neonates. J Pediatr Orthop 13:263, 1993.
22. Drews, JE, Vraciu, JK, and Pellino, G: Range of motion of the joints of the lower extremities of newborns. Phys Occup Ther Pediatr 4:49, 1984.
23. Wanatabe, H, et al: The range of joint motions of the extremities in healthy Japanese people: The difference according to age. Cited in Walker, JM: Musculoskeletal development: A review. Phys Ther 71:878, 1991.
24. Phelps, E, Smith, LJ, and Hallum, A: Normal range of hip motion of infants between 9 and 24 months of age. Dev Med Child Neurol 27:785, 1985.
25. Forero, N, Okamura, LA, and Larson, MA: Normal ranges of hip motion in neonates. J Pediatr Orthop 9:391, 1989.
26. Kozic, S, et al: Femoral anteversion related to side differences in hip rotation. Passive rotation in 1140 children aged 8-9 years. Acta Orthop Scand 68:533, 1997.
27. Ellison, JB, Rose, SJ, and Sahrman, SA: Patterns of hip rotation: A comparison between healthy subjects and patients with low back pain. Phys Ther 70:537, 1990.
28. Boone, DC: Techniques of measurement of joint motion. (Unpublished supplement to Boone, DC, and Azen, SP: Normal range of motion in male subjects. J Bone Joint Surg Am 61:756, 1979.)
29. Walker, JM: Musculoskeletal development: A review. Phys Ther 71:878, 1991.
30. Nonaka, H, et al: Age-related changes in the interactive mobility of the hip and knee joints: A geometrical analysis. Gait Posture 15:236, 2002.
31. Allander, E, et al: Normal range of joint movements in shoulder, hip, wrist and thumb with special reference to side: A comparison between two populations. Int J Epidemiol 3:253, 1974.
32. Walker, JM, et al: Active mobility of the extremities in older subjects. Phys Ther 64:919, 1984.
33. Boone, DC, Walker, JM, and Perry, J: Age and sex differences in lower extremity joint motion. Presented at the National Conference of the American Physical Therapy Association, Washington, DC, 1981.
34. James, B, and Parker, AW: Active and passive mobility of lower limb joints in elderly men and women. Am J Phys Med Rehabil 68:162, 1989.
35. Steinberg, N, et al: Range of movement in female dancers and non-dancers aged 8–16 years. Am J Sports Med 34:814, 2006.
36. Simoneau, GG, et al: Influence of hip position and gender on active hip internal and external rotation. J Orthop Sports Phys Ther 28:158, 1998.
37. Hu, H, et al: Measurements of voluntary joint range of motion of the Chinese elderly living in Beijing area by a photographic method. Intern J Indust Ergonomics 36: 861, 2006.
38. Sanya, AO, and Obi, CS: Range of motion in selected joints of diabetic and non-diabetic subjects. Afr J Health Sci 6:17, 1999.
39. Kettunen, J, et al: Factors associated with hip joint rotation in former elite athletes. Br J Sports Med 34:44, 2000.
40. Escalante, A, et al: Determinants of hip and knee flexion range: Results from the San Antonio Longitudinal Study of Aging. Arthritis Care Res 12:8, 1999.
41. Lichtenstein, MJ, et al: Modeling impairment: Using the disablement process as a framework to evaluate determinants of hip and knee flexion. Aging (Milan) 12:208, 2000.
42. Bennell, K, et al: Hip and ankle range of motion and hip muscle strength in young novice female ballet dancers and controls. Br J Sports Med 33:340, 1999.
43. Bierma-Zeinstra, SMA, et al: Comparison between two devices for measuring hip joint motions. Clin Rehabil 12:497, 1998.
44. Van Dillen, LR, et al: Effect of knee and hip position on hip extension range of motion in individuals with and without low back pain. J Orthop Sports Phys Ther 30:307, 2000.
45. Gilbert, CB, Gross, MT, and Klug, KB: Relationship between hip external rotation and turnout angle for the five classical ballet positions. J Orthop Sports Phys Ther 27:339, 1998.
46. Tyler, T, et al: A new pelvic tilt detection device: Roentgenographic validation and application to assessment of hip motion in professional hockey players. J Orthop Sports Phys Ther 24:303, 1996.
47. Van Mechelen, W, et al: Is range of motion of the hip and ankle joint related to running injuries? A case control study. Int J Sports Med 13:606, 1992.
48. Steultjens, MPM, et al: Range of motion and disability in patients with osteoarthritis of the knee or hip. Rheumatology 39:955, 2000.
49. Mollinger, LA, and Steffan, TM: Knee flexion contractures in institutionalized elderly: Prevalence, severity, stability and related variables. Phys Ther 73:437, 1993.
50. Beissner, KL, Collins, JE, and Holmes, H: Muscle force and range of motion as predictors of function in older adults. Phys Ther 80:556, 2000.
51. Magee, DJ: Orthopedic Physical Assessment, ed 4. WB Saunders, Philadelphia, 2002.
52. The Pathokinesiology Service and the Physical Therapy Department: Observational Gait Analysis Handbook. Ranchos Los Amigos Medical Center, Downey, Cal., 1989.
53. Livingston, LA, Stevenson, JM, and Olney, SJ: Stairclimbing kinematics on stairs of differing dimensions. Arch Phys Med Rehabil 72:398, 1991.
54. McFayden, BJ, and Winter, DA: An integrated biomechanical analysis of normal stair ascent and descent. J Biomech 21:733, 1988.
55. Protopapadaki, A, Drechsler, WI, Cramp, MC, et al: Hip knee and ankle kinematics and kinetics during stair ascent and descent in healthy young individuals. Clin Biomech 22:203, 2007.
56. Oberg, T, Krazinia, A, and Oberg, K: Joint angle parameters in gait: Reference data for normal subjects 10–79 years of age. J Rehabil Res Dev 31:199, 1994.
57. Hemmerich, A, Brown, H, Smith, S, et al: Hip, knee and ankle kinematics of high range of motion activities of daily living. J Orthop Res 24:770, 2006.
58. McWhirk, LB, and Glanzman, AM: Within-session inter-rater reliability of goniometeric measures in patients with spastic cerebral palsy. Pediatr Phys Ther 18:262, 2006.

59. Holm, I, et al: Reliability of goniometric measurements and visual estimates of hip ROM in patients with osteoarthrosis. Physiother Res Int 5:242, 2000.

60. Pandya, S, et al: Reliability of goniometric measurements in patients with Duchenne muscular dystrophy. Phys Ther 65:1339, 1985.

61. Croft, PR, et al: Interobserver reliability in measuring flexion, internal rotation and external rotation of the hip using a pleurimeter. Ann Rheum Dis 55:320, 1996.

62. Kilgour, G, McNair, P and Stott, NS: Intrarater reliability of lower limb sagittal range of motion measures in children with spastic cerebral palsy. Develop Med Child Neurol 45:391, 2003.

63. Mutlu, A, Livanelioglu A, and Gunel, MK: Reliability of goniometric measurements in children with spastic cerebral palsy. Med Sci Monit 13:CR323, 2007.

64. Boone, DC, et al: Reliability of goniometric measurements. Phys Ther 58:1355, 1978.

65. Clapper, MP, and Wolf, SL: Comparison of the reliability of the Orthoranger and the standard goniometer for assessing active lower extremity range of motion. Phys Ther 68:214, 1988.

66. Ekstrand, J, et al: Lower extremity goniometric measurements: A study to determine their reliability. Arch Phys Med Rehabil 63:171, 1982.

67. Cibulka, MT, et al: Unilateral hip rotation range of motion asymmetry in patients with sacroiliac joint regional pain. Spine 23:1009, 1998.

68. Cadenhead, SL, McEwen, IR, and Thompson, DM: Effect of passive range of motion exercises on lower extremity goniometric measurements of adults with cerebral palsy: A single subject study design. Phys Ther 82:658, 2002.

69. Piva, SR, et al: Reliability of measures of impairments associated with patellofemoral pain syndrome. BMC Musculoskelet Disord 7:33, 2006.

70. Cliborne, AV, et al: Clinical hip tests and a functional squat test in patients with knee osteoarthritis: Reliability, prevalence of positive test findings, and short-term response to hip mobilization. J Orthop Sports Phys Ther 234:676, 2004.

71. Owen, J, Stephens, D, and Wright, JG: Reliability of hip range of motion using goniometry in pediatric femur shaft fractures. Can J Surg 50:251, 2007.

72. Sprigle, S, et al: Development of a noninvasive measure of pelvic and hip angles in seated posture. Arch Phys Med Rehabil 83:1597, 2002.

# The Knee

## ⌀ Structure and Function

### Tibiofemoral and Patellofemoral Joints

#### Anatomy

The knee is composed of two distinct articulations enclosed within a single joint capsule: the tibiofemoral joint and the patellofemoral joint. At the tibiofemoral joint, the proximal joint surfaces are the convex medial and the lateral condyles of the distal femur (Fig. 9.1). Posteriorly and inferiorly, the

longer medial condyle is separated from the lateral condyle by a deep groove called the intercondylar notch. Anteriorly, the condyles are separated by a shallow area of bone called the femoral patellar surface. The distal articulating surfaces are the two shallow concave medial and lateral condyles on the proximal end of the tibia. Two bony spines called the intercondylar tubercles separate the medial condyle from the lateral condyle. Two joint discs called menisci are attached to the articulating surfaces on the tibial condyles (Fig. 9.2). At the patellofemoral joint, the articulating surfaces are the posterior surface of the patella and the femoral patellar surface (Fig. 9.3).

The joint capsule that encloses both joints is large, loose, and reinforced by tendons and expansions from the surrounding muscles and ligaments. The quadriceps tendon, patellar ligament, and expansions from the extensor muscles provide anterior stability (see Fig. 9.3). The lateral and medial collateral ligaments, iliotibial band, and pes anserinus help to provide medial–lateral stability, and the knee flexors help to

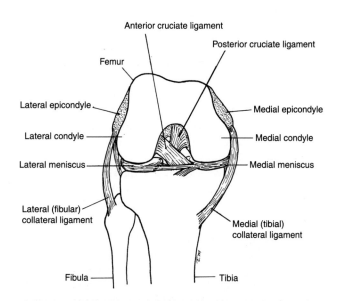

**FIGURE 9.1** An anterior view of a right knee showing the tibiofemoral joint.

**FIGURE 9.2** An anterior view of a right knee in the flexed position showing femoral and tibial condyles, medial and lateral menisci, and cruciate and collateral ligaments.

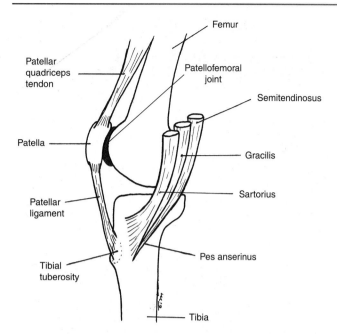

**FIGURE 9.3** A view of a right knee showing the medial aspect, where the cut tendons of the three muscles that insert into the anteromedial aspect of the tibia make up the pes anserinus. Also included are the patellofemoral joint, the patellar ligament, and the patellar tendon.

provide posterior stability. In addition, the tibiofemoral joint is reinforced by the anterior and posterior cruciate ligaments, which are located within the joint (see Fig. 9.2).

## Osteokinematics

The tibiofemoral joint is a double condyloid joint with 2 degrees of freedom. Flexion–extension occurs in the sagittal plane around a medial–lateral axis; rotation occurs in the transverse plane around a vertical (longitudinal) axis.[1] The incongruence and asymmetry of the tibiofemoral joint surfaces combined with muscle activity and ligamentous restraints produce an automatic rotation. This automatic rotation is involuntary and occurs primarily toward the end of extension when motion stops on the shorter lateral femoral condyle but continues on the longer medial condylar surface. During the last portion of active extension range of motion (ROM) automatic rotation produces what is referred to as either the screw-home mechanism, or "locking," of the knee. For example, during non–weight-bearing active knee extension with the tibia moving on the femur, the tibia laterally rotates during the last 10 to 15 degrees of extension to lock the knee.[2] Therefore, in the fully extended position of the knee, the tibia is laterally rotated in relation to the femur. To unlock the knee, either the tibia has to rotate medially or the femur has to rotate laterally to unlock the knee. This rotation is not under voluntary control and should not be confused with the voluntary rotation movement possible at the joint when the knee is flexed.

Passive ROM in flexion is generally considered to be between 130 and 140 degrees. The range of extension beyond 0 degrees is about 5 to 10 degrees in young children, whereas 0 degrees is considered to be within normal limits for adults.[3]

The greatest range of voluntary knee rotation occurs at 90 degrees of flexion; at this point, about 45 degrees of lateral rotation and 15 degrees of medial rotation are possible.

## Arthrokinematics

In non–weight-bearing active motion, the concave tibial articulating surfaces slide on the convex femoral condyles in the same direction as the movement of the shaft of the tibia. The tibial condyles slide posteriorly on the femoral condyles during flexion, and the tibial condyles slide anteriorly on the femoral condyles during extension.

The incongruence of the tibiofemoral joint and the fact that the femoral articulating surfaces are larger than the tibial articulating surfaces dictate that when the femoral condyles are moving on the tibial condyles (in a weight-bearing situation) the femoral condyles must roll and slide to remain on the tibia. In weight-bearing flexion, the femoral condyles roll posteriorly and slide anteriorly. The menisci follow the roll of the condyles by distorting posteriorly in flexion. In extension, the femoral condyles roll anteriorly and slide posteriorly.[1] In the last portion of extension, motion stops at the lateral femoral condyle, but sliding continues on the medial femoral condyle to produce locking of the knee.

The patella slides superiorly in extension and inferiorly in flexion. Some patellar rotation and tilting accompany the sliding during flexion and extension.[1]

## Capsular Pattern

The capsular pattern at the knee is characterized by a smaller limitation of extension than of flexion and no restriction of rotations.[4,5] Fritz and associates[6] found that patients with a capsular pattern, defined as a ratio of extension loss to flexion loss between 0.03 and 0.50, were 3.2 times more likely to have arthritis or arthroses of the knee. Hayes reported a mean ratio of extension loss to flexion loss of 0.40 in a study of 79 patients with osteoarthritis.[7,8]

# RANGE OF MOTION TESTING PROCEDURES: Knee

 Landmarks for Testing Procedures

**FIGURE 9.4** A lateral view of the subject's right lower extremity showing surface anatomy landmarks for goniometer alignment.

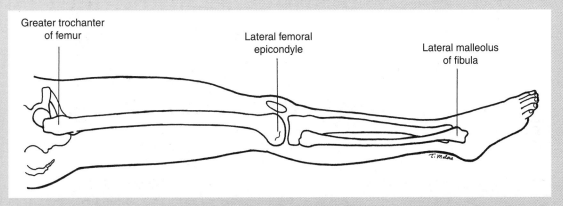

Greater trochanter of femur

Lateral femoral epicondyle

Lateral malleolus of fibula

**FIGURE 9.5** A lateral view of the subject's right lower extremity showing bony anatomical landmarks for goniometer alignment for measuring knee flexion ROM.

# ● KNEE FLEXION

Motion occurs in the sagittal plane around a medial–lateral axis. According to the American Medical Association (AMA),[9] the normal flexion ROM for adults is 150 degrees. According to Boone and Azen,[10] the mean flexion ROM for males age 18 months to 54 years is 142.5 degrees. Roach and Miles[11] found a mean knee flexion range of 132.0 degrees for males and females 25 to 74 years of age. Please refer to Tables 9.1 through 9.4 in the Research Findings section for additional normal ROM values by age and gender.

## Testing Position

Place the subject supine, with the knee in extension. Position the hip in 0 degrees of extension, abduction, and adduction. Place a towel roll under the ankle to allow the knee to extend as much as possible.

## Stabilization

Stabilize the femur to prevent rotation, abduction, and adduction of the hip.

## Testing Motion

Hold the subject's ankle in one hand and the posterior thigh with the other hand. Move the subject's thigh to approximately 90 degrees of hip flexion and move the knee into flexion (Fig. 9.6). Stabilize the thigh to prevent further motion and guide the lower leg into knee flexion. The end of the range of knee flexion occurs when resistance is felt and attempts to overcome the resistance cause additional hip flexion.

## Normal End-Feel

Usually, the end-feel is soft because of contact between the muscle bulk of the posterior calf and the thigh or between the heel and the buttocks. The end-feel may be firm because of tension in the vastus medialis, vastus lateralis, and vastus intermedialis muscles.

## Goniometer Alignment

See Figures 9.7 and 9.8.

1. Center **fulcrum** of the goniometer over the lateral epicondyle of the femur.
2. Align **proximal arm** with the lateral midline of the femur, using the greater trochanter for reference.
3. Align **distal arm** with the lateral midline of the fibula, using the lateral malleolus and fibular head for reference.

**FIGURE 9.6** The right lower extremity at the end of knee flexion ROM. The examiner uses one hand to move the subject's thigh to approximately 90 degrees of hip flexion and then stabilizes the femur to prevent further flexion. The examiner's other hand guides the subject's lower leg through full knee flexion ROM.

**FIGURE 9.7** In the starting position for measuring knee flexion ROM, the subject is supine with the upper thigh exposed so that the greater trochanter can be visualized and palpated. The examiner either kneels or sits on a stool to align and read the goniometer at eye level.

**FIGURE 9.8** At the end of the knee flexion ROM, the examiner uses one hand to maintain knee flexion and also to keep the distal arm of the goniometer aligned with the lateral midline of the leg.

## ● KNEE EXTENSION

Extension occurs in the sagittal plane around a medial–lateral axis and may be described as a return to the 0 starting position from the end of the knee flexion ROM. Knee extension is usually recorded as the starting position for flexion. An extension limitation (inability to reach the 0 starting position) is present when the starting position for flexion ROM does not begin at 0 degrees but in some amount of flexion. When extension goes beyond the 0 starting position, it may be within normal limits in children, but when it exceeds 5 or more degrees in the adult, it is called **hyperextension** or **genu recurvatum**. See Table 9.2 in the Research Findings section for normal extension limitations in neonates, and see Table 9.3 for normal extension beyond 0 in children 0 to 12 years of age.

### Normal End-Feel

The end-feel is firm because of tension in the posterior joint capsule, the oblique and arcuate popliteal ligaments, the collateral ligaments, and the anterior and posterior cruciate ligaments.

## MUSCLE LENGTH TESTING PROCEDURES: Knee

## ● RECTUS FEMORIS: ELY TEST

The rectus femoris is one of the four muscles that make up the muscle group called the quadriceps femoris. The rectus femoris is the only one of the four muscles that crosses both the hip and the knee joints. The muscle arises proximally from two tendons: an anterior tendon from the anterior inferior iliac spine and a posterior tendon from a groove superior to the brim of the acetabulum. Distally, the muscle attaches to the base of the patella by way of the thick, flat quadriceps tendon and attaches to the tibial tuberosity by way of the patellar ligament (Fig. 9.9).

When the rectus femoris muscle contracts, it flexes the hip and extends the knee. If the rectus femoris is short, knee flexion is limited when the hip is maintained in a neutral position. If knee flexion is limited when the hip is in a flexed position, the limitation is not due to a short rectus femoris muscle but to abnormalities of joint structures or short one-joint knee extensor muscles. In a study by Piva and associates, the mean of four tester's measurements of the length of the rectus femoris in 30 patients with patellofemoral pain syndrome aged 14 to 47 years was 138.5 degrees, with a standard deviation (SD) of 12.3 degrees.[12]

### Starting Position

Place the subject prone, with both feet off the end of the examining table. Extend the knees and position the hips in 0 degrees of flexion, extension, abduction, adduction, and rotation (Fig. 9.10).

### Stabilization

Stabilize the hip to maintain the neutral position. Do not allow the hip to flex.

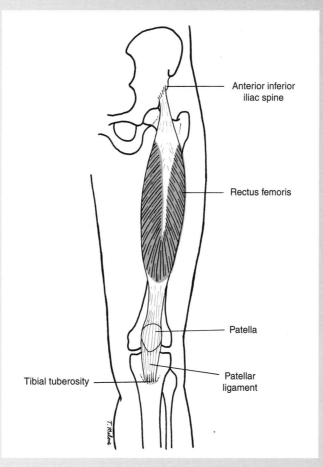

**FIGURE 9.9** An anterior view of the left lower extremity showing the attachments of the rectus femoris muscle.

**FIGURE 9.10** The subject is shown in the prone starting position for testing the length of the rectus femoris muscle.

**FIGURE 9.11** A lateral view of the subject at the end of the testing motion for the length of the left rectus femoris muscle.

**FIGURE 9.12** A lateral view of the left rectus femoris muscle being stretched over the hip and knee joints at the end of the testing motion.

## Testing Motion

Flex the knee by lifting the lower leg off the table. The end of the ROM occurs when resistance is felt from tension in the anterior thigh and further knee flexion causes the hip to flex. If the knee can be flexed to at least 90 degrees with the hip in the neutral position, the length of the rectus femoris is normal (Figs. 9.11 and 9.12).

## Goniometer Alignment

See Figure 9.13.

1. Center **fulcrum** of the goniometer over the lateral epicondyle of the femur.
2. Align **proximal arm** with the lateral midline of the femur, using the greater trochanter as a reference.
3. Align **distal arm** with the lateral midline of the fibula, using the lateral malleolus and the fibular head for reference.

**FIGURE 9.13** Goniometer alignment for measuring the position of the knee.

# ✦ HAMSTRING MUSCLES: SEMITENDINOSUS, SEMIMEMBRANOSUS, AND BICEPS FEMORIS: DISTAL HAMSTRING LENGTH TEST OR POPLITEAL ANGLE TEST

The distal hamstring length test is also called the popliteal angle (PA) test because the angle that is being measured is the popliteal angle between the femur and the lower leg. The hamstring muscles are composed of the semitendinosus, semimembranosus, and biceps femoris. The semitendinosus, semimembranosus, and the long head of the biceps femoris cross both the hip and the knee joints. The proximal attachment of the **semitendinosus** is on the ischial tuberosity, and the distal attachment is on the proximal aspect of the medial surface of the tibia (Fig. 9.14A). The proximal attachment of the **semimembranosus** is on the ischial tuberosity, and the distal attachment is on the medial aspect of the medial tibial condyle (Fig. 9.14B). The **biceps femoris** muscle arises from two heads; the long head attaches to the ischial tuberosity and the sacrotuberous ligament,

whereas the short head attaches along the lateral lip linear aspera, the lateral supracondylar line, and the lateral intermuscular septum. The distal attachments of the biceps femoris are on the head of the fibula, with a small portion attaching to the lateral tibial condyle and the lateral collateral ligament (see Fig. 9.14A).

When the hamstring muscles contract, they extend the hip and flex the knee. In the following test, the hip is maintained in 90 degrees of flexion while the knee is extended to determine whether the muscles are of normal length. If the hamstrings are short, the muscles limit knee extension ROM when the hip is positioned at 90 degrees of flexion.

Gajdosik and associates,[13] in a study of 30 healthy males aged 18 to 40 years, found a mean value of 31 degrees (SD = 7.5 degrees) for passive knee extension during this test with a large range of values from 17 to 45 degrees. Testers noted that knee extension end-feel was firm and easily identified. Intrarater reliability intraclass correlation coefficients (ICCs) for the test were 0.86 when knee extension was performed actively and 0.90 when performed passively. Some researchers have reported the supplementary angles to those noted by Gajdosik and associates. Youdas and colleagues[14] used a 360-degree universal goniometer to measure the

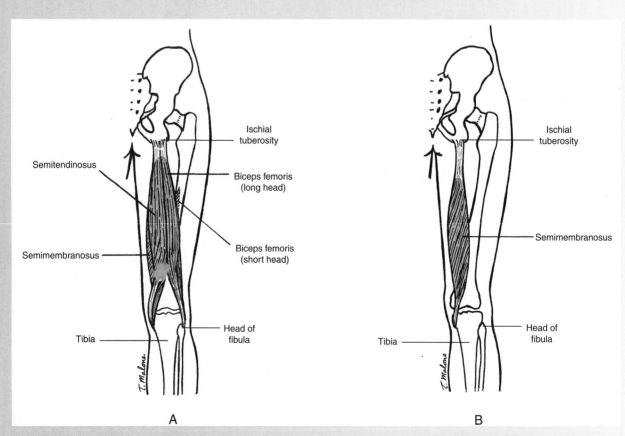

A

B

**FIGURE 9.14 A:** A posterior view of the thigh showing the attachments of the semitendinosus and the biceps femoris muscles. **B:** A posterior view of the thigh showing the attachments of the semimembranosus muscle, which lies under the two hamstring muscles shown in A.

PA in 214 subjects (108 women and 106 men) between the ages of 20 and 79 years. The mean value for the women of 152.0 degrees (SD = 10.6 degrees) was greater than the mean value for men of 141.4 degrees (SD = 8.1 degrees). The supplementary angles of these values for women and men are 28.0 and 38.6 degrees respectively, which is generally consistent with the values noted by Gajdosik and associates.

Two testers in a study by Fredriksen and colleagues[15] found that passive knee extension angle measurements for a single female subject tested 16 times per side ranged from 153 to 159 degrees for the left leg and from 154 to 165 degrees for the right leg. The supplementary angles of these values range from 27 to 21 degrees for the left leg and from 26 to 15 degrees for the right leg. A standardized force using a dynamometer was used to extend the knee, and the pelvis was stabilized by a belt. The hip was positioned in 120 degrees of flexion, which is a considerably larger angle of flexion than the 90 degrees of hip flexion used by both Youdas and associates[14] and Gadjosik and associates.[13]

## Starting Position
Position the subject supine with the hip on the side being tested in 90 degrees of flexion and 0 degrees of abduction, adduction, and rotation (Fig. 9.15). Initially, the knee being tested is allowed to relax in flexion. The lower extremity that is not being tested rests on the examining table with the knee fully extended and the hip in 0 degrees of flexion, extension, abduction, adduction, and rotation.

## Stabilization
Stabilize the femur to prevent rotation, abduction, and adduction at the hip and to maintain the hip in 90 degrees of flexion.

## Testing Motion
Extend the knee to the end of the ROM. The end of the testing motion occurs when resistance is felt from tension in the posterior thigh and further knee extension causes the hip to move toward extension (Figs. 9.16 and 9.17).

## Normal End-Feel
The end-feel is firm owing to tension in the semimembranosus, semitendinosus, and biceps femoris muscles.

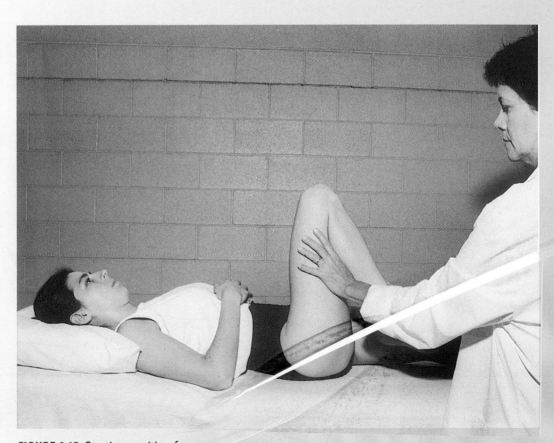

**FIGURE 9.15** Starting position for measuring the length of the hamstring muscles.

**FIGURE 9.16** End of the testing motion for the length of the right hamstring muscles.

**FIGURE 9.17** A lateral view of the right lower extremity shows the hamstring muscles being stretched over the hip and knee joints at the end of the testing motion.

## Goniometer Alignment
See Figure 9.18.

1. Center **fulcrum** of the goniometer over the lateral epicondyle of the femur.
2. Align **proximal arm** with the lateral midline of the femur, using the greater trochanter for a reference.
3. Align **distal arm** with the lateral midline of the fibula, using the lateral malleolus and fibular head for reference.

**FIGURE 9.18** Goniometer alignment for measuring knee position.

## ✐ Research Findings

This section of the chapter includes not only age and gender effects on knee ROM but also the effects of body mass. Also included is the range of functional knee ROM required for stairs and other activities of daily living followed by a sampling of reliability and validity studies in normal and patient populations. Table 9.1 provides knee ROM values from selected sources.[9–11] See Tables 9.2 to 9.4 for additional ROM values by age and gender.

### Effects of Age, Gender, and Other Factors

#### Age

Knee extension limitations at birth are normal and similar to extension limitations found at the hip joint at birth. The term "extension limitation" is used rather than "flexion contracture" because contracture refers to an abnormal condition caused by fixed muscle shortness, which may be permanent.[16] Knee extension limitations in the neonate gradually disappear, and extension, instead of being limited, may become excessive in the toddler. Waugh and colleagues[17] and Drews and coworkers[18] found that newborns lacked approximately 15 to 20 degrees of knee extension. Schwarze and Denton,[19] in a study of 1000 neonates (527 girls and 473 boys) in the first 3 days of life, found a mean extension limitation of 15 degrees. These findings agree with the findings of Wanatabe and associates,[20] who found that newborns lacked 14 degrees of knee extension. The extension limitation gradually disappears, as shown by comparing Tables 9.2 and 9.3.

Broughton, Wright, and Menelaus[21] measured extension limitations in normal neonates at birth and again at 3 months and 6 months. At birth, 53 of the 57 (93 percent) neonates had extension limitations of 15 degrees or greater, whereas only 30 of 57 (53 percent) infants had extension limitations at 6 months of age. The mean reduction in extension limitations was 3.5 degrees per month from birth to 3 months and 2.8 degrees between 3 and 6 months (see Table 9.3). The 2 year olds in the study conducted by Wanatabe and associates[20] (see Table 9.3) had no evidence of a knee extension limitation.

Knee extension beyond 0 degrees (often referred to as hyperextension) is considered to be a normal finding in young children but is not usually observed in adults,[3] who may have slightly less than full knee extension. Wanatabe and associates[20] found that the 2 year olds had up to 5 degrees of extension beyond 0. This finding is similar to the mean of 5.4 degrees of extension beyond 0 noted by Boone[22] for the group of children between 1 year and 5 years of age. Beighton, Solomon, and Soskolne,[23] in a study of joint laxity in 1081 males and females, found that joint laxity decreased rapidly throughout childhood in both genders and decreased at a slower rate during adulthood. The authors used a ROM of greater than 10 degrees of knee extension beyond 0 as one of the criteria of joint laxity. Cheng and colleagues,[24] in a study of 2360 Chinese children, found that the average of 16 degrees of knee extension beyond 0 in children of 3 years of age decreased to 7 degrees by the time the children reached 9 years of age. A comparison of the knee extension beyond 0 mean values for the group aged 13 to 19 years in Table 9.4 with the extension values for the group aged 1 to 5 years in Table 9.3, demonstrates the decrease in extension beyond 0 that occurs in childhood.

| TABLE 9.1 | Knee Flexion Range of Motion: Normal Values in Degrees | | |
|---|---|---|---|
| | AMA[9] | Boone[10] | Roach and Miles[11] |
| | | **Males 18 mos–54 yrs n = 109** | **Males and Females 25–74 yrs n = 1683** |
| **Motion** | | **Mean (SD)** | **Mean (SD)** |
| Flexion | 150 | 142.5 (5.4) | 132.0 (10.0) |

(SD) = standard deviation.

| TABLE 9.2 | Knee Extension Limitations in Neonates 6 Hours to 7 Days of Age: Normal Values in Degrees | | | |
|---|---|---|---|---|
| | Waugh et al[17] | Drews et al[18] | Schwarze and Denton[19] | Broughton et al[21] |
| | **6–65 hrs n = 40** | **12 hrs–6 days n = 54** | **1–3 days n = 1000** | **1–7 days n = 57** |
| **Motion** | **Mean (SD)** | **Mean (SD)** | **Mean** | **Mean (SD)** |
| Extension limitation | 15.3 (9.9) | 20.4 (6.7) | 15.0 | 21.4 (7.7) |

(SD) = standard deviation.
All values were obtained from passive range of motion measurements with use of a universal goniometer.

| TABLE 9.3 | Knee Range of Motion in Infants and Young Children 0 to 12 Years of Age: Normal Values in Degrees | | | | |
|---|---|---|---|---|---|
| | Broughton et al[21] | | Wanatabe et al[20] | Boone[22] | |
| | 3 mos n = 57 | 6 mos n = 57 | 0–2 yrs n = 109 | 1–5 yrs n = 19 | 6–12 yrs n = 17 |
| Motion | Mean (SD) | Mean (SD) | Range of means | Mean (SD) | Mean (SD) |
| Flexion | 145.5 (5.3) | 141.7 (6.3) | 148–159 | 141.7 (6.2) | 147.1 (3.5) |
| Extension | 10.7 (5.1)* | 3.3 (4.3)* | | 5.4 (3.1)† | 0.4 (0.9) |

(SD) = standard deviation.
* Indicates extension limitations.
† Indicates extension beyond 0 degrees.

In Table 9.4 the mean values obtained by Boone[22] are from male subjects, whereas the values obtained by Roach and Miles[11] are from both genders. If values presented for the oldest groups (those aged 40 to 74 years) in both studies are compared with the values for the youngest group (those aged 13 to 19 years), it can be seen that the oldest groups have smaller mean values of flexion. However, with a SD of 11 degrees in the oldest groups, the difference between the youngest and the oldest groups is not more than 1 SD. Roach and Miles[11] concluded that, at least in individuals up to 74 years of age, any substantial loss (greater than 10 percent of the arc of motion) in joint mobility should be viewed as abnormal and not attributable to the aging process. The flexion values obtained by these authors were considerably smaller than the 150-degree average value published by the AMA.[9]

Walker and colleagues[25] studied active ROM of the extremity joints in 30 men and 30 women (ranging in age from 60 to 84 years) from recreational centers. No differences were found in knee ROM between subjects aged 60 to 69 years and subjects aged 75 to 84 years. However, average values indicated that the subjects had an extension limitation (inability to attain a neutral 0-degree starting position). This finding was similar to the loss of extension noted at the hip, elbow, and first metatarsophalangeal (MTP) joints. The 2-degree extension limitation found

at the knee was much smaller than that found at the hip joint. According to the American Association of Orthopaedic Surgeons (AAOS) handbook,[3] extension limitations of 2 degrees are considered to be normal in adults. Extension limitations greater than 5 degrees in adults may be considered as knee flexion contractures. These contractures often occur in the elderly because of disease, sedentary lifestyles, and the effects of the aging process on connective tissues.

Mollinger and Steffan[26] used a universal goniometer (UG) to assess knee ROM among 112 nursing home residents with an average age of 83 years. The authors found that only 13 percent of the subjects had full (0 degrees) passive knee extension bilaterally. Thirty-seven of the 112 subjects (33 percent) had bilateral knee extension limitations of 5 degrees or less bilaterally, which the AAOS considers to be normal in older adults. Forty-seven subjects (42 percent) had greater than 10 degrees of limitations in extension (flexion contractures). Residents with a 30-degree loss of knee extension had an increase in resistance to passive motion and a loss of ambulation.

Steultjens and coworkers[27] found knee flexion contractures in 31.5 percent of 198 patients with osteoarthritis of the knee or hip. (It should be noted that these authors considered knee flexion contractures as an inability to attain the horizontal 0 position

| TABLE 9.4 | Age Effects on Knee Motion in Individuals 13 to 74 Years of Age: Mean Values in Degrees | | | | |
|---|---|---|---|---|---|
| | Boone[22] | | | Roach and Miles[11] | |
| | 13–19 yrs n = 17 | 20–29 yrs n = 19 | 40–45 yrs n = 19 | 40–59 yrs n = 727 | 60–74 yrs n = 523 |
| Motion | Mean (SD) | Mean (SD) | Mean (SD) | Mean (SD) | Mean (SD) |
| Flexion | 142.9 (3.7) | 140.2 (5.2) | 142.6 (5.6) | 132.0 (11.0) | 131.0 (11.0) |
| Extension | 0.0 (0.0) | 0.4 (0.9) | 1.6 (2.4) | | |

(SD) = standard deviation.

starting position for measuring flexion.) Flexion contractures of the knee or hip or both were found in 73 percent of patients. Generally, a decrease in active assistive ROM was associated with an increase in disability but was motion specific. The motions that had the strongest relationship with disability were knee flexion, hip extension, and lateral rotation. Ersoz and Ergun[28] found that in a group of 44- to 76-year-old patients with primary knee osteoarthritis, 33 out of the 40 knees tested (82.5 percent) had extension limitations ranging from 1 to 14 degrees.

Despite the knee flexion contractures found in the elderly by Mollinger and Steffan,[26] many elderly individuals appear to have at least a functional flexion ROM. Escalante and coworkers[29] used a universal goniometer (UG) to measure knee flexion passive ROM in 687 community-dwelling elderly subjects between the ages of 65 and 79 years. More than 90 degrees of knee flexion was found in 619 (90.1 percent) of the subjects. The authors used a cutoff value of 124 degrees of flexion as being within normal limits. Subjects who failed to reach 124 degrees of flexion were classified as having an abnormal ROM. Using this criterion, 76 (11 percent) right knees and 63 (9 percent) left knees were below this value and thus had abnormal (limited) passive ROM in flexion.

Nonaka and colleagues[30] examined age-related changes at the hip and knee in 77 healthy male volunteers aged 15 to 73 years. The authors found that passive range of motion (PROM) of the hip joint decreased with increasing age but the knee joint PROM remained unchanged. However, interactive motion of the hip and knee showed an age-related reduction, which the authors attributed to shortening of muscle and connective tissue.

## Gender

Beighton, Solomon, and Soskolne[23] defined more than 10 degrees of knee extension beyond 0 as hyperextension and included this criterion in a study of joint laxity in 1081 males and females. Females in the study had more joint laxity than males at any age. Loudon, Goist, and Loudon[31] operationally defined knee hyperextension (genu recurvatum) as more than 5 degrees of extension beyond the 0 position. Clinically, the authors had observed that not only was hyperextension more common in females than males, but that the condition might be associated with functional deficits in muscle strength, instability, and poor proprioceptive control of terminal knee extension. The authors cautioned that the female athlete with hyperextended knees may be at risk for anterior cruciate ligament injury. Hall and colleagues[32] found that 10 female patients diagnosed with hypermobility syndrome had alterations in proprioceptive acuity at the knee compared with an age-matched and gender-matched control group.

James and Parker[33] studied knee flexion ROM in 80 men and women who ranged in age from 70 years to older than 85 years. Women in this group had greater ROM in both active and passive knee flexion than men. Overall knee flexion values were lower than expected for both genders, possibly owing to the fact that the subjects were measured in the prone

position, where the two-joint rectus femoris muscle may have limited the ROM.

In contrast to the findings of James and Parker,[33] Escalante and coworkers[29] found that female subjects had reduced passive knee flexion ROM compared with males of the same age. However, the women had on average only 2 degrees less knee flexion than men. The women also had a higher body mass index (BMI) than the men, which may have contributed to their reduced knee flexion.

Schwarze and Denton[19] observed no differences owing to gender in a study of 527 girls and 473 boys aged 1 to 3 days. Likewise, Cleffken and colleagues[34] found no gender differences in active and passive knee flexion and extension ROM in 23 male and 19 female healthy volunteers aged 19 to 27 years.

### Body Mass Index

Lichtenstein and associates[35] found that among 647 community-dwelling elderly subjects (aged 64 to 78 years), those with high BMI had lower knee ROM than their counterparts with low BMI. Elderly subjects who were severely obese had an average loss of 13 degrees of knee flexion ROM compared with their counterparts who were not obese. The authors determined that a loss of knee ROM of at least 1 degree occurred for each unit increase in BMI. Escalante and coworkers[29] found that obesity was significantly associated with a decreased passive knee flexion ROM. Knees of subjects who were overweight had a flexion ROM that was 5 degrees less than subjects who were not obese. Sobti and colleagues[36] found that obesity was significantly associated with the risk of pain or stiffness at the knee or hip in a survey of 5042 Post Office pensioners. Knees of subjects who were overweight had a knee flexion ROM that was 5 degrees less than subjects who were not obese.

## Functional Range of Motion

Table 9.5 provides knee ROM values required for various functional activities. Figures 9.19 to 9.21 show a variety of functional activities requiring different amounts of knee flexion. Of the activities measured by Jevsevar and coworkers[37] (stair ascent and descent, gait, and rising from a chair), stair ascent required the greatest range of knee motion.

Livingston and associates[38] used three testing staircases with different dimensions. Shorter subjects had a greater maximum mean knee flexion range (92 to 105 degrees) for stair ascent in comparison with taller subjects (83 to 96 degrees). Laubenthal, Smidt, and Kettlekamp[39] used an electrogoniometric method to measure knee motion in three planes (sagittal, coronal, and transverse). Stair dimensions used by McFayden and Winter[40] were 22 cm for stair height and 28 cm for stair tread. Similar dimension stairs were used by Protopapadaki and associates,[41] who used a rise height of 18 cm and a stair tread length of 28.5 cm to determine the knee motion during stair ascent and descent of 33 young healthy male and female subjects ranging in age from 18 to 39 years. The mean knee flexion

| TABLE 9.5 | Knee Flexion Range of Motion Necessary for Functional Activities: Normal Values in Degrees | | | | |
|---|---|---|---|---|---|
| | Jevsevar et al*[37] | Livingston et al[38] | Laubenthal et al[39] | McFayden and Winter[40] | Rowe et al[42] |
| | Healthy Subjects (6M, 5F) Mean = 53 yrs n = 11 | Healthy Women Range 19-26 yrs n = 15 | Healthy Men Mean = 25 yrs n = 30 | Healthy Male* n = 1 | Normal Elderly Mean = 67 yrs n = 20 |
| Motion | Mean (SD) | Mean range | Mean range (SD) | Mean range | Mean (SD) |
| Walk on level surfaces | 63.1 (7.7) | | | | 64.5 (5.9) |
| Ascend stairs | 92.9 (9.4) | 2–105.0 | 0–83.0 (8.4) | 10–100.0 | 80.3 (8.1) |
| Descend stairs | 86.9 (5.7) | 1–107.0 | 0–83.0 (8.2) | 20–100.0 | 77.8 (8.3) |
| Rise from chair | 90.1 (9.8) | | | | 89.8 (9.4) |
| Sit in chair | | | 0–93.0 (10.3) | | 91.0 (11.8) |
| Tie shoes | | | 0–106.0 (9.3) | | |
| Lift object from floor | | | 0–117.0 (13.1) | | |

(SD) = standard deviation.
* Sample consisted of one subject measured during eight trials.

**FIGURE 9.19** Descending stairs requires between 86.9[37] and 107[38] degrees of knee flexion depending on the stair dimensions.

**FIGURE 9.20** Rising from a chair requires a mean range of knee flexion of 90.1[37] to 95.0 degrees.[41]

**FIGURE 9.21** Putting on socks requires approximately 117 degrees of knee flexion.[39]

angles were 93.9 degrees for stair ascent and 90.5 degrees for stair descent.

Rowe and associates[42] used a flexible electrogoniometer to measure knee joint motion in gait, stairs, and getting in and out of a chair and a bath. Walking required the least amount of knee flexion for the 20 elderly subjects (aged 54 to 90 years) in the study, whereas getting in and out of a bath required the most knee flexion (135 degrees). The authors suggested that a clinical guideline of at least 110 degrees of flexion is necessary to allow patients to be able to walk, negotiate stairs, and get in and out of chairs. A goal of 90 degrees of knee flexion is not adequate to allow patients to carry out normal activities.

Lark and colleagues[43] compared knee ROM in stair descent in six healthy elderly males (mean age = 64 years) and six height- and weight-matched young males (mean age = 25 years). Knee flexion ROM was 12 percent less in the elderly group than in the younger group, but there was no difference between the groups in knee extension. However, the elderly group used 80 percent to 100 percent of their passive knee ROM, whereas the younger males used only 70 percent to 80 percent.

Oberg, Karsznia, and Oberg[44] used electrogoniometers to measure knee joint motion in midstance and swing phases of gait in 233 healthy males and females aged 10 to 79 years.

Only minor changes were attributable to age, and the authors determined that an increase in knee angle of about 0.5 degrees per decade occurred at midstance and a decrease of 0.5 to 0.8 degrees in knee angle occurred in swing phase. According to Rancho Los Amigos Medical Center,[45] the mean range of values for knee motion in gait on level surfaces is 5 to 60 degrees; however, the age, sex, and health status of the population used to obtain these values is unknown.

Mullholland and Wyss[46] reviewed the literature on the functional range of knee motions that are required in non-Western cultures for normal activities of daily living. The review revealed that in many parts of Asia, chairs were not commonly used and floor sitting, squatting, kneeling, or sitting cross-legged were the preferred positions. Hemmerich and colleagues[47] used an electrogoniometry motion tracking device to determine the range of motion needed to perform some of the activities identified by Mullholland and Wyss.[46] Thirty healthy Indian subjects (10 women and 20 men) with an average age of 48.2 years performed squatting with the heels up and down, cross-legged sitting, and kneeling with ankles dorsiflexed and plantarflexed. The authors found that medial rotation at the knee accompanied hip flexion in all activities. The greatest mean maximum knee medial rotation (33 degrees) was necessary for sitting cross-legged. Mean maximum knee flexion angles reached values greater than 150 degrees for both types of squatting and for kneeling with the ankles dorsiflexed. The maximal angle of knee flexion needed for kneeling with ankles plantarflexed was 144.4 degrees, whereas the mean maximum angle of knee flexion for squatting with the heels up was 156.9 degrees. The ranges of motion results found in this study are far greater than can be accommodated by any existing prostheses and are many degrees more than the clinical guideline of 110 degrees of knee flexion suggested by Rowe and associates.[42]

## Reliability and Validity

Reliability studies of active and passive range of knee motion have been conducted in healthy subjects[48–52] and in patient populations.[53–59] Similar to findings at other joints, the results of knee studies show that intratester reliability is higher than intertester reliability.[48,55] Reliability and ROM values also appear to be affected by measurement instruments and testing positions and by the type of motion (active or passive) tested. Factors that have been shown to improve reliability include training of testers, use of more than one person to assist with stabilization (especially in the presence of spasticity), holding of heavy extremities, and marking of landmarks.

### Reliability: Universal Goniometer in Healthy Populations

Boone and associates[48] had four testers use UGs to measure active knee flexion and extension ROM at four weekly sessions. Intratester reliability was higher than intertester reliability, and the total intratester SD for measurements at the knee was 4 degrees, whereas the intertester SD was 5.9 degrees. The authors recommended that when more than one tester measures the range of knee motion, changes in ROM should exceed 6 degrees to show that a real change has occurred.

Rheault and coworkers[50] found good intertester reliability for the UG (Table 9.6) and the fluid-based inclinometer (r = 0.83) for measurements of active knee flexion. However, significant differences in the ROM values were found between the instruments. Therefore, the authors concluded that, although the universal and fluid-based goniometers each appeared to have good reliability, they should not be used interchangeably in the clinical setting.

Bartholomy, Chandler, and Kaplan[51] had similar findings. These authors compared measurements of passive knee flexion ROM taken with a UG with measurements taken with a fluid-based inclinometer and an Optotrak motion analysis system. Eighty subjects aged 22 to 43 years were measured. Individually, the UG and the inclinometer were found to be reliable instruments for measuring passive knee flexion. ICCs for the UG were 0.97, and ICCs for the fluid inclinometer were 0.98. However, there were significant differences in the ROM values obtained among the three devices used, and the authors caution that these instruments should not be used interchangeably.

Mollinger and Steffan[26] collected intratester reliability data on measurement of knee extension made by two testers using a UG. ICCs for repeated measurements of knee extension were high (see Table 9.6), with differences between measurements averaging 1 degree.

Brosseau and associates[60] used a UG and a parallel goniometer (PG) to measure two flexion-angle positions in the right knees of 60 healthy subjects (44 females and 16 males). Intratester reliability of the smaller-angle (about 20 degrees) and larger-angle (about 100 degrees) positions

| TABLE 9.6 | Intratester and Intertester Reliability: Knee Range of Motion Measured with a Universal Goniometer |

| Author | n | Sample | Motion | Intra ICC | Inter ICC | Intra r | Inter r |
|---|---|---|---|---|---|---|---|
| Boone et al [48] | 12 | Healthy adult males (25–54 yrs) | AROM Flexion | 0.87 | 0.50 | | |
| Brosseau et al[60] | 60 | Healthy adults (mean age 20.6 yrs) | Flexion fixed angles | 0.86–0.97 | 0.91–0.94 | | |
| Rheault et al [50] | 20 | Healthy adults (mean age 24.8 yrs) | AROM Flexion | | | | 0.87 |
| Gogia et al [49] | 30 | Healthy adults (20–60 yrs) | PROM Flexion | | 0.99 | | 0.98 |
| Drews et al [18] | 9 | Healthy infants (12 hrs–6 days) | PROM Flexion | | | | 0.69 left 0.89 right |
| Rothstein et al [53] | 12 | Patients (ages not reported) | PROM Flexion Extension | 0.97–0.99 0.91–0.97 | 0.84–0.99 0.59–0.80 | 0.97–0.99 0.91–0.96 | 0.83–0.92 0.57–0.79 |
| Watkins et al [54] | 43 | Patients (mean age 39.5 yrs) | PROM Flexion Extension | 0.99 0.98 | 0.90 0.86 | | |
| Pandya et al [55] | 150* 21† | Duchenne muscular dystrophy (<1 yr–20 yrs) | PROM Extension | 0.93 | 0.73 | | |
| Mollinger and Steffan [26] | 10 | Nursing home residents | Extension | 0.99 | 0.97 | | |
| Beissner et al [56] | 10 | Nursing home and Independent living residents (mean age 81.0 yrs) | PROM Flexion Extension | | | | 0.70–0.93 0.70–0.93 |

AROM = active range of motion; ICC = intraclass correlation coefficient; PROM = passive range of motion; r = pearson product moment correlation coefficient.
*150 subjects were used to calculate intratester ICC.
†21 subjects were used to calculate intertester ICC.

were good to excellent for the UG and good for the PG. Intertester reliability was lower than intratester reliability for both positions and goniometers, however, the smaller angle had lower intertester reliability compared to the large angle (see Table 9.6).

## Reliability: Universal Goniometer in Patient Populations

Rothstein, Miller, and Roettger[53] investigated intratester, intertester, and interdevice reliability in a study involving 12 patients referred to physical therapy for their knee. Intratester reliability for passive ROM measurements for knee flexion and extension was high. Intertester reliability also was high among the 12 testers for passive ROM measurements for flexion but was lower for knee extension measurements (see Table 9.6). Intertester reliability was not improved by repeated measurements but was improved when testers used the same patient positioning. Interdevice reliability was high for all measurements. Neither the composition of the UG (metal or plastic) nor the size (large or small) had a significant effect on the measurements.

Watkins and associates[54] compared passive ROM measurements of the knees of 43 patients made by 14 physical therapists who used a UG and visual estimates. These authors found that intratester reliability with the UG was high for both knee flexion and knee extension. Intertester reliability for goniometric measurements also was high for knee flexion but only good for knee extension (see Table 9.6). Both intratester and intertester reliability were lower for visual estimation than for goniometric measurement. The authors suggested that therapists should not substitute visual estimates for goniometric measurements when assessing a patient's range of knee motion because of the additional error that is introduced with use of visual estimation.

Pandya and colleagues[55] studied intratester and intertester reliability of passive knee extension measurements in 150 children aged 1 to 20 years who had a diagnosis of Duchenne muscular dystrophy. Intratester reliability with use of the UG was high, but intertester reliability was only fair (see Table 9.6).

McWhirk and Glanzman[57] had two physical therapists measure the knee ROM and the popliteal angle in 46 knees in 25 children (aged 2 to 18 years) with spastic cerebral palsy. The intertester reliability of knee extension measurements was an ICC of 0.78 with a 95% confidence interval (CI) = $\pm1.75$, and the popliteal angle measurement had an ICC of 0.93 with a 95% CI = $\pm1.47$. The therapists helped each other during the measurements by having one or the other either provide support for the test leg or stabilize the other extremity.

In a study by Lessen and associates[58] two physical therapists used a long arm UG to measure active and passive knee flexion and extension in 30 patients within the first 4 days after total knee arthoplasty. Measurements were taken with the patients supine in a hospital bed and in the sitting position on an examination table. The highest levels of agreement between the testers were found for passive flexion and extension in the sitting position. The lowest level of agreement was found for passive flexion in the supine position with 16.2 to

19.0 degrees difference between the two testers. ICC values for intertester reliability were highest for active and passive flexion while sitting.

Kilgour, McNair, and Stott[59] had three pediatric physical therapists measure bilateral knee extension in 25 children with spastic cerebral palsy ranging in age from 6 to 17 years and 25 age- and sex-matched controls. Intrasessional absolute differences ranged from 0 to 2.7 degrees in the control group and 0 to 2.4 degrees in the cerebral palsy (CP) group. Intrasessional ICCs were good in the control group (ICC = 0.79 to 0.87) and excellent in the CP group (ICC = 0.97 to 0.99). Intersessional ICCs were lower for both the control and CP group, but only the control group had unacceptable ICCs (0.34 to 0.67) compared to an ICC of 0.89 to 0.92 for the CP group. The authors concluded that sagittal plane ROM measures have similar levels of reliability in children with spastic CP compared with healthy controls both within and between sessions.

## Reliability: Electronic Digital Inclinometer (CYBEX EDI320)

Cleffken and associates[34] conducted a study to determine both intratester and intertester reproducibility for measurements of active and passive knee flexion and extension in 42 healthy volunteers. Each motion was measured by two testers three times in four measurements sessions. Measurements of passive maximum flexion of the knee resulted in a smaller detectable difference (SDD = $0 \pm 6.4$ degrees) than active knee flexion (SDD = $0 \pm 7.4$ degrees) for intertester comparisons. Intratester reliability showed better reproducibility with SDDs reduced by 0.4 to 1.9 degrees over intertester values.

## Reliability: Electrogoniometer

Piriyaprasarth and colleagues[61] assessed intratester and intertester reliability of measurements using a flexible electrogoniometer of two different fixed flexion angles (45 and 75 degrees) in sitting, supine, and standing positions Thirty-seven healthy volunteers (mean age 31 years) participated in the intratester study, and 35 healthy volunteers (mean age 30 years) participated in the intertester reliability study. Ten repetitions of joint angles were taken by two testers. Intratester reliability of measurements ranged from fair for supine (ICC = 0.75 to 0.76), good in sitting (ICC = 0.86 to 0.87), to very good in standing (ICC = 0.87 to 0.88). Intertester reliability was poor to fair for supine (ICC = 0.58 to 0.71), poor to fair for sitting (ICC = 0.68 to 0.79), and poor to good for standing (ICC = 0.57 to 0.80). The sitting position had larger ICCs and lower standard errors of measurement (SEMs) for both intratester and intertester reliability compared to the supine position. One drawback of the study was that only angles less than 90 degrees were measured. The SEM was less than 1.7 degrees when the same tester repeated the measurements.

## Reliability: Inclinometer

The mean knee flexion ROM for the Ely test was 138.5 degrees for four testers using an inclinometer in a study by Piva and associates.[12] Measurements were taken of 30 patients with patellofemoral pain syndrome ranging in age from 14 to 47 years. The intertester reliability ICC was 0.91.

## Validity: Universal Goniometer

Gogia and colleagues[49] measured knee joint angles between 0 and 120 degrees of flexion. These measurements were immediately followed by radiographs. Intertester reliability was high (Table 9.6). The ICC for validity also was high (0.99). The authors concluded that the knee angle measurements taken with a UG were both reliable and valid.

Enwemeka[52] compared the measurements of six knee joint positions (0, 15, 30, 45, 60, and 90 degrees) taken with a UG with bone angle measurements provided by radiographs. The measurements were taken on 10 healthy adult volunteers (four women and six men) between 21 and 35 years of age. The mean differences ranged from 0.52 to 3.81 degrees between goniometric and radiographic measurements taken between 30 and 90 degrees of flexion. However, mean differences were higher (4.59 degrees) between goniometric and radiographic measurements of the smaller angles between 0 and 15 degrees.

Ersoz and Ergun[28] used a UG with 25-cm arms and 1-degree increments to measure the ROM in both knees of 20 patients with bilateral knee osteoarthritis. Radiographs were taken of tibiofemoral, lateral tibiofemoral, and patellofemoral compartments of the same knees. The authors found a clear relationship between knee ROM measurements of flexion, extension, and medial and lateral rotation taken with a UG and radiographs. For example, limitations in internal rotation ROM provided a prediction of advanced disease in the lateral knee compartment. The authors concluded that measurements of joint ROM were helpful in the determination of the compartment or compartments that were affected by the disease process.

Brousseau and associates[60] measured active knee flexion in two positions in 60 healthy university students (44 females and 16 males) with a mean age of 21 years. Two trained testers alternately used either a universal (UG) or a pendulum (PG) goniometer for the measurements. Eight measurements were taken with the knee flexed in the supine position and eight with the knee in the first 20 degrees of flexion in the supine position. A radiograph was taken of each subject in each knee position. Criterion validity was determined by calculating Pearson product moment correlation coefficients between each goniometric and radiologic measurement. Results showed that both the PGs and UGs had higher validity when measuring the larger fixed knee flexion angle compared to the smaller angle when using radiographs as the gold standard.

Rheault and coworkers[50] investigated the concurrent validity of a UG and an inclinometer for measurements of active knee flexion. Each instrument had good validity, but instruments could not be used interchangeably.

# REFERENCES

1. Levangie, PK, and Norkin, CC: Joint Structure and Function: A Comprehensive Analysis, ed 4. FA Davis, Philadelphia, 2005.
2. Williams, PL (ed): Gray's Anatomy, ed 38. Churchill Livingstone, New York, 1995.
3. Greene, WB, and Heckman, JD (eds): The Clinical Measurement of Joint Motion. American Academy of Orthopaedic Surgeons, Chicago, 1994.
4. Kaltenborn, FM: Mobilization of the Extremity Joints, ed 5. Olaf Norlis Bokhandel, Oslo, 1999.
5. Cyriax, JH, and Cyriax, PJ: Illustrated Manual of Orthopaedic Medicine. Butterworths, London, 1983.
6. Fritz, JM, et al: An examination of the selective tissue tension scheme, with evidence for the concept of a capsular pattern of the knee. Phys Ther 78:1046, 1998.
7. Hayes, KW: Invited commentary. Phys Ther 78:1057, 1998.
8. Hayes KW, Petersen C, and Falcone, J: An examination of Cyriax's passive motion tests with patients having osteoarthritis of the knee. Phys Ther 74:697, 1994.
9. American Medical Association: Guides to the Evaluation of Permanent Impairment, ed 3 (revised). AMA, Chicago, 1990.
10. Boone, DC, and Azen, SP: Normal range of motion of joints in male subjects. J Bone Joint Surg Am 61:756, 1979.
11. Roach, KE, and Miles, TP: Normal hip and knee active range of motion: The relationship to age. Phys Ther 71:656, 1991.
12. Piva, SR, et al: Reliability of measures of impairments associated with patellofemoral pain syndrome. BMC Musculoskelet Disord 7:33, 2006.
13. Gajdosik, RL, et al: Comparison of four clinical tests for assessing hamstring muscle length. J Orthop Sport Phys Ther 18:614, 1993.
14. Youdas, JW, et al: The influence of gender and age on hamstring muscle length in healthy adults. J Orthop Sports Phys Ther 35:246–252, 2005.
15. Fredriksen, H, et al: Passive knee extension test to measure hamstring muscle tightness. Scand J Med Sci Sports 7:279–282, 1997.
16. Rothstein, JM, Roy, SH, and Wolf, SL: The Rehabilitation Specialist's Handbook, ed 2. FA Davis, Philadelphia, 1998.
17. Waugh, KG, et al: Measurement of selected hip, knee, and ankle joint motions in newborns. Phys Ther 63:1616, 1983.
18. Drews, JE, Vraciu, JK, and Pellino, G: Range of motion of the lower extremities of newborns. Phys Occup Ther Pediatr 4:49, 1984.
19. Schwarze, DJ, and Denton, JR: Normal values of neonatal limbs: An evaluation of 1000 neonates. J Pediatr Orthop 13:758, 1993.
20. Wanatabe, H, et al: The range of joint motions of the extremities in healthy Japanese people: The difference according to age. Nippon Seikeigeka Gakkai Zasshi 53:275, 1979 (Cited by Walker, JM: Musculoskeletal development: A review. Phys Ther 71:878, 1991.)
21. Broughton NS, Wright J, and Menelaus, MB: Range of knee motion in normal neonates. J Pediatr Orthop 13:263, 1993.
22. Boone, DC: Techniques of measurement of joint motion. (Unpublished supplement to Boone, DC, and Azen, SP: Normal range of motion in male subjects. J Bone Joint Surg Am 61:756, 1979.)
23. Beighton, P, Solomon, L, and Soskolne, CL: Articular mobility in an African population. Ann Rheum Dis 32:23, 1973.
24. Cheng, JC, Chan, PS, and Hui, PW: Joint laxity in children. J Pediatr Orthop 11:752, 1991.
25. Walker, JM, et al: Active mobility of the extremities in older subjects. Phys Ther 64:919, 1984.
26. Mollinger, LA, and Steffan, TM: Knee flexion contractures in institutionalized elderly: Prevalence, severity, stability and related variables. Phys Ther 73:437, 1993.
27. Steultjens, MPM, et al: Range of motion and disability in patients with osteoarthritis of the knee or hip. Rheumatology 39:955, 2000.
28. Ersoz, M, and Ergun, S: Relationship between knee range of motion and Kellgren-Lawrence radiographic scores in knee osteoarthritis. Am J Phys Med Rehabil 82:110–115, 2003.
29. Escalante, A, et al: Determinants of hip and knee flexion range: Results from the San Antonio Longitudinal Study of Aging. Arthritis Care Res 12:8, 1999.
30. Nonaka, H, Mita, K, Watakabe, M et al: Age-related changes in the interactive mobility of the hip and knee joints: A geometrical analysis. Gait Posture 15:236–243, 2002.
31. Loudon, JK, Goist, HL, and Loudon, KL: Genu recurvatum syndrome. J Orthop Sports Phys Ther 27:361, 1998.
32. Hall, MG, et al: The effect of hypermobility syndrome on knee joint proprioception. Br J Rheumatol 34:121, 1995.
33. James, B, and Parker, AW: Active and passive mobility of the lower limb joints in elderly men and women. Am J Phys Med Rehab 68:162, 1989.
34. Cleffken, B, van Breukelen, G, Brink, P, et al: Digital goniometric measurement of knee joint motion. Evaluation of usefulness for research settings and clinical practice. Knee 14:385–389, 2007.
35. Lichtenstein, MJ, et al: Modeling impairment: Using the disablement process as a framework to evaluate determinants of hip and knee flexion. Aging (Milano) 12:208, 2000.
36. Sobti, A, et al: Occupational physical activity and long term risk of musculoskeletal symptoms: A national survey of post office pensioners. Am J Indust Med 32:76, 1997.
37. Jevsevar, DS, et al: Knee kinematics and kinetics during locomotor activities of daily living in subjects with knee arthroplasty and in healthy control subjects. Phys Ther 73:229, 1993.
38. Livingston, LA, Stevenson, JM, and Olney, SJ: Stairclimbing kinematics on stairs of differing dimensions. Arch Phys Med Rehabil 72:398, 1991.
39. Laubenthal, KN, Smidt, GL, and Kettlekamp, DB: A quantitative analysis of knee motion during activities of daily living. Phys Ther 52:34, 1972.
40. McFayden, BJ, and Winter, DA: An integrated biomechanical analysis of normal stair ascent and descent. J Biomech 21:733, 1988.
41. Protopapadaki, A, Drechsler, WI, Cramp, MC, et al: Hip, knee and ankle kinematics and kinetics during stair ascent and descent in healthy young individuals. Clin Biomech 22:203–210, 2007.
42. Rowe, PJ, et al: Knee joint kinematics in gait and other functional activities measured using flexible electrogoniometry: How much knee motion is sufficient for a normal daily life? Gait Posture 12:143–155, 2000.
43. Lark, SD, et al: Knee and ankle range of motion during stepping down in elderly compared to young men. Eur J Appl Physiol 9:287–295, 2004.
44. Oberg, T, Karsznia, A, and Oberg, K: Joint angle parameters in gait: Reference data for normal subjects, 10–79 years of age. J Rehabil Res Dev 31:199, 1994.
45. The Pathokinesiology Service and Physical Therapy Department: Observational Gait Analysis, ed. 4. Los Amigos Research and Education Institute, Inc. Rancho Los Amigos National Rehabilitation Center, Downey, CA, 2001.
46. Mulholland, SJ, Wyss, UP: Activities of daily living in non-Western cultures: range of motion requirements for hip and knee joints. Int J Rehabil Res 24:191–198, 2001.
47. Hemmerich, A, Brown, H, Smith, S, et al: Hip, knee and ankle kinematics of high range of motion activities of daily living. J Orthop Res 24:770–781, 2006.
48. Boone, DC, et al: Reliability of goniometric measurements. Phys Ther 58:1355, 1978.
49. Gogia, PP, et al: Reliability and validity of goniometric measurements at the knee. Phys Ther 67:192, 1987.
50. Rheault, W, et al: Intertester reliability and concurrent validity of fluid-based and universal goniometers for active knee flexion. Phys Ther 68:1676, 1988.
51. Bartholomy, JK, Chandler, RF, and Kaplan, SE: Validity analysis of fluid goniometer measurements of knee flexion. [Abstr] Phys Ther 80:S46, 2000.
52. Enwemeka, CS: Radiographic verification of knee goniometry. Scand J Rehabil Med 18:47, 1986.
53. Rothstein, JM, Miller, PJ, and Roettger, RF: Goniometric reliability in a clinical setting. Phys Ther 63:1611, 1983.
54. Watkins, MA, et al: Reliability of goniometric measurements and visual estimates of knee range of motion obtained in a clinical setting. Phys Ther 71:90, 1991.
55. Pandya, S, et al: Reliability of goniometric measurements in patients with Duchenne muscular dystrophy. Phys Ther 65:1339, 1985.
56. Beissner K, Collins JE, and Holmes H: Muscle force and range of motion as predictors of function in older adults. Phys Ther 80:556, 2000.
57. McWhirk, LB, Glanzman, AM: Within-session inter-rater reliability of goniometric measures in patients with spastic cerebral palsy. Paedtr Phys Ther 18:262–265, 2006.
58. Lessen, AF, van Dam, EM, Crijns, YH, et al: Reproducibility of goniometric measurement of the knee in the in-hospital phase following total knee arthroplasty. BMC Musculoskeletal Disord 8:83, 2007.
59. Kilgour, G, McNair, PM, Stott, NS: Intrarater reliability of lower limb sagittal range-of-motion measures in children with spastic diplegia. Dev Med Child Neurol 45:391–399, 2003.
60. Brosseau, L, Tousignant, M, Budd, J, et al: Intratester and intertester reliability and criterion validity of the parallelogram and universal goniometers for active knee flexion in healthy adults. Physiother Res Int 2:150–166, 1997.
61. Piriyaprasarth, P, et al: The reliability of knee joint position testing using electrogoniometry. BMC Musculoskelet Disord 9:6, 2008.

# The Ankle and Foot

# Chapter 10

## Structure and Function

### Proximal and Distal Tibiofibular Joints

#### Anatomy
The proximal tibiofibular joint is formed by a slightly convex tibial facet and a slightly concave fibular facet and is surrounded by a joint capsule that is reinforced by anterior and posterior ligaments. The distal tibiofibular joint is formed by a fibrous union between a concave facet on the lateral aspect of the distal tibia and a convex facet on the distal fibula (Fig. 10.1A). Both joints are supported by the interosseous membrane, which is located between the tibia and the fibula (Fig. 10.1B). The distal joint does not have a joint capsule but is supported by anterior and posterior ligaments and the crural interosseous tibiofibular ligament (Fig. 10.1C).

#### Osteokinematics
The proximal and distal tibiofibular joints are anatomically distinct from the talocrural joint but function to serve the ankle. The proximal joint is a plane synovial joint that allows a small amount of superior and inferior sliding of the fibula on the tibia and a slight amount of rotation. The distal joint is a syndesmosis, or fibrous union, but it also allows a small amount of motion.

#### Arthrokinematics
During dorsiflexion of the ankle, the fibula moves proximally and slightly posteriorly (lateral rotation) away from the tibia. During plantarflexion, the fibula glides distally and slightly anteriorly toward the tibia.

#### Capsular Pattern
The capsular pattern is not defined for the tibiofibular joints.

### Talocrural Joint

#### Anatomy
The talocrural joint comprises the articulations between the talus and the distal tibia and fibula. Proximally, the joint is formed by the concave surfaces of the distal tibia and the tibial and fibular malleoli. Distally, the joint surface is the convex dome of the talus. The joint capsule is thin and weak anteriorly and posteriorly, and the joint is reinforced by lateral and medial ligaments. Anterior and posterior talofibular ligaments and the calcaneofibular ligament provide lateral support for the capsule and joint (Fig. 10.2A and B). The deltoid ligament provides medial support (Fig. 10.3).

#### Osteokinematics
The talocrural joint is a synovial hinge joint with 1 degree of freedom. The motions available are dorsiflexion and plantarflexion. These motions occur around an oblique axis and thus do not occur purely in the sagittal plane. The motions cross three planes and therefore are considered to be triplanar. Dorsiflexion of the ankle brings the foot up and slightly lateral, whereas plantarflexion brings the foot down and slightly medial. The ankle is considered to be in the 0-degree neutral position when the foot is at a right angle to the tibia.

#### Arthrokinematics
During dorsiflexion in the non–weight-bearing position, the talus moves posteriorly. During plantarflexion, the talus moves anteriorly. During dorsiflexion, in the weight-bearing position, the tibia moves anteriorly. During plantarflexion, the tibia moves posteriorly.

#### Capsular Pattern
The pattern is a greater limitation in plantarflexion than in dorsiflexion.

### Subtalar Joint

#### Anatomy
The subtalar (talocalcaneal) joint is composed of three separate plane articulations: the posterior, anterior, and middle articulations between the talus and the calcaneus. The posterior articulation, which is the largest, includes a concave facet on the inferior surface of the talus and a convex facet on the body of the calcaneus. The anterior and middle articulations are formed by two convex facets on the talus and two concave facets on the calcaneus. The anterior and middle articulations share a joint capsule with the talonavicular joint; the posterior articulation has its own capsule. The subtalar joint is

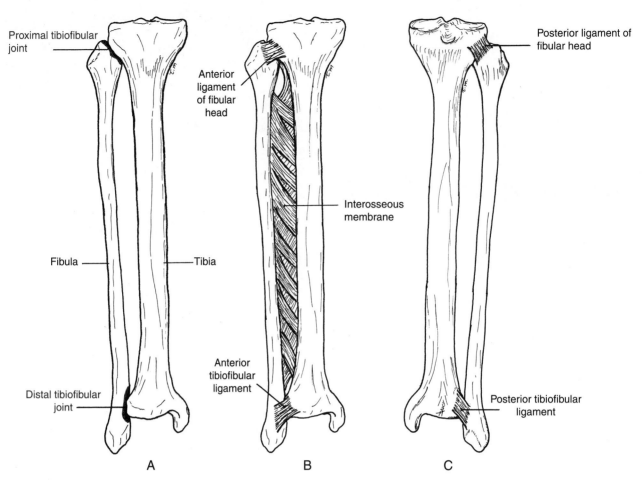

**FIGURE 10.1**  **A:** The anterior aspect of the proximal and distal tibiofibular joints of a right lower extremity. **B:** The anterior tibiofibular ligaments and the interosseous membrane. **C:** The posterior aspect of the tibiofibular joints and the posterior tibiofibular ligaments of a right lower extremity.

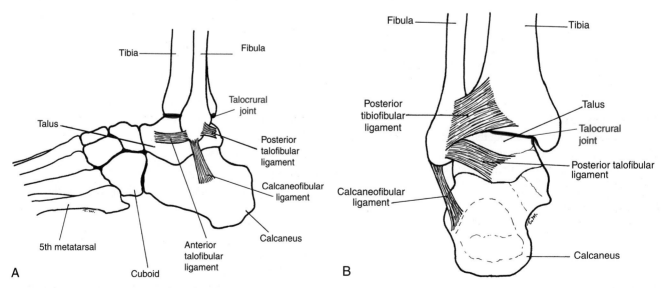

**FIGURE 10.2**  **A:** A lateral view of a left talocrural joint with the anterior and posterior talofibular ligaments and the calcaneofibular ligament. **B:** A posterior view of a left talocrural joint shows the posterior talofibular ligament and the calcaneofibular ligament.

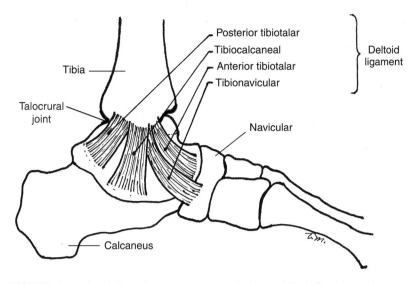

**FIGURE 10.3** The deltoid ligament in a medial view of a left talocrural joint.

reinforced by anterior, posterior, lateral, and medial talocalcaneal ligaments and the interosseus talocalcaneal ligament (Figs. 10.4 and 10.5).

## Osteokinematics

The motions permitted at the joint are inversion and eversion, which occur around an oblique axis. These motions are composite motions consisting of abduction–adduction, flexion–extension, and supination–pronation.[1] During non–weight-bearing inversion, the calcaneus adducts around an anterior–posterior axis, supinates around a longitudinal axis, and plantarflexes around a medial–lateral axis. During eversion, the calcaneus abducts, pronates, and dorsiflexes.

## Arthrokinematics

The alternating convex and concave facets limit mobility and create a twisting motion of the calcaneus on the talus. During inversion of the foot, the calcaneus slides laterally on a fixed talus. During eversion, the calcaneus slides medially on the talus.

### Capsular Pattern

The capsular pattern consists of a greater limitation in inversion.[2]

## Transverse Tarsal (Midtarsal) Joint

### Anatomy

The transverse tarsal, or midtarsal, joint is a compound joint formed by the talonavicular and calcaneocuboid joints (Fig. 10.6A). The talonavicular joint is composed of the large convex head of the talus and the concave posterior portion of the navicular bone. The concavity is enlarged by the plantar calcaneonavicular ligament (spring ligament). The joint shares a capsule with the anterior and middle portions of the subtalar joint and is reinforced by the spring, bifurcate

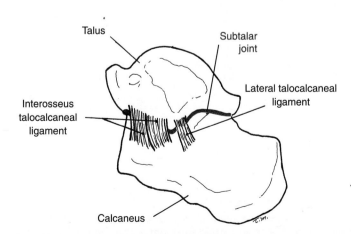

**FIGURE 10.4** The interosseus talocalcaneal and lateral talocalcaneal ligaments in a lateral view of a left subtalar joint.

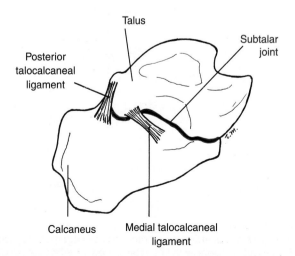

**FIGURE 10.5** The medial and posterior talocalcaneal ligaments in a medial view of a left subtalar joint.

(calcaneocuboid and calcaneonavicular), and dorsal talonavicular ligaments (Fig. 10.6B).

The calcaneocuboid joint is composed of the shallow convex–concave surfaces on the anterior calcaneus and the convex–concave surfaces on the posterior cuboid. The joint is enclosed in a capsule that is reinforced by the bifurcate (calcaneocuboid and calcaneonavicular), dorsal calcaneocuboid, plantar calcaneocuboid, and long plantar ligaments (Fig. 10.6*C*).

### Osteokinematics

The joint is considered to have two axes, one longitudinal and one oblique. Motions around both axes are triplanar and consist of inversion and eversion. The transverse tarsal joint is the transitional link between the hindfoot and the forefoot.

### Arthrokinematics

During inversion in a non-weight-bearing position, the concave navicular slides medially and dorsally on the convex talus. The cuboid slides medially and toward the plantar surface on the calcaneus. During eversion, the navicular slides laterally and toward the plantar surface; the cuboid slides laterally and toward the dorsal surface.

### Capsular Pattern

The capsular pattern consists of a limitation in inversion (adduction and supination). Other motions are full.

## Tarsometatarsal Joints

### Anatomy

The five tarsometatarsal (TMT) joints link the distal tarsals with the bases of the five metatarsals (Fig. 10.7). The concave base of the first metatarsal articulates with the convex surface of the medial cuneiform. The base of the second metatarsal articulates with the mortise formed by the intermediate cuneiform and the sides of the medial and lateral cuneiforms. The base of the third metatarsal articulates with the lateral cuneiform, and the base of the fourth metatarsal articulates with the lateral cunieform and the cuboid. The fifth metatarsal articulates with the cuboid. The first joint has its own capsule,

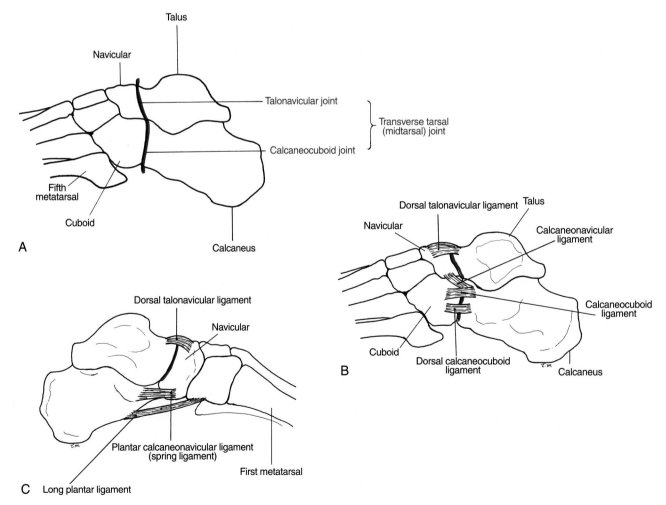

**FIGURE 10.6 A:** The two joints that make up the transverse tarsal joint are shown in a lateral view of a left ankle. **B:** The dorsal talonavicular ligament, the bifurcate ligament (calcaneonavicular and calcaneocuboid ligaments), and the dorsal calcaneocuboid ligament in a lateral view of a left ankle. **C:** The long plantar ligament, the plantar calcaneonavicular ligament, and the dorsal talonavicular ligament in a medial view.

whereas the second and third joints and the fourth and fifth joints share capsules. Each joint is reinforced by numerous dorsal, plantar, and interosseous ligaments.

### Osteokinematics

The TMT joints are plane synovial joints that permit gliding motions, including flexion–extension, a minimal amount of abduction–adduction, and rotation. The type and amount of motion vary at each joint. For example, at the third TMT joint, the predominant motion is flexion–extension. The combination of motions at the various joints contributes to the hollowing and flattening of the foot, which helps the foot conform to a supporting surface.

### Arthrokinematics

The distal joint surfaces glide in the same direction as the shafts of the metatarsals.

## Metatarsophalangeal Joints

### Anatomy

The five metatarsophalangeal (MTP) joints are formed proximally by the convex heads of the five metatarsals and distally by the concave bases of the proximal phalanges (Fig. 10.8A). The first MTP joint has two sesamoid bones that lie in two grooves on the plantar surface of the distal metatarsal. The four lesser toes are interconnected on the plantar surface by the

deep transverse metatarsal ligament (Fig. 10.8B). The plantar aponeurosis helps to provide stability and limits extension.

### Osteokinematics

The five MTP joints are condyloid synovial joints with 2 degrees of freedom, permitting flexion–extension and abduction–adduction. The axis for flexion–extension is oblique and is referred to as the metatarsal break. The range of motion (ROM) in extension is greater than in flexion, but the total ROM varies according to the relative lengths of the metatarsals and the weight-bearing status.

### Arthrokinematics

In flexion, the bases of the phalanges slide in a plantar direction on the heads of the metatarsals. In abduction, the concave bases of the phalanges slide on the convex heads of the

**FIGURE 10.8 A:** The metatarsophalangeal, interphalangeal, and distal interphalangeal joints in a dorsal view of a left foot. **B:** The deep transverse metatarsal ligaments and the plantar plates in a plantar view of a left foot.

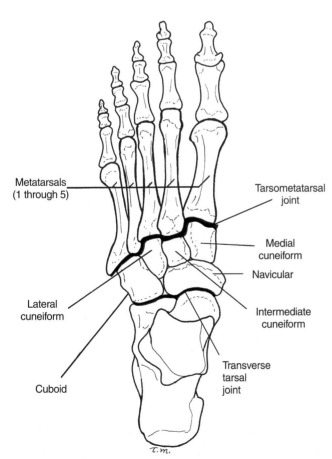

**FIGURE 10.7** The tarsometatarsal joints and transverse tarsal joint in a dorsal view of a left foot.

metatarsals in a lateral direction away from the second toe. In adduction, the bases of the phalanges slide in a medial direction toward the second toe.

### Capsular Pattern

The pattern at the first MTP joint is gross limitation of extension and slight limitation of flexion. At the other joints (second to fifth), the limitation is more restriction of flexion than extension.[2]

## Interphalangeal Joints

### Anatomy

The structure of the interphalangeal (IP) joints of the feet is identical to that of the IP joints of the fingers. Each IP joint is composed of the concave base of a distal phalanx and the convex head of a proximal phalanx (see Fig. 10.8A).

### Osteokinematics

The IP joints are synovial hinge joints with 1 degree of freedom. The motions permitted are flexion and extension in the sagittal plane. Each joint is enclosed in a capsule and reinforced with collateral ligaments.

### Arthrokinematics

The concave base of the distal phalanx slides on the convex head of the proximal phalanx in the same direction as the shaft of the distal bone. The concave base slides toward the plantar surface of the foot during flexion and toward the dorsum of the foot during extension.

# RANGE OF MOTION TESTING PROCEDURES: Ankle and Foot

## Landmarks for Testing Procedures: Talocrural Joint

**FIGURE 10.9** The subject's right lower extremity showing surface anatomy landmarks for goniometer alignment in measurement of dorsiflexion and plantarflexion range of motion.

**FIGURE 10.10** The subject's right lower extremity shows the bony anatomical landmarks for goniometer alignment for measurement of dorsiflexion and plantarflexion range of motion.

# ● DORSIFLEXION: TALOCRURAL JOINT

Motion occurs in the sagittal plane around a medial–lateral axis. The mean dorsiflexion ROM in adults according to both the American Academy of Orthopaedic Surgeons (AAOS)[3,4] and the American Medical Association (AMA)[5] is 20 degrees. The mean active dorsiflexion ROM in the non–weight-bearing position is 12.6 degrees according to Boone and Azen.[6] Refer to Tables 10.1 through 10.7 in the Research Findings section for additional normal ROM values by age and gender.

Dorsiflexion ROM is affected by the testing position (knee flexed or extended) and by whether the measurement is taken in either a weight-bearing or non–weight-bearing position. Dorsiflexion ROM measured with the knee flexed is usually greater than that measured with the knee extended. Knee flexion slackens the gastrocnemius muscles, so passive tension in the muscle does not limit dorsiflexion ROM. Knee extension stretches the gastrocnemius muscle, and ROM measured in this position represents the length of the muscle. Weight-bearing dorsiflexion ROM is usually greater than non–weight-bearing measurements, and these positions should not be used interchangeably.

## Testing Position
Place the subject sitting, with the knee flexed to 90 degrees. The foot should be in 0 degrees of inversion and eversion.

## Stabilization
Stabilize the tibia and fibula to prevent knee motion and hip rotation.

## Testing Motion
Use one hand to move the foot into dorsiflexion by pushing on the bottom of the foot (Fig. 10.11). Avoid pressure on the lateral border of the foot under the fifth metatarsal and the toes. A considerable amount of force is necessary to overcome the passive tension in the soleus and Achilles musculotendinous unit. Often, a comparison of the active and passive ROMs for a particular individual helps to determine the amount of upward force necessary to complete the

**FIGURE 10.11** The subject's left ankle at the end of dorsiflexion range of motion. The examiner holds the distal portion of the lower leg with one hand to prevent knee motion and uses her other hand to push on the palmar surface of the foot to maintain dorsiflexion.

passive ROM in dorsiflexion. The end of the ROM occurs when resistance to further motion is felt and attempts to produce additional motion cause knee extension.

## Normal End-Feel

The end-feel is firm because of tension in the posterior joint capsule, the soleus muscle, the Achilles tendon, the posterior portion of the deltoid ligament, the posterior talofibular ligament, and the calcaneofibular ligament.

## Goniometer Alignment

See Figures 10.12 and 10.13.

1. Center **fulcrum** of the goniometer over the lateral aspect of the lateral malleolus.

2. Align **proximal arm** with the lateral midline of the fibula, using the head of the fibula for reference.

3. Align **distal arm** parallel to the lateral aspect of the fifth metatarsal. Although it is usually easier to palpate and align the distal arm parallel to the fifth metatarsal, an alternative method is to align the distal arm parallel to the inferior aspect of the calcaneus. However, if the latter landmark is used, the full cycle ROM in the sagittal plane (dorsiflexion plus plantarflexion) may be similar to the total ROM of the preferred technique, but the separate ROM values for dorsiflexion and plantarflexion will differ considerably.

**FIGURE 10.12** In the starting position for measuring dorsiflexion range of motion the ankle is positioned so that the goniometer is at 90 degrees. This goniometer reading is transposed and recorded as 0 degrees. The examiner sits on a stool or kneels in order to align the goniometer and perform the readings at eye level.

**FIGURE 10.13** At the end of dorsiflexion range of motion, the examiner uses one hand to align the proximal goniometer arm while the other hand maintains dorsiflexion and alignment of the distal goniometer arm.

### Non–Weight-Bearing Dorsiflexion ROM: Supine Position (Knee Flexed)

Place the subject supine with the knee flexed to 30 degrees and supported by a pillow. Goniometer alignment is the same as that for the seated position.

### Non–Weight-Bearing Dorsiflexion ROM: Prone Position

Position the subject prone with the knee on the side being tested flexed to 90 degrees. Position the foot in 0 degrees of inversion, eversion, and plantarflexion (Fig. 10.14). Goniometer alignment is the same as that for the seated position.

### Weight-Bearing Dorsiflexion ROM: Standing (Knee Flexed)

Usually measurements taken in the standing position are considerably larger than measurements taken in non–weight-bearing positions; therefore, the two positions should not be used interchangeably. Weight-bearing measurements may be able to provide the examiner with information that is relevant to the performance of functional activities such as walking. However, it may be difficult to control substitute motions of the hindfoot and forefoot in the weight-bearing position. Also, some subjects may not have the strength and balance necessary to assume the weight-bearing position.

Position the subject standing with all his or her weight on the leg to be tested. The knee of the test leg should be flexed as far as possible while maintaining the foot flat on the floor. The end of the motion occurs when additional motion causes the heel to raise from the floor (Fig. 10.15). Goniometer alignment is the same as that for the seated position.

FIGURE 10.14 Goniometer alignment at the end of dorsiflexion range of motion. The subject is in an alternative prone position with the knee flexed to 90 degrees.

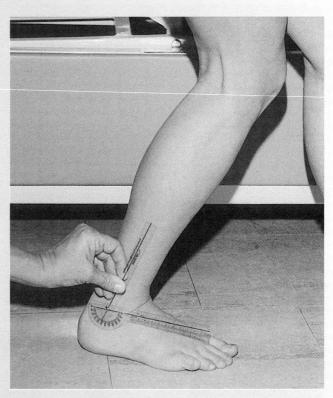

FIGURE 10.15 Goniometer alignment at the end of dorsiflexion range of motion. The subject is in an alternative weight-bearing position with the knee flexed.

## PLANTARFLEXION: TALOCRURAL JOINT

Motion occurs in the sagittal plane around a medial–lateral axis. The ROM is 50 degrees for adults according to the AAOS,[3,4] 40 degrees for adults according to the AMA,[5] and 56.1 degrees for males ages 1 to 54 years according to Boone and Azen.[6] Refer to Tables 10.1 through 10.4 in the Research Findings section for additional normal ROM values by age and gender.

### Testing Position

Place the subject sitting with the knee flexed to 90 degrees. Position the foot in 0 degrees of inversion and eversion. Alternatively, it is possible to place the subject in the supine position.

### Stabilization

Stabilize the tibia and fibula to prevent knee flexion and hip rotation.

### Testing Motion

Push downward with one hand on the dorsum of the subject's foot to produce plantarflexion (Fig. 10.16). Do not exert any force on the subject's toes, and be careful to avoid pushing the ankle into inversion or eversion. The end of the ROM is reached when resistance is felt and attempts to produce additional plantarflexion result in knee flexion.

**FIGURE 10.16** The subject's left ankle at the end of plantarflexion range of motion.

## Normal End-Feel

Usually, the end-feel is firm because of tension in the anterior joint capsule; the anterior portion of the deltoid ligament; the anterior talofibular ligament; and the tibialis anterior, extensor hallucis longus, and extensor digitorum longus muscles. The end-feel may be hard because of contact between the posterior tubercles of the talus and the posterior margin of the tibia.

## Goniometer Alignment

See Figures 10.17 and 10.18.

1. Center **fulcrum** of the goniometer over the lateral aspect of the lateral malleolus.
2. Align **proximal arm** with the lateral midline of the fibula, using the head of the fibula for reference.

3. Align **distal arm** parallel to the lateral aspect of the fifth metatarsal. Although it is usually easier to palpate and align the distal arm parallel to the fifth metatarsal, as an alternative, the distal arm can be aligned parallel to the inferior aspect of the calcaneus. If the alternative landmark is used, full cycle ROM in the sagittal plane (dorsiflexion plus plantarflexion) may be similar to full cycle ROM measurement using the fifth metatarsal as a landmark, but the single cycle ROM values for dorsiflexion and plantarflexion will differ considerably. Measurements taken with the alternative landmark should not be used interchangeably with those taken using the fifth metatarsal landmark.

**FIGURE 10.17** Goniometer alignment in the starting position for measuring plantarflexion range of motion.

**FIGURE 10.18** At the end of the plantarflexion range of motion, the examiner uses one hand to maintain plantarflexion and to align the distal goniometer arm. The examiner holds the dorsum and sides of the subject's foot to avoid exerting pressure on the toes. She uses her other hand to stabilize the tibia and align the proximal arm of the goniometer.

## Landmarks for Testing Procedures: Tarsal Joints

**FIGURE 10.19** An anterior view of the subject's left ankle with surface anatomy landmarks to indicate goniometer alignment for measuring inversion and eversion range of motion.

**FIGURE 10.20** An anterior view of the subject's left ankle with bony anatomical landmarks to indicate goniometer alignment for measuring inversion and eversion range of motion.

# ● INVERSION: TARSAL JOINTS

Inversion is a combination of supination, adduction, and plantarflexion occurring in varying degrees at the subtalar, transverse tarsal (talocalcaneonavicular and calcaneocuboid), cuboideonavicular, cuneonavicular, intercuneiform, cuneocuboid, tarsometatarsal (TMT), and intermetatarsal joints. The functional ability of the foot to adapt to the ground and to absorb contact forces depends on the combined movement of all of these joints. Because of the uniaxial limitations of the goniometer, inversion is measured in the frontal plane around an anterior–posterior axis.

Menadue and colleagues measured active inversion in both ankles in 30 male and female subjects with a mean age of 35 years. Mean values obtained with a universal goniometer ranged from 30 degrees to 35.0 degrees.[7]

## Testing Position

Place the subject in the sitting position, with the knee flexed to 90 degrees and the lower leg over the edge of the supporting surface. Position the hip in 0 degrees of rotation, adduction, and abduction. Alternatively, it is possible to place the subject in the supine position, with the foot over the edge of the supporting surface.

## Stabilization

Stabilize the tibia and the fibula to prevent medial rotation and extension of the knee and lateral rotation and abduction of the hip.

## Testing Motion

Push the forefoot downward into plantarflexion, medially into adduction, and turn the sole of the foot medially into supination to produce inversion (Fig. 10.21). The end of the ROM occurs when resistance is felt and attempts at further motion produce medial rotation of the knee and/or lateral rotation and abduction at the hip.

**FIGURE 10.21** The subject's left foot and ankle at the end of inversion range of motion. The examiner uses one hand on the subject's distal lower leg to prevent knee and hip motion while her other hand maintains inversion.

## Normal End-Feel

The end-feel is firm because of tension in the joint capsules; the anterior and posterior talofibular ligament; the calcaneofibular ligament; the anterior, posterior, lateral, and interosseous talocalcaneal ligaments; the dorsal calcaneal ligaments; the dorsal calcaneocuboid ligament; the dorsal talonavicular ligament; the lateral band of the bifurcate ligament; the transverse metatarsal ligament; and various dorsal, plantar, and interosseous ligaments of the cuboideonavicular, cuneonavicular, intercuneiform, cuneocuboid, TMT, and intermetatarsal joints; and the peroneus longus and brevis muscles.

## Goniometer Alignment

See Figures 10.22 and 10.23.

1. Center **fulcrum** of the goniometer over the anterior aspect of the ankle midway between the malleoli. (The flexibility of a plastic goniometer makes this instrument easier to use for measuring inversion than a metal goniometer.)
2. Align **proximal arm** of the goniometer with the anterior midline of the lower leg, using the tibial tuberosity for reference.
3. Align **distal arm** with the anterior midline of the second metatarsal.

**FIGURE 10.22** Goniometer alignment in the starting position for measuring inversion range of motion.

**FIGURE 10.23** At the end of the range of motion, the examiner uses her one hand to maintain inversion and to align the distal goniometer arm.

# ● Eversion: Tarsal Joints

Eversion is a combination of pronation, abduction, and dorsiflexion occurring in varying degrees at the subtalar, transverse tarsal (talocalcaneonavicular and calcaneocuboid), cuboideonavicular, cuneonavicular, intercuneiform, cuneocuboid, TMT, and intermetatarsal joints. The functional ability of the foot to adapt to the ground and to absorb contact forces depends on the combined movement of all of these joints. Because of the uniaxial limitations of the goniometer, this motion is measured in the frontal plane around an anterior–posterior axis. Menadue and colleagues[7] measured active eversion in both ankles in 30 male and female subjects with a mean age of 35 years. Mean values obtained with a universal goniometer ranged from 11.0 degrees to 12.0 degrees.[7] (Methods for measuring eversion isolated to the rearfoot and the forefoot are included in the sections on the subtalar and transverse tarsal joints.)

## Testing Position

Place the subject in the sitting position, with the knee flexed to 90 degrees and the lower leg over the edge of the supporting surface. Position the hip in 0 degrees of rotation, adduction, and abduction. Alternatively, it is possible to place the subject in the supine position, with the foot over the edge of the supporting surface.

## Stabilization

Stabilize the tibia and fibula to prevent lateral rotation and flexion of the knee and medial rotation and adduction of the hip.

## Testing Motion

Pull the forefoot laterally into abduction and upward into dorsiflexion, turning the forefoot into pronation so that the lateral side of the foot is higher than the medial side to produce eversion (Fig. 10.24). The end of the

**FIGURE 10.24** The left ankle and foot at the end of the range of motion in eversion. The examiner uses one hand on the subject's distal lower leg to prevent knee flexion and lateral rotation. The examiner's other hand maintains eversion.

ROM occurs when resistance is felt and attempts at further motion cause lateral rotation at the knee and/or medial rotation and adduction at the hip.

## Normal End-Feel

The end-feel may be hard because of contact between the calcaneus and the floor of the sinus tarsi. In some cases, the end-feel may be firm because of tension in the joint capsules; the deltoid ligament; the medial talocalcaneal ligament; the plantar calcaneonavicular and calcaneocuboid ligaments; the dorsal talonavicular ligament; the medial band of the bifurcated ligament; the transverse metatarsal ligament; various dorsal, plantar, and interosseous ligaments of the cuboideonavicular, cuneonavicular, intercuneiform, cuneocuboid, TMT, and intermetatarsal joints; and the tibialis posterior muscle.

## Goniometer Alignment
See Figures 10.25 and 10.26.

1. Center the **fulcrum** of the goniometer over the anterior aspect of the ankle midway between the malleoli. (The flexibility of a plastic goniometer makes this instrument easier to use than a metal goniometer for measuring inversion.)
2. Align **proximal arm** of the goniometer with the anterior midline of the lower leg, using the tibial tuberosity for reference.
3. Align **distal arm** with the anterior midline of the second metatarsal.

**FIGURE 10.25** Goniometer alignment in the starting position for measuring eversion range of motion.

**FIGURE 10.26** At the end of the eversion range of motion, the examiner's left hand maintains eversion and keeps the distal goniometer arm aligned with the subject's second metatarsal.

## Landmarks for Testing Procedures: Subtalar Joint (Rearfoot)

**FIGURE 10.27** Surface anatomy landmarks indicate goniometer alignment for measuring rearfoot inversion and eversion range of motion in a posterior view of a subject's left lower leg and foot.

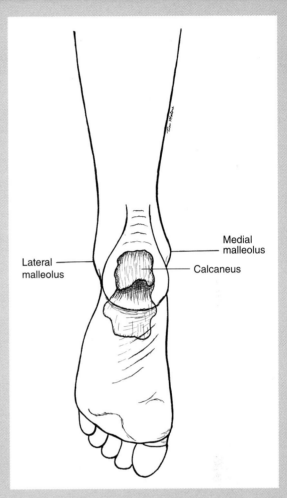

Lateral malleolus

Medial malleolus

Calcaneus

**FIGURE 10.28** Bony anatomical landmarks for measuring subtalar (rearfoot) inversion and eversion range of motion in a posterior view of the subject's left lower leg and foot.

# ● INVERSION: SUBTALAR JOINT (REARFOOT)

Inversion is a combination of supination, adduction, and plantarflexion. Because of the uniaxial limitations of the goniometer, inversion of the subtalar joint is measured in the frontal plane around an anterior–posterior axis. The ROM is about 5 degrees according to the AAOS [3] and a mean ROM of 15 degrees according to Menadue and colleagues,[7] who measured active inversion in 60 ankles in the prone position.

## Testing Position

Place the subject in the prone position, with the hip in 0 degrees of flexion, extension, abduction, adduction, and rotation. Position the knee in 0 degrees of flexion and extension. Position the foot over the edge of the supporting surface.

## Stablization

Stabilize the tibia and fibula to prevent lateral hip and knee rotation and hip adduction.

## Testing Motion

Hold the subject's lower leg with one hand and use the other hand to pull the subject's calcaneus medially into adduction and to rotate it into supination, thereby producing rearfoot subtalar inversion (Fig. 10.29). Avoid pushing on the forefoot. The end of the ROM is reached when resistance to further motion is felt and attempts at overcoming the resistance produce lateral rotation at the hip or knee.

**FIGURE 10.29** The left lower extremity at the end of subtalar (rearfoot) inversion range of motion.

## Normal End-Feel

The end-feel is firm because of tension in the lateral joint capsule; the anterior and posterior talofibular ligaments; the calcaneofibular ligament; and the lateral, posterior, anterior, and interosseous talocalcaneal ligaments.

## Goniometer Alignment

See Figures 10.30 and 10.31.

1. Center **fulcrum** of the goniometer over the posterior aspect of the ankle midway between the malleoli.
2. Align **proximal arm** with the posterior midline of the lower leg.
3. Align **distal arm** with the posterior midline of the calcaneus.

**FIGURE 10.30** Goniometer alignment in the starting position for measuring subtalar (rearfoot) inversion range of motion. Normally, the examiner's hand would be holding the distal goniometer arm, but for the purpose of this photograph, she has removed her hand.

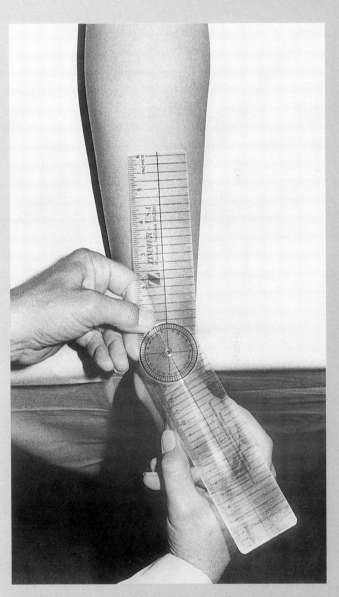

**FIGURE 10.31** At the end of subtalar (rearfoot) inversion, the examiner's hand maintains inversion and keeps the distal goniometer arm in alignment.

## ● EVERSION: SUBTALAR JOINT (REARFOOT)

Eversion is a combination of pronation, abduction, and dorsiflexion. Because of the uniaxial limitations of the goniometer, eversion of the subtalar joint is measured in the frontal plane around an anterior–posterior axis. The ROM is about 5 degrees according to the AAOS[3] and between 8 and 9 degrees for active eversion according to Menadue and colleagues.[7]

### Testing Position
Place the subject prone, with the hip in 0 degrees of flexion, extension, abduction, adduction, and rotation.

Position the knee in 0 degrees of flexion and extension. Place the foot over the edge of the supporting surface.

### Stabilization
Stabilize the tibia and fibula to prevent medial hip and knee rotation and hip abduction.

### Testing Motion
Pull the calcaneus laterally into abduction and rotate it into pronation to produce subtalar eversion (Fig. 10.32). The end of the ROM occurs when resistance to further

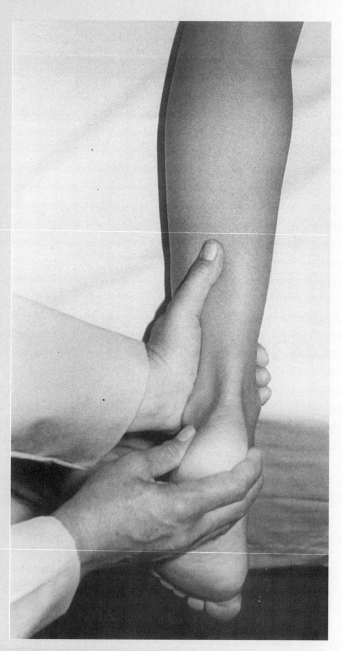

**FIGURE 10.32** The left lower extremity at the end of subtalar (rearfoot) eversion range of motion. One can observe that this subject's eversion is quite limited. The examiner's hand maintains subtalar eversion by pulling the calcaneus laterally.

movement is felt and additional attempts to move the calcaneus result in medial hip or knee rotation.

## Normal End-Feel

The end-feel may be hard because of contact between the calcaneus and the floor of the sinus tarsi, or it may be firm because of tension in the deltoid ligament, the medial talocalcaneal ligament, and the tibialis posterior muscle.

## Goniometer Alignment

See Figures 10.33 and 10.34.

1. Center **fulcrum** of the goniometer over the posterior aspect of the ankle midway between the malleoli.
2. Align **proximal arm** with the posterior midline of the lower leg.
3. Align **distal arm** with the posterior midline of the calcaneus.

**FIGURE 10.33** Goniometer alignment in the starting position for measuring subtalar (rearfoot) eversion.

**FIGURE 10.34** At the end of subtalar eversion, the examiner's hand maintains eversion and keeps the distal goniometer arm aligned.

## ● INVERSION: TRANSVERSE TARSAL JOINT

Most of the motion in the midfoot and forefoot occurs at the transverse tarsal joint which comprises the talonavicular and calcaneocuboid joints. Some additional motion occurs at the cuboideonavicular, cuneonavicular, intercuneiform, cuneocuboid, and TMT joints.

Inversion is a combination of supination, adduction, and plantarflexion. Because of the uniaxial limitation of the goniometer, inversion of the transverse tarsal joint is measured in the frontal plane around an anterior–posterior axis. The normal ROM for adults for forefoot inversion is 35 degrees.[3,6]

### Testing Position
Place the subject sitting, with the knee flexed to 90 degrees and the lower leg over the edge of the supporting surface. The hip is in 0 degrees of rotation, adduction, and abduction, and the subtalar joint is placed in the 0 starting position. Alternatively, it is possible to place the subject in the supine position, with the foot over the edge of the supporting surface.

### Stabilization
Stabilize the calcaneus to prevent dorsiflexion of the ankle and inversion of the subtalar joint.

### Testing Motion
Grasp the metatarsals rather than the toes and push the forefoot slightly into plantarflexion and medially into adduction. Turn the sole of foot medially into supination, being careful not to dorsiflex the ankle (Fig. 10.35). The end of the ROM occurs when resistance is felt and attempts at further motion cause dorsiflexion and/or subtalar eversion.

**FIGURE 10.35** The left lower extremity at the end of transverse tarsal inversion range of motion (ROM). The examiner's hand stabilizes the calcaneus to prevent subtalar inversion. Notice that the ROM for the transverse tarsal joint is less than that of all of the tarsal joints combined.

## Normal End-Feel

The end-feel is firm because of tension in the joint capsules; the dorsal calcaneocuboid ligament; the dorsal talonavicular ligament; the lateral band of the bifurcated ligament; the transverse metatarsal ligament; various dorsal, plantar, and interosseous ligaments of the cuboideonavicular, cuneonavicular, intercuneiform, cuneocuboid, TMT, and intermetatarsal joints; and the peroneus longus and brevis muscles.

## Goniometer Alignment

See Figures 10.36 and 10.37.

1. Center **fulcrum** of the goniometer over the anterior aspect of the ankle slightly distal to a point midway between the malleoli.
2. Align **proximal** arm with the anterior midline of the lower leg, using the tibial tuberosity for reference.
3. Align **distal arm** with the anterior midline of the second metatarsal.

**FIGURE 10.36** Goniometer alignment in the starting position for measuring transverse tarsal inversion.

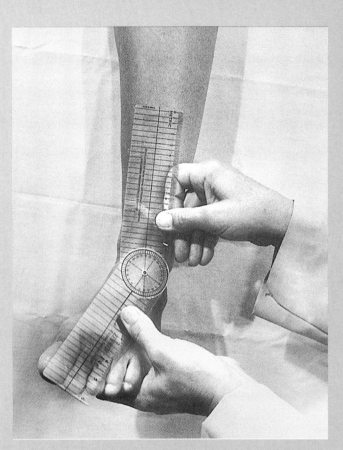

**FIGURE 10.37** At the end of transverse tarsal inversion, one of the examiner's hands releases the calcaneus and aligns the proximal goniometer arm with the lower leg. The examiner's other hand maintains inversion and holds the distal goniometer arm aligned with the second metatarsal.

# ● EVERSION: TRANSVERSE TARSAL JOINT

Eversion is a combination of pronation, abduction, and dorsiflexion. Because of the uniaxial limitations of the goniometer, eversion of the transverse tarsal joint is measured in the frontal plane around an anterior–posterior axis. The normal ROM for forefoot eversion ranges from 15 to 21 degrees.[5,6]

## Testing Position

Place the subject sitting, with the knee flexed to 90 degrees and the lower leg over the edge of the supporting surface. Position the hip in 0 degrees of rotation, adduction, and abduction and the subtalar joint in the 0 starting position. Alternatively, it is possible to place the subject in the supine position, with the foot over the edge of the supporting surface.

## Stabilization

Stabilize the calcaneus and talus to prevent plantarflexion of the ankle and eversion of the subtalar joint.

## Testing Motion

Pull the forefoot laterally into abduction and upward into dorsiflexion. Turn the forefoot into pronation so that the lateral side of the foot is higher than the medial side (Fig. 10.38). The end of the ROM occurs when resistance is felt and attempts to produce additional motion cause plantarflexion and/or subtalar eversion.

**FIGURE 10.38** The end of transverse tarsal eversion range of motion. The examiner's hand stabilizes the calcaneus to prevent subtalar eversion. As can be seen in the photograph, only a small amount of motion is available at the transverse tarsal joint in this subject.

## Normal End-Feel

The end-feel is firm because of tension in the joint capsules; the deltoid ligament; the plantar calcaneo-navicular and calcaneocuboid ligaments; the dorsal talonavicular ligament; the medial band of the bifurcated ligament; the transverse metatarsal ligament; various dorsal, plantar, and interosseous ligaments of the cuboideonavicular, cuneonavicular, intercuneiform, cuneocuboid, TMT, and intermetatarsal joints; and the tibialis posterior muscle.

## Goniometer Alignment

See Figures 10.39 and 10.40.

1. Center **fulcrum** of the goniometer over the anterior aspect of the ankle slightly distal to a point midway between the malleoli.
2. Align **proximal arm** with the anterior midline of the lower leg, using the tibial tuberosity for reference.
3. Align **distal arm** with the anterior midline of the second metatarsal.

**FIGURE 10.39** Goniometer alignment in the starting position for measuring transverse tarsal eversion range of motion.

**FIGURE 10.40** At the end of the transverse tarsal eversion range of motion, one of the examiner's hands releases the calcaneus and aligns the proximal goniometer arm with the lower leg. The examiner's other hand maintains eversion and alignment of the distal goniometer arm.

## Landmarks for Testing Procedures: Metarsophalangeal Joint

See Figures 10.41 A and B and 10.42 A and B.

**FIGURE 10.41 A:** Surface anatomy landmarks for measuring flexion and extension at the first metatarsophalangeal (MTP) joint and first interphalangeal (IP) joint in a medial view of the subject's left foot. **B:** Bony anatomical landmarks for measuring flexion and extension at the first MTP and IP joints.

## Landmarks for Testing Procedures: Metarsophalangeal Joint (continued)

1st metatarsal

Proximal phalanx

Distal phalanx

A

B

**FIGURE 10.42 A:** Surface anatomy landmarks for goniometer alignment for measuring flexion and extension range of motion at the first and second MTP and IP joints and abduction and adduction at the first MTP joint. **B:** Bony anatomical landmarks for flexion and extension at the first and second MTP and IP joints and abduction and adduction at the first MTP joint.

# ● FLEXION:
## METATARSOPHALANGEAL JOINT

Motion occurs in the sagittal plane around a medial–lateral axis. Flexion ROM at the fist MTP joint ranges between 30 degrees[5] and 45 degrees.[3]

## Testing Position

Place the subject in the supine or sitting position, with the ankle and foot in 0 degrees of dorsiflexion, plantarflexion, inversion, and eversion. Position the MTP joint in 0 degrees of abduction and adduction and the IP joints in 0 degrees of flexion and extension. (If the ankle is plantarflexed and the IP joints of the toe being tested are flexed, tension in the extensor hallucis longus or extensor digitorum longus muscle will restrict the motion.)

## Stabilization

Stabilize the metatarsal to prevent plantarflexion of the ankle and inversion or eversion of the foot. Do not hold the MTP joints of the other toes in extension because tension in the transverse metatarsal ligament will restrict the motion.

## Testing Motion

Pull the great toe downward toward the plantar surface into flexion (Fig. 10.43). Avoid pushing on the distal phalanx and causing interphalangeal flexion. The end of the ROM is reached when resistance is felt and attempts at further motion cause plantarflexion at the ankle.

## Normal End-Feel

The end-feel is firm because of tension in the dorsal joint capsule and the collateral ligaments. Tension in the extensor digitorum brevis muscle may contribute to the firm end-feel.

## Goniometer Alignment

See Figures 10.44 and 10.45.

1. Center **fulcrum** of the goniometer over the dorsal aspect of the MTP joint.
2. Align **proximal arm** over the dorsal midline of the metatarsal.
3. Align **distal arm** over the dorsal midline of the proximal phalanx.

## Alternative Goniometer Alignment for First Metatarsophalangeal Joint

1. Center **fulcrum** of the goniometer over the medial aspect of the first MTP joint.
2. Align **proximal arm** with the medial midline of the first metatarsal.
3. Align **distal arm** with the medial midline of the proximal phalanx of the first toe.

**FIGURE 10.43** The left first metatarsophalangeal (MTP) joint at the end of the flexion range of motion. The subject is supine, with her foot and ankle placed over the edge of the supporting surface. However, the subject's foot could rest on the supporting surface. The examiner uses her thumb across the metatarsals to prevent ankle plantarflexion. The examiner's other hand maintains the first MTP joint in flexion.

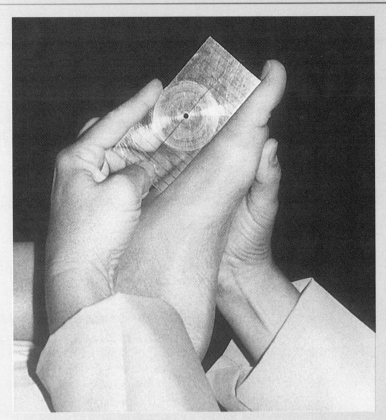

**FIGURE 10.44** Goniometer alignment in the starting position for measuring metatarsophalangeal flexion range of motion. The arms of this goniometer have been cut short to accommodate the relative shortness of the proximal and distal joint segments.

**FIGURE 10.45** At the end of the range of motion, the examiner uses one hand to align the goniometer while her other hand maintains metatarsophalangeal flexion.

# ● EXTENSION:
## METATARSOPHALANGEAL JOINT

Motion occurs in the sagittal plane around a medial–lateral axis. The ROM ranges between 50 degrees[5] and 70 degrees.[3]

## Testing Position

The testing position is the same as that for measuring flexion of the MTP joint. (If the ankle is dorsiflexed and the IP joints of the toe being tested are extended, tension in the flexor hallucis longus or flexor digitorum longus muscle will restrict the motion. If the IP joints of the toe being tested are in extreme flexion, tension in the lumbricalis and interosseus muscles may restrict the motion.)

## Stabilization

Stabilize the metatarsal to prevent dorsiflexion of the ankle and inversion or eversion of the foot. Do not hold the MTP joints of the other toes in extreme flexion because tension in the transverse metatarsal ligament will restrict the motion.

## Testing Motion

Push the proximal phalanx toward the dorsum of the foot, moving the MTP joint into extension (Fig. 10.46). Avoid pushing on the distal phalanx, which causes IP extension. The end of the motion occurs when resistance is felt and attempts at further motion cause dorsiflexion at the ankle.

## Normal End-Feel

The end-feel is firm because of tension in the plantar joint capsule; the plantar pad (plantar fibrocartilaginous plate); and the flexor hallucis brevis, flexor digitorum brevis, and flexor digiti minimi muscles.

## Goniometer Alignment

See Figures 10.47 and 10.48.

1. Center **fulcrum** of the goniometer over the dorsal aspect of the MTP joint.
2. Align **proximal arm** over the dorsal midline of the metatarsal.
3. Align **distal arm** over the dorsal midline of the proximal phalanx.

## Alternative Goniometer Alignment for First Metatarsophalangeal Joint

1. Center **fulcrum** of the goniometer over the medial aspect of the first MTP joint.
2. Align **proximal arm** with the medial midline of the first metatarsal.
3. Align **distal arm** with the medial midline of the proximal phalanx of the first toe.

**FIGURE 10.46** The left first metatarsophalangeal joint at the end of extension range of motion. The examiner places her digits on the dorsum of the subject's foot to prevent dorsiflexion and uses the thumb on her other hand to push the proximal phalanx into extension.

**FIGURE 10.47** Goniometer alignment in the starting position for measuring extension at the first metatarsophalangeal joint.

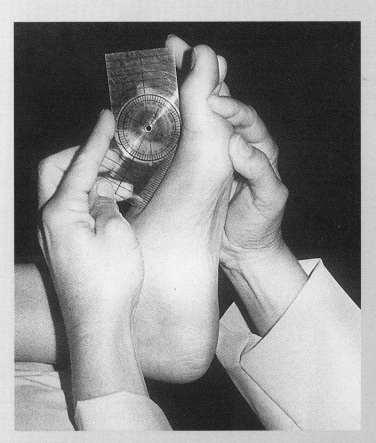

**FIGURE 10.48** At the end of metatarsophalangeal extension, the examiner maintains goniometer alignment with one hand while using the index finger of her other hand to maintain extension.

# ABDUCTION: METATARSOPHALANGEAL JOINT

Motion occurs in the transverse plane around a vertical axis when the subject is in anatomical position.

## Testing Position

Place the subject supine or sitting, with the foot in 0 degrees of inversion and eversion. Position the MTP and IP joints in 0 degrees of flexion and extension. Stabilize the metatarsal to prevent inversion or eversion of the foot.

## Stabilization

Stabilize the metatarsal to prevent inversion or eversion of the foot.

## Testing Motion

Pull the proximal phalanx of the toe laterally away from the midline of the foot into abduction (Fig. 10.49). Avoid pushing on the distal phalanx, which places a strain on the IP joint. The end of the ROM occurs when resistance is felt and attempts at further motion cause either inversion or eversion of the foot.

## Normal End-Feel

The end-feel is firm because of tension in the joint capsule, the collateral ligaments, the fascia of the web space between the toes, and the adductor hallucis and plantar interosseus muscles.

**FIGURE 10.49** The subject's right first toe at the end of abduction range of motion. The examiner uses one thumb to prevent transverse tarsal inversion. She uses the index finger and thumb of her other hand to pull the proximal phalanx into abduction.

## Goniometer Alignment

See Figures 10.50 and 10.51.

1. Center **fulcrum** of the goniometer over the dorsal aspect of the MTP joint.

2. Align **proximal arm** with the dorsal midline of the metatarsal.

3. Align **distal arm** with the dorsal midline of the proximal phalanx.

**FIGURE 10.50** Goniometer alignment in the starting position for measuring metatarsophalangeal abduction range of motion.

**FIGURE 10.51** At the end of metatarsophalangeal (MTP) abduction, the examiner's hand maintains alignment of the distal goniometer arm while keeping the MTP in abduction.

# ● ADDUCTION: METATARSOPHALANGEAL JOINT

Motion occurs in the transverse plane around a vertical axis when the subject is in anatomical position. Adduction is the return from abduction to the 0 starting position and is not usually measured.

# ● FLEXION: INTERPHALANGEAL JOINT OF THE FIRST TOE AND PROXIMAL INTERPHALANGEAL JOINTS OF THE FOUR LESSER TOES

Motion occurs in the sagittal plane around a medial–lateral axis. The ROM is between 30 degrees[5] and 90 degrees for the first toe.[3] See Table 10.2 in the Research Findings section for normal ROM values for the four lesser toes.

## Testing Position

Place the subject supine or sitting, with the ankle and foot in 0 degrees of dorsiflexion, plantarflexion, inversion, and eversion. Position the MTP joint in 0 degrees of flexion, extension, abduction, and adduction. (If the ankle is positioned in plantarflexion and the MTP joint is flexed, tension in the extensor hallucis longus or extensor digitorum longus muscles will restrict the motion. If the MTP joint is positioned in full extension, tension in the lumbricalis and interosseus muscles may restrict the motion.)

## Stabilization

Stabilize the metatarsal and proximal phalanx to prevent dorsiflexion or plantarflexion of the ankle and inversion or eversion of the foot. Avoid flexion and extension of the MTP joint.

## Testing Motion

Pull the distal phalanx of the first toe or the middle phalanx of the lesser toes down toward the plantar surface of the foot. The end of the ROM occurs when resistance is felt and attempts at further flexion cause plantarflexion of the ankle or flexion at the MTP joint.

## Normal End-Feel

The end-feel for flexion of the IP joint of the big toe and the proximal interphalangeal (PIP) joints of the smaller toes may be soft because of compression of soft tissues between the plantar surfaces of the phalanges. Sometimes, the end-feel is firm because of tension in the dorsal joint capsule and the collateral ligaments.

## Goniometer Alignment

1. Center **fulcrum** of the goniometer over the dorsal aspect of the interphalangeal joint being tested.
2. Align **proximal arm** over the dorsal midline of the proximal phalanx.
3. Align **distal arm** over the dorsal midline of the phalanx distal to the joint being tested.

## ● EXTENSION: INTERPHALANGEAL JOINT OF THE FIRST TOE AND PROXIMAL INTERPHALANGEAL JOINTS OF THE FOUR LESSER TOES

Motion occurs in the sagittal plane around a medial–lateral axis. Usually this motion is not measured because it is a return from flexion to the 0 starting position.

## ● FLEXION: DISTAL INTERPHALANGEAL JOINTS OF THE FOUR LESSER TOES

Motion occurs in the sagittal plane around a medial–lateral axis. Flexion ROM is 0 to 30 degrees.[4]

### Testing Position
Place the subject supine or sitting, with the ankle and foot in 0 degrees of dorsiflexion, plantarflexion, inversion, and eversion. Position the MTP and PIP joints in 0 degrees of flexion, extension, abduction, and adduction.

### Stabilization
Stabilize the metatarsal, proximal, and middle phalanx to prevent dorsiflexion or plantarflexion of the ankle and inversion or eversion of the foot. Avoid flexion and extension of the MTP and PIP joints of the toe being tested.

### Testing Motion
Push the distal phalanx toward the plantar surface of the foot. The end of the motion occurs when resistance is felt and attempts to produce further flexion cause flexion at the MTP and PIP joints and/or plantarflexion of the ankle.

### Normal End-Feel
The end-feel is firm because of tension in the dorsal joint capsule, the collateral ligaments, and the oblique retinacular ligament.

### Goniometer Alignment
1. Center **fulcrum** of the goniometer over the dorsal aspect of the distal interphalangeal (DIP) joint.
2. Align **proximal arm** over the dorsal midline of the middle phalanx.
3. Align **distal arm** over the dorsal midline of the distal phalanx.

## ● EXTENSION: DISTAL INTERPHALANGEAL JOINTS OF THE FOUR LESSER TOES

Motion occurs in the sagittal plane around a medial–lateral axis. Usually this motion is not measured because it is a return from flexion to the 0 starting position.

# MUSCLE LENGTH TESTING PROCEDURES: The Ankle and Foot

## 🥚 GASTROCNEMIUS

The gastrocnemius muscle is a two-joint muscle that crosses both the ankle and knee. The medial head of the gastrocnemius originates proximally from the posterior aspect of the medial condyle of the femur, whereas the lateral head of the gastrocnemius originates from the posterior lateral aspect of the lateral condyle (Fig. 10.52). Both heads join with the tendon of the soleus muscle to form the tendocalcaneus (Achilles) tendon, which inserts distally into the posterior surface of the calcaneus. When the gastrocnemius contracts, it plantarflexes the ankle and flexes the knee.

A short gastrocnemius can limit ankle dorsiflexion and knee extension. During the test for the length of the gastrocnemius the knee is held in full extension. A short gastrocnemius results in a decrease in ankle dorsiflexion ROM when the knee is extended. If, however, ankle dorsiflexion ROM is decreased with the knee in a flexed position, the dorsiflexion limitation is due to shortness of the one-joint soleus muscle or other joint structures.

Normal values for dorsiflexion of the ankle with the knee in extension vary. See Tables 10.6 and 10.7 in the Research Findings section for normal ROM values by age and gender.

### Starting Position
Place the subject supine, with the knee extended and the foot in 0 degrees of inversion and eversion.

### Stabilization
Hold the knee in full extension. Usually, the weight of the limb and hand pressure on the anterior leg can maintain an extended knee position.

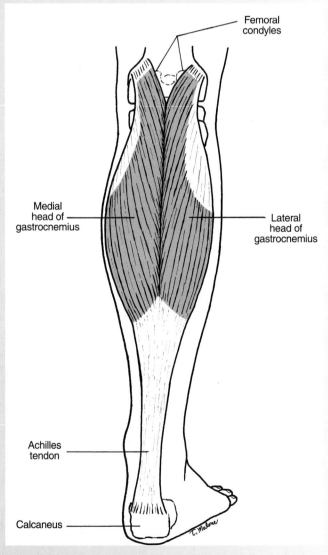

**FIGURE 10.52** A posterior view of a right lower extremity shows the attachments of the gastrocnemius muscle.

## Testing Motion

Dorsiflex the ankle to the end of the ROM by pushing upward across the plantar surface of the metatarsal heads (Fig. 10.53 and Fig. 10.54). Do not allow the foot to rotate and move into inversion or eversion. The end of the testing motion occurs when considerable resistance is felt from tension in the posterior calf and knee and further ankle dorsiflexion causes the knee to flex.

## Normal End-Feel

The end-feel is firm owing to tension in the gastrocnemius muscle.

**FIGURE 10.53** The subject's right ankle at the end of the testing motion for the length of the gastrocnemius muscle.

**FIGURE 10.54** The gastrocnemius muscle is stretched over the extended knee and dorsiflexed ankle.

## Goniometer Alignment
See Figure 10.55.

1. Center **fulcrum** of the goniometer over the lateral aspect of the lateral malleolus.
2. Align **proximal arm** with the lateral midline of the fibula, using the head of the fibula for reference.
3. Align **distal arm** parallel to the lateral aspect of the fifth metatarsal.

**FIGURE 10.55** Goniometer alignment at the end of the testing motion for the length of the gastrocnemius muscle.

# ● GASTROCNEMIUS LENGTH TESTING POSITION: STANDING

Place the subject in the standing position, with the knee extended and the foot in 0 degrees of inversion and eversion. The foot is in line (sagittal plane) with the lower leg and knee. The subject stands facing a wall or examining table, which can be used for balance and support.

## Stabilization

Maintain the knee in full extension, and ensure the heel remains in total contact with the floor. The examiner may hold the heel in contact with the floor.

## Testing Motion

The patient dorsiflexes the ankle by leaning the body forward (Fig. 10.56). The end of the testing motion occurs when the patient feels tension in the posterior calf and knee and further ankle dorsiflexion causes the knee to flex.

## Goniometer Alignment

See Figure 10.57.

1. Center **fulcrum** of the goniometer over the lateral aspect of the lateral malleolus.
2. Align **proximal arm** with the lateral midline of the fibula, using the head of the fibula for reference.
3. Align **distal arm** parallel to the lateral aspect of the fifth metatarsal.

**FIGURE 10.56**  The subject's left ankle at the end of the weight-bearing testing motion for the length of the gastrocnemius muscle.

**FIGURE 10.57**  Goniometer alignment in the alternative testing position.

## ⭗ Research Findings

Tables 10.1 and 10.2 provide ankle and toe ROM values from various sources. The 1994 AAOS[4] edition includes ROM values from various research studies, including the same values from Boone and Azen[6] that are found in Table 10.1, and a few values from the 1965 edition. Boone and Azen,[6] using a universal goniometer, measured active ROM on male subjects.

## Effects of Age, Gender, and Other Factors

### Age

Table 10.3 shows that newborns, infants, and 2 year olds have a larger dorsiflexion ROM than older children. The mean values for dorsiflexion in the youngest age groups are more than double the average adult values presented in Tables 10.1 and 10.4. However, between 1 and 5 years of age, dorsiflexion values show a decrease (Table 10.3). Plantarflexion ROM in newborns is smaller compared to adults, but newborns attain adult values in the first few weeks of life. According to Walker,[11] the persistence in infants of a limited ROM in plantarflexion may indicate pathology.

Table 10.4 provides evidence that decreases in both dorsiflexion and plantarflexion ROM occur with increases in age. However, the difference between dorsiflexion values in the youngest and oldest groups constitutes less than 1 standard deviation (SD). Plantarflexion values in the oldest group are slightly more than 1 SD less than values for the youngest group.

Alanen and colleagues[13] found a wide variation in maximum passive ROM measurements of dorsiflexion and plantarflexion in 245 boys and girls with a mean age of 10 years and an age range of 7 to 14 years. ROM values varied from 5 to 50 degrees for maximum dorsiflexion with the knee extended in the prone position and from 21 to 61 degrees with the knee flexed in the weight-bearing position. Plantarflexion

| TABLE 10.2 | Toe Motion: Values in Degrees from Selected Sources | | | |
|---|---|---|---|---|
| | Extension | | Flexion | |
| Joint | AMA[5] | AAOS[3] | AMA[5] | AAOS[3] |
| MTP 1 | 50 | 70 | 30 | 45 |
| 2 | 40 | 40 | 30 | 40 |
| 3 | 30 | 40 | 20 | 40 |
| 4 | 20 | 40 | 10 | 40 |
| 5 | 10 | 40 | 10 | 40 |
| IP 1 | — | — | 30 | 90 |
| PIP 2–5 | — | — | — | 35 |
| DIP 2–5 | — | — | — | 60 |

AMA = American Medical Association; AAOS = American Associaion of Orthopaedic Surgeons; DIP = distal interphalangeal; IP = interphalangeal; MTP = metatarsophalangeal; PIP = proximal interphalangeal.

values also varied widely, ranging from 30 to 80 degrees. Intraindividual differences of greater than 5 to 10 degrees were found between children's right and left ankles, leading the authors to caution testers about using the ROM in one ankle as a normal ROM for the opposite ankle in this young age group.

Saxena and Kim[14] tested dorsiflexion ROM in 40 high school athletes ages 14 to 17 years. An experienced tester used a goniometer to measure ankle dorsiflexion in the supine position in both ankles with the knees extended and flexed. In contrast to the findings of Alenan and colleagues,[13] no significant differences were found between measurements of right and left ankles or between girls and boys. However, the age groups are considerably different between the two studies. Ankle dorsiflexion in this group of adolescent athletes was

| TABLE 10.1 | Ankle Motion: Values in Degrees from Selected Sources | | | |
|---|---|---|---|---|
| | AAOS[3] | AAOS[4] | AMA[5] | Boone and Azen[*6] |
| *Motion* | | | | *Mean (SD)* |
| Dorsiflexion | 20 | 20 | 20 | 12.6  (4.4) |
| Plantarflexion | 50 | 50 | 40 | 56.2  (6.1) |
| Inversion | 35 | — | 30 | 36.8  (4.5) |
| Eversion | 15 | — | 20 | 20.7  (5.0) |
| Subtalar inversion | 5 | — | — | —  — |
| Subtalar eversion | 5 | — | — | —  — |

AMA = American Medical Association; AAOS = American Association of Orthopaedic Surgeons; SD = standard deviation.
* Subjects were 109 males 1 to 54 years of age.

| TABLE 10.3 | Effects of Age on Ankle Motion in Newborns and Children Aged 6 to 12 Years: Mean Values in Degrees | | | | | |
|---|---|---|---|---|---|---|
| | Waugh et al[8] | | Wanatabe et al[9] | | Boone[10] | |
| | 6–72 hrs n = 40 | 2–4 wks n = 57 | 4–8 mos n = 54 | 2 yrs n = 57 | 1–5 yrs n = 19 | 6–12 yrs n = 17 |
| Motion | Mean (SD) | Mean range | | | Mean (SD) | Mean (SD) |
| Dorsiflexion | 58.9 (7.9) | 0–53.0 | 0–51.0 | 0–41.0 | 14.5 (5.0) | 13.8 (4.4) |
| Plantarflexion | 25.7 (6.3) | 0–58.0 | 0–60.0 | 0–62.0 | 59.7 (5.4) | 59.6 (4.7) |

SD = standard deviation.

found to be 0.35 (SD = 2.2) degrees with the knees extended and just less than 5 degrees with the knees flexed. These values for dorsiflexion are below the normal values and less than the 10 degrees needed for normal gait. The authors did not offer any explanation for the limited ROM, but it is possible that it is related to either developmental changes in this group of adolescents or athletic activities that decreased the extensibility of the gastrocnemius and soleus muscles.

James and Parker[15] found a consistent reduction in both active and passive ROM with increasing age in all ankle joint motions in a group of 80 active men and women ranging in age from 70 to 92 years. The most rapid reduction in ROM occurred for individuals in the ninth decade. Ankle dorsiflexion measured with the knee extended (a test of the length of the gastrocnemius muscle) showed the most marked change. The investigators suggested that the decrease in extensibility of the plantarflexor muscle-tendon unit was due to connective tissue changes associated with the aging process. In another study that examined the effects of aging on dorsiflexion ROM, Gajdosik, VanderLinden, and Williams[16] used an isokinetic dynamometer to passively stretch the calf muscles in 74 females (aged 20 to 84 years). The older women (aged 60 to 84 years) had a significantly smaller mean dorsiflexion angle of 15.4 degrees than the younger women (aged 20 to 39 years), who had a mean of 25.8 degrees, and the middle-aged women, who had a mean of 22.8 degrees. The decrease in dorsiflexion in the older women was associated with a decrease in plantarflexor muscle-tendon unit extensibility.

In a subsequent study, Gajdosik and colleagues[17] compared the passive stretch and release characteristics of the calf muscles of 15 healthy older women with a mean age of 79 years with that of 15 healthy young women with a mean age of 24 years. The right ankles of all subjects were stretched from plantarflexion to maximal dorsiflexion and then released into plantarflexion. Older women had less calf muscle length extensibility, less passive resistive force, less stored passive-elastic energy, and less mean maximum passive dorsiflexion ROM (10.3 degrees) compared to younger women (28.0 degrees).

Nigg and associates[18] found that age-related changes in ankle ROM were motion specific and differed between males and females. The authors measured active ROM in 121 subjects (61 males and 60 females) between the ages of 20 and 79 years. For the entire group of subjects, decreases in active ROM with increases in age occurred in plantarflexion, inversion, abduction, and adduction but not in eversion and dorsiflexion (tested in the sitting position with the knee flexed). Plantarflexion decreased about 8 degrees from the youngest to the oldest group.

### Gender

Gender effects on ROM are joint specific and motion specific and are often related to age. Nigg and associates[18] found gender differences in ankle motion but determined that the differences

| TABLE 10.4 | Effects of Age on Active Ankle Motion for Individuals 13 to 69 Years of Age: Normal Values in Degrees | | | | |
|---|---|---|---|---|---|
| | Boone[10] | | | | Boone et al[11] |
| | 13–19 yrs n = 17 | 20–29 yrs n = 19 | 30–39 yrs n = 18 | 40–54 yrs n = 19 | 61–69 yrs n = 10 |
| Motion | Mean (SD) | Mean (SD) | Mean (SD) | Mean (SD) | Mean (SD) |
| Dorsiflexion | 10.6 (3.7) | 12.1 (3.4) | 12.2 (4.3) | 12.4 (4.7) | 8.2 (4.6) |
| Plantarflexion | 55.5 (5.7) | 55.4 (3.6) | 54.6 (6.0) | 52.9 (7.6) | 46.2 (7.7) |

SD = standard deviation.

changed with increasing age. Only in the oldest group did women have more (8 degrees) plantarflexion than men. The only gender differences noted by Boone, Walker, and Perry[12] were that females in the 1-year-old to 9-year-old group and those in the 61-year-old to 69-year-old group had significantly more ROM in plantarflexion than their male counterparts. Four other studies also found that females had more plantarflexion than males.[13,15,19,20] Alanen and colleagues,[13] in a study of ankle joint mobility in 245 children ages 7 to 14 years (mean age 10 years), found that girls had a significantly greater range of passive plantarflexion compared to the boys in the study. However, according to the authors, the differences were small and probably not of clinical importance.

Bell and Hoshizaki[19] studied 17 joint motions in 124 females and 66 males ranging in age from 18 to 88 years. Females between 17 and 30 years of age had a greater ROM in plantarflexion and dorsiflexion than males in the same age groups. Walker and colleagues[20] studied active ROM in 30 men and 30 women ranging in age from 60 to 84 years. Women had 11 degrees more ankle plantarflexion than men.

James and Parker[15] found that the only motion that showed a significant difference between the genders was plantarflexion measured with the knee extended. Women and men had similar mean values in the group between 70 and 74 years of age, but the reduction in active and passive ROM over the entire age range was greater for men (25.2 percent) than for women (11.3 percent). High-heeled shoe wear has been proposed by Nigg and associates[18] as one reason why women have a greater ROM in plantarflexion than men.

In contrast to the findings that women have greater ROM in plantarflexion than men, a few investigators have found that females have less active and passive dorsiflexion ROM than males.[18,20,21] In a study by Nigg and associates,[18] males in the oldest group had a greater active ROM in dorsiflexion (8 degrees) measured with the knee flexed than females in the same age group (Table 10.5). Females showed a significant decrease in active dorsiflexion ROM with increasing age, from 26.0 degrees in the youngest group to 18.5 degrees in the oldest group. Females also showed a significant decrease in eversion of 5.8 degrees with increasing age. Males, however, had little or no change in either active dorsiflexion or eversion ROM from the youngest to the oldest group. Vandervoort and coworkers[21] experienced similar findings in a study measuring passive dorsiflexion ROM with the knee flexed. The end of the ROM was defined as the maximum degree of dorsiflexion possible before muscle contraction occurred, or when the subject felt discomfort, or when the heel lifted from a floor plate. Females in the study showed a decrease in passive dorsiflexion ROM, from a high of 19.3 degrees in the youngest group (aged 55 to 60 years) to a low of 12.1 degrees in the oldest group (aged 81 to 85 years; Table 10.5). In comparison, male subjects showed a decrease of only 2.3 degrees in dorsiflexion from the youngest group (mean = 15.4 degrees) to the oldest group (mean = 13.1 degrees). Males had greater passive elastic stiffness than females, with 10 degrees of dorsiflexion.

In a study conducted by Baggett and Young[22] of 18 to 66 year olds, males compared to females had less dorsiflexion ROM in non–weight-bearing and a greater ROM in weight-bearing. However the differences in ROM were small between the genders and probably not of clinical importance.

Grimston and associates[23] measured active ROM in 120 subjects (58 males and 62 females) ranging in age from 9 to 20 years. These authors found that females generally had a greater ROM in all ankle motions than males. Both males and females showed a consistent trend toward decreasing ROM with increasing age, but females had a larger decrease than males.

In contrast to the findings of the previously mentioned studies, Saxena and Kim[14] found no differences in dorsiflexion ROM values between 24 boys and 16 girls ages 14 to 17 years. However, the age range in this study was relatively small compared to Grimston's[23] study.

## Testing Position

A variety of positions are used to measure dorsiflexion ROM, including sitting with the knee flexed, supine with the knee either flexed or extended, prone with the knee either flexed or extended, and standing with the knee either flexed or extended. Positions in which the knee is flexed bring the distal and proximal attachments of the gastrocnemius muscle closer together and result in relaxing the muscle so that its effect on dorsiflexion ROM is reduced. Positions in which the knee is extended generally are used for testing the length of the gastrocnemius muscle (Tables 10.6 and 10.7). Dorsiflexion measurements taken in the weight-bearing position are usually greater than measurements taken in non–weight-bearing positions.[22]

McPoil and Cornwall[28] compared dorsiflexion ROM measurements taken with the knee flexed with measurements taken with the knee extended in 27 healthy young adults. As might be expected, the mean dorsiflexion ROM (16.2 degrees) with the knee flexed was greater than the mean (10.1 degrees) with the knee extended (Table 10.7). In a study of dorsiflexion ROM in 7 to 14 year olds, Alanen and colleagues[13] found that dorsiflexion measurements taken with the knee flexed to 90 degrees were 10 to 19 degrees greater than measurements taken with the knee extended.

Riemann and coworkers[29] measured the resistance to passive dorsiflexion from 23 degrees of plantarflexion to 13 degrees of dorsiflexion in 12 physically active men (mean age 22 years) and 12 women (mean age 20 years). Passive movements at a constant angular velocity were applied using a Biodex System 2 Isokinetic Dynamometer in passive mode. Significantly higher stiffness values were found in the knee extended position compared with the knee flexed position. The stiffness values in the gastrocnemius increased significantly as the ankle moved from plantarflexion toward dorsiflexion. Stiffness was defined by the authors as representing the amount of deformation proportional to the load applied.

Moseley, Crosbie, and Adams[24] quantified the passive dorsiflexion ROM resulting from a 12-Nm torque applied by a dynamometer to the soles of both feet of 300 healthy male and

## TABLE 10.5 Effects of Age and Gender on Dorsiflexion Range of Motion in Males and Females Aged 40 to 85 Years: Normal Values in Degrees

| Nigg et al*[18] | | | | Vandervoort et al†[21] | | | |
|---|---|---|---|---|---|---|---|
| 40–59 yrs | | 70–79 yrs | | 55–60 yrs | | 81–85 yrs | |
| Males n = 15 | Females n = 15 | Males n = 15 | Females n = 15 | Males n = 20 | Females n = 16 | Males n = 18 | Females n = 17 |
| Mean (SD) | Mean (SD) | Mean (SD) | Mean (SD) | Mean (SD) | Mean (SD) | Mean (SD) | Mean (SD) |
| 25.0 (7.0) | 26.0 (6.4) | 26.4 (4.7) | 18.5 (4.8) | 15.4 (4.3) | 19.3 (3.2) | 13.1 (3.5) | 12.1 (5.5) |

ROM = range of motion; SD = standard deviation.
* A laboratory coordinate system ROM instrument was used to measure active ROM in subjects sitting with the knee flexed.
† An electric computer-controlled torque motor system was used to produce passive ROM in subjects positioned prone with the knee flexed.

## TABLE 10.6 Dorsiflexion Range of Motion Measured in Non–Weight-Bearing Positions with the Knee Extended in Male and Female Subjects Aged 20 to 85 Years: Normal Values in Degrees

| Gajdosik et al*[16] | | | Moseley et al†[24] | Jonson and Gross‡[25] | Vandervoort et al§[21] | |
|---|---|---|---|---|---|---|
| 20–24 yrs n = 24 | 40–59 yrs n = 24 | 60–84 yrs n = 33 | 15–34 yrs n = 298 | 18–30 yrs n = 57 | 55–60 yrs n = 36 | 80–85 yrs n = 35 |
| Mean (SD) | Mean (SD) | Mean (SD) | Mean (SD) | Mean (SD) | Mean (SD) | Mean (SD) |
| 25.83 (5.5) | 22.8 (4.4) | 15.4 (5.8) | 18.1 (6.9) | 16.2 (3.7) | 20.3 (4.6) | 11.8 (5.2) |

ROM = range of motion; SD = standard deviation.
* All measurements are of passive ROM in female subjects taken in the supine position with a universal goniometer.
† All measurements are of passive ROM in both genders taken in the prone position with use of a protractor and with the application of 12.0 Nm of torque.
‡ All measurements are of active assistive ROM in the prone position.
§ All measurements are of active ROM in the prone position with use of a footplate and a potentiometer.

## TABLE 10.7 Comparison Between Dorsiflexion Range of Motion Measurements Taken With the Knee Flexed and Extended in Subjects Aged 8 to 87 Years: Normal Values in Degrees

| | Bennell et al*[26] | | Ekstrand et al†[27] | | McPoil and Cornwall‡[23] | Mecagni et al§[24] |
|---|---|---|---|---|---|---|
| | 8–11 yrs n = 77 | 8.2–11 yrs n = 49 | 20–25 yrs n = 10 | 22–30 yrs n = 12 | Mean 26.1 yrs n = 56 feet | 64–87 yrs n = 34 |
| | Mean (SD) | Mean (SD) | Mean (SD) | Mean (SD) | Mean (SD) | Mean (SD) |
| Knee flexed | 31.9 (6.8) | 29.2 (6.4) | 26.6 (2.5) | 24.9 (0.8) | 16.2 (3.2) | 10.9 (4.2) |
| Knee extended | 25.0 (7.6) | 25.4 (8.5) | 22.9 (2.5) | 22.5 (0.7) | 10.1 (2.2) | 8.5 (3.1) |

ROM = range of motion; SD = standard deviation.
* All measurements were taken in weight-bearing positions with use of an inclinometer.
† All measurements were taken in weight-bearing positions with use of a Leighton Flexometer (a type of gravity inclinometer). The flexed-knee testing position was greater than 90 degrees.
‡ All measurements were taken by one tester using a masked goniometer. The testing position was not reported, but in the flexed-knee position, the knee was flexed to 90 degrees.
§ All measurements were taken in non–weight-bearing positions with use of an active assistive ROM technique.

female subjects who were in the supine position with the knee extended. Based on the results, the authors proposed a scheme in which application of the same Nm torque would classify passive dorsiflexion ROM less than 4 degrees as hypomobile, 11.2 to 25 degrees as normal, and 32 degrees as hypermobile.

Baggett and Young[22] compared measurements of dorsiflexion ROM taken in the non–weight-bearing supine position with those taken in the standing weight-bearing position in 10 males and 20 female patients aged 18 to 66 years. Both supine and standing measurements were taken with the knees extended. The average dorsiflexion ROM in the supine position was 8.3 degrees, whereas the average dorsiflexion ROM in the standing position was 20.9 degrees. Little correlation was found between measurements taken in the non–weight-bearing position with those taken in the weight-bearing position. Consequently, the authors recommended to examiners that the non–weight-bearing and weight-bearing positions should not be used interchangeably and that the weight-bearing position might be more clinically relevant.

Bohannon, Tiberio, and Waters,[30] in a study involving 11 males and 11 females aged 21 to 43 years, investigated passive ROM for ankle dorsiflexion by means of different goniometer alignments. In one alignment, the arms of the goniometer were arranged parallel with the fibula and the heel. The second alignment used the fibula and a line parallel to the fifth metatarsal. These authors found that passive ROM measurements for dorsiflexion differed significantly according to which landmarks were used.

Menadue and colleagues[7] compared measurements of inversion and eversion in both ankles of 60 male and female patients between the ages of 21 and 59 years. Some of the patients had a past history of a variety of orthopedic ankle conditions. Three testers used universal goniometers to perform the measurements in the sitting and prone positions. Full cycle (inversion-eversion) ROM was 43.1 degrees in the sitting position and 24.2 degrees in the prone position. Naturally, the two positions should not be used interchangeably.

Lattanza, Gray, and Kanter[31] measured subtalar joint eversion in weight-bearing and non–weight-bearing postures in 15 females and 2 males. Measurements of subtalar joint eversion in a weight-bearing posture were found to be significantly greater than those in a non–weight-bearing posture. The authors advocated measurement in both positions.

Nawoczenski, Baumjauer, and Umberger[32] measured active and passive extension ROM of the MTP joint of the first toe in different positions in 14 women and 19 men between the ages of 20 and 54 years. Active and passive toe extension measurements were taken with the subject standing on a platform with toes extending over the edge. Passive measurements were taken in the non–weight-bearing seated position and during heel rise in standing. Mean values in the weight-bearing position were 37.0 degrees for passive MTP extension and 44.0 degrees for active extension, compared with a mean value of 57.0 degrees obtained in the non–weight-bearing seated position and 58 degrees during heel rise in the standing position. Similar to the effects of different testing positions on ankle ROM, the

results showed that the positions could not be used interchangeably, with the exception of the heel rise and seated non–weight-bearing positions.

## Injury/Disease

Wilson and Gansneder[33] measured physical impairments (loss of passive ankle dorsiflexion, plantarflexion ROM, and swelling), functional limitations, and disability duration in 21 athletes with acute ankle sprains. ROM loss was obtained by subtracting the passive ROM total of the affected ankle from the passive ROM measurements taken on the unaffected ankle. The authors found that the combination of ROM loss and swelling predicted an acceptable estimate of disability duration, accounting for one third of the variance. Functional limitation measures alone provided a better estimate of disability duration, accounting for 67 percent of the variance in the number of days the athletes were unable to work after the acute ankle sprain.

Morrison and Kaminski[34] reviewed the literature for the years 1965 to 2005 for information that identified the risk factors for acute and chronic ankle inversion injuries and for the role that the foot played in these types of injuries. The authors found that the most commonly identified risk factors were a high longitudal arch, large foot width, cavovarus foot deformity, open chain large calcaneal eversion ROM in women, subtalar joint instability, and a large ROM in MTP extension. However, the authors suggested that a great deal of research was necessary to adequately evaluate these risk factors.

Kaufman and associates[35] tracked 449 trainees at a Naval Special Warfare Training Center to determine whether an association existed between foot structure and the development of musculoskeletal overuse injuries of the lower extremities. Restricted dorsiflexion ROM was one of the five risk factors associated with overuse injury.

Chesworth and Vandervoort[36] measured dorsiflexion ROM after ankle fractures due to snowboarding accidents. They found that large differences occurred in the maximum passive dorsiflexion ROM between fractured ankles and the contralateral uninvolved ankles. Maximum passive dorsiflexion was defined as that point just prior to the initiation of muscle activity in the plantarflexor muscles. The authors hypothesized that the reflex length-tension relationship was altered in the fractured ankles and that this reflex activity acted as a protective mechanism to prevent overstretching of the fragile plantarflexors after a period of immobilization.

Reynolds and colleagues[37] found that in rats, 6 weeks of immobilization of a healthy hind limb resulted in a significant (70 percent) loss of dorsiflexion ROM when a fixed torque was applied. The authors suggested that loss of extensibility of the musculotendinous unit was probably caused by tissue remodeling that occurred during extended immobilization.

Hastings and coworkers[38] studied a single patient with diabetes mellitus who had received a tendo-achilles lengthening procedure. The operation resulted in an increase in dorsiflexion ROM with the knee extended from a preoperative level of 0 degrees to a 7-month postoperative level of 18 degrees. Plantar pressure during gait was considerably reduced by 55 percent when the patient was wearing shoes, and the patient's scores on the performance of a number of functional tasks was improved by 24 percent.

Salsich, Mueller, and Sahrmann[39] found that patients with diabetes mellitus and peripheral neuropathy demonstrated less dorsiflexion ROM (extensibility of the musculotendinous unit) than a group of age-matched control subjects. Salsich, Brown, and Mueller[40] determined that there was a positive relationship between body size and passive plantar flexor muscle stiffness.

Rao and colleagues[41] compared ankle ROM and stiffness in 25 individuals with diabetes mellitus (mean age 54 years) and 64 people without diabetes who were similar in age and gender. Significantly lower peak dorsiflexion ROM and higher passive ankle stiffness were found in the group with diabetes compared to the controls. Peak dorsiflexion with the knee extended was 13 degrees in the group with diabetes and 21 degrees in the controls. Peak dorsiflexion with the knee flexed was 20 degrees in the group with diabetes and 28 degrees in controls. The authors suggested that the resistance to passive elongation may be attributed to change in the properties of the contractile and elastic elements of the plantarflexors in people with diabetes.

## Functional Range of Motion

An adequate ROM at the ankle, foot, and toes is necessary for normal gait. At least 10[42,43] to 15[44] degrees of dorsiflexion is necessary in the stance phase of gait so that the tibia can advance over the foot (Table 10.8), and 15 degrees of plantarflexion is necessary in preswing phase of gait.[42] Five degrees of eversion is necessary at loading response to unlock the midtarsal joint for shock absorption.[42] When the midtarsal joint is unlocked, the foot is able to accommodate to various surfaces by tilting medially and laterally. In normal walking the first toe extends at every step, and it has been estimated that this MTP extension occurs about 900 times in walking a mile.[45] About 30 degrees of extension is required at the MTP joints in the terminal stance phase of gait. In preswing, extension at the MTP joints reaches a maximum of approximately 60 degrees when the toes maintain contact with the floor after heel rise. The subject standing on her toes in Figure 10.58 has

**FIGURE 10.58** Standing on tiptoe requires a full range of motion in plantarflexion and 58 to 60 degrees of extension[32] at the first metatarsophalangeal joint.

| TABLE 10.8 | Range of Ankle Motion Necessary for Functional Locomotor Activities: Values in Degrees | | |
|---|---|---|---|
| | **Gait Level Surfaces** | **Stair Ascent** | **Stair Descent** |
| Dorsiflexion | 0–10 (Murray)[43] | 14–27 (Livingston et al)*[48] | 21–36 (Livingston et al)*[48] |
| | 0–10 (Rancho Los Amigos)[42] | 15–25 (McFayden and Winter)*[47] | 21.1 (Protopadaki et al)†[49] |
| | 0–15 (Ostrosky et al)[44] | 11.2 (Protopadaki et al)†[49] | |
| Plantarflexion | 15–30 (Murray)*[43] | 23–30 (Livingston et al)*[48] | 24–31 (Livingston et al)*[48] |
| | 0–15 (Rancho Los Amigos)[42] | 15–25 (McFayden and Winter)*[47] | 40.1 (Protopadaki et al)†[49] |
| | 0–31 (Ostrosky et al)[44] | 31.3 (Protopadaki et al)†[49] | |

* Range of maximum mean angles observed during the activity.
† Mean maximum angle observed during the activity.

an adequate extension ROM at the MTP joints for normal gait. If the ROM at the MTP joints is limited, it will interfere with forward progression, and the step length of the contralateral leg will be decreased.[42]

Running requires 0 to 20 degrees of dorsiflexion and 0 to 30 degrees of plantarflexion.[46] These ROMs are similar to the amount of motion required for stair ascent and descent, as shown in Table 10.8. Ascending stairs requires between 11 and 27 degrees of dorsiflexion,[47] whereas descending stairs requires a maximum of between 21 and 36 degrees of dorsiflexion[48] (Fig. 10.59) and between 24 and 40 degrees of plantarflexion.[49] The height of the stair risers will affect the amount of ROM required. Another activity requiring maximum dorsiflexion is rising from a chair (Fig. 10.60).

In a study by Lark and associates,[50] six elderly and six young subjects performed a stepping-down task from a range of stair heights. At all stair heights, the maximum dorsiflexion angle during descent was significantly greater in the elderly than in the younger subjects. The authors determined that the

elderly used 200 percent of their passive dorsiflexion ROM so that they could spend more time in foot flat to increase their stability.

Mecagni and colleagues[51] suggested that decreases in dorsiflexion ROM constituted a risk factor for decreased balance and alteration of movement patterns. Hastings and coworkers[38] identified limited dorsiflexion ROM as a risk factor for increased plantar pressures during walking and decreased functional performance in patients with diabetes mellitus.

Torburn, Perry, and Gronley[52] found that when subjects assumed a relaxed, one-legged standing position in three trials, they stood with the rearfoot in approximately the same everted position (mean of 9.8 degrees). This position of the rearfoot during one-legged standing could be used as an indication of the maximum eversion ROM needed for the single support phase of gait. Garbalosa and associates[53] measured forefoot–rearfoot frontal plane relationships in 234 feet (120 healthy males and females with a mean age of 28.1 years).

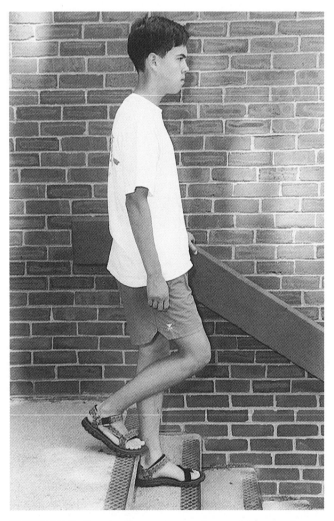

**FIGURE 10.59** Descending stairs requires an average of 21 to 36 degrees of dorsiflexion.[48]

**FIGURE 10.60** Getting out of a chair may require a full dorsiflexion range of motion (ROM), depending on the height of the chair seat. The lower the seat, the greater the ROM required.

Approximately 87 percent of the measured feet had forefoot varus, 8.8 percent had forefoot valgus, and 4.6 percent had a neutral forefoot–rearfoot relationship.

Hemmerich and associates,[54] in a study of activities of daily living in a non-Western culture, found that the largest mean dorsiflexion angle required by 30 Indian subjects was 39.7 degrees for kneeling with the ankles dorsiflexed. Squatting with the heels down required 38.5 degrees of dorsiflexion. These amounts of dorsiflexion are much larger than required for many activities of daily living in Western cultures, such as getting in and out of a chair or bed or walking up and down stairs. Cross-legged sitting on the floor is another common posture assumed in non–Western cultures, and that activity was found to require a maximum angle of 17 degrees of eversion. Because health-care workers are apt to encounter people of many different cultures, it is important that they are aware that other cultures may require different ROM goals for rehabilitation.

## Reliability and Validity

Reliability studies involving one or more motions at the ankle have been conducted on healthy subjects[13,56–60] and on patient populations.[66–68] Also, motions of the subtalar joint, the subtalar joint neutral position, and the forefoot position have been investigated.

In 2004 Martin and McPoil[55] reviewed the existing ankle literature and found ample evidence for intratester reliability for dorsiflexion and plantarflexion ROM, some evidence for intertester reliability of dorsiflexion, but little evidence of intertertester reliability for plantarflexion ROM. The authors also determined that subject diagnosis, with the exception of cerebral palsy, did not appear to affect intratester reliability. Training sessions prior to measurement appeared to have a positive effect on intrarater reliability. However, the authors concluded that on the basis of the literature review, the responsiveness of ankle measurements was uncertain.

### Reliability: Dorsiflexion and Plantarflexion in Healthy Populations

Some joints and motions can be measured more reliably than others. Boone and associates[56] found that intratester reliability for selected motions at the ankle was better than that obtained for hip and wrist motions, but it was not as good as that obtained for selected motions at the shoulder, elbow, and knee.

Clapper and Wolf[57] found that both the universal goniometer and the OrthoRanger (Orthotronics, Daytona Beach, FL) were reliable instruments for measuring dorsiflexion and plantarflexion but that the intraclass correlation coefficients (ICCs) were higher for the universal goniometer. The ICC for measurements of active dorsiflexion for the universal goniometer was 0.92, in comparison with 0.80 for the OrthoRanger. The ICC for the universal goniometer for plantarflexion was 0.96, whereas the ICC for the OrthoRanger was 0.93.

Bennell and colleagues[58] determined intertester and intratester reliability using the weight-bearing lunge method for measuring dorsiflexion. Four examiners used an inclinometer to measure the angle between the anterior border and the vertical border of the tibia and a tape measure to determine the distance of the lunging toe from the wall. Intratester and intertester reliability was extremely high (ICC = 0.97 to 0.99) for the four examiners with both methods of assessment (Table 10.9).

Three testers in a study by Evans and Scutter[60] used visual estimation to assess dorsiflexion ROM in 29 healthy children ages 4 to 6 years. The estimates were made with children in the prone position with the knee both flexed and extended. Intertester reliability of measures in both positions was very poor and highly variable between testers.

Alanen and colleagues[13] used a universal goniometer to assess the ROM of the ankle in 245 healthy children ages 7 to 14 years. Passive dorsiflexion was measured in the prone position with the knee extended and flexed. Plantarflexion was measured in the supine position. Dorsiflexion in the weight-bearing position was measured from photographs. The range of ICCs varied from a low of 0.51 for right eversion to 0.88 for weight-bearing dorsiflexion measurements.

### Reliability: Dorsiflexion and Plantarflexion in Patient Populations

Allington, Leroy, and Doneux[61] had two testers follow a strict protocol to assess intratester and intertester reliability and reproducibility of ankle ROM in 24 children ages 3 to 14 years with cerebral palsy. Pearson's correlation coefficients for intratester and intertester reliability for both the universal goniometer and visual estimates were excellent (r >90) for dorsiflexion with the knee flexed and extended. The Pearson's correlation coefficients for intratester and intertester reliability for plantarflexion for both goniometric and visual estimates were in the good category (r >0.80) and in the fair to good category for inversion and eversion. The SEM for dorsiflexion and plantarflexion was 4 to 5 degrees; the SEM for eversion was 6 to 9 degrees; and the SEM for inversion was 5 to 9 degrees. Even though both goniometric and visual estimates were reliable, the mean measurement error of 5 degrees plus the standard deviation of 5 degrees produced a 0- to 10.degree error that would have to be taken into account in clinical decision-making.

McWhirk and Glanzman[62] assessed intertester reliability of measurements of ankle dorsiflexion in 25 children (ages 2 to 18 years) with spastic cerebral palsy. The two therapists who took the measurements succesively on the same day helped each other hold the limbs at end range. Intertester reliability was very good, with an ICC = 0.87 and a mean absolute difference of 3.6 degrees. The 95 percent confidence interval around the mean absolute difference was ±1.2 degrees.

Mutlu, Livanelioglu, and Gunel[63] assessed the intratester and intertester reliability of goniometric measurements of ankle dorsiflexion that were taken by three therapists in 38 children (ages 18 to 108 months) with spastic cerebral palsy. The therapists used a 360-degree universal goniometer to measure dorsiflexion once in two different sessions a week apart. Intratester reliability was determined using Pearson's

## TABLE 10.9    Intratester and Intertester Reliability: Dorsiflexion

| Authors | n | Sample | Position | Intra ICC | Inter ICC | SEM |
|---|---|---|---|---|---|---|
| Bennell et al[58] | 13 | Healthy adults (mean age 18.8 yrs) | Weight bearing lunge with knee flexed | 0.98 | 0.97 | 1.1° (Intra) 1.4° (Inter) |
| Clapper and Wolfe[56] | 20 | Healthy adults (20–36 yrs) | | 0.92 | | |
| McPoil and Cornwall[28] | 27 | Healthy adults (mean age 26.1 yrs) | Knee flexed to 90° Knee extended | 0.97 0.98 | | |
| Jonson and Gross[25] | 18 | Healthy adults (18–30 yrs) | Knee extended— prone position | 0.74 | 0.65 | |
| Salsich et al[39] | 34 | One-half healthy/ one-half with diabetes mellitus (59–63 yrs) | Knee extended— prone position | 0.95 | | |
| Elveru et al[64] | 43 | Patients with orthopedic or neurological problems (12–81 yrs) | Passive ROM— no standard position used | 0.90 | 0.50 | |
| Youdas et al[65] | 38 | Patients with orthopedic problems (13–71 yrs) | Active ROM— no standard position used* | 0.64–0.96 Median 0.83 | 0.28 | |

ICC = Intertester or intertester correlation coefficient, as noted; ROM = range of motion;
 SEM = standard error of the measurement.
* Knee was extended in 87.7 percent of measurement sessions.

reliability coefficient (r) and ICCs. The r values ranged from 0.65 to 0.81, and ICCs ranged from 0.81 to 0.90, with the most experienced tester obtaining the highest reliability. Intertester reliability r values ranged from 0.65 to 0.75, and the ICC value was very good (0.88). Based on the findings of this study and the previous study, it appears to be possible to obtain reliable goniometric measurements in this population of children with spastic cerebral palsy. The authors suggested that this study needs to be followed with a validity study.

Elveru and associates[64] employed 12 physical therapists using universal goniometers to measure the passive ankle ROM in 43 patients with either neurological or orthopedic problems. The ICCs for intratester reliability for inversion and eversion were 0.74 and 0.75, respectively, and intertester reliability was poor (see Tables 10.9, 10.10, and 10.11). Intertester reliability also was poor for dorsiflexion, and patient diagnosis affected the reliability of dorsiflexion measurements. Sources of error were identified as variable amounts of force being exerted by the therapist, resistance to

movement in neurological patients, and difficulties encountered by the examiner in maintaining the foot and ankle in the desired position while holding the goniometer. It would appear that the latter problem could be solved by having another person either maintain the foot and ankle in position or hold the goniometer.

Youdas, Bogard, and Suman[65] used 10 examiners in a study to determine the intratester and intertester reliability for active ROM in dorsiflexion and plantarflexion. The authors compared measurements made by a universal goniometer with visual estimates on 38 patients with orthopedic problems. Fair to excellent reliability was noted when repeated measurements were made by the same therapist using a goniometer. Reliability was higher using the mean of two repeated measurements than using one measurement. A considerable measurement error was found to exist when two or more therapists made either repeated goniometric or visual estimates of the ankle ROM on the same patient (see Tables 10.9 and 10.10). Therapists used various patient

## TABLE 10.10 Intratester and Intertester Reliability: Plantarflexion

| Author | n | Sample | Type of Motion | Intra ICC | Inter ICC |
|---|---|---|---|---|---|
| Clapper and Wolf[57] | 20 | Healthy adults (20–36 yrs) | Active ROM | 0.96 | — |
| Elveru et al[64] | 43 | Patients with orthopedic or neurological problems (12–81 yrs) | Passive ROM | 0.86 | 0.72 |
| Youdas et al[65] | 38 | Patients with orthopedic problems (13–71 yrs) | Active ROM | 0.47–0.98 Median 0.87 | 0.25 |

ICC = intertester or intratester coefficient, as noted.; ROM = range of motion

positions and goniometer alignment methods. The authors suggested that the same therapist should make two goniometric measurements and record the average value when making repeated measurements of ankle ROM.

### Reliability: Eversion and Inversion

The subtalar joint neutral position, which has been the subject of numerous studies, is not the same as the 0 starting position for the subtalar joint as used in this book and many others, including those of the AAOS,[3,4] the AMA,[5] and Clarkson.[66] The subtalar joint neutral position is defined as one in which the calcaneus inverts twice as many degrees as it everts. According to Elveru and associates,[67] this position can be found when the head of the talus either cannot be palpated or is equally extended at the medial and lateral borders of the talonavicular joint. This is the position usually used in the casting of foot orthotics, but it also has been used for measurement of joint motion. However, Elveru, Rothstein, and Lamb[64] found that referencing passive ROM measurements for inversion and eversion to the subtalar joint neutral position consis-

tently reduced reliability (see Table 10.11). Based on the study of Elveru, Rothstein, and Lamb[64] and information from the following studies, we have decided not to use the subtalar neutral position as defined by Elveru and associates[67] in this text.

Bailey, Perillo, and Forman[68] used tomography to study the subtalar joint neutral position in 2 female and 13 male volunteers aged 20 to 30 years. These authors found that the neutral subtalar joint position was quite variable in relation to the total ROM and that it was not always found at one third of the total ROM from the maximally everted position. Furthermore, the neutral position varied not only from subject to subject but also between right and left sides of each subject.

Picciano, Rowlands, and Worrell[69] conducted a study to determine the intratester and intertester reliability of measurements of open-chain and closed-chain subtalar joint neutral positions. Both ankles of 15 volunteer subjects (with a mean age of 27 years) were measured by two inexperienced physical therapy students. The students had a 2-hour training session using a universal goniometer prior to data collection. The method of taking measurements was based on the work of Elveru and

## TABLE 10.11 Intratester and Intertester Reliability: Inversion and Eversion

| Author | n | Sample | Motion | Intra ICC | Inter ICC |
|---|---|---|---|---|---|
| McPoil and Cornwall[28] | 27 | Healthy adults (mean age 26.1 yrs) | Inversion Eversion | 0.95 0.96 | — |
| Torburn et al[52] | 42 | — | Inversion Eversion | — | 0.37 0.39 |
| Menadue et al[7] | 60 ankles | Nonacute ankle conditions in 11 of the 30 subjects (ages 21–59 years) | Inversion in sitting Eversion in sitting Inversion prone Eversion prone | 0.92, 0.91, 0.96 0.90, 0.82, 0.93 0.94, 0.94, 0.94 0.94, 0.83, 0.88 | 0.73 (0.61–0.82) 0.62 (0.49–0.74) 0.54 (0.33–0.70) 0.41 (0.25–0.56) |
| Elveru et al[64] | 43 | Patients with orthopedic and neurological problems | Inversion Eversion | 0.62* 0.74 0.59* 0.75 | 0.15* 0.32 0.12* 0.17 |

ICC = Intertester and intratester correlation coefficient as noted.
* Referenced to subtalar joint neutral.

associates.[67] Intratester reliability of open-chain measurements of the subtalar joint neutral position was an ICC of 0.27 for one tester and ICC of 0.06 for the other tester. Intertester reliability was 0.00. Intratester and intertester reliability also were poor for closed-kinematic-chain measurements. The authors[69] concluded that subtalar joint neutral measurements taken by inexperienced testers were unreliable; they recommended that clinicians should practice taking measurements and performing repeated measurements to determine their own reliability for these measurements. However, Torburn, Perry, and Gronley[52] suggested that inaccuracy of measurement technique with use of a universal goniometer, rather than the ability of examiners to position the subtalar joint in the neutral position, might be responsible for poor reliability findings for subtalar joint neutral positioning. The ICC for intertester reliability for three examiners was an ICC of 0.76 for positioning the subtalar joint in the neutral position. In this study, the examiners palpated the head of the talus in 10 subjects lying in the prone position while an electrogoniometer was used to record the position (see Table 10.11). already inserted Table 10.11

Keenan, App, and Bach[70] used a prone measurement position system described by Elveru et al[67] to assess the non–weight-bearing subtalar neutral position and subtalar inversion and eversion in 24 healthy subjects. Static and dynamic measurements were made on two different occasions by four experienced clinicians using a universal goniometer. Intertester reliability was poor and so was test-retest reliability for static measurements. Reliability was also poor for visual assessments of dynamic measurements. The most experienced clinician had the highest overall reliability, whereas the clinician with only a year's experience had the lowest reliability. However, the same trend was not evident in static measurements.

In contrast to the low reliability found in the aforementioned studies, McPoil and Cornwall[46] found high intratester reliability for both subtalar inversion and eversion ROM measurements taken by two testers (see Table 10.11).

Menadue and colleagues[7] assessed active inversion and eversion ROM in the prone lying position with the ankle over the edge of the table. The 30 subjects in the study had both ankles measured by three testers using a blinded universal goniometer. Test and retest measurements were made 2 weeks apart. Within-session intratester reliability for inversion was excellent (ICC = 0.94) for all testers, whereas intratester reliability for eversion was slightly lower and ranged from good (ICC = 0.83) to excellent (ICC = 0.96) among the three testers. Intertester reliability ranged from poor (ICC = 0.33) to fair (ICC = 0.70) for inversion and was unacceptable for eversion. Between-sessions measurement error ranged from 4 degrees to 8 degrees. (See Table 10.11 for additional information.)

## Validity: Eversion, Inversion, Dorsiflexion, and Plantarflexion

We are unaware of any studies that compared ankle and foot ROM values measured with a universal goniometer to values measured with radiographs. However, eversion and inversion values measured with a universal goniometer have been compared to values taken with another device. Menadue and colleagues[7] found low correlations between full-cycle active inversion and eversion measurements taken with the 3Space Fastrak electromagnetic tracking system and the universal goniometer. Only 18 percent of the variance in Fastrak measurements could be explained by the goniometric measurements. The discrepancy between the goniometric and Fastrak measurements may be partially explained by the fact that the Fastrak system records motion in all planes, whereas the universal goniometer measures motion in one plane.

Ankle ROM values have been compared to functional assessment measures. Mecagni and coworkers[51] assessed active assistive and passive ankle ROM and balance performance using the Performance Oriented Mobility Assessment (POMA) in 34 healthy elderly women ages 64 to 87 years. Correlations between the POMA gait subtest indicated that all ankle motions contributed to the maintenance of balance during gait: inversion (r = 0.50), dorsiflexion with knee flexed (r = 0.44), plantarflexion (r = 0.42), and eversion (r = 0.32). Active assistive ROM had higher correlations compared to passive ROM. The highest correlation was between active assistive ROM and the POMA gait subtest (r = 0.63).

## Reliability: Metatarsophalangeal Extension

Hopson, McPoil, and Cornwall[71] conducted four static clinical tests to measure extension ROM of the first MTP joint in 20 healthy adult subjects between 21 and 45 years of age. All measurement techniques were found to be reliable but not interchangeable. Approximately 65 degrees of first MTP extension was required for normal walking as determined from video recordings. The values from the four clinical tests of first MTP extension ROM exceeded the amount required for walking.

## Validity: Metatarsophalangeal Extension

No studies were noted that examined the concurrent validity of MTP motions measured with a universal goniometer to radiographs. Construct validity of clinical measures of first MTP extension ROM to indicate ROM during gait have been initally explored.[71,32] Nawoczenski, Baumjauer, and Umberger[32] used four clinical tests to measure the first MTP joint extension: active and passive ROM and heel rise in the weight-bearing position, and passive ROM in the non–weight-bearing position. Test values were compared with measurements of MTP extension during normal walking. Active ROM in the weight-bearing position (44 degrees) and extension measured during heel rise (58 degrees) had the strongest correlations with motion of the MTP joint (42 degrees) during normal walking (r = 0.80 and 0.87, respectively).

# REFERENCES

1. Levangie, PK, and Norkin, CC: Joint Structure and Function: A Comprehensive Analysis, ed 4. FA Davis, Philadelphia, 2005.
2. Cyriax, JM, and Cyriax, PJ: Illustrated Manual of Orthopaedic Medicine. Butterworths, London, 1983.
3. American Academy of Orthopaedic Surgeons: Joint Motion: Method of Measuring and Recording. AAOS, Chicago, 1965
4. Greene, WB, and Heckman, JD (eds): The Clinical Measurement of Joint Motion: American Academy of Orthopaedic Surgeons, Chicago, 1994.
5. American Medical Association: Guides to the Evaluation of Permanent Impairment, ed 3 (revised). AMA, Chicago, 1988.
6. Boone, DC, and Azen, SP: Normal range of motion of joints in male subjects. J Bone Joint Surg Am 61:756, 1979.
7. Menadue, C, et al: Reliabililty of two goniometric methods of measuring active inversion and eversion range of motion at the ankle. BMC Musculoskelet Diord 7:60, 2006.
8. Waugh, KG, et al: Measurement of selected hip, knee and ankle joint motions in newborns. Phys Ther 63:1616, 1983.
9. Wanatabe, H, et al: The range of joint motion of the extremities in healthy Japanese people: The differences according to age. Nippon Seikeigeka Gakkai Zasshi 53:275, 1979. (Cited in Walker, JM: Musculoskeletal development: A review. Phys Ther 71:878, 1991.)
10. Boone, DC: Techniques of measurement of joint motion. (Unpublished supplement to Boone, DC, and Azen, SP: Normal range of motion in male subjects. J Bone Joint Surg Am 61:756, 1979.)
11. Walker, JM: Musculoskeletal development: A review. Phys Ther 71:878, 1991.
12. Boone, DC, Walker, JM, and Perry, J: Age and sex differences in lower extremity joint motion. Presented at the National Conference, American Physical Therapy Association, Washington, DC, 1981.
13. Alanen, JT, et al: Ankle joint complex mobility of children 7-14 years old. J Pediatr Orthop 21:731, 2001.
14. Saxena, A, and Kim,W: Ankle dorsiflexion in the adolescent. J Am Podiatr Med Assoc 93:312, 2003.
15. James, B, and Parker, AW: Active and passive mobility of lower limb joints in elderly men and women. Am J Phys Med Rehabil 68:162, 1989.
16. Gajdosik, RL, VanderLinden, DW, and Williams, AK: Influence of age on length and passive elastic stiffness: Characteristics of the calf muscle-tendon unit of women. Phys Ther 79:827, 1999.
17. Gajdosik, RL, et al: Slow passive stretch and release characteristics of the calf muscles of older women with limited dorsiflexion range of motion. Clin Biomech 19:398, 2004.
18. Nigg, BM, et al: Range of motion of the foot as a function of age. Foot Ankle 613:336, 1992.
19. Bell, RD, and Hoshizaki, TB: Relationships of age and sex with range of motion of seventeen joint actions in humans. Can J Appl Sport Sci 6:202, 1981.
20. Walker, JM, et al: Active mobility of the extremities of older subjects. Phys Ther 64:919, 1984.
21. Vandervoort, AA, et al: Age and sex effects on the mobility of the human ankle. J Gerontol 476:M17, 1992.
22. Baggett, BD, and Young, G: Ankle joint dorsiflexion. Establishment of a normal range. J Am Podiatr Med Assoc 83:251, 1993.
23. Grimston, SK, et al: Differences in ankle joint complex range of motion as a function of age. Foot Ankle 14:215, 1993.
24. Moseley, AN, Crosbie, J, and Adams, R: Normative data for passive plantarflexion-dorsiflexion flexibility. Clin Biomech (Bristol, Avon) 16:514, 2001.
25. Jonson, SR, and Gross, MT: Intraexaminer reliability, interexaminer reliability and mean values for nine lower extremity skeletal measures in healthy midshipmen. J Orthop Sports Phys Ther 25:253, 1997.
26. Bennell, K, et al: Hip and ankle range of motion and hip muscle strength in young female ballet dancers and controls. Br J Sports Med 33:340, 1999.
27. Ekstrand, MD, et al: Lower extremity goniometric measurements: A study to determine their reliability. Arch Phys Med Rehabil 63:171, 1982.
28. McPoil, TG, and Cornwall, MW: The relationship between static lower extremity measurements and rearfoot motion during walking. J Orthop Sports Phys Ther 24: 309, 1996.
29. Riemann, BL, et al: The effects of sex, joint angle, and the gastrocnemius muscle on passive ankle joint complex stiffness. J Athl Train 93:312, 2003.
30. Bohannon, RW, Tiberio, D, and Waters, G: Motion measured from forefoot and hindfoot landmarks during passive ankle dorsiflexion range of motion. J Orthop Sports Phys Ther 13:20, 1991.
31. Lattanza, L, Gray, GW, and Kanter, RM: Closed versus open kinematic chain measurements of subtalar joint eversion: Implications for clinical practice. J Orthop Sports Phys Ther 9:310, 1988.
32. Nawoczenski, DA, Baumhauer, JF, and Umberger, BR: Relationship between clinical measurements and motion of the first metatarsophalangeal joint during gait. J Bone Joint Surg 81:370, 1999.
33. Wilson, RW, and Gansneder, BM: Measures of functional limitation as predictors of disablement in athletes with acute ankle sprains. J Orthop Sports Phys Ther 30:528, 2000.
34. Morrison, KE, and Kaminski, TW: Foot characteristics in association with inversion ankle injury. J Athl Train 42:135, 2007.
35. Kaufman, KR, et al: The effect of foot structure and range of motion on musculoskeletal overuse injuries. Am J Sports Med 27:585, 1999.
36. Chesworth, BM, and Vandervoort, AA: Comparison of passive stiffness variables and range of motion in uninvolved and involved ankle joints of patients following ankle fractures. Phys Ther 75:253, 1995.
37. Reynolds, CA, et al: The effect of nontraumatic immobilization on ankle dorsiflexion stiffness in rats. J Orthop Sports Phys Ther 23: 27, 1996.
38. Hastings, MK, et al: Effects of a tendo-achilles lengthening procedure on muscle function and gait characteristics in a patient with diabetes mellitus. J Orthop Sports Phys Ther 30:85, 2000.
39. Salsich, GB, Mueller, MJ, and Sahrmann, SA: Passive ankle stiffness in subjects with diabetes and peripheral neuropathy versus an age matched comparison group. Phys Ther 80:352, 2000.
40. Salsich, GB, Brown, M, and Mueller, MJ: Relationship between plantarflexor muscle stiffness, strength and range of motion in subjects with diabetes; peripheral neuropathy compared to age-matched controls. J Orthop Sports Phys Ther 30: 473, 2000.
41. Rao, SR, et al: Increased passive ankle stiffness and reduced dorsiflexion range of motion in individuals with diabetes mellitus. Foot Ankle Int 27:617, 2006.
42. Pathokinesiology Service and Physical Therapy Dept: Observational Gait Analysis, ed 4. LAREI, Ranchos Los Amigos National Rehabilitation Center, Downey, CA, 2001.
43. Murray, MP: Gait as a total pattern of movement. Am J Phys Med Rehabil 46:290, 1967.
44. Ostrosky, KM: A comparison of gait characteristics in young and old subjects. Phys Ther 74:637, 1994.
45. Cailliet, R: Foot and Ankle, ed 3. FA Davis, Philadelphia, 1997.
46. McPoil, TG, and Cornwall, MW: Applied sports biomechanics in rehabilitation running. In Zachazewski, JE, Magee, DJ, and Quillen, WS (eds): Athletic Injuries and Rehabilitation. WB Saunders, Philadelphia, 1996.
47. McFayden, BJ, and Winter, DA: An integrated biomechanical analysis of normal stair ascent and descent. J Biomech 21:733, 1988.
48. Livingston, LA, Stevenson, JM, and Olney, SJ: Stairclimbing kinematics on stairs of differing dimensions. Arch Phys Med Rehabil 72:398, 1991.
49. Protopapadaki, A, et al: Hip, knee, ankle kinematics and kinetics during stair ascent and descent in healthy young individuals. Clin Biomech 22:203, 2007.
50. Lark, SD, et al: Knee and ankle range of motion during stepping down in elderly compared to young men. Eur J Appl Physiol 91:287, 2004.
51. Mecagni, C, et al : Balance and ankle range of motion in community-dwelling women aged 64–87 years: A correlational study. Phys Ther 80:1004, 2000.
52. Torburn, L, Perry, J, and Gronley, J-AK: Assessment of rearfoot motion: Passive positioning, one-legged standing, gait. Foot Ankle Int 19:688, 1998.
53. Garbalosa, JC, et al: The frontal plane relationship of the forefoot to the rearfoot in an asymptomatic population. J Orthop Sports Phys Ther 20:200, 1994.
54. Hemmerich, A, Brown, H, Smith, S : Hip, knee and ankle kinematics of high range of motion activities of daily living. J Orthop Res 24:770, 2006.
55. Martin, RRL, McPoil, TG: Reliability of ankle goniometric measurements: A literature review. J Am Podiatr Med Assoc 95:564, 2005.
56. Boone, DC, et al: Reliability of goniometric measurements. Phys Ther 68:1355, 1978.
57. Clapper, MP, and Wolf, SL: Comparison of the reliability of the Ortho-ranger and the standard goniometer for assessing active lower extremity range of motion. Phys Ther 68:214, 1988.

58. Bennell, K, et al: Interrater and intrarater reliability of a weight-bearing lunge measure of ankle dorsiflexion. Aust Physiother 44:175, 1998.

59. Rome, K, and Cowieson, F: A reliability study of the universal goniometer, fluid goniometer, and electrogoniometer for the measurement of ankle dorsiflexion. Foot Ankle Int 17:28, 1996.

60. Evans, AM, and Scutter, SD: Sagittal plane range of motion of the pediatric ankle joint. Am Podiatr Med Assoc 96:418, 2006.

61. Allington, NJ, Leroy, N, Doneux, C: Ankle joint range of motion measurements in spastic cerebral palsy children: Intraobserver and Interobserver reliability and reproducibility of goniometry and visual estimation. J Pediatr Orthop 11:2236, 2002.

62. McWhirk, LB, and Glanzman, AM: Within-session inter-rater reliability of goniometric measures in patients with spastic cerebral palsy. Pediatr Phys Ther 18:262, 2006.

63. Mutlu, A, Livanelioglu, A, and Gunel, MK: Reliability of goniometric measurements in children with spastic cerebral palsy. Med Sci Monit 23:CR323, 2007.

64. Elveru, RA, Rothstein, J, and Lamb, RL: Goniometric reliability in a clinical setting: Subtalar and ankle joint measurements. Phys Ther 68:672, 1988.

65. Youdas, JW, Bogard, CL, and Suman, VJ: Reliability of goniometric measurements and visual estimates of ankle joint range of motion obtained in a clinical setting. Arch Phys Med Rehabil 74:1113, 1993.

66. Clarkson, HM: Musculoskeletal Assessment: Joint Range of Motion and Manual Muscle Strength, ed. 2. Lippincott Williams & Wilkins, Philadelphia, 2000.

67. Elveru, RA, et al: Methods for taking subtalar joint measurements: A clinical report. Phys Ther 68:678, 1988.

68. Bailey, DS, Perillo, JT, and Forman, M: Subtalar joint neutral: A study using tomography. J Am Podiatr Assoc 74:59, 1984.

69. Picciano, AM, Rowlands, MS, and Worrell, T: Reliability of open and closed kinetic chain subtalar joint neutral positions and navicular drop test. J Orthop Sports Phys Ther 18:553, 1993.

70. Keenan, A-M, and Bach, TM: Clinician's assessment of the hindfoot: A study of reliability. Foot Ankle Int 27:451, 2006.

71. Hopson, MM, McPoil, TG, and Cornwall, MW: Motion of the first metatarsophalangeal joint. Reliability and validity of four measurement techniques. J Am Podiatr Med Assoc 85:198, 1995.

# TESTING OF THE SPINE AND TEMPOROMANDIBULAR JOINT

## OBJECTIVES

ON COMPLETION OF PART IV, THE READER WILL BE ABLE TO:

1. **Identify:**
   - Appropriate planes and axes for each spinal and jaw motion
   - Expected normal end-feels
   - Structures (contractile and noncontractile) that have the potential to limit the end of the range of motion

2. **Describe:**
   - Testing positions for motions of the spine and jaw
   - Goniometer, tape measure, and inclinometer alignments
   - Capsular patterns of restrictions
   - Range of motion necessary for functional tasks

3. **Explain:**
   - How age, gender, and other factors may affect the range of motion
   - How sources of error in measurement may affect testing results

4. Perform a range of motion assessment of the cervical spine using the universal goniometer, tape measure, inclinometers (double and single), and cervical range of motion (CROM) device.

Perform a range of motion assessment of the thoracic and lumbar spines using the universal goniometer, tape measure, and inclinometers. Please include the following in your assessment:

- A clear explanation of the testing procedure
- Placement of the subject in the appropriate testing position
- Adequate stabilization of the proximal joint component
- Correct determination of the end of the range of motion
- Correct identification of the end-feel
- Palpation and marking of the correct bony landmarks
- Accurate alignment of the goniometer
- Correct reading and recording

5. Perform a range of motion assessment of the temporomandibular joint using a ruler.

6. Assess the intratester and intertester reliability of measurements of the spine and temporomandibular joint.

7. Discuss the reliability and validity of range of motion measurements using the universal goniometer, tape measure, inclinometers, CROM device, and ruler.

Chapters 11 through 13 present common clinical techniques for measuring gross motions of the cervical, thoracic, and lumbar spine and the temporomandibular joint. Evaluation of the range of motion and end-feels of individual facet joints of the spine are not included.

# The Cervical Spine

## ⬭ Structure and Function

### Atlanto-Occipital and Atlantoaxial Joints

#### Anatomy

The atlanto-occipital joint is composed of the right and left deep concave superior facets of the atlas (C1) that articulate with the right and left convex occipital condyles of the skull (Fig. 11.1).

The atlantoaxial joint is composed of three separate articulations: the median atlantoaxial and two lateral joints. The median atlantoaxial joint consists of an anterior facet on the dens (the odontoid process of C2) that articulates with a facet on the internal surface of the atlas (C1). The two lateral joints are composed of the right and left superior facets of the axis (C2) that articulate with the right and left slightly convex inferior facets on the atlas (C1) (Fig. 11.2).

The atlanto-occipital and atlantoaxial joints are reinforced anteriorly by the anterior-occipital and atlantoaxial membranes (Fig.11.3A) and posteriorly by the posterior atlanto-occipital, atlantoaxial, and tectorial membranes (Fig.11.3B).

#### Osteokinematics

The atlanto-occipital joint is a condylar synovial joint that permits active flexion–extension as a nodding motion.[1] However, a very limited amount of axial rotation and lateral flexion may be produced passively.[1] Flexion–extension takes place in the sagittal plane around a medial–lateral axis. Extremes of flexion are limited by osseous contact of the anterior ring of the foramen magnum with the dens. Normally flexion is limited by tension in the posterior neck muscles and tectorial membrane and by impaction of the submandibular tissues against the throat. Extension is limited by the occiput compressing the suboccipital muscles.[1] Combined flexion–extension is reported to be between 20 degrees[2] and 30 degrees[3] and is usually described as the amount of motion that occurs during nodding of the head. However, according to Cailliet,[4] the range of motion (ROM) in flexion is 10 degrees and the range in extension is 30 degrees. Maximum rotation at the atlanto-occipital joint is between approximately 2.5 percent and 5 percent of the total cervical spine rotation.[5] Lateral flexion is approximately 10 degrees.[2]

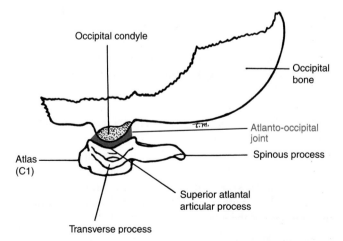

**FIGURE 11.1** A lateral view of a portion of the atlanto-occipital joint shows the superior atlantal articular process of the atlas (C1) and the corresponding occipital condyle. The joint space has been widened to show the articular processes.

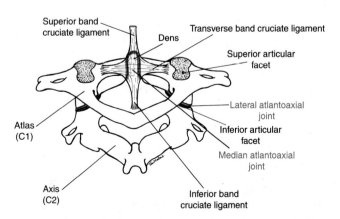

**FIGURE 11.2** A posterior view of the atlantoaxial joint and the superior, inferior, and transverse bands of the cruciate ligament.

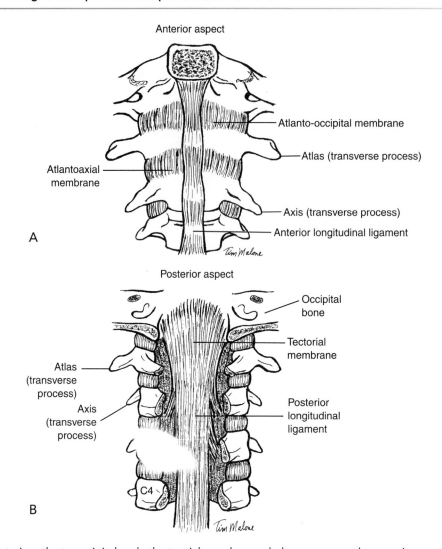

Anterior aspect

Atlanto-occipital membrane

Atlas (transverse process)

Atlantoaxial membrane

Axis (transverse process)

Anterior longitudinal ligament

A

Posterior aspect

Occipital bone

Tectorial membrane

Atlas (transverse process)

Axis (transverse process)

Posterior longitudinal ligament

C4

B

**FIGURE 11.3 A:** The anterior atlanto-occipital and atlantoaxial membranes help to support the anterior aspect of the atlanto-occipital and atlantoaxial joints. **B:** The posterior atlanto-occipital, atlantoaxial, and tectorial membranes help to support the posterior aspect of the atlanto-occipital and atlantoaxial joints. The tectorial membrane is an extension of the posterior longitudinal ligament.

The two lateral atlantoaxial joints are plane synovial joints that allow flexion–extension, lateral flexion, and rotation. The median atlantoaxial joint is a synovial trochoid (pivot) joint that permits rotation. Approximately 55 percent of the total cervical range of rotation occurs at the atlantoaxial joint. Rotation at the median atlantoaxial joint is limited primarily by the two alar ligaments, with minor restraint being provided by the capsules of the lateral atlantoaxial joints.[1] About 45 degrees of rotation to the right and left sides are available. The motions permitted at the three atlantoaxial articulations are flexion–extension, lateral flexion, and rotation.[6]

## Arthrokinematics

At the atlanto-occipital joint when the head moves on the atlas (convex surfaces moving on concave surfaces), the occipital condyles roll in the same direction as the top of the head and glide in the direction opposite to the movement of the top of the head. For example, in flexion, the occipital condyles roll anteriorly and glide posteriorly on the concave articular surfaces of the atlas. In extension, the occipital condyles roll posteriorly and glide anteriorly on the atlas and the back of the head moves posteriorly.[1]

At the lateral atlantoaxial joints the inferior zygapophyseal articular facets of the atlas are convex and articulate with the superior concave articular facets of the axis. At the median joint the atlas forms a ring with the transverse ligament (band) of the cruciate ligament, and this ring rotates around the dens (odontoid process), which serves as a pivot for rotation. The dens articulates with a small facet in the central area of the anterior arch of the atlas.

## Capsular Pattern

The capsular pattern for the atlanto-occipital joint is an equal restriction of extension and lateral flexion. Rotation and flexion are not affected.[2]

# Intervertebral and Zygapophyseal Joints

## Anatomy

The intervertebral joints are composed of the superior and inferior surfaces of the vertebral bodies and the adjacent intervertebral discs (Fig. 11.4). The joints are reinforced anteriorly by the anterior longitudinal ligament, which limits extension (Fig. 11.5), and posteriorly by the posterior longitudinal ligament, ligamentum nuchae, ligamentum flavum, supraspinous and interspinous ligaments (Fig. 11.6), and the back extensors, which help to limit flexion.

The zygapophyseal joints are formed by the right and left superior articular facets (processes) of one vertebra and the right and left inferior articular facets of an adjacent superior vertebra (Fig. 11.7). Each joint has its own capsule and capsular ligaments, which are lax and permit a relatively large ROM. The ligamentum flavum helps to reinforce the joint capsules.

## Osteokinematics

According to White and Punjabi,[7] one vertebra can move in relation to an adjacent vertebra in six different directions (three translations and three rotations) along and around three axes. The compound effects of sliding and tilting at a series of vertebrae produce a large ROM for the column as a whole, including flexion–extension, lateral flexion, and rotation. Some motions in the vertebral column are coupled with other motions; this coupling varies from region to region. A coupled motion is one in which one motion around one axis is consistently associated with another motion or motions around a different axis or axes. For example, left lateral

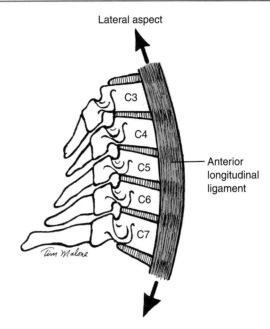

**FIGURE 11.5** The anterior longitudinal ligament reinforces the anterior portion of the discs and helps to prevent extremes of extension.

flexion from C2 to C5 is accompanied by rotation to the left (spinous processes move to the right) and forward flexion. In the cervical region from C2 to C7, flexion and extension are the only motions that are not coupled.[7]

The intervertebral joints are cartilaginous joints of the symphysis type. The zygapophyseal joints are synovial plane joints. In the cervical region, the facets are oriented at 45 degrees to the transverse plane. The inferior facets of the

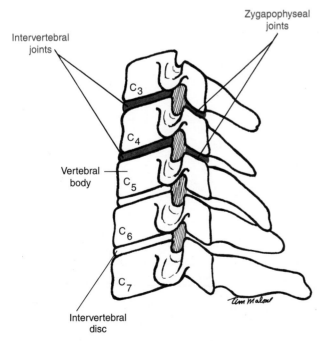

**FIGURE 11.4** The lateral view of the cervical spine shows the intervertebral and zygapophyseal joints from C3 to C7.

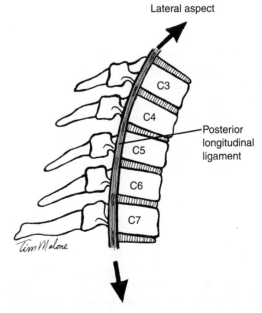

**FIGURE 11.6** The posterior longitudinal ligament reinforces the posterior portion of the discs and helps to prevent extremes of forward flexion.

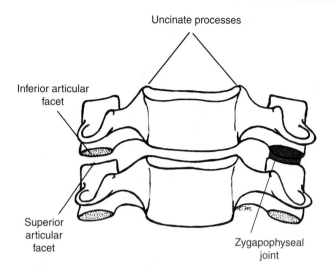

Uncinate processes

Inferior articular facet

Superior articular facet

Zygapophyseal joint

**FIGURE 11.7** An anterior view of the right and left zygapophyseal joints between two cervical vertebrae. The vertebrae have been separated to provide a clear view of the inferior articular facets of the superior vertebra and the superior articular facets of the adjacent inferior vertebra.

superior vertebrae face anteriorly and inferiorly. The superior facets of the inferior vertebrae face posteriorly and superiorly. The orientation of the articular facets, which varies from region to region, determines the direction of the tilting and sliding of the vertebra, whereas the size of the disc determines the amount of motion. In addition, passive tension in a number of soft tissues and bony contacts controls and limits motions of the vertebral column. In general, although regional variations exist, the soft tissues that control and limit extremes of motion in forward flexion include the supraspinous and interspinous ligaments, zygapophyseal joint capsules, ligamentum flavum, posterior longitudinal ligament, posterior fibers of the annulus fibrosus of the intervertebral disc, and back extensors.

Extension is limited by bony contact of the spinous processes and by passive tension in the zygapophyseal joint capsules, anterior fibers of the annulus fibrosus, anterior longitudinal ligament, and anterior trunk muscles. Lateral flexion is limited by the intertransverse ligaments, by passive tension in the annulus fibrosus on the side opposite the motion on the convexity of the curve, and by the uncinate processes. Rotation is limited by fibers of the annulus fibrosus.

## Arthrokinematics

The intervertebral joints permit a small amount of sliding and tilting of one vertebra on another. In all of the motions at the intervertebral joints, the nucleus pulposus of the intervertebral disc acts as a pivot for the tilting and sliding motions of the vertebrae. Flexion is a result of anterior sliding and tilting of a superior vertebra on the interposed disc of an adjacent inferior vertebra. Extension is the result of posterior sliding and tilting.

The zygapophyseal joints permit small amounts of sliding of the right and left inferior facets on the right and left superior facets of an adjacent inferior vertebra. In flexion, the

inferior facets of the superior vertebrae slide anteriorly and superiorly on the superior facets of the inferior vertebrae. In extension, the inferior facets of the superior vertebrae slide posteriorly and inferiorly on the superior facets of the inferior vertebrae. In lateral flexion and rotation, one inferior facet of the superior vertebra slides inferiorly and posteriorly on the superior facet of the inferior vertebra on the side to which the spine is laterally flexed. The opposite inferior facet of the superior vertebra slides superiorly and anteriorly on the superior facet of the adjacent inferior vertebra.

### Capsular Pattern

The capsular pattern for C2 to C7 is recognizable by pain and equal limitation of all motions except flexion, which is usually minimally restricted. The capsular pattern for unilateral facet involvement is a greater restriction of movement in lateral flexion to the opposite side and in rotation to the same side. For example, if the right articular facet joint capsule is involved, lateral flexion to the left and rotation to the right are the motions most restricted.[8]

Measurement of the cervical spine ROM is complicated by the region's multiple joint structure, lack of well-defined and standardized landmarks, lack of an accurate and workable definition of the neutral position, and lack of a standardized method of stabilization to isolate cervical motion from thoracic spine motion. The search for instruments and methods that are capable of providing accurate and affordable measurements of the cervical spine ROM is ongoing. Tables 11.1 through 11.4 in the Research Findings Section provide normal cervical spine ROM values from various sources and with use of a variety of methods. Additional tables and text in the Research Findings section provide ROM values by age and gender. This information is followed by functional ranges of motion and a review of research studies on the reliability and validity of the various instruments used to measure cervical range of motion.

# RANGE OF MOTION TESTING PROCEDURES: Cervical Spine

## Landmarks for Testing Procedures

**FIGURE 11.8** Surface anatomy landmarks for goniometer alignment and tape measure alignment for measuring cervical motions.

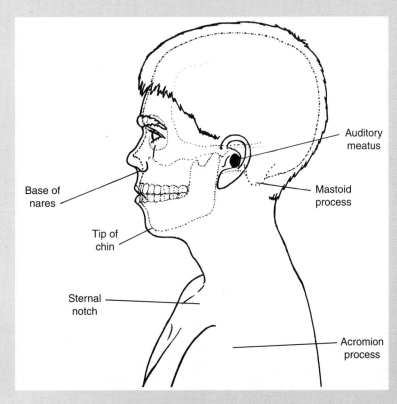

**FIGURE 11.9** Bony anatomical landmarks for goniometer alignment for measuring cervical flexion and extension.

## Landmarks for Testing Procedures (continued)

**FIGURE 11.10** Surface anatomy landmarks used to measure cervical motion with a tape measure: tip of the chin, sternal notch, and acromion process. The mastoid process, which is used to measure lateral flexion, is included in Figure 11.8.

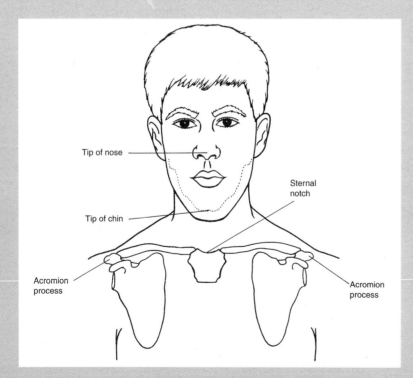

**FIGURE 11.11** Bony anatomical landmarks for measuring cervical spine range of motion with a tape measure and universal goniometer.

## Landmarks for Testing Procedures (continued)

**FIGURE 11.12** A posterior view of the subject's head and cervical spine shows the surface anatomy landmarks used for measuring lateral flexion with a goniometer and flexion and extension with dual inclinometers.

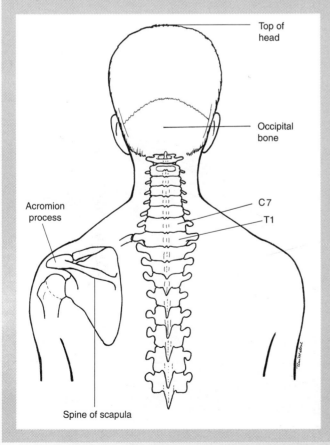

Top of head

Occipital bone

C7

T1

Acromion process

Spine of scapula

**FIGURE 11.13** Bony anatomical landmarks used to align the goniometer, inclinometers, and cervical range of motion device. The goniometer uses the spinous process of the seventh cervical vertebra as a landmark for the measurement of at least one cervical motion. The inclinometers use the spinous process of the T1 vertebra.

## ● CERVICAL FLEXION: UNIVERSAL GONIOMETER

Motion occurs in the sagittal plane around a medial–lateral axis. The mean cervical flexion ROM measured with a universal goniometer is 40 degrees (standard deviation [SD] = 12 degrees) in adults.[9] See Youdas, Carey, and Garrett[9] in Table 11.1 in the Research Findings section for additional normal ROM values by age and gender.

### Testing Position

Place the subject in the sitting position, with the thoracic and lumbar spine well supported by the back of a chair. Position the head in 0 degrees of rotation and lateral flexion.

### Stabilization

Stabilize the shoulder girdle and chest by using a strap because the examiner's hands are involved in the measurement. Have the subject place his or her hands on their knees.

### Testing Motion

Put one hand on the back of the subject's head and, with the other hand, hold the subject's chin. Push gently but firmly on the back of the subject's head to move the head anteriorly. Pull the subject's chin in toward the chest to move the subject through flexion ROM (Fig. 11.14). The end of the ROM occurs when resistance to further motion is felt and further attempts at flexion cause forward flexion of the trunk.

### Normal End-Feel

The normal end-feel is firm owing to stretching of the posterior ligaments (supraspinous, infraspinous, ligamentum flavum, and ligamentum nuchae), posterior fibers of the annulus fibrosus in the intervertebral disks, and the zygapophyseal joint capsules and because of impaction of the submandibular tissues against the throat and passive tension in the following muscles: iliocostalis cervicis, longissimus capitis, longissimus cervicis, obliquus capitis superior, rectus capitis posterior major, rectus capitis posterior minor, semispinalis capitis, semispinalis cervicis, splenius cervicis, splenius capitis, spinalis capitis, spinalis cervicis, and upper trapezius.

**FIGURE 11.14** The subject at the end of cervical flexion range of motion.

## Goniometer Alignment

See Figures 11.15 and 11.16.

1. Center **fulcrum** of the goniometer over the external auditory meatus.
2. Align **proximal arm** so that it is either perpendicular or parallel to the ground.
3. Align **distal arm** with the base of the nares. If a tongue depressor is used, align the arm of the goniometer parallel to the longitudinal axis of the tongue depressor.

▶ **NOTE: The same testing position, testing motion, and stabilization described for measuring flexion using a goniometer are to be used for all of the following alternative methods.**

**FIGURE 11.15** In the 0 starting position for measuring cervical flexion range of motion, the goniometer reads 90 degrees. This reading should be transposed and recorded as 0 degrees.

**FIGURE 11.16** The goniometer reads 135 degrees at the end of the range of motion (ROM) but the ROM should be recorded as 0-45 degrees.

# ● CERVICAL FLEXION: TAPE MEASURE

The mean cervical flexion ROM obtained with a tape measure ranges from 1.0 to 4.3 cm[10,11] for ages 14 to 31 years. See Table 11.2 in the Research Findings section for normal values, but remember that you need to check that the landmarks that are being used by the researchers are the same as the ones that you are using.

## Alignment

Use a skin marking pencil to place marks on the following landmarks: the lower edge of the sternal notch and the middle of the tip of the chin. Ask the subject to tuck his or her chin in and bend his or her head as far forward as possible without moving the trunk.

Measure the distance between the mark on the tip of the chin and the mark at the lower edge of the sternal notch at the end of the ROM. Make sure that the subject's mouth remains closed during the motion (Fig. 11.17).

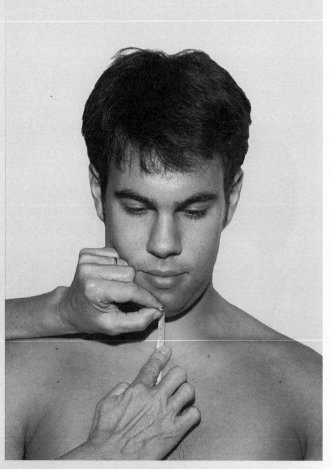

**FIGURE 11.17** The examiner uses a tape measure for cervical flexion by determining the distance from the tip of the chin to the sternal notch.

## ● CERVICAL FLEXION: DOUBLE INCLINOMETERS

The double inclinometer method is included because the fifth edition of the *Guides to Evaluation of Permanent Impairment*[12] published by the American Medical Assocation (AMA) requires the use of double inclinometers for measurements of the spine. However, not enough studies have been done to establish the reliability and validity of this method of measurement and hence to provide normative data.

Both inclinometers must be zeroed after they are positioned on the subject and prior to the beginning of the measurement. To zero the inclinometer, adjust the rotating dial so the bubble or pointer is at 0 degrees on the scale.

### Inclinometer Alignment

1. Place **one inclinometer** directly over the spinous process of the T-1 vertebra, making sure that the inclinometer is adjusted to 0 degrees.
2. Place the **second inclinometer** firmly on the top of the head, making sure that the inclinometer is adjusted to 0 degrees (Fig. 11.18).

### Testing Motion

Instruct the subject to bring the head forward into flexion while keeping the trunk straight (Fig. 11.19). (Note that active ROM [AROM] is being measured.) At the end of the motion, read and record the degrees on the dials of each inclinometer. The ROM is the difference between the readings of the two instruments.

**FIGURE 11.18** Inclinometer alignment in the starting position for measuring cervical flexion range of motion.

**FIGURE 11.19** Inclinometer alignment at the end of cervical flexion range of motion.

## CERVICAL FLEXION: CERVICAL RANGE OF MOTION (CROM) DEVICE

The mean flexion ROM for the CROM device ranges from 64 degrees in subjects aged 11 to 19 years to 40 degrees in subjects aged 80 to 89 years.[13] For additional ROM values by age and gender, refer to Capuano-Pucci[14] and Tousignant[15] in Table 11.1 in the Research Findings section; to Nilsson[16] in Tables 11.5, 11.6, and 11.7; and to Youdas[13] in Tables 11.4, 11.8, and 11.9.

Familiarize yourself with the CROM device prior to beginning the measurement. The CROM device consists of a headpiece that supports two gravity inclinometers and a compass inclinometer. One gravity inclinometer is located on the side of the head in the sagittal plane and is used to measure flexion and extension. The other gravity inclinometer is located over the forehead in the frontal plane and is used to measure lateral flexion. The compass inclinometer has a gravity needle and is situated over the top of the head in the transverse plane and is used to measure rotation. A neckpiece containing two strong magnets is placed around the subject's neck to ensure the accuracy of the compass inclinometer.

The CROM device should fit comfortably over the bridge of the subject's nose. A Velcro strap that goes around the back of the head can be adjusted to make a snug fit. One size instrument fits all, and it is relatively easy for an examiner to fit the device to a subject.[17] Remember to stabilize the subject's trunk to prevent thoracic motion.

### CROM Device Alignment[17]

1. Place the CROM device carefully on the subject's head so that the nosepiece is on the bridge of the nose and the Velcro strap fits snugly across the back of the subject's head (Fig. 11.20).
2. Position the subject's head so that the inclinometer on the side of the head reads 0 degrees.

FIGURE 11.20 The CROM device positioned on the subject's head in the starting position for measuring cervical flexion range of motion. The dial on the gravity inclinometer located on the side of the subjects head is at 0 degrees.

FIGURE 11.21 The examiner is shown stabilizing the trunk with one hand and maintaining the end of the flexion range of motion with her other hand.

## Testing Motion

Push gently but firmly on the back of the subject's head to move it anteriorly and inferiorly through flexion ROM (Fig. 11.21). At the end of the motion, read the dial on the inclinometer on the side of the head and record the reading.

## ● CERVICAL EXTENSION: UNIVERSAL GONIOMETER

Motion occurs in the sagittal plane around a medial–lateral axis. Mean cervical extension ROM measured with a universal goniometer is 50 degrees (SD = 14 degrees)[9] in adults. Refer to Youdas et al[9] in Table 11.1 in the Research Findings section for additional normal ROM values by age and gender.

## Testing Position

Place the subject in the sitting position, with the thoracic and lumbar spine well supported by the back of a chair. Position the cervical spine in 0 degrees of rotation and lateral flexion. A tongue depressor can be held between the teeth for reference.

## Stabilization

Stabilize the shoulder girdle and chest to prevent extension of the thoracic and lumbar spine. Usually, the stabilization is achieved through the cooperation of the patient and support from the back of the chair. A strap placed around the chest and the back of the chair also may be used.

## Testing Motion

Put one hand on the back of the subject's head and, with the other hand, hold the subject's chin. Push gently but firmly upward and posteriorly on the chin to move the head through the ROM in extension (Fig. 11.22). The end of the ROM occurs when resistance to further motion is felt and further attempts at extension cause extension of the trunk.

## Normal End-Feel

The normal end-feel is firm owing to the passive tension developed by stretching of the anterior longitudinal ligament, anterior fibers of the annulus fibrosus, zygapophyseal joint capsules, and the following muscles: sternocleidomastoid, longus capitis, longus colli, rectus capitis anterior, and scalenus anterior. Extremes of extension may be limited by contact between the spinous processes.

**FIGURE 11.22** The end of cervical extension ROM. The examiner helps to prevent cervical rotation and lateral flexion by holding the back of the subject's head. Ideally the examiner's other hand should be on the subject's chin in order to move the head into extension.

## Goniometer Alignment
See Figures 11.23 and 11.24.

1. Center **fulcrum** of the goniometer over the external auditory meatus.
2. Align **proximal arm** so that it is either perpendicular or parallel to the ground.

3. Align **distal arm** with the base of the nares. If a tongue depressor is used, align the arm of the goniometer parallel to the longitudinal axis of the tongue depressor.

▶ **NOTE: The same testing position, testing motions, and stabilization decribed for measuring extension with a goniometer should be used for all of the following alternative measurement methods.**

**FIGURE 11.23** In the 0 starting position for measuring cervical extension range of motion the goniometer reads 90 degrees. This reading should be transposed and recorded as 0 degrees.

**FIGURE 11.24** At the end of cervical extension, the examiner maintains the perpendicular alignment of the proximal goniometer arm and keeps the distal arm aligned with the base of the nares.

## ● CERVICAL EXTENSION: TAPE MEASURE

The mean cervical extension ROM measured with a tape measure ranges from 18.5 to 22.4 cm[10,11] in adults. See Table 11.2 in the Research Findings section for additional normal ROM values by age and gender.

Use a skin marking pencil to place a mark at the lower edge of the sternal notch and on the tip of the chin. Ask the subject to look straight ahead and then move his or her head posteriorly as far as possible, being careful not to extend the trunk. Measure the distance between the mark at the sternal notch and the mark on the tip of the chin at the end of cervical extension ROM (Fig. 11.25). The distance between the two points of reference is recorded in centimeters. Be sure that the subject's mouth remains closed during the measurement.

**FIGURE 11.25** In the tape measure method for measuring cervical extension one end of the tape measure is placed on the tip of the subject's chin; the other end is placed at the subject's sternal notch.

## ● CERVICAL EXTENSION: DOUBLE INCLINOMETERS

### Inclinometer Alignment

1. Place **one inclinometer** directly over the spine of the scapula. Adjust the dial of the inclinometer so that it reads 0 degrees. (If the inclinometer is placed over the first thoracic vertebra, it may contact the back of the head in full extension.)
2. Place the **second inclinometer** firmly on the top of the head, making sure that the inclinometer reads 0 degrees (Fig. 11.26).

### Testing Motion

Instruct the subject to move the head into extension while keeping the trunk straight (Fig. 11.27). (Note that AROM is being measured.) At the end of the motion, read and record the information on the dials of each inclinometer. The ROM is the difference between the readings of the two instruments.

**FIGURE 11.26** Inclinometer alignment in the starting position for measuring cervical extension range of motion. The examiner has zeroed both inclinometers prior to beginning the motion.

**FIGURE 11.27** Inclinometer alignment at the end of cervical extension range of motion.

# ● CERVICAL EXTENSION: CROM DEVICE

The mean cervical ROM in extension measured with the CROM device ranges from 86 degrees in males aged 11 to 19 years and to 49 degrees in males aged 80 to 89 years.[13] For additional normal ROM values by age and gender, refer to ROM values listed under Capuano-Pucci[14] and Tousignant[15] in Table 11.1; to Nilsson[16] in Tables 11.5, 11.6, and 11.7; and to Youdas[13] in Tables 11.8 and 11.9 in the Research Findings section.

## CROM Device Alignment

1. Place the CROM device carefully on the subject's head so that the nosepiece is on the bridge of the nose and the Velcro strap fits snugly across the back of the subject's head (Fig. 11.28).
2. Position the subject's head so that the gravity inclinometer on the side of the head reads 0 degrees.

## Testing Motion

Guide the subject's head posteriorly and inferiorly through extension ROM (Fig. 11.29). At the end of the motion read the dial on the inclinometer on the side of the head.

**FIGURE 11.28** The subject is positioned in the starting position with the CROM device in place. The gravity inclinometer located at the side of the subject's head is at 0 degrees prior to beginning the motion.

**FIGURE 11.29** At the end of cervical extension range of motion (ROM), the examiner is stabilizing the trunk with one hand and maintaining the end of the ROM with her other hand on top of the subject's head.

# ● CERVICAL LATERAL FLEXION: UNIVERSAL GONIOMETER

Motion occurs in the frontal plane around an anterior–posterior axis. The mean cervical lateral flexion ROM to one side, measured with a universal goniometer, is 22 degrees (SD = 7 to 8 degrees) in adults. [9] See Youdas[9] in Table 11.1 in the Research Findings section for additional normal ROM values by age and gender.

## Testing Position

Place the subject sitting with the cervical spine in 0 degrees of flexion, extension, and rotation.

## Stabilization

Stabilize the shoulder girdle and chest to prevent lateral flexion of the thoracic and lumbar spine.

## Testing Motion

Grasp the subject's head at the top and side (opposite to the direction of the motion). Pull the head toward the shoulder. Do not allow the head to rotate, forward flex, or extend during the motion (Fig. 11.30). The end of the motion occurs when resistance to motion is felt and attempts to produce additional motion cause lateral trunk flexion.

## Normal End-Feel

The normal end-feel is firm owing to the passive tension developed in the intertransverse ligaments, the lateral annulus fibrosus fibers, and the following contralateral

**FIGURE 11.30** The end of the cervical lateral flexion range of motion. The examiner's hand holds the subject's left shoulder to prevent lateral flexion of the thoracic and lumbar spine. The examiner's other hand maintains cervical lateral flexion by pulling the subject's head laterally.

muscles: longus capitis, longus colli, scalenus anterior, and sternocleidomastoid.

## Goniometer Alignment

See Figures 11.31 and 11.32.

1. Center **fulcrum** of the goniometer over the spinous process of the C7 vertebra.
2. Align **proximal arm** with the spinous processes of the thoracic vertebrae so that the arm is perpendicular to the ground.
3. Align **distal arm** with the dorsal midline of the head, using the occipital protuberance for reference.

▶ NOTE: The same testing position, testing motion, and stabilization decribed for measuring lateral flexion with a goniometer should be used for all of the following lateral flexion measurement methods.

**FIGURE 11.31** In the starting position for measuring cervical lateral flexion range of motion, the proximal goniometer arm is perpendicular to the floor.

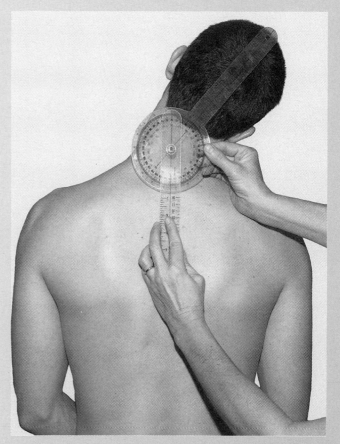

**FIGURE 11.32** At the end of cervical lateral flexion ROM, the examiner maintains alignment of the proximal goniometer arm. In practice, the examiner would have one hand on the subject's head to maintain lateral flexion.

## ● CERVICAL LATERAL FLEXION: TAPE MEASURE

The mean cervical lateral flexion ROM measured with a tape measure ranges from 10.7 to 12.9 cm for subjects 14 to 31 years of age. Refer to Table 11.2 in the Research Findings section for additional normal ROM values by age and gender.

Use a skin marking pencil to place marks on the subject's mastoid process and on the lateral tip of the acromial process. Measure the distance between the two marks at the end of cervical lateral flexion ROM (Fig. 11.33).

**FIGURE 11.33** The subject is shown at the end of cervical lateral flexion range of motion.

## ● CERVICAL LATERAL FLEXION: DOUBLE INCLINOMETERS

### Inclinometer Alignment

1. Position **one inclinometer** directly over the spinous process of the T1 vertebra. Adjust the rotating dial so that the bubble is at 0 on the scale.
2. Place the **second inclinometer** firmly on the top of the subject's head and adjust the dial so that it reads 0 (Fig. 11.34).

### Testing Motion

Instruct the subject to move the head into lateral flexion while keeping the trunk straight (Fig. 11.35). (Note that AROM is being measured.) The ROM is the difference between the two instruments.

**FIGURE 11.34** In the starting position for measuring cervical lateral flexion range of motion, one inclinometer is positioned at the level of the spinous process of the first thoracic vertebra. A piece of tape has been placed at that level to help align the inclinometer. The examiner has zeroed both inclinometers prior to beginning the motion.

**FIGURE 11.35** Inclinometer alignment at the end of lateral flexion range of motion. At the end of the motion, the examiner reads and records the information on the dials of each inclinometer. The range of motion is the difference between the readings of the two instruments.

## ● CERVICAL LATERAL FLEXION: CROM DEVICE

The ROM in lateral flexion using the CROM device ranges from a mean of 45 degrees in subjects aged 11 to 19 years to a mean of 24 in male subjects and 26 degrees in female subjects aged 80 to 89 years.[13] For additional normal ROM values by age and gender, see Capuano-Pucci[14] and Tousignant[15] in Table 11.1; and Nilsson[16] in Tables 11.4, 11.5, and 11.6; and Youdas[13] in Tables 11.7 and 11.8 in the Research Findings section.

## CROM Device Alignment[17]

1. Place the CROM device on the subject's head so that the nosepiece is on the bridge of the nose and the band fits snugly across the back of the subject's head.
2. Position the subject in the testing position so that the gravity inclinometer on the front of the CROM device reads 0 degrees (Fig. 11.36).

## Testing Motion

Guide the subject's head into lateral flexion (Fig.11.37). At the end of the motion, read the dial located in front of the forehead and record the number of degrees.

**FIGURE 11.36** The subject is placed in the starting position for measuring cervical lateral flexion range of motion so that the inclinometer located in front of the subject's forehead is zeroed before starting the motion.

**FIGURE 11.37** At the end of lateral flexion range of motion (ROM), the examiner is stabilizing the subject's shoulder with one hand and maintaining the end of the ROM with her other hand on the subject's head.

# ● CERVICAL ROTATION: UNIVERSAL GONIOMETER

Motion occurs in the transverse plane around a vertical axis. The mean cervical ROM in rotation measured with a universal goniometer is 49 degrees to the left (SD = 9 degrees) and 51 degrees to the right (SD = 11 degrees) in adults.[9] See Youdas[9] in Table 11.1 in the Research Findings section for additional normal ROM values by age and gender. Magee[2] reports that the ROM in rotation is between 70 and 90 degrees but cautions that cervical rotation past 50 degrees may lead to kinking of the contralateral vertebral artery. The ipsilateral artery may kink at 45 degrees of rotation.[2]

## Testing Position

Place the subject sitting, with the thoracic and lumbar spine well supported by the back of the chair. Position the cervical spine in 0 degrees of flexion, extension, and lateral flexion. The subject may hold a tongue depressor between the front teeth for reference.

## Stabilization

Stabilize the shoulder girdle and chest to prevent rotation of the thoracic and lumbar spine. A strap across the chest may be used to keep the trunk from rotating.

## Testing Motion

Grasp the subject's chin and rotate the head by moving the head toward the shoulder, as shown in Figure 11.38. The end of the ROM occurs when resistance to movement is felt and further movement causes rotation of the trunk.

## Normal End-Feel

The normal end-feel is firm owing to stretching of the alar ligament, the fibers of the zygapophyseal joint capsules, and the following contralateral muscles: longus capitis, longus colli, and scalenus anterior. Passive tension in the ipsilateral sternocleidomastoid may limit extremes of rotation.

## Goniometer Alignment

See Figures 11.39 and 11.40.

1. Center **fulcrum** of the goniometer over the center of the cranial aspect of the head.
2. Align **proximal arm** parallel to an imaginary line between the two acromial processes.
3. Align **distal arm** with the tip of the nose. If a tongue depressor is used, align the arm of the goniometer parallel to the longitudinal axis of the tongue depressor.

**FIGURE 11.38** The end of the cervical rotation range of motion. One of the examiner's hands maintains rotation and prevents cervical flexion and extension. The examiner's other hand is placed on the subject's left shoulder to prevent rotation of the thoracic and lumbar spine.

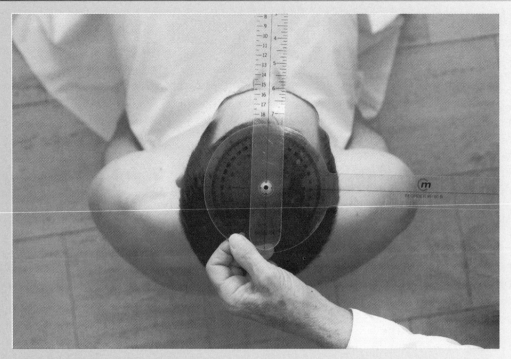

**FIGURE 11.39** To align the goniometer at the starting position for measuring cervical rotation range of motion, the examiner stands in back of the subject, who is seated in a low chair.

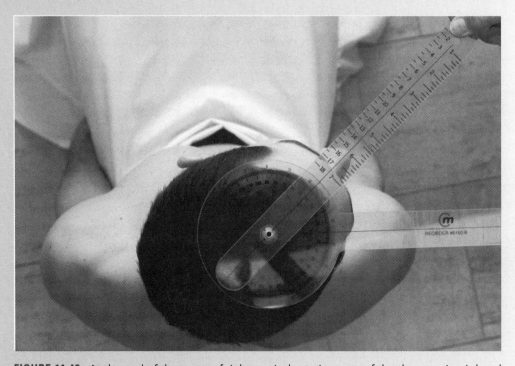

**FIGURE 11.40** At the end of the range of right cervical rotation, one of the the examiner's hands maintains alignment of the distal goniometer arm with the tip of the subject's nose. The examiner's other hand keeps the proximal arm aligned parallel to the imaginary line between the acromial processes.

## ● CERVICAL ROTATION: TAPE MEASURE

The mean cervical rotation ROM to the left measured with a tape measure ranges from 11.0 to 13.2 cm[10,11] in 14 to 31 year olds. See Table 11.2 in the Research Findings section for additional normal ROM values by age and gender.

Use a skin marking pencil to place marks on the tip of the chin and the acromial process. Have the subject look straight ahead and then turn his or her head to the right as far as possible without rotating the trunk. Measure the distance between the two marks at the end of the motion (Fig. 11.41). Have the subject return his or her head to the neutral starting position and then turn the head as far to the left as possible wihtout rotating the trunk.

## ● CERVICAL ROTATION: INCLINOMETER

The normal ROM for rotation using an inclinometer is 80 degrees to each side, according to the AMA.[12]

### Testing Position
Place the subject supine with the head in neutral rotation, lateral flexion, flexion, and extension.

### Inclinometer Alignment
1. Place the inclinometer in the middle of the subject's forehead, and zero the inclinometer (Fig. 11.42).
2. Hold the inclinometer firmly while the subject's head moves through rotation ROM (Fig. 11.43).

### Testing Motion
Instruct the subject to roll the head into rotation. The ROM can be read on the inclinometer at the end of the ROM.

**FIGURE 11.41** At the end of the right cervical range of motion, the examiner is using a tape measure to determine the distance between the tip of the subject's chin and her right acromial process.

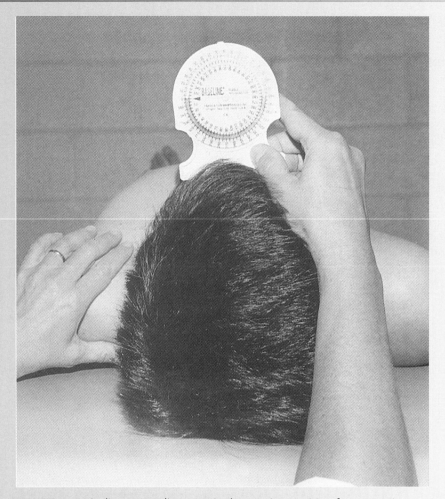

**FIGURE 11.42** Inclinometer alignment in the starting position for measuring cervical rotation range of motion. Only one inclinometer is used for this measurement.

**FIGURE 11.43** Inclinometer alignment at the end of cervical rotation range of motion (ROM). The number of degrees on the dial of the inclinometer equals the ROM in rotation.

# ● CERVICAL ROTATION: CROM DEVICE

The mean ROM in right rotation with use of the CROM device varies from 75 degrees in female subjects aged 11 to 19 years to 46 degrees in male subjects aged 80 years.[13] For additional ROM values by age and gender, refer to Capuano-Pucci[14] and Tousignant[15] in Table 11.1; to Nilsson[16] in Tables 11.4, 11.5, and 11.6; and to Youdas[13] in Tables 11.7 and 11.8 in the Research Findings section.

## CROM Device Alignment[17]

1. Place the CROM device on the subject's head so that the nosepiece is on the bridge of the nose and the band fits snugly across the back of the subject's head. The arrow on the magnetic yoke should be pointing north (Fig. 11.44).
2. To ensure that the compass inclinometer is level, adjust the position of the subject's head so that both gravity inclinometers read 0 degrees (Fig. 11.45).
3. After leveling the compass inclinometer, turn the rotation meter on the compass inclinometer until the pointer is at 0 degrees.

## Testing Motion

Guide the subject's head into rotation and read the inclinometer at the end of the ROM.

**FIGURE 11.44** The compass inclinometer on the top of the CROM device has been leveled so that the examiner is able to zero it prior to the beginning of the motion.

**FIGURE 11.45** At the end of right rotation range of motion (ROM), the examiner is stabilizing the subject's shoulder with one hand and maintaining the end of rotation ROM with the other hand. The examiner will read the dial of the inclinometer on the top of the CROM device. Rotation ROM will be the number of degrees on the dial at the end of the ROM.

# Research Findings

Measurement of the cervical spine ROM is complicated by the region's multiple joint structure and lack of well-defined landmarks, a workable definition of the neutral position, and a standardized method of stabilization to isolate cervical motion from thoracic motion. The search for instruments and methods capable of providing accurate and affordable measurements of the cervical spine is ongoing. At this time the universal goniometer appears to be the most commonly used instrument in the clinic, although relatively few research studies are available to provide normative data and to attest to the goniometer's reliability and validity. ROM values from one study are presented in Table 11.1. The tape measure also is used in the clinical setting and ROM values can be found in Table 11.2. Single inclinometer values are found in Table 11.3.

## Effects of Age, Gender, and Other Factors on Cervical Range of Motion Measurements

### Age

A large number of researchers have investigated the effects of age on active cervical ROM,[13,16,20–36] but differences between the populations tested and the wide variety of instruments and procedures employed in these studies make it difficult to compare results. Generally, most researchers agree that in adults a tendency exists for cervical ROM to decrease with increasing age. The only exception that has been found by some authors is that axial rotation (occurring primarily at the atlantoaxial joint) has been shown either to stay the same or to increase with increasing age to compensate for an age-related decrease in rotation in the lower cervical spine.[22,29] Age may not account for a large amount of the variance in cervical ROM, but age appears to have a stronger effect than gender.

O'Driscoll and Tomenson[20] studied cervical ROM across age groups using a type of inclinometer. They measured 79 females and 80 males ranging in age from 0 to 79 years and found that ROM decreased with increasing age and differences existed between males and females. In another study that included a relatively large number of subjects (250) and a large age range (from 14 to 70 years), Feipel and colleagues[28] found a significant decrease in all cervical motions with increasing age. Kulman[30] compared the range of motion of 42 subjects aged 70 to 90 years and 31 subjects aged 20 to 30 years and found that the elderly group had significantly less motion than the younger group for all motions measured, including rotation. Sforza and coworkers,[35] who studied the effects of age on ROM in 20 male adolescents (mean age 16 years), 30 young adult males (mean age 23 years), and 20 middle-aged men (mean age 37 years) also found that all cervical AROMs decreased between the youngest group and the oldest group.

Pellachia and Bohannon[26] found that the mean values for lateral flexion in subjects younger than 30 years of age exceeded 42 degrees, whereas mean values for lateral flexion in subjects older than 79 years of age were less than 25 degrees. Nilsson, Hartvigsen, and Christensen,[16] in a study of 90 healthy men and women aged 20 to 60 years, concluded that the decrease in half cycle cervical passive range of motion (PROM) with increasing age could be explained by using a simple linear regression of ROM as a function of age. Chen and colleagues,[27] in a detailed review of the literature regarding the effects of aging on cervical spine ROM, concluded that active cervical ROM decreased by 4 degrees per decade. This finding is very close to the 5-degree decrease found by Youdas and associates.[13]

## TABLE 11.1  Cervical Spine Range of Motion: Normal Values in Degrees

| | Lantz, Chen, and Buch[34] | AMA†[12] | Capuano-Pucci et al[14] | Youdas et al[9] | Tousignant et al[15] |
|---|---|---|---|---|---|
| | CA-6000 Spine Motion Analyzer Ages 20–39 yrs n = 63 | Inclinometer | CROM Mean age = 23.5 yrs n = 20 | Universal Goniometer Mean age = 59.1 yrs n = 20 | CROM Mean age = 51.5 yrs n = 55 |
| *Motion* | *Mean (SD)* | | *Mean (SD)* | *Mean (SD)* | *Mean (SD)* |
| Flexion | 60 (8) | 50 | 51 (9) | 40 (12) | 47 (11) |
| Extension | 56 (11) | 60 | 70 (9) | 50 (14) | 50 (14) |
| Right lateral flexion | 43 (8) | 45 | — | 22 (8) | 30 (9) |
| Left lateral flexion | 41 (7) | 45 | 44 (8) | 22 (7) | 33 (9) |
| Right rotation | 72 (7) | 80 | — | 51 (11) | 56 (10) |
| Left rotation | 73 (6) | 80 | 71 (5) | 49 (9) | 56 (12) |

CROM = cervical range of motion device; ROM = range of motion; SD = standard deviation.

| TABLE 11.2 | Cervical Spine Range of Motion Measured With a Tape Measure: Normal Values in Centimeters | | |
|---|---|---|---|
| | Hsieh and Yeung*[10] | | Balogun et al[†11] |
| | Ages 14–31 yrs | | Ages 18–26 yrs |
| | Tester 1 n = 17 | Tester 2 n = 17 | n = 21 |
| **Motion** | Mean (SD) | Mean (SD) | Mean (SD) |
| Flexion | 1.0 (1.7) | 1.8 (1.6) | 4.3 (2.0) |
| Extension | 22.4 (1.6) | 20.8 (2.4) | 18.5 (2.0) |
| Right lateral flexion | 11.0 (1.9) | 11.5 (2.1) | 12.9 (2.4) |
| Left lateral flexion | 10.7 (1.9) | 11.1 (2.1) | 12.8 (2.5) |
| Right rotation | 11.6 (1.7) | 12.6 (2.5) | 11.0 (2.5) |
| Left rotation | 11.2 (1.9) | 13.2 (2.4) | 11.0 (2.5) |

CI = confidence interval; r = Pearson product moment correlation coefficient; SD = standard deviation.
* 99% CI of measurement error ranged from 1.4 cm to 2.6 cm for tester 1 (experienced).
  CI ranged from 1.9 cm to 3.3 cm for tester 2 (inexperienced).
† r values ranged from 0.26 to 0.88 for intratester reliability and from 0.30 to 0.92 for intertester reliability.

In Table 11.4 the mean values for active neck flexion in the two oldest groups of males and females ages 80 to 90 years have about 20 degrees less motion than the youngest group of 1 to 19 year olds. Both men and women were measured using the CROM device; therefore, the values presented in the table should be used for reference only if the examiners are using the CROM as their measuring instrument. Ideally, the examiner should use norms that are appropriate to the method of measurement and the age and gender of the individuals being examined.

Hole, Cook, and Bolton[33] determined that the loss of cervical mobility equals to approximately 4 percent per decade in flexion and lateral flexion and 6 to 7 percent for extension. The decrease in extension, lateral flexion, and rotation occurred between 20 and 29 year olds and 30 and 39 year olds in their study of 84 asymptomatic men and women. Demaille-Wlodyka,[32] in a study of 232 healthy volunteers ranging in age from 15 to 65 years of age or older, found that all cervical motions decreased after age 25 and that the age effect was significant. Nilsson and associates[16] measured PROM using the CROM device in 90 healthy men and women with a mean age of 39 years and an age range of 21 to 60 years. The authors determined that the decrease in PROM as age increases could be described by a simple linear regression. See Tables 11.5, 11.6, and 11.7.

Other investigators have postulated that the effects of age on ROM may be motion specific and age specific; however,

| TABLE 11.3 | Cervical Spine ROM Measured With the Myrin Single Inclinometer: Normal Values in Degrees | | |
|---|---|---|---|
| | Balogen et al[11] | Malstrom et al[18] | Alaranta et al[19] |
| | Healthy young people Mean age = 22 yrs n = 21 | Healthy men and women Ages 22–58 yrs n = 60 | White and blue collar employees Ages 35–54 yrs n = 508 |
| **Motions** | Mean (SD) | Mean (SD) | Mean (SD) |
| Extension | 64 (17) | 67 (12) | 120* (16) |
| Flexion | 32 (13) | 65 (8) | — |
| Left lateral flexion | 41 (9) | 41 (7) | 37† (6) |
| Right lateral flexion | 42 (9) | 42 (7) | — |
| Left rotation | 64 (17) | 76 (8) | 75 (7) |
| Right rotation | 68 (15) | 76 (9) | — |

* Full cycle (flexion plus extension)
† Mean of two measurements

| TABLE 11.4 | Age Effects on Active Cervical Flexion ROM in Males and Females Aged 11 to 89 Years: Normal Values in Degrees Using the CROM Device |
| --- | --- |

| 11–19 yrs n = 40 | 20–29 yrs n = 42 | 30–39 yrs n = 41 | 40–49yrs n = 42 | 50–59 yrs n = 40 | 60–69 yrs n = 40 | 70–79 yrs n = 40 | 80–89 yrs n = 38 |
| --- | --- | --- | --- | --- | --- | --- | --- |
| Mean (SD) | Mean (SD) | Mean (SD) | Mean (SD) | Mean (SD) | Mean (SD) | Mean (SD) | Mean (SD) |
| 64 (9) | 54 (9) | 47 (10) | 50 (11) | 46 (9) | 41 (8) | 39 (9) | 40 (9) |

SD = standard deviation; CROM = cervical range of motion device.
Adapted from Youdas, JW, et al[13]: Reprinted from Physical Therapy with the permission of the American Physical Therapy Association.

the evidence appears to be somewhat controversial. Trott and colleagues[25] found a significant decrease in the means of all motions (flexion–extension, lateral flexion, and axial rotation) with increasing age, but they determined that most coupled motions were not affected by age. In contrast to Trott's findings, Damaille-Wlodyka[32] found that lateral flexion, which was always coupled with axial rotation, decreased with increasing age, whereas axial rotation increased. In fact, these authors found that coupled motions showed a tendency to decrease with age in all three planes.

Pearson and Walmsley[23] and Walmsley, Kimber, and Culham[24] were the only authors to include the cervical spine motions of retraction and protraction in their studies. Pearson and Walmsley[23] found that the older age groups had less ROM in retraction but that they showed no age difference in the neutral resting position. In contrast to Pearson and Walmsley's[23] findings, Walmsley, Kimber, and Culham[24] found age-related decreases in both protraction and retraction.

Lantz, Chen, and Buch,[34] in a study of 52 matched males and females, found a significant age effect, with subjects in the third decade having greater ROM in rotation and flexion–extension than subjects in the fourth decade. Dvorak and associates[22] determined that the most dramatic decrease in ROM in 150 healthy men and women (aged 20 to 60 years and older) occurred between the 30-year-old group and the 40-year-old group. A somewhat similar result was found by Peolsson and colleagues,[36] who investigated the age effects on cervical motion in 101 volunteers including 51 men ages 25 to 63 years and 50 women ages 25 to 60 years. These authors found that AROM in all planes decreased by about 30 degrees from the 25- to 34-year-old group to the 55- to 64-year-old group. The decrease in AROM was statistically significant in all planes but was most pronounced in extension and least evident in flexion (0.3 degrees/year).

In contrast to the findings of Dvorak and associates[22] and Peolsson and colleagues,[36] Trott and colleagues[25] found that

| TABLE 11.5 | Age and Gender Effects on Cervical Lateral Flexion ROM: Normal Values in Degrees* |
| --- | --- |

| Age Groups | Nilsson et al[†16] Males n = 31 Mean (SD) | Dvorak et al[‡22] Males n = 86 Mean (SD) | Castro et al[§29] Males n = 71 Mean (SD) | Nilsson et al[16] Females n = 59 Mean (SD) | Dvorak et al[22] Females n = 64 Mean (SD) | Castro et al[29] Females n = 86 Mean (SD) |
| --- | --- | --- | --- | --- | --- | --- |
| 20–29 yrs | 122 (4) | 101 (13) | 92 (14) | 116 (18) | 100 (9) | 90 (13) |
| 30–39 yrs | 111 (12) | 95 (10) | 89 (23) | 108 (14) | 106 (18) | 86 (18) |
| 40–49 yrs | 102 (15) | 84 (14) | 74 (15) | 99 (11) | 88 (16) | 77 (12) |
| 50–59 yrs | 104 (12) | 88 (29) | 70 (12) | 97 (7) | 76 (10) | 69 (15) |
| 60–69 yrs | — | 74 (14) | 65 (14) | — | 80 (18) | 68 (12) |
| 70–79 yrs | — | — | 47 (12) | — | — | 70 (14) |
| 80+ yrs | — | — | — | — | — | 50 (18) |

SD =standard deviation.
* The values in this table represent the combined total of right and left lateral flexion range of motion.
† Nilsson et al used the cervical range of motion (CROM) device to measure passive range of motion.
‡ Dvorak et al used the CA-6000 Spine Motion Analyzer to measure passive range of motion.
§ Castro et al used an ultasound-based coordinate measuring system, the CMS 50, to measure active range of motion.

TABLE 11.6 Age and Gender Effects on Cervical Flexion–Extension ROM: Normal Values in Degrees*

| | Nilsson et al[†16] | Dvorak et al[‡22] | Castro et al[§29] | Nilsson et al[16] | Dvorak et al[22] | Castro et al[29] |
|---|---|---|---|---|---|---|
| | Males n = 31 | Males n = 86 | Males n = 71 | Females n = 59 | Females n = 64 | Females n = 86 |
| Age Groups | Mean (SD) | Mean (SD) | Mean (SD) | Mean (SD) | Mean (SD) | Mean (SD) |
| 20–29 yrs | 129 (6) | 153 (20) | 149 (18) | 128 (12) | 149 (12) | 152 (15) |
| 30–39 yrs | 120 (8) | 141 (11) | 135 (26) | 120 (12) | 156 (23) | 141 (12) |
| 40–49 yrs | 110 (6) | 131 (19) | 129 (21) | 114 (10) | 140 (13) | 125 (13) |
| 50–59 yrs | 111 (8) | 136 (16) | 116 (14) | 117 (19) | 127 (15) | 124 (24) |
| 60–69 yrs | — | 116 (19) | 110 (16) | — | 133 (8) | 117 (15) |
| 70–79 yrs | — | — | 102 (13) | — | — | 121 (21) |
| 80+ yrs | — | — | — | — | — | 98 (11) |

SD = standard deviation.
* The values in this table represent the combined total of flexion and extension range of motion.
† Nilsson et al used the cervical range of motion device (CROM) to measure passive range of motion.
‡ Dvorak et al used the CA-6000 Spine Motion Analyzer to measure passive ROM.
§ Castro et al used an ultasound-based coordinate measuring system, the CMS 50, to measure active range of motion.

the greatest decrease in flexion–extension ROM in 60 healthy men and women (aged 20 to 59 years) occurred between the 20-year-old group and the 30-year-old group. The decrease in ROM as one ages after adulthood appears to be different in young children. Arbogast[31] found that in 67 young children AROM in cervical flexion and right and left rotation measured by the CROM device actually increased slightly between 3 and 12 years of age.

## Gender

Many of the same researchers who looked at the effects of age on cervical ROM also studied the effects of gender, but the results of these studies appear to be more inconsistent and controversial than the results of the age studies. In some studies, the trend for women to have a greater ROM than men was apparent, although differences were small and generally not significant. Also, in some instances, the effects of gender

TABLE 11.7 Age and Gender Effects on Cervical Rotation ROM: Normal Values in Degrees*

| | Nilsson et al[†16] | Dvorak et al[‡22] | Castro et al[§29] | Nilsson et al[16] | Dvorak et al[22] | Castro et al[29] |
|---|---|---|---|---|---|---|
| | Males n = 31 | Males n = 86 | Males n = 71 | Females n = 59 | Females n = 64 | Females n = 86 |
| Age Groups | Mean (SD) | Mean (SD) | Mean (SD) | Mean (SD) | Mean (SD) | Mean (SD) |
| 20–29 yrs | 174 (13) | 184 (12) | 161 (16) | 174 (13) | 182 (10) | 160 (14) |
| 30–39 yrs | 166 (12) | 175 (10) | 156 (32) | 167 (13) | 186 (10) | 150 (15) |
| 40–49 yrs | 161 (21) | 157 (20) | 141 (15) | 170 (10) | 169 (14) | 142 (15) |
| 50–59 yrs | 158 (10) | 166 (14) | 145 (11) | 163 (12) | 152 (16) | 139 (19) |
| 60–69 yrs | — | 146 (13) | 136 (18) | — | 154 (15) | 126 (14) |
| 70–79 yrs | — | — | 121 (14) | — | — | 135 (16) |
| 80+ yrs | — | — | — | — | — | 113 (21) |

SD = standard deviation.
* The values in this table represent the combined total of right and left rotation range of motion.
† Nilsson et al used the cervical range of motion device (CROM) to measure passive range of motion.
‡ Dvorak et al used the CA-6000 Spine Motion Analyzer to measure passive ROM.
§ Castro et al used an ultasound-based coordinate measuring system, the CMS 50, to measure active range of motion.

appeared to be motion specific and age specific in that some motions at some ages were affected more than others.

Castro[29] was one of the authors who found significant gender differences in cervical ROM, but this author noted that the differences occurred primarily in the motions of lateral flexion and flexion–extension in subjects between the ages of 70 and 79 years (see Tables 11.5, 11.6, and 11.7). Women older than 70 years of age were on the average more mobile in flexion–extension than men of the same age. Nilsson, Hartvigsen, and Christensen[16] found a significant difference between genders in lateral flexion ROM, but, in this study, males were more mobile than females, as seen in Table 11.6. Lantz, Chen, and Buch[34] studied a total of 56 healthy men and women aged 20 to 39 years. The authors found no difference between genders in total combined left and right lateral flexion, but women had greater ranges of active and passive axial rotation and flexion–extension than men of the same age. Women had an average of 12.7 degrees more active flexion–extension and an average of 6.50 degrees more active axial rotation than men of the same age. Women also had greater passive ROM in all cervical motions. Dvorak and associates[22] found that women between 40 and 49 years of age had greater ROM in all motions than men in the same age group. However, within each of the other age groups—20 to 29 years, 60 to 69 years, 70 to 79 years, and 80 to 89 years—no differences in cervical ROM were found between genders. Tables 11.8 and 11.9 contain information from a study by Youdas and associates[13] that shows that females in almost all age groups appear to have greater mean values for active cervical motion than males. Ferrario and associates[37] used a digital optoelectronic instrument to measure cervical motion in 30 women and 30 men and found that the women had greater ROM in all motions than the men. More support for a gender difference comes from Demaille-Wlodyka,[32] who found that of 232 healthy subjects aged 15 to 79 years, females had greater range of motion in flexion–extension and lateral flexion than males but not in axial rotation.

Youdas and associates[13] found a significant gender effect in all motions except flexion and determined that both males and females lose about 5 degrees of active extension and 3 degrees of active lateral flexion and rotation with each 10-year increase in age. If the measurements using the CROM device are valid, one can expect to find approximately 15 degrees to 20 degrees less active neck extension in a healthy 60-year-old individual compared with a healthy 20-year-old individual of the same gender.

In contrast to the preceding studies, a number of investigators concluded that gender had no effect on cervical ROM.[24,25,27,28,33] Ordway and associates[38] found a nonsignificant gender effect, and Pellachia and Bohannon,[26] in a study of 135 subjects aged 15 to 95 years with a history of neck pain, concluded that neither neck pain nor gender had any effect on ROM. Arbogast and coworkers[31] also found no effects of gender in the 67 children tested between the ages of 3 and 12. Hole, Cook, and Bolton[33] determined that gender had no significant effect on cervical range of motion in a group of 84 healthy men and women 20 to 69 years of age. Mannion[39] also found no effects of gender in 10 men and women whose AROM was measured in all cervical motions.

## Active Versus Passive ROM

The AMA's fifth edition of the *Guides to the Evaluation of Permanent Impairment* recommends that AROM be performed.[12] The authors of the *Guides* are aware that a number of factors may affect a person's performance of AROM, such as pain, fear of injury, and motivation; therefore, they stress that a patient must be encouraged to put forth a maximal effort. They also state that AROM is probably much closer than PROM to the type of motion that a patient would use functionally and therefore is more relevant to impairment. Furthermore, PROM is dependent on the amount of force applied by the examiner, and a patient could be at risk of injury. Also, if a patient can perform a full ROM actively, then there is no reason to perform PROM.[12]

Other reasons for using AROM rather than PROM have been investigated by the following researchers, who have found that AROM is more reliably measured than PROM and has less variability. Assink and coworkers[40] determined that the intraclass correlation coefficients (ICCs) of AROM measurements were higher than the ICCs of PROM measurements in 30 symptomatic and 30 unsymptomatic volunteers. In asymptomatic subjects, PROM was generally larger than in AROM. In symptomatic subjects, the percentage of paired observations within 5 degrees varied from a low of 17 percent for PROM in extension to a high of 60 percent for AROM in rotation.

Nilsson[41] used the CROM device to measure half cycle PROM in 14 asymptomatic volunteers (seven men and seven women between the ages of 23 and 45 years). All motions were measured by two testers from neutral 0, and intratester reliability was found to be acceptable to the author, ranging from an r of 0.61 for right lateral flexion to an r of 0.85 for extension. Intertester reliability was unacceptable because the correlation coefficients fell below 0.60 in four out of the six directions, ranging from an r of 0.29 for left rotation to an r of 0.71 for flexion.

Nilsson, Christensen, and Hartvigsen[42] conducted a study to correct any problems with the previous study. More extensive training was arranged for the testers, and the number of subjects was increased from 14 to 35 (17 men and 18 women) who ranged in age from 20 to 28 years. Intertester reliability still was unacceptable for half cycle PROM because three out of six measurements fell below an r of 0.60. Intertester reliability for full cycle PROM was much better with r values in three planes ranging from 0.61 to 0.88. It appears as if the half cycle motions may be contributing more than the passive range of motion to the poor intertester reliability.

Bergman and associates[43] found that the highest variation in both 58 subjects in the symptomatic group and the 48 men and women in the asymptomatic group occurred in PROM testing versus AROM testing. The variation over a 12-week period ranged from 20.4 degrees for passive lateral flexion in

**TABLE 11.8  Age and Gender Effects on Half Cycle Active Cervical Spine Motion in Males and Females Aged 11 to 49 Years: Normal Values in Degrees Using the CROM Device**

| | Ages 11–19 yrs | | Ages 20–29 yrs | | Ages 30–39 yrs | | Ages 40–49 yrs | |
| --- | --- | --- | --- | --- | --- | --- | --- | --- |
| | Males n = 20 | Females n = 20 | Males n = 20 | Females n = 20 | Males n = 20 | Females n = 21 | Males n = 20 | Females n = 22 |
| Motion | Mean (SD) | Mean (SD) | Mean (SD) | Mean (SD) | Mean (SD) | Mean (SD) | Mean (SD) | Mean (SD) |
| Extension | 86 (12) | 84 (15) | 77 (13) | 86 (11) | 68 (13) | 78 (14) | 63 (12) | 78 (13) |
| Right lateral flexion | 45 (8) | 49 (7) | 45 (7) | 46 (7) | 43 (9) | 47 (8) | 38 (11) | 42 (9) |
| Left lateral flexion | 46 (7) | 47 (7) | 41 (7) | 43 (5) | 41 (10) | 44 (8) | 36 (8) | 41 (9) |
| Right rotation | 74 (8) | 75 (10) | 70 (6) | 75 (6) | 67 (7) | 72 (6) | 65 (10) | 70 (7) |
| Left rotation | 72 (7) | 71 (10) | 69 (7) | 72 (6) | 65 (9) | 66 (8) | 62 (8) | 64 (8) |

SD = standard deviation; CROM = cervical range of motion device.
Adapted from Youdas, JW, et al[13]: Reprinted from *Physical Therapy* with the permission of the American Physical Therapy Association.

**TABLE 11.9  Age and Gender on Half Cycle Active Cervical Spine Motion in Subjects Aged 50 to 89 Years: Mean Values in Degrees Using the CROM Device**

| | Ages 50–59 yrs | | Ages 60–69 yrs | | Ages 70–79 yrs | | Ages 80–89 yrs | |
| --- | --- | --- | --- | --- | --- | --- | --- | --- |
| | Males n = 20 | Females n = 20 | Males n = 20 | Females n = 20 | Males n = 20 | Females n = 20 | Males n = 20 | Females n = 18 |
| Motion | Mean (SD) | Mean (SD) | Mean (SD) | Mean (SD) | Mean (SD) | Mean (SD) | Mean (SD) | Mean (SD) |
| Extension | 60 (10) | 65 (16) | 57 (11) | 65 (13) | 54 (14) | 55 (10) | 49 (11) | 50 (15) |
| Right lateral flexion | 36 (5) | 37 (7) | 30 (5) | 33 (10) | 26 (7) | 28 (7) | 24 (6) | 26 (6) |
| Left lateral flexion | 35 (7) | 35 (6) | 30 (5) | 34 (8) | 25 (8) | 27 (7) | 24 (7) | 23 (7) |
| Right rotation | 61 (8) | 61 (9) | 54 (7) | 65 (10) | 50 (10) | 53 (9) | 46 (8) | 53 (11) |
| Left rotation | 58 (9) | 63 (8) | 57 (7) | 60 (9) | 50 (9) | 53 (9) | 47 (9) | 51 (11) |

SD = standard deviation; CROM = cervical range of motion device.
Adapted from Youdas, JW, et al[13]: Reprinted from *Physical Therapy* with the permission of the American Physical Therapy Association.

the asymptomatic group to 85.2 degrees for passive rotation in the symptomatic group. The fact that a substantial amount of variation occurred in PROM measurement prompted the authors to question whether PROM should be used as an outcome measure in intervention studies. Demaille-Wlodyka and colleagues[32] recommended that PROM should not be used because it overestimates a subject's mobility.

### Testing Position

The lack of a well-defined neutral cervical spine position is thought to be responsible for the lower reliability of cervical spine motions starting in the neutral position (**half cycle motions**) compared with those starting at the end of one ROM and continuing to the end of another ROM (**full cycle motions**). An example of a half cycle motion is flexion, whereas an example of a full cycle motion is flexion-extension.

Studies that have attempted to better define the neutral position have used either radiographs[38,44] or motion analysis systems.[45,46] In the radiographic study conducted by Ordway and associates,[38] the authors determined that when the cervical spine is in the neutral position, the upper segments are in flexion and the lower segments have progressively less flexion; therefore, at C6 to C7, the spine is in a considerable amount of extension. Miller, Polissar, and Haas,[44] in the other radiographic study, found that the cervical spine is in the neutral position when the hard palate is in the horizontal plane. Although these findings are of considerable interest, they provide little help to the average clinician, who does not have access to radiographs for patient positioning.

Two studies that are more clinically relevant used the CA-6000 Spine Motion Analyzer.[45,46] This motion analysis system is capable of giving the location of neutral 0 position as coordinates in three dimensions corresponding to the three planes of motion. Christensen and Nilsson[45] found that the ability of 38 young (20 to 30 years of age) subjects to reproduce the neutral spine position with eyes and mouth closed was very good. The mean difference from neutral 0 in three motion planes was 2.7 degrees in the sagittal plane, 1.0 degrees in the horizontal plane, and 0.65 degrees in the frontal plane. Possibly, patients may be able to find the neutral position on their own, but the subjects in this study were healthy individuals, and the ability of patients to reproduce the neutral position is unknown. Solinger, Chen, and Lantz[46] attempted to standardize a neutral head position when measuring cervical motion in 20 subjects. For flexion and extension, the authors described a neutral position as one in which the corner of the eye was aligned with the upper angle of the ear, at the point where it meets the scalp. For lateral flexion, neutral was defined as the point at which the axis of the head was perceived to be vertically aligned. Compared with data collected using a less stringent head positioning, Solinger, Chen, and Lantz[46] demonstrated that by standardizing head position they obtained increases in reliability of 3 percent to 15 percent for rotation and lateral flexion but showed a decrease in reliability of up to 14 percent for flexion–extension.

Demaille-Wlodyka and colleagues[32] determined that neither age nor gender affected the 232 healthy volunteers'

ability to return their heads to a self-defined neutral position after performing a cervical ROM. However, Owens,[47] who used a computer interface electrogoniometer to measure head position in 48 students (36 males and 12 females) with a mean age of 28 years, found that active contractions of the posterior neck muscles caused subjects to undershoot their target neutral position by 2.1 degrees. This finding demonstrated that a recent history of cervical paraspinal muscle contraction can influence head repositioning in flexion–extension.

In a study using the 3Space Isotrak System, Pearson and Walmsley[23] found a significant difference in the neutral resting position (it became more retracted) after repeated neck retractions performed by 30 healthy subjects, but no statistically significant difference was found in the neck retraction ROM.

Another potential positional problem that testers need to be aware of has been identified by Lantz, Chen, and Buch.[34] These authors found that ROM measurements of the cervical spine taken in the seated position were consistently about 2.6 degrees greater than measurements taken in the standing position in all planes of motion. Greater differences occurred between seated and standing positions when flexion and extension were measured as half cycle motions starting in the neutral 0 position as opposed to measurement of full cycle motions. For axial rotation there was no significant difference in half cycle motions between sitting and standing.

### Body Size

Castro[29] found that patients who were obese were not as mobile as patients who were not obese. Mean values for motions in all planes decreased with increasing body weight. Chibnall, Duckro, and Baumer,[48] in a study of 42 male and female subjects, found that body size reflected by distances between specific anatomical landmarks (e.g., between the chin and the acromial process) influenced ROM measurements taken with a tape measure. Any variation in body size among subjects resulted in an underestimation of ROM for subjects with large distances between landmarks and an overestimation of ROM for subjects with small distances between landmarks. The authors concluded that the use of **proportion of distance** (POD) should be used when comparing testing results among subjects. The use of POD (calculated by dividing the distance between the at-rest value and the end-of-range value by the at-rest value) helps to eliminate the effect of body size on ROM values obtained with a tape measure. Obviously, calculation of POD is not necessary if the progress of only one subject is measured. Peolsson and colleagues[36] found no significant correlation between body mass index (BMI) and AROM, with the exception of extension for both men and women and flexion for men.

## Functional Range of Motion

Motion of the cervical spine is necessary for most activities of daily living and for most recreational and occupational activities. Bennett and asssociates[49] used the CROM device to determine the range of cervical motion required for 13 daily tasks performed by 28 college students. The greatest amount of motion was required by the following activities: backing up a car, tying shoes, and crossing the street. Relatively small amounts of flexion, extension, and rotation are required for eating, reading, writing, and using a computer. Drinking requires more cervical extension ROM than eating, and stargazing or simply looking up at the ceiling requires a full ROM in extension (Fig. 11.46). Using a telephone requires lateral flexion and rotation. Bathing and grooming require a considerable amount of motion.[49]

Sports activities such as serving a tennis ball, catching or batting a baseball, canoeing, and kayaking may require a full ROM in all planes. Different types of sports activities may have effects on ROM. For example, Guth[50] compared cervical rotation ROM in a group of 40 swimmers with that in 40 nonathletic volunteers. The swimmers, aged 14 to 17 years, had a mean total rotation ROM that was 9 degrees greater than the ROM of those aged 14 to 17 years in the control group. Certain occupational activities such as house painting or wallpapering require a full range of cervical extension and, possibly, a full

**FIGURE 11.46** One needs at least 40 to 50 degrees of cervical extension range of motion (ROM) to look up at the ceiling.[2] If cervical extension ROM is limited, the person must extend the entire spine in an effort to place the head in a position whereby the eyes can look up at the ceiling.

range of flexion. A full ROM in cervical rotation is essential for safe driving of cars or trucks (Fig. 11.47).

## Reliability and Validity

An article by Jordan[51] provides an excellent review of reliability studies and the instruments and methods used to evaluate cervical range of motion. The author identifies a number of problems with studies, including among others, the lack of an adequate sample size, appropriate statistical methods, and standardized protocols for measurement and for performance of the motions. These deficits make it difficult to compare studies and to be able to use the data that they generate.

Many different methods and instruments have been employed to assess motion of the head and neck. Similar to other areas of the body, intratester reliability generally is better than intertester reliability, no matter what instrument is used. Also, some motions seems to be more reliably measured than others. For example, the full cycle motions such as flexion–extension and right–left lateral flexion measured from one extreme of the range to the other appear to be more reliably measured than half cycle motions such as flexion measured from the neutral position.[18,32,40–43,52] This finding may be owed to the variability of the neutral position and the lack of a standardized method that an examiner can use for placing a subject's head in the neutral position. However, the problem with only measuring full cycle motions is that full cycle measurements do not provide any information about where unilateral limitations in motion occur.

Nilsson[41] found that intratester reliability was good when measuring half cycle motions, but intertester reliability was poor. Nilsson, Christensen, and Hartvigsen[42] found that the intertester reliability of passive range of motion measurements of half cycle motions was poor (r = 0.39 to 0.70), but the intertester reliability of passive range of motion measurements of full cycle motions was acceptable (r = 0.61 to 0.70). Jordan and colleagues,[52] who used the three-dimensional Fastrak system to measure cervical ROM, also found that the intertester reliability of full cycle motions (intraclass correlation coefficients [ICCs] = 0.81 to 0.89) was better than the reliability of half cycle motions (ICCs = 0.61 to 0.80) in 40 healthy subjects with two testers. The same was true for intratester reliability in which the ICCs for full cycle motions ranged from 0.76 to 0.82, whereas the ICCs for half cycle motions ranged from 0.54 to 0.70 in 32 healthy subjects with one tester on three occasions.

Malstrom and colleagues,[18] using both the Zebris ultrasonic system and the Myrin inclinometer, found that the full cycle motions showed less variability than the half cycle motions in 60 healthy volunteers (25 men and 35 women) 22 to 58 years of age. The ICCs ranged from 0.92 to 0.97 for full cycle motions and from 0.88 to 0.93 for half cycle motions. The full cycle motions also showed better concurrent validity with the Zebris than did half cycle measurements.

Damaille-Wlodyka,[32] in a study of 232 subjects, determined that full cycle motions had better validity than half cycle motions but half cycle motions allow for better assessment of unilateral limitations. Piva and associates,[53] using a

**FIGURE 11.47** One needs a minimum of 60 to 70 degrees of cervical rotation to look over the shoulder.[2] If cervical rotation range of motion is limited, the person has to rotate the entire trunk to position the head to check for oncoming traffic.

single gravity goniometer to measure half cycle motions in 30 patients with neck pain, found that the standard error of measurement (SEM) ranged from 3.7 degrees for right lateral flexion to 5.6 degrees for extension. ICCs ranged from 0.78 for flexion to 0.91 for axial rotation, and intertester reliability was moderate to substantial for measuring active ROM in the sagittal and transverse planes of motion.

According to Chen and colleagues,[27] it is not possible to obtain a true validation of cervical ROM measurements because radiographic measurement has not been subjected to reliability and validity studies. Therefore, no valid gold standard exists. The only option available for investigators at the present time is to conduct concurrent validity studies to obtain agreement between instruments and procedures.[27] However, many researchers still consider radiographic measurement to be the gold standard.

Some of the studies that have been conducted to assess reliability or validity (or both) of the various instruments and methods are reviewed in the following section. The terms high, good, fair, poor, and unacceptable are used to designate different degrees of reliability. High reliability refers to ICCs of 90 to 99, good reliability refers to ICCs of 80 to 89, fair reliability refers to ICCs of 70 to 79, low or poor reliability is an ICC of 60 to 69, and unacceptable reliability is an ICC of less than 0.60. These definitions of reliability appear to be the most commonly used terms in the following studies, although a few authors have used the interpretation by Portney and Watkins[54] in which correlation coefficients higher than

0.75 indicate good reliability and coefficients of less than 0.75 indicate poor to moderate reliability.

### Reliability: Universal Goniometer

Tucci and coworkers[55] found that the ICCs for intertester reliability of cervical spine motion ranged from –0.08 for flexion to 0.82 for extension for measurements taken with the universal goniometer by two experienced testers on 10 volunteer subjects.

Youdas, Carey, and Garrett[9] measured half cycle AROM in 60 patients with orthopedic problems ranging in age from 21 to 84 years. The patients were divided into three groups of 20 people. Each subject performed five repetitions of the motion in each plane to increase the compliance of the neck's soft tissues. Intratester reliability was good for flexion (ICC = 0.83), extension (ICC = 0.86), right lateral flexion (ICC = 0.85), left lateral flexion (ICC=0.84 and right rotation (ICC=0.90). Intratester reliability was fair for left rotation (ICC=0.78). Intertester reliability was fair (ICC=0.72 to 0.79) for extension, left lateral flexion, and right lateral flexion. Intertester reliability was poor (ICC = 0.54 to 0.62) for flexion and left and right rotation.

Pile and associates[56] used a universal goniometer to measure half cycle lateral flexion and flexion and extension in 10 patients with ankylosing spondylitis with minimal disease activity and ranging from 28 to 73 years of age. The testers included a rheumatologist, a rheumatology registrar, and three physical therapists. For intratester reliability each tester measured one patient four times. The authors did not present intratester reliability coefficients. The intertester reliability coefficient for right lateral flexion was 0.74; for left lateral flexion it was 0.68. The landmarks used for the lateral flexion measurement were the sternal notch as the axis and a line through the nose and forehead for the proximal arm. Flexion and extension were measured in the same way as the goniometer is used in this text. The intertester reliability coefficient for flexion was unacceptable (0.21), whereas the coefficient for extension was somewhat better (0.59).

Maksymowych and colleagues[57] measured full cycle rotation AROM using a plastic universal goniometer in 44 patients with ankylosing spondylitis with a mean age of 42.7 years. All measurements were taken by two testers (a trained clinical nurse and a rheumatologist) in mid-morning to avoid the effects of early morning stiffness. Intratester reliability was high for two testers (ICC = 0.98 and 0.97), and intertester reliability also was high (ICC = 0.95).

## Validity: Universal Goniometer

In a search of the literature, no validity studies were found for the universal goniometer in which radiographs were used as the gold standard.

## Reliability: Tape Measure

The fact that the landmarks used to obtain the measurements varied from study to study diminishes the usefulness of some of the following information. Landmarks and methods need to be standardized to make valid comparisons. The landmarks and results of studies by the authors[10,11] in Table 11.2 and by others are described in the following paragraphs.

Hsieh and Young[10] used two testers (one experienced and one inexperienced) to measure half cycle AROM in 34 healthy volunteers (27 men and 7 women) with an average age of 18 years. The landmarks used in the study for flexion and extension were the sternal notch and the chin. The landmarks for rotation were the acromial process and the chin, and the landmarks for lateral flexion were the acromion process and the lowest point of the earlobe. One tester measured 17 subjects, and the other tester measured a different group of 17 subjects. Intratester reliability coefficents (Pearson's r) ranged from 0.80 to 0.95 for the experienced tester and from 0.78 to 0.91 for the inexperienced tester. Measurement error for the experienced tester at the 99 percent confidence interval (CI) was approximately ±1 cm for sagittal motions and ± 2 cm for other motions. The inexperienced tester had a higher measurement error of approximately ±2 to 3 cm for sagittal motions and ±3 cm for other motions.

Balogen and associates[11] employed three physical therapists to measure half cycle AROM in 21 physical therapy students. The test-retest interval ranged from 4 to 110 days. The landmarks used to measure cervical flexion were the tip of the chin and the sternal notch. Landmarks for measuring lateral flexion were the anterior dimples in the shoulder to the lowest point of the earlobe. For rotation, the landmarks were the tip of the chin and the anterior dimples in the shoulder. Intratester reliability coefficients (r) for measuring neck flexion was poor for all three therapists. Intratester reliability for extension was very good for two therapists and fair for one therapist. The intratester values for left and right rotation ranged from an r of 0.58 to 0.86. The fact that the interval between the first and second sessions was so long may have had an adverse effect on the intratester values. Intertester values ranged from an r of 0.35 to 0.90 in Session I and from an r of 0.47 for left lateral flexion to an r of 0.92 for extension in Session II.

Haywood and associates[58] used a plastic tape measure for measuring half cycle AROM in 159 patients with ankylosing spondylitis. The authors used the tip of the nose and the acromioclavicular joint as landmarks to measure right and left cervical rotation. The ROM was the difference between the tape measurement in the neutral position and the measurement in maximal ipsilateral rotation. Fifty-five patients participated in the reliability study. The intratester reliability (test-retest at 2-week interval) was high (ICC >0.90), but intertester reliability was unacceptable for the neutral starting position.

Maksymowych and coworkers[57] measured full cycle rotation AROM on 263 patients with ankylosing spondylitis from three different countries. Forty-four of the patients were involved in the reliability study. Landmarks used for measuring rotation were the tragus of the right ear and the supersternal notch. Measurements were taken with a tape-based tool at full right rotation (D1) and at full left rotation (D2). Full cycle rotation was defined as the distance between the two measurements (D1-D2). Intratester reliability was good for the two testers (ICC = 0.80 and 0.89); intertester reliability also was good (ICC = 0.82).

Viitanen and associates[59] measured cervical lateral flexion and rotation in a series of 52 male patients with idiopathic ankylosing spondylitis with a mean age of 45 years. Testing was done by two physical therapists. Intratester aand intertester reliability coefficients for tape measurements were excellent for cervical lateral flexion (ICCs = 0.96 and ICC = 0.97, respectively) and for rotation (ICC = 0.98 and ICC = 0.97, respectively).

## Validity: Tape Measure

Balogun and associates[11] compared measurements taken with a tape measure with measurements taken with a Myrin Reference Goniometer (Inclinometer). The r values of each of the three testers were higher for the tape measuring method than for the inclinometer method. Therefore, the authors recommended that the tape measure method be used more widely.

Viitanen and associates[59] compared cervical rotation and lateral flexion tape measurements with radiologic changes such as changes in the apophyseal joints, calcification of discs, and ossification of spinal ligaments. Cervical rotation and lateral flexion measurements correlated significantly with cervical radiologic changes and, therefore, according to the authors, the tape measure was an appropriate method for assessing disease severity and progression.

Maksymowych and coworkers[57] compared measurements of cervical AROM taken with a tape measure with measurements of cervical rotation AROM taken with a plastic universal goniometer. The authors found that the tape measure approach was comparable to the universal goniometer, which the authors used as the gold standard.

## Reliability: Inclinometer

Viitanen and associates[59] used the Myrin Gravity Reference Goniometer to measure AROM in 52 male patients with ankylosing spondylitis with a mean age of 44.7 years. Two physical therapists measured patients on successive days. Both intratester reliability and intertester reliability were high with ICCs of 0.89 to 0.98.

Balogun and coworkers[11] employed three testers to use the Myrin Gravity Reference Goniometer to measure the AROM of half cycle motions. Twenty-one healthy students were measured over a period of several days (between 4 and 110). Intratester reliability coefficients (r) values for all motions ranged from unacceptable (r = 0.31) for flexion to good (r = 0.86) for extension. Intertester reliability coefficients across two testing sessions ranged from unacceptable (r = 0.26) for left rotation to good (r = 0.84) for extension.

Alaranta and associates[19] used a liquid single inclinometer, the MIE (Medical Research Ltd, London), which they attached by Velcro to a cloth helmet to the top of the subject's head to measure half cycle AROM flexion and extension and lateral flexion. A gravitational inclinometer was attached to the helmet, and the subject was placed in a supine position to measure rotation. Ninety-nine subjects participated in the intratester reliability part of the study in which one physiotherapist measured all subjects twice at an interval of 1 year. The correlation coefficient values for half cycle motions were an r of 0.68 for flexion and extension, r of 0.61 for lateral flexion, and unacceptable (r = 0.37) for rotation. Forty-eight subjects participated in the intertester reliability study in which two physiotherapists did the testing at a 1-week interval. The values for full cycle motions ranged from an r of 0.69 for flexion-extension to an r of 0.86 for left-right rotation.

Hole, Cook, and Bolton[33] also had two testers use an MIE single inclinometer to measure AROM in 30 healthy volunteers ages 20 to 69 years. Intratester reliability for flexion-extension, right lateral flexion, and right rotation was high (ICC = 0.93 to 0.94) and intratester reliability for left lateral flexion and left rotation was good (ICC = 0.84 to 0.88). Intertester reliability was good (ICC = 0.81 to 0.86) for flexion-extension, both right and left lateral flexion as well as left rotation. However, intertester reliability was only fair for right rotation (ICC = 0.76).

Hoving and associates[60] used a Cybex Electronic Digital Inclinometer-320 (EDI-320) to measure full cycle AROM in 32 patients 18 to 70 years of age with neck pain, neck stiffness, or both. Intratester reliability was high for motions in three planes, with values ranging from an ICC of 0.93 for lateral flexion for both raters to an ICC of 0.97 for flexion-extension for one rater. Intertester reliability was good to high with ICCs of 0.89 and higher. The smallest detectable differences (SDDs) based upon intratester agreement results for one of the testers were 11.1 degrees for flexion-extension, 10.4 degrees for lateral flexion, and 13.5 degrees for rotation.

Therefore, only changes greater than these values can be detected beyond measurement error when a single therapist performs the measurements. The SDD values were higher if two different raters performed the measurements.

Piva and coworkers[53] measured half cycle AROM with a gravity goniometer (MIE) in 30 patients ages 18 to 75 years of age who had symptoms in their neck, scapula, or head. ICC values ranged from fair to high (ICC = 0.78 to ICC = 0.91). The minimal detectable change (MDC) the authors considered to be adequate for clinical use ranged from 9 degrees for left rotation in flexion to 16 degrees for the motions of flexion and extension. The SEM was as follows: extension = 5.6 degrees, flexion = 5.8 degrees, left lateral flexion = 4.2 degrees, right lateral flexion = 3.7 degrees, left rotation = 4.1 degrees, and right rotation = 4.8 degrees.

Malstrom and associates[18] used the Myrin Gravity Reference Goniometer to measure both full and half cycle AROM in 60 "neck healthy" volunteers (35 women and 25 men) ranging in age from 22 to 58 years of age (Table 11.10). Intratester reliability was high, with ICCs of 0.90 and higher for full cycle flexion–extension, lateral flexion, and rotation. Intratester reliability was lower for half cycle motions, with the ICC ranging from 0.69 for left rotation to 0.89 for extension.

Bush and associates[61] evaluated the reliability of the following inclinometers: a single inclinometer, double inclinometers, and a single inclinometer with stabilization. Six Gerhardts Uni-Level pendulum inclinometers were used by 34 practicing physical therapists to take half cycle measurements of AROM of neck motions in three healthy models. The reliability between the three methods was unacceptable, with ICC values of 0.13 for extension, 0.31 for right lateral flexion, and 0.20 for left lateral flexion.

## Validity: Inclinometer

Herrmann[62] took radiographic measurements of passive ROM of neck flexion–extension in 16 individuals aged 2 to 68 years. The radiographic measurements were compared with those obtained by means of a pendulum goniometer (inclinometer). ICCs of 0.98 indicated a good agreement between the two methods.

Lanz, Chen, and Buch[34] compared the double inclinometer Dualer digital dual inclinometer and the CA-6000 electrogoniometer. Simultaneous measurements by the two instruments were performed twice over a 1-week interval. Concurrent validity of the two instruments showed almost identical mean values for flexion, extension, and lateral flexion. The ICC for between-instrument comparison in the same session was high.

Malstrom and associates[18] compared the Myrin Gravity Reference Goniometer with a three-dimensional ultrasound motion device—the Zebris, CMS 30/70P system (Zebris Medizintechnik GmbH, Isny, Germany). Both instruments were used to measure full cycle AROM in 60 healthy volunteers (35 women and 25 men) ranging in age from 22 to 58 years of age. The test and retest ICC was high, greater than 0.90 for intradevice reliability. The ICC was greater than 0.93 for concurrent validity. The authors concluded that their research supports the continued use of the Myrin in routine clinical work.

# TABLE 11.10 Cervical Range of Motion (CROM) Device: Intratester and Intertester Reliability

| Author | Tester n | Subject n | Mean Age | Sample | Motions | Intra ICC | Inter ICC | Intra r | Inter r | SEM |
|---|---|---|---|---|---|---|---|---|---|---|
| Cupuano-Pucci et al[14] | 2 | 20 | 23.5 yrs | Healthy | Flexion | | | | | |
| | | | | | Tester 1 | | | 0.63 | | |
| | | | | | Tester 2 | | | 0.91 | | |
| | | | | | Extension | | | | | |
| | | | | | Tester 1 | | | 0.90 | | |
| | | | | | Tester 2 | | | 0.82 | | |
| | | | | | Right lateral flexion | | | | | |
| | | | | | Tester 1 | | | 0.79 | 0.84 | |
| | | | | | Tester 2 | | | 0.89 | | |
| | | | | | Right rotation | | | | | |
| | | | | | Tester 1 | | | 0.85 | 0.84 | |
| | | | | | Tester 2 | | | 0.62 | | |
| Youdas et al[13] | 5 | 6 (Intratester) 20 (Intertester) | 27.2 yrs 33.0 yrs | Healthy | Flexion | 0.88 | 0.83 | | | |
| | | | | | Extension | 0.94 | 0.90 | | | |
| | | | | | Right lateral flexion | 0.88 | 0.87 | | | |
| | | | | | Right rotation | 0.82 | 0.82 | | | |
| Nilsson[41] | 2 | 14 | 20–45 yrs | Healthy | Flexion | | | 0.76 | 0.71 | 6°* |
| | | | | | Extension | | | 0.85 | 0.47 | 5° |
| | | | | | Right lateral flexion | | | 0.61 | 0.58 | 5° |
| | | | | | Right rotation | | | 0.75 | 0.66 | 6° |
| Nilsson et al*[42] | 2 | 35 | 20–28 yrs | Healthy | Flexion | | 0.65 | | 0.70 | |
| | | | | | Extension | | 0.54 | | 0.55 | |
| | | | | | Right lateral flexion | | 0.64 | | 0.70 | |
| | | | | | Right rotation | | 0.41 | | 0.41 | |
| | | | | | Flexion–extension | | 0.60 | | 0.61 | |
| | | | | | Right–left lateral flexion | | 0.69 | | 0.71 | |
| | | | | | Right–left rotation | | 0.88 | | 0.88 | |

Continued

## TABLE 11.10    Cervical Range of Motion (CROM) Device: Intratester and Intertester Reliability—cont'd

| Author | Tester n | Subject n | Mean Age | Sample | Motions | Intra ICC | Inter ICC | Intra r | Inter r | SEM |
|---|---|---|---|---|---|---|---|---|---|---|
| Rheault et al[63] | | 22 | 37.4 yrs | Hx of cervical spine pathology | Flexion | | 0.76 | | | |
| | | | | | Extension | | 0.98 | | | |
| | | | | | Right lateral flexion | | 0.87 | | | |
| | | | | | Right rotation | | 0.81 | | | |
| Peolsson et al[36] | 2 | 31 | 32.3 yrs | Healthy | Flexion-extension | 0.91 | 0.90 | | | 2° |
| | | | | | Right and Left lateral flexion | 0.94 | 0.90 | | | 3° |
| Olson et al[72] | 4 | 12 | 21-47 yrs | Healthy | Flexion | 0.88 | 0.58 | | | 4°[†] |
| | | | | | Extension | 0.99 | 0.97 | | | 3° |
| | | | | | Right lateral flexion | 0.98 | 0.96 | | | 2° |
| | | | | | Right rotation | 0.99 | 0.96 | | | 3° |
| Youdas et al[9] | 11 | 20 | 55.9 yrs | Orthopedic disorders | Flexion | 0.95 | 0.86 | | | |
| | | | | | Extension | 0.90 | 0.86 | | | |
| | | 20 | 60.7 yrs | | Right lateral flexion | 0.92 | 0.88 | | | |
| | | 20 | 60.8 yrs | | Left lateral flexion | 0.93 | 0.92 | | | |

ICC = intraclass correlation coefficient, r = Pearson product moment correlation coefficient; SEM = standard error of measurement.
* 95% confidence interval for single subject measurement.
† Represents intertester SEM.

Bush and associates[61] compared three methods of inclinometry measurements of sagittal and frontal plane cervical motion with radiographic measurements. Transverse plane motion measurements were compared with computed tomography scan measurements. The authors defined validity as those inclinometry measurements that fell within ±5 degrees of radiographic measurements. Using this standard, only the single and double inclinometer methods were valid for measuring flexion; only the single and single stabilization methods were valid for measuring extension. No methods were valid for measuring either lateral flexion or rotation. The single inclinometer method had the highest validity among the three methods.

## Reliability: CROM Device

Capuano-Pucci[14] in 1981 conducted one of the earliest studies on the CROM device in which two testers took measurements of each half cycle AROM performed by 20 subjects (16 women and 4 men) with a mean age of 23.5 years. The author found good intratester reliability for four out of six half cycle motions for one tester and for five out six motions for the second tester. All correlation coefficients were greater than 0.80 for intertester reliability, which was slightly higher than intratester reliability. This unusual finding was attributed to the fact that the time interval between testers was only minutes, whereas the time interval between the first and second trials by one tester was 2 days. More detailed information about this study and other studies in the section can be found in Table 11.10.

In the 1991 study by Youdas, Carey, and Garrett,[9] 11 volunteer physical therapists were given a 1-hour training session on the CROM device prior to measuring half cycle AROM in 60 patients (39 women and 21 men) with orthopedic disorders. The patients, ranging in age from 21 to 84 years, were divided into groups of 20 and were tested twice by two therapists. The results of the testing showed high intratester reliability and good intertester reliability for both flexion and extension. Intratester reliability was good for left neck lateral flexion (ICC = 0.84) and was high for right lateral flexion (ICC = 0.92). Intertester reliability was fair for left lateral flexion and good for right lateral flexion. Intratester reliability was high for both left and right rotation, and intertester reliability for rotation ranged from good for left rotation to high for right rotation.

Youdas and associates[13] used five testers to measure half cycle AROM in 337 healthy subjects (171 women and 166 men) who were 11 to 97 years of age. Each subject performed three repetitions of each motion, and each subject was tested by three testers within minutes of each other. Intratester reliability was low for flexion (ICC = 0.76), high for extension (ICC = 0.94), and good for left and right lateral flexion. Intratester reliability for rotation also was good, with ICCs of 0.84 for left rotation and 0.80 for right rotation. The intertester reliability of all half cycle neck motion measurements was good except for left rotation, which was poor (ICC = 0.66).

Nilsson[41] measured half cycle PROM on 14 volunteers 23 to 45 years of age. Each subject was measured three times at 20-minute intervals. Intratester reliability was considered to be acceptable (r = 0.61 to 0.86). Intertester reliability was unacceptable (r = 0.29 to 0.66) based on the mean of five repeated measures and the fact that in four out of six motions the r was less than 0.60.

Hole, Cook, and Bolton[33] selected 30 of 84 asymptomatic subjects for the reliability portion of a study of full cycle AROM. Intratester reliability was high (ICC = 0.96) for the full cycle combined motion of flexion and extension, and intertester reliability was good (ICC = 0.88). Intratester reliability was high (ICC = 0.96) for full cycle right-left lateral flexion, and intertester reliability was good (ICC = 0.84). Both intratester and intertester reliability were high (ICC = 0.92) for the full cycle motion of left-right rotation.

Nilsson, Christiansen, and Hartvigsen[42] measured half and full cycle PROM on 17 males and 18 females 20 to 28 years of age. Subjects were asked to close their eyes and position their heads in neutral while the dials on the CROM device were set to 0. Intertester reliability was acceptable (r = 0.61 to 0.88) for full cycle motions, but intertester reliability for measuring single cycle motions was an r of 0.39 to 0.70. Rheault and colleagues[63] found only small mean differences ranging from 0.5 degrees to 3.6 degrees between two testers who measured half cycle extension AROM with the CROM device.

Lindell, Eriksson, and Strender[64] compared the performance of a medically untrained tester with an experienced physical therapist using the therapist as the gold standard. The untrained tester received 4 hours of training and practice in 10 tests including measurements of half cycle cervical flexion and extension and rotation taken with the CROM device. The subjects in the study included 30 patients with neck and back pain and 20 healthy subjects. In the interrater reliability study, all 50 subjects were tested once by each tester. In the intertester study, each tester measured neck motions twice in 10 of the 20 healthy subjects. Intratester reliability for the therapist was good for flexion (ICC = 0.86) and high for extension (ICC = 0.98), with an SEM of 2 degrees for each measurement. The ICCs for intratester reliabilty for the other tester were 0.62 for flexion and 0.80 for extension. The ICC for the therapist for right rotation was high; for left rotation the ICC was good. The other tester had good ICCs for both right and left rotation and slightly higher SEMs compared to the therapist. Cervical flexion and extension had poor intertester reliability, which the authors attributed to the need for manual stabilization. Other tests that required manual stabilization also had poor intertester reliability, but overall, the medically untrained tester was able to perform acceptably in 7 out of 10 tests.

## Validity: CROM Device

Ordway and coworkers[65] simultaneously measured full cycle AROM of combined flexion-extension with the CROM device, 3Space system, and radiographs in 20 healthy volunteers (11 women and 9 men) between 20 and 49 years of age. The authors found no significant difference between CROM device measurements and the radiographic angle between the occipital line and the vertical body, nor between the 3Space system and radiographic angle between the occipital line and the C7 vertebral body. However, there was a significant difference between flexion and extension measurements taken with the CROM device and the 3Space system. Therefore, these methods could not be used interchangeably. The authors determined that full cycle flexion–extension could be reliably measured by all three methods but that standardization of positioning was required to minimize upper thoracic motion with the CROM device. Protraction and retraction measured with the 3Space system were in agreement with the radiographic measurements but differed significantly from the measurements taken with the CROM device The CROM device's advantages over the 3Space system were lower cost and ease of use.

Tousignant[66] used radiographs to determine the criterion validity of the CROM device for measuring half cycle flexion and extension on 31 healthy participants who were 18 to 25 years of age. CROM measurements were highly correlated with measurements obtained by the radiographic method for extension (r = 0.98, P <0.001) and flexion (r = 0.97, P <0.001) so that the validity of the CROM device for measuring flexion and extension was supported.

Tousignant and associates[67] determined that the CROM measurements of half cycle AROM of lateral flexion demonstrated a very good linear relationship with radiographic measurements. A physiotherapist who had received 4 hours of instruction in using the CROM device measured right and left lateral flexion in 24 patients with neck pain. The measurements of left lateral flexion and right lateral flexion were compared with radiographic measurements as the gold standard. The correlation between the CROM device and radiographic measurements was good for both left (r = 0.82) and right (r = 0.84) lateral flexion. Therefore, the criterion validity of the CROM device for measuring lateral flexion was supported.

Tousignant and associates,[15] in another criterion validity study, compared half cycle AROM measurements taken with the CROM device with measurements taken with the Optotrak (an optoelectronic system). Subjects in the study included 34 women (21 to 85 years of age) and 21 men (19 to 80 years of age) recruited from the community. The results showed a very strong linear relationship between cervical rotation measured with the CROM device and the values obtained with the Optotrak. Pearson correlation coefficients (r) between CROM values and Optotrak values were good to excellent for rotation and for all other cervical motions. Based on their findings, the authors concluded that the validity of the CROM device was supported for the measurement of half cycle rotation in healthy individuals.

Hole, Cook, and Bolton[33] compared measurements of full cycle AROM taken with the CROM device to measurements taken with a single gravity inclinometer (MIE) to determine the reliability and concurrent validity of the two instruments for measuring cervical motion. Eighty-four asymptomatic subjects were included in the study. There was good agreement between the two instruments when measuring AROM in the sagittal and coronal planes, and concurrent validity was supported for flexion–extension and for right–left lateral flexion, but there was no agreement when measuring rotation in the transverse plane because, according to the authors, motion was consistently overestimated by the MIE.

## Reliability: CA-6000 Electrogoniometer

Lantz, Chen, and Buch[34] measured active and passive half cycle motions in healthy students with the CA-6000. Intratester reliability ICC ranged from fair (0.76) to high (0.97) for AROM for full cycle motions and from poor (0.58) to high (0.95) for PROM for full cycle motions. Intertester ICCs for full cycle AROM were higher, ranging from good (0.84) to high (0.91), compared to ICCs for full cycle PROM, which were fair (0.74) to good (0.86).

Solinger, Chen, and Lantz[46] measured half and full cycle AROM in 20 healthy volunteer subjects (9 men and 11 women) ranging in age from 20 to 40 years. Each subject's ROM was measured twice by two experienced testers. Intertester and intratester reliability for full cycle motions of rotation and lateral flexion had high ICCs, ranging from 0.93 to 0.97, whereas intertester and intratester reliability ICCs for half cycle motions ranged from good (0.83) to high (0.95). Reliability values were consistently lower for measurements beginning in the neutral position compared with full cycle motions. The ICCs indicated that the electrogoniometer performed very reliably for rotation and lateral flexion but only at an acceptable level for flexion–extension (0.75 to 0.93). Flexion from the neutral position was the least reliable measurement even when taken by a single tester.

Christensen and Nilsson[68] found good intratester and intertester reliability for measurements of AROM in 40 individuals tested by two testers. Intratester reliability was also good for PROM, but intertester reliability was good only for full cycle motions.

## Validity: CA-6000 Spine Motion Analyzer Electrogoniometer

Mannion and associates[39] compared cervical CROM measurements taken with the CA-6000 Spine Motion Analyzer with measurements taken with a three-dimensional ultrasound motion device called the Zebris CMS System. Initial measurements by both systems were taken in 19 healthy volunteers, and the same measurements were taken 3 days later. Test-retest reliability was good for each instrument, but a small significant difference (1 to 10 percent) between the values obtained by each instrument occurred.

Petersen and coworkers[69] determined that there was a large difference between the measurements obtained with the CA-6000 Spine Motion Analyzer and radiographs.

## Reliability: Visual Estimation

The reliability of visual estimates has been studied by Viikari-Juntura[71] in a neurological patient population and by Youdas, Carey, and Garrett[9] in an orthopedic patient population. In the study by Viikari-Juntura,[71] the subjects were 52 male and female neurological patients ranging in age from 13 to 66 years who had been referred for cervical myelography. Intertester reliability between two testers of visual estimates of cervical ROM was determined by the authors to be fair. The weighted kappa reliability coefficient for intratester agreement in categories of normal, limited, or markedly limited ROM ranged from 0.50 to 0.56.

In the study by Youdas, Carey, and Garrett,[9] the subjects were 60 orthopedic patients ranging in age from 21 to 84 years. Intertester reliability for visual estimates of both active flexion and extension was poor (ICC = 0.42). Intertester reliability for visual estimates of active neck lateral flexion ROM was fair. The ICC for left lateral flexion was 0.63; for right lateral flexion it was 0.70. The intertester reliability for visual estimates of rotation was poor for left rotation (ICC = 0.69) and good for right rotation (ICC = 0.82).

## Summary

Each of the techniques for measuring cervical ROM discussed in this chapter has certain advantages and disadvantages. The universal goniometer and tape measure are the least inexpensive and easiest to obtain, transport, and use, and therefore may be more acceptable clinically than other instruments. Generally, intratester reliability is better than intertester reliability. Therefore, if these methods are used to determine a patient's progress, repeated measurements should be taken by a single therapist. However, both the universal goniometer and tape measure require more extensive research to validate their continued use in the clinic.

In consideration of the cost and availability of the various instruments for measuring cervical ROM, and because of the fact that the intratester reliability of the universal goniometer and tape measure appears comparable with that of measurements taken with other instruments, we have retained the universal goniometer and tape measure methods in this edition, but we added methods using the double inclinometer and the CROM device. We included the double inclinometer because this method is advocated for measuring the cervical spine by the American Medical Association, although research on the reliability and validity of this method is lacking. The reliability and validity of the CROM device has been very well researched, as presented in this section. If the tape measure is being used to compare ROM among subjects, calculation of proportion of distance (POD) should help to eliminate the effects of different body sizes on measurements (refer to Body Size in the Research Findings section).[48]

# REFERENCES

1. Bogduk, N, and Mercer, S: Biomechanics of the cervical spine, I: Normal kinematics. Clin Biomech 15:633, 2000.

2. Magee, DJ: Orthopedic Physical Assessment, ed 4. WB Saunders, Elsevier Science USA, Philadelphia, 2002.

3. Goel, VK: Moment-rotation relationships of the ligamentous occipito-atlanto-axial complex. J Biomech 8:673, 1988.

4. Cailliet, R: Soft Tissue Pain and Disability, ed 3. FA Davis, Philadelphia, 1991.

5. Crisco, JJ, Panjabi, MM, and Dvorak, J: A model of the alar ligaments of the upper cervical spine in axial rotation. J Biomech 24:607, 1991.

6. Dumas, JL, et al: Rotation of the cervical spinal column. A computed tomography in vivo study. Surg Radiol Anat 15:33, 1993.

7. White, AA, and Punjabi, MM: Clinical Biomechanics of the Spine, ed 2. JB Lippincott, Philadelphia, 1990.

8. Hertling, D, and Kessler, RM: Management of Common Musculoskeletal Disorders, ed 3. JB Lippincott, Philadelphia, 1996.

9. Youdas, JW, Carey, JR, and Garrett, TR: Reliability of measurements of cervical spine range of motion: Comparison of three methods. Phys Ther 71:2, 1991.

10. Hsieh, C-Y, and Yeung, BW: Active neck motion measurements with a tape measure. J Orthop Sports Phys Ther 8:88, 1986.

11. Balogun, JA, et al: Inter- and intratester reliability of measuring neck motions with tape measure and Myrin gravity-reference goniometer. J Orthop Sports Phys Ther 10:248, 1989.

12. American Medical Association: Guides to the Evaluation of Permanent Impairment, ed 5. AMA, Chicago, 2000.

13. Youdas, JW, et al: Normal range of motion of the cervical spine: An initial goniometric study. Phys Ther 72:770, 1992.

14. Capuano-Pucci, D, et al: Intratester and intertester reliability of the cervical range of motion device. Arch Phys Med Rehabil 72:338, 1991.

15. Tousignant, M, et al: Criterion validity study of the Cervical Range of Motion (CROM) Device for rotational range of motion on healthy adults. J Orthop Sports Phys Ther 36:242, 2006.

16. Nilsson, N, Hartvigsen, J, and Christensen, HW: Normal ranges of passive cervical motion for women and men 20–60 years old. J Manipulative Physiol Ther 19:306, 1996.

17. CROM Procedure Manual: Procedure for Measuring Neck Motion with the CROM. Performance Attainment Association, St Paul, MN.

18. Malstrom, EM, et al: Zebris versus Myrin: A comparative study between a three-dimensional ultrasound movement analysis and an inclinometer/compass method: Interdevice reliability, concurrent validity, intertester comparison, intertester reliability, and intraindividual variability. Spine 28:E433, 2003.

19. Alaranta, H, et al: Flexibility of the spine: Normative values of goniometric and tape measurements. Scand J Rehab Med 26:147, 1994.

20. O'Driscoll, SL, and Tomenson, J: The cervical spine. Clin Rheum Dis 8:617, 1982.

21. Keske, J, Johnson, G, and Ellingham, C: A reliability study of cervical range of motion of young and elderly subjects using an electromagnetic range of motion system (ENROM) (abstract). Phys Ther 71:S94, 1991.

22. Dvorak, J, et al: Age and gender related normal motion of the cervical spine. Spine 17:S-393, 1992.

23. Pearson, ND, and Walmsley, RP: Trial into the effects of repeated neck retractions in normal subjects. Spine 20:1245, 1995.

24. Walmsley, RP, Kimber, P, and Culham, E: The effect of initial head position on active cervical axial rotation range of motion in two age populations. Spine 21:2435, 1996.

25. Trott, PH, et al: Three dimensional analysis of active cervical motion: The effect of age and gender. Clin Biomech 11:201, 1996.

26. Pellachia, GL, and Bohannon, RW: Active lateral neck flexion range of motion measurements obtained with a modified goniometer: Reliability and estimates of normal. J Manipulative Physiol Ther 21:443, 1998.

27. Chen, J, et al: Meta-analysis of normative cervical motion. Spine 24:1571, 1999.

28. Feipel, V, et al: Normal global motion of the cervical spine: An electrogoniometric study. Clin Biomech (Bristol, Avon) 14:462, 1999.

29. Castro, WHM: Noninvasive three-dimensional analysis of cervical spine motion in normal subjects in relation to age and sex. Spine 25:445, 2000.

30. Kulman, KA: Cervical range of motion in the elderly. Arch Phys Med Rehabil 74:1071, 1993.

31. Arbogast KB, et al: Normal cervical range of motion in children 3–12 years old. Spine 12:E309, 2007

32. Demaille-Wlodyka S, et al: Cervical range of motion and cephalic kinesthesis: Ultrasonographic analysis by age and sex. Spine 32:E254, 2007.

33. Hole DE, Cook JM, and Bolton JE: Reliability and concurrent validity of two instruments for measuring cervical range of motion: Effects of age and gender. Manual Therapy 1:36, 1995.

34. Lantz, CA, Chen, J, and Buch, D: Clinical validity and stability of active and passive cervical range of motion with regard to total and unilateral uniplanar motion. Spine 11:1082, 1999.

35. Sforza, C, et al:Three dimensional analyses of active head and cervical spine range of motion: Effect of age in healthy male subjects. Clin Biomech 17:611, 2002.

36. Peolsson, A, et al: Intra- and inter-tester reliability and range of motion of the neck. Physiother Canada Summer:233, 2000

37. Ferrario VF, et al: Active motion of the head and cervical spine: A three-dimensional investigation in healthy young adults. J Othop Res 20:122, 2002.

38. Ordway, NR, et al: Cervical flexion, extension, protrusion and retraction. A radiographic segmental analysis. Spine 24:240, 1999.

39. Mannion, AF, et al: Range of global motion of the cervical spine: Intraindividual reliability and the influence of measurement device. Eur Spine J 9:379, 2000.

40. Assink N, et al: Interobserver reliability of neck-mobility measurements by means of the flock of birds electromagnetic tracking system. J Manipulative Physiol Ther 28:408, 2005.

41. Nilsson N: Measuring passive cervical motion: A study of reliability. J Manipulative Physiol Ther 18:293, 1995

42. Nilsson N, Christensen, HW, and Hartvigsen, J: The interexaminer reliability of measuring passive cervical range of motion. J Manipulative Physiol Ther 19:302, 1996.

43. Bergman GJ, et al: Variation in the cervical range of motion over time measured by the "flock of birds" electromagnetic tracking system. Spine 30:650, 2005.

44. Miller, JS, Polissar, NL, and Haas, M: A radiographic comparison of neutral cervical posture with cervical flexion and extension ranges of motion. J Manipulative Physiol Ther 19:296, 1996.

45. Christiansen, HW, and Nilsson, N: The ability to reproduce the neutral zero position of the head. J Manipulative Physiol Ther 22:26, 1999.

46. Solinger, AB, Chen, J, and Lantz, CA: Standardized initial head position in cervical range-of-motion assessment: Reliability and error analysis. J Manipulative Physiol 23:20, 2000.

47. Owens, EF, et al: Head repositioning erors in normal student volunteers: A possible tool to assess the neck's neuromuscular system. Chirop Osteopat 14:5, 2006.

48. Chibnall, JT, Duckro, PN, and Baumer, K. The influence of body size on linear measurements used to reflect cervical range of motion. Phys Ther 74:1134, 1994.

49. Bennett, SE, Schenk, RJ, Simmons, ED: Active range of motion utilized in the cervical spine to perform daily functional tastks. J Spinal Disord Tech 15:307, 2002.

50. Guth, EH: A comparison of cervical rotation in age-matched adolescent competitive swimmers and healthy males. J Orthop Sports Phys Ther 21:21, 1995.

51. Jordan, K: Assessment of published reliability studies for cervical range of motion measurement tools. J Manipulative Physiol Ther 23:180, 2000.

52. Jordan K, et al: The reliability of the three-dimensional FASTRAK measurement system in measuring cervical spine and shoulder range of motion in healthy subjects. Rheumatol 39:382, 2000.

53. Piva SR, et al: Inter-tester reliability of passive intervertebral and active movements of the cervical spine. Man Ther 11:321, 2006.

54. Portney, L and Watkins, M: Foundations of Clinical Research: Applicaions to Practice, ed 2. Prentice-Hall, Upper Saddle River, NJ, 2000.

55. Tucci, SM, et al: Cervical motion assessment: A new, simple and accurate method. Arch Phys Med Rehabil 67:225, 1986.

56. Pile, K,D, et al: Clinical assessment of ankylosing spondylitis: A study of observer variation in spinal measurements. Br J Rheumatol 30:29,1991.

57. Maksymowych WP, et al: Development and validation of a simple tapebased measurement tool for recording cervical rotation in patients with ankylosing spondylitis: Comparison with a goniometer-based approach. J Rheumatol 33:2242, 2006.

58. Haywood KL, et al: Spinal mobility in ankylosing spondylitis: reliability, validity and responsiveness, Rheumatology (Oxford) 43:750, 2004.

59. Viitanen JV, et al: Clinical assessment of spinal mobility measurements in ankylosing spondylitis: A compact set for follow-up trials? Clin Rheumatol 19:131, 2000.

60. Hoving JL, et al.: Reproducibility of cervical range of motion in patients with neck pain. BMC Musculoskelet Dis 6:59, 2005.

61. Bush, KW, et al: Validity and intertester reliability of cervical range of motion using inclinometer measurements. J Manual Manipul Ther 8:52, 2000.

62. Herrmann, DB: Validity study of head and neck flexion-extension motion comparing measurements of a pendulum goniometer and roentgenograms. J Orthop Sports Phys Ther 11:414, 1990.

63. Rheault, W, et al: Intertester reliability of the flexible ruler for the cervical spine. J Orthop Sports Phys Ther Jan:254, 1989.

64. Lindell O, Eriksson L, and Strender L-E: The reliability of a 10-test package for patients with prolonged back and neck pain: could an examiner without formal medical education be used without loss of quality? A methodological study. BMC Musculoskelet Dis 8:31, 2007.

65. Ordway, NR, et al: Cervical sagittal range of motion. Analysis using three methods: Cervical range-of-motion device. 3. Space and radiography. Spine 22:501, 1997.

66. Tousignant, MA: Criterion validity of the cervical range of motion (CROM) goniometer for cervical flexion and extension. Spine 25:324, 2000.

67. Tousignant M, et al: Validity study for the Cervical Range of Motion Device used for lateral flexion in patients with neck pain. Spine 27:812, 2002.

68. Christensen, HW, and Nilsson, N: The reliability of measuring active and passive cervical range of motion: An observer blinded and randomized repeated measures design. J Manipulative Physiol Ther 21:341, 1998.

69. Petersen CM, et al: Agreement of measures obtained radiographically and by the OSI CA-8000 Spine Motion Analyzer for cervical spine motion. Man Ther 13:200, 2008.

70. Defibaugh, JJ: Measurement of head motion. Part II: An experimental study of head motion in adult males. Phys Ther 44:163, 1964.

71. Viikari-Juntura, E: Interexaminer reliability of observations in physical examination of the neck. Phys Ther 67:1526, 1987.

72. Olson, SL, et al: Tender point sensitivity, range of motion, and perceived disability in subjects with neck pain. J Ortho Sports Phys Ther 30:13, 2000.

# The Thoracic and Lumbar Spine

## ⟠ Structure and Function

### Thoracic Spine

#### Anatomy of the Vertebrae

The 12 vertebrae of the thoracic spine form a curve that is convex posteriorly (Fig. 12.1A). These vertebrae have a number of unique features. Spinous processes slope inferiorly from T1 to T10 and overlap from T5 to T8, whereas the spinous processes of T11 and T12 take on the horizontal orientation of the lumbar region's spinous processes. The transverse processes from T1 to T10 are large, with thickened ends that support paired costal facets for articulation with the ribs. Paired demifacets (superior and inferior costovertebral facets), also for articulation with the ribs, are located on the posterolateral corners of the vertebral bodies from T2 to T9.

#### Anatomy of the Joints

The intervertebral and zygapophyseal joints in the thoracic region have essentially the same structure as described for the cervical region, except that the superior articular zygapophyseal facets face posteriorly, somewhat laterally, and cranially. The superior articular facet surfaces are slightly convex, whereas the inferior articular facet surfaces are slightly concave. The inferior articular facets face anteriorly and slightly medially and caudally. In addition, the joint capsules are tighter than those in the cervical region.

The costovertebral joints are formed by slightly convex costal superior and inferior demifacets (costovertebral facets) on the head of a rib and corresponding demifacets on the vertebral bodies of a superior and an inferior vertebra (Fig. 12.1B). From T2 to T8, the costovertebral facets articulate with concave demifacets located on the inferior body of one vertebra and on the superior aspect of the adjacent inferior vertebral body. Some of the costovertebral facets also articulate with the interposed intervertebral disc, whereas the 1st, 11th, and 12th ribs articulate with only one vertebra. A thin, fibrous capsule, which is strengthened by radiate ligaments (see Fig. 12.1B) and the posterior longitudinal ligament, surrounds the costovertebral joints. An intra-articular ligament lies within the capsule and holds the head of the rib to the annulus pulposus.

The costotransverse joints are the articulations between the costal tubercles of the 1st to the 10th ribs and the costal facets on the transverse processes of the 1st to the 10th thoracic vertebrae. The costal tubercles of the 1st to the 7th ribs are slightly convex, and the costal facets on the corresponding transverse processes are slightly concave. The articular surfaces of the costal and vertebral facets are quite flat from about T7 to T10. The costotransverse joint capsules are strengthened by the medial, lateral, and superior costotransverse ligaments.

#### Osteokinematics

The zygapophyseal articular facets lie in the frontal plane from T1 to T6 and therefore limit flexion and extension in this region. The articular facets in the lower thoracic region are oriented more in the sagittal plane and thus permit somewhat more flexion and extension. The ribs and costal joints restrict lateral flexion in the upper and middle thoracic region, but in the lower thoracic segments, lateral flexion and rotation are relatively free because these segments are not limited by the ribs. In general, the thoracic region is less flexible than the cervical spine because of the limitations on movement imposed by the overlapping spinous processes, the tighter joint capsules, and the rib cage.

#### Arthrokinematics

In flexion, the body of the superior thoracic vertebra tilts anteriorly, translates anteriorly, and rotates slightly on the adjacent inferior vertebra. At the zygapophyseal joints, the inferior articular facets of the superior vertebra slide upwards on the superior articular facets of the adjacent inferior vertebra. In extension, the opposite motions occur: the superior vertebra tilts and translates posteriorly and the inferior articular facets glide downward on the superior articular facets of the adjacent inferior vertebra.

In lateral flexion to the right, the right inferior articular facets of the superior vertebra glide downward on the right superior articular facets of the inferior vertebra. On the

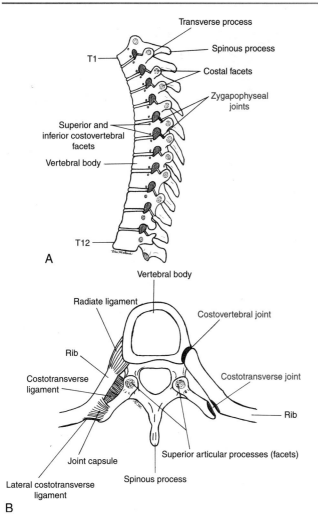

**FIGURE 12.1  A:** A lateral view of the thoracic spine shows the costal facets on the enlarged ends of the transverse processes from T1 to T10 and the costovertebral facets on the lateral edges of the superior and inferior aspects of the vertebral bodies. The zygapophyseal joints are shown between the inferior articular facets of the superior vertebrae and the superior articular facets of the adjacent inferior vertebra.
**B:** A superior view of a thoracic vertebra shows the articulations between the vertebra and the ribs: the left and right costovertebral joints, the costotransverse joints between the costal facets on the left and right transverse processes, and the costal tubercles on the corresponding ribs.

contralateral side, the left inferior articular facets of the superior vertebra glide upward on the left superior articular facets of the adjacent inferior vertebra.

In axial rotation, the superior vertebra rotates on the inferior vertebra, and the inferior articular surfaces of the superior vertebra impact on the superior articular surfaces of the adjacent inferior vertebra. For example, in rotation to the left, the right inferior articular facet impacts on the right superior articular facet of the adjacent inferior vertebra. Rotation and gliding motions occur between the ribs and the vertebral bodies at the costovertebral joints. A slight amount of rotation is possible between the joint surfaces of the ribs and the transverse processes at the upper costotransverse joints, and more

rotation is allowed in the gliding that occurs at the lower joints (T7 to T10). The movements at the costal joints are primarily for ventilation of the lungs but also allow some flexibility of the thoracic region.

## Capsular Pattern

The capsular pattern for the thoracic spine is a greater limitation of extension, lateral flexion, and rotation than of forward flexion.[1]

# Lumbar Spine

### Anatomy of the Vertebrae

The bodies of the five lumbar vertebrae are more massive than those in the other regions of the spine in order to support the weight of the trunk. Spinous processes are broad and thick and extend almost horizontally (Fig. 12.2A). The fifth lumbar vertebra differs from the other four vertebrae in having a wedge-shaped body, with the anterior height greater than the posterior height. The inferior articular facets of the fifth vertebra are widely spaced for articulation with the sacrum.

### Anatomy of the Joints

The surfaces of the superior articular facets at the zygapophyseal joints are concave and face medially and posteriorly. The inferior articular facet surfaces are convex and face laterally and anteriorly. Joint capsules are strong and ligaments of the region are essentially the same as those for the thoracic region, except for the addition of the iliolumbar ligament and thoracolumbar fascia and the fact that the posterior longitudinal ligament is not well developed in the lumbar area. The supraspinous ligament is well developed only in the upper lumbar spine. However, the intertransverse ligament is well developed in the lumbar area, and the anterior longitudinal ligament is strongest in this area (Fig. 12.2B). The interspinous ligaments connect one spinous process to another, and the iliolumbar ligament helps to stabilize the lumbosacral joint and prevent anterior displacement.

### Osteokinematics

The zygapophyseal articular facets of L1 to L4 lie primarily in the sagittal plane, which favors flexion and extension and limits lateral flexion and rotation. However, flexion is more limited than extension. During combined flexion and extension, the greatest mobility takes place between L4 and L5, whereas the greatest amount of flexion takes place at the lumbosacral joint, L5-S1. Lateral flexion and rotation are greatest in the upper lumbar region, and little or no lateral flexion is present at the lumbosacral joint because of the orientation of the facets.

### Arthrokinematics

According to Bogduk,[2] flexion at the lumbar intervertebral joints consistently involves a combination of 8 to 13 degrees of anterior rotation (tilting), 1 to 3 mm of anterior translation (sliding), and some axial rotation. The superior vertebral body rotates, tilts, and translates (slides) anteriorly on the adjacent inferior vertebral body. During flexion at the zygapophyseal the superior vertebra slide upward on the left superior facets of the adjacent inferior vertebra.

In axial rotation, the superior vertebra rotates on the inferior vertebra, and the inferior articular surfaces of the superior vertebra impact on the superior articular facet surfaces of the adjacent inferior vertebra. In rotation to the left, the right inferior articular facet impacts on the right superior facet of the adjacent inferior vertebra.

### Capsular Pattern

The capsular pattern for the lumbar spine is a marked and equal restriction of lateral flexion followed by restriction of flexion and extension.[1]

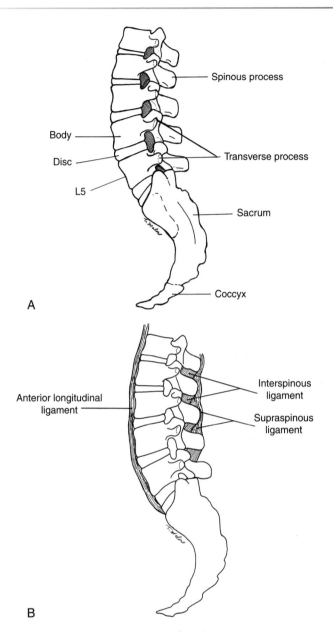

**FIGURE 12.2 A:** A lateral view of the lumbar spine shows the broad, thick, horizontally oriented spinous processes and large vertebral bodies. **B:** A lateral view of the lumbar spine shows the anterior longitudinal, supraspinous, and interspinous ligaments.

joints, the inferior articular facets of the superior vertebra slide upward on the superior articular facets of the adjacent inferior vertebra. In extension, the opposite motions occur: the vertebral body of the superior vertebra tilts and slides posteriorly on the adjacent inferior vertebra, and the inferior articular facets of the superior vertebra slide downward on the superior articular facets of the adjacent inferior vertebra.

In lateral flexion, the superior vertebra tilts and translates laterally on the adjacent vertebra below. In lateral flexion to the right side, the right inferior articular facets of the superior vertebra slide downward on the right superior facets of the adjacent inferior vertebra. The left inferior articular facets of

# RANGE OF MOTION TESTING PROCEDURES

Measurement of the thoracic and lumbar spines is complicated by the regions' multiple joint structure, lack of well-defined landmarks, and difficulty separating thoracic and lumbar motion from hip motion. These difficulties have given rise to the variety of different methods used to measure ROM. The testing procedures presented in this section include the tape measure method, the Modified Schober technique (MST) as described by Macrae and Wright,[3] the Modified–Modified Schober Test (MMST), the universal goniometer (UG) method, and the double inclinometer method. The first four methods were selected because they are inexpensive, are relatively easy to use, and have acceptable reliability. The double inclinometer method has been included in this edition because the fifth edition of the American Medical Association's (AMA) *Guides to the*

*Evaluation of Permanent Impairment*[4] requires that this method be used to obtain reliable spinal mobility measurements for disability determination. According to the *Guides,* full ROM is interpreted as no impairment, and restriction of movement in one or more directions is interpreted as a degree of impairment.

Normal thoracic and lumbar spine ROM values using a variety of instruments are located in the Research Findings section, where Tables 12.1 to 12.5 provide information about the effects of age and gender on thoracic and lumber ROM. This information is followed by functional ranges of motion and a review of research studies on the reliability and validity of the various instruments and methods used to measure thoracic and lumbar ROM (see Tables 12.6 to 12.8 in the Research Findings section). Note that in the following testing procedures we are measuring active range of motion (AROM).

## Landmarks for Testing Procedures

**FIGURE 12.3** Surface anatomy landmarks for tape measure, universal goniometer, and inclinometer alignment for measuring the thoracolumbar spine motion. The dots are located over spinous processes of C7, T1, T12, L1, L5, and S2 and over the right and left posterior superior iliac spines (PSIS).

**FIGURE 12.4** Bony anatomical landmarks for tape measure, universal goniometer, and inclinometer alignment for measuring thoracolumbar spine motion.

## ● THORACOLUMBAR FLEXION

Motion occurs in the sagittal plane around a medial–lateral axis.

### Testing Position

Place the subject standing with feet shoulder width apart and with the cervical, thoracic, and lumbar spine in 0 degrees of lateral flexion and rotation.

### Stabilization

Stabilize the pelvis to prevent anterior tilting.

### Testing Motion

Direct the subject to bend forward gradually while keeping the arms relaxed (Fig. 12.5) and the knees straight. The end of the motion occurs when resistance to additional flexion is experienced by the subject and the examiner feels the pelvis start to tilt anteriorly.

### Normal End-Feel

The normal end-feel is firm owing to the stretching of the posterior longitudinal ligament (in the thoracic region), the ligamentum flavum, the supraspinous and interspinous ligaments, and the posterior fibers of the annulus pulposus of the intervertebral discs and the zygapophyseal joint capsules. Passive tension in the thoracolumbar fascia and the following muscles may contribute to the end-feel: spinalis thoracis, semispinalis thoracis, iliocostalis lumborum and iliocostalis thoracis, interspinales, intertransversarii, longissimus thoracis, and multifidus. The orientation of the zygapophyseal facets from T1 to T6 restricts flexion in the upper thoracic spine.

▶ NOTE: Use the same testing position, stabilization, testing motion, and normal end-feel described in the Thoracolumbar Flexion section above for the following flexion measurement methods unless changes are noted.

**FIGURE 12.5** The subject is shown at the end of thoracolumbar flexion ROM. The examiner is shown stabilizing the subject's pelvis to prevent anterior pelvic tilting.

## ● THORACOLUMBAR FLEXION: TAPE MEASURE

Four inches (10 cm) is considered to be an average measurement for healthy adults.[5]

### Procedure

1. Mark the spinous processes of the C7 and S2 vertebrae using a skin marking pencil, with the subject in the standing position. The spinous process of S2 is on a horizontal level with the posterior superior iliac spines [PSIS]. We have chosen to use the spinous process of S2 for a landmark as it is easier to identify than the spinous process of S1, and there is no motion between S1 and S2.
2. Align the tape measure between the two spinous processes and record the distance at the starting of the ROM (Fig. 12.6).
3. Hold the tape measure in place as the subject performs flexion ROM. (Allow the tape measure to unwind and accommodate the motion.)
4. Record the distance at the end of the ROM (Fig. 12.7). The difference between the first and the second measurements indicates the amount of thoracolumbar flexion ROM.

**FIGURE 12.6** Tape measure alignment in the starting position for measuring thoracolumbar flexion ROM.

**FIGURE 12.7** Tape measure alignment at the end of thoracolumbar flexion ROM. The metal tape measure case (not visible in the photo) is in the examiner's right hand.

## THORACOLUMBAR FLEXION: FINGERTIP-TO-FLOOR

In a study by Quack and associates, the fingertip-to-floor distance was 0.1 cm for 70 healthy females with a mean age of 53 years.[8] In another study the ROM was 2.2 cm for 6 males and 14 females ranging in age from 22 to 55 years.[9]

According to Perret and associates,[10] this test has excellent intratester and intertester reliability (intraclass correlation coefficient [ICC] = 0.99) and validity. However, this test only can be used to assess general body flexibility[11–13] because it combines spinal and hip flexion, making it impossible to isolate either motion.

### Procedure

1. Ask the subject to slowly bend forward as far as possible in an attempt to touch the floor with the fingers while keeping the knees extended and feet together.
2. No stabilization is provided by the examiner.
3. At the end of the motion, measure the perpendicular distance between the tip of the subject's middle finger and the floor either with a tape measure or ruler (Fig. 12.8).

**FIGURE 12.8** At the end of trunk and hip flexion the examiner measures the distance between the tip of the subject's middle finger and the floor with either a centimeter ruler or a tape measure.

# ● THORACOLUMBAR FLEXION: DOUBLE INCLINOMETER

## Procedure

1. Use a skin marking pencil to mark the spinous process of the T1 vertebra and the spinous process of the S2 vertebra (which is on a level with the posterior superior iliac spines [PSIS]), with the subject in the standing position.
2. Position **one inclinometer** over the spinous process of T1 and the **second inclinometer** over the sacrum at the level of S2. Then **zero** both inclinometers (Fig. 12.9).
3. At the end of the motion, read and record the values on both inclinometers (Fig. 12.10). The difference between the two inclinometers indicates the amount of thoracolumbar flexion ROM.

**FIGURE 12.9** The starting position for measuring thoracolumbar flexion with both inclinometers aligned and zeroed.

**FIGURE 12.10** Inclinometer alignment at the end of thoracolumbar flexion ROM.

# THORACOLUMBAR EXTENSION

Motion occurs in the sagittal plane around a medial–lateral axis.

## Testing Position

Place the subject standing with feet shoulder width apart and with the cervical, thoracic, and lumbar spine in 0 degrees of lateral flexion and rotation.

## Stabilization

Stabilize the pelvis to prevent posterior tilting.

## Testing Motion

Ask the subject to extend the spine as far as possible (Fig. 12.11). The end of the extension ROM occurs when the pelvis begins to tilt posteriorly.

## Normal End-Feel

The end-feel is firm owing to stretching of the zygapophyseal joint capsules, anterior fibers of the annulus fibrosus, anterior longitudinal ligament, rectus abdominis, and external and internal oblique abdominals. The end-feel also may be hard owing to contact by the spinous processes and the zygapophyseal facets.

▶ **NOTE: Use the same testing position, stabilization, testing motion, and normal end-feel described in the Thoracolumbar Extension section above for the following extension measurement methods unless changes are noted.**

**FIGURE 12.11** At the end of thoracolumbar extension ROM, the examiner uses her hands on the subject's iliac crests to prevent posterior pelvic tilting. If the subject has balance problems or muscle weakness in the lower extremities, the measurement can be taken in either the prone or side-lying position.

# ● THORACOLUMBAR EXTENSION: TAPE MEASURE

## Procedure

1. Mark the spinous processes of the C7 and S2 vertebrae using a skin marking pencil, with the subject in the standing positon.
2. Align the tape measure between the two spinous processes and record the measurement (Fig. 12.12).
3. Keep the tape measure aligned during the motion and record the measurement at the end of the ROM (Fig. 12.13). The difference between the measurement taken at the beginning of the motion and that taken at the end indicates the amount of thoracic and lumbar extension.

**FIGURE 12.12** Tape measure alignment in the starting position for measurement of thoracolumbar extension. When the subject moves into extension, the tape slides into the tape measure case in the examiner's hand.

**FIGURE 12.13** At the end of thoracolumbar extension ROM, the distance between the two landmarks is less than it was in the starting position.

# THORACOLUMBAR EXTENSION: DOUBLE INCLINOMETERS

## Procedure

1. Mark the spinous processes of the T1 and S2 vertebrae using a skin marking pencil, with the subject in the standing position.
2. Position **one inclinometer** over the spinous process of T1 and the second **inclinometer** over the sacrum at the level of S2. Then **zero** both inclinometers. (Fig. 12.14).

3. At the end of the motion, read and record the values on both inclinometers (Fig. 12.15). The difference between the two inclinometers indicates the amount of thoracolumbar extension ROM.

**FIGURE 12.14** The starting position for measuring thoracolumbar extension with both inclinometers aligned and zeroed.

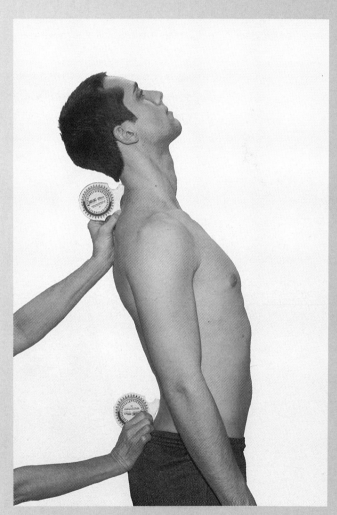

**FIGURE 12.15** Inclinometer alignment at the end of thoracolumbar extension.

# THORACOLUMBAR LATERAL FLEXION

## Testing Position

Place the subject standing with the feet shoulder width apart and the cervical, thoracic, and lumbar spine in 0 degrees of flexion, extension, and rotation.

## Stabilization

Stabilize the pelvis to prevent lateral tilting.

## Testing Motion

Ask the subject to bend the trunk to one side while keeping the arms in a relaxed position at the sides of the body. Keep both feet flat on the floor with the knees extended (Fig. 12.16). The end of the motion occurs when the heel begins to rise on the foot opposite to the side of the motion and the pelvis begins to tilt laterally.

## Normal End-Feel

The end-feel is firm owing to the stretching of the contralateral fibers of the annulus fibrosus, zygapophyseal joint capsules, intertransverse ligaments, thoracolumbar fascia, and the following muscles: external and oblique abdominals, longissimus thoracis, iliocostalis lumborum and thoracis lumborum, quadratus lumborum, multifidus, spinalis thoracis, and serratus posterior inferior. The end-feel may also be hard owing to impact of the ipsilateral zygapophyseal facets (right facets when

**FIGURE 12.16** The end of thoracolumbar lateral flexion ROM. The examiner places both hands on the subject's pelvis to prevent lateral pelvic tilting.

bending to the right) and the restrictions imposed by the ribs and costal joints in the upper thoracic spine.

▶ NOTE: Use the same testing position, stabilization, testing motion, and normal end-feel described in the Thoracolumbar Lateral Flexion section above for the following lateral flexion measurement methods unless changes are noted.

## ● THORACOLUMBAR LATERAL FLEXION: UNIVERSAL GONIOMETER

According to the American Academy of Orthopaedic Surgeons (AAOS),[6] the ROM is 35 degrees to each side (see Table 12.1 in the Research Findings section). Fitzgerald and associates[14] found that normal values ranged from a mean of 37.6 degrees (in a group of 20 to 29 year olds) to 18.0 degrees (in a group of 70 to 79 year olds). See Table 12.2 in the Research Findings section for additional information.[14] According to Sahrmann,[15] more than three-fourths of thoracic and lumbar lateral flexion ROM takes place in the thoracic spine.

### Procedure

1. Mark the spinous processes of C7 and S2 vertebrae using a skin marking pencil.
2. Center **fulcrum** of the goniometer over the posterior aspect of the spinous process of S2 (Fig. 12.17).
3. Align **proximal arm** so that it is perpendicular to the ground.
4. Align **distal arm** with the posterior aspect of the spinous process of C7 (Fig. 12.18).

FIGURE 12.17 The subject is shown with the goniometer aligned in the starting position for measurement of thoracolumbar lateral flexion.

FIGURE 12.18 At the end of thoracolumbar lateral flexion, the examiner keeps the distal goniometer arm aligned with the subject's C7 vertebra. The examiner makes no attempt to align the distal arm with the subject's vertebral column. As can be seen in the photograph, the lower thoracic and upper lumbar spine become convex to the left during right lateral flexion.

# THORACOLUMBAR LATERAL FLEXION: FINGERTIP-TO-FLOOR

The normal values for females with a mean age of 53 years was determined to be 15.9 cm for right lateral flexion and 16.9 cm for left lateral flexion.[8] One problem with this method is that it will be affected by the subject's body proportions. Therefore, it should be used only to compare repeated measurements for a single subject and not for comparing one subject with another subject.

## Procedure

1. Have the subject stand with feet shoulder width apart and arms hanging freely at the sides of the body. Ask the subject to bend to the side as far as possible while keeping both feet flat on the ground with knees extended.
2. At the end of the ROM, make a mark on the leg level with the tip of the middle finger and use a tape measure or ruler to measure the distance between the mark on the leg and the floor (Fig. 12.19).

**FIGURE 12.19** At the end of thoracolumbar lateral flexion range of motion, the examiner is using a tape measure to determine the distance from the tip of the subject's third finger to the floor. Lateral pelvic tilting should be avoided.

# THORACOLUMBAR LATERAL FLEXON: FINGERTIP-TO-THIGH

This method is a variation of the fingertip-to-floor method, designed to account for differences in body size.[16] The normal ROM values for children ages 11 to 16 years were 21.0 cm for both right and left lateral flexion.[17] ROM values derived from 39 healthy adults were 21.6 cm.[16] Lindell and associates[9] found similar values for 20 healthy adults ages 22 to 55 years. Right lateral flexion was 21.2 cm, and left lateral flexion was 21.0 cm. Alaranta and colleagues,[18] in a study of 119 blue and white collar workers ages 35 to 59 years, found a mean value of 19.1 cm. See Table 12.7 in the Research Findings section for reliability information on this procedure.

## Procedure

1. Have the subject stand with his or her back against the wall with feet shoulder width apart and arms hanging freely at the sides of the body.
2. Place a mark on the thigh where the tip of the subject's third finger rests (Fig. 12.20).
3. Ask the subject to bend to the side as far as possible while keeping the back and shoulders against the wall and both feet flat on the ground with knees extended.
4. At the end of the ROM, make a second mark on the leg level with the tip of the middle finger (Fig. 12.21).
5. Use a tape measure or ruler to measure the distance between the first mark on the leg and the second mark on the leg (Fig. 12.22). The distance between the two marks is the value for thoracolumbar lateral flexion ROM.

**FIGURE 12.20** In the starting position for measuring thoracolumbar lateral flexion the examiner marks the thigh at the level of the tip of the subject's middle finger.

**FIGURE 12.21** At the end of thoracolumbar lateral flexion the examiner places a second mark on the thigh on a level with the new position of the tip of the subject's middle finger.

**FIGURE 12.22** The examiner uses a tape measure or ruler to measure the distance between the two thigh marks to obtain the ROM.

# THORACOLUMBAR LATERAL FLEXION: DOUBLE INCLINOMETER

## Procedure

1. Mark the spinous processes of the T1 and S2 vertebrae using a skin marking pencil, with the subject in the standing position.
2. Place **one inclinometer** over the T1 spinous process and the **second inclinometer** over the sacrum at the level of S2. Then **zero** both inclinometers (Fig. 12.23).
3. Ask the subject to bend to the side as far as possible while keeping both knees straight and both feet firmly on the ground (Fig. 12.24).
4. At the end of the ROM, read and record the information on both inclinometers. Subtract the degrees on the sacral inclinometer from the degrees on the thoracic inclinometer to obtain the lateral flexion ROM.
5. Repeat the measurement process to measure lateral flexion ROM on the other side.

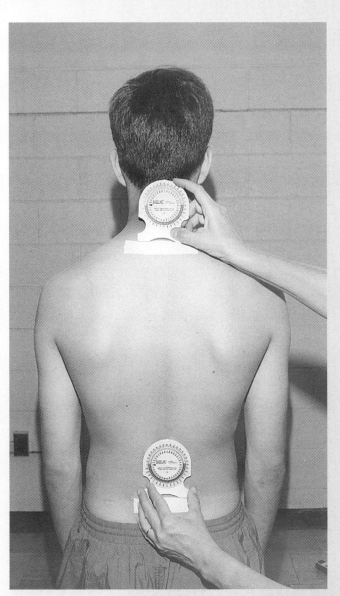

**FIGURE 12.23** The subject is in the starting position for measurement of thoracolumbar lateral flexion with both inclinometers aligned and zeroed.

**FIGURE 12.24** Inclinometer alignment at the end of thoracolumbar lateral flexion ROM.

## ● THORACOLUMBAR ROTATION

Motion occurs in the transverse plane around a vertical axis.

### Testing Position

Place the subject sitting, with the feet on the floor to help stabilize the pelvis. A seat without a back support is preferred so that rotation of the spine can occur freely. The cervical, thoracic, and lumbar spine are in 0 degrees of flexion, -extension, and lateral flexion.

### Stabilization

Stabilize the pelvis to prevent rotation. Avoid flexion, extension, and lateral flexion of the spine.

### Testing Motion

Ask the subject to turn his or her body to one side as far as possible, keeping the trunk erect and feet flat on the floor (Fig. 12.25). The end of the motion occurs when the examiner feels the pelvis start to rotate.

### Normal End-Feel

The end-feel is firm owing to stretching of the fibers of the contralateral annulus fibrosus and zygapophyseal joint capsules; costotransverse and costovertebral joint capsules; supraspinous, interspinous, and iliolumbar ligaments; and the following muscles: rectus abdominis, external and internal obliques and multifidus, and semispinalis thoracis and rotatores. The end-feel may also be hard owing to contact between the zygapophyseal facets.

▶ **NOTE: Use the same testing position, stabilization, testing motion, and normal end-feel described in the Thoracolumbar Rotation section above for the following rotation measurement methods unless changes are noted.**

## ● THORACOLUMBAR ROTATION: UNIVERSAL GONIOMETER

According to the AMA, the normal ROM value for thoracolumbar rotation using the universal goniometer is 45 degrees.[6] See Figures 12.26 and 12.27.

### Procedure

1. Center **fulcrum** of the goniometer over the center of the cranial aspect of the subject's head.
2. Align **proximal arm** parallel to an imaginary line between the two prominent tubercles on the iliac crests.
3. Align **distal arm** with an imaginary line between the two acromial processes.

**FIGURE 12.25** The subject is shown at the end of the thoracolumbar rotation ROM. The subject is seated on a low stool without a back rest so that spinal movement can occur without interference. The examiner positions her hands on the subject's iliac crests to prevent pelvic rotation.

**FIGURE 12.26** In the starting position for measurement of rotation range of motion, the examiner stands behind the seated subject. The examiner positions the fulcrum of the goniometer on the superior aspect of the subject's head. One of the examiner's hands is holding both arms of the goniometer aligned with the subject's acromion processes. The subject should be positioned so that the acromion processes are aligned directly over the iliac tubercles.

**FIGURE 12.27** At the end of rotation, one of the examiner's hands keeps the proximal goniometer arm aligned with the subject's iliac tubercles while keeping the distal goniometer arm aligned with the subject's right acromion process.

## ● THORACOLUMBAR ROTATION: DOUBLE INCLINOMETER

### Procedure

1. Mark the spinous processes of the T1 and S2 vertebrae using a skin marking pencil
2. Place the subject in a forward flexed standing position so that the subject's back is parallel to the floor.
3. Place **one inclinometer** over the spinous process of T1 and the **second inclinometer** over the sacrum at the level of S2. Then **zero** both inclinometers (Fig. 12.28).

4. Ask the subject to rotate the trunk as far as possible without moving into extension (Fig. 12.29). The examiner needs to hold the inclinometers firmly against the subject's back during the motion.
5. Note the degrees shown on the inclinometers at the end of the motion. The difference between inclinometer readings is the rotation ROM.

**FIGURE 12.28** The subject is in the starting position for measurement of thoracolumbar rotation with inclinometers aligned and zeroed.

**FIGURE 12.29** The subject is shown with the inclinometers aligned at the end of thoracolumbar range of motion.

## LUMBAR FLEXION

### Testing Position
Place the subject standing, with the cervical, thoracic, and lumbar spine in 0 degrees of lateral flexion and rotation.

### Stabilization
Stabilize the pelvis to prevent anterior tilting.

### Testing Motion
Ask the subject to bend forward as far as possible while keeping the knees straight.

### Normal End-Feel
The end-feel is firm owing to stretching of the ligamentum flavum; posterior fibers of the annulus fibrosus and zygapophyseal joint capsules; thoracolumbar fascia; illiolumbar ligaments; and the multifidus, quadratus lumborum, and iliocostalis lumborum muscles. The location of the following muscles suggests that they may limit flexion, but the actual actions of the interspinales and intertransversaii mediales and laterales are unknown.[2]

## LUMBAR FLEXION: MODIFIED–MODIFIED SCHOBER TEST[19,20] OR SIMPLIFIED SKIN DISTRACTION TEST[21]

In the original Schober method, the examiner made only two marks on the subject's back. The first mark was made at the lumbosacral junction, and the second mark was made 10 cm above the first mark on the spine. Macrae and Wright[3] decided to modify the Schober method (Modified Schober test) because they found that skin movement was a problem in the original method. They believed that the skin was more firmly attached in the region below the lumbosacral junction and therefore decided to use three marks—the first mark at the lumbosacral junction, the second mark 10 cm above the first mark, and the third mark 5 cm below the lumbosacral junction. The tape measurement is placed between the most superior and the most inferior marks. However, difficulty in correctly identifying the lumbosacral junction led to another modification of the original Schober test, called the Modified–Modified Schober Test (or MMST), which was proposed by van Adrichem and van der Korst.[20] The MMST is sometimes referred to as the simplified skin distraction test[21] and is described in the next paragraph.

The MMST uses two marks: one over the sacral spine on a line connecting the two PSISs and the other mark over the spine 15 cm superior to the first mark. Because the PSISs are much easier to identify than the lumbosacral junction, van Adrichem and van der Korst[20]

were able to eliminate one potential source of error in the original Schober and Modified Schober tests.

Normal values for the MMST for subjects between 15 and 18 years of age are 6.7 cm for males and 5.8 cm for females in the same age group.[20] Jones and associates[17] found a slightly larger normal value of 7.7 cm in a study of 89 healthy children between the ages of 11 and 16 years.

### Procedure
1. Use a ruler to locate and place a **first mark** at a midline point on the sacrum that is level with the posterior superior iliac spines (this mark will be over the spinous process of S2). Make a **second mark** 15 cm above the midline sacral mark (Fig. 12.30).
2. Align the tape measure between the superior and inferior marks (Fig. 12.31). Ask the subject to bend forward as far as possible while keeping the knees straight. Maintain the tape measure against the subject's back during the motion, but allow the tape measure to unwind to accommodate the motion.
3. At the end of flexion ROM, note the distance between the two marks (Fig. 12.32). The ROM is the difference between 15 cm and length measured at the end of the motion.

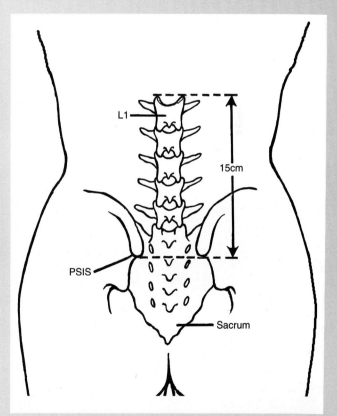

**FIGURE 12.30** A line is drawn between the two posterior superior iliac spines and the point at which the lower end of the tape measure should be positioned. The location of the 15-cm mark shows that all five of the lumbar vertebrae in this subject are included.

**FIGURE 12.31** The tape measure is aligned between the upper and the lower landmarks at the beginning of lumbar flexion range of motion. Paper tape was placed over the skin marking pencil dots to improve visibility of landmarks for the photograph.

**FIGURE 12.32** The tape measure is stretched between the upper and the lower landmarks at the end of lumbar flexion range of motion.

# LUMBAR FLEXION:MODIFIED SCHOBER TEST

Macrae and Wright[3] found an average of 6.3 cm of flexion in healthy adults, and Battie and coworkers[22] found an average of 6.9 cm in a similar group of subjects.

## Procedure

1. Place the **first mark** at the lumbosacral junction with a skin marking pencil. Place a **second mark** 10 cm above the first mark. Place a **third mark** 5 cm below the first mark at the lumbosacral junction.
2. Align the tape measure between the most superior and the most inferior marks. Ask the subject to bend forward as far as possible while keeping the knees straight.
3. Maintain the tape measure against the subject's back during the movement, and note the distance between the most superior and the most inferior marks at the end of the ROM. The ROM is the difference between 15 cm and the length measured at the end of the motion.

# LUMBAR FLEXION: DOUBLE INCLINOMETER

The normal adult ROM is 60 degrees according to the AMA[4,6] and 0 to 66 degrees (for males 15 to 30 years of age) according to Loebl.[23] Ng and associates[24] found a mean value of 52 degrees for 35 healthy men with a mean age of 29 years.

## Procedure

1. Mark the spinous processes of the T12 and S2 vertebrae using a skin marking pencil, with the subject in the standing position.
2. Place **one inclinometer** over the spinous process of T12 and the **second inclinometer** over the sacrum at the level of S2. **Zero** both inclinometers (Fig. 12.33).
3. Ask the subject to bend forward as far as possible while keeping the knees straight. Maintain the inclinometers firmly against the spine during the motion.
4. Note the information on the inclinometers at the end of flexion ROM (Fig. 12.34). Calculate the ROM by subtracting the degrees on the sacral inclinometer from the degrees on T12 inclinometer. The degrees on the sacral inclinometer are supposed to represent hip flexion ROM, and that is why they are subtracted.[21]

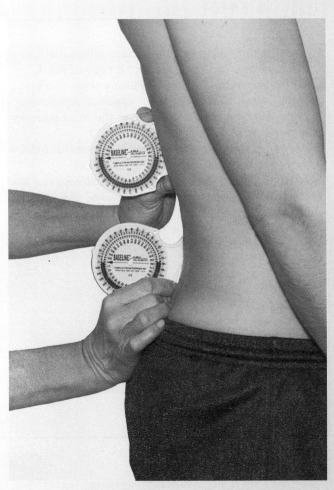

**FIGURE 12.33** The starting position for measurement of lumbar flexion range of motion, with inclinometers aligned and zeroed.

**FIGURE 12.34** The end of lumbar flexion range of motion, with inclinometers aligned over the spinous processes of T12 and S2.

# ● LUMBAR EXTENSION

## Testing Position
Place the subject standing, with the cervical, thoracic, and lumbar spine in 0 degrees of lateral flexion and rotation.

## Stabilization
Stabilize the pelvis to prevent posterior tilting.

## Testing Motion
Ask the subject to extend the spine as far as possible. The end of the extension ROM occurs when the pelvis begins to tilt posteriorly.

## Normal End-Feel
The end-feel is firm owing to stretching of the anterior longitudinal ligament, anterior fibers of the annulus fibrosus, zygapophyseal joint capsules, rectus abdominis, and external and internal oblique muscles. The end-feel may also be hard owing to contact between the spinous processes.

▶ **NOTE: Use the same testing position, stabilization, testing motion, and normal end-feel described in the Lumbar Extension section above for the following extension measurement methods unless changes are noted.**

# ● LUMBAR EXTENSION: SIMPLIFIED SKIN ATTRACTION TEST MODIFIED-MODIFIED SCHOBER TEST (MMST)

## Procedure[21]
1. Hold a ruler between two posterior superior iliac spines (PSIS) and place a **first mark** on a midline point of the sacrum that is on a level with the PSIS; this will be over the spinous process of S2. A second mark should be made on the lumbar spine that is 15 cm above the first mark.
2. Align the tape measure between the first and **second marks** on the spine (Fig. 12.35), and ask the subject to bend backward as far as possible.
3. At the end of the ROM, note the distance between the superior and the inferior marks (Fig. 12.36). The ROM is the difference between 15 cm and the length measured at the end of the motion.

# ● LUMBAR EXTENSION: MODIFIED SCHOBER TEST

Battie and coworkers[22] found a normal value of 1.6 cm in 100 healthy adults.

## Procedure
1. Use a skin-marking pencil to place a **first mark** at the lumbosacral junction. Place a **second mark** 10 cm above the first mark. Place a **third mark** 5 cm below the first mark (lumbosacral junction).
2. Align the tape measure between the most superior and the most inferior marks.
3. Ask the subject to put the hands on the buttocks and to bend backward as far as possible.
4. Note the distance between the most superior and the most inferior marks at the end of the ROM, and subtract the final measurement from the initial 15 cm. The ROM is the difference between 15 cm and the length measured at the end of the motion.

**FIGURE 12.35** Tape measure alignment in the starting position for measurement of lumbar extension range of motion with use of the simplified skin distraction method (modified–modified Schober method).

**FIGURE 12.36** Tape measure alignment at the end of lumbar extension range of motion, with use of the simplified skin distraction method.

## ● LUMBAR EXTENSION: DOUBLE INCLINOMETER

The normal ROM values for young-adult males (15 to 30 years) is 38 degrees, whereas the value for middle-age males (31 to 60 years) is 35 degrees. In males older than age 60 years the ROM is 33 degrees. In young-adult females the ROM is 42 degrees, in middle-aged females the ROM is 40 degrees, and in females older than 60 years the ROM is 36 degrees.[23] According to the AMA,[6] the normal ROM for adults is from 20[7] to 25[4] degrees; both of these values are considerably less than the values that were found by Loebl.[23]

## Procedure

1. Mark the spinous processes of the T12 and S2 vertebrae using a skin marking pencil, with the subject in the standing position.
2. Place **one inclinometer** over the spinous process of T12 and the **second inclinometer** over the midline of the sacrum at S2. Then **zero** both inclinometers (Fig 12.37).

3. Ask the subject to bend backward as far as possible. Maintain the inclinometers firmly against the spine during the motion (Fig. 12.38).
4. Read and record the degrees from both inclinometers at the end of the motion. Subtract the degrees on the sacral inclinometer from the degrees on the T12 inclinometer to obtain the lumbar extension ROM.

**FIGURE 12.37** Starting position for measuring lumbar extension range of motion with double inclinometers placed over the T12 and S2 spinous processes.

**FIGURE 12.38** At the end of the lumbar extension range of motion (ROM), read and record the degrees on both inclinometers. Subtract the degrees on the sacral inclinometer from the T12 reading to obtain the ROM.

# LUMBAR LATERAL FLEXION

## Testing Position
Place the subject standing with the feet shoulder width apart and the cervical, thoracic, and lumbar spine in 0 degrees of lateral flexion and rotation.

## Stabilization
Stabilize the pelvis to prevent lateral tilting.

## Testing Motion
Ask the subject to bend to the side as far as possible. The end of the lateral flexion ROM occurs when the pelvis begins to tilt laterally.

## Normal End-Feel
The end-feel is firm owing to stretching of the contralateral band of the iliolumbar ligament, contralateral thoracolumbar fascia, contralateral fibers of the annulus fibrosus, and zygapophyseal joint capsules. The following contralateral muscles may contract eccentrically to control and resist lateral flexion when gravity begins to affect the motion: quadratus lumborum, interspinales, and iliocostales lumborum. The end-feel could be hard due to contact of the ipsilateral apophyseal joints.

▶ NOTE: **Use the same testing position, stabilization, testing motion and normal end-feel described in the Lumbar Lateral Flexion section above for the following lateral flexion measurement methods unless changes are noted.**

# ● LUMBAR LATERAL FLEXION: DOUBLE INCLINOMETER

According to the AMA, the ROM value is 25 to 30 degrees to each side.[4,7]

## Procedure

1. Mark the spinous processes of the T12 and S2 vertebrae using a skin marking pencil, with the subject in the standing position.
2. Position **one inclinometer** over the T12 spinous process and the **second inclinometer** over the sacrum at the level of S2. Then, **zero** both inclinometers (Fig. 12.39).

3. Ask the subject to bend the trunk laterally while keeping both feet flat on the ground and the knees straight (Fig. 12.40).
4. Read and record the degrees on both inclinometers. Subtract the degrees on the sacral inclinometer from the degrees on the T12 inclinometer to obtain the lumbar lateral flexion ROM to one side.
5. Repeat the measurement process to measure lumbar lateral flexion ROM on the other side.

FIGURE 12.39 Starting position for measuring lumbar lateral flexion range of motion with double inclinometers placed over the spinous processes of T12 and S2.

FIGURE 12.40 At the end of lumbar lateral flexion range of motion (ROM), read and record the degrees on each inclinometer. Subtract the degrees on the sacral inclinometer from the T12 reading to obtain the ROM.

## ◌ Research Findings

Table 12.1 shows thoracolumbar spine ROM values from the AAOS and lumbar spine ROM values from the AMA.

### Effects of Age, Gender, and Other Factors

#### Age

Many instruments and methods have been used to determine the range of thoracic, thoracolumbar, and lumbar motion. Therefore, comparisons between studies are difficult. As is true for other regions of the body, conflicting evidence exists regarding the effects of age on ROM. However, the majority of studies appear to indicate that age-related decreases in spinal ROM occur and that these changes may affect certain motions more than others at the same joint or region.[3,18,23–33]

The following two studies with relatively large numbers of subjects and extended age ranges arrived at similar conclusions regarding the motions that showed the greatest and least decrease in ROM with increasing age. Extension was one of the motions that showed the greatest decrease, and axial rotation showed the least decrease.

McGregor, McCarthy, and Hughes[29] found that, although age had a significant effect on all planes of motion, the effect varied for each motion, and age accounted for only a small portion of the variability seen in the 203 normal subjects studied. Maximum extension was the most affected motion, with significant decreases between each decade. Lateral flexion decreased after age 40 and each decade thereafter. Flexion decreased initially after age 30 years but stayed the same until an additional decrease after age 50 years. No similar decreases or trends were found in axial rotation.

The findings of Troke and associates[31,32] were similar in that these authors found no change in lumbar axial rotation in 405 asymptomatic subjects (196 females and 209 males) ages 16 to 90 years. Likewise, lumbar extension showed the greatest decline in ROM (approximately 76 percent). Male and female lumbar spine flexion range of motion declined considerably less, by about 40 percent over the age span, and right and left lateral flexion each declined about 43 percent. These authors used the CA-6000 Spine Motion Analyzer to measure half cycle motions at different times of the day to account for diurnal variations.

In another fairly large study, Moll and Wright[26] used skin markings and a plumb line to measure the range of lumbar extension in a study involving 237 subjects (119 men and 118 women) aged 20 to 90 years. These authors found a wide variation in normal values but detected a gradual decrease in lumbar extension in subjects between 35 and 90 years of age.

Van Herp and associates,[33] in a study of 100 healthy male and female subjects 20 to 77 years of age, used the 3Space System to measure lumbar ROM from T12 to S1. The authors found a constant decrease with increasing age in all lumbar motions except for flexion in 50- to 59-year-old males.

Fitzgerald and associates[14] determined that the oldest group had considerably less motion than the youngest group in all motions except for flexion. Also, the coefficients of variation (CV) indicated that a greater amount of variability existed in the ROM in the oldest groups (Table 12.2).

Alaranta and coworkers[18] used both a tape measure and an inclinometer to assess lumbar ROM in 508 males and females 35 to 45 years of age. Some of these subjects had either neck or back pain, but all were actively employed. Lumbar flexion showed more than a 10 percent decrease when comparing the youngest to the oldest subjects, but lateral flexion showed an even greater decrease (19 percent) with increasing age. This

## TABLE 12.1 Thoracolumbar and Lumbar Spine Motion: Normal Values for Adults in Inches and Degrees From Selected Sources

| Instrument<br><br>Motion<br>Authors<br>Sample | Tape Measure &<br>Goniometer<br>Thoracolumbar<br>AAOS*[5] | Double<br>Inclinometers<br>Lumbar<br>AMA†[6] | BROM II<br><br>Lumbar<br>Breum et al[70]<br>18–38 years | 3Space<br>isotrak system<br>Lumbar<br>VanHerp et al[33]<br>20–29 years | Inclinometer<br><br>Lumbar<br>Ng et al[24]<br>30 yrs |
|---|---|---|---|---|---|
| *Motion* | | | *Mean (SD)* | *Mean (SD)* | *Mean (SD)* |
| Flexion | 4 inches | 60 degrees | 56.3 (1.3) degrees | 56.4 (7.1) degrees | 52 (90) degrees |
| Extension | 20–30 degrees | 25 degrees | 21.5 (8.2) degrees | 22.5 (7.8) degrees | 19 (9) degrees |
| Right lateral flexion | 35 degrees | 25 degrees | 33.3 (5.9) degrees | 26.2 (8.4) degrees | 31 (6) degrees |
| Left lateral flexion | 35 degrees | 25 degrees | 33.6 (6.2) degrees | 25.8 (7.8) degrees | 30 (6) degrees |
| Right rotation | 45 degrees | | | 14.4 (5.1) degrees | 33 (9) degrees |

AAOS = American Association of Orthopaedic Surgeons; AMA = American Medical Association.
* Flexion measurement in inches was obtained with a tape measure with use of the spinous processes
  of C7 and S1 as reference points. The remaining motions were measured with a universal goniometer and are in degrees.
† Lumbar motion was measured from sacrum (S1) to T12.

**TABLE 12.2** Age Effects on Lumbar and Thoracolumbar Spine Motion in 20- to 79-Year-Old Adults: Normal Values in Centimeters and Degrees

| Sample / Motion | 20–29 yrs n = 31 Mean (SD) | 30–39 yrs n = 42 Mean (SD) | 40–49 yrs n = 16 Mean (SD) | 50–59 yrs n = 43 Mean (SD) | 60–69 yrs n = 26 Mean (SD) | 70–79 yrs n = 9 Mean (SD) |
|---|---|---|---|---|---|---|
| Flexion* | 3.7 (0.7) | 3.9 (1.0) | 3.1 (0.8) | 3.0 (1.1) | 2.4 (0.7) | 2.2 (0.6) |
| Extension | 41.2 (9.6) | 40.0 (8.8) | 31.1 (8.9) | 27.4 (8.0) | 17.4 (7.5) | 16.6 (8.8) |
| Right lateral flexion | 37.6 (5.8) | 35.3 (6.5) | 27.1 (6.5) | 25.3 (6.2) | 20.2 (4.8) | 18.0 (4.7) |
| Left lateral flexion | 38.7 (5.7) | 36.5 (6.0) | 28.5 (5.2) | 26.8 (6.4) | 20.3 (5.3) | 18.9 (6.0) |

SD = standard deviation.
* Flexion measurements were obtained with use of the Schober method and are reported in centimeters.
All other measurements were obtained with use of a universal goniometer and are reported in degrees.
Adapted from Fitzgerald, GK, et al: Objective assessment with establishment of normal values for lumbar
 spine range of motion. Phys Ther 63:1776, 1983.[14] With the permission of the American Physical Therapy Association.

decrease in lateral flexion is similar to the findings of McGregor, McCarthy, and Hughes,[29] who found that lateral flexion showed a slightly higher decrease in ROM (43 percent) than the decrease in forward flexion (40 percent).

In other studies the authors reported that both flexion and extension ROM were found to decline with increasing age, but in some of the studies the motions were full cycle motions, so it is difficult to tell whether the decrease was in flexion or in extension.

In one of the earlier studies, in 1967 Loebl[23] used an inclinometer to measure active sagittal plane ROM of the thoracic and lumbar spine of 126 males and females between 15 and 84 years of age. He found age-related effects for both males and females and concluded that both genders should expect a loss of about 8 degrees of spinal ROM per decade with increases in age.

In a more recent study, Sullivan, Dickinson, and Troup[25] used double inclinometers to measure sagittal plane lumbar motion in 1126 healthy male and female subjects. These authors found that when gender was controlled, flexion and extension decreased with increasing age. The authors suggested that the ROM thresholds that determine impairment ratings should take age into consideration.

In 1969 Macrae and Wright[3] used a modification of the Schober technique to measure forward lumbar flexion in 195 women and 147 men (18 to 71 years of age). The authors found that active flexion ROM decreased with age.

Anderson and Sweetman[27] used a device that combined a flexible rule and a hydrogoniometer to measure the ROM of 432 working men aged 20 to 59 years. Increasing age was associated with a lower total lumbar spine ROM (flexion and extension) in this group of subjects.

The preceding studies are fairly consistent in concluding that both thoracolumbar and lumbar ROM decreases with increasing age, and that extension and lateral flexion may be affected more than flexion. Axial rotation was not measured in the majority of studies, but when it was measured, no age-related changes in ROM were found.

The following two studies investigated segmental mobility. Gracovetsky and associates[28] found a significant difference between young and old in a group of 40 subjects aged 19 to 64 years. Older subjects had decreased segmental mobility in the lower lumbar spine compared with younger subjects. To compensate for the decrease in mobility, the older subjects increased the contribution of the pelvis to flexion and extension.

Wong and colleagues[35] assessed intervertebral lumbar flexion and extension in 100 healthy volunteers (50 males and 50 females) ages 20 to 76 years. The results showed that all segmental lumbar spinal motion profiles within the ROM of 10 degrees of extension to 40 degrees of flexion did not change as age increased until subjects were 51 years of age or older. Subjects in the oldest age group had a decrease in maximum flexion and extension ROM, but an increase in the slopes of the intervertebral flexion-extension curves at each lumbar segment.

### Gender

Investigations of the effects of gender on lumbar spine ROM indicate that the effects may be motion specific and possibly age specific, but controversy still exists concerning which motions are affected, and some authors report that gender has no effects. The fact that investigators used different instruments and methods makes comparisons between studies difficult. However, the following five studies appear to agree that the ROM in flexion is greater in males than in females, at least in subjects 15 to 65 years of age. This difference in flexion ROM between males and females is apparent even in children between the ages of 5 to 11 years.[30] At the other end of the age spectrum, this difference between the genders in flexion ROM may have evened out by the time men and women were in their 80s.[31,32]

Macrae and Wright[3] found that females had significantly less forward flexion than males across all age groups. Sullivan, Dickinson, and Troup[25] also found that when age was controlled, mean flexion ROM was greater in males. However, mean extension ROM and total ROM were significantly greater in females. Subjects in the study were 1126 healthy male and female volunteers aged 15 to 65 years. The authors noted that, although female total ROM was significantly greater than male total ROM, the difference of 1.5 degrees was not clinically relevant. Age and gender combined accounted for only 14 percent of the variance in flexion, 25 percent in extension, and 20 percent of the variance in total ROM (Table 12.3). Alaranta and associates,[18] in a study of 508 males and females ages 35 to 45 years, also determined that men had greater flexion ROM than women. However, these authors found no difference between the sexes in extension ROM. Kondratek and associates,[30] in a study of 116 girls and 109 boys aged 5 to 11 years of age, found a statistically significant difference between the youngest and oldest subjects in active lumbar flexion in girls and active lumbar lateral flexion and rotation in both girls and boys. The older girls, aged 11 years, consistently demonstrated less motion in forward flexion and right and left lateral flexion than the boys. Extension varied very little in either gender. Troke and colleagues[31,32] found that men had greater ROM in flexion at 16 years than women, but in the final decade (80 to 90 years) men and women were equal.

Moll and Wright's[26] findings are directly opposite to the findings of the previous three studies in that Moll and Wright determined that male mobility in extension significantly exceeded female mobility by 7 percent. Differences in findings between studies may have resulted from the fact that Moll and Wright[26] did not control for age. These authors measured the range of lumbar extension in a study involving 237 subjects (119 males and 118 females) aged 15 to 90 years, who were clinically and radiologically normal relatives of patients with psoriatic arthritis (Tables 12.4 and 12.5).

Van Herp and associates,[33] in an investigation of lumbar range of motion in 100 subjects (50 male and 50 female) 20 to 77 years of age, found that females consistently showed greater flexibility than males in lumbar flexion–extension, lateral flexion, and axial rotation throughout the age range. Because flexion was not separated from extension, it is difficult to know which motion was responsible for the increase.

In contrast to the preceding authors, the following three studies reported no significant effects for gender on lumbar spine ROM. Loebl[23] found no significant gender differences between the 126 males and females aged 15 to 84 years of age for measurements of lumbar flexion and extension. Bookstein and associates[34] used a tape measure to measure the lumbar extension ROM in 75 elementary school children aged 6 to 11 years. The authors found no differences for age or gender, but they found a significant difference for age–gender interaction in the 6-year-old group. Girls aged 6 years had a mean range of extension of 4.1 cm, in contrast to the 6-year-old boys, who had a mean range of extension of 2.1 cm. Wong and colleagues[35] used an electrogoniometer and videofluoroscopy to assess the flexion–extension profile of the lumbar spine in different genders and age groups. A total of 100 healthy volunteers (50 females and 50 males) ages 21 to 51 years and older participated in the study, but no statistically significant differences in the pattern of motion were found between the genders.

## Diurnal Effects

Ensink and coworkers [36] determined that the average increase in height in the morning after 8 hours of bed rest was 2 mm, with 40 percent of the increase occurring in the lumbar spine. The increase in height was due to the hydration of the discs that occurred during bed rest. Lumbar spine ROM in flexion was decreased in the morning but increased during the day as water was squeezed out of the discs. ROM in extension was not affected. Consequently, examiners should try to test and retest lumbar flexion ROM during the same time of day.

## Occupation and Lifestyle

Researchers have investigated the following factors among others in relation to their effects on lumbar ROM: occupation,[37] lifestyle,[29,37–39] time of day,[36] and disability.[25,40–44] Similar to the findings related to age and gender, the results have been controversial.

Sughara and colleagues,[37] using a device called a spinometer, studied age-related and occupation-related changes in thoracolumbar active ROM in 1071 men and 1243 women aged 20 to 60 years. Subjects were selected from three occupational groups: fishermen, farmers, and industrial workers. Although both flexion and extension were found to decrease with increasing age, decreases in the extension ROM were

| TABLE 12.3 | Age and Gender Effects on Lumbar Motion in Individuals 15 to 65 Years Old: Normal Values in Degrees Using a Fluid-Filled Inclinometer | | | | | |
|---|---|---|---|---|---|---|
| Sample | 16–24 yrs Male n = 122 | 15–24 yrs Female n = 161 | 25–34 yrs Male n = 295 | 25–34 yrs Female n = 143 | 35–65 yrs Male n = 269 | 35–65 yrs Female n= 136 |
| Motion | Mean (SD) | Mean (SD) | Mean (SD) | Mean (SD) | Mean (SD) | Mean (SD) |
| Flexion | 33 (9) | 26 (9) | 31 (8) | 24 (8) | 27 (8) | 22 (8) |
| Extension | 54 (10) | 63 (9) | 52 (9) | 60 (10) | 47 (9) | 53 (9) |

SD = standard deviation.
Adapted from Sullivan, MS, Dickinson, CE, and Troup, JDG: The influence of age and gender on lumbar spine sagittal plane range of motion: A study of 1126 healthy subjects. Spine 19:682, 1994.[40]

**TABLE 12.4** Age and Gender Effects on Lumbar and Thoracolumbar Motion in Individuals Ages 15 to 44 Years: Normal Values in Centimeters

| Sample | 15–24 yrs | | 25–34 yrs | | 35–44 yrs | |
|---|---|---|---|---|---|---|
| | Male n = 21 | Female n = 10 | Male n = 13 | Female n = 16 | Male n = 14 | Female n = 18 |
| *Motion* | *Mean (SD)* | *Mean (SD)* | *Mean (SD)* | *Mean (SD)* | *Mean (SD)* | *Mean (SD)* |
| Flexion* | 7.23 (0.92) | 6.66 (1.03) | 7.48 (0.82) | 6.69 (1.09) | 6.88 (0.88) | 6.29 (1.04) |
| Extension* | 4.21 (1.64) | 4.34 (1.52) | 5.05 (1.41) | 4.76 (1.53) | 3.73 (1.47) | 3.09 (1.31) |
| Right lateral flexion† | 5.43 (1.30) | 6.85 (1.46) | 5.34 (1.06) | 6.32 (1.93) | 4.83 (1.34) | 5.30 (1.61) |
| Left lateral flexion† | 5.06 (1.40) | 7.20 (1.66) | 5.93 (1.07) | 6.13 (1.42) | 4.83 (0.99) | 5.48 (1.30) |

Adapted from Moll, JMH, and Wright, V: Normal range of spinal mobility: An objective clinical study. Ann Rheum Dis 30:381, 1971.[26] The authors used skin markings and a plumb line on the thorax for lateral flexion.
SD = standard deviation.
*Lumbar motion.
†Thoracolumbar motion.

greater than decreases in flexion. Decreases in active extension ROM were less in fishermen and their wives than in the other occupational groups in the study. The researchers concluded that because both fishermen and their wives had more extension than other groups, other variables than the physical demands of fishing were affecting the maintenance of extension ROM.

Sjolie[39] compared low-back strength and low-back and hip mobility between a group of 38 adolescents living in a community without access to pedestrian roads and a group of 50 adolescents with excellent access to pedestrian roads. Low-back mobility was measured by means of the modified Schober technique. The results showed that adolescents living in rural areas without easy access to pedestrian roads had less low-back extension and hamstring flexibility than their counterparts in urban areas. The hypothesis that negative associations would

exist between school bus use and physical performance was confirmed. The distance traveled by the school bus was inversely associated with hamstring flexibility and other hip motions but not with low-back flexion. Walking or bicycling to leisure activities was positively associated with low-back strength, low-back extension ROM, and hip flexion and extension.

Freidrich and colleagues[38] conducted a comprehensive examination of spinal posture during stooped walking in 22 male sewer workers aged 24 to 49 years. Working in a stooped posture has been identified as one of the risk factors associated with spinal disorders. Five posture levels corresponding to standardized sewer heights ranging in decreasing size from 150 to 105 cm were taped by a video-based motion analysis system. The results showed that the lumbar spine abruptly changed from the usual lordotic position in normal

**TABLE 12.5** Age and Gender Effects on Lumbar and Thoracolumbar Motion in Individuals Ages 45 to 74 Years: Normal Values in Centimeters

| Sample | 45–54 yrs | | 55–64 yrs | | 65–74 yrs | |
|---|---|---|---|---|---|---|
| | Male n = 19 | Female n = 23 | Male n = 34 | Female n = 30 | Male n = 14 | Female n = 14 |
| *Motion* | *Mean (SD)* | *Mean (SD)* | *Mean (SD)* | *Mean (SD)* | *Mean (SD)* | *Mean (SD)* |
| Flexion* | 7.17 (1.20) | 6.02 (1.32) | 6.87 (0.89) | 6.08 (1.32) | 5.67 (1.31) | 4.93 (0.90) |
| Extension* | 3.88 (1.19) | 3.12 (1.36) | 3.56 (1.28) | 3.57 (1.32) | 3.41 (1.56) | 2.72 (0.95) |
| Right lateral flexion† | 4.71 (1.35) | 5.37 (1.54) | 5.05 (1.30) | 5.10 (1.85) | 4.44 (1.03) | 5.56 (2.04) |
| Left lateral flexion† | 4.55 (0.94) | 5.14 (1.54) | 4.94 (1.22) | 4.88 (1.61) | 4.38 (0.98) | 5.55 (2.16) |

Adapted from Moll, JMH, and Wright, V: Normal range of spinal mobility: An objective clinical study. Ann Rheum Dis 30:381, 1971.[26] The authors used skin markings and a plumb line on the thorax for lateral flexion.
SD = standard deviation.
*Lumbar motion.
†Thoracolumbar motion.

upright walking to a kyphotic position in mild, 150-cm head-room restriction. As ceiling height decreased, the neck progressively assumed a more extended lordotic position; the thoracic spine extended and flattened, becoming less kyphotic; and the lumbar spine became more kyphotic. As expected, the older workers showed decreased segmental mobility in the lumbar spine and an increase in cervical lordosis with decreasing ceiling height.

## Disability

The relationship between ROM findings and disability is a topic of considerable interest and importance to health professionals. Researchers have reported conflicting results, so that there appears to be no clear relationship between range of motion and disability at the present time.

Sullivan, Dickinson, and Troup[25] used dual inclinometers to measure lumbar spine sagittal motion in 1126 healthy individuals. The authors found a large variation in measurements and suggested that detection of ROM impairments might be difficult because 95% confidence intervals yielded up to a 36-degree spread in normal ROM values. Sullivan, Shoaf, and Riddle[40] examined the relationship between impairment of active lumbar flexion ROM and disability. The authors used normative data to determine when an impairment in flexion ROM was present and used the judgment of physical therapists to determine whether flexion ROM impairment was relevant to the patient's disability. Low correlations between lumbar ROM and disability were found, and the authors concluded that active lumbar ROM measurements should not be used as treatment goals.

Nattrass and associates[43] used a long-arm goniometer to measure thoracolumbar ROM and dual inclinometers to measure low-back ROM in 34 patients aged 20 to 65 years with chronic low-back pain. ROM for all subjects was compared with ratings on commonly used impairment and disability indexes. Only flexion measured with the goniometer demonstrated greater than 50 percent of the variance in common with one of the disability measues. The authors concluded that lumbar ROM alone is not enough to represent impairment and, therefore, the AMA *Guides to the Evaluation of Permanent Impairment* should not limit impairment ratings to ROM because ROM seems to represent only one aspect of impairment.

However, Lundberg and Gerdle,[41] who investigated spinal and peripheral joint mobility and spinal posture in 607 female home care employees (mean age 40.5 years), found that lumbar sagittal hypomobility alone was associated with higher disability, and a combination of positive pain provocation tests and lumbar sagittal hypomobility was associated with particularly high disability levels. Peripheral joint mobility, spinal sagittal posture, and thoracic sagittal mobility showed low correlations with disability.

Kujala and coworkers[42] conducted a 3-year longitudinal study of lumbar mobility and occurrence of low-back pain in 98 adolescents. The subjects included 33 nonathletes (16 males and 17 females), 34 male athletes, and 31 female athletes. Participation in sports and low maximal lumbar flexion predicted low-back pain during the follow-up in males, but accounted for only 16 percent of the variance between groups with and without low-back pain. A decreased ROM in the lower lumbar segments, low maximal ROM in extension, and high body weight were predictive of low-back pain in females and accounted for 31 percent of the variability between groups.

Alaranta and associates,[18] in a study of 508 male and female white and blue collar employees ages 35 to 54 years, found that the strongest connections were between trunk lateral flexion ROM and low-back pain during the preceding year.

## Functional Range of Motion

Hsieh and Pringle[45] used a CA-6000 Spinal Motion Analyzer (Orthopedic Systems, Inc., Hayward, CA) to measure the amount of lumbar motion required for selected activities of daily living performed by 48 healthy subjects with a mean age of 26.5 years. Activities included stand to sit, sit to stand, putting on socks, and picking up an object from the floor. The individual's peak flexion angles for the activities were normalized to the subject's own peak flexion angle in erect standing. Stand to sit and sit to stand (Fig. 12.41) required approximately 56 percent to 66 percent of lumbar flexion. The mean was 34.6 degrees for sit to stand and 41.8 degrees for stand to sit. Putting on socks (Fig. 12.42) required 90 percent of lumbar flexion ROM (mean 56.4 degrees), and picking up an object from the floor (Fig. 12.43) required 95 percent of lumbar flexion (mean 60.4 degrees). In view of these findings, one can understand how limitations in lumbar ROM may

**FIGURE 12.41** Sit to stand requires an average of 35 degrees of lumbar flexion.[45]

**FIGURE 12.42** Putting on socks requires an average of 56 degrees of lumbar flexion.[45]

**FIGURE 12.43** Picking up an object from the floor requires an average of 60 degrees of lumbar flexion.[45]

affect an individual's ability to independently carry out dressing and other activities of daily living.

Levine and associates[46] conducted a study with 20 healthy women (mean age 23.4 years) from a university student population to determine changes in lumbar spine motion in standing, walking, and running on a treadmill at three different gradients. According to results obtained from the Vicon Motion Analysis System, total lumbar spine ROM was greater during running than during walking, and greater walking downhill than walking uphill or on a level surface. However, the maximum amount of lumbar extension (anterior pelvic tilt) was found in standing at the three gradients.

## Reliability and Validity

The following section on reliability and validity has been divided according to the instruments and methods used to obtain the measurements. However, some overlap occurs between the sections because several investigators have compared different methods and instruments within one study.

Littlewood and May[47] conducted a systematic review of 86 ROM studies to determine what low tech measurement methods were valid for measuring lumbar spine ROM. Only four studies—those by Samo and colleagues,[48] Saur and colleagues,[49] Williams and colleagues,[19] and Tousignant and colleagues[50]—were found to meet the criteria of English language only, evaluated validity by comparison to radiographs, included adult subjects with non-specific low back pain, and included measurement accuracy to enable judgement on validity. All failed to meet the criteria of blinding the examiners. Double inclinometers were used in three of the four studies, and the Modified-Modified-Schober Test (MMST) was used in the other study. Littlewood and May[4] performed a qualitative analysis but did not perform a meta-analysis. In regard to the double inclinometer method, they concluded that there was only limited positive supporting evidence for the validity of measuring total lumbar ROM in comparison to radiographic analysis; there was conflicting evidence for the validity of measuring lumbar flexion ROM; and there was limited positive evidence for the lack of validity of measuring lumbar extension. In regard to the

MMST they determined that there was limited positive evidence for the lack of validity for measuring lumbar flexion ROM. The authors concluded that there is a need for scientific evidence on the validity of these measurement procedures.

In another review, Essendrop and colleagues[51] screened databases from 1980 to 1999 for reliability studies regarding the measurement of low-back ROM, strength, and endurance. Seventy-nine studies were located, 6 of which met the predetermined criteria for a quality study and focused on the measurement of low back ROM. Noting the difficulty in making definite conclusions based on these limited studies, the authors reported that the tape measure was the most reliable instrument for flexion measurements. Reliable extension measurements were difficult to achieve with any of the reviewed instruments. The tape measure and Cybex EDI 320 goniometer were reliable for trunk lateral flexion when comparing groups but not individuals. Trunk rotation measurements were the most unreliable for all instruments including the double inclinometer, Myrin inclinometer, tape measure, and universal goniometer.

## Reliability:Inclinometer

The AMA *Guides to the Evaluation of Permanent Impairment*[4] states that "measurement techniques using inclinometers are necessary to obtain reliable spinal mobility measurements." However, in a study by Williams and coworkers[19] that compared the measurements of the inclinometer with those of the tape measure, the authors found that the double inclinometer technique had questionable intertester reliability (Table 12.6). Reliability problems with the use of double inclinometers are often related to difficulty in identifying landmarks and in holding the inclinometers correctly. Other problems include too long a time period between test and retest and lack of sufficient practice to familiarize the examiner with the instruments.

Loebl[23] has stated that the only reliable technique for measuring lumbar spine motion is radiography. However, radiography is expensive and may pose a health risk to the subject; moreover, the validity of radiographic assessment of ROM is unreported. Loebl[23] used an inclinometer to measure flexion and extension in nine subjects. He found that in five repeated active measurements, the ROM varied by 5 degrees in the most consistent subject and by 23 degrees in the most inconsistent subject. Variability decreased when measurements were taken on an hourly basis rather than on a daily basis. Patel,[52] who used the double inclinometer method to measure lumbar flexion on 25 subjects aged 21 to 37 years, found intratester reliability to be high (r = 0.91), but intertester reliability was considerably lower (r = 0.68).

Mayer and associates[53] compared repeated measurements of lumbar ROM of 18 healthy subjects taken by 14 different examiners using three different instruments: a fluid-filled inclinometer, the kyphometer, and the electrical inclinometer. The three instruments were found to be equally reliable, but significant differences were found between examiners. Poor intertester reliability was the most significant source of variance. The authors identified sources of error as being caused by differences in instrument placement among examiners and inability to locate the necessary landmarks.

Saur and colleagues[49] used Pleurimeter V inclinometers to measure lumbar ROM in 54 patients with chronic low-back pain who were between 18 and 60 years of age. Measurements were taken with and without radiographic verification of the T12 and S1 landmarks used for positioning the inclinometers. Intertester reliability of the inclinometry technique for full cycle flexion–extension in a subgroup of 48 patients was high (r = 0.94) and half cycle flexion was good (r = 0.88), but half cycle extension was poor (r = 0.42). The authors concluded that the Pleurimeter V was a reliable and valid method for measuring lumbar ROM and that with use of this instrument it was possible to differentiate lumbar spine movements from hip movements.

Chen and associates[54] investigated intertester and intratester reliability using three health professionals to measure lumbar ROM using a Pleurimeter V (double inclinometer), a carpenter's double inclinometer, and a computed single-sensor inclinometer. Intertester reliability was poor, with all ICCs less than 0.75; with a single exception, intratester reliability was less than 0.90. The authors determined that the largest source of measurement error was attributable to the examiners and associated factors and concluded that these three surface methods had only limited clinical usefulness.

Mayer and colleagues[55] used a Cybex EDI-320 (Lumex, Ronkonkoma, NY), a computed inclinometer with a single sensor, to measure lumbar ROM in 38 healthy individuals. Full cycle sagittal ROM was the most accurate measurement, and extension was the least accurate. Clinical utility of lumbar sagittal plane ROM measurement appeared to be highly sensitive to the training of the test administrator in aspects of the process such as locating bony landmarks of T12 and S1 and maintaining inclinometer placement without rocking on the sacrum. Device error was negligible relative to the error associated with the test process itself. The authors found that practice was the most significant factor in eliminating the largest source of error when inexperienced examiners were used.

Nitschke and colleagues[56] compared the following measurement methods in a study involving 34 male and female subjects with chronic low-back pain and two examiners: dual inclinometers for lumbar spine ROM (flexion, extension, and lateral flexion) and a plastic long-arm goniometer for thoracolumbar ROM (flexion, extension, lateral flexion, and rotation). Intertester reliability was poor for all measurements except for flexion taken with the long-arm goniometer (Table 12.6). The dual inclinometer method had no systematic error, but there was a large random error for all measurements. The authors concluded that the standard error of measurement might be a better indicator of reliability than the ICC.

Reynolds[57] compared intratester and intertester reliability with use of a spondylometer, a plumb line and skin distraction, and an inclinometer. Intertester error was calculated by comparing the results of two testers taking 10 repeated measurements of lumbar flexion, extension, and lateral flexion on 30 volunteers with a mean age of 38.1 years. Highly significant positive correlations were found between flexion–extension

**TABLE 12.6** Intratester and Intertester Reliability for Thoracolumbar and Lumbar ROM

| Author | Subject n | Sample | Instrument | Motions | Intra ICC | Inter ICC | Intra r | Inter r |
|---|---|---|---|---|---|---|---|---|
| Fitzgerald[14] | 17 | Healthy adults | Tape measure* (Schober) | Flexion | | | | 1.0 |
| | | | Universal goniometer+ | Extension | | | | 0.88 |
| | | | | R. lat. flexion | | | | 0.76 |
| | | | | L. lat. flexion | | | | 0.91 |
| Nitschke et al[56] | 34 | Patients with back pain 20–65 yrs | Universal goniometer+ | Flexion | 0.92 | 0.84 | | |
| | | | + | Extension | 0.81 | 0.63 | | |
| | | | | R. lat. flexion | 0.76 | 0.62 | | |
| | | | | Flexion | 0.90 | 0.52 | | |
| | | | Dual inclinometers* | Extension | 0.70 | 0.35 | | |
| | | | | R. lat. flexion | 0.90 | 0.18 | | |
| Williams et al[19] | 15 | Patients with CLBP | Dual inclinometers* | Flexion | | 0.60 | 0.13 – 0.87 | |
| | | | | Extension | | 0.48 | 0.28 – 0.66 | |
| Madson et al[67] | 40 | Healthy adults 20–40 yrs | BROM* | Flexion | 0.67 | | | |
| | | | | Extension | 0.78 | | | |
| | | | | R. lat. flexion | 0.95 | | | |
| | | | | R. rotation | 0.93 | | | |
| Kachingwe and Phillips[68] | 91 | Healthy adults mean age = 28 yrs | BROM* | Lat. flexion | 0.83 – 0.85 | | | |
| | | | | Flexion | 0.79 – 0.84 | | | |
| Kondratek et al[30] | 15 | Healthy Children 5–11 yrs | BROM II* | Flexion | 0.53 – 0.71 | | | |
| | | | | Extension | 0.82 – 0.94 | | | |
| Petersen et al[70] | 21 | Healthy subjects 10–79 yrs | OSI CA-6000+ | Flexion | 0.90 | 0.85 | | |
| | | | + | Extension | 0.96 | 0.96 | | |
| | | | | R. lat. flexion | 0.89 | 0.85 | | |
| | | | | R. rotation | 0.95 | 0.90 | | |

BROM = Back Range of Motion Device; OSI CA-6000 = Spine Motion Analyzer.
* Lumbar ROM.
+ Thoracolumbar ROM.

ROM measured with the inclinometer and that measured with the spondylometer. The inclinometer had acceptable intertester reliability, with the highest reliability for measurement of lateral flexion to the right.

## Validity: Double Inclinometers

Saur and colleagues[49] found that the correlation of radiographic ROM measurements with inclinometer ROM measurements demonstrated an almost linear correlation for flexion (r = 0.98) and total lumbar flexion–extension ROM (r = 0.97), but extension did not correlate as well (r = 0.75).

In contrast to the findings of Saur and colleagues,[49] Samo and coworkers[48] reported poor criterion validity with the use of inclinometers. Samo and coworkers[48] compared radiographic measurements of lumbar ROM in 30 subjects with measurements taken with the following three instruments: a Pleurimeter V (double inclinometer), a carpenter's double inclinometer, and a computed single-sensor inclinometer. All ICCs between radiographs and each method were less than the 0.90 established by the authors as the criterion. Therefore, the authors judged that each method had poor validity.

## Reliability: Universal Goniometer

Nitschke and colleagues[56] compared lumbar spine ROM measurements taken with the universal goniometer and the double inclinometer in a study involving 34 males and females with low-back pain. The goniometer was used to measure all ranges of lumbar spine motion. Intertester reliability was poor for all measurements for both instruments except for flexion using the goniometers (see Table 12.6).

Fitztgerald and associates[14] used the universal goniometer to measure thoracolumbar lateral flexion and extension. Two testers measured half cycle motions in 17 volunteers who were physical therapy students. The intertester reliability was high for left lateral flexion (r = 0.91), good for extension (r = 0.88), and fair for right lateral flexion (r = 0.76).

## Validity: Universal Goniometer

Nattrass and coworkers[43] compared measurements of the thoracolumbar spine taken with the universal goniometer and measurements of the lumbar spine with the Dualer Electric Inclinometer with three measures of impairment. Thirty-four patients between 20 and 65 years of age with chronic low-back pain were the subjects for the study. The results showed that only flexion ROM measured with the goniometer demonstrated greater than 50 percent of the variance in common with one of the disability measures.

## Reliability: Schober Test

Fitzgerald and associates[14] used the Schober technique to measure lumbar flexion and the universal goniometer to measure thoracolumbar lateral flexion and extension. Intertester reliability was calculated from measurements taken by two testers on 17 volunteers who were physical therapy students. Pearson reliability coefficients were calculated on paired results of the two testers (see Table 12.6). Intertester reliability using the Schober Test was excellent with an r value of +1.0.

## Reliability: Modified Schober Test

Many of the following reliability studies were conducted on patient populations that usually have lower reliability scores than healthy populations. However, one can see by looking at Table 12.7 that some of the intrareliability and interreliability coefficients for the modified Schober test (MST) are in the good to excellent category for patient populations.

Haywood and colleagues[58] used the MST to evaluate the measurement properties of spinal mobility in 159 patients with ankylosing spondylitis (133 males and 26 females, 20 to 74 years of age). Fifty-one patients participated in the reliability study in which both intratester (ICC = 0.94) and intertester (ICC = 0.90) reliability were high. Also, the MST had a strong relationship with all mobility measures.

Viitanen and associates[59] employed two physical therapists to use the MST to measure lumbar flexion ROM in 52 patients with ankylosing spondylitis with a mean age of 45 years. Repeat tests were performed within 72 hours from entry on successive days at the same time of day. Intratester

reliability was excellent (ICC = 0.94) and so was intertester reliability (ICC = 0.96).

Jones and associates[17] conducted a repeated measures study of 119 children aged 11 to 16 years to assess the measurement error associated with spinal mobility measures. Thirty children in the sample reported recurrent low-back pain, and 89 children were asymptomatic (Table 12.8). The correlation coefficient for lumbar flexion using the MST was 0.99 for the asymptomatic group and 0.93 for the symptomatic group. Little systematic error was present, but the 95 percent limits of agreement showed that all measures exhibited random error, which was greater in the symptomatic group and could affect the reliability of spinal mobility tests in children with back pain.

Reynolds[57] calculated intertester error by comparing the results of two testers taking 10 repeated measurements of lumbar flexion and extension on 30 volunteers with a mean age of 38.1 years. The MST had acceptable intertester reliability only for extension.

Pile and colleagues[60] had five testers (three physical therapists, a rheumatologist, and a rheumatology registrar) use the MST to measure lumbar flexion twice in each of 10 patients with ankylosing spondylitis. Intertester reliability was fair (r = 0.78).

Lindell and coworkers[9] conducted a study with one medically trained physiotherapist and one medically untrained tester (research assistant) using the MST to measure lumbar flexion in 50 subjects (30 patients with low-back or neck pain, and 20 healthy participants). The intratester reliability was an ICC of 0.87 with a standard error of the measurement (SEM) of 0.3 cm for the medically trained tester, and an ICC of 0.79 with a SEM of 0.7 cm for the other tester. Intertester reliability ranged from an ICC of 0.94 (SEM=0.4 cm) when testing patients to an ICC of 0.22 (SEM=1.0 cm) when testing healthy participants. The intertester ICC for all subjects was 0.79 (SEM=0.7 cm). The authors concluded that reliable measurements could be taken by medically untrained testers using tests like the MST, forward bending fingertip-to-floor test, and lateral bending fingertip-to-thigh test that did not require manual stabilization.

Gill and coworkers[37] compared the reliability of four methods of measurement including fingertip-to-floor distance, the Modified Schober technique, the two-inclinometer method, and a photometric technique. The subjects of the study were 10 volunteers (5 men and 5 women) aged 24 to 34 years. Repeatability of the fingertip-to-floor method was poor (coefficient of variation (CV) = 14.1 percent). Repeatability of the inclinometer for the measurement of full flexion was also poor (CV = 33.9 percent). The MST yielded a CV of 0.9 percent for full flexion and a CV of 2.8 percent for extension.

## Validity: Schober and Modified Schober Tests

Macrae and Wright[3] tested the validity of both the original two-mark Schober technique and a three-mark modification of the Schober technique (modified Schober). The authors

**TABLE 12.7** Reliability of Schober Tests: Modified Schober Test (MST) and Modified–Modified Schober Test (MMST)

| Test Author | MST Lindell et al[9] | | MST Haywood et al[58] | | MST Jones et al[17] | | MST Pile et al[60] | MMST Williams et al[19] | | MMST Tousignant et al[50] | |
|---|---|---|---|---|---|---|---|---|---|---|---|
| Sample | 20 healthy and 30 patients with back/neck pain 20–63 yrs n = 20  n = 50 | | Patients with ankylosing spondylitis (AS) 18–75 yrs n = 26  n = 51 | | 89 healthy and 30 patients with LBP 11–16 yrs n = 30  n = 89 | | Patients with AS 26–73 yrs n = 10 | Patients with CLBP 25–53 yrs n = 15 | | Patients with LBP Mean age = 44 yrs n = 31 | |
| Motion | Intra ICC | Inter ICC | Intra ICC | Inter ICC | Inter r | Inter r | Inter | Intra r | Inter ICC | Intra ICC | Inter ICC |
| Flexion | 0.87 | 0.79 | 0.90 | 0.94 | 0.94 | 0.94 | 0.78 | 0.78 - 0.89 | 0.72 | 0.95 | 0.91 |
| Extension | | | | | | | | 0.69 - 0.91 | 0.76 | | |

CLBP = chronic low-back pain; LBP = low-back pain. ICC = intraclass correlation coefficient; r = pearson product moment correlation coefficient; Intra = intratester reliability; Inter = intertester reliability.

found a linear relationship between measurements of lumbar flexion obtained by these methods and radiographic measurements. The correlation coefficient was 0.90 between the Schober technique and radiographs (x-rays), with an SE of 6.2 degrees. The correlation coefficient was 0.97 between the modified Schober measurement and the radiographic measurements, with an SE of 3.25 degrees. Clinical identification of the lumbosacral junction was not easy, and faulty placement of skin marks seriously impaired the accuracy of the unmodified Schober technique. Placement of marks 2 cm too low led to an overestimate of 14 degrees. Marks placed 2 cm too high led to an underestimate of 15 degrees. In the MST, the same errors in placement led to overestimates and underestimates of 5 and 3 degrees, respectively.

**TABLE 12.8** Reliability of Thoracolumbar Lateral Flexion ROM: Tape Measure

| Test Author | Fingertip-to-Thigh Alaranta et al[18] | | Fingertip-to-Thigh Lindell et al[9] | | Fingertip-to-Thigh Jones et al[17] | | Fingertip-to-Floor Haywood et al[58] | | Fingertip-to-Floor Pile et al[60] |
|---|---|---|---|---|---|---|---|---|---|
| Sample | 508 employed workers* 35–45 yrs n = 34  n = 93 | | 20 healthy and 30 patients with back/neck pain 22–55 yrs n = 20  n =30 | | 89 healthy and 30 patients with LBP 11–16 yrs n = 89  n = 30 | | Patients with AS 18–75 yrs n=26  n=51 | | Patients with AS† 28–73 yrs n= 10 |
| Motion | Intra r | Inter r | Intra ICC | Inter ICC | Intra r | Intra r | Intra ICC | Inter ICC | Inter |
| Right and Left | 0.81 | 0.91 | | | | | | | |
| Right | | | 0.99 | 0.93 | 0.99 | 0.93 | 0.98 | 0.98 | 0.83 |
| Left | | | 0.94 | 0.95 | 0.99 | 0.95 | 0.95 | 0.95 | 0.79 |

AS = ankylosing spondylitis; ICC = intraclass correlation coefficient; LBP = low-back pain; r = Pearson product moment correlation coefficient; Intra = intratester reliability;  Inter = intertester reliability.
* Some workers had back or neck pain, and some had no pain.

Viitanen and associates[59] found that the MST, thoracolumbar lateral flexion, and fingertip-to-floor test using a tape measure had the most significant correlations with thoracolumbar changes seen on x-ray (calcifications of discs, ossification of liagments, and changes in the apophyseal joints).

In contrast to the preceding studies, the following two studies did not find good evidence for the validity of the Schober and the MST. Portek and colleagues[63] compared the MST and two other clinical methods with each other and with radiographs. These authors found little correlation either among the measurements obtained by two testers using three clinical techniques to measure lumbar flexion in 11 subjects or among the three clinical techniques and radiographs. A Pearson's reliability coefficient of 0.43 was found between the MST and the radiographic measurement. The intertester error for the MST for lumbar flexion showed significant differences between testers according to paired t-tests. However, intertester error was calculated between 10 measurements on 10 different days, and the authors attributed the error to difficulties in reestablishing a neutral starting position and the mobility of the skin over the landmarks.

Quack and colleagues,[8] in a study involving 112 female subjects with a mean age of 53 years, compared the MST with magnetic resonance imaging (MRI) findings. The authors did not find any statistically significant findings between the MST and MRI findings. Therefore, the validity for the MST with respect to segmental lumbar degeneration was questioned.

## Reliability: Modified–Modified Schober Test

Williams and coworkers[19] measured flexion and extension on 15 patient volunteers with a mean age of 36 years who had chronic low-back pain. The authors compared the MMST,[20] which is also referred to as the simplified skin distraction method,[21] with the double inclinometer method. Intratester Pearson correlation coefficients for the MMST were an r of 0.89 for tester 1, an r of 0.78 for tester 2, and an r of 0.83 for tester 3. Intertester Pearson correlation coefficients between the three physical therapist testers were an r of 0.72 for flexion and an r of 0.77 for extension with use of the MMST. The therapists underwent training in the use of standardized procedures for each method prior to testing. According to the testers, the MMST was easier and quicker to use than the double inclinometer method. The only disadvantage to using the MMST method is that norms have not been established for all age groups.

Tousignant and associates[50] used the MMST to obtain lumbar flexion ROM measurements in 31 patients with low-back pain. The authors found excellent intratester reliability (ICC = 0.95) and very good intertester reliability (ICC = 0.91).

## Validity: Modified–Modified Schober Test

The ease of finding landmarks for measuring lumbar flexion and extension with the MMST appears to make this method a better choice over the Schober and MST; however, more studies need to be performed to confirm its validity. Tousignant and associates[50] used the MMST to obtain lumbar flexion ROM measurements in 31 patients with low-back pain. The authors compared these measurements with measurements calculated on x-rays as the gold standard. The comparison showed that the MMST had moderate validity (r = 0.67; 95% confidence interval = 0.44 to 0.84). The minimum metrically detectable change (MMDC) of 1 cm was determined to be excellent in this group of patients, but because of the moderate validity finding, the authors suggest that further studies need to be perfomed to establish the test's validity.

## Reliability: Prone Press-Up (for Extension)

Bandy and Reese[64] compared the reliability of the prone press-up to measure lumbar extension under two conditions: with and without a strap to control pelvic motion. Sixty-three unimpaired individuals with a mean age of 26 years participated as subjects in the study. Measurements of extension ROM were taken by an experienced group and a student group using a tape measure. Intratester reliability was excellent for the experienced group in both the strapped (ICC = 0.91) and unstrapped (ICC = 0.90) conditions and good for the student group. Intertester reliability for both the strapped and unstrapped conditions was good (ICC = 0.87 and ICC = 0.85, respectively).

## Reliability and Validity: Fingertip-to-Floor Test (for Forward Flexion)

Perret and colleagues[10] included 32 patients with low-back pain with a mean age of 52 years in a reliability study. Intratester and intertester reliability were excellent (ICC = 0.99). Ten patients with low-back pain (mean age of 42 years) participated in the validity study. Two lateral radiographs were taken: one of the dorsal spine with the patients in the neutral standing position and one taken in full trunk flexion. Spearman's correlation coefficient for this validity test of trunk flexion was excellent (r = 0.96). Seventy-two patients with low-back pain participated in the responsiveness study. High values were found for responsiveness for the fingertip-to-floor method, which showed that the fingertip test has very good sensitivity to change.

Haywood and colleagues[58] also assessed reliability, validity, and responsiveness of the fingertip-to-floor forward flexion test in 77 patients with ankylosing spondylitis. The authors found both intratester and intertester reliability to be excellent, with ICCs between 0.94 and 0.99. Also, the test was the most responsive to self-perceived changes in health at 6 months. Authors recommended this test for clinical practice and research.

Viitanen and associates[59] found that the fingertip-to-floor test had significant correlations with thoracolumbar changes seen on x-ray (calcifications of disc, ossification of ligaments, and changes in apophyseal joints).

Pile and associates[60] found that the sagittal plane fingertip-to-floor test had an excellent intertester reliability (ICC = 0.95) in a study in which three physical therapists, a rheumatologist, and a rheumatology registrar measured 10 patients twice.

Lindell and coworkers[9], in a study of 50 subjects (30 patients with low-back or neck pain, and 20 healthy participants), found intratester reliability to be excellent with an ICC = 0.95 and SEM=0.9 cm for both an experienced physiotherapist and a medically untrained research assistant. Intertester reliability was also excellent with ICC values greater than 0.95 and SEM values ranging from 0.9 to 1.2 cm.

Gauvin, Riddle, and Rothstein[65] used a modified version of the fingertip-to-floor test by placing subjects on a stool and then measuring the distance from the tip of the subject's middle finger to the stool. Seventy-three patients with low-back pain participated in the study, and both intratester (ICC = 0.98) and intertester (ICC = 0.95) reliability were excellent. The modified version of the test is supposed to account for the fact that many people can reach the floor, and in this study 27 percent of the subjects were able to reach the top of the stool or beyond the top.

In contrast to the preceding studies, the following study did not find acceptable retest reliability. Gill and coworkers[61] compared the reliability of four methods of measurement including fingertip-to-floor distance, the Modified Schober technique, the two-inclinometer method, and a photometric technique. The subjects of the study were 10 volunteers (5 men and 5 women) aged 24 to 34 years. Repeatability of the fingertip-to-floor method was poor (CV = 14.1 percent). Repeatability of the inclinometer for the measurement of full flexion was also poor (CV = 33.9 percent).

### Reliability: Fingertip-to-Thigh Test (for Lateral Flexion)

Alaranta and associates,[18] in a study involving 508 white and blue collar workers between the ages of 35 and 54 years, found that the intertester reliability was high at an interval of 1 week for the fingertip-to-thigh method of assessing thoracolumbar lateral flexion. Intratester reliability at the interval of 1 year was remarkably good for the large time interval between tests (see Table 12.8).

Jones and colleagues,[17] in a study of 119 children ages 11 to 16 years (30 children with low-back pain and 89 asymptomatic children), found excellent correlation coefficients for right and left lateral flexion in the low-back pain group (r = 0.93 to 0.95) and in the asymptomatic group (r = 0.99). Limits of agreement, expressed as the mean difference between test and retest $\pm$ 1.96 $\times$ SD of the difference between test and retest, were 0.16 mm $\pm$ 6.78 for right lateral flexion for the asymptomatic children but much larger for the symptomatic group (0.50 mm $\pm$ 16.93 mm). The authors concluded that there was very little systematic bias but all measures exhibited random error, which was larger in the symptomatic group (see Table 12.8).

Lindell and coworkers[9] conducted a study of 50 subjects (30 patients with low-back or neck pain, and 20 healthy subjects) who were tested by two examiners. The intratester reliability for the fingertip-to-thigh test for lateral bending was excellent for the experienced physiotherapist (ICC = 0.94-0.99, SEM = 0.5-1.0 cm) and fair for the medically untrained tester (ICC = 0.73-0.86, SEM = 1.4-1.6 cm). Intertester reliability was fair to excellent depending on the group and side tested, with ICCs ranging from 0.79 to 0.98 and SEMs ranging from 0.9 to 1.5 cm.

### Reliability: Back Range of Motion Device

Reliability results are inconclusive, and it appears that additional research needs to be done on this method of measurement to warrant the expenditure involved in purchasing the back range of motion (BROM) device. The BROM II device (Performance Attainment Associates, Roseville, MN) is a revised and improved version of the original BROM. Two groups of researchers investigating the reliability of the BROM II device agreed that the instrument had high reliability for measuring lumbar lateral flexion and low reliability for measuring extension. However, the two groups differed regarding the reliability of the BROM II device for measuring flexion and rotation. Breum, Wiberg, and Bolton[66] concluded that the BROM II device could measure flexion and rotation reliably, whereas Madson, Youdas, and Suman[67] determined that rotation but not flexion could be reliably measured (see Table 12.6). Potential sources of error identified by the authors[67] included slippage of the device over the sacrum during flexion and extension and variations in the identification of landmarks from one measurement to another.

Kondratek and colleagues[30] used the BROM II to conduct one of the few studies on lumbar ROM in children. The subjects were 225 normally developing children ages 5 to 11 years of age. Two physical therapists experienced working with children were trained in the use of the BROM II. Intrarater reliability on 15 childern was good to excellent for one tester for all half cycle motions except for flexion, which was unacceptable (ICC = 0.53). The intratester reliability for the second tester ranged from an ICC of 0.71 for flexion and an ICC of 0.76 for right lateral flexion, to an ICC of 0.91 for right rotation.

Kachingwe and Phillips[68] employed two testers to use the BROM to measure lumbar motions in 91 healthy men and women with a mean age of 28 years. Intratester reliability for lateral flexion was good (ICC = 0.85 to 0.83), forward flexion was good to fair (ICC = 0.84 to 0.79), and extension and rotation was fair to poor (ICC = 0.76 to 0.58). Intertester reliability was fair to poor for all lumbar motions and for pelvic inclination (ICC = 0.76 to 0.58).

### Reliability: Motion Analysis Systems

A number of researchers have investigated the reliability of motion analysis systems including, among others, the CA-6000 Spine Motion Analyzer,[14,29] the SPINETRAK,[71] and the FASTRAK (Polhemus, Colchester, VT).[69] Two research groups found that intratester reliability for measuring lumbar flexion was very high with use of the CA-6000.[29,45] In one of the studies, both intratester and intertester reliability ranged from good to high for lumbar forward flexion and extension, but intratester and intertester reliability were poor for rotation.[29]

In a study using the SPINETRAK,[72] ICCs were 0.89 or greater for intratester reliability. ICCs for intertester reliability ranged from 0.77 for thoracolumbar flexion to 0.95 for thoracolumbopelvic flexion. Steffan and colleagues[69] used the FASTRAK system to measure segmental motion in forward lumbar flexion by tracking sensors attached to Kirschner wires that had been inserted into the spinous processes of L3 and L4 in 16 healthy men. Segmental forward flexion showed large intersubject variation.

Van Herp and associates[33] used the Polhemus Navigation Sciences 3 Space System to measure ROM in 100 healthy subjects (50 male and 50 female subjects) ranging in age from 20 to 77 years of age. Recorded ranges of motion including flexion, extension, lateral flexion and rotation showed a level of agreement with x-ray data indicating good concurrent validity.

## Summary

The sampling of studies reviewed in this chapter reflects the amount of effort that has been directed toward finding reliable and valid methods for measuring spinal motion. Each method reviewed has advantages and disadvantages, and clinicians should select a method that appears to be appropriate for their particular clinical situation.

# REFERENCES

1. Cyriax, JH, and Cyriax, P: Illustrated Manual of Orthopaedic Medicine. Butterworths, London, 1983.
2. Bogduk, N: Clinical Anatomy of the Lumbar Spine and Sacrum, ed 3. Churchill Livingstone, New York, 1997.
3. Macrae, IF, and Wright, V: Measurement of back movement. Ann Rheum Dis 28:584, 1969.
4. American Medical Association: Guides to the Evaluation of Permanent Impairment, ed 5. Cocchiarella, L, and Andersson, GBJ (eds). AMA, Chicago, 2000.
5. American Academy of Orthopaedic Surgeons: Joint Motion: Method of Measuring and Recording. AAOS, Chicago, 1965.
6. American Medical Association: Guides to the Evaluation of Permanent Impairment ed 3. Chicago, 1988.
7. Gerhardt, J, Cocchiarella, L, and Lea, R: The Practical Guide to Range of Motion Assessment. AMA, Chicago, 2002.
8. Quack, C, et al: Do MRI findings correlate with mobility tests? An explorative analysis of the test validity with regard to structure. Eur Spine J 16:803, 2007.
9. Lindell, O, Eriksson, L, and Strender, L-E: The reliability of a 10-test package for patients with prolonged back and neck pain: Could an examiner without formal medical education be used without loss of quality? A methodological study. BMC Musculoskelet Dis 8:31, 2007.
10. Perret, C, et al: Validity, reliability, and responsiveness of the fingertip-to-floor test. Arch Phys Med Rehabil 82:1566, 2001.
11. Kraus, H, and Hirschland, RP: Minimum muscular fitness tests in school children. Res Q Exerc Sport 25:178, 1954.
12. Nicholas, JA: Risk factors, sports medicine and the orthopedic system: An overview. J Sports Med 3:243, 1975.
13. Brodie, DA, Bird, HA and Wright,V: Joint laxity in selected athletic populations. Med Sci Sports Exerc 14:190, 1982.
14. Fitzgerald, GK, et al: Objective assessment with establishment of normal values for lumbar spine range of motion. Phys Ther 63:1776, 1983.
15. Sahrmann, SA: Diagnosis and Treatment of Movement Impairment Syndromes. Mosby, St. Louis, 2002.
16. Mellin, GP: Accuracy of measuring lateral flexion of the spine with a tape measure. Clin Biomech 1:85, 1986.
17. Jones, MA, et al: Measurement error associated with spinal mobility measures in children with and without low-back pain. Acta Paediatr 91:1339, 2002.
18. Alaranta, H, et al: Flexibility of the spine: Normative values of goniometric and tape measurements. Scand J Rehab Med 26:147, 1994.
19. Williams, R, et al: Reliability of the modified–modified Schober and double inclinometer methods for measuring lumbar flexion and extension. Phys Ther 73:26, 1993.
20. Van Adrichem, JAM, and van der Korst, JK: Assessment of the flexibility of the lumbar spine. A pilot study in children and adolescents. Scand J Rheumatol 2:87, 1973.
21. Greene, WB, and Heckman, JD (eds): The Clinical Measurement of Joint Motion. American Academy of Orthopaedic Surgeons. Rosemont, IL, 1994.
22. Battie, MC, et al: The role of spinal flexibility in back pain complaints in industry. A prospective study. Spine 15:768, 1990.
23. Loebl, WY: Measurement of spinal posture and range of spinal movement. Ann Phys Med 9:103, 1967.
24. Ng, JK, et al: Range of motion and lordosis of the lumbar spine: Reliability of measurement and normative values. Spine 26:53, 2001.
25. Sullivan, MS, Dickinson, CE and Troup, JDG: The influence of age and gender on lumbar spine range of motion. A study of 1126 healthy subjects. Spine 19:682, 1994.
26. Moll, JMH, and Wright, V: Normal range of spinal mobility: An objective clinical study. Ann Rheum Dis 30:381, 1971.
27. Anderson, JAD, and Sweetman, BJ: A combined flexi-rule hydrogoniometer for measurement of lumbar spine and its sagittal movement. Rheumatol Rehabil 14:173, 1975.
28. Gracovetsky, S, et al: A database for estimating normal spinal motion derived from non-invasive measurements. Spine 20:1036, 1995.
29. McGregor, AH, McCarthy, D and Hughes, SP: Motion characteristics of the lumbar spine in the normal population. Spine 20:2421, 1995.
30. Kondratek, M, et al: Normative values for active lumbar range of motion in children. Pediatr Phys Ther 19:236, 2007.
31. Troke, M, et al: A normative database of lumbar ranges of motion. Man Ther 10: 198, 2005.

32. Troke, M, et al: A new comprehensive normative database of lumbar spine ranges of motion. Clin Rehabil 15:371, 2001.
33. Van Herp, G, et al: Three dimensional lumbar spine kinematics: a study of range of movement in 100 healthy subjects aged 20 to 60+ years. Rheumatology 39:1337, 2000.
34. Bookstein, NA, et al: Lumbar extension range of motion in elementary school children. Abstr Phys Ther 72:S35, 1992.
35. Wong, KWN, et al: The flexion–extension profile of lumbar spine in 100 healthy volunteers. Spine 29:1636, 2004.
36. Ensink, FB, et al: Lumbar range of motion. Influence of time of day and individuals factors on measurements. Spine 21:1339, 1996.
37. Sughara, M, et al: Epidemiological study on the change of mobility of the thoraco-lumbar spine and body height with age as indices for senility. J Hum Ergol (Tokyo) 10:49, 1981.
38. Freidrich, M, et al: Spinal posture during stooped walking under vertical space constraints. Spine 25:1118, 2000.
39. Sjolie, AN: Access to pedestrian roads, daily activities and physical performance of adolescents. Spine 25:1965, 2000.
40. Sullivan, MS, Shoaf, LD, and Riddle, DL: The relationship of lumbar flexion to disability in patients with low back pain. Phys Ther 80:240, 2000.
41. Lundberg, G, and Gerdle, B: Correlations between joint and spinal mobility, spinal sagittal configuration, segmental mobility, segmental pain symptoms and disabilities in female homecare personnel. Scand J Rehab Med 32:124, 2000.
42. Kujala UM, et al: Lumbar mobility and low back pain during adolescence. A longitudinal three-year follow-up study in athletes and controls. Am J Sports Med 25:363, 1997.
43. Nattrass, CL, et al: Lumbar spine range of motion as a measure of physical and functional impairment: An investigation of validity (abstract). Clin Rehabil 13:211, 1999.
44. Shirley, FR, et al: Comparison of lumbar range of motion using three measurement devices in patients with chronic low back pain. Spine 19:779, 1994.
45. Hsieh, CY, and Pringle, RK: Range of motion of the lumbar spine required for four activities of daily living. J Manipulative Physiol Ther 17:353, 1994.
46. Levine, D, et al: Sagittal lumbar spine position during standing, walking and running at various gradients. J Athlet Train 42:29, 2007.
47. Littlewood, C, and May, S: Measurement of range of movement in the lumbar spine: What methods are valid? A systematic review. Physiother 93:201, 2007.
48. Samo, DG, et al: Validity of three lumbar sagittal motion measurement methods: Surface inclinometers compared with radiographs. J Occup Environ Med 39:209, 1997.
49. Saur, PMM, et al: Lumbar range of motion: Reliability and validity of the inclinometer technique in the clinical measurement of trunk flexibility. Spine 21:1332, 1996.
50. Tousignant, M, et al: The Modified-Modified. Schober test for range of motion assessment of lumbar flexion in patients with low back pain: A study of criterion validity, intra-and inter-rater reliability and minimum metrically detectable change. Disabil Rehabil 27:553, 2005.
51. Essendrop, M, et al: Measures of low back function: A review of reproducibility studies. Clin Biomech 17:235, 2002.
52. Patel, RS: Intratester and intertester reliability of the inclinometer in measuring lumbar flexion. Phys Ther 72:S44, 1992.
53. Mayer, RS, et al: Variance in the measurement of sagittal lumbar range of motion among examiners, subjects, and instruments. Spine 20:1489, 1995.
54. Chen, SP, et al: Reliability of the lumbar sagittal motion measurement methods: Surface inclinometers. J Occup Environ Med 39:217, 1997.
55. Mayer, TG, et al: Spinal range of motion. Accuracy and sources of error with inclinometric measurement. Spine 22:1976, 1997.
56. Nitschkje, JE, et al: Reliability of the American Medical Association Guides' Model for Measuring Spinal Range of Motion. Its implication for whole-person impairment ratings. Spine 24:262, 1999.
57. Reynolds, PMG: Measurement of spinal mobility: A comparison of three methods. Rheumatol Rehabil 14:180, 1975.
58. Haywood, KL, et al: Spinal mobility in ankylosing spondylitis: Reliability, validity and responsivenesss. Rheumatol 43:750, 2004.
59. Viitanen, JV, et al: Clinical assessment of spinal mobility measurements in ankylosing spondylitis: A compact set for follow-up and trials? Clin Rheumatol 19:131, 2000.
60. Pile, KD, et al: Clinical assessment of ankylosing spondylitis: A study of observer variatioin in spinal measurements. Br J Rheumatol 30:29, 1991.

61. Gill, K, et al: Repeatability of four clinical methods for assessment of lumbar spinal motion. Spine 13:50, 1988.

62. Miller, MH, et al: Measurement of spinal mobility in the sagittal plane: New skin distraction technique compared with established methods. J Rheumatol 11:4, 1984.

63. Portek, I, et al: Correlation between radiographic and clinical measurement of lumbar spine movement. Br J Rheumatol 22:197, 1983.

64. Bandy, WD, and Reese, NB: Strapped versus unstrapped technique of the prone press-up for measurement of lumbar extension using a tape measure: Differences in magnitude and reliability of measurements. Arch Phys Med Rehabil 85:99, 2004.

65. Gauvin, MG, Riddle, DL, and Rothstein, JM: Reliability of clinical measurements of forward bending using the modified fingertip-to-floor method. Phys Ther 70:443, 2000.

66. Breum, J, Wiberg, J, and Bolton, JE: Reliability and concurrent validity of the BROM II for measuring lumbar mobility. J Manipulative Physiol Ther 18:497, 1995.

67. Madson, TJ, Youdas, JW and Suman, VJ: Reproducibility of lumbar spine range of motion measurements using the back range of motion device. J Orthop Sports Phys Ther 29:470, 1999.

68. Kachingwe, AF, and Phillips, BJ: Inter and Intrarater reliability of a back range of motion instrument. Arch Phys Med Rehabil 86:2347, 2005.

69. Steffan, T, et al: A new technique for measuring lumbar segmental motion in vivo: Method, accuracy and preliminary results. Spine 22:156, 1997.

70. Petersen, CM, et al: Intraobserver and interobserver reliability of asymptomatic subject's thoracolumbar range of motion using the OSI CA-6000 Spine Motion Analyzer. J Orthop Sports Phys Ther 220:207, 1997.

71. Robinson, ME, et al: Intrasubject reliability of spinal range of motion and velocity determined by video motion analysis. Phys Ther 73:626, 1993.

# Chapter 13

# The Temporomandibular Joint

## ⬭ Structure and Function

### Temporomandibular Joint

#### Anatomy

The temporomandibular joint (TMJ) is the articulation between the mandible, the articular disc, and the temporal bone of the skull (Fig. 13.1A, B). The disc divides the joint into two distinct parts, which are referred to as the upper and lower joints. The larger upper joint is formed by the convex articular eminence, concave mandibular fossa of the temporal bone, and the superior surface of the disc. The lower joint consists of the convex surface of the mandibular condyle and the concave inferior surface of the disc.[1-3] The articular disc helps the convex mandible conform to the convex articular surface of the temporal bone.[2]

The TMJ capsule is described as being thin and loose above the disc but taut below the disc in the lower joint. Short capsular fibers surround the joint and extend between the mandibular condyle and the articular disc and between the disc and the temporal eminence.[3] Longer capsular fibers extend from the temporal bone to the mandible.

The primary ligament associated with the TMJ is the temporomandibular ligament. The stylomandibular and the sphenomandibular ligaments (Fig. 13.2) are considered to be accessory ligaments.[4,5] The muscles associated with the TMJ are the medial and lateral pterygoids, temporalis, masseter, digastric, stylohyoid, mylohyoid, and geniohyoid.

#### Osteokinematics

The upper joint is an amphiarthrodial gliding joint, and the lower joint is a hinge joint. The TMJ as a whole allows motions in three planes around three axes. All of the motions except mouth closing begin from the resting position of the joint in which the teeth are slightly separated (freeway space).[3,6] The amount of freeway space, which usually varies from 2 mm to 4 mm, allows free anterior, posterior, and lateral movement of the mandible.

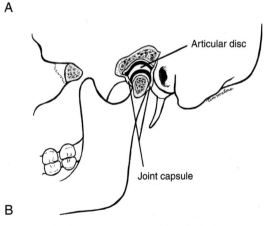

**FIGURE 13.1  A:** Lateral view of the skull showing the temporomandibular joint (TMJ) and surrounding structures. **B:** A lateral view of the TMJ showing the articular disc and a portion of the joint capsule.

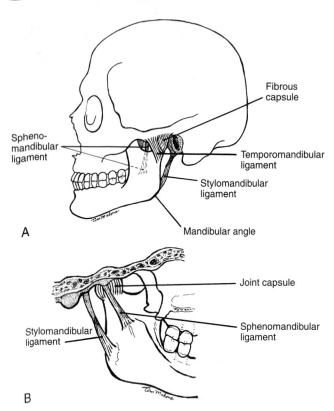

**FIGURE 13.2 A:** A lateral view of the temporomandibular joint showing the oblique fibers of the temporomandibular ligament and the stylomandibular and sphenomandibular ligaments. **B:** A medial view of the temporomandibular joint showing the medial portion of the joint capsule and the stylomandibular and sphenomandibular ligaments.

The functional motions permitted are mandibular depression (mouth opening), mandibular elevation (mouth closing), protrusion (anterior translation; Fig.13.3) and retrusion (posterior translation; Fig.13.4), and right and left lateral excursion or laterotrusion (lateral deviation; Fig. 13.5). Maximal contact of the teeth in mouth closing is called centric occlusion.

Reinforcement of the TMJ is provided primarily by the temporomandibular ligament, which limits mouth opening, retrusion, and lateral excursion. The functions of the stylomandibular and sphenomandibular ligaments are somewhat controversial, but these ligaments appear to help suspend the mandible from the cranium.[4] According to Magee,[7] the ligaments keep the condyle, disc, and temporal bone in close approximation. These ligaments also may prevent excessive protrusion, but their exact function has not been verified.

The inferior head of the lateral pterygoid muscles and the digastric muscles produce mandibular depression (mouth opening),[1,3–7] whereas the mylohyoid and geniohyoid muscles assist in the motion, especially against resistance.[3,7] Mandibular elevation (mouth closing) is produced by bilateral contractions of the temporalis, masseter, and medial pterygoid muscles.[1,3–7] Mandibular protrusion is a result of bilateral action of the masseter,[1,7] medial,[1,3,7] and lateral[3–8] pterygoid muscles, which may be assisted by the mylohyoid, stylohyoid, and digastric muscles.[7] Retrusion is brought about by bilateral action of the posterior fibers of the temporalis muscles[1,3–7]; by the digastric,[1,3–7] middle, and deep fibers of the masseter[3,7]; and by the stylohyoid, mylohyoid,[1,7] and geniohyoid[1,3,7] muscles. Mandibular lateral excursion is produced by a unilateral contraction of the medial and lateral pterygoid muscles,[1–7] which produce contralateral motion, whereas a unilateral contraction of the temporalis muscle causes lateral motion to the same side.

Cervical spine muscles may be activated in conjunction with TMJ muscles because of the close functional relationship that exists between the head and the neck.[1,4–11] Extension of the head and neck has been found to occur simultaneously with mouth opening, whereas flexion of the head and neck accompanies mouth closing. These coordinated and parallel movements at the TMJ and cervical spine joints have been observed in studies, and researchers suggest that preprogrammed neural commands may simultaneously activate both jaw and neck muscles.[9–11]

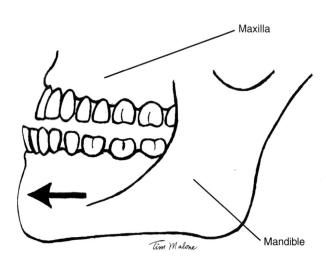

**FIGURE 13.3** Protrusion is an anterior motion of the mandible in relation to the maxilla.

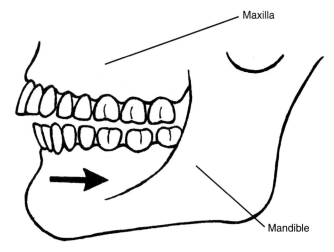

**FIGURE 13.4** Retrusion is a posterior motion of the mandible in relation to the maxilla.

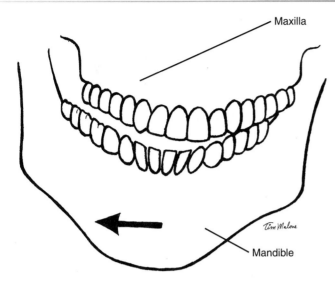

**FIGURE 13.5** Lateral excursion is a lateral motion of the mandible to either side.

## Arthrokinematics

Mandibular depression (mouth opening) occurs in the sagittal plane and is accomplished by rotation and sliding of the mandibular condyles. Condylar rotation is combined with anterior and inferior sliding of the condyles on the inferior surface of the discs, which also slide anteriorly (translate) along the temporal articular eminences. Mandibular elevation (mouth closing) is accomplished by rotation of the mandibular condyles on the discs and sliding of the discs with the condyles posteriorly and superiorly on the temporal articular eminences.

In protrusion, the bilateral condyles and discs translate together anteriorly and inferiorly along the temporal articular eminences. The movement takes place at the upper joint, and no rotation occurs during this motion. In lateral excursion, one mandibular condyle and disc slide inferiorly, anteriorly, and medially along the articular eminence. The other mandibular condyle rotates about a vertical axis and slides medially within the mandibular fossa. For example, in left lateral excursion, the left condyle spins and the right condyle slides anteriorly.

## Capsular Pattern

In the capsular pattern, mandibular depression is limited.[7]

# RANGE OF MOTION TESTING PROCEDURES: Temporomandibular Joint

## Landmarks for Testing Procedures

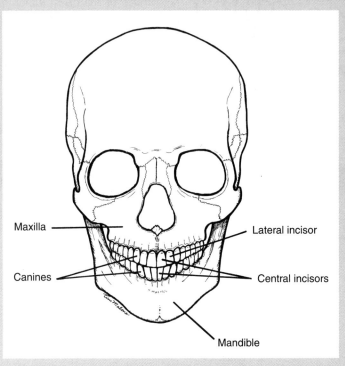

**FIGURE 13.6** The adult has between 28 and 32 permanent teeth, including 8 incisors, 4 canines, 8 premolars, and 8 to 12 molars. The central incisors serve as landmarks for ruler placement.

## ● DEPRESSION OF THE MANDIBLE (MOUTH OPENING)

Motion occurs in the sagittal plane around a medial–lateral axis. Functionally, the mandible is able to depress approximately 35 mm to 50 mm so that the subject's three fingers or two knuckles can be placed between the upper and the lower central incisor teeth.[7] According to the consensus judgments of the Permanent Impairment Conference in 1995, the normal range of motion (ROM) for mouth opening ranges between 40 mm and 50 mm.[12] See Table 13.1 in the Research Findings section for additional normal values. The mean ROM for depression of the mandible in Table 13.1 ranges from 41 mm to 58.6 mm.

The Research Diagnostic Criteria for Temporomandibular Disorders (RDC/TMD) recommends that the examiner observe pain-free active mouth opening and describe fully any deviations of the mandible that take place during the motion.[13] The observation of active mouth opening should be followed with measurements of maximal active mouth opening and passive mouth opening.

## Testing Position

Place the subject sitting, with the cervical spine in 0 degrees of flexion, extension, lateral flexion, and rotation.

## Stabilization

Stabilize the posterior aspect of the subject's head and neck to prevent flexion, extension, lateral flexion, and rotation of the cervical spine.

## Testing Motions

### Active Pain Free Mouth Opening

Ask the subject to open his or her mouth slowly and as far as possible without pain. Observe the motion for any lateral excursion of the mandible. In normal active movement, no lateral mandibular motion occurs during mandibular depression (Fig. 13.7). If lateral excursion does occur, it may take the form of either a C-shaped or an S-shaped curve. With a C-shaped curve, the lateral excursion is to one side and should be noted on the recording form (Fig. 13.8). With an S-shaped curve, the lateral excursion occurs first to one side and then to the opposite side.[7] Include a description of the deviation on the recording form (Fig. 13.9).

### Active Mouth Opening

Ask the subject to make an effort to open his or her mouth as wide as possible even if pain is present.

**FIGURE 13.7** Normal maximal active mouth opening.

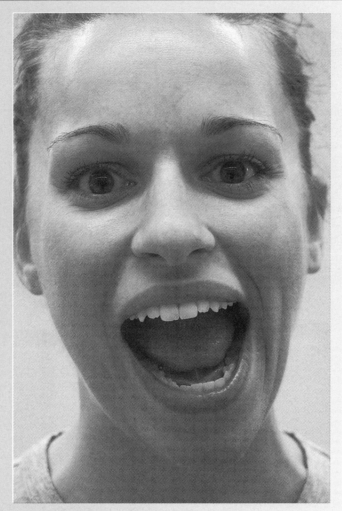

**FIGURE 13.8**  Abnormal mouth opening with lateral deviation to the left.

**FIGURE 13.9**  Examples of recording temporomandibular motions. **A:** Lateral deviation R and L on opening, maximal opening is 4 cm; lateral excursions are equal and 1 cm in each direction; protrusion on functional opening (dashed line). **B:** Opening limited to 1 cm; deviation to the left on opening; lateral excursion greater to the R than to L. **C:** Protrusion is 1 cm; lateral deviation to R on protrusion (indicates weak pterygoid on opposite side). Adapted from Magee, DJ: Orthopedic Physical Assessment, ed 3. WB Saunders, Philadelphia, 1997, p. 165, with permission.

## Testing Motions

### Passive Mouth Opening

Grasp the mandible so that it fits between the thumb and the index finger, and pull the mandible inferiorly (Fig. 13.10). The subject may assist with the motion by opening the mouth as far as possible. The end of the motion occurs when resistance is felt and attempts to produce additional motion cause the head to nod forward (cervical flexion).

### Normal End-Feel

The end-feel is firm owing to stretching of the joint capsule; retrodiscal tissue; the temporomandibular ligament; and the masseter, temporalis, and medial pterygoid muscles.[6,7]

### Measurement Method

Use a millimeter ruler to measure the vertical distance between the edge of the upper central incisor and the corresponding edge of the lower central incisor. The correct ruler placement is shown in Figure 13.11.

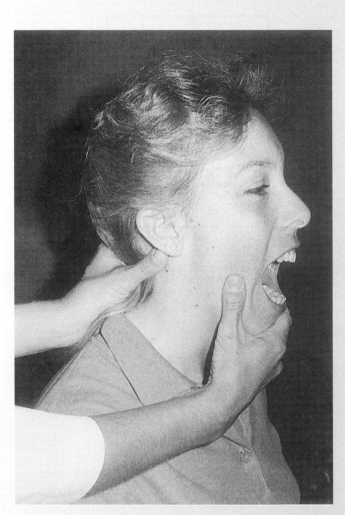

**FIGURE 13.10** At the end of passive mandibular depression (mouth opening), one of the examiner's hands maintains the end of the range of motion by pulling the jaw inferiorly. The examiner's other hand holds the back of the subject's head to prevent cervical motion.

**FIGURE 13.11** Use a millimeter ruler to measure the vertical distance between the edge of a lower central incisor and the edge of the opposing upper central incisor to measure mouth opening.

## ● OVERBITE

**Overbite,** which is the amount that the upper teeth extend over the lower teeth when the mouth is closed, is usually added to the mouth opening measurements. This addition provides a more accurate measurement of mouth opening ROM, especially in persons with a large overbite. Most normal values published from research studies add the amount of overbite to mouth opening values as recommended by the RDC/TMD criteria.

## Measurement Method

When the person's mouth is closed, use a nontoxic marking pencil to make a horizontal line on the lower central incisors at the bottom edge of the overlapping upper central incisors[14] (Fig.13.12). After the line is drawn and the person's mouth is opened, measure the amount of overbite between the horizontal line and upper edge of the mandibular central incisors (Fig.13.13).

**FIGURE 13.12** To measure the amount of overbite that is present use a nontoxic marking pencil to draw a horizontal line across the lower central incisors where the upper central incisors overlap when the mouth is closed.

**FIGURE 13.13** Ask the subject to open the mouth slightly so that it is possible to measure the amount of overbite as the distance from the horizontal line drawn on the lower central incisors to the top edge of the lower incisors.

## ● PROTRUSION OF THE MANDIBLE

Protrusion of the mandible is a translatory motion that occurs in the transverse plane. Normally, the lower central incisor teeth are able to protrude 6 mm to 9 mm beyond the upper central incisor teeth. However, the normal ROM for adults may range from 3 mm[7] to 10 mm.[6] See Table 13.2 in the Research Findings section for additional normal values and the effects of age and gender on ROM.

### Testing Position

Place the subject sitting, with the cervical spine in 0 degrees of flexion, extension, lateral flexion, and rotation. The TMJ is opened slightly.

### Stabilization

Stabilize the posterior aspect of the head and neck to prevent flexion, extension, lateral flexion, and rotation of the cervical spine.

### Testing Motion
#### Active Protrusion

Have the subject push the lower jaw as far forward as possible without moving the head forward.

#### Passive Protrusion

Grasp the mandible between the thumb and the fingers from underneath the chin. The subject may assist with the movement by pushing the chin anteriorly as far as possible. The end of the motion occurs when resistance is felt and attempts at additional motion cause anterior motion of the head (Fig. 13.14).

### Normal End-Feel

The end-feel is firm owing to stretching of the joint capsule; stylomandibular and sphenomandibular ligaments; and the temporalis, masseter, digastric, stylohyoid, mylohyoid, and geniohyoid muscles.[3,7]

### Measurement Method

Measure the distance between the lower central incisor and the upper central incisor teeth with a tape measure or ruler (Fig. 13.15). Alternatively, two vertical lines drawn on the upper and lower canines or lateral incisors may be used as the landmarks for measurement.[14]

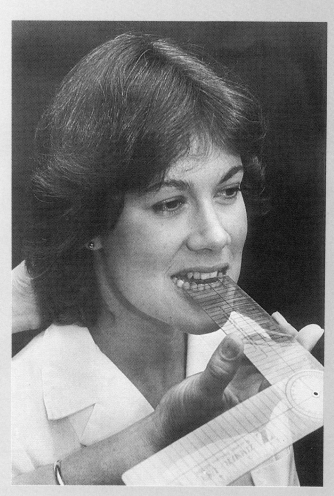

**FIGURE 13.14**  At the end of passive mandibular protrusion range of motion, the examiner uses one hand to stabilize the posterior aspect of the subject's head while her other hand moves the mandible into protrusion.

**FIGURE 13.15**  At the end of mandibular protrusion range of motion, the examiner uses the end of a plastic goniometer to measure the distance between the subject's upper and lower central incisors. The subject maintains the position.

# ● LATERAL EXCURSION OF THE MANDIBLE

This translatory motion occurs in the transverse plane. The amount of lateral movement to the right and left sides is not usually symmetrical, and there is some evidence that movement to the left is greater than to the right.[15] The normal ROM for adults is between 10 mm and 12 mm[2] but may range from 10 mm to 15 mm.[7] According to the consensus judgment of the Permanent Impairment Conference, the normal ROM is between 8 mm and 12 mm.[12] See Table 13.2 in the Research Findings section for additional normal values and the effects of age and gender on ROM.

## Testing Position

Place the subject sitting, with the cervical spine in 0 degrees of flexion, extension, lateral flexion, and rotation. The TMJ is opened slightly so that the subject's upper and lower teeth are not touching prior to the start of the motion.

## Stabilization

Stabilize the posterior aspect of the head and neck to prevent flexion, extension, lateral flexion, and rotation of the cervical spine.

## Testing Motion

### Active Lateral Excursion

Have the subject slide his or her lower jaw as far to the right as possible. Have the subject move the lower jaw as far to the left as possible.

### Passive Lateral Excursion

Grasp the mandible between the fingers and the thumb and move it to the side. The end of the motion occurs when resistance is felt and attempts to produce additional motion causes lateral cervical flexion (be careful to avoid depression, elevation, and protrusion and retrusion during the movement; Fig. 13.16).

## Normal End-Feel

The normal end-feel is firm owing to stretching of the joint capsule; the temporomandibular ligaments; and the temporalis, medial, and lateral pterygoid muscles.

## Measurement Method

Measure the lateral distance between the center of the lower incisors and the center of the upper central incisors with a millimeter ruler (Fig. 13.17). The distance that the mandible has moved laterally in relation to the maxilla is evident by comparing the position of the upper and lower central incisors in Figures 13.17 and 13.18.

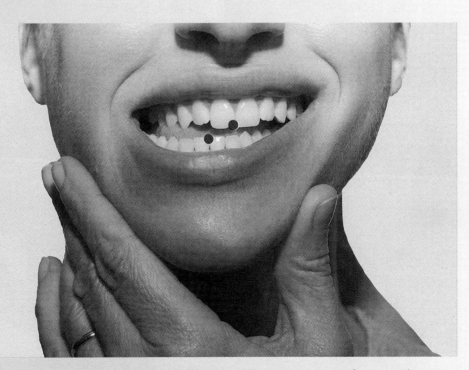

**FIGURE 13.16** At the end of passive mandibular lateral excursion range of motion, the examiner uses one hand to prevent cervical motion and the other hand to maintain a lateral pull on the mandible.

**FIGURE 13.17** The examiner uses a millimeter ruler to measure the lateral distance between the center of the two upper incisors and the center of the two low incisors. Align the ruler with the upper incisors first as these teeth have not moved during the motion.

**FIGURE 13.18** Note the difference between the alignment of the lower and upper central incisors in the neutral position compared to alignment of these incisors at the end of lateral excursion as shown in Figs. 3.16 and 3.17.

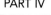

# Research Findings

The search for normative ROM values for TMJ joint motions is ongoing and includes various age groups of males and females in different populations and ethnic groups. A sampling of these studies is included in this section and in the sections that follow on the effects of age and gender on TMJ ROM.

In one of the few studies conducted to determine reference values for children, Cortese, Oliver, and Biondi[16] found that the normal range of mouth opening in boys and girls with a mean age of 4.6 years was 38.6 mm. For children in the study with a mean age of 6.9 years, the ROM was found to be 42.0 mm.[16] Hirsch and colleagues,[17] in a study involving children and adolescents 10 to 17 years old, found that the mean ROM for mouth opening was 50.6 mm.

Functional mouth opening is a distance sufficient for the subject to place two or three flexed proximal interphalangeal joints within the opening. That distance in adults may range from 35 mm to 50 mm, although an opening of only 25 mm to 35 mm is needed for normal activities.[7] A slightly more restricted normal range of adult values (40 to 50 mm) was arrived at by consensus judgments made at a 1995 Permanent Impairment Conference by representatives of all major societies and academies whose members treat TMJ disorders.[12] Similar normative mean values for adult mouth opening, from a low of 41 mm to a high of 58.6 mm, are presented in Table 13.1. Normal mean values for the ROM in protrusion and lateral excursive motions are presented from four sources in Table 13.2.

Dijkstra and coworkers[18] investigated the relationship between vertical and horizontal mandibular ROM in 91 healthy subjects (59 women and 32 men) with a mean age of 27.2 years. A mean ratio was found ranging from 6.0:1 to 6.6:1 between vertical and horizontal ROM. Therefore, based on the results of this study, the authors concluded that the 4:1 ratio between vertical and horizontal ROM that has been used as a standard in the past[19] should be replaced by the approximately 6:1 ratio found in this study. However, the authors found that the ratio has poor predictive value.

## Effects of Age, Gender, and Other Factors

### Age

Temporomandibular joint ROM in children tends to show an increase in ROM as age increases between the ages of 3 and 17 years.[16,17] Similar to other areas of the body, the ROM in adults tends to decrease rather than increase as age increases from ages 16 or 17 years onward. Also, like other areas of the body, some TMJ motions appear to be affected by age more than other TMJ motions in both adults and children.

Cortese, Oliver, and Biondi[16] determined ROM values in a sample of 212 boys and girls ages 3 to 11 years of age. The ROM in mouth opening and lateral excursion was found to be smaller in young children (3 to 4 years) compared to slightly older children (11 years), but no change in protrusion ROM was observed.

In a population-based study involving 1011 German male and female children and adolescents between the ages of 10 and 17 years, Hirsch and colleagues[17] also found an increase in the ROM of some motions as age increased. A significant difference occurred between maximum active mouth opening in the 10- to 13-year-old group and in the 14- to 17-year-old group, with the older adolescent group having a greater range of mouth opening. The authors determined that maximal unassisted mouth opening increased by 0.4 mm per year of age. Lateral excursion and protrusion also were influenced by age, with lateral excursion

| TABLE 13.1 | Maximum Active Mouth Opening ROM in Subjects 10 to 99 Years of Age: Normal Linear Distance in Millimeters* | | | | | | | |
|---|---|---|---|---|---|---|---|---|
| Author | Hirsch et al[17] | Marklund and Wunman[20] | Goulet et al[21] | Celic et al[22] | Gallagher et al[23] | | Turp et al[15] | |
| Sample | Male and female German school children | Male and female Swedish dental students | Male and female volunteers | Male Croatian dental students | Males and females from population in Ireland | | Male and female German dental students and staff | |
| | 10–17 yrs | 18–48 yrs | Mean age 29 yrs | 19–28 yrs | 16–99 yrs | | Mean age 26.1 yrs | |
| | | | | | Males | Females | Males | Females |
| | n = 1011 | n = 371 | n = 36 | n = 60 | n = 657 | n = 856 | n = 58 | n = 83 |
| | Mean (SD) | Mean (SD) | Mean (SD) | Mean (SD) | Mean | Mean | Mean (SD) | Mean (SD) |
| ROM | 50.6 (6.4) | 55.3 (6.1) | 52.6 (6.3) | 50.8 (5.0) | 43 | 41 | 58.6 (7.1) | 54.6 (7.9) |

SD = standard deviation;.

* All measurements were obtained with a millimeter ruler, and all measurements include the amount of overbite except for measurements taken by Gallagher et al.

| TABLE 13.2 | Mandibular Protrusion and Lateral Excursion Range of Motion: Normal Linear Distance in Millimeters* | | | | | | | |
|---|---|---|---|---|---|---|---|---|
| Author | Hirsch et al[17] | | Celic et al[22] | | Walker et al[14] | | Turp et al[15] | |
| Sample | 486 male and 525 female students 10–17 yrs n = 1011 | | Males and females 19–28 yrs n = 60 | | 3 males and 12 females 21–61 yrs n = 15 | | Male and female students and staff Mean age = 26.1 yrs n = 141 | |
| | | | | | | | Male | Female |
| Motion | Mean (SD) | Range | Mean (SD) | Range | Mean (SD) | Range | Mean (SD) | Mean (SD) |
| Protrusion | 8.2 (2.5) | 1–22 | 7.9 (2.5) | 3–13 | 7.1 (2.3) | 4–11 | — | |
| Left lateral excursion | 10.6 (2.3) | 3–21 | 10.1 (3.0) | 3–15 | 8.6 (2.1) | 5–12 | 12.1 (2.3) | 11.5 (2.4) |
| Right lateral excursion | 10.2 (2.2) | 3–17 | 10.0 (2.8) | 4–15 | 9.2 (2.6) | 6–14 | 11.0 (2.6) | 10.9 (2.1) |

SD = standard deviation.
* All measurements were obtained with a millimeter ruler.

increasing 0.1 mm per year of age and protrusion decreasing 0.1 mm per year of age.

Gallagher and coworkers[23] conducted a population-based study of mouth opening in 1513 Irish adults ages 16 to 99 years. Maximum mouth opening showed a decrease in ROM from 45 mm in the 16- to 24-year-old group of males to 41 mm in the 65- to 99-year-old group of males. A similar decrease in mouth opening ROM occurred in females from the youngest to the oldest group. Thurnwald[24] also found that mouth opening decreased with increasing age. The decrease was about 5 mm from a mean of 59.4 mm in the 17-year-old group to 54.3 mm in the 65-year-old group. In fact, active ROM in all TMJ motions except for retrusion decreased with increasing age in the 100 subjects in the study.

In contrast to the preceding studies Hassel, Rammelsberg, and Schmitter,[25] in a comparison of ROM between a group of 44 young adults ages 18 to 45 years and a group of 43 elderly patients ages 68 to 96 years, found that mouth opening ROM did not decrease from the youngest to the oldest groups. However, the ROM in protrusion and lateral excursion followed the normal pattern and decreased from the youngest to the oldest group.

## Gender

A definite gender difference appears to be present in adults 16 to 99 years of age, with males having larger ROM in mouth opening than females.[23,24,26] Studies also have found that male adults have a larger ROM in lateral excursion than females.[15,24] Furthermore, Hirsch and colleagues[17] detected a gender effect in 10 to 17 year olds, with males having a significantly larger (1.8 mm) ROM in maximum active mouth opening than females. However, according to Cortese, Oliver, and Biondi,[16] the gender effect on mouth opening does not appear to be present in young children 3 to 11 years of age.

Gallagher and coworkers,[23] in a study of mouth opening in 1513 Irish males and females, determined that the 657 males 16 to 99 years of age had greater maximum active mouth opening ROM compared to the 856 females in the study.

Thurnwald[24] found that the subject's gender significantly affected both mouth opening and lateral excursion. The 50 males in this study had a greater mean range of mouth opening (59.4 mm) than the 50 females (54.0 mm). The males also had a greater mean ROM in right lateral excursion, but the difference between genders in this instance was small. The healthy 26-year-old males in a study by Turp, Alpaslan, and Gerds[15] had significantly larger maximum ROM in mouth opening and in both right and left lateral excursion in comparison to healthy females of the same age (see Table 13.1). Lewis, Buschang, and Throckmorton[26] determined that males had significantly greater mouth opening ROM (mean = 52.1 mm) than females (mean = 46.0 mm).

However, when mouth opening was measured as the angular displacement of the mandible in relation to the cranium (angle of mouth opening), Westling and Helkimo[27] found that maximal jaw opening in adolescents was slightly larger in females than in males. This finding might have been influenced by the fact that females generally reach adult ROM values by 10 years of age, whereas males do not reach adult ROM values until 15 years of age.[28]

## Mandibular Length

The ROM in mouth opening appears to be related to the length of the mandible. Dijkstra and colleagues,[29] in a study of mouth opening in 13 females and 15 males, found that the linear distance between the upper and the lower incisors during mandibular depression was significantly influenced by mandibular length. In a subsequent study, Dijkstra and associates[30] investigated the relationship between incisor distances, mandibular length, and angle of mouth opening in 91 healthy subjects (59 women and 32 men) ranging from 13 to 56 years of age (mean 27.2 years). Mouth opening was influenced by both mandibular length and angle of mouth opening. Therefore, it is possible that subjects with the same mouth opening distance may differ from each other in regard to TMJ mobility. Lewis, Buschang, and Throckmorton[26] found that mandibular length accounted for some of the gender differences in mouth opening and for most of the gender differences in condylar translation in mouth opening. Westling and Helkimo[27] found that passive mouth opening ROM was strongly correlated to mandibular length.

To adjust for mandibular length, Miller and coworkers[31] developed a "mouth opening index," called the temporomandibular opening index (TOI), which was determined by using the following formula: TOI = (PO − MVO/PO + MVO) × 100. PO is passive opening, and MVO refers to maximal voluntary opening. In a subsequent study, Miller and associates[32] compared the TOI in patients with a temporomandibular disorder (TMD) with the TOI in a control group of individuals without TMDs. Based on the results of the study, the authors concluded that the TOI appeared to be independent of age, gender, and mandibular length. Moipolai, Karic, and Miller,[33] in a study of 42 asymptomatic patients, used analysis of covariance to assess the association between the TOI and age, gender, ramus length, and gonial angle. No relationship between the variables and the TOI was found. In a more recent study, Miller[34] found that the TOI was able to distinquish between two groups of patients with myogenous TMD, a finding that should make the TOI valuable as a diagnostic tool.

### Head and Neck Positions and Motions

Head and neck positions and motions are closely linked with mouth opening and closing movements. Also, the ROM of mouth opening is affected by the static position of the head and neck, so examiners need to be aware of the subject's head and neck position during measurements of the TMJ. According to Zafar,[9,10] there is a functional linkage between the temporomandibular and craniocervical regions, with head and neck extension movements being an integral part of natural active mouth opening and head and neck flexion being an integral part of mouth closing.

Higbie and associates[35] investigated the effects of static head positions (forward, neutral, and retracted) on mouth opening in 20 healthy males and 20 healthy females between 18 and 54 years of age. Mouth opening ROM measured with a millimeter ruler was significantly different among the three positions. Mouth opening was greatest (mean = 44.5 mm, standard deviation [SD] = 5.3) in the forward head position, which includes extension of the upper cervical region; it was less in the neutral head position (mean = 41.5 mm, SD = 4.8); and it was least (mean = 36.2 mm, SD = 4.5) in the retracted head position, which includes cervical flexion. Day-to-day reliability was found to vary from an r value of 0.90 to 0.97, depending on head position, and the standard error of measurement (SEM) ranged from 0.77 to 1.69 mm, also depending on head position. As a result of the findings, the authors concluded that the head position should be controlled when mouth opening measurements are taken. However, the authors found that an error of 1 mm to 2 mm occurred regardless of the position in which the head was placed.

### Temporomandibular Disorders (TMDs)

The structure of the TMJs and the fact that these joints get so much use predisposes the joints, associated ligaments, and musculature to injury, mechanical problems, and degenerative changes. For example, the articular disc may become entrapped, deformed, or torn; the capsule may become thickened; the ligaments may become shortened or lengthened; and the muscles may become inflamed, contracted, and hypertrophied. These problems may give rise to a variety of symptoms and signs that are included in the TMD classification.

Restricted mouth opening ROM is considered to be one of the important signs of TMD.[36] Popping or clicking noises (or both) in the joint during mouth opening and/or closing and deviation of the mandible during mouth opening and closing may be present.[36–39] Other signs and symptoms include facial pain; muscular pain[36]; tenderness in the region of the TMJ, either unilaterally or bilaterally; headaches; and stiffness of the neck. TMDs appear to be more prevalent in females of all ages after puberty, although the actual percentages of women affected varies among investigators.[36,39–43]

A number of studies have investigated TMJ disorders in populations of children, adolescents, and elderly individuals.[17,20,22,25,39,44–46] Celic and colleagues[22] investigated the range of mandibular movements in a young male population of 180 patients with TMD disorders and 60 control subjects. A significant difference was found in maximal active mouth opening and active lateral excursion and protrusion between the controls and patients with TMD, but the authors concluded that it was not possible to discriminate among the following three patient groups: myogenous, disc, and combined myogenous and disc.

Cooper and Kleinberg [47] reviewed the records of 4528 men, women, and children patients between the ages of 11 and 70 years and found that the prevalence of TMDs was highest between the ages of 21 and 50 years of age. The authors also found a gender difference in that 77 percent of the patients were females.

In a study of 114 males and 194 female university students with a mean age of 23 years, Marklund and Wanman[20] found that the persistence of signs and symptoms over the period of a year was higher in female students. However, the 1-year incidence of TMJ signs and symptoms (12 percent) was not significantly different between men and women.

Possible reasons for a gender preference have been attributed to a number of factors including, among others, greater stress levels in women,[42] hormonal influences,[43] and habits of adolescent girls that are extremely harmful to the temporomandibular joints (e.g., intensive gum chewing, continuous arm leaning, ice crushing, nail biting, biting foreign objects, jaw play, clenching, and bruxism).[37,38]

## Reliability and Validity

As is the case in other areas of the body, some TMJ motions appear to be more reliably measured than other motions in both asymptomatic and symptomatic subjects. Mouth opening (active and passive) measured with a millimeter ruler as the vertical distance between the upper and lower central incisors has consistently demonstrated good to excellent reliability (see Table 13.3).[14,35,47–50] Measurements of protrusion have also shown good reliability, but lateral excursion has consistently shown poor to good reliability.[25,48,50–53]

Walker, Bohannon, and Cameron[14] determined that all six TMJ motions measured with a millimeter ruler were reliable. Measurements were taken by two testers at three sessions, each of which were separated by a week. The 30 subjects who were measured included 15 patients with a TMJ disorder (13 females and 2 males with a mean age of 35.2 years) and 15 subjects without a TMJ disorder (12 females and 3 males with a mean age of 42.9 years). The intratester reliability intraclass correlation coefficients (ICCs) for tester 1 ranged from 0.82 to 0.99, and the intratester reliability for tester 2 ranged from 0.70 to 0.90. However, only mouth opening measurements had construct validity and were useful for discriminating between subjects with and without TMJ disorders. The technical error of measurement (difference between measurements that would have to be exceeded if the measurements were to be truly different) was 2.5 mm for mouth opening measurement in subjects without a TMJ disorder.

Higbie and associates[35] also found that ROM measurements of mouth opening were highly reliable with the use of a millimeter ruler. Twenty males and 20 females with a mean age of 32.9 years were measured by two examiners. Intratester, intertester, and test-retest reliability ICCs ranged from 0.90 to 0.97, depending on head position. SEM values indicated that an error of 1 mm to 2 mm existed for the measurement technique used in the study.

Kropmans and colleagues[48] found similar high reliability in a study of mouth opening involving 5 male and 20 female patients with painfully restricted TMJs. Intratester, intertester,

and test-retest reliability varied between 0.90 and 0.96. However, in contrast to the findings of Walker, Bohannon, and Cameron[14] and those of Higbie and associates,[35] the authors found that the smallest detectable difference of maximal mouth opening in this group of subjects varied from 9 mm to 6 mm. Based on these results, a clinician would have to measure at least 9 mm of improvement in maximal mouth opening in this group of patients to say that improvement had occurred.

Reliability appears to be improved when examiners participate in a calibration training program in which examiners are calibrated to a standarized set of examination procedures and criteria, as described by the RDC/TMD. Lobbezoo and colleagues[52] found that calibration training resulted in good to excellent interexaminer reliability of both active and passive mouth opening measurements and protrusion ROM. Only lateral excursion ROM measurements had fair interexaminer reliability.

In a study by Leher and colleagues,[51] no significant difference was found in the reliability of ROM measurements between inexperienced dental students and experienced practitioners who had participated in a calibration program. The authors concluded that calibration training was more important than experience. However, both groups had unacceptable reliability scores for lateral excursive motions. Lausten, Glaros, and Williams[53] compared nonexpert and expert examiners' ability to measure TMJ ROM following calibration training. The nonexperts were able to measure maximum active mouth opening ROM with a high degree of reliability, but, similar to Leher's results, neither group was able to measure lateral excursive motions reliably.

| TABLE 13.3 | Intertester Reliability of Mandibular Measurements Using a Millimeter Ruler | | | |
|---|---|---|---|---|
| Author | Goulet et al[21] | Walker et al[14] | Walker et al[14] | John et al[50] |
| Testers Sample | 5 experienced 10 males and 62 females; 36 patients with TMD and 36 without TMD Mean age 29 yrs n = 72 | 2 experienced 2 male and 13 female patients with TMD 20–52 yrs n = 15 | 2 experienced 3 males and 12 females without TMD 21–61 yrs n = 15 | 4 experienced 11 patients with TMD and 25 without TMD 17–71 yrs n = 36 |
| | ICC | ICC | ICC | ICC |
| Mouth opening | 0.87 | 0.99 | 0.98 | 0.93 |
| Right lateral excursion | 0.59 | 0.96 | 0.90 | 0.73 |
| Left lateral excursion | 0.68 | 0.94 | 0.95 | 0.79 |
| Protrusion | — | 0.98 | 0.95 | 0.91 |

ICC = intraclass correlation coefficient; TMD = temporomandibular disorder.

# REFERENCES

1. Hoover, D, and Ritzline, P: The temporomandibular joint. In Levangie, PK, and Norkin, CC (eds): Joint Structure and Function: A Comprehensive Analysis, ed 4. FA Davis, Philadelphia, 2005.
2. Iglarsh, ZA, and Synder-Mackler, L: The temporomandibular joint and the cervical spine. In Richardson, JK, and Iglarsh, ZA (eds): Clinical Orthopaedic Physical Therapy. WB Saunders, Philadelphia, 1994.
3. Williams, PL: Gray's Anatomy, ed 38. Churchill Livingstone, New York, 1995.
4. Neumann, DA: Kinesiology of the Musculoskeletal System: Foundations for Physical Rehabilitation. Mosby, Inc., St. Louis, 2002.
5. Otis, CA: Kinesiology: The Mechanics and Pathomechanics of Human Movement. Lippincott William and Wilkins, Philadelphia, 2004.
6. Harrison, AL: The temporomandibular joint. In Malone, TR, McPoil, T, and Nitz, AJ (eds): Orthopedic and Sports Physical Therapy, ed 3. CV Mosby, St. Louis, 1997.
7. Magee, DJ: Orthopedic Physical Assessment, ed 3. WB Saunders, Philadelphia, 1997.
8. Cailliet, R: Soft Tissue Pain and Disability, ed 3. FA Davis, Philadelphia, 1996.
9. Zafar, H, Nordh, E, and Eriksson, PO: Temporal coordination between mandibular and head-neck movements during jaw opening-closing tasks in man. Arch Oral Biol 45:675, 2000.
10. Zafar, H: Integrated jaw and neck function in man. Studies of mandibular and head-neck movements during jaw opening-closing tasks. Swed Dent J 143(Suppl):1, 2000.
11. Eriksson, PO, et al: Co-ordinated mandibular and head-neck movements during rhythmic jaw activities in man. J Dent Res 79:1378, 2000.
12. Phillips, DJ, et al: Guide to evaluation of permanent impairment of the temporomandibular joint. J Craniomandibular Pract 15:170, 1997.
13. Dworkin, SF, and Le Resche, L: Research diagnostic criteria for temporomandibular disorders. J Craniomandib Disord 6:301,1992.
14. Walker, N, Bohannon, RW, and Cameron, D: Discriminant validity of temporomandibular joint range of motion measurements obtained with a ruler. J Orthop Sports Phys Ther 30:484, 2000.
15. Turp, JC, Alpaslan, C, and Gerds, T: Is there a greater mandibular movement capacity towards the left? Verification of an observation from 1921. J Oral Rehabil 32:242, 2005.
16. Cortese, SG, Oliver, LM, and Biondi, AM: Determination of mandibular movements in children without temporomandibular disorders. J Craniomandibular Practice 25:200, 2007.
17. Hirsch, C, et al: Mandibular jaw movement capacity in 10–17-yr-old children and adolescents: Normative values and the influence of gender, age, and temporomandibular disorders. Eur J Oral Sci 114:465, 2006.
18. Dijkstra, PU, et al: Ratio between vertical and horizontal mandibular range of motion. J Oral Rehabil 25:353, 1998.
19. Hockstedler, JL, Allen, JD, and Follmar, MA: Temporomandibular joint range of motion: a ratio of intercisal opening to excursive movement in a healthy population. Cranio 14:296, 1996.
20. Marklund, S, and Wanman, A: Incidence and prevalence of temporomandibular joint pain and dysfunction. A one-year prospective study of university students. Acta Odontologica Scandanavia 65:119, 2007.
21. Goulet, J-P, et al: The reproducibility of muscle and joint tenderness detection methods and maxumum mandibular movement measurement for the temporomandibular system. J Orofacial Pain 12:17, 1998.
22. Celic, R, et al: Measurement of mandibular movement in patients with temporomandibular disorders and in asymptomatic subjects. Coll Antropol Suppl 2:43, 2003.
23. Gallagher, C, et al: The normal range of mouth opening in an Irish population. J Oral Rehabil 31:110, 2004.
24. Thurnwald, PA: The effect of age and gender on normal temporomandibular joint motion. Physiother Theory Pract 7:209, 1991.
25. Hassel AJ, Rammelsberg, P, and Schmitter, M: Inter-examiner reliability in the clinical examination of temporomandibular disorders: Influence of age. Community Dent Oral Epidemiol 34:41, 2006.
26. Lewis, RP, Buschang, PH, and Throckmorton, GS: Sex differences in mandibular movements during opening and closing. Am J Orthod Dentofacial Orthop 120:294, 2001.
27. Westling, L, and Helkimo, E: Maximum jaw opening capacity in adolescents in relation to general joint mobility. 19:485, 1992.
28. Wright, DM, and Moffat, BC, Jr: The postnatal development of the human temporomandibular joint. Am J Anat 141:235, 1974.
29. Dijkstra, PU, et al: Temporomandibular joint mobility assessment: A comparison between four methods. J Oral Rehabil 22:439, 1995.
30. Dijkstra, PU, et al: Influence of mandibular length on mouth opening. J Oral Rehabil 26:117, 1999.
31. Miller, VJ, et al: A mouth opening index for patients with temporomandibular disorders. J Oral Rehabil 26:534, 1999.
32. Miller, VJ, et al: The temporomandibular opening index (TOI) in patients with closed lock and a control group with no temporomandibular disorders (TMD): An initial study. J Oral Rehabil 27:815, 2000.
33. Moipolai, P, Karic, VV, and Miller, VJ: The effect of gonial angle, ramus length, age and gender on temporomandibular opening index. J Oral Rehabil 30:1195, 2003.
34. Miller, VJ, Karic, VV, and Myers, SL: Differences in initial symptom scores between myogenous TMD patients with high and low TOI scores. J Craniomandib Pract 24:25, 2006.
35. Higbie, EJ, et al: Effect of head position on vertical mandibular opening. J Orthop Sports Phys Ther 29:127, 1999.
36. Esposito, CJ, Panucci, PJ, and Farman, AG: Associations in 425 patients having temporomandibular disorders. J Kentucky Med Assoc 98:213, 2001.
37. Gavish, A, et al: Oral habits and their association with signs and symptoms of temporomandibular disorders in adolescent girls. J Oral Rehabil 27:22, 2000.
38. Winocur, E, et al: Oral habits among adolescent girls and their association with symptoms of temporomandibular disorders. J Oral Rehabil 28:624, 2001.
39. Rauhala, K, et al: Facial pain and temporomandibular disorders: An epidemiological study of the northern Finland 1966 birth cohort. J Craniomandib Pract 18:40, 2000.
40. Hiltunen, K, et al: Prevalence of signs of temporomandibular disorders among elderly inhabitants of Helsinki, Finland. Acta Odontol Scand 53:20, 1995.
41. La Resche, L: Epidemiology of temporormandibular disorders: Implications for the investigation of etiologic factors. Crit Rev Oral Biol Med 8:291, 1997.
42. Kutilla, M, et al: TMD treatment need in relation to age, gender, stress and diagnostic subgroup. J Orofac Pain 12:67, 1998.
43. Warren, MP, and Fried, JL: Temporomandibular disorders and hormones in women. Cells Tissues Organs 169:187, 2000.
44. Sonmez, H, et al: Prevalence of temporomandibular dysfunction in Turkish children with mixed and permanent dentition. J Oral Rehabil 28:280, 2001.
45. Alamoudi, N, et al: Temporomandibular disorders among school children. J Clin Pediatr Dent 22:323, 1998.
46. Nilsson, IM: Reliability, validity, incidence and impact of temporomandibular pain disorders in adolescents. Swed Dent J Suppl 183:7, 2007.
47. Cooper, BC, and Kleinberg, I: Examination of a large patient population for the presence of symptoms and signs of temporomandibular disorders. J Craniomandibular Pract 25:115, 2007.
48. Kropmans, T, et al: Smallest detectable difference of maximal mouth opening in patients with painfully restricted temporomandibular joint function. Eur J Oral Sci 108:9, 2000.
49. List, T, et al: Recalibration improves inter-examiner reliability of TMD examination. Acta Odontologica Scandinavia 64:146, 2006.
50. John, MT, and Zwignenberg, AJ: Interobserver variables in assessment of signs of TMD. Intl J Prosthodontics 14:265, 2001
51. Leher, A, et al: Is there a difference in the reliable measurement of temporomandibular disorder signs between experienced and inexperienced examiners ? J Orofac Pain 19:58, 2005.
52. Lobbezoo, F, et al: Use of the research diagnostic criteria for temporomandibular disorders for multinational research: Translation efforts and reliability assessments in the Netherlands. J Orofac Pain 19:301, 2005.
53. Lausten, LL, Glaros, AC, and Williams, K: Inter-examiner reliability of physical assessment methods for assessing temporomandibular disorders. Gen Dent 52:509, 2004.

# Normative Range of Motion Values

| TABLE A.1 | Shoulder, Elbow, Forearm, and Wrist Motion: Mean Values in Degrees |
| --- | --- |

| | Wanatabe et al*[1] | Boone and Azen[2] | Green and Wolf[3] | Walker et al[4] | Downey et al[5] | AAOS[6] | AMA[7] |
| --- | --- | --- | --- | --- | --- | --- | --- |
| | 0–2 yrs n = 45 | 1–54 yrs n = 109 | 18–55 yrs n = 20 | 65–85yrs n = 60 | 61–93 yrs n = 106 | | |
| Motion | | (M) | (10 M, 10 F) | (30 M, 30 F) | (60 M, 140 F shoulders) | | |
| **Shoulder Complex** | | | | | | | |
| Flexion | 172–180 | 167 | 156 | 165 | 165 | 180 | 180 |
| Extension | 78–89 | 62 | — | 44 | — | 60 | 50 |
| Abduction | 177–187 | 184 | 168 | 165 | 158 | 180 | 180 |
| Medial rotation | 72–90 | 69 | 49 | 62 | 65 | 70 | 90 |
| Lateral rotation | 118–134 | 104 | 84 | 81 | 81 | 90 | 90 |
| **Elbow and Forearm** | | | | | | | |
| Flexion | 148–158 | 143 | 145 | 143 | — | 150 | 140 |
| Extension | — | 1 | 0 | 4[†] | — | 0 | 0 |
| Pronation | 90–96 | 76 | 84 | 71 | — | 80 | 80 |
| Supination | 81–93 | 82 | 77 | 74 | — | 80 | 80 |
| **Wrist** | | | | | | | |
| Flexion | 88–96 | 76 | 73 | 64 | — | 80 | 60 |
| Extension | 82–89 | 75 | 65 | 63 | — | 70 | 60 |
| Radial deviation | — | 22 | 25 | 19 | — | 20 | 20 |
| Ulnar deviation | — | 36 | 39 | 26 | — | 30 | 30 |

AAOS = American Association of Orthopaedic Surgeons; AMA = American Medical Association;
  M = males; F = females.
All values obtained with a universal goniometer.
* Values in this column represent a range of means.
† Value refers to extension limitation.

| TABLE A.2 | Glenohumeral Motion: Mean Values in Degrees | | | |
|---|---|---|---|---|
| Author | Ellenbecker et al[8] | Ellenbecker et al[8] | Boon & Smith[9] | Lannan et al[10] |
| | 11–17 yrs n = 113 | 11–17 yrs n = 90 | 12–18 yrs n = 50 | 21–40 yrs n = 60 |
| *Motion* | *(M)* | *(F)* | *(18 M, 32 F)* | *(20 M, 40 F)* |
| Glenohumeral | | | | |
| Flexion | — | — | — | 106 |
| Extension | — | — | — | 20 |
| Abduction | — | — | — | 129 |
| Medial rotation | 51 | 56 | 63 | 49 |
| Lateral rotation | 103 | 105 | 108 | 94 |

M = males; F = females.
Values obtained with a universal goniometer.

| TABLE A.3 | Finger Motions: Mean Values in Degrees | | | | | |
|---|---|---|---|---|---|---|
| Author | Skarilova & Plevkova*[,11] | Mallon et al‡[, 12] | Smahel & Klimova*[,13,14] | Hume et al†[,15] | AAOS[6] | AMA[7] |
| | 20–25 yrs n = 200 | 18–35 yrs n = 120 | 18–28 yrs n = 101 | 26–28 yrs n = 35 | | |
| *Motion* | *(100 M, 100 F)* | *(60 M, 60 F)* | *(52 M, 49 F)* | *(M)* | | |
| Finger MCP | | | | | | |
| Flexion | 91 | 95 | 92 | 100 | 90 | 90 |
| Extension | 26 | 20 | 25 | — | 45 | 20 |
| Finger PIP | | | | | | |
| Flexion | 108 | 105 | 111 | 105 | 100 | 100 |
| Extension | — | 7 | — | 0 | 0 | 0 |
| Finger DIP | | | | | | |
| Flexion | 85 | 68 | 81 | 85 | 90 | 70 |
| Extension | — | 8 | — | 0 | 0 | 0 |

CMC = carpometacarpal; IP = interphalangeal; MCP = metacarpophalangeal; AAOS = American Association of Orthopaedic Surgeons; AMA = American Medical Association; F = females ; M = males.
* Values obtained with a metallic slide goniometer on dorsal aspect.
† Values obtained with a computerized Greenleaf goniometer.
‡ Values obtained with a gonimeter applied to the dorsal aspect.

| TABLE A.4 | Thumb Motions: Mean Values in Degrees |
|---|---|

| Author | Skarilova and Plevkova*,11 | Skarilova and Plevkova*,11 | Jenkins et al†,16 | DeSmet et al‡,17 | AAOS6 | AMA7 |
|---|---|---|---|---|---|---|
| | 20–25 yrs n = 200 (100 M, 100 F) | 20–25 yrs n = 200 (100 M, 100 F) | 16–72 yrs n = 119 (50 M, 69 F) | 16–83 yrs n = 101 (43 M, 58 F) | | |
| Motion | Active | Passive | Active | | | |
| Thumb CMC | | | | | | |
| Abduction | — | — | — | — | 70 | — |
| Flexion | — | — | — | — | 15 | — |
| Extension | — | — | — | — | 20, 80 | 35§ |
| Thumb MCP | | | | | | |
| Flexion | 57 | 67 | 59 | 54 | 50 | 60 |
| Extension | 14 | 23 | — | — | 0 | 40 |
| Thumb IP | | | | | | |
| Flexion | 79 | 86 | 67 | 80 | 80 | 80 |
| Extension | 23 | 35 | — | — | 20 | 30 |

DIP = Distal interphalangeal; MCP = metacarpophalangeal; PIP = proximal interphalangeal;
AAOS = American Association of Orthopaedic Surgeons; AMA = American Medical Association; M = Males; F = females.
* Values obtained with a metallic slide goniometer on dorsal aspect.
† Values obtained with a universal goniometer on lateral aspect.
‡ Values obtained with a digital goniometer on dorsal aspect.
§ Range of motion value of 35 degrees is the difference between the minimal angle (15 degrees)
  of separation between first and second metacarpals and the maximal angle (50 degrees) of separation.

| TABLE A.5 | Hip and Knee Motions: Mean Values in Degrees |
|---|---|

| Author | Waugh et al18 | Drews et al 19 | Schwarze and Denton20 | Wanatabe et al1 | Phelps et al21 | Boone and Azen2 | Roach and Miles22 | AAOS6 | AMA7 |
|---|---|---|---|---|---|---|---|---|---|
| | 6–65 hrs n = 40 | 12 hrs– 6 days n = 54 | 1–3 days n = 1000 | 4 weeks n = 62 | 9 mos n = 25 | 1–54 yrs n = 109 | 25–74 yrs n = 1683 | | |
| Motion | | (26 M, 28 F) | (473 M, 527 F) | | (M and F) | (109 M) | (821 M, 862 F) | | |
| Hip | | | | | | | | | |
| Flexion | — | — | — | 138 | — | 122 | 121 | 120 | 100 |
| Extension | 46* | 28*† | 20* | 12* | 10* | 10 | 19 | 20 | 30 |
| Abduction | — | 55‡ | 78‡ | 51 | — | 46 | 42 | | 40 |
| Adduction | — | 6‡ | 15‡ | — | — | 27 | — | | 20 |
| Medial rotation | — | 80‡ | 58 | 24 | 52 | 47 | 32 | 45 | 50 |
| Lateral rotation | — | 114‡ | 80 | 66 | 47 | 47 | 32 | 45 | 50 |
| Knee | | | | | | | | | |
| Flexion | — | — | 150 | — | — | 142 | 132 | 135 | 150 |
| Extension | 15* | 20* | 15* | — | — | — | — | 10 | — |

AAOS = American Association of Orthopaedic Surgeons; AMA = American Medical Association;
  M = males; F = females.
* Values refer to extension limitations.
† Tested witth subjects in sidelying position
‡Tested with subjects in supine position

## TABLE A.6 — Ankle and Foot Motions: Mean Values in Degrees

| Author | Waugh et al[18] | Wanatabe et al[1] | Boone and Azen[2] | McPoil and Cornwall[25] | Mecagni et al[24] | AAOS[6] | AMA[7] |
|---|---|---|---|---|---|---|---|
| | 6–65 hrs n = 40 | 4–8 mos n = 54 | 1–54 yrs n = 109 | 26.1 yrs n = 27 (54 feet) | 64–87 yrs n = 34 | | |
| *Motion* | *(18 M, 22 F)* | | *(M)* | *(9 M, 18 F)* | *(F)* | | |
| **Ankle** | | | | | | | |
| Dorsiflexion | 59 | 51 | 13 | 16 | 11 | 20 | 20 |
| Plantar flexion | 26 | 60 | 56 | — | 64 | 50 | 40 |
| Inversion | — | — | 37 | 19 (Subtalar) | 26 | 35 | 30 |
| Eversion | — | — | 21 | 12 (Subtalar) | 17 | 15 | 20 |
| **First MTP** | | | | | | | |
| Flexion | — | — | — | — | — | 45 | 30 |
| Extension | — | — | — | 86 | — | 70 | 50 |

AAOS = American Association of Orthopaedic Surgeons; AMA = American Medical Association;
 M =males; F = females.
All range of motion values in the table obtained with a universal goniometer.

## TABLE A.7 — Cervical Spine Motions: Mean Values in Centimeters and Degrees

| Author | Youdas et al[*,26] | | | | | | Lantz et al[†,27] | | Hsieh and Young[‡,28] | Balogun et al[§,29] | | AAOS[6] | AMA[7] |
|---|---|---|---|---|---|---|---|---|---|---|---|---|---|
| | 11–19 yrs n = 40 (20M, 20F) | | 30–39 yrs n = 41 (20 M, 21 F) | | 70–79 yrs n = 40 (20 M, 20 F) | | 20–39 yrs n = 63 | | 14–31 yrs n = 34 (27 M, 7 F) | 18–26 yrs n = 21 (15 M, 6 F) | | 26–39 yrs n = 63 | |
| *Motion* | *M* | *F* | *M* | *F* | *M* | *F* | *Active* | *Passive* | | | | | |
| Flexion | 64 | — | 47 | — | 39 | — | 60 | 74 | 1.0 cm | 4.3 cm | 32 | 45 | 50 |
| Extension | 86 | 84 | 68 | 78 | 54 | 55 | 56 | 53 | 22 cm | 19 cm | 64 | 45 | 60 |
| Right lateral flexion | 45 | 49 | 43 | 47 | 26 | 28 | 43 | 48 | 11 cm | 13 cm | 41 | 45 | 45 |
| Right rotation | 74 | 75 | 67 | 72 | 50 | 53 | 72 | 79 | 12 cm | 11 cm | 64 | 60 | 80 |

AAOS = American Association of Orthopaedic Surgeons; AMA = American Medical
 Association; F = female; M = male.
 \* Values in degrees were obtained for active range of motion using the cervical range
  of motion (CROM) instrument.
 † Values in degrees were obtained for active and passive range of motion with use of
  the OSI CA-6000 Spinal Motion Analyzer.
 ‡ Values in centimeters were obtained with a tape measure.
 § Values in centimeters obtained with a tape measure appear in the last column, whereas values in
  degrees obtained with a Myrin gravity-referenced goniometer appear in the second column.
 NB: AMA values in degrees were obtained with use of a universal goniometer, and AAOS
  values in degrees were obtained with use of an inclinometer.

| TABLE A.8 | Thoracic and Lumbar Spine Motions: Mean Values in Centimeters and Degrees | | | | | | | | | | | |
|---|---|---|---|---|---|---|---|---|---|---|---|---|

| Author | Haley et al*,30 | Moll and Wright*,31 | Van Adrichem and van der Korst†,32 | | Breum et al‡,33 | | McGregor et al§,34 | | Fitzgerald et al¶,35 | AAOS6 | AMA7 | |
|---|---|---|---|---|---|---|---|---|---|---|---|---|
| | 5–9 yrs n = 282 (140 M, 142 F) | 15–75 yrs n = 237 (119 M, 118 F) | 15–18 yrs n = 66 (34 M, 32 F) | | 18–38 yrs n = 47 (27 M, 20 F) | | 50–59 yrs n = 41 (21 M, 20 F) | | 20–82 yrs n = 172 (168 M, 4 F) | | | |
| Motion | | | M | F | M | F | M | F | | M | F | |
| Flexion | 6–7 cm | 5–7 cm | 7 cm | 6 cm | 56 | 54 | 55 | 60 | — | 80 | 60 | |
| Extension | — | — | — | — | 22 | 21 | 21 | 18 | 16–41 | 25 | 25 | |
| Right lateral flexion | — | — | — | — | 33 | 31 | 30 | 30 | 18–38 | 35 | 25 | |
| Right rotation | — | — | — | — | 8 | 8 | 26 | 26 | — | 45 | 30 | |

AAOS = American Association of Orthopaedic Surgeons; AMA = American Medical Association; F = female; M = male.
* Lumbar values obtained with use of the Modified Schober method.
† Lumbar values obtained using the Modified–Modified Schober (simplified skin distraction) method.
‡ Lumbar values in the first column were obtained with the BROM II. Lumbar values in the second column were obtained with double inclinometers.
§ Lumbar values obtained with the OSI CA-6000.
¶ Range of motion (ROM) values for thoracolumbar extension and lateral flexion were obtained with a universal goniometer. Lower values are for ages 70–79 years and higher values are for ages 20–29 years.
NB: AAOS values for thoracolumbar motions were obtained with a universal goniometer. AMA values were obtained with use of the two-inclinometer method for lumbar motions of flexion, extension, and lateral flexion. The AMA value for rotation is for the thoracic spine.

| TABLE A.9 | Tempomandibular Motions: Mean Values in Millimeters | | | | | | |
|---|---|---|---|---|---|---|---|

| Author | Walker et al*,36 | Hirsch et al*,37 | | Thurnwald†,38 | | | |
|---|---|---|---|---|---|---|---|
| | 21–61 yrs n = 15 (3 M, 12 F) | 10–17yrs n = 1011 (486 M, 525 F) | | 17–25 yrs n = 50 (25 M, 25 F) | | 50–65 yrs n = 50 (25 M, 25 F) | |
| Motion | | M | F | M | F | M | F |
| Opening | 43 | 51 | 51 | 61 | 55 | 58 | 51 |
| Left lateral excursion | 9 | 11 | 10 | 9 | 8 | 8 | 6 |
| Right lateral excursion | 9 | 10 | 10 | 10 | 9 | 7 | 9 |
| Protrusion | 7 | 8 | 8 | 5 | 5 | 5 | 4 |

* Values were obtained for active range of motion (ROM) with an 11-cm plastic ruler marked in millimeters.
† Values were obtained for active ROM with Vernier calipers as the measuring instrument.

# REFERENCES

1. Wanatabe, H, et al: The range of joint motion of the extremities in healthy Japanese people: The differences according to age. (Cited in Walker, JM: Musculoskeletal development: A review. Phys Ther 71:878, 1991.)

2. Boone, DC, and Azen, SP: Normal range of motion of joints in male subjects. J Bone Joint Surg 61:756, 1979.

3. Greene, BL, and Wolf, SL: Upper extremity joint movement: Comparison of two measurement devices. Arch Phys Med Rehabil 70:288, 1989.

4. Walker, JM, et al: Active mobility of the extremities in older subjects. Phys Ther 4:919, 1984.

5. Downey, PA, Fiebert, I, and Stackpole-Brown, JB: Shoulder range of motion in persons aged sixty and older. (abstract). Phys Ther 71:S75, 1991.

6. American Academy of Orthopaedic Surgeons: Joint Motion: Method of measuring and recording. American Academy of Orthopaedic Surgeons, Chicago, 1965.

7. Cocchiarella, L and Andersson, GBJ (eds) American Medical Association: Guides to the Evaluation of Permanent Impairment, ed 5. AMA, Chicago 2001.

8. Ellenbecker, TS, et al: Glenohumeral joint internal and external rotation range of motion in elite junior tennis players. J Orthop Sports Phys Ther 24:336, 1996.

9. Boon, AJ, and Smith, J: Manual scapular stabilization: Its effect on shoulder rotational range of motion. Arch Phys Med Rehabil 81:978, 2000.

10. Lannan, D, Lehman, T, and Toland, M: Establishment of normative data for the range of motion of the glenohumeral joint. Master of Science thesis, University of Massachusetts, Lowell, 1996.

11. Skarilova, B, and Plevkova, A: Ranges of joint motion of the adult hand. Acta Chir Plast 38:67, 1996.

12. Mallon, WJ, Brown, HR, and Nunley, JA: Digital ranges of motion: Normal values in joung adults. J Hand Surg 16A:882, 1991.

13. Smahel, Z and Klimova, A: The influence of age and exercise on the mobility of hand joints 1: metacarpophalangeal joint of the three-phalangeal fingers. Acta Chirurgiae Plasticae 46:81, 2004.

14. Smahel, Z and Klimova, A: The influence of age and exercise on the mobility of hand joints 2: interphalangeal joints of the three-phalangeal fingers. Acta Chirurgiae Plasticae 46:122, 2004.

15. Hume, M, et al: Functional range of motion of the joints of the hand. J Hand Surg 15A:240, 1990.

16. Jenkins, M, et al: Thumb joint motion: What is normal? J Hand Surg 23B:796, 1998.

17. DeSmett, L, et al: Metacarpophalangeal and interphalangeal flexion of the thumb: Influence of sex and age, relation to ligamentous injury. Acta Orhtop Belg 59:37, 1993.

18. Waugh, KG, et al: Measurement of selected hip, knee and ankle joint motions in newborns. Phys Ther 63:1616, 1983.

19. Drews, JE, Vraciu, JK, and Pellino, G: Range of motion of the lower extremities of newborns. Phys Occup Ther Pediatr 4:49, 1884.

20. Schwarze, DJ, and Denton, JR: normal values of neonatal limbs: An evaluation of 1000 neonates. J Pediatr Orthop 13:758, 1993.

21. Phelps, E, Smith, LJ, and Hallum, A: Normal ranges of hip motion of infants between 9 and 24 months of age. Dev Med Child Neurol 27:785, 1985.

22. Roach, KE, and Miles, TP: Normal hip and knee active range of motion: The relationship of age. Phys Ther 71: 656, 1991.

23. Greene, WB, and Heckman, JD (eds): The Clinical Measurement of Joint Motion. American Academy of Orthopaedic Surgeons, Rosemont, Ill. 1994.

24. Mecagni, C, et al: Balance and ankle range of motion in community dwelling women aged 64–87 years: A correlational study. Phys Ther 80:1004, 2000.

25. McPoil, TG, and Cornwall, MW: The relationship between static lower extremity measurements and rearfoot motion during walking. Phys Ther 24:309, 1996.

26. Youdas, J, et al: Normal range of motion of the cervical spine: An initial goniometric study. Phys Ther 72:770, 1992.

27. Lantz, CA, Chen, J, and Buch, D: Clinical validity and stability of active and passive cervical range of motion with regard to total and uniplanar motion. Spine 24:1082, 1999.

28. Hsieh, C-Y and Yeung, BW: Active neck motion measurements with a tape measure. J Orthop Sports Phys Ther 8:88, 1986.

29. Balogun, JA, et al: Inter-and intratester reliability of measuring neck motions with tape measure and Myrin Gravity-Reference Goniometer. J Orthop Sports Phys Ther 9:248, 1989.

30. Haley, SM, Tada, WL, Carmichael, EM: Spinal mobility in young children. Phys Ther 66:1697, 1986.

31. Moll, JMH, and Wright, V: Normal range of spinal mobility: An objective clinical study. Ann Rheum Dis 30:381, 1971.

32. van Adrichem, JAM, and van der Korst, JK: Assessment of flexibility of the lumbar spine. A pilot study in children and adolescents. Scand J Rheumatol 2:87, 1973.

33. Breum, J, Wiberg, J, and Bolton, JE: Reliability and concurrent validity of the BROM II for measuring lumbar mobility. J Manipulative Physiol Ther 18:497, 1995.

34. Mcgregor, AH, MacCarthy, ID, and Hughes, SP: Motion characteristics of the lumbar spine in the normal population. Spine 20:2421, 1995.

35. Fitzgerald, GK, et al: Objective assessment with establishment of normal values for lumbar spine range of motion. Phys Ther 63:1776, 1983.

36. Walker, N, Bohannon, RW, Cameron, D: Validity of temporomandibular joint range of motion measurements obtained with a ruler. J Orthop Sports Phys Ther 30:484, 2000.

37. Hirsch,C, John, MT, Lautenschlager,C, List, T: Mandibular jaw movement capacity in 10-17-yr-old children and adolescents;normative values and the influence of gender,age, and temporomandibular disorders. Eur. J Oral Sci 114:465-470, 2006.

38. Thurnwald, PA: The effect of age and gender on normal temporomandibular joint movement. Physiother Theory Pract 7:209, 1991.

# Joint Measurements by Body Position

| | Prone | Supine | Sitting | Standing |
|---|---|---|---|---|
| Shoulder | Extension | Flexion<br>Abduction<br>Medial rotation<br>Lateral rotation | | |
| Elbow | | Flexion | | |
| Forearm | | | Pronation<br>Supination | |
| Wrist | | | Flexion<br>Extension<br>Radial deviation<br>Ulnar deviation | |
| Hand | | | All motions | |
| Hip | Extension<br>Medial rotation††<br>Lateral rotation†† | Flexion<br>Abduction<br>Adduction | Medial rotation<br>Lateral rotation | |
| Knee | | Flexion | | |
| Ankle and foot | Subtalar inversion<br>Subtalar eversion | Dorsiflexion<br>Plantar flexion<br>Inversion<br>Eversion<br>Midtarsal inversion<br>Midtarsal eversion | Dorsiflexion<br>Plantar flexion<br>Inversion<br>Eversion<br>Midtarsal inversion<br>Midtarsal eversion | |
| Toes | | All motions | All motions | |
| Cervical spine | | Rotation* | Flexion<br>Extension<br>Lateral flexion<br>Rotation† | |
| Thoracic and lumbar spine | | | Rotation | Flexion<br>Extension<br>Lateral flexion |
| Temporomandibular joint | | | Depression (opening)<br>Protrusion<br>Lateral excursion<br>Overbite | |

* Measurement position using single inclinometer.
† Measurement position using universal goniometer, tape measure, and cervical range of motion device (CROM).
††Alternative position.

# Numerical Recording Forms

| | | | Range of Motion—Temporomandibular Joint and Spine | | | |
|---|---|---|---|---|---|---|
| **Patient's Name:** | | | | Date of Birth | | |
| **Left** | | | | **Right** | | |
| | | | Date | | | |
| | | | Examiner's Initials | | | |
| | | | **Temporomandibular Joint** | | | |
| | | | Depression (opening) | | | |
| | | | Protrusion | | | |
| | | | Lateral Excursion | | | |
| | | | Overbite | | | |
| | | | Comments: | | | |
| | | | **Cervical Spine** | | | |
| | | | Flexion | | | |
| | | | Extension | | | |
| | | | Lateral Flexion | | | |
| | | | Rotation | | | |
| | | | Comments: | | | |
| | | | **Thoracolumbar Spine** | | | |
| | | | Flexion | | | |
| | | | Extension | | | |
| | | | Lateral Flexion | | | |
| | | | Rotation | | | |
| | | | Comments: | | | |
| | | | **Lumbar Spine** | | | |
| | | | Flexion | | | |
| | | | Extension | | | |
| | | | Lateral Flexion | | | |
| | | | Comments: | | | |

**Range of Motion—Upper Extremity**

Patient's Name:_____ Date of Birth _____

| Left | | | | Right | | |
|---|---|---|---|---|---|---|
| | | | **Date** | | | |
| | | | **Examiner's Initials** | | | |
| | | | **Shoulder Complex** | | | |
| | | | Flexion | | | |
| | | | Extension | | | |
| | | | Abduction | | | |
| | | | Medial Rotation | | | |
| | | | Lateral Rotation | | | |
| | | | Comments: | | | |
| | | | **Glenohumeral** | | | |
| | | | Flexion | | | |
| | | | Extension | | | |
| | | | Abduction | | | |
| | | | Medial Rotation | | | |
| | | | Lateral Rotation | | | |
| | | | Comments: | | | |
| | | | **Elbow and Forearm** | | | |
| | | | Flexion | | | |
| | | | Supination | | | |
| | | | Pronation | | | |
| | | | Comments: | | | |
| | | | **Wrist** | | | |
| | | | Flexion | | | |
| | | | Extension | | | |
| | | | Ulnar Deviation | | | |
| | | | Radial Deviation | | | |
| | | | Comments: | | | |

| | | | Range of Motion—Hand | | | |
|---|---|---|---|---|---|---|
| Patient's Name: | | | | Date of Birth | | |
| Left | | | | | Right | |
| | | | Date | | | |
| | | | Examiner's Initials | | | |
| | | | **Thumb** | | | |
| | | | CMC Flexion | | | |
| | | | CMC Extension | | | |
| | | | CMC Abduction | | | |
| | | | CMC Opposition | | | |
| | | | MCP Flexion | | | |
| | | | IP Flexion | | | |
| | | | IP Extension | | | |
| | | | **Index Finger** | | | |
| | | | MCP Flexion | | | |
| | | | MCP Extension | | | |
| | | | MCP Abduction | | | |
| | | | PIP Flexion | | | |
| | | | DIP Flexion | | | |
| | | | **Middle Finger** | | | |
| | | | MCP Flexion | | | |
| | | | MCP Extension | | | |
| | | | MCP Radial Abduction | | | |
| | | | MCP Ulnar Abduction | | | |
| | | | PIP Flexion | | | |
| | | | DIP Flexion | | | |
| | | | **Ring Finger** | | | |
| | | | MCP Flexion | | | |
| | | | MCP Extension | | | |
| | | | MCP Abduction | | | |
| | | | PIP Flexion | | | |
| | | | DIP Flexion | | | |
| | | | **Little Finger** | | | |
| | | | MCP Flexion | | | |
| | | | MCP Extension | | | |
| | | | MCP Abduction | | | |
| | | | PIP Flexion | | | |
| | | | DIP Flexion | | | |
| | | | Comments: | | | |

**Range of Motion—Lower Extremity**

Patient's Name:_____ Date of Birth_____

| Left | | | | Right | | |
|---|---|---|---|---|---|---|
| | | | **Date** | | | |
| | | | **Examiner's Initials** | | | |
| | | | **Hip** | | | |
| | | | Flexion | | | |
| | | | Extension | | | |
| | | | Abduction | | | |
| | | | Adduction | | | |
| | | | Medial Rotation | | | |
| | | | Lateral Rotation | | | |
| | | | **Knee** | | | |
| | | | Flexion | | | |
| | | | **Ankle** | | | |
| | | | Dorsiflexion | | | |
| | | | Plantarflexion | | | |
| | | | Inversion—Tarsal | | | |
| | | | Eversion—Tarsal | | | |
| | | | Inversion—Subtalar | | | |
| | | | Eversion—Subtalar | | | |
| | | | Inversion—Midtarsal | | | |
| | | | Eversion—Midtarsal | | | |
| | | | **Great Toe** | | | |
| | | | MTP Flexion | | | |
| | | | MTP Extension | | | |
| | | | MTP Abduction | | | |
| | | | IP Flexion | | | |
| | | | **Toe _____** | | | |
| | | | MTP Flexion | | | |
| | | | MTP Extension | | | |
| | | | MTP Abduction | | | |
| | | | PIP Flexion | | | |
| | | | DIP Flexion | | | |
| | | | Comments: | | | |

| | | | **Muscle Length** | | | |
|---|---|---|---|---|---|---|
| | | | | | | |

Patient's Name:_____ Date of Birth _____

| **Left** | | | | **Right** | | |
|---|---|---|---|---|---|---|
| | | | **Date** | | | |
| | | | **Examiner's Initials** | | | |
| | | | **Upper Extremity** | | | |
| | | | Biceps Brachii | | | |
| | | | Triceps Brachii | | | |
| | | | Flexor Digitorum Profundus and Superficialis | | | |
| | | | Extensor Digitorum, Indicis, and Digiti Minimi | | | |
| | | | Lumbricals, Palmar and Dorsal Interossei | | | |
| | | | Comments: | | | |
| | | | **Lower Extremity** | | | |
| | | | Hip Flexors—Thomas Test | | | |
| | | | Rectus Femoris—Ely Test | | | |
| | | | Hamstrings—SLR | | | |
| | | | Hamstrings—Distal Hamstring Length Test | | | |
| | | | Tensor Fascia Lata—Ober Test | | | |
| | | | Gastrocnemius | | | |
| | | | Comments: | | | |

# Index